SECOND PROMISED LAND

Second Promised Land

Migration to Alberta and the Transformation of Canadian Society

HARRY H. HILLER

McGill-Queen's University Press
Montreal & Kingston • London • Ithaca

ISBN 978-0-7735-3517-6 (cloth)
ISBN 978-0-7735-3526-8 (paper)

Legal deposit second quarter 2009
Bibliothèque nationale du Québec

Printed in Canada on acid-free paper that is 100% ancient forest free (100% post-consumer recycled), processed chlorine free

This book has been published with the help of a grant from the Canadian Federation for the Humanities and Social Sciences, through the Aid to Scholarly Publications Programme, using funds provided by the Social Sciences and Humanities Research Council of Canada.

McGill-Queen's University Press acknowledges the support of the Canada Council for the Arts for our publishing program. We also acknowledge the financial support of the Government of Canada through the Book Publishing Industry Development Program (BPIDP) for our publishing activities.

Library and Archives Canada Cataloguing in Publication

Hiller, Harry H., 1942–
Second promised land : migration to Alberta and the transformation of Canadian society / Harry H. Hiller.

Includes bibliographical references and index.
ISBN 978-0-7735-3517-6 (bound). – ISBN 978-0-7735-3526-8 (pbk.)

1. Migration, Internal – Canada. 2. Alberta – Population. 3. Alberta – Economic conditions – 1991–. 4. Alberta—Social conditions – 1991–. I. Title.

HB3530.A6H54 2009 304.80971 C2008-907726-1

Typeset by Jay Tee Graphics Ltd. in 10.5/13 Sabon

To my extended family
On both the maternal and paternal side
Who taught me the meaning and significance of migration for Canada
Through their own experiences and through my own observations

and

To my mother and my immediate family
Who have provided love, joy, and belonging

and

To my wife Edna
Who shares my life with grace and beauty

Contents

Preface

One of the tasks of sociologists is to analyze and interpret social change as it occurs. Sometimes things happen so fast that it is unclear how momentous something is until it is over.

Such was my previous experience in Alberta. The late 1970s and early 1980s were heady times in the province. The construction of high-rise office buildings were transforming the downtowns of Calgary and Edmonton. The demand for housing was unparalleled and people were arriving by the thousands to take advantage of the new opportunities. Optimism was everywhere and shrewd investors were making big money just on the basis of rising prices due to demand. There was a feeling in the air that the West, and Alberta in particular, was finally having its day in the sun. I remember attending a conference entitled "Power Shift West," which examined the possibilities that, for the first time, a new phoenix might be rising in the Canadian West and that the structure of Canada might be in the process of revision. But no one who was in Alberta at that time could ever forget how the National Energy Policy played a pivotal role in bringing this new-found growth and expectations about the future to a halt. Investment in property had caused many people to overextend themselves with financing that could not be sustained once the boom turned into a bust. Many people walked away from their homes and mortgages as property was devalued to less than existing mortgages. Office building construction was halted and many buildings remained in a state of partial completion for a long time. In-migration not only slowed to a trickle but was surpassed by out-migration, meaning that the bloom had fallen off the "wild rose" (the provincial flower). As a sociologist living in Alberta I watched all this happen, and, after it was over, I lamented the fact that it was gone, never to be recovered, and that an important piece of

Canadian history had been lost (only to be recovered, perhaps, through post-event reconstruction years later).

In the late 1990s, anyone living in Alberta could not help but notice that the province was undergoing a similar kind of change. The first tip to a local resident involved seeing cars with out-of-province licence plates everywhere one went. When talking with people in the community, whether new neighbours, clerks in the store, fellow employees, or people in a wide variety of service professions, newcomers to the province were constantly encountered. For many Alberta residents, there was a clear sense of déjà vu. This looked like the wave previously experienced happening all over again, and I was determined not to let it happen without some attempt to research and chronicle it.

I am very grateful to the Social Sciences and Humanities Research Council of Canada for its timely financial support of this project known as the Alberta In-Migration Study. The only problem is that there was no clear end to the in-migration or the boom at the time of writing that would be equivalent to what occurred in 1981–82, when the economy went into a steep decline. Instead, the expansion of the oil sands in northern Alberta, beginning around 2004, intensified the economic development to the point where labour shortages became a major issue. While the economic growth in Alberta had been intense but more gradual and manageable up until that time, and house prices and construction costs were more or less under control, 2005 marked a new time period when the economy had become overheated. House prices soared and availability of housing and office space became a major problem. Too much construction activity, undertaken to meet the needs of expansion, caused costs to soar, and, at the time of writing, the boom was almost out of control, with no end in sight. Just prior to publication, the unexpected recession that struck the United States and the world in 2008 created new uncertainties whose outcome is unknown. Nevertheless, the study had to have defined boundaries for purposes of data collection. A lull in the in-migration growth was observable in 2003, prior to the boom-like conditions of the next few years so the primary period of investigation became 1996 to 2002. The rationale I developed to justify this time frame is discussed later. It needs to be understood, then, that this study provides a snapshot of migration to Alberta at a particular point in time. At other times things may have been quite different. In fact, the desperate need for labour after 2005 both changed the appeal of Alberta for unsponsored migrants (due to the problems of an overheated economy) and forced employers to create numerous incentives to encourage migration to Alberta, which was in a vastly different situation from what it was a few years earlier.

There are many aspects to understanding periods of rapid economic growth. From a sociological perspective, one of the most intriguing elements of this growth has been the migration of people to Alberta. Migration is almost always motivated by expectations that the destination holds more promise than the place of current residence; thus, the destination serves as a type of "promised land." The idea of a "promised land" involves not only heightened expectations and anticipation but also the rather sudden movement of large numbers of people into a new area. The title of this book reflects the fact that Alberta has been a rapid migration destination more than once. It is possible to refer to the first rush of settlers who arrived around the turn of the twentieth century and the following two decades as those seeking a promised land (Berton 1984; Francis and Kitzan 2007). Immigrants from Europe and the United States were part of that migration but so also were residents of eastern Canada who moved into the thinly populated territory of the West that eastern interests were seeking to integrate into the new Canadian nation. Alberta was just part of the western interior undergoing rapid settlement at that time and so was not the only province to receive a strong migration flow. From this perspective, it is possible to understand what occurred in Alberta during the first part of the twentieth century as the first movement of in-migration, while what occurred towards the end of that century may be understood as the second movement of in-migration.

It is also possible to understand Alberta as a second promised land if we divide the more recent migration into two waves; 1975 to 1982 and the post-1996 period. In these two migration flows, Alberta became a promised land once again largely because a specific natural resource (energy hydrocarbons) fuelled expectations of a positive migration outcome. What was particularly noteworthy about these two migration surges was that most of the migrants were movers from within Canada (or domestic migrants), for whom relocation was much less cumbersome than was the case with international migrants. Consequently, the migration seemed to serve as an important reflection of significant macro (structural) and micro (individual) issues occurring within Canadian society. What was it that propelled people to leave their place of residence in an advanced capitalist society in search of something better elsewhere within their own nation-state? This study, then, seeks to place migration to Alberta within a national framework, and it focuses specifically on the second migration wave of the contemporary period.

Words cannot adequately express the impact that this research has had on me personally. It was impossible to interact with in-migrants, to hear their stories, and to listen to people who have been affected by this migration, particularly in the communities from which these migrants came, without being personally moved. Our research team met with people in their homes, in coffee shops, in hotel meeting rooms, and many other places. We met entire families, individual representatives of families, and single persons, some for whom the move was successful and some for whom it was very difficult. I saw people living with minimal furniture, people who spent much of their income on telephone bills back home, and people who experienced both feelings of elation and sadness when recounting their migration experiences. Many interviewees in Alberta had an intense personal interest in this research, and this paved the way for people back in their region of origin to welcome me warmly when I did research there. The wonderful home-cooked meals and warm hospitality in places like Grand Le Pierre, Newfoundland; Sydney and St Peter's, Nova Scotia; and Kinkora, Prince Edward Island; will always be a fond memory. I will never forget driving across the Canso Causeway into Cape Breton at Port Hawkesbury (thousands of kilometres from Alberta) only to be greeted by a big sign in front of a Canadian Tire store wishing the managers well on their move to Calgary ("Good Luck Bob and Judy in Calgary"). The first talkshow on this topic in which I participated was in St John's, Newfoundland, and the flood of calls that were received was overwhelming. These two experiences made it clear to me that migration to Alberta was indeed a major grassroots issue all over the country. And these intensely human interchanges with people who experienced the full effects of migration in deeply personal ways made me aware that migration was much more than numbers and statistics regarding how many were moving and their demographic characteristics. Data collection was anything but a dry and tedious task; rather, it was an emotional encounter with other human beings, and this encounter gave me a greater appreciation of the diversity of people and regional cultures in Canadian society and helped me to avoid understanding migration in a purely analytical way. Furthermore, it became clear to me that this migration really was not just about Alberta (the view from Alberta) but also about the regions and social contexts from which people had come.

One of the intriguing things about this research was that, because the expanding economy of Alberta and its role as a magnet destination was a significant public issue in Canada, input was received in many ways beyond the formal sample of respondents. A very interesting symbiotic relationship with the media emerged at an early stage in that they were interested in discussing the topic long before there were any study results to be contemplated. Media encounters almost always resulted in numerous other contributions from the general public. Audiences would often call our toll-free number with corroboratory or corrective comments reflecting their own experiences and often give me many new ideas. Questions from the media often caused me to think of this phenomenon in new ways, and having to articulate my own observations and analyses in public forums assisted greatly in the progression of my thinking. Another interesting informal input to the study came from my own interactions with people in the community who were migrants but whom I encountered in service positions or elsewhere in the community in my daily routines. This type of interaction provided continuous feedback into my thinking and, again, enlarged the input beyond the formal sample.

A large number of people and organizations helped to make this study possible. The base funding was provided by the Social Science and Humanities Research Council of Canada. Along the way, other support was provided by the Faculty of Social Sciences at the University of Calgary, which awarded me a Faculty of Social Science Research Fellowship for this project. Part of the analysis and writing for the book was also conducted while I was a Sproul Fellow at the University of California, Berkeley, and I am thankful for the hospitality of Thomas Barnes and Rita Ross. Many colleagues made suggestions from time to time, but I would specifically like to recognize the assistance of Herb Emery and Nathan Hiller. Some of the conclusions presented here have been developed in more detail and for a specialist audience in professional journals, in particular the *Canadian Review of Sociology and Anthropology*, *New Media and Society*, *Prairie Forum*, and the *Journal of Social and Personal Relationships*.

Throughout this study, I have had a number of research assistants, including Ralph Fidel, Allison Millar, Linda DiLuzio, Letishia Knuttila, Serena Wall, Colleen Will, Pui Hong, and Tracy Simmons. Three people who deserve particular commendation served as research assistants and office manager successively over the course of this work: Tara Franz, Kendall McCaig, and Christina Leung. Kendall McCaig was with the project the longest and over the most critical period and played a key role in bringing all of the data together to facilitate its completion. I am especially grateful for her capable and enthusiastic support but thank all the others as well. My thanks to Joanne Richardson, whose work as copy editor resulted in a much more polished manuscript. And the timely work of my cartograph Shawn Muallen is also gratefully acknowledged. I am forever grateful to my family for their support over the years as this project unfolded.

SECOND PROMISED LAND

1

Migration to Alberta in Perspective

"If I don't move to Alberta, my children will so I might as well move now." These were the words of a migrant from Atlantic Canada who moved to Alberta because of the perception that the dynamics of Canadian society were shifting westward. While such a viewpoint might be considered extreme, it struck at a truth that often lurked beneath the surface. How is it that a hinterland region could emerge from its minor status in a national system to become a major player and a magnet migration destination? And would this development lead to a reconfiguration of Canadian society?

As one of the largest countries in the world, Canada possesses a huge territory in which the railroad was originally conceived as the tie that would bind a spatially challenged nation together. It was the railroad that played an especially vital role in settling the western part of the country and linking it with the centres of finance and industry in central Canada. The railroad supported an unbalanced yet symbiotic relationship linking east and west, in which western Canada served a useful role as a hinterland within the national hierarchy of power and control. This study, in contrast to the role of the railroad in the early development of the region, moves forward almost one hundred years to discover that the highway, and also to some degree the airplane, has replaced the railroad and contributed to the restructuring of Canada, primarily through the redistribution of its people. While the highway itself is not my focus, the automobile is symbolic of the migration of people who made their own choices about relocating to another region of Canada. Most of these migrants moved independently with U-hauls, half-ton trucks and trailers, and packed cars to take advantage of what they considered to be better prospects in "the promised land" of Alberta. These migrants are sometimes referred to as "car people" in contrast to "boat people" (who arrived from places like Vietnam), all of whom took great personal risks to start over again in a new place. The Trans-Canada Highway became a migration pipeline as people from other parts of Canada travelled to and from Alberta in response to unparalleled economic opportunity in the late twentieth- and early twenty-first centuries.

To a considerable degree driven by energy hydrocarbons, Alberta represented an anomaly in the Canadian context. Its political life, its economy, and its worldview appeared to be different from those of the rest of Canada, and migration to Alberta, coupled with the province's sudden ascendance into national (if not international) prominence, was surprising and disturbing both to Albertans and to Canadians in other regions. The critical story, though, is not just oil prices and capital flows but ordinary Canadians relocating in response to changing economic environments both at home and in Alberta. In important ways, the emergence of a new Alberta and the migration flows that it created threatened to change the Canadian status quo in important ways. *Second Promised Land* seeks to make a contribution to understanding that transformation.

What is this place called Alberta? On the one hand, it is just one of ten provinces in Canada. It was not made a province until 1905 (along with Saskatchewan), when settlement began in earnest, and, in that sense, its history within Confederation has been shorter than that of all other provinces (except Newfoundland, which was a late addition in 1949). With a comparatively small population and little economic or political power, the province possessed a hinterland mentality, or a sense of colonial inferiority, that was shaped by its frontier experience. But, on the other hand, and perhaps even because of this background, Alberta has possessed a somewhat renegade attitude. It was the first of the western provinces to mount a challenge to the "eastern" establishment through the successive elections of third parties – the United Farmer's of Alberta (1921) and Social Credit (1935). While some thought this political experimentation was merely the result of a province in transition from its beginnings to maturity, much later in the twentieth century Alberta also became the base for new political innovations such as the Reform Party and the Canadian Alliance, which again challenged the national status quo. Ultimately, in the 1990s, the phrase "The West Wants In" was replaced by "The Alberta Advantage," which became the edgy slogan suggesting that times were changing and that Alberta no longer had the same sense of outsider status as it had had previously. This unsettled position within Confederation has played a large part in creating the impression that Alberta is, indeed, different from other Canadian provinces and possesses a unique "state of mind" (Sharpe, Gibbins, Marsh, and Edwards 2005).

The Alberta of the first half of the twentieth century certainly was very different from the Alberta of the last half of the century. The maturation and specialization of agriculture and food processing (e.g., Alberta became the focal point of the beef industry in Canada); the expansion of the province's two major cities (Calgary and Edmonton) beyond their regional role, with growing international links and populations that were reaching towards one million inhabitants each; and, especially, the development of the energy industry in response to global demand and higher prices were all symbols of a province in continuing transition. By the turn of the century (2001), Alberta stood out from the other provinces in a number of ways. For the last three decades it had had the highest employment rate in Canada. It had the lowest percentage of residents who depended on government transfer payments (8.7 percent), and its social assistance rate (1.7 percent) was considerably below the national average (5.9 percent). Alberta had the lowest median age (thirty-five) among the provinces and the lowest percentage of those over sixty-five (10.4 percent). It had the most even sex ratio (99.9 males per 100 females) in the country and the highest proportion of the population that had been born elsewhere in Canada (27.6 percent). In the 2001 census, Alberta had the fastest growth rate in the country (10.3 percent since 1996) and the highest percentage of the population that, five years ago, had lived in another province (8.8 percent). Alberta was also distinctive in other ways. It had the lowest rate of unionization in Canada and the lowest percentage of its labour force working in public administration (4.6 percent). It had a higher percentage of its labour force engaged in construction (7.7%) and mining and oil and gas extraction (5.1%) than did any other province. As a challenge to previous stereotypes, Alberta (23.6 percent) was second only to British Columbia (35.9 percent) in terms of the percentage of its population that claimed to have no religion. Both these percentages are considerably higher than those in other provinces (e.g., Ontario 16 percent, Nova Scotia 11.6 percent).

The unique attributes of Alberta are not limited to those listed above, but there does seem to be evidence to support the notion that Alberta is different from other provinces in Canada. One of the key elements in the evolution of this difference has been migration – especially migration from within the country. It is not primarily the migration of the settlement period but, rather, the migration of more recent years that is central to this transformation of the changing role of Alberta within

Canada and the alteration of regional dynamics within Canadian society. The primary objective of *Second Promised Land* is to explore the nature and role of the internal migration that Alberta experienced around the turn of the twenty-first century and that has contributed to the evolution of Alberta as a unique place within Canadian society.

THE ROLE AND MEANING OF INTERNAL/DOMESTIC MIGRATION

This has been called the "age of migration" (Castles 2003). Millions of people are moving from one country to another at a rate unparalleled in human history and in a manner that is transforming the world order (Castles and Davidson 2000). Migration has also been declared "the single most powerful force" shaping Canadian society (Messamore 2004, 1). In all of these discussions, migration focuses on its international form, particularly immigration. In an attempt to monitor, evaluate, and adapt to these shifting currents, the multi-country Metropolis Project (http://canada.metropolis.net/index_e.html) was established in 1998 to assist receiving societies deal with the transformations that they were experiencing due to issues relating to migration policy and socio-economic and cultural integration.

Lost in the more high-profile shuffle of people from country to country has been the internal movement of population, which can also transform national societies by creating new growth poles or, conversely, regions of decline. Relocations within a country are perhaps considered more natural, as less threatening, than international relocations and are less likely to be viewed as connected with state policy. On the other hand, international migration usually sparks all kinds of national debate over appropriate policy, including size of flows and source of migration flows. Since residents of a particular country presumably have unfettered access to any part of that country to which they choose to move, internal movements of population are usually understood to be either a response to natural forces of labour demand and supply or just plain personal choice. Such a view is partially true, but it is also unquestionably naïve as there are a host of complex factors that lead people to seek an alternate location of residence. In fact, state policy and corporate decision making play a major role in population relocation, and amenities and opportunities affect personal choices made by migrants themselves. What differentiates internal migration from international migration is the fact that formal barriers are largely absent with regard to the former, thereby making primary migration (initial move to a new location), return migration (moving back to the place of origin), onward migration (moving from one location to another), and hyper mobility (multiple moves) much easier and less available to monitoring.

It has been argued that Canada and the United States are "restless nations" in which migration is part of a life strategy (Weeks 1996, 246; Jasper 2000) more common among their residents than among those of other Western nations (Long 1988). Since both countries have so many immigrants, relocation might be a behaviour pattern that is repeatedly experienced as immigrants and their children seek the most appropriate place of residence within their new society. Internal migration might also be important for the native-born in search of a more suitable environment or perhaps as a means of "moving up," with employee transfers and national job searches serving as mechanisms of upward mobility. Moving companies, relocation assistance firms, and moving rental equipment companies all reflect a thriving industry to accommodate a society constantly on the move. Believing in the possibilities of "fresh starts," people also relocate because of perceptions of new opportunities elsewhere (Jasper 2000, 5, 246). An individualist ethos within our culture has provided legitimacy to family members who desire to strike out on their own, to make their own way, and to attain personal objectives through relocation. With family members scattered all over the continent, loyalty to place of birth or place of childhood development sometimes appears to be an out-dated concept. Congested airports and highways at important holidays attest to the fact that dispersed families need to come together from time to time, even if only briefly.

These perceptions of a country on the move have produced numerous analyses in which internal migration was thought to generate a particular kind of society, with disruptive and alienating effects. Vance Packard (1972) saw this kind of mobility as producing a "nation of strangers." Moves that are more local may have slowed in recent years in both Canada and the United States, but interstate/interprovincial moves continue to be significant. Fischer (2002) examined residential mobility data in the United States from 1950 to 1999 and concluded that local moves had actually declined, while rates for longer-distance moves remained more or less constant at about 7 percent.[1] Schachter (2004) notes that, in comparison to other types of moves, interstate migration in the United States is increasing slightly. In Canada, relocations have also been declining, largely as the result of an aging population, but about 13 percent of the population (3.5 million people) changed municipalities and 3.5 percent of the population (one million people) relocated across provincial borders from 1996 to 2001. In both countries, internal migration involves higher volumes than international migration, and in that sense it is numerically more significant (Vachon and Vaillancourt 1999, 101). The question of why internal migration occurs is intriguing because it sheds light on changes and trends within a national society. This is particularly so with longer-distance migration. The volume, direction, and destination of migration are indicators of societal change that cannot be ignored.

MIGRATION AS NORMAL OR DEVIANT?

In the debate about the consequences of migration, there is often lack of clarity regarding how to interpret it (Jackson 1969, 3; Jansen 1970, 52–3). What is the natural condition for human life? Is it to be sedentary or is it to be mobile? If a static society is normal, then any movement can be considered deviant. If the normal thing is for people to stay in their community or region of origin (Beaujot and Kerr 2004, 140), then any migration away from that location is not only non-normative behaviour but reflects a problem. From this perspective, the problem is with the potential individual migrant who chooses to leave and therefore deviates from the expected pattern. But the problem may also be with the community or region itself, where conditions may force the resident to consider other options.

Analysts are keenly aware that migration always involves some kind of disruption to existing patterns and that this demands evaluation. Measuring the economic costs and consequences of migration may be a matter of statistical calculation, but assessing the social costs and consequences of migration is much more difficult. At the root of negative evaluations of migration is the assumption that it tears people from long-standing social ties in the community of origin and places them in largely alien territory. This makes migration almost a form of anomic behaviour. Migration can also be viewed as a form of dissent in that it implies a rejection of a community of origin, which, for one reason or another, is no longer considered adequate. Because the migrant has no guarantee of the outcome of the migration, relocation is also risk-taking behaviour. All of these interpretations imply a social problems perspective in which there is an implicit assumption that staying in your own community is what should be considered normal.

On the other hand, humans have been migrating since the beginning of time. Migration for food and water, to avoid enemies or persecution, or for trade has a long-standing history. Most of these migrations occurred in groups as whole communities often moved together. What appears to be more recent are relocations of individuals or isolated nuclear family units. While this form of migration often has more social supports than it appears to, self-interest has clearly become a more prominent motivating element in migration than group interest. Thus, in a world of heightened individualism, and in a world of constant change, the idea of a static society indeed seems to be a myth, and migration cannot be interpreted as abnormal. While there may still be some barriers to international migration, domestic migration has become typical behaviour as people seek more suitable locations for their material and social interests at varying stages of the lifecycle. Single young adults may relocate for reasons that are very different from seniors, and moving for work may represent a very different reason for relocation than moving in search of amenities or for climate preferences. While migration flows to particular destinations might involve large numbers of people, these moves are primarily the result of individual choices rather than the relocation of entire groups of people.

Short-distance relocations are typically rather frequent. Often referred to as residential mobility, this type of relocation is often highly symbolic of a status shift. It might be a rite of passage such as changing houses upon leaving the parental home, buying a more elaborate home reflecting one's socio-economic mobility, or making larger or smaller accommodations at different stages of one's lifecycle. Relocations, then, might be considered normal adaptations to changing circumstances. However, staying within a general regional area, regardless of how it is defined, is not normally considered migration. Longer-distance moves, defined as relocations between larger jurisdictional entities such as provinces/states, are much less typical but have been facilitated by new developments in communication and transportation that make migration much less foreboding and permanent. When a potential migrant no longer feels satisfied with life in her/his community of origin, short-distance moves may do little to change the situation and a longer-distance move within a nation-state may be deemed preferable.

In contrast to international migration, in most industrial/post-industrial societies domestic migration can be considered normal – and, sometimes, even expected – behaviour. For example, when labour pools are considered to be national in scope, unemployment in one region may be expected to be a cause of migration to another region. There are usually fewer formal constraints to moving within a national territory and, conversely, there are also forces supporting continuity. Practical constraints may include factors of distance and cost, family obligations, or skill levels; however, the portability of national programs such as health care, pensions, or employment assistance support domestic migration, which, unlike international migration, does not require advance government approval. Furthermore, once migration has begun, it is possible to relocate internally from destination to origin at any time (return migration), to go back and forth between the place of origin and destination either occasionally or repeatedly (circular migration), or even to move on to new destinations (onward migration). Citizenship guarantees the right of free access, which supports mobility that may occur at any time. In a society with a "high mobility ethic," or where migration is viewed as part of a "life strategy," internal migration is considered normative adaptive behaviour. If this migration is the result of individual decisions, the question that needs to be answered is: what leads some people to move while others remain where they are? Furthermore, how do people come to the decision to relocate and how do they choose where to relocate?

The decisions about long-distance migration may reflect personal choices, but they do not occur in a vacuum. They occur within specific socio-economic contexts, which shape and constrain choices. The macro question, then, is also important. Why is it that some regions experience considerable out-migration while other regions experience repeated waves of in-migration? What is it about the way a national society is structured that contributes to uneven migration flows? From this perspective, migration flows serve as a barometer for measuring important tensions, contradictions, or inequalities within a society. The political economy of migration serves as an important contextual backdrop for understanding the movement of people. Migration is not so much natural or normal as it is a response to the way a society is structured, which gives advantages to some regions over other regions. It is imperative, then, that we understand the context of migration because this is what reveals important dynamics within nation-states.

In Canada, the most typical migration-defining boundary (MDB) is the province. With the exception of the three maritime provinces on the East Coast, which are small and clustered together, and the City of Ottawa, which is located on the Quebec/Ontario border, the provinces are large enough and their populations separated enough so that movement between them serves as a meaningful unit of analysis of long-distance moves that may be identified as internal migration.

THEMATIC CONTOURS OF INTERNAL MIGRATION

The two most widely recognized experiences of internal migration on the North American continent are the westward shift of the population through the settlement of the West and the rural-urban migration of the agricultural population. While the settlement of the West involved some immigration from abroad, the fact that it occurred from east to west across the country also gave it the character of an internal movement as residents of the east were part of the migration stream. In any case, long distances were involved, which meant movement across political (state/province) boundaries into weakly populated areas. Rural-urban migration, on the other hand, occurred later and reached its apex in the post-Second World War period as agriculture went through a massive transformation and urban opportunities beckoned. This migration may or may not have crossed state/province boundaries as masses of people who were largely native-born moved to the cities. One of the significant movements of people in the United States from about 1890 to the 1970s involved millions of Afro-Americans who moved from the South into the industrialized North in what is often referred to as the Great Migration (Lemann 1991). Cities like Detroit, Philadelphia, and Pittsburgh were significantly transformed by this migration and the economic activity that supported it. Muller and Espenshade (1985, 23) argue that the most intensive internal migration in the history of the United States was the movement of three million people to California from 1941 to 1945. The State of California had received a disproportionate share of defence contracts at that time, which supported a migration that increased its population by one-third.[2] More recently, other migration shifts have taken place from the frost belt/rust belt to the sunbelt in the American South and Southwest. The urbanization of the population to the largest cities has also continued producing urban sprawl and creating urban regions (rather than just single cities). Each of these shifts has resulted in important changes within American society.

Canada, like the United States, was also settled from east to west as a result of both internal and international migration (Whitely 1932). In the United States, the geographic centre of the population has been moving steadily westward from Maryland in 1790 to St Louis, Missouri, by 2000 (United States 2003, 20). This shift is also evident in Canada, although natural westward expansion was blocked by the Canadian Shield until the late 1800s, when settlement of the interior plains began to take place in earnest. The rapid influx of people into the western interior had a mixed effect in that it initially created a burgeoning population in the region, but after thirty to forty years of growth, rural depopulation occurred as the result of the Depression and changing agricultural practices. This rural-urban shift occurred everywhere but was particularly dramatic on the agricultural plains. Alberta and

British Columbia were the primary beneficiaries of this shift in the postwar period in the western region, and the strong industrial economy of Ontario ensured that that province and its cities were also major recipients of this migration. From 1951 to 2001, Ontario's share of the national population increased from 34 percent to 38 percent, while the share of the national population in all provinces east of Ontario as well as in Manitoba and Saskatchewan declined. In contrast, the share of the national population in Alberta increased from 7 percent to 10 percent and in British Columbia from 8 percent to 13 percent. While there has been a shift westward in terms of the increasing share of the Canadian population living in the two most westerly provinces, this has not occurred at the expense of Ontario (at least until recently), which has retained its dominant position so that it (along with Quebec) preserved its role as both a geographic centre and the fulcrum of the national society.

The rural-urban shift is not just a shift from rural areas to the closest cities but also a shift to the provinces with the biggest cities, which then also includes urban-to-urban migration. The dramatic growth of the City of Toronto, which became Canada's largest city, is of special interest. Toronto has always served as a magnet for internal migrants but, by the turn of the twenty-first century, its growth had been stimulated more by international migration. Toronto, with 44 percent of its population foreign-born by 2001, had truly become "a world in a city" (Anisef and Lanphier 2003), possessing the second highest foreign-born population (Miami had the highest) of any city in the world. By 2006, it had the highest percentage of foreign-born population of any city in the world. Canada's largest cities (including Vancouver and Montreal) have been particularly attractive to immigrants, which has created a significant cultural gulf between them and non-immigrant receiving areas. While it is readily acknowledged that international migration is changing Canadian society, internal migration continues to have a huge impact and its role ought not to be minimized. Sending provinces are deeply affected by the loss of population, which affects the structure of local communities and represents a deficit of generational cohorts of young adults. Receiving provinces replenish and strengthen their labour pool, which facilitates further economic expansion and forces adjustment to rapid growth. These domestic shifts in population foster and reflect regional differences and inequalities and, indeed, often intensify such disparities even further. Internal migration, then, plays an important role in transforming Canadian society.

THREE SPECIFIC INTERNAL MIGRATION FLOWS CHANGING CANADIAN SOCIETY

In addition to the two broad forms of internal migration that have already been mentioned, three more specific migration flows of some significance can be identified. The first is the development of a stronger population base on the West Coast, which has always been accomplished through a combination of internal migration and international migration. The ocean-going ports of British Columbia made its cities very accessible to immigrants, and its relatively mild climate also made it attractive to internal migrants. As the Pacific Rim has grown in importance with regard to Canada's national interests, and as trade with Asia has become more significant, the Lower Mainland (i.e., the Vancouver metropolitan region) in particular has become an important growth pole in the Canadian economy and has supported more internal migration. Later I show that, in recent years, immigration has become more important to this region's growth than internal migration; however, overall, internal migration has been and continues to be important to this region's increasing significance within the national fabric.

The second internal movement of population within Canada of some significance is the out-migration from Quebec, which produced net internal migration losses for that province. Since the mid-1970s, anglophones in particular have increasingly migrated out of Quebec, and the number of anglophones moving into the province has withered (Newbold 1996a; Lo and Teixiera 1998). Internal migration, therefore, has had the effect of solidifying Quebec as a francophone province. In conjunction with low fertility, it has also contributed to Quebec's shrinking share of the national population, from 29 percent in 1951 to 24 percent in 2001. These demographic changes symbolize a shifting role and position for Quebec within Canadian society.

The third and more recent form of internal migration that has affected Canadian society has been the movement of people to the western landlocked province of Alberta. In contrast to the other provinces of the western interior (Saskatchewan and Manitoba), which built their economies on agriculture and then began to experience out-migration, this province has had a very different trajectory.

Migration to Alberta was initially significant because of its role in the peopling of the province, particularly from 1890 to 1911. From 1901 to 1905 alone, 40,000 homesteads were granted in Alberta, which required settlement on a farm site and breaking the land for a minimum three-year period in order to establish ownership (Alberta Agriculture 1997, 6). The years from 1912 to 1914 were optimistic boom years for the province. A promotional pamphlet described "the Great Alberta," the "Empire of Fulfillment," "the land where opportunities are unlimited." It went on to predict that Edmonton "must inevitably become the largest city in Canada," to describe Calgary as "the city of business and bustle by the Bow," and Medicine Hat as potentially "the Minneapolis of Canada (Collins 1994, 2–3). Alberta was described as the "wonder child of Canada," where populations of 5 million or even 20 million were expected. Regarding the population of Calgary,

> In 1900 it stood at 5,000, a decade later at over 40,000, and after 1910 newcomers were pouring in at the rate of 1,000 a month. By the end of 1912 it was edging 75,000 people and promoters talked of a half-million by the 1930's. Every day, carpenters, bricklayers and surveyors stepped off the train with families in tow. Meanwhile, land speculation was the city's biggest industry ... 358 real estate agents against 166 grocery stores, 17 banks, and 27 hardware stores. (Hutchinson 1994, 88)

Its growth from 5,000 to 75,000 people in twelve years supported endless optimism about the future of Calgary and created a sense of boom times that was soon shattered by the war years and the tough economic times that followed. As with other frontiers, the buoyancy and expectations of new life in Alberta was limited by its agricultural economy, which underwent considerable change after the Depression. Growth was halted and even reversed in some areas, and growth in the cities was moderate at best.

The movement of people into the western Canadian interior was part of the federal government's broader policy objective to "claim the West" in what was known as the National Policy. Other than this initial settlement period, and until the 1970s, Alberta's growth was slow and not always steady, and it depended considerably on rural-urban migration within the region. However, a new thrust of expansion and development within the province thanks to internal migration is most often associated with energy hydrocarbons. From the mid-1970s to the early 1980s, Alberta once again felt like a frontier because of the rush of people into the province, which was then followed by an out-migration in a classic boom-and-bust cycle that earned the province considerable notoriety. No other province, or even similar American states like Oklahoma and Texas, experienced such volatility (Mansell and Percy

1990). Because economic booms are stimulants to internal migration, the influx of people to the province during the good times resulted in considerable national attention, but so did its reversal in the mid-1980s, when many left the province. Even though Alberta still experienced net growth and its economy matured greatly, the fact that the growth was predicated on an oil boom helped to perpetuate frontier-like images of risk-takers and wealth-seekers in search of black gold. These images were considerably overdrawn and even unfamiliar to most Albertans, but the overheated economy and significant recession were a reality with which all had to cope. On the other hand, this boom marked the dawn of a new era for the province, which may have only been the beginning of the transformation of its national role. It was ironic, though, that the images of Alberta that were originally created during its settlement period – that is, as one of the Prairie provinces in a region often described as barren, harsh, inhospitable, isolated, and prone to economic depression (e.g., Britnell 1939; Francis 1989a) – should, by the latter part of the same century, become so radically different.

By the last decade of the twentieth century, Alberta had become a different place. In spite of the boom-and-bust cycle of the late-1970s and early 1980s, a recovery occurred that built on the energy industry but that began to be shaped around Alberta's commitment to free enterprise principles. This ideology clearly differentiated the province from neighbouring provinces at that time and was expected to be a tool to attract more inward investment supporting economic diversification. Around 1996, a second wave of in-migration entered into an economy that clearly benefited from rising energy prices but that also showed strength in other sectors, such as logistics and transportation as well as business services. The growth of Calgary was particularly dramatic, and the transfer of the head offices of several prominent corporations to the city (in addition to those already there) was viewed as a symbol of a new era, in which Alberta as a destination of choice intensified. How a province could shift from being a hinterland of agricultural migrants to being a magnet for highly educated internal migrants is a phenomenon worthy of explanation and analysis and is the subject of this book.[3]

ALBERTA IN COMPARATIVE PERSPECTIVE

Alberta is certainly not unique on the North American continent with regard to being a less well-known province/state that experienced dramatic growth and positive in-migration flows. The United States has seen significant regional fluctuations in that the once powerful magnetic industrial northeast lost more people through internal migration from 1995 to 2000 than any other region (Franklin 2003). Most Midwestern states also experienced net losses through internal migration. In contrast, a whole new set of states became significant destinations. Nevada, for example, had the highest net internal migration rate of any state. Colorado, Arizona, North Carolina, and Georgia also had strong in-migration gains. Colorado, which topographically has the most in common with Alberta, grew from just over 2 million people in 1970 to over 4 million people in about thirty years, roughly doubling its population. Nevada grew from less than half a million in 1970 to over 2 million in 2000. Arizona grew from less than 2 million in 1970 to over 5 million in 2000. Similarly, Alberta grew from around 1.5 million in 1971 to around 3 million in 2001, roughly doubling the population in thirty years. Alberta, then, has a similar demographic trajectory to these other mountain states. Alberta also shares a similarity with these states in that at least some of the in-migration was from high-cost states/provinces and states/provinces with bigger, more diverse, and more densely populated cities.

However, Alberta differs significantly from these states in important ways. First of all, it is part of a country that has one-tenth the population of the United States, meaning that the potential size of migration flows is much bigger south of the border. On the other hand, the impact of a strong migration flow in Canada is likely to be much more significant, given the smaller total population and the smaller number of jurisdictions (i.e., ten provinces), half of whom have a population of less than 1 million people, than it is in the United States. Ontario is by far the province with the largest population, and it is the single most important migration magnet (i.e., migration of all types) in the country. In the United States, even though California has the largest population, there are far more options for migration than there are in Canada because there are many states with substantial populations (e.g., New York, Florida, Texas, etc.). Second, Ontario has had a stranglehold on both economic and population growth in Canada, and the emergence of a new alternative has a dramatic effect in that it apparently challenges this dominance. The historic supremacy of central Canada has been a fact of life for a long time, and the emergence of an upstart and ascendant province "on the Prairies" has huge implications for the status quo. Most provinces have been losing more population than they have been gaining through internal migration, which makes the case of Alberta stand out all the more. East/west distances across Canada are huge, and any movement across the Canadian Shield is much more cumbersome than is long-distance migration in the United States, which is supported by many interstate highways. Any migration, especially from the Atlantic provinces, that skips over Ontario overcomes a major hurdle that truly breaks traditional migration patterns. Third, migration to Alberta is less likely to be based on climatic factors such as those occurring in the American South, and there are no intervening variables such as massive illegal migration from Mexico to compound population growth. In short, while migration to Alberta is not new, any large-scale movement to this province breaks traditional patterns and expectations and potentially transforms the society in significant ways. It is important, then, to examine more carefully what has been happening in Alberta.

STUDY TIMELINES

At the time of writing, Alberta's economy became overheated. No longer was it traditional means of oil extraction that was driving the economy but, rather, beginning in 2003, the new investments made in the oil sands, which had a dramatic effect on the tone of growth, fuelling what could be called hyper-growth. By 2005, the incremental growth that Alberta had experienced reached a new feverish pace, in which job creation exceeded the rate of migration. "Boom-time" was the only term to describe what was happening. Statistics Canada declared that Alberta was in the midst of "the strongest period of economic growth ever recorded by any province in Canada's history," with the tightest labour market in North America (Cross and Bowlby 2006). Migration flows became distorted by employer-induced migration through elaborate recruitment strategies and pay and benefit incentives. Special arrangements were made to foster greater international migration. Home prices, which had been affordable in comparison to other major centres in Canada, suddenly increased exponentially. In fact, in one year's time, home prices in Calgary increased by 50 percent (Toneguzzi 2006). Infrastructure deficits such as in roads, road interchanges, schools, and hospital beds became much more obvious, and the province appeared to be in a state of partially controlled crisis. Oil sands expansion in northern Alberta was the catalyst of this growth, primarily because oil sands construction and investment were much more long term and on a grander scale than conventional oil extraction, which had been declining. This suggested that the period of strong economic growth was likely to be sustained much longer than had been thought. Servicing an expanding population (e.g., the need for teachers, medical personnel, etc.) was, in itself, also contributing to exponential economic growth. At the same time, considerable apprehension emerged about the future in light of what appeared to be unsustainable growth as rising costs, infrastructural deficits, and labour shortages produced an increasing sense of crisis. At the very least, the uncontrolled pace of growth increasingly came to be viewed as having deleterious effects and, in particular, as producing a widening gap between the rich and the poor due to income inequity, which especially affected independent migrants (as opposed to corporate transfers). It remains to be seen where this boom is going and how long it will last before an economic correction occurs.

The characteristics of a boom are much different from those of an expanding economy. Booms create anxiety and fear caused by factors such as suddenness, uncontrollability, and extremes. On the other hand, expanding economies are more easily processed and absorbed because the growth is slower and more incremental. The focus of *Second Promised Land* is on the period from 1996 to 2002, which encompasses the years of economic expansion that occurred before growth took on a different character and appeared to spiral out of control. By 2006, net interprovincial migration to Alberta reached an unprecedented peak. In some ways, this growth should be included in this analysis. However, since, at the time of writing, the trajectory of this growth was unknown, I made an arbitrary decision not to include it. My rationale is that the existence of severe labour shortages and an overheated economy results in a very different kind of migration. This migration is more directly employer-driven, involving significant recruitment outside the province involving employer inducements and other incentives to relocate, and these were not present to the same degree at the time I conducted this study. Furthermore, boom conditions resulted in much more apprehension regarding moving to Alberta as people now had to consider the reality of rising costs. Such conditions also affected the ability of migrants to remain in the province and increased the likelihood that others would want to leave. In short, an overheated economy changed the dynamics of migration in significant ways from what I had observed earlier. For this reason, my analysis distinguishes between an expanding economy and a boom-time economy. The data upon which the Alberta In-Migration Study was based are rooted in an expanding economy. The dynamics of boom conditions, on the other hand, are much more explosive and precarious and, perhaps, are a subject unto itself. Once the boom conditions ease, we will be in a better position to assess the full cycle.

I do not focus on in-migration, the theme of this book, to celebrate it; rather, I do so because the movement of people to Alberta provides macro-level evidence of how societies are continuously being restructured. Much of the micro-level data that are presented provide evidence pertaining to how individuals make decisions and to how they navigate changes within their own communities. The movement of people from one region to another is not just about the redistribution of labour; indeed, I show that migration is more complex than purely economic forces would indicate. But it does demonstrate how capital investment and global economic forces contribute to the transformation of a nation. This study was undertaken not merely to analyze losers and winners in the interregional migration shuffle but also to understand how societies experience change through migrations from within. In short, the thesis of *Second Promised Land* is that migration to Alberta must be understood as part of a broader reconfiguration of Canadian society.

2

The Old West and the New West

Something new has been stirring in the Canadian West. The old notion was that the West was divided in two: the Prairie West (including the three "Prairie provinces" of Manitoba, Saskatchewan, and Alberta) and the Coastal West (British Columbia). What both regions had in common through the first half of the nineteenth century was that they were recently settled, with relatively small populations, and that they were hinterlands to central Canada. The National Policy of 1879 clearly conceived of the West as a hinterland that would benefit central Canada (Fowke 1957). As Hall (1977, 84) has pointed out, there was no vision of the Prairie West, in particular, as anything other than an agriculturally based society that, though it may have a West Coast port, was intricately tied to the industries of central Canada. If Morton (1973) is correct in positing that, initially, it was migration from Ontario that settled the western interior and gave it its institutions, it soon became clear that later immigration and the experiences of living on the frontier were producing a society that was both tied to Ontario and, due to its own process of society-building, resistant to it. The question is whether in the process of society-building a New West has been created – one that is radically different and in which the Prairie West has been transformed, with new divisions having been created as the sense of agricultural unity has disappeared. As we will see, it is primarily what has happened in Alberta that has created a new dynamic both in western Canada and in Canada as a whole.

The distinctiveness of the Prairie West as a region is part history and part myth. Much of the imagery is built from similar settlement patterns at a particular point in time (Gray 1979) and the politics of a wheat economy. Prior to the rush of migration for settlement, the region was known as the Northwest. Here fur trading shaped the economy, which was located in the more northerly regions (Fort Edmonton was its hub) and along the major rivers. The term "Prairies" came to represent a new stage in the evolution of the western interior, in which farming and land ownership became the magnet for migration. In contrast to the more northern character of the fur economy, agriculture was thought to be more appropriate to the plains because they required less clearing of trees – an endeavour that had been painstaking and difficult in Ontario. The decision to run the new transcontinental railroad line (the Canadian Pacific Railway, which was completed in 1885) through the southern part of the region then ensured that the early agrarian settlement would occur on the plains. The railway shifted both economic activity and population southward, which enhanced Calgary's role since it was located on the rail line (Palmer 1990, 50–1). Thus emerged the conception of the West as "the Prairies," which were associated with the attempt to profit from agriculture on arid, bleak, windswept, and treeless terrain while fighting the demons of pestilence and erosion (especially in those early years). This led many to reconsider their decision to build their long-term future on the land.[1]

The question, of course, is whether this imagery any longer describes the reality of the region's inhabitants. If it is no longer appropriate, then the idea of the Prairie West being "a cultural region" (Thompson 1998, ix) with a common set of myths about what it is and what its goals are is questionable. Allen (1973) argues that a region is a mental construct and that most of the constructs of the Prairie region have not been born there but, rather, have been imposed from without. If that is so, then it is time that this region be examined to determine whether or not these constructs are appropriate. As a land-locked region with no easy access to the Canadian population in the St Lawrence Lowlands or on the West Coast, the Prairie region is also unique in that its settlement reaches much farther north than does settlement in other regions of Canada, whose populations are huddled near the American border. Perhaps this fact more than any other has given birth to the conception of the Prairie West as homogeneous and distinct.

It is true that there is a similarity among the three Prairie provinces; this is because the Laurentian Shield to the east and the Rocky Mountains to the west serve both as barriers and as boundaries, resulting in a rough similarity of climate that contrasts sharply with that of the St Lawrence Lowlands and the West Coast. Further, the period of settlement at the end of the eighteenth and beginning of the nineteenth centuries was roughly similar within the Prairie region and was rooted in the wheat economy. Thus, "Prairie provinces" became a convenient way to refer to one of the sections of Canada, and this way of looking at the region has endured in regional myths as well as aggregated statistics. For example, Alberta, Saskatchewan, and Manitoba are often lumped together in data presentations at the national level, with the result that Ontario, Quebec, and British Columbia are contrasted with the Atlantic provinces and the Prairie provinces. This always eventuates in misleading conclusions because, whatever similarities the three provinces may have had in the past, these have been radically altered, particularly by the ascendance of Alberta. Besides, the region is far more complex than the imagery conjured by the phrase "Prairie provinces" suggests.

There are a number of reasons, then, why we might want to challenge this characterization of the region as a homogeneous unit. One is that the wheat economy no longer represents the region the way it once did as other agricultural pursuits and natural resources are now playing more dominant roles. Second, a fertile belt known as "parkland," not "prairie," is now where crop-based agriculture is the most productive. Third, due to rural depopulation and urbanization, most people who live in the region no longer live "on the prairies." Saskatchewan may have retained more of its rural character than the other two provinces, but Manitoba's population is overwhelmingly urban and is located in Winnipeg. Fourth, Alberta's population has grown much faster than has that of the other two provinces, to the point where the province now has a larger population (over 2 million more residents) than the other two provinces combined, and its two major cities (Edmonton and Calgary) are unsurpassed in size within the region. Even the eastern half of Alberta, which is the most prairie-like, has been radically depopulated. The southern rural portion has been transformed by feedlots, meatpacking, and commercial agrifood production and processing (e.g., potatoes, corn). Fifth, growth that is occurring in northern cities such as Grand Prairie and Fort McMurray is in heavily wooded areas (not prairies), where lumbering and hydrocarbons form the basis of the economy. Even Red Deer (halfway between Edmonton and Calgary) is in the greenbelt area and not really on the prairies. All of this suggests that the old concept of "the Prairies" as an agricultural-based region is no longer adequate.

The term "Prairies" is misleading: a more appropriate designation for the area incorporating the three western provinces of Manitoba, Saskatchewan, and Alberta would be "the western interior."[2] "Prairies" no longer define what these three provinces are all about, perhaps with the exception of Saskatchewan, which is closest to being a "true" Prairie province, though only in the sense that living and working on the land or in smaller cities is more typical there than in the other provinces. When Winnipeg served as the gateway to the entire region, which was seen as a newly settled area of agriculturalists, it made sense to refer to it as the Prairies. However, the emergence of Edmonton and Calgary as the dominant cities of the region symbolizes a transformation that the imagery associated with "the Prairies" no longer accurately captures. Whatever homogeneity the Prairie image may have conveyed can no longer hide the diversity and change occurring in the region. The concept of the Prairies is dated and no longer expresses the realities of the region. Above all, it no longer applies to Alberta.

THE EVOLUTION OF REGIONAL TRANSFORMATION

In 1901, only 419,000 people lived in the Prairie West, and over 60 percent of these people lived in one province – Manitoba (Dawson and Yonge 1940, 28). From 1901 to 1911, the regional population increased dramatically (by over 300 percent) to 1,328,000. Saskatchewan was the primary beneficiary of this growth, and, for the next forty years, it was the most populated province in the entire West and the third most populous province in Canada. It was not until 1951 that Alberta and British Columbia surpassed Saskatchewan in population size. Thus, until that time, Saskatchewan played a key role in defining the West (Britnell 1939). Winnipeg, on the other hand, was the administrative and service centre for the West. From 1951 to 1971, British Columbia's population grew by 92 percent to 2.2 million, Alberta's grew by 77 percent to 1.7 million, while Saskatchewan's and Manitoba's grew by 12 percent and 29 percent, respectively, to around 1 million people each. In short, 1951 marks the beginning of the great divide between the Old West and the New West. If, in the West, the first half of the twentieth century was marked by provincial populations of less than 1 million each, and all provinces were of roughly the same size by mid-century, the second half saw much stronger growth in Alberta and British Columbia than anywhere else. In fact, whereas Manitoba and Saskatchewan grew by only 44 percent and 18 percent, respectively, in the fifty years from 1951 to 2001, Alberta grew by 217 percent and British Columbia grew by 335 percent. By 2001, British Columbia (3.9 million) and Alberta (3 million) had almost four-fifths (77 percent) of the West's 9 million people. Thus, in one century, growing from a combined population of just over half a million people, the balance of power in the West had shifted to the Far West and the Mountain West.

While in the Old West the Prairie West could be clearly distinguished from the Coastal West (British Columbia), in the New West the westward shift of population included both British Columbia and Alberta as growth poles. The Continental Divide notwithstanding, Alberta then joined British Columbia as part of the strategic change in the West, but, at the same time, it was also part of the western interior; this is distinct from British Columbia, which has been referred to as "a geographic region apart" (Resnick 2000, 4).[3] Thus, we include British Columbia in our discussions of the West but not in our discussions of the Western Interior.

ASSESSING THE CONCEPT OF "THE PRAIRIES"

It is instructive to examine the so-called "Prairie West" to determine its continued usefulness as a concept.[4] Traditionally, as we have noted, it has included the three provinces of Manitoba, Saskatchewan, and Alberta, which are isolated by the eastern barrier of the Canadian Shield and the western barrier of the Rockies, making the region geographically discrete. It was from the southern part of each province, known as the grasslands, that the region received its stereotype as flatlands with howling winds and little moisture. This was where settlement initially occurred since this was where the Canadian Pacific Railway ran through the territory, facilitating settlement and development through spur lines to adjacent areas. Labelled contradictorily as both a barren wasteland and a "garden of Eden," "agrarian paradise," or "promised land" (Warkentin 1973; Owram 1980; Francis 1992), climate and topography provided a trying context for this region, where high expectations and the harsh realities of settlement clashed (Burnet 1951). This is the origin of the myth that the Prairies form a natural physiographic area consisting of dryland grain farming – a description that is most characteristic of the area between Portage La Prairie, Manitoba, and Drumheller, Alberta (Stabler and Olfert 2002). According to this myth, the topography of the region consists of a few trees and short grass, with extreme temperatures in summer and winter, farmers struggling to survive under tough conditions of drought and/or poor market prices, and grain elevators (the sentinels of the Prairies) acting like beacons for small farming communities spread throughout the area. Among the many issues encountered here is the fact that many settlers knew little about farming and even less about dryland farming.[5] It was no surprise that many farmers gave up and moved elsewhere. And, if they did not, their adult children, for whom there was not enough income, did.

The grasslands served a major role in defining the region as they were part of the Great Plains extending south from Canada to the Texas Panhandle. Sometimes referred to as "the Great American Desert," the Canadian portion was, at one point, called the Palliser Triangle. This was due to a report written by Captain John Palliser, who declared that the region was unsuited for agriculture. In addition to the three Canadian provinces, this "desert" included all or parts of ten states from the Missouri River in the east to the Rocky Mountains in the west. All of North Dakota, South Dakota, Nebraska, and Kansas are part of the Great Plains, in addition to the eastern parts of Montana, Wyoming, Colorado, New Mexico, and parts of Texas and Oklahoma. While there is considerable variation within the region, it is generally known as a treeless area with lots of sunshine and semi-arid conditions, and it is firmly held that, under the right conditions, it would support a crop economy. Part of the area is conducive to the growing of corn and soybeans, but most of it supports a wheat economy. At one time, custom combiners would start in Kansas, where the wheat matured earlier, and then work their way north into the Dakotas and the Prairie provinces, combining for farmers as they followed the crop cycle. In other words, the wheat economy defined the region (Fowke 1957, 282).

The Great Plains region is the least densely populated area on the continent. States that have retained agriculture as their dominant industry have experienced little growth. All states and provinces that are part of the plains region generally have weak economies and constantly lose people to other regions and/or bigger cities. There is no city in the entire Great Plains region that is now as big as either Edmonton or Calgary (assuming these two cities even belong to that region). The only exception is metropolitan Oklahoma City (which is about the same size as Calgary or Edmonton) and places at the boundaries of the region, such as Denver or Dallas-Fort Worth. The plains side of Colorado has experienced little growth, but the urban centres in the foothills (e.g., Denver, Colorado Springs) are experiencing explosive growth. It is therefore interesting that Alberta, which is at least partially a part of the Great Plains region, located at its northern extremities, should have experienced the growth that it has.

The agrarian foundation of plains life in the Canadian western interior is indisputable. Eighty percent of Canada's total arable land is located in this region which is significant in view of the fact that only 7 percent of Canada's land surface is suitable for agriculture. The average Prairie farm is now at least three times larger than farms located elsewhere in the country, and 50 percent of all farms in Canada are located in this region. Ontario and Quebec have 40 percent of all farms in the country but only 13 percent of all farmland, which indicates that the size of farms there is much smaller than are those in the Prairies (*National Atlas of Canada*). The Canadian plains were originally settled on the assumption that crop farming would be the major source of income, with wheat as the dominant crop (this was often referred to as a wheat monoculture) along with some oats and barley. With the exception of some ranching in southern Alberta, livestock was not a primary source of income, and cattle were primarily raised for home consumption. After the Second World War, growing grains as livestock feed (particularly barley) became more important as livestock became an important exportable commodity. By 1958, cattle had become the single largest source of income for farmers in Alberta, replacing wheat (Minister of Industry 2004, 247–56). Diversification into new crops such as canola, sunflower seed, mustard seed, peas, and beans was motivated by new export markets.

Even though these three western interior provinces have 80 percent of the farmed land in the country, there are vast differences between them. Saskatchewan has 39.1 percent of all agricultural land in Canada, followed by Alberta with 30.9 percent, and Manitoba with 11.4 percent. About one-sixth of the Province of Manitoba (14.5 percent) is covered with water and much of the rest consists of the forest-covered escarpment of the Cambrian Shield. The province's fertile belt is primarily in the south and on the western borders, such as the Swan River Valley, most of which is devoted to crops rather than to pasture. Saskatchewan also has the majority of its land devoted to crops and a much lower percentage devoted to pasture. Alberta is distinct in that the proportion of land devoted to crops is almost equal to the proportion devoted to pasture, and this is reflected in the fact that about 40 percent of all of Canada's beef cattle industry is located in that province, with Saskatchewan next at about 18 percent. The northern part of all three interior provinces is boreal forest (see the map in figure 1). Even here Alberta is distinctive in that it has more territory available for settlement than any other province, primarily because people are able to engage in agriculture in the Peace River country to the north. In contrast, 90 percent of British Columbia is actually Crown land, much of which is licensed for forestry and mining, and agriculture is more limited (Friesen 1999, 75).

Saskatchewan, sometimes referred to as the breadbasket of the world, is the province with the highest wheat production. Its reliance on

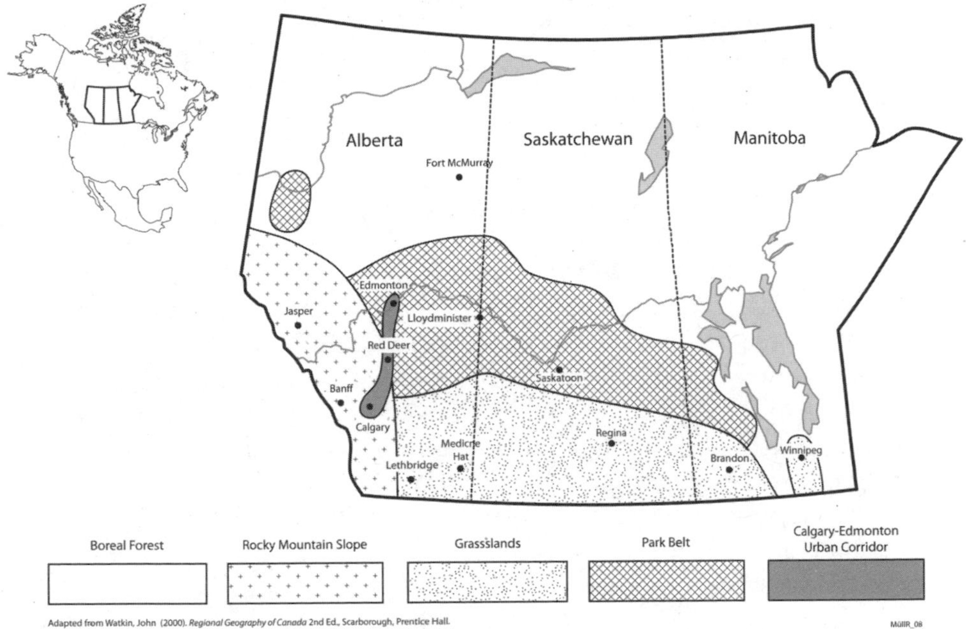

Figure 1
SOURCE: Adapted from John Warkentin. *A Regional Geography of Canada*, 2nd ed. (Scarborough: Prentice Hall, 2000).

wheat as a cash crop contrasts considerably with Alberta and Manitoba, both of which have much more mixed farming. Even as early as 1921, Manitoba field crops were less than 50 percent wheat, and Alberta had even more mixed farming, with the large production of barley, canola, vegetables, dairying, and livestock (Proudfoot 1972, 59–62). Thus as farms grew in size due to the mechanization of agriculture, Saskatchewan was affected more dramatically than were the other two provinces, and this resulted in less demand for labour, which, in turn, resulted in a smaller population. In contrast, the population growth poles were located in the other two provinces as Winnipeg, Edmonton, and Calgary became the three largest cities of the region.

If the imagery of the Prairies is based on the grasslands and the wheat economy, it is important to know that this economy and its environment no longer best represents the region and its residents. Figure 1 shows that Saskatchewan has the largest grasslands area of the three provinces,[6] but only about 12 percent of the population of the western interior lives or works in areas that have these topographical characteristics. Considerably different from the grasslands in the south and the forests in the north is a Parkland belt that is transitional between the two topographies. Here one finds a sedimentary basin of fertile soil, rolling hills, and clusters of trees, where there is mixed farming and more crop diversity. Whereas the grasslands had no river to tie the region together, the parkland area is structured around the Saskatchewan River. Almost 40 percent of the population of the western interior is found here, including centres such as Red Deer, Edmonton, Lloydminster, Saskatoon, and Yorkton. This is not the arid, shortgrass prairie but, rather, a fertile belt that supports diverse agricultural activity.[7] Well over half of Alberta's agricultural production occurs in this parkland area rather than on the prairie (Ironside 1984, 101). A fourth topographical area within the western interior is known as the Rocky Mountain Slopes. This encompasses the foothills and the mountains themselves, including not only the mountain communities of Banff and Jasper but also the Crowsnest Pass, Canmore, Calgary, and the area up to Lethbridge. Here about 25 percent of the population of the western interior region is located. This area, which is significantly different from the grasslands, is known for Chinook winds, coal, two-thirds of all irrigated crop production in Canada, feedlots, and tourism and recreation. Clearly, the region and its landscape is much more diverse than the term "Prairies" suggests.

The Dominion Lands Act had assumed that farm size of one-quarter section was the ideal, and yet that size seldom provided enough land to keep a farm economically viable (Voisey 1988, 128). Even at that, the thinness of the population on large and isolated homesteads made the region particularly difficult to govern (Bantjes 2005). Saskatchewan's demographic strength in the first half of the twentieth century was due to the fact that most of its population were farmers. However, the evolution of farming has truly transformed the region. If the concept of the Prairies or the plains is based on the physiography of the grasslands, that image no longer reflects the reality of life for most people in the western interior. Most people in the region no longer live on "the Prairies" but, rather, on parkland or the mountain slopes. Furthermore, most people in the region are not engaged in agriculture and now live in cities. Over 60 percent of the population of Manitoba now live in Winnipeg, a city of almost 700,000, and 63 percent of the population of Alberta live in Calgary and Edmonton, each with a population of 1 million. Only about 6 percent of the populations of Manitoba and Alberta live on farms or are engaged in agriculture. The level of urbanization is the lowest in Saskatchewan, which has smaller cities and a larger rural population (13 percent) than the other two western interior provinces, although even this low number represents a dramatic change from earlier years.

In 1941, there were almost 300,000 farms on the Canadian plains, but this number declined to 210,000 by 1961 and 125,000 by 2001. Rural depopulation was the natural result of the need for larger farms to ensure efficiency and sustainability, especially with the close of the pioneer era. Saskatchewan had almost as many farms as Manitoba and Alberta together, but after 1941, the decline in the number of farms was much sharper in that province than in the other two (table 14). Between 1941 and 1971, the number of farms in Saskatchewan dropped from 139,000 to 77,000, and by 2001 it had dropped to 51,000. At the same time, the size of farms increased from 175 hectares (432 acres) in 1941 to 342 hectares (845 acres) in 1971 to 519 hectares (1,283 acres) in 2001. By 2001, the number of farms in Saskatchewan and Manitoba had shrunk from their peak by about 175 percent, whereas the number of farms in Alberta had only shrunk by 85 percent, with the result that Alberta had more farms than either of the other two provinces. Saskatchewan had fewer farms, but they were now the largest in Canada by a considerable margin. With this kind of change, it is no wonder that the rural depopulation of Saskatchewan has been so dramatic and so continuous. The transformation of the old Prairie region is demonstrated yet again by the fact that the average size of farms in the western interior was now 424 hectares (1,048 acres), whereas the average size of farms elsewhere in Canada was only 109 hectares (269 acres).

Hilda, Alberta: Rural Settlement and Rural Depopulation

The hamlet of Hilda, Alberta, serves as a useful illustration of the growth and decline of a particular concept of the western interior. The rush of settlers into the region suggested that agriculture would be an anchor to a particular way of life that would dominate the area and support flourishing towns. However, changes that were never anticipated by these settlers eventually led to the collapse of the robust patterns that were initially established.

Located in the southeastern part of the province 80 kilometres northeast of Medicine Hat, and close to the Saskatchewan border, the Hilda area was originally home to indigenous peoples whose nomadic way of life meant that they had no permanent settlements. In the late nineteenth century ranchers moved into the area, but it was not until the early twentieth century that intense settlement whose purpose was the farming of what was essentially shortgrass virgin land began to occur. This was truly "the Prairies," and the railway played a key role in opening them up. Settlers were required to work hard and live frugally, albeit with the promise of future rewards.

Homesteading and land ownership were particular attractions for the settlers, many of whom were German immigrants who had migrated from Russia. The years between 1910 and 1913 saw the largest influx of people, so that by 1921 the region in which Hilda was located (Improvement District #1) had grown to almost 10,000 people, and the immediate Hilda area itself had 1,400 residents. In 1923, the coming of the railroad to the town helped to support further growth so that at its peak, Hilda had six grain elevators and twenty-two businesses. These included lumber yards, implement dealers, general stores, a shoe repair, hardware stores, a lawyer, a blacksmith, a tailor, a watch repair, a bank, a hotel, and, ultimately, gas stations. It also had seven churches and a number of schools.

The community weathered the tough years of drought from 1917 to 1919, but the Depression of the 1930s began to take its toll and the process of rural depopulation began. The region was at its peak by the 1930s, but slowly the community lost its vitality as young people left and the process of farm consolidation began. Businesses in the community remained reasonably strong until the 1950s, and then they too began to collapse. The construction of Highway 41 to Medicine Hat shortened the travel time to larger centres, and local businesses could not compete. By 1951, Improvement District #1 had only 5,000 people left from the previous 10,000. Hilda itself only had sixty-five residents by 1986, and the area only had about two persons per 2.59 square kilometres (1 square mile). Whereas the Hilda area had once had 1,400 inhabitants, there were only about 200 by the turn of the millennium. There were virtually no businesses left, no schools, and only two churches.

Homesteading provided the incentive for thousands of people to flock into the Prairie region as agriculturalists, but it was only a short-term settlement for many, and it lasted, at most, for one generation. A combination of factors pertaining to changes in farming methods, economics, new agricultural technologies, and new urban opportunities meant that the dreams of many for a strong rural western interior would be significantly altered. Much of the imagery of the "Prairie West" is based on the early years of rural settlement and vitality; however, this imagery has undergone a considerable metamorphosis.

Source: Based on material from the Southeast Alberta Regional Planning Commission, Regional Population Study (1980) and Welcome to Hilda, 3rd ed. (2000).

I have already shown that the emphasis on the geographical characteristics of the region is misleading because it focuses on one particular physiographic trait – the shortgrass prairie, even though, within the region, there are significant differences in everything from topography to precipitation, temperatures, vegetation, humidity, and minerals (Card 1960:1). These differences have played an enormous role in changing settlement patterns and developing economies. For example, places close to the mountains are deemed to be more preferable for habitation than are flatlands, while locations devoted to mineral extraction have drawn larger labour pools than have agricultural places. These examples show that the region consists of created space (i.e., space constructed by human decisions) as well as geographic space. Calgary, for instance, was created as a result of the Canadian Pacific Railway's decision to have a terminus there; Winnipeg's location on a railroad line resulted in its becoming a centre of investment in manufacturing and regional distribution. Later technologies (e.g., air travel) and new ports and shipping possibilities (e.g., through the Panama Canal) took much of this dynamic away from Winnipeg. While oil is found in all of the western provinces, investment and administration of the oil industry are sited in Alberta, and this has had a particularly profound effect on that province. Furthermore, the timing of oil's discovery and the changing demands for it have also played a role in creating differences within the region. Clearly, there is considerable variation within the region not only as the result of natural factors but also as the result of investment, political decisions, and international factors.

The western interior region has undergone a major transformation. Almost 60 percent of the population of the region now lives in one province – Alberta. Throughout the region, urbanization has transformed what was once an orientation to rural agricultural grasslands. In other words, the concept of "the Prairies" no longer reflects the dominant way of life in this region.

THE NATURE AND STRUCTURE OF THE OLD WEST

Much of the Old West needs to be understood as rooted in the pioneer economy and as adjusting to its aftermath. In pioneer areas, people were sometimes referred to as "sodbusters" (van Herk 2001) and often settled without the right skills or backgrounds to enhance the likelihood of success. Voisey (1988, 33–52) has demonstrated that one of the major attractions of migration to the Canadian West was the prospect of land appreciation, which encouraged speculation. The assumption was that as a community matured, land values would rise and produce economic gain regardless of whether farming was a success. Voisey discovered townships in which half of the original settlers were gone in less than ten years, and only one-quarter of these settlers were left twenty-five years later. Transiency and mobility were much more typical than is often thought, suggesting that the optimism that was part of this settlement period was clearly countered by flux and change amidst challenges and difficulties. Thus, the promise of the West was experienced by people in different ways, and perseverance and abandonment were countervailing forces among the settlers.

McGinnis (1977) viewed 1936 as the apogee of the pioneer economy that had held for thirty years but then began to crumble. For example, in Alberta, since 1900, 14.6 million hectares (36 million acres) of land had been occupied for the first time, 1,216 grain elevators were built (an average of forty per year), and 105,550 rural dwelling units were constructed. By 1936, 63 percent of the population of Alberta was considered rural, and 52 percent of the labour force was actively engaged in agriculture. In the next fifteen years, there was a massive exodus from farms and villages (over 150,000 persons left), and the number of people employed in agriculture declined by 27 percent. Rather than view these agriculturalists as independent farmers (as Macpherson [1953] does), McGinnis notes that they were either marginal undercapitalized farmers or farm labourers who sought any means possible to supplement their meagre incomes as pioneers searching for cash. Farms were often too small and crops unpredictable. If families did not leave the farm, then their children certainly did in the form of surplus labour. Thus, while a large labour pool was needed in the initial settling of the land, the consolidation of farm size was largely the result of the inability of farmers to sustain themselves, with many having to leave. The Depression merely served as the catalyst to provoke an exodus whose root cause lay in an overexpansion of the agricultural sector (Burnet 1951).

As has been stated, Winnipeg was the gateway city to the Old West. In comparison to other cities in the western interior, Winnipeg was transversed by both transcontinental railway lines and, before amalgamation, as many as twenty-four railway lines serviced it (Friesen 1984, 275). Symbolic of its critical function as "bull's eye of the Dominion" were the Grain Exchange, the Grain Grower's Guide, the financial district (with its imposing stone structures), warehousing (particularly with regard to hardware companies like Ashdowns and Marshall Wells), catalogue goods (as represented by Eaton's), railroad marshalling yards with thousands of cars, and the arts and entertainment district. The intersection of "Portage and Main" was a locational coordinate well known to every westerner and represented big-city prestige in the form of banking, finance, investment, and wholesaling. The sense of Winnipeg's being a big city was reflected in the clashes between workers and large organizations that produced the Winnipeg General Strike in 1919 as well as in the prophets of the social gospel, such as William Woodsworth, who advocated a society in which the poor and disadvantaged should have an opportunity to succeed. Winnipeg may have begun as a hinterland city, but it grew to become the "Chicago of the North," with large mansion-like dwellings as well as acute poverty (especially among immigrants in the North End), suggesting an urban centre with typical urban problems. Winnipeg became the third largest city in Canada, and, by 1951, its population was larger than all Prairie cities combined.

Vancouver, because of its internodal capabilities as the terminus for the railroad and as a Pacific port, challenged Winnipeg's role. The opening of the Panama Canal in 1914 allowed Vancouver to be another outlet for Prairie wheat, with the result that it was no longer necessary to depend entirely on moving eastward from Winnipeg to Port Arthur and Fort William (now Thunder Bay) through the Great Lakes to the Atlantic. British Columbia was unique not only in having much more racial diversity than other provinces in Canada but also in having a working class even more strident than that of Winnipeg. Mining, forestry, and shipping were tasks that involved people working for large organizations in a situation in which profits were unpredictable and union solidarity was strong. Between Vancouver and Winnipeg, and particularly east of the Continental Divide, however, the West remained primarily a rural-oriented society in that residents either lived on the land or provided services for the rural economy.

TRANSITION FROM THE OLD WEST TO THE NEW WEST

The years between 1951 and 1971 form the transitional period between the Old West and the New West. Whereas agriculture had once defined the western interior and most people were engaged in it, the rural non-farm population and the urban population began to grow more rapidly during this period as people moved off of marginal farm operations (Hay 1992). In 1941, almost 60 percent of Saskatchewan's population and 48 percent of Alberta's population were farm-based;

however, by 2001, that number dropped to 13 percent and 6 percent, respectively. The farm population in Saskatchewan in 1941 was just over half a million, but that number dropped to fewer than 125,000 by 2001. In short, the agricultural transformation in Saskatchewan had a much more devastating impact on that province than the agricultural transformation in Alberta had on that province. Whereas, in 1931, two-thirds of the population of the Prairie West had been agriculturalists, by 1951 that number had dropped to less than 40 percent. On the other hand, the rural non-farm and urban population increased substantially. Whereas, in 1941, Winnipeg had a larger population than all of the other major urban centres in the region combined, by 1971, Edmonton had almost caught up with it, and Calgary was not far behind.

Because the Homestead Act had required that people settle on the land in order to own it, the Old West was characterized by a whole series of small towns strung together along railroad lines, with a grain elevator, a few stores, a school, and a church or two (Mackintosh 1934). There were 2,423 such villages strung across the region in 1930, two-thirds of which had fewer than ten stores (Zimmerman and Moneo 1971, 3, 28). Improvements in transportation (e.g., the automobile and highways) lessened dependence on the railroad and allowed some communities to play more of a retail function. By 1966, there were 11 Prairie cities, 164 trading communities, and 1,401 dependent villages in the region. Small communities had difficulty surviving and retail centres grew by servicing the farm community. Thus emerged small farm cities like Brooks, Stettler, Dauphin, Altona, Estevan, Kindersley, and Melfort, which consolidated smaller communities into larger ones. As farms became larger and schools were consolidated, and as transportation improvements continued to make longer trips possible, even these communities faced pressure from the increasingly dominant bigger cities. Many places that had once served as "hometowns" centred on schools and local businesses had become minimum convenience centres as busing took children to schools in larger centres that also had better shopping and other service facilities. Nowhere is this more noticeable than in Saskatchewan, where many places that had served as partial or complete shopping centres had lost that function. Whereas there were 271 minimum convenience centres in 1961, that number had climbed to 500 in 1995 as many communities lost their structural stability (Stabler and Olfert 1996). One of the indicators of this transformation was the abandonment of rail lines, which was the result of replacing grain elevators with centralized grain terminals owned by large integrated companies like Agricore. This process began in the 1970s and reached a crescendo in the 1990s with the abolishment of the Crow freight rates. Not only had rail service been discontinued in many rural areas, but railroad tracks were being removed leaving no trace of the earlier era.

The transition from the Old West to the New West took place over a number of years and was related to several important changes. To begin with, 1951 marks the first year that the size of the urban population surpassed that of the rural population. Thus began the continuing process of the region's becoming overwhelmingly urban (Lamont and Proudfoot 1975). From 1951 to 1971, the growth of Alberta's two major cities outstripped the growth of other Prairie cities, and this growth occurred primarily as the result of rural-urban migration from within the region. Between 1941 and 1971, the number of occupied farms declined by 41 percent, while the amount of land dedicated to farming increased by 11 percent (Gibbins 1980, 78–9), suggesting that farming was now becoming a highly capitalized business rather than a traditional way of life. Crop diversification was also increasing, and cattle production had become more prominent. Rural depopulation was encouraged not only as the result of the mechanization of agriculture, or because farms needed to become larger in order to be economically viable, but also as a response to the employment and educational opportunities of urban life (Weir 1972, 97–8). From 1941 to 1956, 79 percent of the 7,237 townships in the Prairie region lost population (Weir 1972, 96). And, of the population that remained in the rural areas by the end of the century, only about one-quarter of it was still engaged in farming as off-farm employment had become increasingly common (Stabler and Olfert 2002). Gibbins (1980, 93) argues that, by the 1970s, the sense of a distinct and homogeneous Prairie culture consisting of agrarians had been largely eroded.

Another factor in this transition to a New West was the crystallization of distinct provincial identities.[8] In spite of the fact that the Prairie experience may have bred a particular personality type consisting of courageous pragmatists and individualists devoted to hard work (Lautt 1973, 128–30), each province developed a very different political history. Born in the tough times of crop failures, market fluctuations, and the Depression, Alberta and Saskatchewan, in particular, developed their own traditions both of protest and of internal cooperation (Brym 1978). In Alberta, the emergence of governments led by the United Farmers of Alberta in 1921 and Social Credit in 1935 began a tradition of protest and alienation from central Canada. This tradition galvanized support against external control by using the provincial state as an instrument of power within a context of free enterprise. Using a somewhat different model, the people of Saskatchewan elected a Co-operative Commonwealth Federation (CCF) government in 1944, which expressed their alienation through a unique form of cooperation known as agrarian socialism (Lipset 1968). By the fiftieth anniversary of both provinces in 1955, each had already made its distinct political mark on the Canadian landscape through their respective divergent ideologies. The political dimensions of British Columbia and Manitoba were different yet again, suggesting that a New West was emerging in which political traditions and cultures demonstrated considerable variability in spite of whatever else they may have held in common (Wiseman 1996). Thus, while the Old West was divided into two regions, the Prairies and the Coast ("the West and the Far West" [British Columbia sometimes being referred to as "the West beyond the West"]), where wheat contended with lumbering and fishing, and Winnipeg and Vancouver were the major cities, the New West was becoming much more complex and was defined by increasingly unique provincial political cultures, all of which detracted from a sense of regional commonality.

A third factor in this transitional phase was the shift to new industries. If in the Old West the goal was to settle the West as an agricultural community, the transitional years sought to stabilize that community through various government supports such as the Canadian Wheat Board. But the New West experienced a shift away from agriculture as the focus moved to new nodes of employment based on resources and services. Nickel mining in Manitoba and potash mining in Saskatchewan are two examples of a new employment generator. The discovery of vast deposits of hydrocarbons in Alberta in the late 1940s started a process of development that slowly began to transform that province. Alberta also began to build on advantages that it had already developed in the manufacturing sector – advantages that Saskatchewan did not have (Emery and Kneebone 2005). The 1950s and 1960s, then, were stabilizing yet momentum-building transitional years, especially for Alberta, and they set the stage for a restructured West within Canadian society.

THE NEW WEST

Natural resources played the most critical role in reconfiguring the West. More specifically, the discovery of oil in Leduc in 1947 eventually completely reorganized the regional economy (Barr 1972) and gave

Alberta a strategic advantage over the rest of the West. While Leduc may have been the symbolic beginning of the oil boom, the full impact of that development did not begin until the 1970s, when the Organization of the Petroleum Exporting Countries (OPEC)-induced energy crisis led to a dramatic increase in oil prices. Thus, if the 1950s and 1960s were transitional years between the Old West and the New West, the latter begins in the 1970s, when Alberta took the momentum.

In Alberta, at the political level, the emergence of the New West is most distinctly linked to the election of Peter Lougheed's Progressive Conservative Party in 1971. Social Credit, which had been in power since 1935, had stood for a rural-based Alberta, and it came to power representing the interests of agriculturalists in a fight against eastern domination and big business. The long-standing premier Ernest Manning had led the province through the early years of the oil era but had now retired, and his party was struggling to find its way with voters who were now overwhelmingly urban. The election of the Lougheed government represented the rise of a new urban-educated voter who was middle class and whose goals resonated with the dreams of new elites who saw the possibilities for a different kind of Alberta. Lougheed's policies sought to capture more of the resource royalties for province-building, aimed to enlarge the petrochemical industry to capture more of the forward-processing opportunities from oil and gas, and also wanted to support the building of local capital pools and local entrepreneurship.

THE DEMOGRAPHIC BASIS OF THE NEW WEST

After the initial settlement period (1901–1931), during which Alberta's population grew tenfold in thirty years, from 73,000 to 732,000, the province experienced a net migration loss from 1931 to 1941 as the impact of the Depression, drought, and poor cash prices for grain led many to leave their agricultural way of life and seek new residential alternatives. However, in comparison to the other provinces in the western interior, which continued to lose population through out-migration in subsequent years, Alberta recovered somewhat. And, particularly after the Second World War, its cities became a popular destination for those leaving the land throughout the region. Therefore, while, in 1931, Manitoba had a similar population (700,000) to Alberta's (732,000), and Saskatchewan's was even bigger (922,000), by the 1950s, Alberta's population began to grow at a different pace from that of the other western provinces. At the beginning of the twentieth century, Manitoba had the largest population of all the western provinces. However, it was surpassed by Saskatchewan, whose population remained the largest of the western provinces until 1941, after which a decline set in followed by slow growth for the rest of the century. By the turn of the twenty-first century, Manitoba's population was just over 1 million (1.1 million), while Saskatchewan's population was just under 1 million. In comparison to Manitoba and Saskatchewan, the population of Alberta continued to grow, particularly after 1951, to over 3 million by the end of the century.

British Columbia's population size was similar to that of the other western provinces until 1951, after which it grew at an even more brisk pace than theirs. The westward shift of population became clear. Manitoba's and then Saskatchewan's population dominance at the beginning of the twentieth century was completely reversed by the end of the century, when British Columbia had the highest population (4 million) followed by Alberta (3 million). At the end of century the Canadian West was a very different place from what it was at the beginning of the century as the population balance shifted from the two eastern provinces to the two western provinces. Manitoba's and Saskatchewan's share of the West's population declined after 1951, while Alberta's and British Columbia's increased (see figure 2).

The primary reason for the growth differential among the four western provinces as the Old West shifted to the New West was that, by the 1930s, migration no longer served as a positive determining factor in the growth of Manitoba and Saskatchewan. From 1941 onwards, both of these provinces consistently experienced population losses through out-migration. A relatively high birth rate contributed to population growth, but this did not stop the leakage due to out-migration. Winnipeg experienced some population growth in the postwar years through immigration; however, generally speaking, Manitoba and Saskatchewan lost population in the domestic migration trade. In contrast, Alberta and British Columbia became major recipients of interprovincial migration, especially from Manitoba and Saskatchewan.

If Saskatchewan and Manitoba experienced little population growth, what accounts for the growth rates of Alberta and British Columbia? Three dimensions of population growth are relevant to this analysis: (1) growth by births minus deaths, which provides a rate of natural increase; (2) growth by interprovincial migration, including that between in-migrants and out-migrants, yielding a net interprovincial migration rate; and (3) growth through international migration.

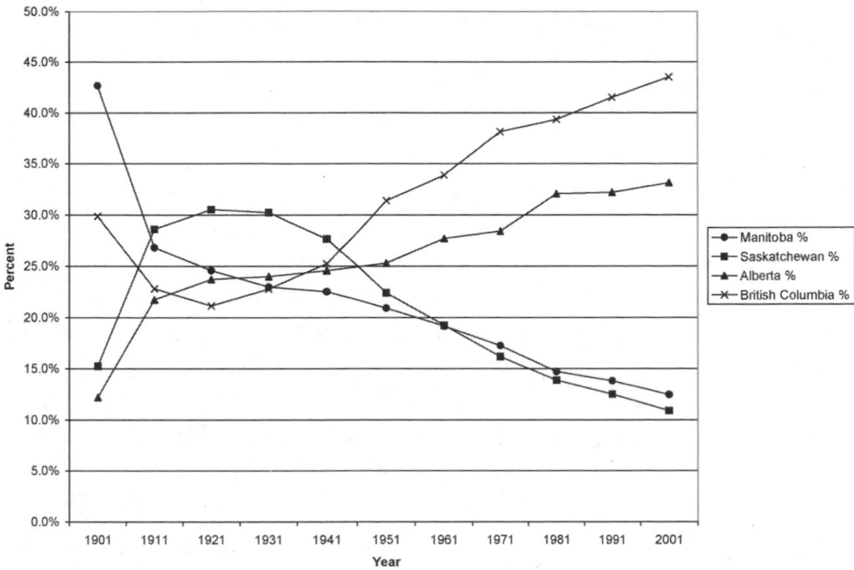

Figure 2 Population of Each Western Province as a Percentage of Total Western Population, 1901–2001

SOURCE: Census of Canada, 1931, Vol. 1, Table 1a; 1996 Census, Nation Series, catalogue #93F0022XDB96002; 2001 Census, catalogue #93F0050XCB01012.

One of the striking things about Alberta is that it has a long history of having one of the highest birth rates, if not the highest, in Canada.[9] One of the major reasons for this is that Alberta has been more likely than the other provinces to attract young in-migrants and less likely to lose young people through out-migration. In comparing Alberta's growth with that of British Columbia's, it is notable that Alberta's birth rate has always been higher than has that of British Columbia, and this has been the case since 1972 (see table 15). Furthermore, over the same time span, British Columbia's death rate has been higher than Alberta's. Since Alberta has a higher birth rate and a lower death rate, its rate and volume of natural increase is much higher than British Columbia's (compare the mean rates at the bottom of table 15 and total growth in table 16). Fully 55 percent of Alberta's growth was due to natural increase, whereas only 33 percent of British Columbia's growth was due to this factor (see table 16). So, natural increase has clearly been a more important determinant of Alberta's growth than it has of British Columbia's.

The second difference of note pertains to interprovincial migration. Alberta and British Columbia have the highest net growth of interprovincial migrants in the country. Alberta took in over 140,000 more internal migrants (of the more than 2 million migrants received) than did British Columbia in the thirty-year period between 1972 and 2002; but British Columbia's retention (net migration) was about 130,000 persons higher than Alberta's (see table 1). At that point, British Columbia had an edge in growth attributable to interprovincial migration. While Alberta was the destination for more interprovincial migrants (2.1 million) than was British Columbia (1.97 million) during this period, internal migration had a greater relative impact on Alberta because its population base (3 million) was much smaller than British Columbia's (4 million). When comparing the rates of interprovincial migration for the two provinces, one finds considerable volatility in both, and a high rate for one province is often countered by a low rate for the other province (see table 15). Both provinces had nine years of negative net migration and both had almost the same number of years (seven/eight) of net migration of over 30,000 (see table 3), but Alberta had even more volatility, so that peaks were higher (see table 2) and losses were greater than was the case in British Columbia (see table 5). Interprovincial migration has been important in both western provinces, but it has had stronger peaks and valleys in Alberta.

The major difference between the two provinces is in international migration for at no time in the last thirty years of the twentieth century (1972 to 2002) has Alberta ever attracted more international migrants than British Columbia, and, in fact, British Columbia has far surpassed Alberta in volume and rate (see table 15 and table 16). Almost 40 percent of British Columbia's growth has been the result of net international migration, whereas only 20 percent of Alberta's growth came from that source (see table 16). In real numbers, net growth from international migration was almost 700,000 people for British Columbia and only 280,000 for Alberta. The result was that, in 2001, 26 percent of British Columbia's population had been born outside the country compared to only 15 percent of Alberta's. Similarly, in comparing the percentages of visible minorities in the two provinces (a key reflection of the more recent immigration), in 2001, 22 percent of British Columbia's population consisted of visible minorities, whereas only 11 percent of Alberta's population did so.

From 1975 to 1982, British Columbia' population growth was more evenly spread between the above three sources of population growth, while Alberta grew primarily due to interprovincial migration and secondarily through natural increase (see figure 3). From 1996 to 2002, British Columbia lost population through interprovincial migration, with its growth being due primarily to international migration (see

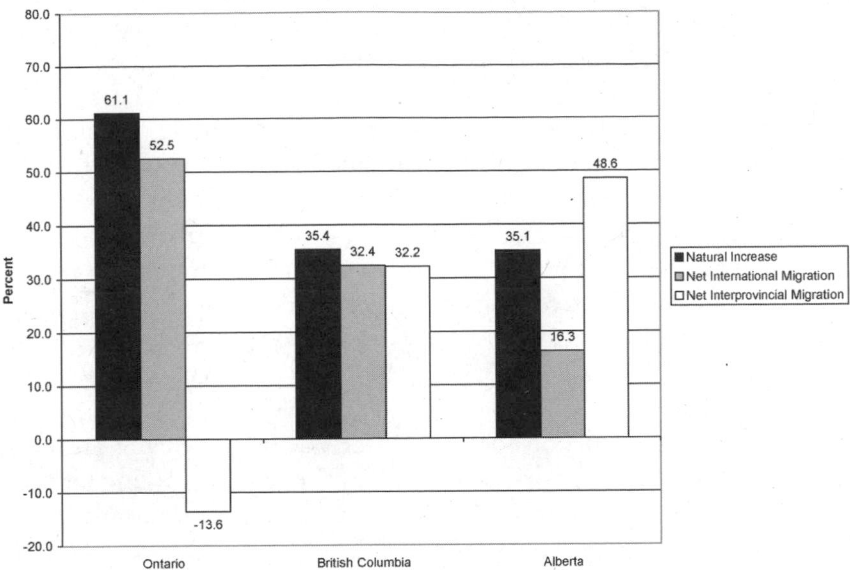

Figure 3 First Wave: Percent Contribution of Natural Increase, Net International Migration, Net Interprovincial Migration to Total Growth, Ontario, Alberta, British Columbia, 1975–1982

SOURCE: Computed from Statistics Canada, CANSIM Table 051-0004 and 051-0033.

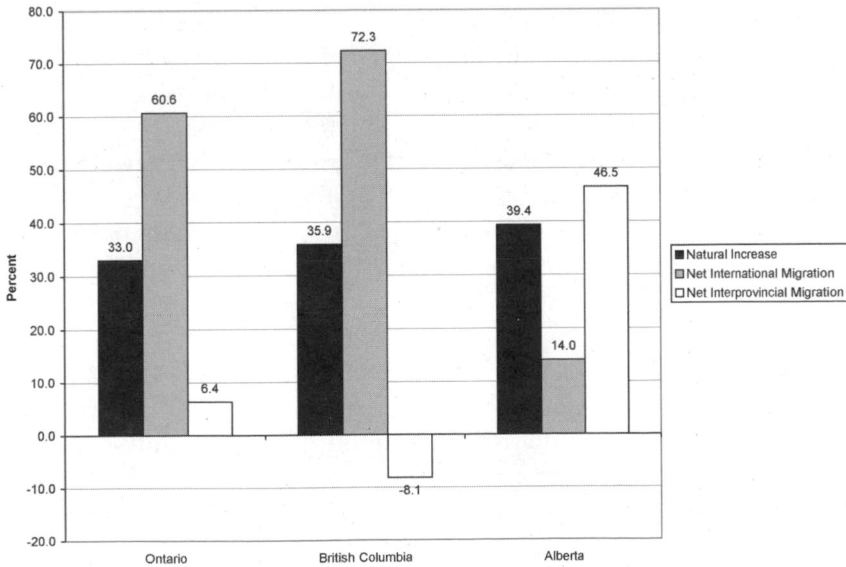

Figure 4 Second Wave: Percent Contribution of Natural Increase, Net International Migration, Net Interprovincial Migration to Total Growth, Ontario, Alberta, British Columbia, 1996–2002

SOURCE: Computed from Statistics Canada, CANSIM Table 051-0004 and 051-0033.

figure 4). International migration has never been as important to Alberta as it has to British Columbia. However, having said that, it is important to note that immigration from 1975 to 1982 did increase, with over 100,000 international migrants coming to Alberta. Almost as many immigrants also came to the province between 1996 and 2002. So it was not that immigration to Alberta did not occur but, rather, that it was proportionately a much less significant cause of growth than was internal migration. In contrast, in British Columbia, immigration (particularly the second wave) overwhelmed domestic migration, which suddenly showed significant losses.

In sum, if the balance of power in the New West has indeed shifted west from Manitoba and Saskatchewan to Alberta and British Columbia, it has done so with considerably different inputs. During the study period, Alberta and British Columbia stand out not only in the West but also within Canada as the poles of growth for internal migration. With regard to this growth, both provinces have shown considerable variation from year to year. However, what makes British Columbia different from Alberta is that it is a more prominent recipient of immigrants. This has meant that British Columbia's migrants are proportionately more likely to be international migrants, whereas Alberta's are proportionately more likely to be internal migrants. As we have already seen, this internal migration to Alberta involves a much younger population, and this contributes to a higher birth rate than is found among domestic migrants to British Columbia, who tend to be older. So when age and nativity are taken into consideration, the end result is a significantly different demographic tone in each of the two western provinces. The fact that Manitoba and Saskatchewan have not participated to a significant degree in either internal migration gains or immigration gains also contributes to major differences between them and the two far western provinces.

CHARACTERISTICS OF THE NEW WEST

What then are the characteristics of the New West? In addition to the demographic factors identified above, there are six characteristics that must be considered. First, the agricultural way of life continued its transformation through the unrelenting depopulation of rural areas and the emergence of agribusinesses, which had the effect of reorganizing rural life.[10] One of the oft-neglected elements of this shift is the social/psychological costs to farmers, who experienced considerable stress, discouragement, and pessimism about their future – all of which supported a continuing exodus from farms (Diaz and Gingrich 1992). Grain elevators were demolished and new grain bins were built, and these were no longer located in small villages on railroad spur lines. In 1933, there were 5,474 grain elevators in the three interior provinces. But, by 1981, that number had shrunk to 3,117, and by 2002 to 412 (Minister of Industry 2004, 257). Corporate farming and contract farming replaced the family farm, which was no longer considered a viable way of life. Intensive livestock operations (ILOs) such as mega-barns for hogs or feedlots for beef now became major industries in Manitoba and Alberta, respectively (Epp and Whitson 2001). Farm cooperatives (e.g., the Alberta Wheat Pool) were replaced by larger entities such as Agricore United; the Saskatchewan Wheat Pool sold shares on the Toronto Stock Exchange; and the United Grain Growers sold part of its stock to an American conglomerate. Integrated American companies like ConAgra and Cargill became dominant players in the new agricultural economy (Basran and Hay 1988; Warnock 2003, 312–16). By the turn of the twenty-first century, 60 percent of all of Canada's beef processing occurred in Alberta (primarily at two sites, one in High River and one in Brooks, owned by large integrated companies), with about 30 percent of that production exported to the United States. Symbolic of the transformation to a new agricultural economy was the dismantling of the old Crowsnest Pass Agreement in the 1990s, which had earlier been the guarantee that farmers could ship their grain out of the region cheaply. Yet, at the same time, the productivity of farms reached record levels, even though costs increased and prices fluctuated greatly. In other words, the former agricultural way of life centred on the family farm had been transformed, and the rural economy was being rebuilt around a new form of corporate capitalism.

The second characteristic of the New West is the fact that the population had not only become urban but was also increasingly concentrated in a few large cities. Portage and Main no longer served as the dominant symbol of urbanism, once known by every westerner. Smaller urban centres that had once been vital coordinates for a more heavily populated rural community had been superseded by regional retail centres with big box retailers. Regina and Saskatoon increasingly served as the retail centres for all of Saskatchewan, and Winnipeg became the singular focus for Manitoba.[11] But, above all, Edmonton and Calgary became the dominant cities in the western interior. Observers sometimes spoke of the Lower Mainland urban region of British Columbia and the Calgary-Edmonton urban corridor as the "economic tigers" of the New West.[12]

Increasing urbanization meant not only an increase in population in preferred urban destinations but also a general change in attitude towards cities and urban living. Rural living became increasingly integrated into the orbit of urban life (Smith 1972, 99). Rural areas, whether on the plains, in parkland, or on the rocky mountain slopes, were now considered important because of their recreational value for urbanites (e.g., in the form of golf resorts or country homes), and a process of gentrification began to occur in these areas (Epp and Whitson 2001). Rural areas also became part of urban regions as urban dwellers sought lower-cost housing or lower-density living environments at significant distances from big cities.

The third characteristic of the New West that needs to be considered concerns how the new, more complex economy contributed to the restructuring of power between provinces and how this was related to the restructuring of the labour force. While primary production in agriculture was still a critical lynchpin in the economy of the region, new activity in resource production transformed the region, as I have already noted. Oil and gas strengthened the economy of the entire region but created new divisions in which Manitoba benefited less than Saskatchewan and British Columbia, but Alberta, as the core location for the industry, benefited the most (Conway 1983, 179–26). Furthermore, the energy industry, in comparison to other forms of mineral extraction, required a very diverse and professional labour force, which, overall, provided high rewards. The demand for highly skilled and professional workers within the energy industry elevated per capita incomes, and the decision by many of the large companies in this industry to locate their corporate headquarters in the region, especially in Calgary, reaffirmed the growth of a well-paid upper middle class as well as a class of technical and managerial elites. Furthermore, the support services required by this industry provided employment in a wide range of areas, from retailing to leisure to finance. A multiplier effect became obvious, with construction and real estate leading the way.

Employment demands required a better educated labour force, which then also resulted in higher incomes. Postsecondary education became routine and was viewed as a tool of upward mobility. Cities, particularly the biggest ones, not only provided employment diversity but also higher incomes, which supported the growth of a large white-collar middle class (Statistics Canada 89–613-MIE–009). By 2001, at least half of the workforce over twenty-five years of age in the western provinces possessed at least some postsecondary education. Calgary led the way, with 61 percent of its labour force having that level of education, but

Edmonton and Saskatoon were right behind. About one-quarter of the population in the Calgary-Edmonton urban corridor had a university education. Thus, big cities represented higher levels of education and became even bigger because they were magnets for others who either had or were seeking advanced education. Calgary and Edmonton, in particular, became sites of capital accumulation, where strategic elites emerged and became strong regional boosters. Calgary had the highest percentage of high-income earners (over $100,000) in the country. Conversely, Regina, Saskatoon, and Winnipeg had a higher percentage of low-income earners, as did their respective provinces, indicating a clear hierarchy of income outcomes within the region. Economic power, then, had not only shifted to the cities of the region but also to the biggest cities of Alberta.

The fourth characteristic of the New West involves the beginning of the free trade era, which began with the release of the Macdonald Royal Commission report in 1985, and general trends towards globalization, which facilitated a more international orientation than had previously existed in the West. Prairie farmers, of course, were accustomed to the vagaries of international prices for wheat, but free trade exposed all aspects of the Canadian economy to the pressures of international commerce and the dispute-regulating agencies that had been established to sustain the rules for the free movement of goods. For example, in 1995 the General Agreement on Tariffs and Trade played a major role in cancelling the Crowsnest freight rate agreement because it was viewed as an unfair export subsidy. Agriculture was now subject to international rules as well as international prices. Beef and pork production were now increasingly for export to US markets, and American agribusinesses became more prominent in Canada. I later discuss how international oil cartels played a major role in revaluing western oil production. In the New West, lumbering and pulp and paper expanded from being solely a British Columbia industry to also being an Alberta industry. Communities like Hinton and Grande Prairie experienced growth in pulp and paper largely for the purposes of foreign export. Perhaps the most significant consequence of these developments was that the earlier east-west trade orientation of the western economy had been transformed into a much greater north-south trade orientation with the United States (Roach 2002).

This international orientation was also reflected in the fact that the urban region of the Lower Mainland of British Columbia became even more important as a destination for immigrants and capital from Asia, especially in the last two decades of the twentieth century (White,

Michalowski, and Cross 2006). Thus, Vancouver's role as "Gateway" to the Pacific Rim and Asia became more pronounced not just for Canada-to-Asia movement but also for the reverse. The result of this development was to minimize British Columbia's dependency on the Canadian economy while also making it a pivotal link between Canada and the Pacific. British Columbia was important as a transshipment point for the landlocked western interior, and it facilitated the internationalization of the region.

The end result of these changes was that the New West was no longer a simple captive to central Canadian interests, serving as its hinterland: now it was an actor in its own right within the international economy. Whereas Europe was once the main market for western Canadian production, now the United States became the most important export destination not only for hydrocarbons but also for agricultural products. And Asia had become a more prominent partner in trade. Of special interest was the fact that the vagaries of the petroleum industry had increasingly become driven by global forces, which gave Alberta a new role in the international economy.

The fifth characteristic of the New West that we need to consider is the fact that a new wave of immigration began to transform the West from being almost exclusively European and Caucasian into a region with much greater racial diversity. Numerous European immigrant groups were part of the original settlement of the Old West (often as blocs), and, in the early 1970s, their presence as a "third force" convinced the Royal Commission on Bilingualism and Biculturalism that Canada should be considered multicultural rather than bicultural. Western Canada had initially been viewed as a fragment of western Europe and central Canada. Immigrants from Russia and the Ukraine were initially viewed with great caution, and immigration from China and Japan was restricted. All of this changed dramatically beginning in the 1970s as the New West experienced a selective transformation through immigration from various parts of Asia. Whereas Vancouver was once an outpost of British settlers, by 2001 about 40 percent of its population consisted of visible minorities from all over Asia. This migration made the Lower Mainland of British Columbia considerably different from the rest of the West. However, the cities of the western interior also experienced some of the same migration, though to a lesser degree. Calgary's population consisted of 18 percent visible minorities, Edmonton's 15 percent, and Winnipeg's 13 percent. Regina's and Saskatoon's visible minority population was lower still, at around 5 percent each. Clearly, then, not all parts of the West were equally affected by this migration: the bigger cities were affected more than the smaller cities, and rural areas were not affected at all. In addition, the increasing urbanization of the Aboriginal population also added a new dimension to urban life, particularly in Winnipeg, Edmonton, Regina, and Saskatoon, that had not been so evident in the Old West. Thus, if the New West was increasingly defined by big city life, racial diversity was a significant part of that new world, but with uneven effects.

The sixth characteristic of the New West is that Alberta intensified its articulation of policies supportive of free enterprise and province building in a manner that distinguished it from other western provinces. While there were clearly common interests across the region,[13] differences became much more pronounced in the 1990s. For one thing, Alberta consistently elected right-wing governments while all three of the other western provinces had strong left-wing traditions and frequently elected left-wing governments.[14] As long as agriculture was the defining characteristic of the Prairie West, there was a deep sense of common interest, in spite of different provincial political histories.[15] Gibbins (1980) argues that the Old West was distinct from the rest of Canadian society because it was demographically and socio-economically different, but that, by the latter part of the century, it had become integrated into the Canadian fabric. As has already been noted, different strategies of province-building produced significant differences between provinces. These differences, in combination with inequalities of resources and other developmental advantages, produced a definite power differential among provinces in the New West, in which Alberta often had the highest profile.[16] In fact, while ideological differences between Alberta and the other western provinces were both implicit and explicit at various times in the past, the Klein government, particularly in its early years, embraced policies that clearly articulated a sense of difference from these provinces. The Klein Revolution, beginning in 1993, established, more clearly than ever before, the fact that free enterprise and conservative ideology is what made Alberta different: and it did this while the three other western provinces had left-wing governments.[17] In fact, the ideological stridency in British Columbia, which eventually led to the defeat of the NDP in 2001 (Carroll and Ratner 2005), played a major role in reinforcing the path that Alberta had taken. Thus, in the New West, Alberta became clearly distinct, and, with its economic advantages, played a major role not only in the West but also in national political thinking (Cooper and Kanji 2000).[18] While the political culture of each western province was different, Alberta stood in sharp contrast to these other provinces in the New West, as well as those in the rest of Canada, even though, over time, all provinces tended to develop some similar policies.[19] There was also often tension between Alberta and the other western provinces when, as a federal power broker, Alberta sometimes assumed the role of speaking for the entire West.

The Klein Revolution was exceedingly painful and, in many ways, debilitating in that it demanded huge cuts in the public sector (including health care and education), which had ripple effects throughout the province (Harrison and Laxer 1995; Taft 1997; Lisac 1995; Smith 2001; Archer and Gibbins 1997). One of the mantras of the Klein government was that it was attempting to create an "Alberta Advantage," meaning a favourable climate for business, by building on the natural advantages of agriculture, forests, and oil and gas but, it was hoped, moving beyond those staples through a free market economy. This was to be done by having a low tax regime, including continuing the policy of no provincial sales tax or payroll taxes, having less government regulation than other provinces, striving to eliminate the provincial debt, and being generally supportive of the entrepreneurial business community. Much of this was done with the clear awareness that the other provinces in the region (if not the rest of Canada) had higher taxes, provincial debt, and more government regulation. This neoconservative agenda, for the first time, made it explicit to a new generation just how Alberta was different from other provinces.[20] The goal was to encourage investment, to compete internationally, and to create more diversification in the labour force. This opened up the potential for persons who were sensitive to ideological swings in their own provinces to consider relocating to Alberta, where a conservative strategy prevailed. No formal estimate has been made of how many firms actually did move to Alberta during the Klein era, but there is no question that many did, particularly in its early years. Some companies moved all their operations to Alberta, while some only moved their registered office or home residence. Reports of condominium sales in Edmonton and Calgary often reflected this transference of assets through establishing residence in Alberta.

THE CONTOURS OF URBANIZATION IN THE TRANSFORMATION OF THE WEST

In the post-1951 period, the reshaping of the West was especially felt in very different patterns of urbanization. This provides an interesting contrast between Alberta and Saskatchewan, both of which became provinces in 1905. By 1951, they were relatively similar in population size, although Alberta had for the first time edged ahead of Saskatchewan. Both provinces had two major cities, although Edmonton and Calgary were slightly bigger than Saskatoon and Regina. Both provinces only had two other cities of over 10,000 people, and all were similar in size: (Prince Albert (17,000) and Moose Jaw (24,000) in Saskatchewan and Medicine Hat (16,000) and Lethbridge (23,000) in Alberta. Alberta only had one city between 5,000 and 9,999 people (Red Deer), while Saskatchewan had four cities (Weyburn, Yorkton, Swift Current, and North Battleford) that all had around 7,000 people. Thus, the majority of the population in both provinces was still typically "Old West" in that it was generally rural or living in small towns and villages.

By 2001, the situation had changed dramatically. Edmonton and Calgary had grown towards the 1 million mark and had spawned numerous satellite cities, which were also developing larger populations. For example, four communities around Edmonton only had around 1,000 people in 1951 but, after 1971, grew to form an Edmonton urban region: St Albert (53,000), Leduc (15,000), Ft Saskatchewan (13,000), and Spruce Grove (16,000).[21] In Calgary, the situation was even more dramatic as a number of communities whose populations were less than 1,000 in 1951 also experienced a population surge after 1971, resulting in an urban region consisting of Airdrie (20,000), Cochrane (12,000), Okotoks (12,000), High River (9,000), and Strathmore (8,000), all of which continued to expand during the first decade of the twenty-first century. In addition, while the old second-tier cities of Lethbridge (67,000) and Medicine Hat (51,000) had tripled in size, other small towns, such as Grande Prairie (37,000), Fort McMurray (41,000), and Red Deer (68,000), had grown from 1,000 or 2,000 to city status. Rural regional centres such as Camrose (15,000) and Wetaskiwin (11,000) retained their vitality and continued to grow slowly through this fifty-year period, and specialty centres related to oil extraction (e.g., Cold Lake [12,000], Lloydminster [13,000]), meatpacking (Brooks [12,000]), and tourism (Canmore [11,000]) grew more dramatically in the post–1971 period. In the under 10,000 category, other communities in the Edmonton-Calgary urban corridor, such as Lacombe (9,000), Innisfail (7,000), Sylvan Lake (7,000), and Olds (7,000) – and specialty centres in pulp and paper and mining, such as Hinton (9,000), Edson (6,000), and Whitecourt (8,000) – were viable, growing communities.

In sum, by 2001, Alberta and Saskatchewan both had two census metropolitan areas, but the difference in size between their cities was dramatic because Alberta's two cities were five times larger than Saskatchewan's (Regina and Saskatoon, which only had populations of around 200,000 each). Furthermore, Alberta now had eighteen other cities of over 10,000 people, whereas Saskatchewan only had six. In the 5,000 to 9,999 category, Alberta had twenty-seven communities and Saskatchewan had only four. While some of this growth in Alberta's communities was continuous over the fifty-year time period, most communities experienced more dramatic growth after 1971, suggesting that the last thirty years of the twentieth century were particularly momentous for Alberta with regard to establishing its new role in the West.

Urbanization in Alberta also needs to be juxtaposed with the City of Winnipeg, which was the third largest city in Canada in the early part of the twentieth century and played a pivotal role in the West for many years. Winnipeg was the largest city in the West until 1931, when Vancouver barely surpassed it in size. Even by 1951, Vancouver had only grown to around half a million people, while Winnipeg was 350,000 strong. In the same year, Edmonton and Calgary had considerably fewer than 200,000 each, indicating that Winnipeg's role in the western interior was still holding strong. It was not until 1981 that Calgary and Edmonton finally overtook Winnipeg's population, and this occurred primarily as a result of growth due to migration in the previous decade. This trend had been developing for some time. For example, Calgary and Edmonton had virtually doubled their populations between 1951 and 1961, while Winnipeg, though with a larger base, had increased by only 34 percent. From 1961 to 1971, Winnipeg grew by 64,000 in ten years, whereas Calgary grew by 124,000 and Edmonton expanded by 158,000. This trend became still stronger in the next decade (1971 to 1981), when Winnipeg grew by 50,000 but Calgary expanded by 223,000 and Edmonton by 245,000. Because of the differences in in-migration, by 2001, Winnipeg's population was under 700,000 whereas the two Alberta cities had about 1 million people each. Clearly, this stands as demographic evidence that urbanization had transformed the patterns established earlier in the twentieth century.

THE RISE OF EDMONTON AND CALGARY AS DOMINANT METROPOLES

It is also important to understand how Calgary and Edmonton grew in relation to each other. Calgary had been bigger than Edmonton until 1931, and, after that, the latter became progressively bigger than the former, with the largest gap between the two cities occurring in 1971, when Edmonton had half a million people, which gave it almost 100,000 more people than Calgary. Through the 1970s and 1980s, both cities grew at a similar rate, though there was still a significant difference between them in size, with Edmonton being considerably bigger. However, by the turn of the twenty-first century, Calgary had surpassed Edmonton in size. While both of these cities had risen to a position of pre-eminence in the western interior, by the end of the twentieth century, they had taken on very different yet complementary roles. It is imperative to understand the basis of these two different patterns of urban development.

As we have seen, Winnipeg was at one time the most dominant city of the western interior. It defined the Old West, which was structured on an east-west axis. While Winnipeg has continued to grow, Edmonton and Calgary have grown much faster because of their north-south linkages. These two cities surpassed Winnipeg in size and significance as the latter lost its pivotal function in relation to the agrarian economy.[22] The two Alberta cities now have the dominant position in the New West. In addition to the discovery of oil in the Edmonton region, which made a significant difference to that city, Edmonton's rise to prominence is also related to other factors, such as its position as "Gateway to the North" – especially between the 1940s and 1950s.

Edmonton's serving as Gateway to the North was partly related to the settlement of parts of the North (e.g., the Peace River region, which was also available for agriculture). Edmonton became significant because it was the source of administration, transportation, and supplies for the northern reaches of the province as well as the Northwest Territories (Wetherell and Kmet 2000). But the Far North had become important for defence reasons as well. During the Second World War, Canada, and particularly the North, played a key role in American defence strategies in relation to the threat from Japan (Hesketh 1996; Grant 1988, 271–73). The Alaska Highway (Coates 1985) made Edmonton the strategic point for the construction of the road, bringing millions of dollars and thousands of troops and civilians to build it (1,965 kilometres [1,221 miles] of the road was in Canada) in about one year (1942). The US military had established a series of airfields through the North to Alaska, known as the Northwest Staging Route. Edmonton was the most important airbase between Great Falls, Montana, and Fairbanks, Alaska, and its expansion supported a large Canadian labour force. Between 1942 and 1945, thousands of US troops and civilians made Edmonton their headquarters (MacGregor 1967, 264–66; Gilpin 1984, 178–80). The American construction of the Canol pipeline from Norman Wells to Whitehorse also enhanced the role of Edmonton as a supply centre and as a beachhead for the expansion of technology and capitalism into the North. The war became a stimulus to the economic development of the North, in which Edmonton had a strategic function. The role that Canada played as a buffer between the United States and Russia during the Cold War in the 1950s also enhanced the importance of the North, and Edmonton played a strategic role having to do with weather stations and radar lines (Grant 1988, 211–37). When these factors are added to Edmonton's important role in providing medical services and supplies to Aboriginal communities in the North, it becomes obvious that Edmonton's role differed from those of other cities in the western interior.

Edmonton's strategic role in the development of the North, emphasized by its geographically central location, meant that the city grew more rapidly than did Calgary. The arrival of a new transcontinental railway in Edmonton in 1905, the Canadian Northern Railway, ensured that Calgary's initial advantage of being located on the Canadian Pacific Railway line would not arrest its development (Smith 1984, 19). Edmonton was also the provincial capital and, until 1966, the home of the province's only university (Stamp 1984, 10–11).

The discovery of oil in Leduc in 1947, just south of Edmonton, affected the city greatly. Within the next few years, literally hundreds of wells were drilled within an eighty-kilometre (fifty-mile) radius of Edmonton, in what became known as the Redwater Field, the Pembina Field, and the Leduc-Woodbend Field. Instead of grain elevators and railroads serving as the basis for community formation, oil companies established towns such as Devon, Redwater, Swan Hills, and Drayton Valley, and Edmonton served as an operational centre. The discovery of the new fields in the Edmonton region also led to the transference of refinery capacity to Edmonton from Calgary, which the city has retained to this day. It has been argued that, during the 1960s, if it had not been for oil, Edmonton's population would have been half of what it became (MacGregor 1967, 295).

Edmonton then had a number of strategic advantages that Calgary did not, and these enhanced its opportunities for growth. Other major urban areas in the western interior, such as Winnipeg and Saskatoon, were not affected by their new-found roles in the same way as was Edmonton. The uranium in northern Saskatchewan, the potash in southern Saskatchewan, and the nickel in northern Manitoba may have provided an economic stimulant to those provinces, but, unlike what occurred in Edmonton, they did not support a large urban workforce.

Edmonton's growth solidified during the transitional period between the New West and the Old West (the 1950s and 1960s), which accentuated the difference in size between the two largest Alberta cities. By 1975, Calgary's population was 450,000 and Edmonton's was 540,000 (Statistics Canada, Cansim Table 051–0014 and 051–0030). However, over the next eight years (up until 1982), Calgary's population increased by 171,000 people (38 percent) while Edmonton's grew by only 140,000 (26 percent). Edmonton's population was now 680,000 and Calgary's was 621,000. After several years of flat growth, the populations of both cities began to grow again by the late 1980s through to the mid-1990s, when growth accelerated again beginning in 1996. At that time, Edmonton's population was 883,208 and Calgary's was 843,112. By 2002, the Calgary census metropolitan area (CMA) had surpassed Edmonton in size and exceeded the 1 million mark (1,000,165) as the result of a 19 percent growth rate. The Edmonton CMA grew by 10 percent to 991,000. Thus, from 1975 to 2002, Calgary more than doubled its population in twenty-eight years (122 percent), while Edmonton grew by 81 percent. In comparison, during the same period metropolitan Toronto grew by 83 percent, Vancouver grew by 84 percent, and Winnipeg grew by 19 percent. This growth not only catapulted the two Alberta cities into a position of dominance in the western interior but also moved them up in the national urban hierarchy to be the fifth and sixth largest cities in the country, with Calgary holding the fifth position. As is discussed later, it was internal migration that caused both cities to grow so rapidly, and it is what vaulted Calgary past Edmonton.

Calgary had clearly undergone its own transformation. The arrival of the railroad in 1883 solidified its role as a service centre for ranchers and new settlers, and its rail yards provided significant employment (Rasporich and Klassen 1975). Agriculture, ranching, and meat packing served as the basis for the local economy of the city that was not chosen to be the seat of government or the location of a university. However, just as the discovery of oil at Leduc was important to Edmonton, so the discovery of oil at Turner Valley (just south of Calgary) in 1914 set the stage for Calgary's position as the administrative centre for Alberta's oil and gas industry. Throughout the twentieth century, the infusion of capital and the importation of expertise to develop the oil industry in the western sedimentary basin went through Calgary. The Alberta Stock Exchange was established in the city to provide risk capital to a host of western-based resource enterprises, particularly oil and gas. Over time the Calgary became the command centre for the industry as it became the corporate headquarters for most energy companies. Companies that were previously located in Toronto and Montreal moved their offices to Calgary: these included Petro-Canada in the early 1980s, Shell in 1984, Suncor in 1995, and Imperial Oil in 2005.[23] Regulatory bodies such as the National Energy Board moved to Calgary in 1991. Another corporate relocation of considerable significance involved the transfer of the headquarters of the Canadian Pacific Railway from Montreal to Calgary in 1996. This corporate concentration in a city outside of central Canada, even though it was a city dominated by one industry, made Calgary stand out among cities in the West.[24]

Employment growth in both Calgary and Edmonton from 1994 to 2004 can be analyzed and contrasted in terms of sectors of employment strength (see table 17). In the ten-year period under review, Calgary experienced 19 percent more job growth than Edmonton. For both cities, employment in the services-producing sector far exceeded employment in the goods-producing sector. Within the goods-producing sector, Calgary has considerably more jobs in the resource sector, which is primarily oil and gas. Both cities have a similar number of jobs in construction and manufacturing (Calgary was considerably behind Edmonton in 1994 but almost caught up by 2004). Most of the employment in these two cities is in the services-producing sector, and business services has demonstrated substantial growth in both cities. Calgary has many more jobs in professional, scientific, and technical services (where the greatest growth has occurred) than Edmonton; however, Edmonton has the edge over Calgary in public administration, health care, and educational services.

An emergent industry sector for Calgary is in the field of transportation and logistics (warehousing). In 1974, the Province of Alberta purchased a controlling interest in Vancouver-based Pacific Western Airlines, which then moved its corporate office to Calgary (and later sold its shares to private investors). This was the beginning of the development of a strong airline transportation sector, which evolved through to Canadian Airlines and then WestJet, both of which became the nation's second largest carriers.[25] Calgary also took on a role as a regional airline hub in the 1990s, with the result that passengers were brought to the city from throughout the region for direct flights to Europe and many US destinations, considerably elevating passenger volume and international access. Notwithstanding Vancouver's prominence as an airline gateway to the Pacific, Calgary had the highest volume of passengers of any city in the western interior.

With regard to logistics, by the early years of the new millennium, Calgary had become a western distribution centre for national retailers. All forms of shipping, from trucking to rail to air freight, required a logistics industry to deal with the transport, storage, and distribution of consumer products. Within the western region, Calgary came to be viewed as a central location that could conveniently service all retailers. Companies like Wal-Mart, Canadian Tire, Sears, Staples, and Shoppers Drug Mart built huge warehouses in Calgary for this task.[26]

While Vancouver was clearly the biggest city in the West by the start of the twenty-first century, and possessed numerous locational advantages, it was noteworthy that two landlocked cities on the other side of the Rockies had experienced such dramatic growth. In 2002, Calgary supplanted Vancouver in terms of the number of corporate head offices (Statistics Canada, the *Daily*, 8 December 2003) and was taking on new roles based on its central location in the West. Its role as the administrative centre of a strategic resource also increased its global links, as evidenced by the differences in international air service between Calgary and Edmonton. Edmonton played a key role in servicing the North, which, due to its location, is not likely a function that will ever be lost. It continues its role as the service centre for the oil industry and has been particularly affected by the growth of the oil sands industry. All of these factors ensure that these two Alberta cities will continue to be dominant within the region.

Within the national context, Edmonton and Calgary had become arriviste cities (Hiller 2007). As upstart cities challenging the status quo in Canada, they possessed a brash tone, reflecting a new sense of power that was nascent and emerging but still somewhat uncertain. They possessed new capital pools with local, national, and international connections, and they had also developed labour pools of technical expertise not only for local consumption but also for export. In being arriviste, they were breaking out of their previous hinterland and regional role but remained considerably less dominant than megacities like Toronto. The resurgence of Edmonton and Calgary is one more indication of Alberta's changing role of Alberta within Canadian society.

CONCLUSION: THE ROLE OF ALBERTA IN THE NEW WEST

Whereas wheat played a key role in creating a sense of region in the Old West, oil and gas was key in the New West. If the Old West consisted of a homogeneous Prairie West and a marginalized British Columbia, the New West is made up of contrasting powerhouses in British Columbia and Alberta, with Manitoba and Saskatchewan in lesser roles. While British Columbia has been building on its strengths as part of the Pacific Rim, the collapse of fishing, limited employment in mining, and lumber export problems, combined with limits to urban expansion due to high housing prices and limited available land, created a window of opportunity for other jurisdictions in the regional economy. The dynamic created by expansion in the oil industry (particularly the oil sands) has supported Alberta as a new western alternative for investment, even beyond the energy industry.

As we see in this chapter, Alberta has been catapulted into economic growth. It has the most arable land of any western province, and it has a more diversified economy, even within agriculture, from grains to livestock production and processing. It has a rapidly growing population that, increasingly, has had an agglomeration effect on a wide range of services and manufacturing. Rather than being a limitation, its geographic position within the west has now made it a hub for the entire region. Its younger, more educated labour force provides a strong tax base of employed persons, many of whom are well paid. The growth of a managerial and technical class, and the profits produced within the region, has created an economic elite with capital and influence (Richards and Pratt 1979). Alberta's general prosperity, founded on the oil industry but having expanded beyond it, gives the provincial government advantages with regard to providing infrastructure and services that other provinces in the region do not have. Alberta has presented its political/economic policies as a differentiating factor that promotes stability, and it has increasingly taken on roles related to becoming a regional/demographic centre for the West. Since the 1970s, and in spite of periods of stunted growth, the role of Alberta as a magnet for capital and labour has intensified. Alberta clearly has come to play a pivotal, if not dominant, role in the New West.

The role of Alberta within the New West has also meant that it now has a different role within the country as a whole. Symbolic of how far the province has moved from its hinterland position is the fact that, by the late 1990s, Alberta was the single largest net importer of university students from other provinces as more people were coming to study there than were leaving to study elsewhere (Junor 2004).[27] The growth of a class of knowledge workers, demanded by an expanding economy, limited the brain drain that had previously occurred and replaced it with a brain gain or labour gain – another indication that Alberta's position within Canada had shifted.

When the wheat economy defined the region, the east-west ties required by that economy integrated the region and the province firmly into the Canadian nation, albeit in an unequal and dependent position. In the New West, however, with the existence of free trade and the rise of oil and gas, Alberta has resisted its old sense of dependency and feels a sense of empowerment. Alberta no longer defines itself solely within the Canadian context, from which its historic grievances had arisen, but now sees itself as a major player on the North American continent – one with global links. The fiscal policies of the Klein Revolution not only had an impact throughout Canada but also symbolized Alberta's entry into the process of globalization (Smith 2001). Thus, the rise of a changed Alberta has not only contributed to a New West but has also resulted in an evolving new role for the province in Canada and the world.

3

The Two Waves of In-migration

The twentieth century was clearly a lively period for the Province of Alberta as its population changed from being newly settled agriculturalists and those serving the agricultural community to being highly urban. The dynamics of power and growth that occurred altered the western region considerably over that time and changed the position of Alberta both within the West and within Canada. As has already been suggested, one of the pivotal aspects of this transformation was migration, particularly internal migration from other parts of Canada. The goal of this chapter is to describe and analyze the pattern of migration that contributed to the rearrangement of regional relations.

Alberta was well known for the rapid influx of people that occurred in the 1970s, followed by a reversal of fortunes in 1982, which led to a substantial out-migration from the province. This boom-and-bust phenomenon led some analysts to refer to being in Alberta as being like "riding a tornado" (see the National Film Board documentary entitled *Riding the Tornado*). After a decade of marginal population growth through migration, another influx of people occurred towards the end of the century. Alberta had experienced cumulative population growth for some time, but it was the last thirty years of the twentieth century, especially the period between 1972 and 2002 and the period between 2005 and 2006 (which was ongoing at the time of writing), that caught the attention of the nation. As noted earlier, my analysis focuses on the period between 1972 and 2002. What was the nature of this in-migration?

THE PRIMARY DESTINATION PROVINCES FOR INTERNAL MIGRANTS

In the Canadian context, it is important to note that internal migration is unbalanced. Some provinces consistently lose population through interprovincial migration, and only Ontario, British Columbia, and Alberta have had large positive net interprovincial migration flows, particularly since the Second World War. These three provinces received almost three-quarters of all interprovincial migrants from 1972 to 2002 (see table 1). Overall, Ontario received more internal migrants than any other province, but Alberta surpassed Ontario at two particular points: between 1979 and 1982, and between 1997 and 1998 (see table 2). Slightly more people moved to Alberta than to British Columbia during this period (1972 to 2002), but this was primarily because Alberta was a more important magnet than British Columbia from 1975 to 1984, and from 1997 to 2002. Thus, of the thirty-one years in my selected time frame, Alberta received more internal migrants than any other province for six of them and more than British Columbia for eighteen of them (and the trend continued for the next few years as well). Perhaps of even greater importance is the fact that, of the three destination provinces, the impact of in-migration was most strongly felt by Alberta because it had the smallest population. This is demonstrated by the ratio of interprovincial in-migrants to total population, which was highest for Alberta at .66, lower for British Columbia at .49, and lower still for Ontario at .21. When out-migrants are deducted from in-migrants, Alberta's net growth from interprovincial migration is particularly strong from 1975 to 1982 and from 1996 to 2002 (see table 3). Later, these are discussed as the two waves of in-migration.

What is striking among these three provinces is how interprovincial migration transfers ebb and flow with gains and losses; and, contrary to popular perceptions, this phenomenon is not limited to Alberta. For example, since 1972, Ontario has had the largest number of internal migrants of any province (see table 1), peaking at 108,000 per year and averaging 83,000 per year (see table 2), but it has also had twelve years of negative net migration, indicating that, at particular points in time, it has lost more people than it has gained through internal migration (see table 3). In comparison, British Columbia has had nine years of negative net migration, with a peak annual inflow of only 82,000, while Alberta has had ten such years, with a peak inflow of 114,000. The mean inflow for the entire study period is 68,000 for Alberta and 63,000 for British Columbia. Interestingly enough, periods of net loss for one province coincide with periods of higher net gains for the other two provinces. For example, in the 1970s, when Ontario was experiencing net losses of migrants, Alberta and British Columbia were both gaining (see table 3). Similarly, in the early 1990s, Ontario's net losses (though sometimes small) were countered by large gains in British Columbia. And when

Alberta was gaining population, either Ontario or British Columbia were losing people through interprovincial migration.

While, overall, Ontario is a major magnet for internal migration, its net gains and losses were also associated with what was occurring in Alberta and British Columbia. Note that while Ontario had taken in more than 2.5 million interprovincial migrants in this thirty-year period, its net gain when considering out-migration is much smaller than is that of Alberta and British Columbia, which each took in around 2 million internal migrants and had a higher net gain (see table 1). Thus, while Ontario accepted more interprovincial migrants during this period than did the other two provinces, its net gain was considerably lower in absolute numbers than was British Columbia's and Alberta's, indicating that internal migration has contributed to a westward shift of population within Canada. This evidence also serves as a corrective to the notion that only Alberta has experienced large gains and losses (see table 3). Outside of these three destination provinces, all other provinces registered net losses through internal migration (with the exception of Prince Edward Island, which showed a minimal gain). This focus on net migration (number of in-migrants minus number of out-migrants), of course, should not obscure the fact that Canadians are constantly moving to and from all provinces (see table 2).

The uniqueness of the two periods, which have been identified as particularly strong surges in interprovincial migration growth in Alberta, can be clarified by comparing the sources of population growth across all provinces (see table 4). In the first period (1975 to 1982), Alberta's in-migration rate is considerably higher than that of any other province, with most provinces exhibiting a negative rate. Alberta's rate of natural increase is also comparatively very high. In the second period (1996 to 2002), Alberta is once again strikingly different in that the rate of interprovincial migration is much stronger than it is in any other province, the rate of natural increase is the highest in Canada, and the immigration rate is much lower than it is in either Ontario or British Columbia, the principle destinations for immigrants. Overall, then, during these periods Alberta stands out among the provinces in having a high growth rate attributable to a high in-migration (internal migration) rate followed by a high rate of natural increase, with immigration being considerably less important.

MIGRATION EXCHANGES

The internal dynamic of migration refers to the transfer of people that occurs when units within an entity exchange persons from one unit to another. It is a form of trade in which there is often little equality. The *principle of migration exchange* is that, unless new people are brought in from the outside (immigration), gains by one unit can only take place because another unit(s) is losing people. Theoretically, the process of trading people could be equal; but, in reality, the internal migration exchange is a zero sum game in which some units gain at the expense of others. This implies that a province can only have a net gain if other provinces are losing population. These internal population shifts indicate that there must be catalysts to both leaving a province (out-migration) and relocating to another province (in-migration) that support this transfer of people. In other words, internal migration is a commentary on both the place of origin and the destination.

It is significant that, among the three provinces that have benefited the most from this population exchange, not only did other provinces contribute to their population gain but they also exchanged gains and losses among each other. Thus, in the late 1970s–early 1980s, when Alberta's population grew rapidly due to internal migration, Ontario actually had negative net internal migration and was a primary contributor of people to Alberta. By the mid- to late 1980s, when Ontario experienced high levels of in-migration, both Alberta and British Columbia experienced low levels of in-migration, or negative net interprovincial migration (see table 2 and table 3), and Ontario was a major recipient of that flow. In the late 1990s, when British Columbia experienced its highest levels of out-migration and negative net migration in years, both Alberta and Ontario demonstrated high levels of in-migration from that province. This reaffirms the principle that internal gains and losses are seldom equal, are episodic, and produce cycles of intake and, sometimes, decline as population exchanges rise and fall. When one or two of the three high-destination provinces experience high levels of in-migration, at least one of them shows either low net migration or negative net interprovincial migration, which affirms the linkages between them. Other provinces, of course, are also part of this migration exchange, but they are lower-order destinations and primarily experience negative net migration. All of this suggests that the peaks and valleys in the internal transfer of population is a critical indicator of the socio-economic changes occurring within any national society.

THE TWO WAVES

As has already been noted, internal migration is not smooth and continuous; that is, movement from province to province occurs in fits and starts, often with large gains followed by years of losses. It is this volatility that begs for an explanation and presents an interesting commentary on the dynamics within Canadian society. Nowhere is this better expressed than in the case of internal migration to Alberta. Detailed data on interprovincial migration were not available until the 1960s, and it was not until 1972 that they became available on an annual basis.[1] Prior to the 1960s, there was data support for the fact that, while Alberta gained population from other parts of Canada through the settlement period until the 1920s, it lost population through migration after that, even though it experienced net growth as the result of a high birth rate (Alberta 1961, 28; Government of Alberta, Graphs of Growth, 1961, 28; Statistics Canada 1971, catalogue 99–701, table 11 and table 14). This was clearly the case in the 1930s, when the Depression and Dust Bowl years drove many farmers from their land and from the region, and this trend continued until after the Second World War. In the 1950s, migration to Alberta rebounded, and while the first half of the 1960s showed that interprovincial migration was somewhat slower, it became stronger towards the end of the decade. All of this shows that, while Alberta lost population in the 1930s and 1940s as a result of the economic and agricultural crisis, the postwar years indicated continued population growth through internal migration – the majority of which, at this point, came from within the region (Manitoba and Saskatchewan) rather than from across the country (George 1970, table 6.2).

By the 1970s, the influx of people through interprovincial migration was exceeding the influx even of the initial settlement period. In 1972, the year we first have annual and more accurate data, Alberta had interprovincial in-migration of more than 60,000 persons for a single year, though with out-migration it only had a net gain of 4,000 to 5,000 people (see table 2 and table 3). From 1975 to 1982, in-migration to Alberta reached new heights in annual transfers of people, ranging from 81,000 to 114,000 people per year. Net migration through interprovincial sources reached unprecedented levels, peaking at 46,000 in 1981. From this perspective, the period from 1975 to 1982 can be identified as the first wave of interprovincial migration to Alberta. This influx, though, suddenly tailed off, with negative migration flows or population losses for the next seven years, beginning in 1983. One analyst noted that Alberta's motto at that time should have been "easy come, easy go" (Tepperman 1983). Thus, the beginning and ending of the in-migration wave is very clear and serves as demographic evidence of what is often referred to as a boom-and-bust cycle in Alberta. The total number of in-migrants for the whole wave from 1975 to 1982 was 720,000, meaning that .75 million people flooded a province with, in 1981, a total population of only 2.2 million. Even though out-migration involved 450,000 people, leading to a net gain of 270,000 persons, it is clear that the province had to deal with a sudden influx of new residents.[2] If we consider changes in the total population of Alberta during the eight years of the first wave, it grew from 1.8 million to 2.4 million, a 31 percent increase (attributable not only to migration but also to natural increase). In comparison, British Columbia grew by 15 percent and Saskatchewan increased by 7.6 percent in the same time period.

In the next thirteen years (1983 to 1995), instead of continuous large gains, Alberta experienced significant migration losses (such as in 1984 and 1987) and a few years of net migration gains in the 7,000 to 9,000 range; however, in general it was a mixed period of marginal gains and losses through interprovincial migration (see table 3). The years between 1983 and 1989 saw a particularly heavy period of out-migration from Alberta, with almost half a million people leaving, and three of those years saw an annual out-migration exceeding 70,000 people. Throughout this era, Alberta's population kept growing because of the birth rate, but it was most noticeable that the wave had ended and that some people had left. Although the net migration was lower (and even negative), it is also important to point out that, during this time, in-migration continued at the mean rate of about 53,000 people per year (see table 2), indicating that Alberta continued to be a migration magnet. It was just that more people were leaving than coming in.

Beginning in 1996, a new wave of in-migration began. This wave crested quite early at 86,000 in-migrants in 1998. The length of the second wave is open to some debate because the first wave was easily identifiable by its sudden end in 1982. The second wave, on the other hand, has been given a somewhat arbitrary end in 2002, based on several pieces of evidence. It is acknowledged, however, that a longer time-line is needed to evaluate the duration of this wave. In-migration was still strong in 2003 and 2004, but out-migration increased, yielding smaller net growth in those years (see table 2 and table 3). There is no ready explanation for this trend because the economy of Alberta continued to be strong. It is possible that push factors elsewhere might not have been as acute, particularly in the Province of British Columbia but also in places like Newfoundland, and, of course, some return migration also undoubtedly occurred. In any case, while there is no sense that the wave ended after 2002, there was considerably smaller incremental growth until 2005–06.

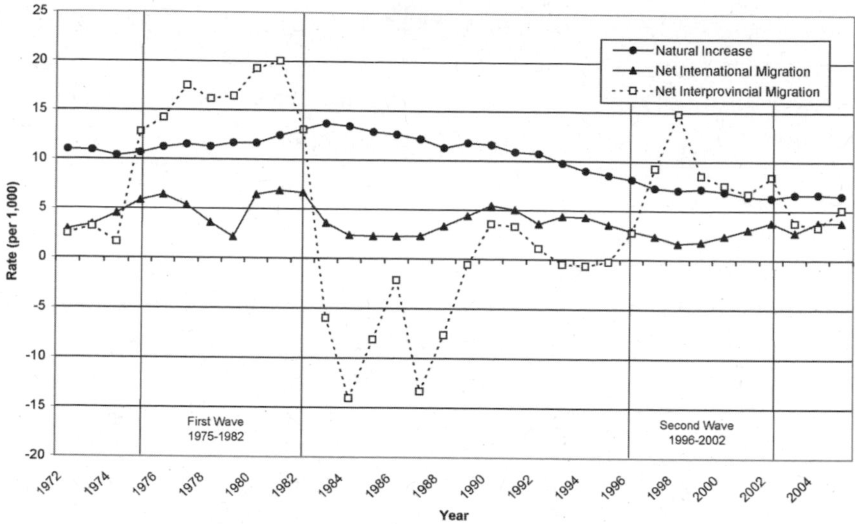

Figure 5 Rates of Natural Increase, Net International Migration, and Net Interprovincial Migration for Alberta, 1972–2004.
SOURCE: Computed from Statistics Canada, CANSIM Tables 051-001, 051-0004 and Annual Demographic Statistics 2004, Table 1.11

Until a longer time period has elapsed, the selection of 2002 as the year ending the wave can be justified from another perspective as well. The significant reduction in net interprovincial migration occurred at the same time that net international migration was increasing (see figure 5). In fact, for 2004, net international migration exceeded net interprovincial migration for the first time since the beginning of the second wave. Indeed, net international migration had exceeded net interprovincial migration through the entire interregnum period between the first and second wave. Even though the number of internal migrants was considerably larger than the number of international migrants, the turnover from out-migration increased the importance of international migration in net population gains for the province. In short, there is some tentative justification for identifying 2002 as the end of the second wave, a lull in that wave, or a shift to a different type of wave (as reflected by a spike in growth in 2005–06).

The two waves are shown in figure 6. The peak of the first wave in 1981 is certainly stronger than the peak of the second wave in 1998. However, if the wave were extended, the dramatic rise in in-migration in 2006 would rival the peak in 1981. If net migration is a possible indicator of the end of a wave because fewer people are coming in and more are leaving, then 2003 and 2004 display a definite drop in positive

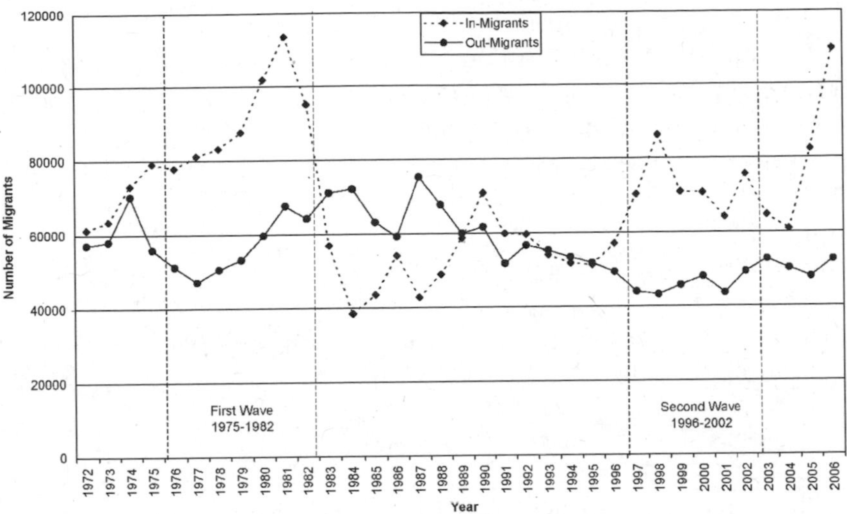

Figure 6 Number of Interprovincial In-migrants and Out-migrants for Alberta, 1972–2006
SOURCE: Statistics Canada, CANSIM Table 051-0012 and Annual Demographic Statistics 2004, Table 1.11.

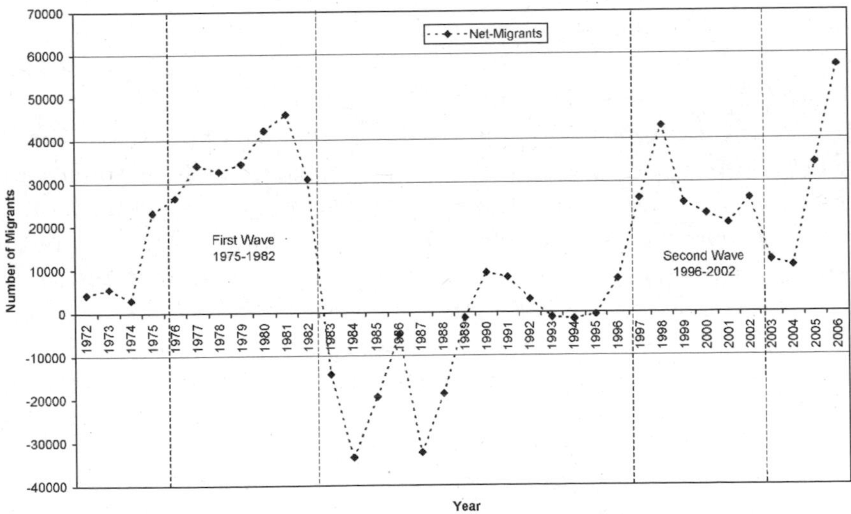

Figure 7 Net Interprovincial Migration for Alberta, 1972–2006
SOURCE: Statistics Canada, CANSIM Table 051-0012 and Annual Demographic Statistics 2004, Table 1.11.

migration flows – a significant drop below the levels of the first wave (see figure 7). On the other hand, the net migration for 2006 totally surpasses previous highs, which is very important. Figure 7 also clarifies the fact that what happened after the first wave had an even more important impact as almost half a million people left the province between 1983 and 1989, resulting in seven consecutive years of net interprovincial migration losses and either small net gains or small net losses for the next six years (until 1995). If we stay with the seven years of the second wave itself, then we see that Alberta's population grew from 2.8 million to 3.1 million – a 12 percent increase – the result of a combination of a high in-migration rate and a high rate of natural increase (see table 4). Again, in comparison, British Columbia's population increased by 6.2 percent and Saskatchewan's decreased by 2.4 percent during the same time period.

OUT-MIGRATION AND MOBILITY

At this point, a brief discussion of the meaning of out-migration is appropriate as it has already been made clear that, in the process of migration exchange, receiving units are also sending units. Figure 6 reveals that increases in in-migration tend to be followed by elevated periods of out-migration. This does not mean that those who leave are necessarily the same persons as those who come in. As I demonstrate later, relocation outside a province of residence occurs for a variety of reasons (e.g., education, family, work, adventure). It is true, though, that for at least some persons, internal migration means only temporary relocation, and multiple moves back and forth are possible. In fact, the ease of relocation within the country facilitates just that kind of short-term or medium-term move. So there is always an element of the population that is coming and going, especially young adults, for whom relocation is a lifecycle issue. As the literature shows, if you have moved once, the chances are great that you will move again, and migration itself conveys no implication of permanence.

The three provinces with the largest in-migration gains also show high levels of out-migration losses, which suggests a constant movement or churning of the population. There is no better example of this than Ontario, which has had not only the highest levels of in-migration but also the highest levels of out-migration (see table 5). Out-migration from that province was particularly high in the 1970s. Out-migration from British Columbia was particularly high in the mid-1970s and late 1990s. As we have seen, Alberta's out-migration was highest in the mid-1980s. Throughout our study period – 1972 to 2002 – Ontario had a mean annual out-migration of 79,000 people, while British Columbia and Alberta had an annual mean level of out-migration of 48,000 and

57,000 respectively. It was the substantial migration losses that Alberta experienced after the first wave that made the difference between the two western provinces as Alberta had a *net* gain of almost 350,000 and British Columbia gained almost 500,000 during the study period. During the same time, Ontario gained only 125,000 (see table 3). In other words, out-migration is as important a part of the migration story as is in-migration. This is because one province's losses are related to another province's gains. For example, Alberta had more in-migrants than British Columbia from 1972 to 2002, but its net gain was less than British Columbia's because of the out-migration that occurred after the first wave. To compare, Ontario had considerably more in-migrants than did Alberta during the same period, but it also had a considerably lower net gain because out-migration was so strong.

SOURCES OF GROWTH

When considering all of the different components of population growth, how important has interprovincial in-migration been to Alberta's growth? Figure 5 shows how important interprovincial migration has been as a component of population growth during the time frame of this analysis. What is striking is that the rate of net international migration has been rather stable; the natural increase rate also demonstrates no sharp changes (though it continues to gradually decline); but it is interprovincial migration that contributes to big swings in population growth. This is in sharp contrast to Ontario and British Columbia, where immigration played a very strong role in population growth during both waves. Figure 3 (first wave) and figure 4 (second wave) show that immigration was a more dominant source of growth for both of these provinces than it was for Alberta, particularly in the second wave, where interprovincial migration was either the weakest source of growth or even resulted in population loss. Ironically, Ontario had a negative interprovincial flow in the first wave, and British Columbia had a similar negative flow in the second wave. Alberta, in contrast, has grown primarily because of high interprovincial migration in both waves, which, ironically, given that the in-migrants are typically young adults, also contributes to the high birth rate as a source of growth.

This is not to minimize the role that immigration has played in Alberta's growth, for the province attracted almost 100,000 immigrants during the second wave. But in comparison to British Columbia (19 percent) and particularly Ontario (56 percent), Alberta only received 6 percent of all immigrants who came to Canada from 1996 to

2002. We also cannot discount the fact that immigrants might have moved to Alberta sometime after they had initially established residency in another province (secondary migration).[3] Nevertheless it is clear that Alberta's growth can be explained most satisfactorily as a result of domestic migration from within Canada. This phenomenon has a close parallel with demographic shifts in the United States as the places that have been attracting the largest number of immigrants are different from the places that have been attracting the largest number of internal migrants. Frey (1996, 1999, 2002) has demonstrated that the high immigration states (California, New York, Texas, New Jersey, Illinois) and their cities are quite different from the high domestic migration receiving states (Georgia, North Carolina, Arizona, Washington, Colorado, Nevada) and their cities. The fact that California became a major destination for immigrants at the same time that it lost more people than it gained through internal migration (Johnson 2002) raises intriguing questions about the nature of the link between these two forms of migration, especially whether there is a causal link between them. It is beyond the scope of *Second Promised Land* to evaluate this question thoroughly for Canada. However, it is interesting that Ontario and British Columbia were the destinations of choice for 75 percent of immigrants to Canada during this time period. The situation is considerably different in the case of internal migration. Alberta received about as many internal migrants as Ontario (about 25 percent of all interprovincial migrants) and more than British Columbia, which received about 17 percent of all such migrants. However, when considering the net internal migration that accrued to these provinces during that time period, Alberta's net growth through interprovincial migration was considerably higher than Ontario's (more than 100,000), while British Columbia experienced a net loss. Clearly, then, Alberta became the dominant destination of choice for internal migrants. Throughout this book I explore some of the reasons for this choice.

WHAT ARE THE CHARACTERISTICS OF MIGRANTS TO ALBERTA?

Statistics Canada not only has data on the volume of migration and its direction but also on the characteristics of internal migrants.[4] The most important characteristics for this analysis of the migration flow to Alberta are age, gender, education, income, and race. It is also important to know where migrants go in Alberta.

Age

The literature is clear that mobility declines with age (Dupuy, Mayer, and Morissette 2000, 6), and young adults, typically between the ages of 20 to 35, are the most likely to migrate. The analysis of migration to Alberta in terms of age supports this conclusion (Finnie 1999a).

The age profiles of migrants are generally similar in all years, though there is a small but interesting difference between the first wave and the second wave.[5] The peak years of each wave (first wave 1981, second wave 1998) have been analyzed (see table 6), and two-thirds of the cohort representing the first wave were between 15 and 34 years of age, confirming that young adults are the most likely to migrate. The cohort representing the second wave was somewhat less likely to be in that age group, although they were still the majority (54 percent). The most dominant category in both waves was the 20–to–24 age group, almost one-quarter of the first wave and one-fifth of the second wave. Interestingly, the next largest categories were those under 15 years of age, which, combined, accounted for 20 percent of the in-migrants in both waves. Thus, three-quarters (74.2 percent) of all in-migrants in the second wave can be accounted for by all those 34 years of age and under. This percentage is somewhat higher in the first wave at 83.3 percent. The pattern is clear then that people who migrate to Alberta are either young adults with no children or young families with small children. The fact that proportionately more of the migrants in the first wave were younger suggests that this group may have also been somewhat less established upon its arrival in Alberta (since it arrived in 1981 and the bust took place in the next year or so). This made it easier to leave, thereby contributing to higher levels of out-migration. The mean age of all Albertans in 1998 was 34.6 years, and the mean age for all Canadians was 36.8 years, so it is intriguing to know that interprovincial migrants were much younger, with a mean age of 28.5, with migrants to Alberta being younger still at 27.3 years. Migrants were much younger than non-migrants, and migrants to Alberta were younger than other interprovincial migrants in Canada. Clearly, this migration played a huge role in making Alberta the youngest province in Canada. The median age in Alberta was 35 in 2001, which was about two years lower than that in the next youngest province and 2.6 years younger than the national median age.

In comparison to in-migrants, out-migrants were somewhat more likely to be over age 35 (see table 6). A higher percentage of the in-migrants in 1998 (25.9 percent) were over 35 than was the case in 1981 (16.6 percent), and the same pattern held for out-migrants in 1998 (29.9 percent) compared to 1981 (22.3 percent). Why in-migrants and out-migrants should be somewhat older in 1998 is unclear. One possible explanation is that in-migrants in the second wave knew that the Alberta economy required a skilled labour force, and such persons were more likely to be a bit older, or perhaps they were surplus skilled labour in their region of origin. It is also possible that there were more employee transfers in the second wave, although we have no way of knowing that for certain. But in both years, out-migrants tended to be older than in-migrants. This may be a reflection of the fact that some of these out-migrants were also in-migrants and were now returning or relocating elsewhere as older people (even if only by a year or two). It is also clear from the "net exchange" column that, in the first wave, Alberta had a net loss of those over 55; however, the same pattern does not hold for the second wave. Whereas in the first wave, Alberta's largest gain was among young adults (between 15 and 25), in the second wave, the gain was distributed more among all age groups, including older adults. This was confirmed by our interviews, which found that many older adults had come to settle in Alberta because their children had previously settled here. This, of course, does not change the observation that the major contribution of the net exchange comes from those under 35 years of age.

Another interesting question is whether there are any differences in the ages of migrants from different provinces (see table 7). Some significant observations stand out. First, the Atlantic provinces provide a significantly higher proportion of out-migrants to Alberta in the 20-to-29-year-old category than does any other province. This might be a commentary on the job market for young people in those provinces, but it is also likely to be due to the fact that younger people are more willing than older people to migrate over greater distances, especially when it is at their own expense. The corollary of this observation is that provinces closer to Alberta are somewhat more likely to attract people beyond the young adult years. Second, when we compare the 40-to-49-year age category among all provinces, we see that the provinces with the largest populations (British Columbia, Ontario, and Quebec) provide the greatest share of that age category to Alberta. Migrants from these provinces include those who are older and are perhaps more likely to have been transferred by their employers or who have job experience that makes the move beneficial. While the numbers are not high, migrants to Alberta who are over 70 are more likely to be from Quebec than from any other province. In fact, migrants to Alberta who are over 55 are more likely to be from Quebec or from the provinces to the west of Quebec than from the Maritime provinces. It is likely that older people moving to Alberta may be going to join their children who moved there earlier. Overall, the net gain to Alberta is highest in the 20–to–24-year age group and next highest in the 25–to–29-year age group, confirming the importance of the in-migration of younger people to the province.

Gender

To the extent that some people may view Alberta as a resource- driven hinterland, one would expect that more males would be drawn to the province than females. The sex ratios of in-migrants to Ontario and British Columbia were calculated, and indeed the sex ratios of migrants to Alberta were higher (data not shown). For Alberta, table 8 shows that, in the first wave, the sex ratio averaged 117.5, meaning that men were much more strongly represented in the migration stream (in a sex ratio, any number over 100 means that men are overrepresented). In the second wave, the ratio was reduced to 110.9, meaning that men were overrepresented but considerably less so than was the case during the first wave. The implication is that men were somewhat more likely to migrate to Alberta than women, which confirms a point already known in the literature about the greater male disposition to migrate. There is no ready explanation for variations in the sex ratio from year to year, except perhaps to suggest that, in the peak years of in-migration, the sex ratio was higher because, when in-migration increased, it was men who were quickest to decide to relocate. Note, however, that men were more likely to migrate interprovincially than were women in Canada as a whole (see table 8, column 3). The sex ratio of out-migrants from Alberta was also over 100 (110.9 in the first wave and 106.7 in the second wave) but was less than the ratio for in-migrants. In short, the overall contribution of in-migration to Alberta increased the proportion of men, which created a more equal gender balance than elsewhere in Canada. The national sex ratio in Canada in 2001 was 96.1, and Alberta had the most even sex ratio in the country at 99.9 (compare Ontario at 95.6 and British Columbia at 96.5). Note also that, particularly in the peak years of each wave, the sex ratio of Alberta migrants is elevated in comparison to those of other Canadian migrants. Thus it seems that men were somewhat more likely to be drawn by the opportunities in Alberta than were women.[6]

Another measure of gender and migration uses census data based on province of residence five years ago in 1981 and 2001, respectively – roughly comparable with the first and second waves (see table 10). Again, the striking thing is that the sex ratio of the first wave (115.7) is much higher than that of the second wave (105.9) regardless of the former province of residence. The only provinces of origin that do not have a lower sex ratio in the second wave are Prince Edward Island and British Columbia. Overall, though, males were more likely to come to Alberta in the first wave than in the second wave, and, in the case of one province, Saskatchewan, more women moved to Alberta than men. Distance also seems to be a factor that influences the likelihood of male migration. The sex ratio from the Atlantic provinces is particularly strong in both waves, even though it is somewhat reduced in the second wave. The decline in the sex ratio of migrants from Quebec, Ontario, and Manitoba from the first to the second wave is quite dramatic because it was high in the former (as high as 126) and was much closer to equality (around 104) in the latter. The sex ratio of Saskatchewan and British Columbia migrants was much closer to being equal in both the first and second waves, even though British Columbia's ratio increased somewhat in the second wave.

To sum up, interprovincial migrants to Alberta were somewhat more likely to be men when compared to the overrepresentation of women in the total Canadian population (see table 9). Migrants who travelled a longer distance in both waves were even more likely to be men, although this was attenuated somewhat in the second wave. The sex ratios were higher even from the neighbouring provinces but were more likely to be lower in the second wave from Quebec westward. When combining these observations with the results of our analysis of gender, the migrants in the second wave were somewhat older and less male dominant (i.e., they constituted a population somewhat closer to the norm).

Foreign-born and Visible Minorities

Interestingly, 9.8 percent of all interprovincial migrants to Alberta are foreign born, which of course means that an overwhelming 90 percent of all migrants are native born. Among foreign-born migrants who were interprovincial migrants in Canada in 2001, 18.9 percent moved to Alberta. Since Alberta received 21 percent of all interprovincial migrants, this means that the foreign born were somewhat underrepresented in the migration exchange. In contrast, British Columbia was overrepresented in the migration exchange of this group in that it received 23.6 percent of these migrants while receiving 19.6 percent of all migrants. British Columbia, then, had a somewhat stronger pull among foreign-born interprovincial migrants than did Alberta. In comparison, Ontario, as an internal destination for foreign-born interprovincial migrants, was even stronger at 39.2 percent of all such migrants, which considerably overrepresents Ontario's share of 25.7 percent of all interprovincial migrants. These three provinces together account for over 80 percent of all foreign-born interprovincial migrants, but Ontario plays a much more dominant role than the other two. In the exchange of foreign-born persons between provinces, Ontario is the preferred destination, followed by British Columbia and then Alberta.

Only 6.9 percent of all interprovincial migrants to Alberta were visible minorities. Of all visible minorities who were interprovincial migrants, Alberta received 17.6 percent, whereas it received 21 percent of all interprovincial migrants. On the other hand, British Columbia was again overrepresented in this category as it received 24 percent of all visible minority interprovincial migrants. In the migration exchange between Alberta and British Columbia, visible minorities were weakly represented in the move to Alberta and somewhat more strongly represented in the move to British Columbia, but visible minorities played a very minor role in the migration flow. So in the interprovincial migration trade, Alberta was less likely than British Columbia to receive both foreign-born and visible minorities. But again, the difference with Ontario is striking as that province received 41.6 percent of all visible minority interprovincial migrants, which overrepresents its share of all interprovincial migrants (25.7 percent).

Another way of looking at this involves examining the destinations of native-born interprovincial migrants. Ontario received 24.5 percent of all native-born interprovincial migrants, which is roughly equivalent to its share of all migrants. British Columbia, on the other hand, received less (15.6 percent) than its share (19.6 percent), while Alberta received more (28.1 percent) than its share (21 percent). The evidence is clear that, while these three provinces are destinations for interprovincial migration, between 1996 and 2001 Alberta was more attractive for native-born migrants, while Ontario and British Columbia were more attractive for interprovincial migrants who were foreign born and visible minorities.

When foreign-born visible minority populations are considered, Alberta is less likely than is British Columbia to have such persons who migrated to Canada since 1991. In fact, when considering the raw numbers, the difference between the two provinces is not even close. However, when the proportion of the total provincial population is considered, foreign-born visible minorities who are interprovincial migrants to Alberta are much higher only if these migrants immigrated to Canada between 1991 and 1996. This suggests that there was some *secondary migration* from other provinces to Alberta in the post-1996 period from among those who immigrated to Canada earlier in the decade. However, foreign-born migrants were a much smaller proportion (9.8 percent) of Alberta's interprovincial gain as about 90 percent of all of migrants were native born. Thus, while some secondary migration contributed to Alberta's growth, direct immigration to Alberta appears to have been a more important source of the province's growth than was the secondary migration of recent immigrants. Overall, however, the internal migration of native-born migrants was the most important source of Alberta's growth during this period.

Education

The Public Use Microdata File, using a 10 percent sample, provides some indication of the educational level of interprovincial migrants. The question is whether migrants are better educated than those already resident in the province. We can begin by looking at those with university degrees: 15 percent of the Canadian population has university degrees, but 25 percent of all interprovincial migrants had university degrees. This suggests that completed advanced postsecondary education fosters migration. At the other end of the spectrum, those who have less than a high school diploma constitute 33 percent of the Canadian population (persons 15 years of age and over), but only 22 percent of interprovincial migrants are in that category. So, when we compare interprovincial migrants with the national population, the differences are particularly dramatic at the lowest and highest levels of education. There were few differences at mid-range levels of education or in the trades, but the best educated were much more likely to migrate interprovincially, while the lowest educated were least likely to do so.

However, when only interprovincial migrants to Alberta are examined, a somewhat different picture emerges. Alberta was more likely to attract people with less than a high school education as well as those with only a high school education or trade school education. Persons with a university degree were underrepresented in the migration pool to Alberta, which suggests that there was a strong demand for semi-skilled and skilled labour. This would be consistent with the need for skilled labour in construction and workers in retailing and services. Trade school education would be an especially desirable preparation for such a move. It is also possible that young adult migrants completed their education in Alberta, to which postsecondary educational institutions operating at full capacity at least partially attested. The well educated were clearly also in demand and were part of the migration stream, something that shows up in nuanced differences in the migration exchange from different regions. For example, migrants from Newfoundland were more likely to have less than a high school education, while migrants from Ontario were more likely to be the most highly educated people.

Income

In general, around 80 percent of all interprovincial migrants in Canada, including those going to Alberta, had individual incomes below \$50,000. Since these data are obtained from those who migrated in the five years previous to 2001, they tend to support the assumption that most interprovincial migrants are not likely to be persons who have been transferred by employers and compensated accordingly; rather, they tend to support the assumption that most of these migrants arrive looking for work and receive low pay, at least in the initial years.

The incomes of interprovincial migrants can be compared both in terms of size of income and source of income. The problem with the income data is that they do not reflect "a before-and-after" scenario; that is, we cannot use census data to tell what the income of an interprovincial migrant was before the move and after the move. The data that are available only tell the income level after the migration of an interprovincial migrant, which makes it impossible to tell whether migration produced an increase in income. In general, the income profile of these migrants varies little from that of the general provincial population. Migrants to Alberta are somewhat overrepresented in the \$30,000-to-50,000 category and slightly underrepresented in the higher-income categories. By comparison, interprovincial migrants to British Columbia are slightly overrepresented in the income range above \$90,000 and slightly underrepresented in the lower-income ranges, suggesting that that province is somewhat less likely to attract low-income persons and somewhat more likely to attract high-income persons (who are also undoubtedly older). Again, by comparison, interprovincial migrants to Saskatchewan had lower income levels after migration than did migrants to either Alberta or British Columbia.

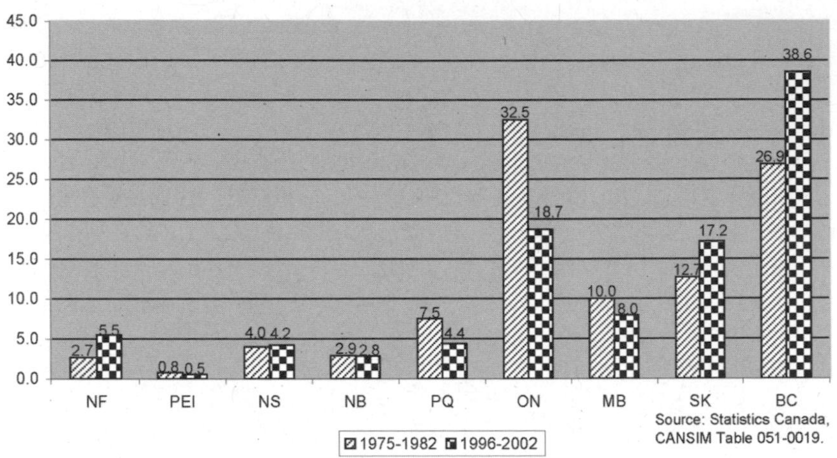

Figure 8 Percent Contribution to Alberta's Internal Migration Growth by Province of Origin, 1975–1982 and 1996–2002

The most striking thing in the comparison of source of income is that interprovincial migrants to Alberta receive a smaller share of their income from transfer payments than do migrants to the other two provinces. Interprovincial migrants in Alberta receive 83.2 percent of their family incomes from wages and employment, whereas only 74.5 percent and 70.8 percent of migrants to Saskatchewan and British Columbia, respectively, receive their income from this source. One possible explanation for this may be that British Columbia attracts more seniors, who receive government transfer payments. A possible but unproven explanation for Saskatchewan may be that interprovincial migrants to that province may require income supports due to the absence of adequate employment or to living in a lower-wage environment. In any case, migrants to Alberta are less likely to depend on transfer payments, which suggests that migrants move to Alberta for the work opportunities.

Province of Origin of Alberta In-migrants

Where are people who are migrating to Alberta coming from? Figure 8 illustrates how much each province contributed to the growth of Alberta in each wave. It is noteworthy that Ontario and British Columbia have contributed approximately three-fifths of the growth in each wave, and their shifting roles in these waves is particularly striking. In the first wave, Ontario (228,000) is the largest contributor (33 percent) to Alberta's growth, but in the second wave that number drops to 90,000 and the proportion drops to 19 percent (see table 11). This is a massive reduction, in absolute numbers, of 138,000 people. The total number of migrants to Alberta is smaller in the second wave than in the first wave, so it is interesting that the total number of migrants from British Columbia to Alberta is roughly similar in absolute numbers in both waves. However, what is significant is that British Columbia reverses position with Ontario in terms of its proportional contribution to Alberta's growth. In the first wave, British Columbia (188,000) was second to Ontario, contributing 26.9 percent of all in-migrants, whereas in the second wave, British Columbia (185,000) was not only higher than Ontario (90,000) but dramatically higher, with a spread of twenty percentage points to 39 percent of all migrants (see table 10). When we examine the absolute numbers, the major difference between the two waves is that, in the first wave, Ontario contributed many more migrants to Alberta than it did in the second wave. In fact, 63 percent of the decrease in total migrants from the first to second wave can be accounted for by the reduction in migrants from Ontario.

It might be expected that Quebec, being Canada's second most populous province, would have played a more major role in migration to Alberta, at least in absolute numbers. In reality, the evidence shows that when Quebecers left their province, they were more likely to move to Ontario; and about two-thirds of out-migrants did just that during the time of the two waves (see table 10). While language and political factors may have reduced the out-migration of francophones, these same factors served as a catalyst to out-migration among anglophones (although francophones also migrated to Alberta). The neighbouring province of Ontario provided a convenient option for those who did migrate but who wanted to be closer to Quebec. Other provinces were only secondary destinations, though it is interesting that, for Quebecers who relocated to a province other than Ontario, Alberta was the second destination of choice in the first wave and was a close third to British Columbia in the second wave.

The three provinces with the largest populations (Ontario, Quebec, and British Columbia) have each had a different impact on migration to Alberta. However, less populated and/or smaller provinces have also made an important contribution to interprovincial migration to Alberta. Alberta's closest neighbour to the east, Saskatchewan, has always been an important place of origin for Alberta's growth by migration, even before the current study period. Saskatchewan supplied over 80,000 migrants in each wave, though that contribution is proportionately more important in the second wave (from 13 percent to 17 percent; see table 10 and figure 8). The other regional province with which Alberta has had strong ties is Manitoba, and what is striking is that this province provided many more people to Alberta in the first wave (70,000) than it did in the second wave (38,000), but its proportional contribution to Alberta's in-migration growth was only slightly smaller in each wave (going from 10 percent to 8 percent). It is also interesting to note that Alberta is the second most popular destination (Ontario is first) for migrants from the Atlantic provinces, being considerably more popular than British Columbia. The most dramatic shift between the two waves, however, involves the substantial increase of migrants to Alberta from Newfoundland. About 8,000 more migrants came to Alberta from that province in the second wave (27,000) than did in the first, and Newfoundland's proportion of the total in-migration increased to almost 6 percent. Largely because of this increase of in-migrants from Newfoundland, the proportion of migrants to Alberta from the Atlantic provinces increased from 10 percent in the first wave to 13 percent in the second.

When people from a particular province decide to migrate to another province, where does Alberta stand in the choice hierarchy? During the first wave, Alberta was the most dominant choice of migrants from all provinces from Ontario west to British Columbia (see table 11; see table 10 for the raw data). Alberta's two neighbouring provinces, British Columbia and Saskatchewan, sent almost 50 percent of their out-migrants to Alberta, while Manitoba and Ontario sent about 30 percent, and the eastern provinces (from Quebec east) contributed around 16 percent of their interprovincial migrants to Alberta. In the second wave, Alberta slipped to third place for migrants from Ontario but still remained the most popular choice for Saskatchewan, Manitoba, and British Columbia. In both waves, more Atlantic migrants chose Ontario than any other province, as did most Quebec migrants. It is interesting that, when we compare Alberta with British Columbia as ranked choices, we see that, in both waves, British Columbia was slightly more likely to be the destination for people from Ontario and Quebec but that, for people from all other provinces, the destination was most likely to be Alberta.

Furthermore, in spite of the fact that, overall, the first wave was much stronger than the second wave, the proportion of domestic migrants who chose Alberta had increased in all provinces except Ontario and Quebec (see table 11). This helps to explain why people in Atlantic Canada had the sense that more of their people were going to

Alberta than ever before. In addition, the fact that more Saskatchewan residents were choosing Alberta in the second wave is also related to the drop in British Columbia's attractiveness as a possible destination during that time period.

Destinations in Alberta

Where in Alberta did migrants settle? What destinations were chosen most often? Again, a snapshot approach (1981 and 2001) needs to be used. This, of course, does not give any indication of whether in-migrants tried more than one destination in the province but, rather, simply indicates where they were settled at a particular point in time. However, in the two years identified as representing the two waves, it is clear that most of the migration went to the biggest cities. In the first wave, 38 percent went to the Calgary metropolitan region and 29 percent went to the Edmonton metropolitan region (see table 12). Together, these two destinations accounted for two-thirds of all interprovincial migrants to Alberta. In the second wave, a somewhat higher percentage (40 percent) went to the Calgary region and a lower percentage (25 percent) went to the Edmonton region. Smaller centres like Grande Prairie, Red Deer, Brooks, and Medicine Hat received a slightly larger percentage of those who migrated in the second wave.[7] So the second wave is somewhat different from the first wave in that Calgary was even more likely to be the preferred destination of in-migrants (especially when compared to Edmonton), but some dispersal to smaller centres also occurred.

From a proportional perspective, the impact of in-migration was much more dramatic in the first wave as 15 percent of those living in Alberta at that time had moved to the province in the five years preceding 1981, but that number dropped to 8 percent in 2001. This decline can largely be attributed to the fact that the population had increased, but this does give us a sense of the overall impact of migration on the host society. This trend is also significant when looking at cities. In Calgary, for example, one in every five persons living in the city in 1981 had moved there in the preceding five years, whereas in 2001, it was only one in every ten (see table 12). Among Fort McMurray's residents in the first wave, almost one in every two persons had moved to Alberta in the preceding five years, whereas in the second wave that proportion had dropped to one in every five persons. In general, then, as the populations of all of these communities grew, the proportion that relocated to Alberta in the preceding five years tended to drop. And, of course, since the 1981 and 2001 data do not fully encompass either wave, these numbers probably underestimate the impact of in-migration. Communities like Camrose, Wetaskiwin, and Lethbridge had much smaller percentages of migrants in 1981 than did growth poles like Lloydminster, Grande Prairie, Brooks, Red Deer, and Fort McMurray. However, even with the growing stabilization of the population, these latter centres continued to lead the way in 2001. When we consider that out-migration also occurred and that these cities had a small base population to begin with, as well as the fact that many people moving to them may have been transient, we see that the role of interprovincial migration in the life of these communities is enormous.

From a national perspective, even in 2001, these growing communities in Alberta had a much higher percentage of persons who had relocated to the province in the preceding five years than did comparable communities elsewhere in Canada (2001 Census, catalogue no. 97F0008XCB01001). For example, 10 percent of the populations of Calgary, Red Deer, Fort McMurray, Grande Prairie, Cold Lake, Lloydminster, and Brooks had lived in another province five years previously. In contrast, only Halifax, a regional growth pole for interprovincial migrants in Atlantic Canada, had a high percentage of recent migrants (9.4 percent) among census metropolitan areas. While the absolute numbers of recent interprovincial migrants to Vancouver and Toronto may have been higher, the impact on these cities (as measured by percentages of their total population [Vancouver 3.5 percent, Toronto 2 percent]) was not nearly as dramatic as it was on cities in Alberta. When we compare provinces, we see that Alberta had a far higher percentage (8.8 percent) of recent interprovincial migrants than did the other provinces (e.g., British Columbia 4.1 percent, Ontario 2.3 percent; see figure 9).

Another good measure of the role that interprovincial migration played in the communities of Alberta can be discovered by examining how many residents in each community were born in another province. More than one in every four persons in Alberta, both in 1981 (29.2 percent) and in 2001 (27.6 percent), were born in another province. Of all provinces, Alberta had the highest percentage of its population born in another province (compare Ontario at 8.8 percent and British Columbia at 24.7 percent). Most of the Alberta urban centres identified in table 12 (third column) have much higher percentages of persons born in another province than is reflected in the provincial average, thereby confirming that most of the interprovincial migrants selected urban locations in Alberta. Fully 40 percent of Calgary's population in 1981

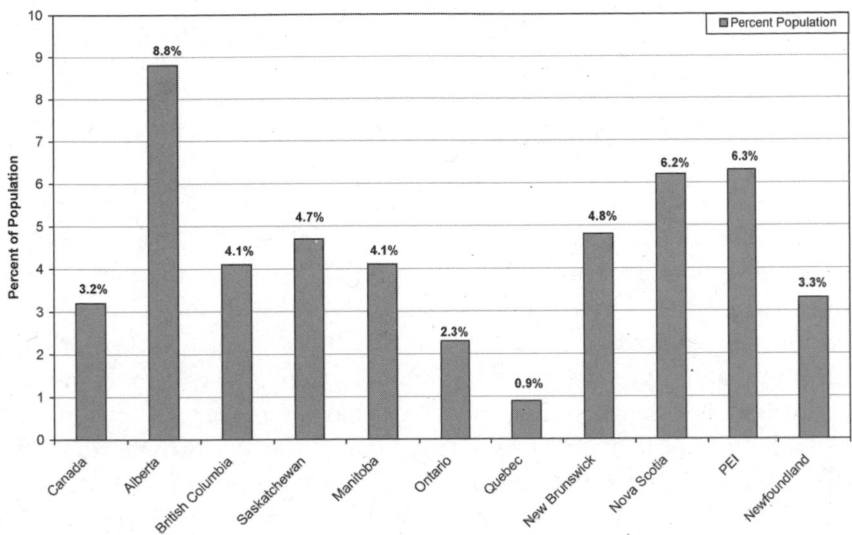

Figure 9 Percentage of Provincial Population Living in Another Province Five Years Ago, 2001
SOURCE: Calculated from Statistics Canada 2001 Census Cat. No. 97F0008XCB2001001

and one-third of its population in 2001 were born in anther province. One-half of Edmonton's population in 1981 was born in another province, but that number dropped to one-quarter by 2001. Two smaller places – Wetaskiwin (25.5 percent) and Camrose (21.7 percent) – are included for purposes of comparison because, even though they were not growth poles for this migration and the percentages of people living in them who were born elsewhere in Canada were below the provincial average, these percentages are still substantial. All the other urban centres mentioned, with the exception of Edmonton in 2001, have higher percentages of those born in another province than is reflected in the provincial average. Of particular note is the fact that Brooks (40 percent) and Lloydminster (70 percent) stand out, having even higher percentages of those born in another province in 2001 than in 1981.

In sum, whether considering place of birth elsewhere in Canada or place of residence five years previously, it is clear that Alberta, particularly its cities, has been more deeply affected by interprovincial migration during the two time periods under consideration than has any other place in Canada. The province's two largest cities, Edmonton and (particularly) Calgary, have been particularly affected. The fact that a large portion of the population of the province and its major cities consists of people who were born in another province indicates that interprovincial migration has been a continuous phenomenon. The impact of this type of migration was particularly dramatic in the first wave and somewhat muted, although still substantial, in the second wave.

EVALUATING THE IMPACT OF MIGRATION: HYPERMOBILITY

The disadvantage of census data is that it they represent snapshot of a particular moment in time. This is a problem when looking at populations because, of course, populations are always on the move. People are constantly moving between provinces, and even provinces that have net population losses are always gaining some people (see table 2, table 3, and table 5). Conversely, a province that has a net population gain through migration always loses some people to other provinces. As we have already seen, provinces with high levels of in-migration also have high levels of out-migration. Clearly, people do not just move one way; return migration and outward migration are common.

The implication of this movement is that, while all provinces experience the effects of in-migration and out-migration, some must deal with the effects of population decline while others must deal with the effects of population increase. Migration introduces an element of instability and change. Clearly, provinces that have smaller populations will be more disturbed by population gains and losses than will provinces with large populations. To demonstrate the extent to which Alberta as an entity had to make dramatic adjustments to the population flux caused by rapid in-migration and out-migration we need to look at a hypermobility index (see table 13). By taking into account the size of the provincial population, this index measures the extent to which all interprovincial shifts, both in and out, affect that province. The index provides a quantifiable measure of population flux and change through entry and departure (regardless of origin or destination) and allows this to be contrasted with other units. In comparing Alberta with other provinces, we see that Alberta's index is the highest by a considerable margin in both time periods. The shaded cells refer to locations that registered net losses and, therefore, were dealing with adjustments due to population decline through interprovincial migration. Alberta stands alone in both periods as a province with high gains as well as with high movements in and out (as revealed by high index numbers). It is intriguing to compare Alberta with Quebec because the latter has the second largest population in Canada and yet it has the lowest index scores of any province. This is a reflection of the fact that, in recent years, Quebec has not participated in the interprovincial exchange to any significant extent. Most other provinces (e.g., Newfoundland, Nova Scotia, and Saskatchewan) with high index numbers are dealing with population decline through interprovincial migration (cell boxes are shaded). Ontario, on the other hand, absorbs the in- and out-migration much more easily than these provinces because its population base is larger and therefore produces lower hypermobility scores.

Since so much interprovincial migration is to urban areas, census metropolitan areas have been differentially affected by interprovincial in-migration and out-migration, as measured by the hypermobility index (see table 13). Note that interprovincial migration is a much smaller factor not only for the provinces of Ontario and Quebec (as revealed by low index scores) but also for the major cities of Toronto, Montreal, and Quebec City. Halifax is the only city with scores that approach those of that of Alberta's cities, and this is because it is the major metropolitan area for the Atlantic region and is located adjacent to spatially smaller provinces, from which in-migration occurs very easily. Otherwise, the high index scores for all Alberta's urban centres are not only consistently higher than are those of other provinces but they are also positive, meaning that Alberta's cities were dealing with considerable growth and population instability related to both in- and out-migration. This demographic shock was stronger in the first wave than it was in the second wave (see table 13), but in both waves, Alberta stands out as a unique province grappling with the impact of population growth and change as the result of internal migration.[8]

OTHER VALIDATING EVIDENCE OF THE TWO WAVES

The discovery and verification of the existence of two waves of interprovincial migration to Alberta is an important theme in this book. While there is some question about the end point of the second wave, there is no question about that of the first wave; and the existence of a second wave, even with an unknown endpoint, has been lively and significant. To this point, my analysis has involved the use of demographic data generated by Statistics Canada. But is there any other evidence that such waves existed?

Applications for driver's licence transfers from other provinces provide a useful indicator of the extent of interprovincial migration. Data were available only since 1989/90, but they do clearly show the existence of an increase in driver's licence transfers beginning in 1997/1998 (see figure 10). If the wave began in 1996, it is likely that internal migrants delayed a bit in securing new licences until they knew that their stay would be more permanent. While this was the peak of such applications, it is clear that the number of such transfers continued to be much higher in the succeeding years than it had been in the first half of the 1990s. Driver's licence transfer applications, then, support the existence of a wave of in-migration to Alberta from other Canadian provinces.

A second measure involves apartment vacancy rates, and data are available as far back as 1971. Vacancy rates are a much more complicated indicator than are driver's licence transfer applications because they depend not only on demand but also on whether other housing stock exists, interest rates, and other options that may encourage owning rather than renting. But low vacancy rates do reflect the demand for housing, particularly rental housing, and can occur as the result of in-migration. New migrants (especially independent ones) are more likely to rent on arrival. Figure 11 indicates that, in both Calgary and Edmonton, the vacancy rate plummeted by the middle of the 1970s, suggesting a very hot housing market due to demand. The dramatic rise in the vacancy rate from 1982 to 1984 is consistent with high levels of out-migration, which signalled the end of the wave. Similarly, from 1998 to 2002, the vacancy rate dropped again, indicating that the demand for rental housing had increased. It is important to note that housing conditions at the end of both waves were diametrically opposed in that, in 1983, mortgage rates were at historic highs, whereas, in 2003, they were very low and therefore encouraged home ownership. The combination of high interest rates after the first wave and declining economic conditions played a major role in supporting out-migration: many walked away from their housing investment, having found that the values of overpriced houses were no longer equivalent to the size of their mortgages. The situation during the second wave encouraged home ownership rather than rental as interest rates were low and economic conditions were strong. So the existence of a period of low vacancy rates from 1998 to 2002 supplies evidence of the existence of a migration wave.

If pressure on rental housing provides one kind of evidence of in-migration, this can also be mediated by the construction of new housing. Particularly if mortgage rates are low (and indeed they were especially low during the second wave), there is little incentive for people to stay in rental accommodation as they can build up equity in a strong housing market and pay for their accommodation by taking advantage of low interest rates and monthly payments that are similar to rents. Figure 12 compares housing starts per capita for each of the

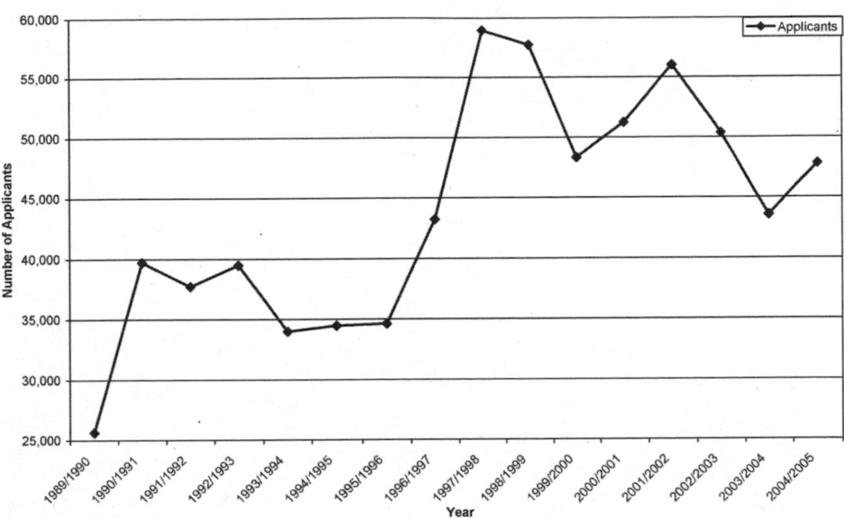

Figure 10 Driver's Licence Transfer Applications in Alberta, 1989/1990 to 2004/2005
SOURCE: Data provided by Alberta Transportation, Driver Safety and Research Branch

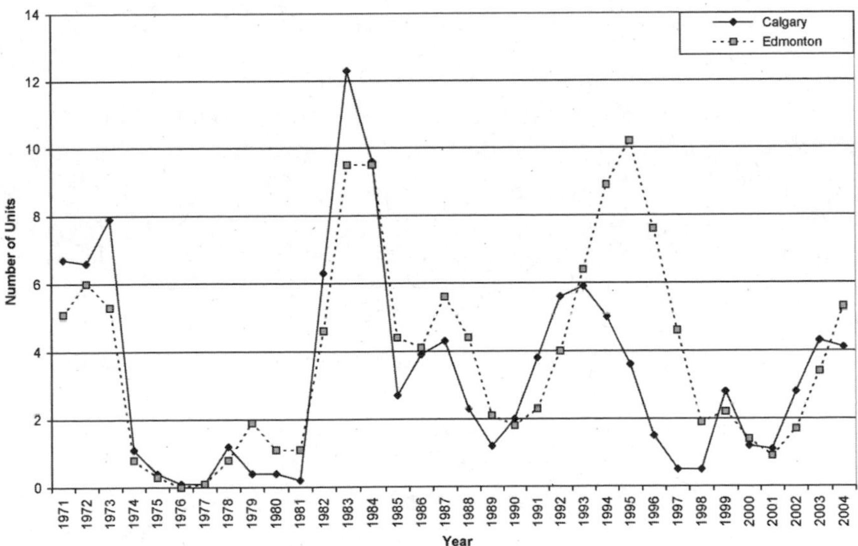

Figure 11 Vacancy Rates For Apartment Structures Six Units and Over for Calgary and Edmonton, 1971–2004
SOURCE: Statistics Canada, CANSIM Table 027-0011

three largest provinces since 1971. From 1976 to 1982, Alberta clearly stands out, with much higher housing starts per capita than Ontario and British Columbia. This suggests that new home construction

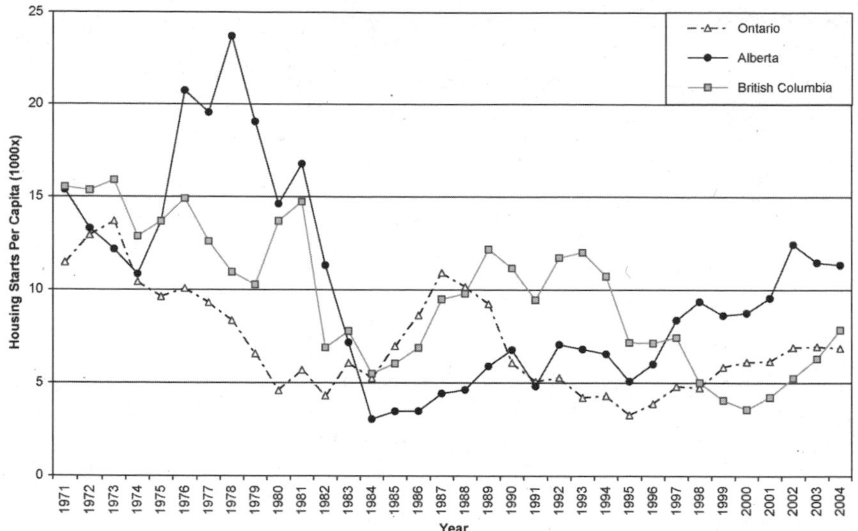

Figure 12 Housing Starts Per Capita for Alberta, Ontario, and British Columbia, 1971–2004
SOURCE: Calculated from Statistics Canada, CANSIM Tables 027-009 and 051-0001

occurred to support the influx of people. The drop in housing starts in the mid- to late 1980s confirms the existence of a less buoyant economy. While the peak is not nearly as strong after 1996 as it was in the first wave, it is clear that housing starts per capita had increased in Alberta (especially in comparison to the other provinces), suggesting that a new population wave was pushing this construction. The rise and fall of housing starts for British Columbia is also consistent with our knowledge of in-migration and out-migration patterns for that province.

There is, then, corroborative evidence that the migration waves identified through the use of demographic data do exist. They are confirmed in Alberta's motor vehicle licence transfers, vacancy rates, and housing starts – all of which are important indicators that migration flows are real and that they their effects are felt within the province.

CONCLUSION

In this chapter I identify a thirty-year period that includes two waves of in-migration to Alberta and that contributed to a high level of flux. While the two other high-destination provinces (Ontario and British Columbia) also experienced similar types of change, what is unique about what occurred in Alberta is that this change was strongly driven by migration from within Canada. Furthermore, the fact that these population surges occurred in a province with a smaller population than the other two meant that the impact was much greater than it would have been in Ontario or British Columbia.

These two in-migration waves provide structure to what occurred and identify specific time periods during which in-migration and out-migration can be analyzed through the use of macro-level contextual factors. For example, price shocks in oil and gas, and increasing world demand for these resources, played a major role in facilitating migration outcomes (see chapter 4). The identification of these waves also provides time points that enable me to analyze the characteristics of internal migrants. Overall, in-migrants to Alberta were more likely to be under 35 and were somewhat more likely to be men than women. They were overwhelmingly born in Canada and were considerably less likely to be foreign born or visible minorities. Persons with high levels of education did choose Alberta, but most of the migrants were persons with high school or trade school educations who were more likely to have moderate incomes in the initial years after arrival. Ontario and British Columbia played a dominant but changing role in this migration exchange, although Alberta was a preferred destination for migrants from all provinces from Ontario westward, and a second choice for those from Quebec eastward. Edmonton and Calgary were the primary destinations for these migrants, although smaller centres also experienced an influx. The first wave appeared to involve younger people, more men, and more people from Ontario. The second wave involved persons who were somewhat better educated, a little older, more women (though, overall, there were still more men than women), and more people from British Columbia.

Thus far, I have used secondary data to verify the existence, extent, and nature of migration flows to the Province of Alberta. However, the emphasis on waves and periods of gains or losses reduces human action to mass movements devoid of personal meaning. There is no sense of how migration is a decision-making process or how the migrant is both an individual and a member of a community. Demographic data do not reveal how migration is created by the actions of individuals. The relationship between the sending and receiving communities needs closer examination, and the process of becoming a migrant and being a migrant needs to be assessed in order to understand what makes relocation possible. In short, migration is about people, not simply economic forces. What leads some people to migrate while others resist that option? The secondary data utilized so far do not provide answers to this question. What is required is primary data – data that allow migrants to become human actors rather than just statistical aggregates.

Before moving to this level, it is important to discuss the contextual factor that has been such a catalyst to the Alberta economy – energy hydrocarbons. To what extent can these resources and the global macro-level perspective that they require serve as a straightforward explanation for what has occurred in Alberta?

4

The Role of Energy Hydrocarbons

Given Alberta's relatively short history as a settled community and its existence as a hinterland to the industrial ambitions of central Canada, what propelled its significant growth and expansion? The easiest and most typical answer is oil. The fact that Alberta appears to have won the geographical lottery in that the majority of Canada's known reserves of oil and gas are located here clearly gives it an undisputed advantage. As we have already seen, the role of Alberta in the New West is more complex than can be accounted for by oil and gas, but there is no denying the power of energy hydrocarbons in transforming the province.

Oil and gas have obviously been present under the surface in the province for a long time. Early settlers had a limited understanding of its existence, but it was not critical to Alberta until the demand for fossil fuels increased in what is known as the "age of oil." Whereas steam power was the most important energy driver of the early industrial period, later industrialism came to depend highly on petroleum and petroleum products as both an energy source and a lubricant (grease). The primary use of oil during the nineteenth century was limited to its role in illumination or as a lubricant. It was not until the twentieth century, when oil began to be used in its processed form – gasoline – in cars, factory machinery, tractors, and airplanes, that oil was transformed into a high demand commodity, thereby creating both upstream (exploration and production) and downstream (processing and retailing) industries. Another petroleum product, natural gas (and its components methane, ethane, butane, propane, and various pentanes), also played a huge role in heating, the production of electricity, and the emergence of petrochemical industries. Oil was critical to industrial economies because it replaced the role of animal power, steam power, and coal, while natural gas derivatives led to the production of a wide range of synthetic commodities such as plastics, toys, rubber, nylon, mouldings, and various other synthetic fibres and products used in everyday life.

Alberta did not participate in energy production to any significant extent until the 1950s. Even though oil and gas had been formally discovered in Alberta in 1914, distance from markets combined with low demand and low prices made the province's location a production disadvantage. It was not until consumption increased and prices rose that Alberta's energy largesse made a significant difference to it. It was in the 1970s that Alberta's economy went into high drive for the first time as the result of higher prices and increased demand for hydrocarbons, and this triggered a rapid in-migration, which has already been noted. There is, then, a strong argument to be made for the correlation between energy and provincial growth. Whether it is the only factor in this growth needs to be more carefully explored. Yet it is true that oil has made the economy of Alberta both so dynamic and so vulnerable.

While it has been argued that the world's first commercial oil well was drilled in southern Ontario in 1858 (McKenzie-Brown, Jaremko, and Finch 1993, 14), it was the United States that, through its capital and expertise, initially developed oil production in large fields for its own industrial apparatus and burgeoning automobile industry. As industrialism swept Europe, it soon became clear that there was a significant difference between energy-consuming nations and energy-producing nations, and even the United States had a production deficit that required petroleum imports. The industrial heartland of Canada – Ontario and Quebec – initially imported most of what it needed from outside the country. By the end of the twentieth century, much of the industrial activity in North America had shifted to Asia, resulting in new demands for energy consumption there. In both cases, industrial and postindustrial economies became high energy consumers, thereby globalizing the petroleum industry in a new way: the search for oil became a worldwide preoccupation. Given the fact that hydrocarbons are a non-renewable energy source, their scarcity amidst escalating demand elevated the global importance of energy-producing areas. Thus, as a depository for hydrocarbons, which are a strong staple ("strong" meaning scarcity and high demand combine to command high prices), Alberta automatically began to become part of the global economy in a way that provinces that relied on wheat, which is a much weaker staple, could not. Oil is perhaps the largest and most international of all industries in the world, and its role as a strategic commodity enhanced its significance for Alberta (Parra 2004, 1).

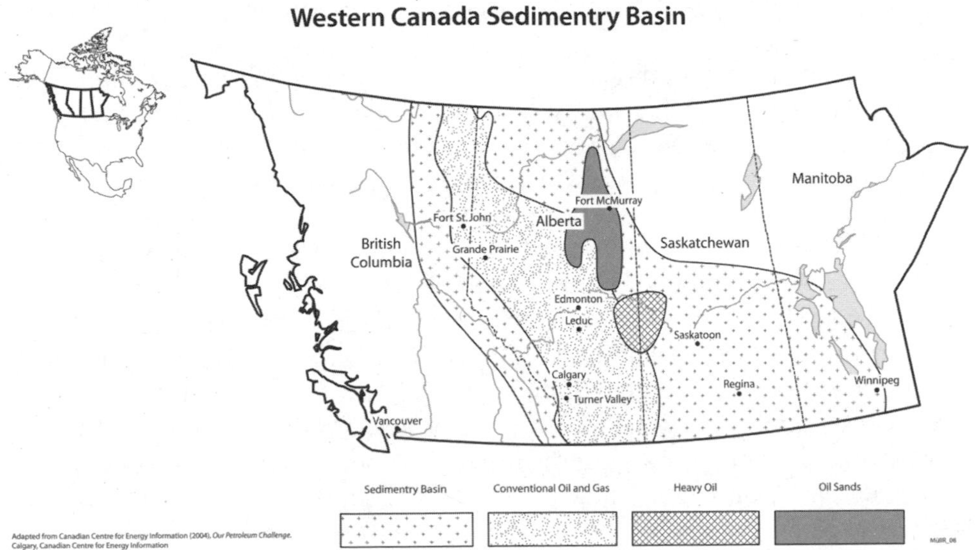

Figure 13

THE EVOLUTION OF THE OIL AND GAS INDUSTRY IN ALBERTA

Alberta is located on a land mass consisting of sand, silt, and the hardened remains of plants and animals in what is known as the Western Canadian Sedimentary Basin (see figure 13). While the Basin includes all four of the western provinces, most of its known reserves of oil and gas are located in Alberta. The first oilfield discovered in Alberta in 1914 at Turner Valley. While it was suspected that there might be more oil elsewhere in the province, distance from markets, among other factors, reduced commercial interest in further exploration. The Second World War played a big role in elevating the importance of oil, and, in the postwar period, there was renewed interest in exploring for oil in Alberta. After drilling 133 legendary "dry holes," Imperial Oil discovered oil at Leduc (just south of Edmonton) in 1947, and in the succeeding years it discovered other fields in the area as well (e.g., Redwater and the Pembina/Drayton Valley). These discoveries almost instantly transformed Canada into an oil-rich country, though their national significance was reduced by their distance from central Canadian markets, which continued to rely on cheaper imported oil.

The 1950s saw a flurry of pipeline construction from Alberta, which attempted to overcome the problem of distance. The first crude oil pipeline was the Interprovincial Pipeline, which was built from Edmonton to Superior, Wisconsin, in 1950 and was extended to Sarnia, Ontario, in 1953 (Bott 2004). This, of course, opened the door for the marketing of Alberta oil in the American Midwest in addition to in Ontario. Similarly, the first oil pipeline westward was built from Edmonton to Vancouver in 1953, and Westcoast Energy began carrying natural gas to the Pacific Northwest in 1957. The first cross-Canada gas pipeline was built by TransCanada Pipelines in 1958. American markets in Chicago and California have always been critically important to the Alberta industry, but until the 1970s the United States produced more oil than it consumed, so Alberta's production for export was limited (unless it significantly lowered its prices). Even in Canada, from Montreal east, imported oil was still preferred due to price and availability, and it was only west of the Ottawa Valley that Alberta oil was important. Thus was placed in motion a pattern in which Alberta benefited from the production of oil but at a much lower level than was to be the case by the end of the century. Mid-century oil producers in the province were eagerly seeking markets and customers for a commodity with relatively low prices and low demand. Energy hydrocarbons, for the first time, began to place Alberta within a continental framework because American markets were needed in order to develop the industry.

While Imperial Oil (a Canadian subsidiary of an American-owned company now known as Exxon-Mobil) was initially the most active explorer and producer of Alberta oil, there were other Canadian companies, such as British American, McColl-Frontenac, and Royalite, among the six hundred or so companies that suddenly sprang up. However, the major integrated American oil companies (e.g., Texaco, Shell, Mobil, and Standard Oil), which also had a significant international presence, were also active in the province. As Hanson (1958, 268) has noted, it was largely American capital, technology, and expertise that sustained the petroleum industry in western Canada during these formative years. The post-Leduc era meant the Americanization of the oil industry in Alberta – a fact that was largely applauded within the province due to its perceived key role in lifting Alberta out of its backwater frontier/hinterland position, which had been established by Canada's National Policy in 1879.

FROM LOCAL PRODUCT TO GLOBAL COMMODITY: PHASE 1

The post-Leduc era meant that the one-industry agricultural economy of Alberta had, in the 1950s, become a dual economy in which the petroleum industry was roughly equal to agriculture in importance

(Hanson 1958, 259). It was not just royalties that contributed to the provincial economy but also a wide range of investments, from drilling to pipelines to housing. The importance of petroleum, however, took a quantum leap forward in the 1970s as the result of global factors that increased its value and strategic importance. The first significant development involved the Arab oil embargo in 1973, and the second involved the Iranian Revolution and the Iran-Iraq war in 1978–79 (Bott 2004). Economists use the term "shocks" to refer to events or activities that destabilize the economy at specific points in time, and these were clearly shocks in that oil prices rose dramatically. From a consumer point of view, higher oil prices affected users negatively, particularly the industrial users in central Canada. However, from a producing province point of view, higher prices were a huge catalyst to economic development, investment, and employment. Alberta oil, for the first time, was no longer a local commodity begging for markets but, rather, a global commodity in high demand, particularly in North American markets concerned about security of supply.

Consumption of petroleum products had been dramatically increasing through the war years, and even in the postwar years, but prices had remained low. By the 1950s, automobiles and trucks, with their single combustion engines, had supplanted the railroad trains as the dominant mode of transportation, and, in combination with the aviation industry's rising need for jet fuel, this had strongly increased the demand for refined oil products. However, crude oil prices ranged from $2 to $3 a barrel in spite of the fact that demand was increasing (Emery 2005). When, in 1973, Syria and Egypt attacked Israel in the Yom Kippur War, the Arab states placed an embargo on oil that was headed for countries that supported Israel, and this led to an increase in the price of oil, pushing it up to $12 a barrel. A few years later, the Iranian Revolution, in conjunction with Iraq's invasion of Iran in 1979–80, contributed to a supply problem that pushed prices up even further, to $35, in 1981. These developments were often referred to as instigators of a world energy crisis because they challenged the economy and lifestyle of energy-consuming countries. The formation of the Organization of Petroleum Exporting Countries (OPEC), largely made up of Middle Eastern nations, played a huge role in controlling supply and price, and this only accentuated the vulnerability of non-OPEC countries, especially those that were major consumers (Parra 2004). The end result of these developments was that Alberta suddenly found itself in possession of a commodity that was of increasing value and of global importance.

The Canadian government's response to the price and supply issue was to embark on new policy initiatives. One goal was to try to keep the price of Canadian-produced oil below the dramatically increasing world prices. Another goal was to establish incentives for the production of oil elsewhere in the country, such as in the North and offshore in the Atlantic region. This was laid out in what was known as the National Energy Program (NEP) in 1980 (Doern and Toner 1985). NEP also had other goals, such as to reduce the foreign presence in the Canadian oil industry by strengthening Canadian ownership (particularly through federal involvement in PetroCanada, initially a Crown corporation) and increasing federal revenue yields through export taxes on oil sent to the United States from Alberta. While the goal of these actions was to protect energy consumers in Canada, there was no doubt that the major location of this energy consumption was in the industrial centre of the country, which, of course, meant that energy-producing provinces, particularly Alberta, were being denied world prices so that the heartland would not be adversely affected. In short, NEP resurrected the old heartland-hinterland antagonisms in the West, and particularly in a resurgent Alberta.

The effect of NEP was to bring the expansion of the petroleum industry in Alberta to a grinding halt, primarily through a massive reduction in investment expenditures. Mansell and Percy (1990, 32) estimate that Alberta lost about $11.5 billion in investment expenditures as the result of NEP and that this provoked a negative multiplier effect throughout the provincial economy. At the same time, interest rates were climbing while oil prices were slumping, and together these factors produced a massive recession in the province. Jobs were lost, real estate values depreciated, and business investments that had been based on an expanding economy fell apart. Between 1982 and 1987, the number of residential mortgage foreclosures increased dramatically to 28,000 final foreclosure orders, and 45,000 statements of claim were filed (Mansell and Percy 1990, 12). Downsizing and streamlining was the response to a changed market environment. New local banks (such as Northland Bank and the Canadian Commercial Bank) and mortgage companies (such as Dial Mortgage and Tower Mortgage), which had risen on the crest of a strong economy, collapsed in this changed environment. Even Canadian oil companies like Home, Dome, and Nova, which had impressive high-rise office towers in downtown Calgary, eventually folded under their debt load (Gray 2005, 458). By 1986, the price of oil had dropped to $10 a barrel, though it picked up later in the decade to around $15 (Emery 2005).

In response to these outcomes, the federal government, with the Western Accord, deregulated oil prices in Canada in 1985 and, ultimately, privatized PetroCanada in 1991. The net effect was to dismantle virtually all of the actions that had been taken by NEP. But prices remained relatively low throughout the decade and even into the early 1990s. Thus, it appeared that the ascendancy and economic robustness that Alberta had experienced had been seriously curtailed. Energy royalties and employment were still putting money into the pockets of the Alberta government and some of its residents, but the expansionist dynamic had been lost. Residents were keenly aware that $15 a barrel was the break-even point for stability in the industry, and even that was not enough for the expansion of more costly production, such as was needed for the oil sands. Albertans were clearly better off for having oil and gas, but their role in restructuring the national economy had been muted.

The dark side of government budgets based on volatile energy royalties was that spending exceeded revenues when prices were low. By 1993, Alberta had a budget deficit of $3.4 billion and an accumulated debt of $25 billion – down from an asset position of 12.6 billion in 1985 (Mansell 1997). The failure of government investments such as Magcan and Novatel left a legacy that exacerbated these losses. The government's spending program had been predicated on higher royalties than were materializing, and there was a widespread perception that Alberta faced a fiscal crisis (Kneebone and McKenzie 1997). In 1993, Premier Klein introduced a massive reduction in government expenditures – 20 percent over three years – which included huge reductions to employment in the public sector. It also meant the privatization of some government services and the goal of lowering taxes to establish a competitive advantage over other provinces. This initiative is often referred to as the Klein Revolution because it was a clear articulation of a neoconservative agenda. While there was considerable negative reaction to the swiftness of the cutbacks, there was also widespread support for the overall goal of eliminating government debt. The deficit was eliminated by 1995, and, largely due to higher royalties, the provincial debt was eliminated by 2005. The irony of experiencing the pain of cutbacks and the euphoria of government surpluses – all in the same ten-year period – only re-emphasized the roller-coaster nature of the economy. But it also created a culture of mixed messages, in which less government became the preferred model even though, if growth and expansion occurred, more government involvement was required to facilitate the provision of services and infrastructure.

ALBERTA AND THE GLOBALIZATION OF THE OIL INDUSTRY: PHASE 2

Through the 1990s and the early years of the new century, energy prices continued to show volatility due to an array of factors. For example, the Asian currency crisis was an issue in the first part of this period and depressed prices, but later the demand for oil in Asia, and particularly China and India, increased significantly and contributed to higher prices. The OPEC countries were often in disarray, with no mechanism to enforce quotas, and some oil-producing countries, like Russia, were so dependent on oil revenues that price was not a factor in production volumes. Prices briefly dropped to $10.35 in 1998, so many producing countries slashed production. However, by 2000, prices hit $37 early, dropped to $26 by December, but climbed past $40 and even higher, to $60, in 2004–05 in response to hurricanes and troubles in the Middle East. Thus, alternating periods of low prices and historic high prices meant volatility, which produced uncertainty, even amidst prosperity, in a province that had learned a valuable lesson through the severe recession and "bust" of the 1980s. If energy hydrocarbons were the economic engine of the province, Albertans had learned that changes in price created an uncertain environment and made long-term planning difficult.

On the other hand, two factors created continuous investment optimism in Alberta. First, while the reserves of conventional oil in the Western Canadian Sedimentary Basin had been depleting, natural gas had become even more important. The deregulation of natural gas exports in 1993–94 helped to increase the volume of gas exports, and gas then yielded more revenue to the province than oil. The significant price increases in natural gas, particularly in 1998, contributed greatly to the performance of the economy. Second, higher oil prices in combination with scarcity of supply made the oil sands deposit in northern Alberta in the Fort McMurray area, and the heavy oil around Cold Lake, a much more viable investment. It has often been pointed out that the discovery at Leduc ushered in a new age of oil production in Alberta that helped transform the province. This form of oil recovery is often referred to as "conventional oil" because it uses traditional methods to produce sweet crude. But if Leduc was symbolic of the traditional period of oil production, then the oil sands served as the symbol of a new era and as a catalyst for new forms of oil extraction and production. In comparison to conventional oil recovery, the oil sands was much more labour and capital intensive, and it required greater technological innovation.

Interest in developing the oil sands had intrigued researchers and entrepreneurs for many years, going back at least to the 1920s (Chastko 2004). The first large-scale oil sands production company at Fort McMurray began operations in 1967 and was initially known as the Great Canadian Oil Sands (GCOS), now Suncor, and a second plant (Syncrude) was brought on stream in 1978. By the late 1980s, improvements in technology had reduced the cost of production of this oil from CDN$35 to CDN$13 per barrel. About 20 percent of the known recoverable oil was surface mineable using what was called the "truck-and-shovel" method to scoop out the mixture and transport it for processing. But 80 percent (or more) of the oil was too deep for mining, and it needed to be recovered by new methods. One of the technological innovations developed involved the use of steam to separate the oil from the sand below the surface, where it was referred to as being "in situ." The heavy oil upgrader activity at Lloydminster/Cold Lake (1992) also represented technological innovation in the processing of oil. While people had known about these non-conventional deposits of oil for some time, it was not until early 2000 that the Energy Utilities Board of Alberta formally announced a major increase in proven reserves on the basis of the capabilities of new technologies to recover oil from the oil sands. In December 2002, the prestigious *Oil and Gas Journal*, which serves as an international clearinghouse of information and statistics on the global industry, announced the extent of the deposit, which then made an enormous difference to world reserves and elevated Canada's position as a global oil producer. Thus the optimism that had been developing within the industry throughout the 1990s now had a global impact and set off a new wave of investment in Alberta.

Not only had Alberta now been declared as the location of the second largest hydrocarbon reserve in the world (Saudi Arabia has the largest), but higher prices made costly mining and processing possible. When OPEC announced production cutbacks in 1998 and 1999, and as the demand in energy markets in Asia become more dramatic, the rise in prices that resulted made expensive oil extraction more profitable. A new royalty regime between government and industry had been negotiated in 1996. This regime was generic (i.e., rather than having been negotiated individually with each company, it followed a standard policy), which increased the return on investment. In short, conditions were right for a wave of fresh investment that created employment both directly in the industry and indirectly in a wide range of services. It especially created a burst of new construction activity in the oil sands. By the end of the twentieth century, new production sites/operations in the Fort McMurray area, with names like Muskeg River, Firebag, Fort Hills, Horizon, Jackfish, Long Lake, Mackay River, and Northern Lights, were being developed. Around the beginning of the new millennium, production from the oil sands had superseded production from conventional oil in Alberta, indicating that the oil sands was the new engine for the economy.

Highway 63: The Road to Nowhere Goes Somewhere Significant

The existence of the oil sands has been known for a long time, and some commercial extraction took place in the 1930s. However, significant oil sands development began in the late 1960s. The two giants in the industry at Fort McMurray are Suncor and Syncrude. Suncor, which originally operated as Great Canadian Oil Sands, first began with a mine and upgrader in 1967, and Syncrude followed, beginning operations in 1978. There are also oil sands in the Cold Lake region, where Imperial Oil has been active, and there are deposits in the Peace River region that have not yet been developed. The industry languished through the 1980s, hampered primarily by high production costs but also affected by low prices and an uncertain market, inefficient technologies, and a poor return on investment.

A conglomerate of business interests formed the National Oil Sands Task Force in 1993 and issued its report in 1995, which laid out a vision for oil sands development, particularly in the light of declining domestic crude production. One of the key elements of this report involved a change in the fiscal terms for the development of the oil sands with regard to both the provincial and federal governments. There were two issues. One was that royalty agreements had previously been negotiated individually, which meant that there was not a level playing field for development. The second issue was that the return on investment was only in the 6 percent-to-8 percent range, which was not enough to encourage new investment. In 1996, the governments of Alberta and Canada announced a new fiscal regime that was generic and that changed the return on investment fro 6 percent-to-8 percent to 11 percent-to-13 percent. Previously, about 70 cents of every dollar went to the government; now it was 60 cents. Prime Minister Chretien made the announcement, which initiated a new era of development, at McDonald Park. The industry then had new incentive to expand its operations, and, in combination with unexpected higher prices for crude oil and world demand, this led to an almost unbelievable expansion of existing facilities and the proposal and approval of new oil sands production on the part of new players in the area.

The year 1996 then became the benchmark against which all future developments were judged. From 1996 to 2002, $2.3 billion was spent on construction, and this amount increased dramatically in the following years. The two original dominant players expanded their own production, which Suncor called the Millennium expansion (which moved into production in 2002) and Syncrude called Syncrude 21. Numerous other companies also began their own projects, such as the Albian Sands Muskeg River Mines (Shell, Chevron), MacKay River (PetroCanada), Christina Lake (EnCana) as well as several others in progress. Interest from Chinese companies like the China National Offshore Oil Corporation (CNOOC) and Sinopec made it clear that oil sands development had truly entered a new era.

The impact of this spending has been enormous not only in Fort McMurray (in the form of the development of residential construction and retail growth) but also in Edmonton (which provides various forms of fabricated material). Highway 63 was a virtual runway for wide-load transport as pipes and steel structures were taken to Fort McMurray from Edmonton. Every Sunday evening seventy-five bus loads of workers arrived in Fort McMurray from Edmonton to work ten-hour shifts from Monday to Thursday, after which they returned to Edmonton. Work camps north of Fort McMurray accommodated about ten thousand workers for the huge labour needs of the construction phases. Air Canada began direct flights from Fort McMurray to Toronto and Newfoundland. The Horizon project, seventy kilometres north of Fort McMurray, even built its own airstrip to fly workers directly into the site via 737s from Atlantic Canada (or from wherever they could locate the requisite skilled workers).

In addition to this key catalyst to the oil sands industry, there were also significant changes in operating technology. The use of draglines and bucketwheel reclaimers for open pit mining was labour intensive, utilized a lot of expensive electricity, and led to real concerns about the viability of the industry. In fact, there were rumours that management at Suncor, in particular, was seriously considering shutting down the operation, and layoffs were numerous in the early 1990s. But a major cost reduction was found by changing from open pit mining to a truck-and-shovel operation, which reduced costs by about one-half. Hydrotransport methods were developed that were both efficient and economical, and less energy was utilized in the extraction methods. Above all, developing hydotransport made it possible to move the tar sands in various stages of the production process via pipes, which meant that production was not limited to one place (e.g., Syncrude was able to open the Aurora mine at some distance from the main plant, and Shell opened the Scottford upgrader near Fort Saskatchewan). Altogether, production costs were reduced from $30 per barrel to $13 per barrel (National Energy Board 2000, 2). In addition, surface mining was increasingly being supplemented by mining in situ which allowed petroleum recovery at deeper levels, where open pit mining was not feasible. Cyclic steam stimulation (CSS), horizontal well technology, and Steam Assisted Gravity Drainage (SAGD) enhanced recovery techniques, which allowed for expansion into deposits not accessible through open pit methods.

The Athabasca Oil Sands Deposit is about 40,000 square kilometres in size, which is about the size of the Province of New Brunswick, or twice the size of the State of Connecticut or the State of Hawaii. By 2003, about 25 percent of all crude oil used in Canada was produced by oil sand recovery, but that number was projected to be between 50 percent to 60 percent within ten years. Oil sands development raises many environmental concerns, from disturbing the land to reclaiming it; to the industrial pollutants produced by, and high energy costs of, the separation process; to the heavy use of water. Unchecked expansion of oil sands development only increases the impact of these concerns.

The 1990s, then, ushered in a new level of economic growth for Alberta, in which the Canada-US free trade agreement, the deregulation of gas exports, the spike in gas prices, and the strength of the American economy in combination with the depreciated Canadian dollar (which meant exporting in American dollars and spending in Canada in devalued Canadian dollars) played a huge role in increased spending in that province. In addition, investment in the oil sands intensified as the century turned and oil prices rose. At first, this resulted in much more managed growth (i.e., lower debt-equity ratios) than what had occurred in the 1970s, which led Mansell and Schlenker (2006) to resist speaking of this time period as a boom. It was also notable that the impact of the public-sector cutbacks demanded by the Alberta government in 1993–94 had considerably abated by 1996, just as other jurisdictions began their process of fiscal restraint. Alberta then possessed all of the characteristics of an economy that was, once again, expanding.

STRUCTURAL IMPLICATIONS OF AN EVOLVING HYDROCARBON INDUSTRY

As the fossil fuel industry evolved and matured, it changed the context for Alberta in significant ways. A stronger Canadian presence within the industry, the production and dissemination of knowledge, the globalization of capital, adaptations within the industry, and the geographical distribution of industry functions all had an impact on the province.

Canadianization within the Industry

The energy industry experienced a major restructuring after the 1970s that had clear implications for Alberta. From the oil industry's emergence in the 1920s, it has been dominated by seven large companies, often referred to as the "seven sisters" (Mobil, Gulf, Esso, Texaco, Standard of California, Shell, and British Petroleum), that are vertically integrated from exploration/production to retailing. The leading company in Canada was Imperial Oil, which had its roots in Ontario but it had been purchased by American-based Standard Oil (now Exxon Mobil) in 1899. By 1970, about 80 percent of the petroleum industry in Canada was controlled by American companies (Laxer 1983, 7–8). There was a lack of venture capital for this activity in Canada, and larger, highly capitalized, and technically experienced American companies filled the void. The result was that the industry in Canada was run like a branch plant of the American industry, with capital pools, technology, and expertise merely being transferred to Canada. Key positions in the industry in Alberta were filled by Americans. However, as the result of the expansion of the industry in the 1970s, and the experience that Canadians gained within the industry (often working for these major companies at home or abroad), upward mobility opportunities meant that the labour force became increasingly Canadian (House 1980, 5), including at its highest levels. The rise of new Canadian companies also mean that Canadian expertise and management somewhat moderated American domination.

The activity in the industry in Alberta in the 1970s led to enormous growth for Canadian companies such as Dome Petroleum, Nova, Hudson's Bay Oil and Gas (HBOG), and PetroCanada; however, other Canadian companies were also on the rise, such as Pan Canadian, Home Oil, Norcen, Canterra, Husky Oil, and Bow Valley. Canadians who became giants in the industry included people like Robert Blair, Jack Gallagher, and Bill Richards. Gerry Maier, who led HBOG, was originally from Regina but was a petroleum engineer graduate of the University of Alberta. Jack Gallagher of Dome was a graduate of the University of Manitoba. Manitoba-born Jack Armstrong became president of Imperial Oil in 1970, and Alberta-born Arne Nelson was already president of Mobil Canada in 1967. The Canadian Petroleum Hall of Fame provides ample evidence of the expertise and leadership in the industry within Canada. Symbolic of this maturation of the industry in Canada during the 1970s was the addition to the Calgary skyline of high-rise office buildings in which to headquarter the industry. Between 1973 and 1984, downtown office space in Calgary grew from 5 million square feet (464,500 square metres) to 28 million square feet (2,601,200 square metres) (Mansell 2002, 89). Buildings were named after the big companies that served as the principle occupants, but literally hundreds of so-called "junior" Canadian oil companies involved in exploration and production also sprang up.

It was not that the industry lost its American ties or foreign links but, rather, that it had matured to the degree where there were more opportunities for Canadians at all levels, including management and ownership. It also meant that the industry became more concentrated and centralized in Alberta. The last plank in this process involved the relocation of Imperial Oil from Toronto to Calgary in 2005. The 2006 announcement by EnCana, another Canadian giant in the industry, of the construction in Calgary of the tallest building in Canada west of Toronto also had immense symbolic value.

Knowledge Production and Dissemination

Alberta became the undisputed centre of oil and gas activity and administration in Canada, but it also became a centre for technological expertise and innovation in the industry. Extraction and refining through the use of imported methods no longer defined the industry in Alberta as the production of new knowledge became prominent (Smart 2001, 181). The need for more sophisticated technologies, such as 3-D seismic GPS-guided horizontal drilling, became evident, and various forms of computer modelling software and automated control systems were utilized and refined in Alberta. The oil sands, in particular, required enhanced oil recovery methods (EOR). Steam-assisted gravity drainage (SAGD), which was the innovation of University of Calgary professor Roger Butler); toe-to-heel air injection (THAI); vapour-assisted petroleum extraction (VAPEX); multiphased superfine atomized residue (MSAR); and initiatives in coalbed methane extraction (i.e., the process of extracting natural gas from coal) were all the result of scientific research and development, much of which was generated in Alberta. Thus it would be a mistake to view the impact of the oil and gas industry as simply involving the extraction of raw materials for export and, as with the mining of coal or nickel, relying on the predominance of blue-collar jobs. Rather, this primary sector resource base supported a wide range of white-collar jobs, from those in finance (accountants and capital fund organizers) and administration (human resources, project managers) to those in earth sciences (e.g., geologists, geophysicists, and many different kinds of engineer [structural, chemical, mechanical, corrosion]). It offered jobs for highly trained people, from seismic explorers to surveyors to operational technicians. Even jobs in the trades, such as those requiring heavy equipment operation and welding, had above-average wage levels, often propelled even higher by a shortage of skilled labour. Alberta had become a prominent destination for graduates from a wide diversity of geo-science programs in Canadian universities and other postsecondary institutions. Clear evidence of this can be found in the fact that, in 1994, the Association of Petroleum Engineers and Geologist and Geophysicists of Alberta (APEGGA) had 27,000 members, which increased to 42,000 by 2004.

As a result of these developments within the industry in Alberta, the expertise that emerged and the technologies that were developed could be exported to other parts of the world. Almost all of the larger companies operating in Alberta had operations elsewhere in the world, and some informal estimates suggest that, at any given time, 15 percent to 20 percent of oil industry employees in Calgary were working on international projects. At the very least, many oil companies based in Alberta had themselves become involved in oil recovery operations all over the world, which meant that Canadian expertise was usually sent to these locations to direct operations. This global involvement applied to exploration, production, and servicing. At one time, Nowsco (now owned by BJ Services), an Alberta well service company that specialized in cementing, simulation, and coiled tubing, had operations in thirty foreign countries. Thus the Canadian oil industry was not just

Alberta-based; rather, it was a player in many places around the globe.[1] The fact that Alberta hosted the World Petroleum Congress in Calgary for the first time in 2000, with representatives attending from over eighty countries, attested to the different role that Alberta was now playing in the industry. Calgary in particular became the clearing house for the development of new technologies and the locus of decision making and the coordination of capital pools. The downtown Petroleum Club was the symbol of this power. In other words, Alberta had become not just a location for the extraction of a marketable resource; rather, it had become the Canadian centre and, in some respects, a global centre for the oil and gas industry.

New Global Capital Ties

Initially, the creation of OPEC had challenged the seven sisters, but other developments were also occurring. The nationalization of the oil industry in a number of countries (e.g., Pemex in Mexico) and/or the increasing role of the state in oil development within producing countries (PDVSA in Venezuela), and the increasing production of oil in non-OPEC countries (e.g., Norway, Malaysia) brought a new global dynamic to the industry that altered the role of the seven sisters. These companies changed as the result of acquisitions or mergers: Exxon and Mobil became ExxonMobil; British Petroleum swallowed up Sohio, Amoco, and Arco; Chevron took over Gulf and Texaco; and large companies typically had operations in many different countries. Oil was now produced in many places and was being sponsored by many different entities. By 2003, for example, the French oil company Total SA had become one of the largest integrated companies in the world and operated in over one hundred countries. In 2003, it began a heavy investment program in Alberta's oil sands. New companies and partnerships were also created, and, in Canada, that meant that ownership became much more international as companies were particularly lured by the oil sands. Companies from Japan, France, and China entered the Canadian oil industry for the first time. Renaissance Energy, a powerhouse in the early 1990s, became part of Husky and was purchased by Hong Kong entrepreneur Li Kai Shing. Even oil companies owned by foreign governments (e.g., Norway's StatoilHydro and China's PetroChina) became active investors in Alberta. Imperial Oil's pre-eminence had been diffused, and new Canadian companies such as EnCana (merging Alberta Energy and Pan Canadian), Talisman Energy (formerly BP Canada), and Nexen (formerly Canadian Occidental) joined Canadian

Natural Resources as strong Canadian players in the oil industry. Ownership groups bought and sold, but what is key is the fact that the industry in Canada was no longer one-sidedly American.

While Canadian companies became more global, Alberta itself became embedded in exchanges of global capital. The impetus for this came from increasing demand for oil elsewhere in the world, especially from heavily populated countries such as China and India, where energy consumption jumped dramatically. The fallout of the attack on the World Trade Center and the subsequent "war on terror" also made "security of supply" a global issue among energy consumers. Consequently, the oil sands aroused new interest in Alberta as an important site for international pools of capital and drew the province more directly into the global economy.

Industry Adaptations

One of the remarkable things about the oil industry is that it is constantly changing. Mergers and acquisitions change the appearance of the industry, and many of the companies that were strong in the 1970s, for example, no longer exist: Dome, Home Oil, Pan Canadian, and many more have all disappeared. The industry is in constant flux, and its personnel are remarkably resilient as they often move from salaried positions to consultant positions and from big companies to small companies.[2] For example, layoffs due to cutbacks and restructuring seldom lead people to leave the industry; instead, they resurface in other positions. There are literally hundreds of small oil companies in Alberta.[3] The existence of so many "junior" oil companies is usually the result of people leaving a large company and essentially starting over, often with a small two- or three-person operation, which may eventually become much larger (Doern and Toner 1985, 246). Larger companies often divest themselves of small fields that are no longer economical to operate, and smaller companies can pick them up and run them profitably. Conversely, smaller companies build themselves up with the hope of being bought out by bigger companies. People working within the industry often have information that they are able to exploit with smaller capital pools or are able to provide services to the industry as consultants (House 1980, 87). In fact, the industry, especially at professional levels, makes heavy use of consultants, who work under contract (non-professional workers and support staff are often more vulnerable). Mansell and Percy (1990, 55) point out that two out of three small businesses that started up in the 1980s did so in response to a negative situation such as job loss and that, at one point during the decade, Alberta led all provinces in the rate at which it incorporated new business. Many of these new businesses were in the oil industry or supported it in some way. Thus, there is a resilience, a flexibility within the industry that seems to enable it to weather the storms of change. Unlike other industries, in which large companies squeeze out smaller companies, the oil industry supports a diversity of entity-types, and its personnel move around and mobilize capital for a variety of functions.

Spatial Effects

The oil industry is not randomly distributed throughout the Province of Alberta but is spatially arranged according to specific functions. Figure 13 indicates that conventional oil and gas is found throughout the province as well as in southwestern Saskatchewan and northeastern British Columbia. Shallow gas is more typical of the Medicine Hat area. Heavy oil is found in the Lloydminster/Cold Lake area, and the oil sands are found not only in northeastern Alberta in the Fort McMurray region but also in the Peace region. Red Deer and Nisku (between Edmonton and Leduc)[4] are the centres for oil and gas servicing, and Edmonton/Fort Saskatchewan is the primary location for refining (here is where we find Canada's largest oil refining complex) and, along with Red Deer (Nova Chemicals, Agrium), is the centre of the petrochemical industry (e.g., Dow Chemical, Shell Upgrader, Sherritt International, Imperial Oil). Edmonton tends to serve as the staging area for the industry not only with regard to providing site workers and tradespeople but also with regard to providing fabricated products and supplies – especially for the oil sands and other oil activity to the north. Calgary, on the other hand, serves as the administrative centre for the industry and is the location of the head offices for virtually all of the oil companies doing business in Canada. It is the focus of the professional, technical, and managerial classes and provides all of the support services that they need. Because of this role, Calgary also serves as the command centre for other oil industry activity elsewhere in Canada (e.g., offshore Atlantic) as well as, increasingly, in other places in the world.[5] By the turn of the twenty-first century, Calgary was home to the second largest number of corporate head offices (seventy-eight) in Canada, most of which were in the energy sector. Oil and gas, then, restructured the human ecology of the province.

The oil and gas industry played a major role in restructuring the urban form of Alberta. First of all, its two major cities, Edmonton and

Calgary, have grown at a much faster rate than might otherwise have occurred, and their metropolitan areas now account for approximately two-thirds of the province's population. Both cities have spawned growing satellite municipalities like St Albert (56,000) and Airdrie (29,000).[6] Second, with the growth of Red Deer, the Calgary-Edmonton urban corridor has begun to take a more distinct shape. Located almost equidistant between Edmonton and Calgary, Red Deer had a population of 30,000 in 1975, but this increased dramatically to 50,000 by the end of the first wave of in-migration. By 1996, Red Deer had 60,000 residents, but that number increased significantly to 83,000 by 2006, making it the third largest city in Alberta. Red Deer displaced Lethbridge from that position largely because of its role in oil and gas servicing along with a growing petrochemical industry. Companies based in Red Deer, like Haliburton and Collicutt Hanover, played a huge role in well servicing and the manufacturing of gas compression equipment. Perhaps of even more importance was the 1997 decision by Nova Chemicals, Union Carbide, and BP Amoco to expand the petrochemical plants at Joffre.

The third development that affected the urban form of the province was the growth of new cities in northern Alberta, particularly Grande Prairie and Fort McMurray. Fort McMurray receives most of the attention because it is largely a creation of the oil sands; technically, however, it is not a city but an urban municipality called Wood Buffalo. Its rather remote location, 435 kilometres northeast of Edmonton, has meant that it is almost totally dependent on oil extraction activities. The fact that it has grown so rapidly, from only a couple of thousand people in 1966 to around 80,000 in 2006, has made it an urban force in the province's north.[7] The other burgeoning city in the north, Grande Prairie, is 465 kilometres northwest of Edmonton. Located in the Peace River District, and often spoken of as the "last best west" because it was the last frontier of agricultural settlement (which began in the 1930s), and, even as late as the 1950s, about 90 percent of the people in the area were agriculturalists. By the late 1990s, however, only 25 percent of the county's population were agriculturalists. The key to this reversal and to the community's growth was the construction of a major pulp mill in the early 1970s and the expansion of the oil and gas industry in the late 1970s. New exploration activity in oil and gas just across the border in northern British Columbia (e.g., the Dawson Creek area) and the areas north of Grande Prairie contributed to even faster growth, particularly around the mid-1990s. By 2006, Grande Prairie had 45,000 residents and had become a major regional retail centre. In short, oil and gas had opened up the provincial north for urban development in a manner that has not occurred in any other province.

The New Alberta North

It was a hot July day in Grande Prairie. I stood at the front of my big-chain hotel on a four-lane by-pass highway. In this town of 45,000, it seemed like I was on the outskirts of a major city. Around me was a power centre of retailing, with outlets from all the major chains, including Wal-Mart, Costco, fast food franchises, and numerous retail shops and grocery outlets. And still more of the same under construction.

Here I was – a five-hour drive northwest of Edmonton, close to the BC border and not far from the start of the Alaska Highway. Locals cannot believe how their community has changed – and it is not just because of the increase in population but because of the growth of amenities to service that population. Grande Prairie has truly become the heart of the formerly agricultural Peace River country.

As I stood in front of my hotel and watched the heavy traffic on the four-lane highway, I was intrigued by the appearance of vehicles and the shapes of their cargoes. There were pump trucks, vacuum trucks, trucks with inverted tanks, haulers in all shapes and sizes, flatbeds – some with heavy equipment, some bearing frames and structures, others campsite offices and structures. There were also logging trucks, some empty and some full. In between were sprinkled motor homes on their way to Alaska. It was a frenetic pace of activity.

The feeling of optimism was clearly in the air. Everybody talked about rumours of how the population would double in the next five years, and it was intriguing to hear people debate the size of the current population. Someone tells me 36,000, and someone corrects her, saying that it is 37,000. Someone else says 50,000. Bigger is clearly better and is a badge of new-found significance.

Boom time in the Alberta north, though, cannot be compared to the gold rush. It uses airplanes, sophisticated equipment and technical processes, and large capital pools rather than horsepacks, primitive technology, and fly-by-night operations. Its magic draws people from all over the country, particularly those eager for new opportunities and those who have faced years of underemployment. The euphemism here for doing well is “making good money.” The oil patch represents an agglomeration of services to the oil and gas industry, which is time sensitive and high cost. People are paid well and work long hours. Even the poorly educated can do well if they are willing to work. The spinoff effects of this industry in other fields make the town buzz.

This is the new Alberta north.

FOSSIL FUELS AND ALBERTA'S CHANGING ROLE

Energy hydrocarbons gave Alberta a position of comparative advantage in relation to other provinces. Since 70 percent of Canada's crude oil production and 80 percent of its natural gas production is based in Alberta (Gibbins and Vander Ploeg 2005), Alberta has control of a strategic resource, particularly since underground minerals are owned by the province. While conventional oil initiated Alberta into the continental oil supply, the oil sands has given it a much more dominant position because it has about 80 percent of all proven reserves of crude oil in North America and 17 percent of all proven reserves of natural gas. The fact that about three-quarters of all spending in the petroleum industry in Canada is taking place in Alberta, and that about 80 percent of all upstream jobs in oil and gas in Canada are located there, means that the province is home to a concentration of industry skills and its commensurate salaries, which have ricocheted throughout the provincial economy. Furthermore, before 1980, most petrochemical activity in Canada took place in Sarnia, Ontario, and in Montreal. By the turn of the century, Alberta was the largest producer of petrochemicals in the country and had four petrochemical plants, including world-scale plants in Joffre and Fort Saskatchewan. Value-added upgrading, particularly from natural gas, was largely based in the province, though the consumer products that resulted, such as tires and toys, were manufactured elsewhere. The collection, transmission, and export of petroleum means that there are 332,000 kilometres of pipelines in the province, with more pipelines on the drawing board. Around 300,000 people are directly or indirectly employed in the energy sector in Alberta (about 120,000 jobs are directly involved with energy), which means that about one in every six workers in the province has a job related to the petroleum industry.

The total value of production of oil and gas in Alberta from 1971 to 2004 was over $1 trillion (constant 2005 dollars), with investment expenditures of about $350 billion (Mansell and Schlenker 2006). Royalties to the Alberta government over that time period were around

$150 billion (2005 dollars). Mansell and Schlenker (2006) argue that, with oil and gas, Alberta's GDP growth was about 1 percent higher than the national average during that time (though around the new millennium it was 20 percent to 30 percent above the national average) and that, without oil and gas, it would have been about 42 percent smaller.

The concentration of the oil and gas industry in one province clearly not only gave Alberta a distinctive dominant industry but also an industry that gave it a clear comparative advantage. This advantage pertained to royalties, which allowed the provincial government to eliminate its debt, keep taxes low, and, with unexpected ballooning surpluses (over $6 billion in 2006), to engage in supplemental discretionary spending. From 1971 to 2004, the Alberta government received over $150 billion in royalties and rents from energy (Mansell and Schlenker 2006). No other province had an industry with that kind of cash flow. Furthermore, the existence of a highly skilled workforce, including managers and entrepreneurs with higher wage returns than was typical in other industries, not only affected consumer spending but also yielded more tax revenue.

The existence of hydrocarbons as a revenue producer in Alberta also affected the federal government through various forms of taxation, which became another factor in transforming the way in which Alberta was perceived within Confederation. Oil and gas forced the rest of Canada to see Alberta as a different kind of player, both within the nation and on the continent, than it had been before. Figure 14 illustrates how pipelines originating in Alberta reached into the continent and offers hard evidence of this new role. At the national level, Alberta's largesse changed Canada from being a petroleum-importing nation to a petroleum-exporting nation and had a huge impact on national economic accounts. The oil industry also played a huge role in the development of a large managerial/entrepreneurial class in the province – a class located in the biggest cities (Mansell 1997, 20). The industry provided key players in the development of a regional bourgeoisie of owners and managers of Alberta-based corporations, senior government bureaucrats, and upper-income professionals who sought to influence the development of the province (Richards and Pratt 1979, 166–8) and, ultimately, the direction of the nation.

OIL AND MULTIPLIER EFFECTS

Is it too simplistic to say that Alberta's economic growth is only the result of oil? With such a dominant and high revenue-producing indus-

Canadian and US Crude Oil Pipelines

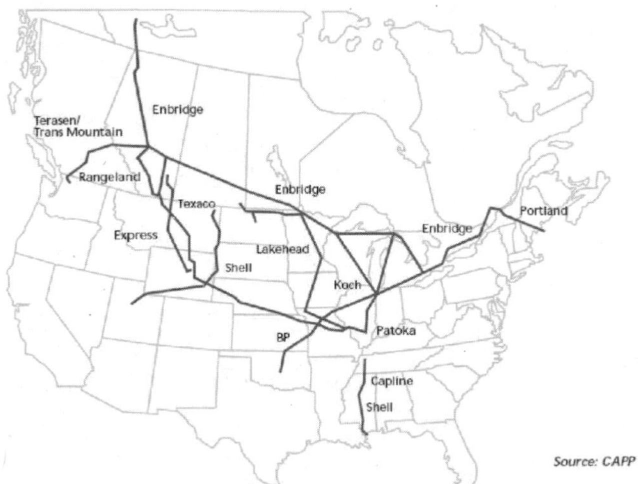

Canadian and US Natural Gas Pipelines

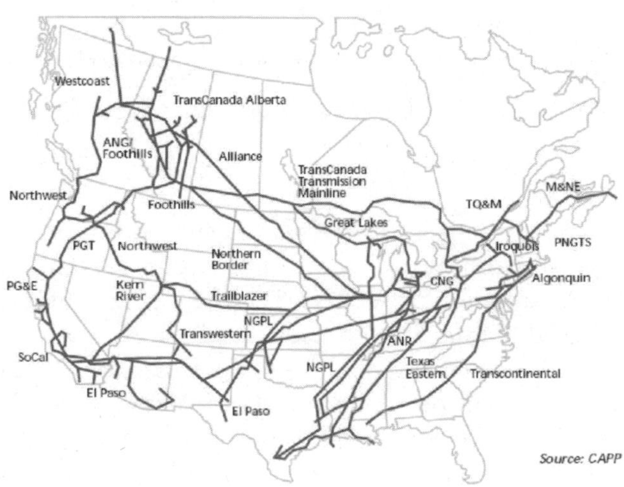

Figure 14

try, it is difficult to separate its effects from what else is going on in the larger economy. A variety of forward and backward linkages with multiplier effects for other businesses and public-sector services did occur, and this served to propel expansion in many different sectors.

Private investment is a strong indicator of economic growth in the Canadian economy. Figure 15 demonstrates that there have been two periods of high per capita private investment in Alberta in comparison to Ontario, which normally has high levels of private investment. These two periods occurred in the mid- to late 1970s and the late 1990s and early 2000s, and, they coincide well with the two waves of in-migration identified earlier as well as with the two periods of energy

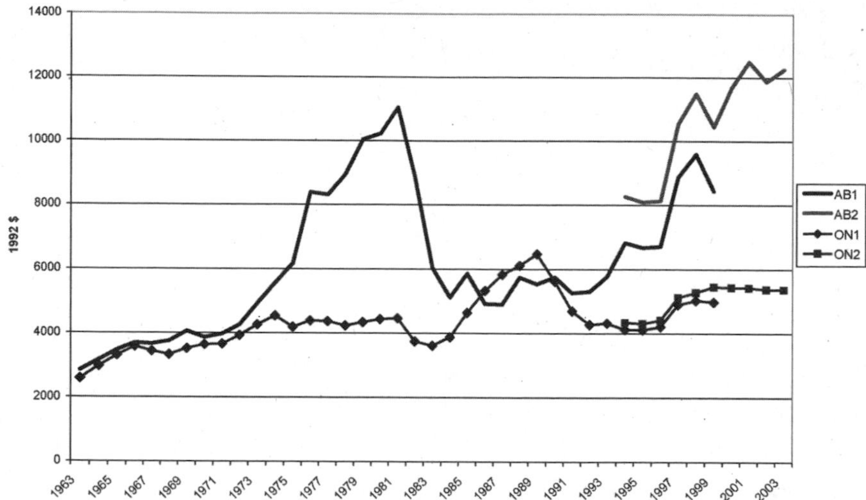

Figure 15 Per Capita Private Investment (1992 $), Alberta and Ontario, 1963–2003
NOTE: A different data series is used for the most recent years and is represented by ON2 and AB2. However, the pattern is simillar in both series.
J.C.H. Emery assisted in the preparation of this graph.
Source: CANSIM II Table 032-0002

price escalations. Clearly, there is a relationship between increased private investment, the energy industry, and in-migration.

The question, of course, is: what sectors of the economy are most affected by this type of investment? In the 1994–2004 time period, the number of jobs increased by almost 400,000, or 36.5 percent (see table 18). Of these jobs, 32 percent were in the goods-producing sector and 68 percent were in the service-producing sector. With regard to employment in the goods-producing sector, the largest number of jobs was in construction, where employment increased by almost 100 percent over the ten-year period. Residential construction had the largest percentage increase, but all types of construction combined showed that the largest group of employees were the goods-producing sector. Related to construction was the significant increase in employment in the manufacturing of wood products (such as doors and window frames), fabricated metal, and machinery. Increased private investment undoubtedly meant more activity in the oil and gas industry, which produced more employment in construction and in the production of goods needed to support construction. This would indicate that any decrease in private investment would make these industry sectors particularly vulnerable to the kind of decline that occurred in the early 1980s (Mansell and Percy 1990, 31).

However, as has already been noted, the largest number of jobs was created in the service-producing sector, which suggests that activity in oil and gas has ripple effects throughout the economy or that other sectors experienced growth as the population increased. The largest number of new jobs was created in retail trade as a growing and more affluent population contributed to more consumer spending (see table 18). Significant new employment was also created in wholesale trade and transportation/warehousing. What was perhaps most remarkable was the increase in the services sector, particularly the doubling of the workforce in administrative services and professional, scientific, and technical services. Health care, food services, and educational services were always major employers, and they demonstrated the type of increase in employment that would follow population growth. "Demand shocks" are created by strong population increases, which channel capital flows to housing, education, and health (Chambers 2001). Not surprisingly, more employment was also created in real estate, finance, and insurance. A larger population also meant an increase in jobs in the arts, entertainment, and recreation. The only sector in which employment decreased during that time period was public administration, and most of that decline was at the federal and provincial levels rather than at the municipal level. In short, there is synergy between an expanding economy and a growing population that leads to new employment options in a diversity of fields.

The relationship between energy hydrocarbons and the Alberta economy is well known. However, it is merely a background factor to most residents, who carry out their lives without any involvement in the oil patch at all.[8] People are involved in education or health care or the arts or business, and they generally lack knowledge about the energy industry. Above all, it is important to know that many people migrate to Alberta for a variety of reasons that may have nothing to do with oil or gas. People come to work as teachers, in sales, as technicians, or to take up a wide variety of administrative positions that have nothing to do with energy. For most migrants, there is not a direct relationship between energy and their decision to move to Alberta.

Yet it is clear that the agglomeration effects of expenditures in the oil industry have multiplier effects in the provincial economy. The government of the province sought diversification, and some applications can be transferred from the oil industry to other uses. One example of the economic and technical spinoffs from the oil industry is an Alberta company known as BW Technologies, which was first established in 1987 and was first traded on the Toronto Stock Exchange in 1999. This company initially built its reputation by creating a portable gas detection device (called a Rig Rat) that could be worn by workers in the oil industry and that would detect toxic fumes and explosive gases. The technology was later expanded to a whole variety of confined-space applications (e.g., in sewers, mines, or parkades, or virtually anywhere where poisonous gases could be a problem). A variety of gas detection instruments was created that had broad application to other industries, and sales soon became worldwide.

Another type of diversification utilized oil revenues to develop a strong research sector in medicine, science, and engineering. In 1980, the Alberta government established the Alberta Heritage Foundation for Medical Research with an endowment of $300 million; by 2004, that endowment had grown to $900 million. Over the course of the first twenty-five years of its operation, the foundation invested at least $800 million dollars in medical research in Alberta. If, in 1980, medicine in Alberta was primarily clinical with some research, twenty-five years later the province had developed its research profile considerably by attracting medical researchers in specialized fields. For example, a heart institute was established in Edmonton, a bone and joint institute was created in Calgary, and major breakthroughs by Alberta researchers in the treatment of diabetes and sleep apnea served as magnets for the further development of medical research and treatment specialists. The massive expansion of health sciences facilities in both major cities reflected this significant change. In 2000, the Alberta Heritage Foundation for Science and Engineering Research (known as Alberta Ingenuity) was established with an endowment of $500 million to attract and develop expertise in Alberta. In short, petrodollars were being used to develop professional skills inside the province but outside the oil industry. This significant increase in professional, scientific, and communication services employment was an important indicator of Alberta's growing resiliency and diversification.

Nevertheless, the primary pitfall of a staples economy that exports raw materials for value-added activity is that it essentially supports the economies of other jurisdictions by creating jobs there. Given the fact that oil is a strategic commodity for both industrial and postindustrial economies, Alberta has depended on the sale of its hydrocarbons to other jurisdictions for its own prosperity, but without conducting enough value-added activity in the province. For example, the growth of the petrochemical industry in Alberta did not lead to the emergence of a significant plastics industry to replace or compete with that in central Canada. If anything, there has been more specialization and con-

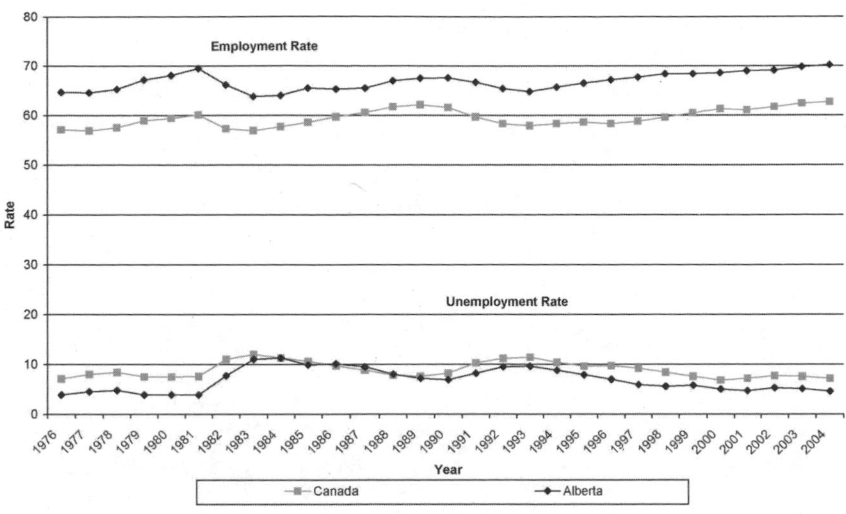

Figure 16 Employment and Unemployment Rates in Canada and Alberta, 1976–2004
SOURCE: Statistics Canada, CANSIM Table 282–0002.

centration in the upstream oil and gas sector in Alberta than ever before as voracious markets eagerly buy the raw materials while energy companies and government look for the fastest payout. The sale of these resources to places of large industrial capacity and large populations negates the intention to create value-added activity within the province (Norrie 1992, 703). In general, though, attempts at diversification have had scattered successes in specialized sectors such as telecommunications and biotechnology.

Much of the dynamic for population growth in the province has emerged from the fact that there is not a surplus pool of labour. In fact, since the 1970s, Alberta has had the highest employment rate in Canada – always considerably above the Canadian average (see figure 16). Given the low median age of the population, this means that a higher proportion of the Alberta population is actually in the labour force. While there were a few years in the mid- to late 1980s when Alberta's unemployment rate was closer to the national rate, for most of the last thirty years, Alberta's unemployment rate was also the lowest in the country.[9] This means that migrants to Alberta have had a reasonable chance of being successful in the job market without the province's having to make major changes through more activist diversification – something that had been an earlier provincial strategy (Richards and Pratt 1979).

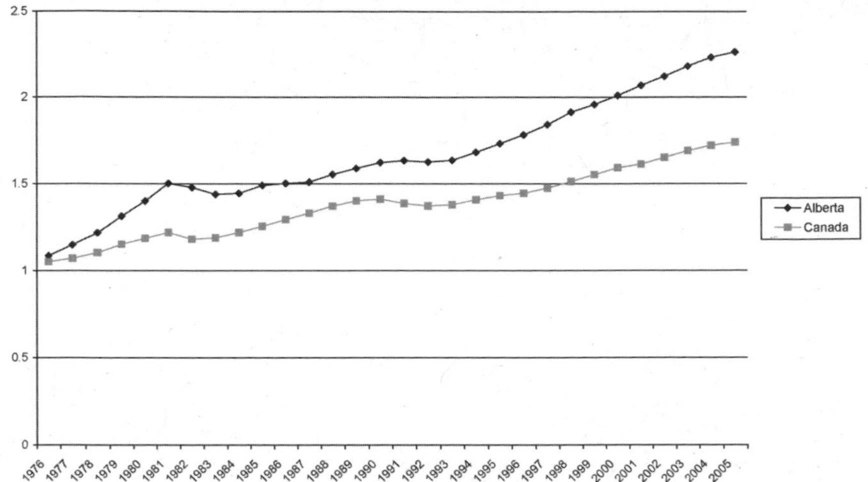

Figure 17 Employment Index, Alberta and Canada, 1976 to 2005 (1976=1)
NOTE: The employment index is a measure of employment growth for workers age fifteen and over using 1976 as the base point.
J.C. Herb Emery assisted in the preparation of this graph.
SOURCE: Statistics Canada, CANSIM II SERIES V2064890, Table 2820087 and Series V2096751, Table 282001

The relationship between in-migration and employment seems obvious when employment growth is measured in an employment index. Figure 17 shows that, since the 1970s, employment growth in Alberta has increased at a faster rate than that in the country as a whole, using 1976 as a benchmark. Employment growth increased particularly rapidly in the late 1970s and early 1980s, and then again from the mid-1990s. Throughout the entire period, employment in Alberta, as indexed, almost doubled employment growth in Canada as a whole. This clearly establishes a framework for my analysis of migration to Alberta: employment opportunities provided the occasion for relocation. It must be remembered, however, that migration and a larger population also increased employment (Chun 1996).[10]

CONCLUSION

In recent years, the oil industry in Alberta has moved from being a branch plant to being a strong player in the global energy industry. It is not just that enhanced recovery methods in the oil sands resulted in Alberta's having the second largest oil deposit in the world, but that, in the province, there emerged the technical and administrative expertise to support new capital pools in oil exploration and production both in Canada and elsewhere in the world. Increased private investment in Alberta led to a significant expansion of employment, and job creation in the province has exceeded that in other jurisdictions in Canada. This has meant a variety of induced and indirect effects, such as home construction, financial services, and retail trade, but it has also had a multiplier effect and an agglomeration effect as the population of the province has grown. Alberta, then, has become unique in that it has one particular industry that provides high rewards both to the government and to employees within the industry (from upper-level management and professional to workers in the field). The oil industry has changed the province both internally and with regard to its relations with the rest of Canada. It is not the sole cause of the province's growth, but its presence has been overwhelming because oil has become such a strategic resource. The bigger question for the future, of course, concerns what will sustain the economy of a province that has been so energized by a non-renewable resource.

It is now clear how and why Alberta developed an advantage unparalleled in Canadian history – an advantage that served as a magnet for Canadians who chose to relocate within Canada. None of this, however, tells us anything about who moves to Alberta, their motivations for doing so, and/or the implications of their doing so. In other words, saying that people move for employment is self-evident, but using employment as the sole explanation for migration hides the micro-level (personal and family) and macro-level (community, regional, and national) factors that affect the movement and relocation of people within a national society.

5

Migration as Voluntaristic Behaviour

The evidence presented in the last chapter suggests that there is a simple explanation for why Alberta became a high-destination province: jobs. Economists and other analysts assume that job opportunities are the drivers of in-migration (Tepperman 1985). Even for Albertans, there is a sense that in-migration simply means that Alberta and its robust economy are what explains the growing population. If the answer were that straightforward, however, there would be little need to write this book. Clearly, people do not migrate to places where there is no work or where the economy is weak. That much is self-evident. This, however, puts the emphasis on the receiving area and its employment opportunities. Perhaps the more critical prior question ought to be: what released migrants from their community of origin? How does someone come to the decision to migrate? When looked at in this light, the focus is more on what occurred in the region of origin than what was available at the destination.

In many ways, this is just another way of debating the old push-pull theories of migration. What is needed instead is a theory that bridges both sides of the debate. In other words, it is obvious that both a push and a pull of some kind must occur. While a push might be more dominant than a pull, or vice versa, we need to link both place of origin and destination. This chapter analyzes existing approaches to the study of migration and shows why the focus needs to be on the individual migrant as a human actor. This lays the groundwork for the methodology utilized (including the focus on the independent unsponsored migrant) as well as for theory-building.

INTERPRETING MIGRATION: THE NEED FOR REVISION

There are two major reasons why interpretations of migration are often problematic: first, the emphasis on the economic explanations for migration minimizes other non-economic motivations for migration; second, the fact that migration is understood more as an act than as a process leads to quantitative analyses at the aggregate level that fail to understand migrants as human actors whose migration behaviour is filled with individual meaning.

Explanations of migration have been overwhelmingly dominated by the presupposition that employment is the primary driver of population movements (Pandit and Withers 1999; Sjaastad 1962; Harris and Todaro 1970; Nakosteen and Zimmer 1982; Robinson and Tomes 1982; Greenwood, Mueser, Plane, and Schlotmann 1991; Cadwallader 1992; Bartram 2005, 8–14). While migration for other reasons, such as retirement (Sandefur 1985), education, family reunification, political asylum/refuge/exile (Berry 2000; Richmond 1993, 12), or even access to natural amenities (Thrush 1999) are recognized, macro theories of migration are usually discussed in terms of labour migration, with the causes of migration being measured in terms of economic outcomes. This is particularly the case for internal migration, where relocation of some individuals may be acknowledged to occur for many non-economic reasons, but larger movements are clearly understood as economically motivated.[1] In discussing interprovincial migration in Canada, economist Thomas J. Courchene (1970, 574) accentuates this point by declaring: "migration is an economic variable, this much is clear." Migration is viewed as a "labour force adjustment" and is measured through "net return minus costs" and "expected earnings." Economists tend to think of migration as an investment in which the outcomes in income can be measured. The literature on internal migration in Canada is replete with studies showing that migration occurs from regions of low per capita income and high unemployment to regions of higher per capita income and low unemployment (Stone 1969; Seldon 1973; Vandercamp and Grant 1976; Shaw 1985; Finnie 1998a, 1998b, 1999a, and 1999b; Hou and Beaujot 1995; Helliwell 1996). And, when migration does not occur this way, the drag on it is understood to be government transfer payments, which encourage people to remain in place (Winer and Gauthier 1982). Non-economic factors are often hard to analyze statistically, and when they are included in the analysis, factors like distance are interpreted in terms of transportation costs, while psychic costs are operationalized in terms of expenditures in communication and costs of return visits to see family and friends (Greenwood 1975). In other words, non-economic factors are reconfigured in economic terms. Furthermore, when these objective economic measures are correlated with migration, subjective motives are often "imputed" to the migrant (e.g., women who migrate with men are "followers") (Shaw 1985, 11), which leaves us with two questions: First, is migration only an economic variable (and, if it is not, then what is it)? Second, how can we know what migration really is if we do not understand the migrant's perspective? Imputing motives to a migrant may lead to inaccuracies and a lack of fairness. At best, it is insensitive to the nuances of migration decision making.

Much internal migration indeed is related to different levels of economic development or economic opportunity within a country (Portnov 1999), and it is nonsensical to think that large numbers in the workforce would move to a place where there was no work or where wages were lower than where they came from (Chun 1996). But the employment outcomes and the economic evaluation of migration, blinds us to the complexities of its meanings and motivations. Just because a migrant obtains employment at her/his destination does not mean that employment is the primary reason for the move. Or just because employment is a stated reason for the move does not mean that other factors may not be just as prominent or even more prominent (Newbold 1998). Perhaps it is just that employment is the most legitimate and socially acceptable reason for migration. In the long run, we are perplexed that some people decide to migrate and others, in similar situations, decide not to migrate (Winson and Leach 2002, 148–51). Obviously, using the catch-all explanation of employment masks a much more complex process in which non-economic factors are present (Jobes, Stinner, and Wardwell 1992).

The place to start is with the individual migrant, not aggregate-level data. In many studies, motivations for migration are inferred from demographic correlates of observed flows (the inferred motivation approach) (Long 1988, 228–9). Age, gender, marital status, education, and employment status of migrants are analyzed, and motivations for migration are inferred from this demographic data. For example, the predominance of young single males in a migrant pool provides no firm evidence regarding why there is a difference in migration behaviour between males and females, but an explanation is developed based on assumptions beyond the data. A second approach, which can be called a "reasons-for-moving" or declared motivation approach, is common in the literature and asks migrants their reasons for moving. Typically, employment is one option of many on a list of fixed reasons for moving provided to a study respondent; and, since a nuanced discussion is impossible, employment has a high likelihood of being chosen. Even when respondents are given an open-ended question regarding why they chose to relocate, employment is the easiest answer. These responses are then accepted as simple and straightforward. But migration decisions are much more complex, as is evidenced by the fact that some people decide to relocate and some people do not, that some people remain at a destination and others return. In short, unless we spend more time examining the factors that went into the migration decision, it is difficult to make sense out of what happens later. This suggests that much more attention needs to be paid to the individual migrant and to how migrants understand and interpret their own behaviour (Sell and DeJong 1978). In moving to the aggregate level too fast (Newbold 1998; Frey 1996; Frey and Alden 1988, Stimson and Minnery 1998), we miss the most basic building block of the migration process – the individual migrant.

The second reason why economically driven interpretations of migration are problematic is that migration is understood as an act rather than as a process (Sell and DeJong 1983). As an act, migration has a "before" and "after" with measurable consequences. Perhaps the most typical approach to migration is either to measure outcomes through occupational and income data before and after migration or to compare the migrant with others in the host society. But migration is not just a matter of outcomes; it is a process filled with ambiguities and dilemmas that begin long before migration occurs and that continue long after arrival at the destination (Munton 1990; Luo and Cooper 1990). Furthermore, there are different expectations of migration, from duration of stay to criteria of success, and these are also ignored. It might be argued that, especially with internal migrants, the ease of movement facilitates a casual approach to relocation, the success of which can be measured in multiple ways. Individual migrants each have their own way of assessing and analyzing the move, and this assessment may change over time. For example, migrants who have children while away may change their assessment of the move from what it had been when they were younger and childless. In other words, an understanding of migration as a process with mixed motivations and consequences, many of which are non-economic, is sacrificed when we view migrants as economic reward-seekers who have simply changed jurisdictional domains. In seeing migration as a process, departure and arrival is not simply a beginning and an ending; rather, they involve a complex and continuous series of behavioural choices and evaluations that affect further decision making.

The approach developed here rejects the stimulus-response form of determinism (Moon 1995) that is typical of the current models of labour migration. It also avoids the rational actor approach, which looks at economic costs and benefits as the precursor of migration. Rather, I perceive migration as the result of an ongoing sequence of perceptions, evaluations, and interpretations on the part of the migrant, both before and after relocation. From a sociological point of view, at all phases of the migration process migrants are both social actors and inhabitants of social contexts in which interpretations are subject to change and re-evaluation. What is necessary is a social-psychological approach to migrating in which the migrant is the unit of analysis throughout the process.[2] Without understanding the meaning of migration from the migrant's perspective, interpretations and explanations of migration risk being either false or superficial (Fielding 1992, 207).

It is not surprising that economists would focus on the economic returns of migration, but it should be acknowledged that this has much legitimacy in the popular mind as well. If employment is considered to be the most frequent reason for migration of distances beyond the local municipality, then it would seem obvious that economic outcomes are the most important data. But behaviourists have challenged these economic interpretations because they see migration as more than an economic process; rather, it involves many personal and contextual factors (Liaw 1990a). Halfacree and Boyle (1993), for example, call for the rejection of linear models that emphasize rationalization and, instead, call for contextualizing migration within "biographically rooted intentions." Wolpert (1965) was one of the first to acknowledge that it was not economic circumstances in themselves that prompted migration but the subjective evaluation of place. Given this, understanding the migrant as an active agent in the evaluation process ought to be our starting point. To reiterate, there is an uneasy tension between economic models and behavioural models because, on the surface, employment appears to be the most dominant factor in explaining migration behaviour. But migration is much more complicated than this implies, and it requires a fresh attempt to theorize it.

THEORY: REVIEW AND EVALUATION

In the field of migration, theory has been shaped more by international migration than by internal migration. Perhaps the most influential review of migration theory in recent years was undertaken by Massey and associates (Massey et al. 1994; Massey et al. 1998; Massey 1999).[3] Using their discussion of international migration as a base, the major theoretical models can be assessed for their contribution to our understanding of internal migration and its application to Alberta.

Neoclassical Economic Models

Neoclassical economic models understood migration as rooted in geographic differences in labour supply and demand, with a shift from low-wage job-scarce regions to high-wage job-rich regions occurring until such time as a corrective equilibrium was reached. Migrants were rational actors in this scheme as their decision to move was predicated on cost-benefit calculations regarding how to maximize their returns. This is as "micro" as this approach gets. Economic returns were the prime motive for migration, which made it easy to aggregate all migrants since they all aimed to obtain the same results; other factors in the migration process were ignored. We have already seen the limitations of this approach.

A further problem with this approach is that it assumed that increased wages per se was the primary objective of the migrant. Such a pattern may represent a central motivation among international migrants from developing countries, where low wages/no wages may make subsistence (food and shelter) and survival a primary concern. But in the case of internal migration in a developed country, where social welfare schemes are present, it is seldom the case that increased wages alone is the issue. Indeed, in a low-wage region typically the cost of living is also low so that migrants who move just for wage reasons may complain that their net gain is not great due to the higher cost of living in a high-wage region. Receiving unemployment insurance ensures that subsistence concerns are met. But what unemployment or underemployment (i.e., working in a job with little challenge, no future, or for which the employee is overqualified) may reflect may not be so much an economic matter as a matter of personal usefulness, personal development, or skill utilization. Migration may be undertaken not so much for increased wages as for better labour opportunity. While increased wages might be an outcome of this process, the primary goal may be personal career development. And this is increasingly the case in Western countries, where educational programs stress postsecondary career training and job specialization, with the result that the pool of unskilled, poorly educated labour has shrunk. Monetary reward may be an outcome of the migration process, but obtaining *more meaningful labour*[4] may its driving force. Clearly, the motivations behind migration can only be uncovered through interviews with the individual migrant; they cannot be inferred from wage differentials.

New Economics of Migration

The focus of this approach shifts from migrants as individuals to migrants as members of households who collectively decide to send one or more members abroad (especially from a developing country to a developed one) as a means of stabilizing or increasing family income through remittances back home. This model has limited relevance with reagard to understanding internal migration in Canadian society, which, when it does occur, does so for one major reason. There is a long tradition of seasonal internal migration in Canada from low employment regions, whether to work "out West" or "up North" or even "on the (Great) Lakes." Frontier expansion, agricultural tasks, railroad or shipping work, oil exploration, and/or construction labour have often required seasonal workers. The largest pool of people crossing interprovincial boundaries for such work has been comprised of people from Atlantic Canada whose families were well established at home and had no desire for permanent relocation (Burrill 1992). Thus, making money and sending it back home, as well as returning home after the season with unemployment benefits, was a fairly widespread pattern.[5] Another pattern is found among people in construction. This is because construction jobs come and go, and, rather than moving an entire family, a residence is maintained in the home province and the construction worker commutes on a monthly or semi-monthly basis. Numerous construction workers in Alberta had families who lived in Saskatchewan or British Columbia. However, as the sense that there was permanent work in Alberta increased, many of these workers began moving their families to that province. In general, though, in Canada there is considerable acceptance of the fact that nuclear families often move independently, a phenomenon that disperses extended families across the country – families that have few fiduciary obligations between them.

Segmented Labour Market Theory

This theory maintains that immigrants are brought to a new location because they will accept jobs with low wages that native-born workers will not accept, thereby creating a split labour market. There is little evidence that such a pattern exists among internal migrants in Canada. While it is true that some recently arrived migrants often accept whatever job is available upon arrival in order to support themselves, there is considerable evidence that, in an expanding economy, the possibilities of movement to a better job and better pay exist everywhere. In fact, this is one of the major attractions of relocating into an expanding economy as employers offering menial jobs with low pay often discover that worker retention is difficult (e.g., fast food franchises in Fort McMurray). The only place where a split labour market may have emerged in Alberta is in the meat-packing plants, particularly at Brooks and High River, where unskilled immigrants who were unable to find employment elsewhere in Canada came to work at a difficult task that was avoided by the local labour market. In general, though, internal migrants were not part of a separate labour pool in Alberta, and they entered the labour market at all levels.

World Systems Theory

World systems relate regionalized dependency and underdevelopment to forces of global capital, and they distinguish between "core" countries (which are centres of power) and "peripheral" countries (which are subordinate hinterlands). A global market economy dislocates populations in peripheral regions, which makes them susceptible to migration to core regions. In other words, places of capital and investment concentration serve as magnets in population movements. While world systems theory has other implications that are less relevant to internal migration, there is no doubt that peripheral regions also exist *within* countries such as Canada and that these regions are losing/have lost population to more core regions. Core regions have advantages in that they have more employment variety and higher-paying jobs than do peripheral regions. While the periphery is likely to have more employment in the primary sector (such as agriculture and natural resource extraction), the core is more likely to have the value-added as well as the administrative, finance, and product development jobs. For this reason, core-periphery relations may be a very significant factor in internal migration. In Canada, for example, there is no question that all aspects of the national economy, from the arts and culture to material production and investment, have been controlled by core urban regions, particularly Toronto. But there is another side to this core-periphery link. The labour pool of the periphery can be understood as a "reserve army of labour" to be summoned when the core requires it. When their labour is no longer needed, these migrants are conditioned to return to the periphery, where they are supported by a variety of forms of government transfer payments. It has sometimes been said that the social welfare system in regions with weaker economies has been an impediment to the free flow of labour that might have occurred through migration to stronger economic regions (Courchene 1970; Day 1989). If this is true, periphery-to-core migration might even have been stronger were these supports not in place. Internal migration, then, is stimulated by the continual assessment of life chances in the place of residence, especially in the periphery, compared to life chances in potential destinations in the core regions of the country, which provide better life chances and to which persons technically have free access.

As a hinterland agricultural province, for years Alberta had lost many residents through internal migration to more urban centre, particularly in central Canada. However, with the growth of its own cities, signalled by the burgeoning energy industry, Alberta has begun to shed its reputation as a hinterland. As the population base, along with pools of capital and expertise within the province, has increased, the province has developed greater economic capacity, which has increased the range of opportunities and attracted a broader pool of migrants. The end result is that Alberta has been moving away from its once peripheral position in the national hierarchy to become a destination province. In truth, Alberta has been struggling with a type of interstitial position between core and periphery – a struggle that has not been without ambiguities and conflict – but the role that oil has played as a strategic resource with international ties has clearly elevated the place of the province in the national hierarchy. Thus, migration to Alberta needs to be understood in terms of the changing role that this province has played in both the national and the global economies.

Social Capital Theory

This theory emphasizes the role of interpersonal ties in reducing the risks and costs of migration in order to facilitate a successful relocation, and even to instigate the move in the first place. The role of social networks has long been acknowledged in international migration, but its presence in internal migration is less well known. The role that earlier migrants from place of origin play in destination selection and the importance of clustering at destination among internal migrants are also seldom discussed. In short, it is important to understand the role that social capital plays in the migration process among internal migrants.

Cumulative Causation

Because each act of migration makes subsequent migration decisions more likely, cumulative causation emphasizes how the migration option occurs within a sending society. The role of exemplars and established migration patterns to specific destinations are both important and obvious when there is a migration stream from an origin to a destination. The role of such cumulative influences has been understudied in cases of internal migration, particularly in terms of how it affects the sending community. But the migrant must also be understood in terms of the receiving community. The impact of disengagement and attempts at re-engagement remain important elements in the migration process. These are the critical social contexts of migration and must be part of any migration theory.

The purpose of this selective review of migration theory is not to analyze them in detail or even to discuss them thoroughly but, rather, to point out some themes in the study of migration that might be relevant to a theory of internal migration. It is clear from this review that the social aspects of migration have been recognized and that migration is not just driven by economic factors. As Massey et al. (1999, 47, 50) note, these theoretical perspectives are not necessarily contradictory, and embracing only one of them would undoubtedly produce an incomplete understanding of migration. While it can be acknowledged that the causes and motivations of migration are complex (Beaman and D'Arcy 1980), either explicitly or implicitly economic factors are understood as more causal while social factors are understood as more facilitative (Clark 1998, 3–5). The exploration of this issue has depended heavily on the study of international migration, and what is needed is a theoretical perspective that is especially relevant to the analysis of internal migration.

To sum up, the goal of this book is to understand domestic migration through the eyes of the migrant. Rather than clustering migrants into aggregates, I want to establish the migrant's perception of the meaning of her/his own behaviour, motivations, and goals. Furthermore, I attempt to examine the non-economic factors in migration – factors that have been acknowledged as of importance but that have seldom been probed (Hunt and Mueller 2004, 241).

MIGRATION AS VOLUNTARY OR INVOLUNTARY BEHAVIOUR?

If the starting point in the analysis of migration is the individual migrant, an important issue that must be faced is whether migration consists of voluntary or involuntary behaviour. In a free society, and especially within one's own country, it is often thought that migration is the result of free choice. Yet almost all migration is at least partially a response to circumstances within the community of origin over which one might have little control (van Hear 1998, 42). In that sense, migration may not be the preferred option at all, and the migrant may feel forced to relocate.

There is no reason to relocate unless the current domain is problematic in some way and a new location is anticipated to be more suitable in some respect. Even the individual with wanderlust is propelled by the fact that her current community seems too small and there is more of the world out there to be explored. More freedom, better economy, better job, better climate, more independence, cheaper housing, and so on all serve to suggest that there is a push from the place of origin that makes the pull of a destination appealing. But the forces of push and pull are not as mechanical and straightforward as is often presumed. The push factors are usually complex and are the result of nuanced interpretation and negotiation. The migrant is only too aware of the mixed bag of gains and losses that migration may entail. In addition, the migration process begins long before migration ever takes place as the potential migrant weighs alternatives and begins a decision-making process that involves considerable reflection, second-guessing, and even reversals. The tension between staying and leaving continues even after settlement at the destination. No mechanistic push-pull theory helps us to understand the dilemmas that individual migrants experience.

In truth, then, all migration is constrained by circumstances that shape choices. Since migration is not just an act but also a process, it is filled with perceptions, interpretations, re-evaluations, and, above all, changing circumstances at each step of its trajectory. Particularly in the case of domestic migration, there is often a sense of tentativeness and transience to such moves for there is a choice to be made not only about whether to move but also about when and where to move. Personal needs and social obligations, the availability of resources, and alternatives all vary at different points in time (Fischer 1977, 184). Thus volition is involved in considering available options in the continuous assessment of costs and consequences. Migration is neither one-dimensional behaviour nor one-directional behaviour; nor is it once-for-all behaviour. In a society in which individual choice is valued and family obligations exist (albeit in muted form), migration is essentially voluntary behaviour. On the other hand, there is an inertia to long-distance migration that encourages the resolution of unsatisfactory issues in the community of residence and/or the acceptance of the status quo. The greatest intrigue in migration is found in this nexus of staying or going, where the dilemmas of constraint and choice are played out simultaneously.

TWO FORMS OF INTERNAL MIGRATION: SPONSORED AND UNSPONSORED

One of the ways in which the issue of choice/constraint plays out in migration is in the distinction between migration sponsored by an employer and migration that is not sponsored by an employer. In Western countries, internal migration is often induced by employers who sponsor/request a relocation and pay the costs associated with the move. This is often referred to as "being transferred," and many employers have deliberate policies to move employees to different places in order to broaden the employee's work experiences, to respond to the changing needs of the organization, and/or to facilitate expansion or new initiatives (Hendershott 1995; Brett 1982). When Vance Packard (1972) wrote his book, this form of corporate-sponsored migration implied that geographic mobility was related to social mobility. Corporate-sponsored migrants were typically white-collar workers with high education and high incomes for whom relocation meant advancement and upward mobility (Sell 1992; Kanter 1977; Rosenbaum 1983). These moves involved considerable corporate support, including all-expenses-paid pre-move visits to the destination for house-hunting, assistance with home sales, the payment of all moving expenses, including various forms of compensations, enticements, and adjustment support.[6] Of course, such moves also implied a guaranteed job at the destination. For example, the branch banking system in Canada (and its need to preserve security, staff remote locations, and provide a wide range of banking experience and training for its management staff) historically required repeated moves by employees and their families. Other employers only engage in such transfers strategically or on request. In truth, corporate movers often have limited choices and their decisions to relocate are constrained by obligations to the company, career investments, and financial considerations such as pensions (Brett and Reilly 1988; Brett, Stroh, and Reilly 1993; Munton, Forster, Altman, and Greenbury, 1993). Another form of sponsored migration (sometimes called contracted migration) occurs through national recruitment outside the organization. In most cases of sponsored migration, the relocation of an existing employee or recruited employee involves other members of a family and often occurs over a considerable distance and at considerable expense. Expensive national moving companies offering "full pack and unpack" services are evidence of this kind of move.

However, there is another category of internal migrant for whom a long-distance move is independent and, indeed, speculative. No company has asked this person to move, there is no financial support for the relocation, and there is no guaranteed job at the destination. This type of migrant is referred to as an unsponsored, or independent, migrant because her/his decision to move is made of her/his own volition, at her/his own expense, and with considerable risk. Available migration statistics do not reveal what percentage of internal migrants are sponsored and unsponsored, but when a migration stream is strong to a place with a vibrant economy, it is likely that there are many more unsponsored migrants than sponsored migrants.[7] Unsponsored migrants are more likely to have lower incomes before moving and perhaps to be less educated than sponsored movers, who already have jobs with employers who value their services. However, unsponsored movers should not necessarily be considered uneducated or unskilled; the migration literature notes that migrants are more likely to be those who have better education and skills, and what they are searching for is a better opportunity. The dynamics of migration for this group are totally different from those of the sponsored migrant, and we need a theory that is able to account for how and why someone in an advanced Western society will relocate at great personal risk and expense.

The unsponsored migrant has much in common with the traditional immigrant in that the move involves risks and considerable personal sacrifice. A family that moved to Alberta from British Columbia illustrates this type of migration, and a family member describes their experience as follows: "We came with nothing. It was almost like being a homesteader. We had to start over. You don't move a family with three children and no job and no home without feeling like that." Various forms of self-moving, especially the U-Haul trailer or truck, are the stock-in-trade of unsponsored movers. The unsponsored domestic migrant is different from the unsponsored foreign immigrant in that, for the former, there are lower administrative costs to relocation. There are no admission requirements and no approvals must be given. The unsponsored migrant can move freely within a country and can be as mobile as he or she wants to be, encumbered only by personal possessions and personal ties. Above all, return migration is possible with smaller risks than would be faced by the foreign migrant. On the other hand, there are almost no agencies available to assist the unsponsored domestic migrant in the adjustment process, and it is assumed she/he is capable of handling all aspects of the relocation independently.

There is no way of ascertaining what percentage of migrants to Alberta in either wave were sponsored and what percentage were not.[8] However, the overwhelming sense we gained in our fieldwork was that what made the waves so dynamic (and unpredictable) was the fact that by far the majority of in-migrants (and out-migrants) were unsponsored migrants who moved independently and who assumed all the risks of relocation. The sudden heavy demand on rental companies specializing in moving equipment serves to confirm this.[9] Given the fact that the dynamics of sponsored migration are so radically different from those of the independent migrant, and given the fact that unsponsored migration was the more typical form of migration in the migration waves under consideration, a theory of internal migration must be constructed based upon the experience of the independent mover.

STUDY DESIGN

If it is true that an expanding economy in one region of a country will attract large numbers of migrants from other regions of the country, migrants who engage in their own decision making, take action of their own volition, and relocate at their own expense, then it would be prudent to make this type of unsponsored migrant the focus of a study on in-migration to Alberta. Furthermore, if it is important to understand migration from the perspective of the individual migrant, then in-depth interviews are required. A study design was developed that involved a three-stage process. In Phase I, interviews were conducted with people who had migrated independently to Alberta from 1996 to 2002. In Phase II, the impact on communities of origin of out-migration was assessed and Alberta migrants who had returned to those communities were interviewed. In Phase III, which occurred two years later, all participants were subject to follow-up data collection in order to determine their assessment of their migration experience. Participants had to have paid their own expenses for relocation and could not have been recruited with incentives to migrate.[10] In Phase I, 341 persons took part in semi-structured, one-hour interviews and it is they who served as the core study group. However, data were also obtained through a variety of other means, and this helped me to evaluate individual migration experiences. The Appendix describes the methodology of the study design in some detail. The following chapters present the data and the emergent theory that resulted from this research.

6

The Migrant and the Migration Process

One of the basic questions in the study of migration is: what leads some people to become migrants? Demonstrating that large numbers of people have migrated from one place to another may identify a migration stream, but it does not tell us why an individual decides to migrate. We can identify waves of migration to Alberta by examining economic conditions, but this does not explain what leads some people to migrate while others stay. The only way to answer this question is to begin with the individual migrant. While migration often consists of networked behaviour in which interpersonal relations influence, shape, and structure the migration process, it is at root a decision taken by individuals who exist in familial and community contexts.

The goal of this chapter is to understand the migration process from the perspective of the individual migrant. It is the social location of the migrant in the departing community and the receiving community that is at the core of this analysis.[1] What leads people to begin the process of uprooting in the first place, and what explains the decision to migrate? We would not expect people who are employed and involved in the community, who own their own home and whose children are deeply rooted in the community, and who are comfortable with their social ties to have any reason to migrate (compare Uhlenberg 1973). I argue that the key to the decision to migrate may be found in feelings of dissatisfaction with social location.

SOCIAL POSITION AND MARGINALITY

Taking a sociological perspective, the study of migration is primarily a study of how social position is perceived, experienced, and negotiated by the potential/actual migrant in the sending and receiving communities.[2] An established, stable, and acceptable position within a community allows a person to feel integrated into it. An unacceptable, precarious, or uncertain position in a community makes a person feel marginal to it. What are the conditions under which some people feel integrated while others feel marginalized? My thesis is that the migrant is someone who feels some form of marginalization in the sending community and seeks to resolve it by migrating to a new community. However, by virtue of being a new member of a different community, the migrant enters it as a marginal person and struggles to become integrated. Thus, at both origin and destination, there is *tension between integration and marginality* as the migrant attempts to relate personal objectives to social location. This tension is often a response to lifecycle issues, shifting economic conditions, changing values and ambitions, and altered relationships and responsibilities. Unsponsored migrants are the most likely to struggle with this process as migration is a clear declaration that something was unsatisfactory in the region of origin. Migration then represents a personal effort to find a more suitable role and position at a new destination. This search may involve employment, but it involves more than that. It involves understanding who one is in relation to a social context – what Brubaker (2004, 44) calls "situated objectivity," which is evaluated either positively or negatively. A satisfactory social location involves a combination of roles, identities, status, values, lifestyle, and relationships. Social location then blends objective elements of social structure with subjective elements of personal evaluation, identified here as satisfaction/dissatisfaction. Because of the complexity of these factors, migration may resolve some aspects of marginality, but it may also create new dilemmas.

Understanding the migration process begins with looking at the social location of the potential migrant in the community of origin. In order for migration to occur, life in the community of origin must be perceived to be unsatisfactory in some way (Speare, Kobrin, and Kingkade 1982; Moon 1995, 512). Seldom does this dissatisfaction involve a complete rejection of the community. Instead, some aspect of life in the community is deemed unsatisfactory, and this establishes an openness to new options. Eisenstadt (1954, 2) refers to these feelings as "unfulfilled expectations," suggesting that the individual anticipated a role that appeared unattainable or that was lost in the place of origin. Taylor (1969, 109–16) speaks of a "search for alternatives," which implies unhappiness with current roles/situations and a desire for something new. Yet a third way in which this dissatisfaction has been expressed is through "stress" (Clark 1981; Wolpert 1966). Personal psychic tension may arise from conditions at the place of origin, but social stress may also be the product of unhappiness with one's social ties within the community of origin. Stress may also emerge from structural upheavals and transformations (e.g., recessions, plant closings) that may produce dislocations (Akerman 1978, 301).

Box 1: Dissatisfaction and Desire for Change

We were spending more and more time working in our own business and we didn't like that lifestyle. That got us thinking that we needed a change in our lives. (Saskatchewan)

I thought about leaving for about a year and I felt I needed a change in environment. I felt I was suffocating and that I needed a geographical change. I had been around the same people for so long and if I changed my surroundings that would be the impetus to make some different decisions. I needed to make a big change. I was getting tired of Ottawa and I wanted to have different opportunities. (Ontario)

I have a lot of friends who stay at home and have kids and are happy and I'm not making a judgment about that, but that wasn't what I wanted. I got an e-mail from a friend out here who told me about a job here and I said why not try it. I had very little tying me down, so I said why not? Alberta is the land of milk and honey. (Nova Scotia)

When things were declining, there was lots of grumbling. They blamed the government for the fishing policy, they blamed the pulp mill, and they blamed the fish companies ... There was always talk about projects and studies about projects but nothing ever happened. We were far away from the centre of power in Victoria and the lobbies were down there. If you were not from there, you were the tail of the dog. If you [didn't] live in Victoria or Vancouver you were off in the hinterland. It just made me unhappy living where I was. (British Columbia)

We did have a decent life there in spite of the economic limitations, but we were not growing as people. (Ontario)

It was just time to leave Nova Scotia. I was very close to my family and I did a lot with them. But it was time to break from that mould and they encouraged me to make a new life for myself ... A lot of people have their feet planted on the ground back there and live in their own little bubble. And that's great. But some of us have more of a sense of adventure and want to see what else is out there. I think a lot of those people are stuck in a rut. Why don't they get out and experience something instead of being stuck at home with two kids? Try something new. You can always go back home. (Nova Scotia)

I was sick of my job and decided within two weeks to leave the small town that I grew up in Saskatchewan. I had been there all my life and wanted a change to a better lifestyle. The small community pressures had little freedom and I needed a larger pool to swim in. (Saskatchewan)

I had heard about things here and I was going through a few things at the time so I quit my job as a maintenance worker and came out. My job at home was fine, but I was going through some things so I thought it would be good to come out. (Nova Scotia)

I think I just got fed up with living in a small town and everyone knowing everything that you're doing. My sister had moved to Alberta so I called her up and said I was coming. (New Brunswick)

When you grow up in one place and you reach a certain age, you want something more. And a growing city offers you more and gives you a chance to grow. I wanted to get away from my home town for awhile because I knew I could always go back ... the fact that everyone knows everyone is a great way to grow up, but I decided I needed a change. (Manitoba)

We had been married for a year and we just had no money and it was very stressful ... We were living across the road from our parents in an old rundown farmhouse that was expensive to heat. Our parents would often bring us groceries. We were making $238 a week and my wife was trying to take courses and draw UI. Lots of people were working in government-subsidized jobs like I was, where the government pays for half of your wage. It is hard to grow up when you are so dependent. (Prince Edward Island)

I didn't like my job. I didn't like our town in Ontario because it was too small. Our landlord went back on all her promises. Rents in

Toronto were insane. We looked in Niagara Falls but the house deal fell through. (Ontario)

The basis of dissatisfaction must be understood in its social context. From this perspective, the emphasis is on roles and the relationships that may have become problematic and for which migration becomes a possible solution. The term used to describe this situation is "disembedded," meaning that when a person's embedded place in a social context becomes awkward, it prompts the need for change (Granovetter 1985; Sinclair, Squires, and Downton 1999). This personal perception of unsatisfactory social position creates a sense of marginalization. *Marginalization is the sociological correlate of dissatisfaction, the result of which is that a person no longer feels comfortable with her/his position (roles, relationships, status) within a community.* Feeling marginalized is not so much a matter of what a community does to an individual as how the individual understands her/his place in the community. This perception may have evolved over time, may be of long-standing, or may have only recently emerged. It is this social/psychological condition that leads individuals to assess their life chances in a community in such a way that migration becomes both an option and a reality.

How and why does social dislocation or dissatisfaction with social position occur? In some instances, it is the result of changes within the local community, but sometimes it is also the result of changes within the individual. The most typical form of dislocation is often thought to be caused by unemployment or underemployment. Losing one's job has not only economic consequences but also social consequences in that the person no longer has a position in the social economy of the community. Restructuring an industry or closing it down represents a structural change over which an individual may have little control and that clearly has an unsettling effect. In either case, the person no longer perceives her/his role in the community as being either productive or comfortable, and this produces a sense of marginalization. Marginalization may be seen as objective in that it may be perceived as the result of a lost, unsatisfactory, or unattainable position within a community, but it may also be seen as subjective in that the potential migrant perceives it as an unsatisfactory situation.

What is critical here is that employment issues need to be understood in terms of their sociological implications. Or, to put it another way, employment has social meanings. Having no job may result in the strongest feeling of marginalization, but having a job with little status when one is qualified to do other things also has a significant marginalizing effect. Having a job that offers little opportunity for advancement may also lead to a person's feeling dissatisfied with her/ his position within a community. Relocation may allow the individual to break out of an employment role and to find new options. In this sense, it is not just moving for work but moving in anticipation of employment that would positively affect one's social position that is important.

Dislocation may occur as a personal response to changing life conditions that have had a marginalizing effect. For example, lifecycle issues emerge when a child or student becomes an adult and is no longer satisfied with his/her role in the community. He/she no longer wants to be viewed as a dependent ("the son or daughter of ___") and desires more autonomy and freedom from familial ties and obligations. Instead of viewing these ties as assets, the child/student often views them as restricting her/his own personal growth. Even the desire for adventure and the desire to explore new places can be seen as a response to the sense of confinement represented by one's community of origin,[3] which is often viewed as being "too small." Obtaining training in a particular field only to discover that the appropriate jobs are not available also results in a feeling of marginalization.

Persons may have aspirations that cannot be met where they currently live, or they may feel restless and trapped. For example, home ownership may be a desired goal, but high costs or lack of an appropriate job may make that unattainable in the community of origin. Strained or broken relationships can produce sharp dissatisfaction with one's place in a community. All of this may lead to marginalization, which results in people no longer being satisfied with their position within their community and, thus, having an intense desire to change it. It is not just one's understanding of the social context but one's understanding of oneself, both cognitively and emotionally, that is affected (Brubaker 2004). Small business failures, marriage and divorce, births and deaths change people's social position in intense ways, but they also change the way in which people think about themselves. Persons may develop special interests or prefer specific lifestyles that become critical to who they are, and these things may not be available or appropriate in their existing community. While some persons prefer the same patterns throughout their lifetime, others seek change, advancement, or growth. Still others are shocked into change through deaths or job loss. The point is, there are many experiences that may make a person's position in a community less acceptable than it had once been. Dissatisfaction may also be increased through the recognition that a realistic alternative is available elsewhere (McHugh 1984). The migration process, then, is a form of transitioning from an unsatisfactory personal position in one community to what is hoped will be a satisfactory personal position in another.

THE RELEASING PROCESS

If migration is a process that involves transitioning, then it cannot simply be reduced to origin and destination; rather, it must begin with how a person becomes a migrant in the first instance and how she/he experiences the destination after arrival. The decision to migrate, in itself, involves not just a departure but also a releasing process that takes place over time; that is, it is an evolving recognition that relocation might be a solution to feelings of dissatisfaction and perceptions of marginality. This process cannot be reduced to a simple common cause. It is individual and personal, and it involves assessing one's present social position in relation to one's aspirations, goals, and various constraints. This is an important point because, when migration is primarily understood as labour migration caused by underemployment or unemployment, it leaves us in the position of being unable to account for the fact that not all unemployed/underemployed people choose to migrate. In fact, migration may be prompted by other factors, with employment issues merely functioning to seal the decision. This is especially so for unsponsored migrants who would not leave their community of origin for an uncertain future without the existence of significant releasing factors. Humans are actors who are engaged in meaning-seeking behaviour; therefore, the process of becoming a migrant requires developing a justification for relocation that facilitates the process of release. Not only is this rationale important with regard to validating one's decision to leave, but it is also important with regard to publicly justifying one's behavioural choices.

Box 2: Releasing Factors

[There were an unbelievable number of personal factors that served as releasing mechanisms for migrants. Some of these include: personal struggles of various kinds, divorces, failed relationships, ex-spouse problems, bankruptcies, timing issues, and physical ailments that made it impossible to work in an old job.]

When my mother died, our family fell apart, so I had no regret in leaving. (Manitoba)

I said that the biggest factor was not having a job that paid well enough, but in reality there were some personal factors pertaining to a previous woman in my life that really made me do it. (Nova Scotia)

Our nuclear families are in Ottawa, and frankly I would prefer to be further distant from them until the quality of our relationship improves. That was part of the impetus for us to go elsewhere. (Ontario)

I had been dating a guy for eight or nine years and he became my fiancée, but we split up and I was looking for a new start. I had just graduated so that was the right time. I now have a new fiancée who I met here, but he is from a town one hour from where I grew up. But I never met the man before in my life till I moved here. (Nova Scotia)

Due to a mid-life crisis and divorce situation I decided on a career change, and there was a new career opportunity in Alberta. I would have stayed in British Columbia but there was no money there. But I didn't choose Alberta for any reason. It was just that there were no opportunities anywhere there. It was not a political issue for me, but when the NDP government screwed up, it reduced opportunities in BC. (British Columbia)

My decision to leave Montreal started a long time ago. But you get to the point that you get so fed up with the political situation. I tried to get a transfer to Toronto and so did my husband, but his heart wasn't in it and neither of us could get transferred. A year later I was divorced and I only had to worry about myself. (Quebec)

I had some personal experiences that made me ready for a change, just retired and just separated from my husband. I was looking for a house that was charming and economical, and I made a quick decision because my children were here. The prices in Vancouver were so astronomical that I could not find anything there I could afford that I liked. (British Columbia)

We were living in the Lower Mainland and paying high rent. We had small children and were taking in students to help offset costs. And we still did not have enough money. My wife's father passed away and that meant her mother was living alone in Edmonton. Six weeks from the day we decided to move, we packed up and moved to Edmonton. Mom did some renovating and moved to the basement, so now we had a home to move to. (British Columbia)

I wanted to distance myself from my mother. (British Columbia)

I had an argument with my family, and I said you can argue by yourself, I'm leaving. (Quebec)

I had worked on Hibernia and Sable Island and Terra Nova, but after that there was nothing on the project horizon for me. By this time, all of my children were working in Alberta. I had never been in the West before and now that our family was here, it made sense to come here because I knew there were opportunities here. But my wife and I are of two minds about how long we are staying. (Nova Scotia)

I had gone to Ottawa to go to school and I found work there. But it was a job that wasn't worth staying at. My husband was offered a buyout at his job and the place where we were living was sold, so it seemed to be the best time to move. We knew we couldn't make a living in Nova Scotia where we had lived for a time before so we knew we had to go out West. I had a sister in Edmonton and we could stay with her while we tried to get established. (Ontario)

When I graduated from high school, I assumed I would be moving away. But when I entered into a relationship with a man, I allowed myself to get stuck there. So when that relationship ended, I realized what I wanted to do in the first place, and this made it easier to leave. I purposely didn't want to leave home until I was back on my feet. If I had left one year earlier, I would have been running away. I had gone through worse things before I came here, and when I felt depressed here, I knew I could weather the storm and just keep going. (Prince Edward Island)

I just didn't want to be in the same job for more than eleven years and stay in the same community where I grew up. But it was also my mom passing away … I refused to be from and live and die in Cambridge, Ontario, and not experience something else. (Ontario)

I operated a business in Sudbury, Ontario, and the business went bankrupt after I had an accident. I lost everything – my house, my wife – and had a lot of stress. So I was looking for a new start in life and was offered a job in Saskatoon. When that ended I was going to go back to Ontario, but then I decided to try Alberta. Business was very difficult in Sudbury, with a lot of unemployment, and there was little use in going back there when the economy was better in Alberta. (Ontario)

I am not a radical socialist but Vancouver is turning into a rich and poor place, and I felt like Edmonton was much more of a blue-collar place, which I liked. Vancouver has turned into a place for the rich and a subclass of servants. We lived in Vancouver['s] West End. There was a condo across the street from us that was worth $7 million, and here we were across the street in a 500-square-foot hovel paying $1,000 a month. People were coming to Vancouver to live the life of luxury, and I had to hold down two jobs to make ends meet. (British Columbia)

When my company was sold, that's when I decided to search elsewhere. I did apply for jobs in Winnipeg but I received little response. So I took a week of holiday and flew to Alberta and got a hotel room while I was here. I brought my wife's resume as well, which I took around. I called a real estate agent who took me around to look at houses. Because I was getting all these offers, I knew something was going to fall into place, so I thought I better look at houses. Before I left I got a firm job offer. It wasn't exactly the job I wanted but I saw it as a stepping stone until I found something else. My wife even got a call to Winnipeg for an interview, and she came out and looked at the house and liked it. So I put my house up for sale and in three days it was gone, so then I had to go through with it. (Manitoba)

I did some research on my genealogy and I traced my ancestors back to 1630, so I am proud to be French Canadian. Most Quebecers that I know here want to stay here because they are sick and tired of hearing of the referendum. That is why we left. (Quebec)

The seemingly self-evident reason for moving to Alberta was initially confirmed in interviews with people who had relocated from another province. When participants were asked why they had moved to

Alberta, the answer was invariably for employment.[4] But in response to the question "how did you come to the decision to relocate?" the first answer was qualified with comments about various circumstances, and this identified deeper reasons for relocation. Respondents talked about soured relationships, the need for more autonomy, restlessness, career ambitions or employment issues, the problems of small-town culture, the rejection of long commutes, or the high price of housing as catalysts in their decision to consider migration. Often respondents explored these push factors in some depth, even to the point where they either qualified their initial response about jobs or where they substituted what they had initially said about why they migrated with a different reason altogether. What emerged from my interviews was the fact that, while employment at the destination was always a factor in migration, there were intensely personal releasing factors present, and these were what enabled migration to be considered in the first place. These factors were invariably related to the migrants' assessment of their position in the community of origin.

The interplay of these factors, which served as releasing mechanisms, was discovered through the in-depth interviews. Personal/family issues were often not mentioned publicly but were very important privately. The response of a 23-year-old male from New Brunswick gets at the heart of this issue.

> I couldn't admit to my parents that I really needed to get away from their influence, so I dressed up my reason in all kinds of other things, like I needed to get a job that would give me experience in my field, reasons that were more acceptable to them and their friends. In fact, I think that this is the first time that I have even admitted this to myself – because I do love my parents. (male, 23, New Brunswick)

Two things emerge in this statement. One is that there is a difference between this person's public rationale and his private rationale for migration; the second is that reasons for migration operate at both a fully conscious and articulated level and at a subterranean level. Migrants often talked about being driven by inner factors. For example, a Quebec francophone talked about the fact that, while she had a good job in Quebec, she had a driving ambition to prove that she could make it in an anglophone business environment. A migrant from Ontario volunteered that, while he had never admitted this even to himself, down deep the real reason he wanted to move was to get away from interfering parents-in-law. Another migrant from the Atlantic provinces spoke about the culture of dependency that prevailed in his home town and said that he could not tolerate it. None of these people felt that they could openly discuss these issues, so employment was their standard answer when asked why they were migrating. Employment was certainly part of the equation, but the releasing factor was intensely personal and discussing it required both a "safe" context and a lengthy interactive interview.

The process whereby, as the interview unfolded, the respondent came to articulate a rationale for migration that included basic motivations that were not typical "stock-in-hand" responses may be described as "reflexive progression."[5] The typical answer to the question of why relocation was considered was always jobs or employment. It was as though this was what the interviewee thought was expected or what was acceptable (especially to people back home); but, at best, this represented only part of the story. It was not acceptable to talk publicly about problem relationships, family conflicts, community of origin issues, or personal goals, and it was easier to give a simple general response – jobs. This was particularly the case because perceptions that contributed to a sense of marginalization could not be discussed publicly without the interviewee's appearing to be critical of the community of origin. But there was always a more personal answer to the question of why migration occurred, and this usually contained within it the releasing factor that made migration possible. Without this releasing factor, no migration would have occurred regardless of how many jobs were waiting at a destination.

The difficulty in uncovering primary and secondary motivations for migration, and the need for migrants to articulate their reasons for migration in a way that is publicly acceptable, can be illustrated in another example in which employment was not the primary reason for migration. A woman from Saskatchewan had this to say:

> It is true that the primary reason we moved is because of the needs of our disabled child but I guess I was predisposed to move because there is a different attitude here. I wanted a more entrepreneurial environment and I guess that explains why we moved and others with similar problems did not. But I don't think I even admitted that outwardly to myself or to others. It was just easier to say it was because of our daughter and people could accept that better. And it's sort of startling to put that on the table now because it was just lurking in the background before. (Saskatchewan)

Migrants were often careful not to give the impression that their departure was in any way a rejection of their departure community. Furthermore, their motivations were often mixed and somewhat confusing to the migrants themselves. What they learned to say publicly may or may not have really explained what released them from their community of origin, and the key to their release was usually found in the more private sphere.

Another point of some significance in the releasing process was the fact that life in a migrant's place of origin was almost always described as problematic in some way. Many respondents went out of their way to lament the fact that they "had to leave." Especially in retrospect, respondents often spoke of the good things about their community of origin. And yet, when it was tied to *their own* explanations of why they left, negative observations often suggested different images of the place of origin. How was it possible to reconcile the co-existence of negative and positive images of the community of origin? When later interviews were conducted in many of these communities of origin, instead of seeing the negative conditions that were described by the migrant, we often found an active and thriving community, and people frequently displayed a satisfaction with life that went against what we had been led to expect. Of course, when respondents were describing conditions in their place of origin, they were describing conditions *as they pertained to them or as they perceived them* – not as how it appeared to those who remained there. In other words, either the migrants had different experiences than did those who remained, or they interpreted circumstances from a different personal perspective. In short, in almost every instance, the decision to migrate was a personal decision that took place in a social context but that reflected individual assessments of life chances in the community of origin.[6] In many instances, those assessments were kept fairly private; when they were released, they were presented in a form that was considered to be palatable to the audience to whom it was delivered. Because the decision to relocate was a life-changing act,[7] it did not occur without some intense inner struggles that were not always publicly shared. These inner struggles and personal motivations, not jobs, were the critical releasing factors in relocation.

THE MIGRATION TRAJECTORY

It should now be clear that migration is not simply a matter of departure and arrival; rather, it is an evaluative process that that begins even before the decision to leave is made. This process has social, psychological, and cognitive dimensions, and it allows the migrant to consider (or imagine) alternatives at both the place of origin and the destination. Information is constantly being processed as a way of establishing a personal road map.[8] We are now in a position to demonstrate how this occurs.

The Experience in the Community of Origin

To summarize, marginalization occurs in the community of origin when a person is increasingly dissatisfied with some aspect of her/his status, role, or ties in the community. Unemployment might be one cause of marginalization, but its social meaning is just as important as its economic meaning. This is because being unemployed means that the individual no longer has a productive place in her/his community. The stigma associated with being unemployed creates a form of marginalization (even when unemployment is widespread) in which the unemployed persons (and even their families) no longer have a role in the social economy. Also, people may discover that they have ideas that differ from those prevalent in their community of origin, and this may make them feel uncomfortable. Broken or strained relationships (within families, marriages, workplaces) contribute to another form of marginalization. These feelings refer to particular situations that touch the individual and marginalizes her/him in some specific way, thereby triggering a sense of *dissatisfaction* (see figure 18).

Box 3: Situational Marginalization

[Note the social context in each example and how several factors often came together in one response.]

I had wanted to leave ever since my friends left. There weren't a lot of jobs and I had no close friends there anymore. I was bored by what I was doing and felt I needed to move to a larger city where there were more options. I wanted a real career and I wanted a real job. I knew others who were talking about leaving for their careers. When people heard what we were thinking, they all said, "Oh, you must be going to Alberta" because that is where all the jobs are. (Nova Scotia)

I was in a rut. All my friends had gotten married and were having kids, and that put me increasingly outside their social circle ... I was

Figure 18 The Migration Trajectory

MIGRATION:	A continuous process of evaluation, interpretation, and negotiation of social position by individuals who relocate from community of origin to destination *Not* just an act of relocation but an ongoing process from pre-migration to post-migration
PERSPECTIVE:	Social/Psychological/Cognitive Understands migration through the eyes of the migrant as an actor who *evaluates* place through *social position* within a community
MARGINALIZATION THESIS:	Migration occurs as the result of individuals feeling dissatisfied with their social position in a community which produces a sense of marginalization. The migrant seeks to obtain a more satisfactory position at the destination which results in either partial integration or migrating again

MIGRATION AS A PROCESS

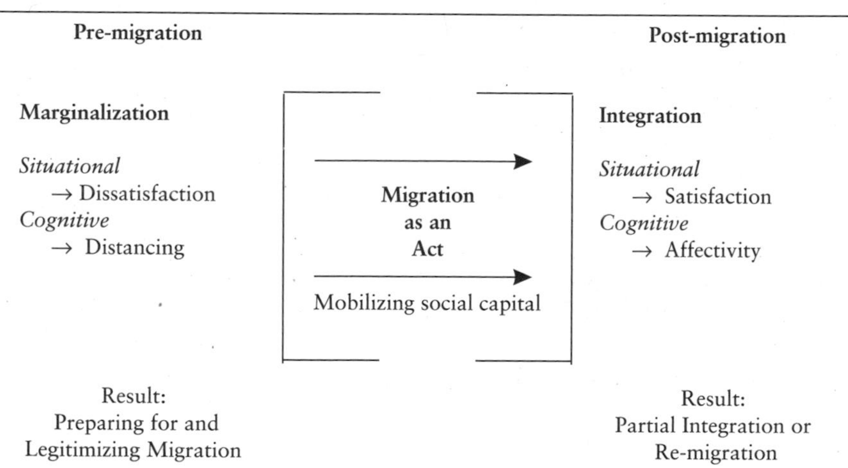

more career driven rather than relationship driven, so I decided to move. (Saskatchewan)

Almost everybody who was leaving was doing so because of the language. Montreal is a beautiful city but I often wanted to just move it out of that province. The thing is that you had no choice. If you don't like it, leave. (Quebec)

We were basically killing ourselves working hard to make ends meet. We realized we couldn't get to where we wanted to be in life compared to how we grew up living there. We couldn't afford to buy a home. (British Columbia)

Anglophones from northern New Brunswick leave because of their linguistic limitations, so there is nothing to stay for or go back to. Bilingual capacity enhances your chances to stay in the region. They even had an ad in the paper for a dog catcher who had to be bilingual. (New Brunswick)

We were kind of pressured by our children to move here when we retired. Three of our six children live in Calgary and one in Edmonton. We were the only members of our family left in Ontario, though we had lots of friends there. (Ontario)

Things never changed in Saskatchewan from year to year. It was always "pay attention to the news" to see how the crops were growing, see if the government deficit was growing, or whether there would be more taxes. Corporations were leaving town because of the taxes, and it was always an environment of pessimism – like a depressing feel. You go to the coffee shop and you hear people complaining about the government and the taxes all the time. As a young guy, it made me feel like I didn't want to be part of it. It leads young people to say they want to get out of there and go somewhere where things are better. (Saskatchewan)

My family is very backwoods French Acadian. Yet the slang of my French is not readily accepted by the separatists. I can relate well to working-class people but the more schooled were detrimental to my sense of self-worth and my ideas were different from the leaders of the Parti Quebecois. (Quebec)

I am French and I did not have as much opportunity when I was growing up because I was French. So I brought the children up English and it backfired because now, while they are bilingual, they are not French enough, and I think that means that none of us belongs. (New Brunswick)

Prince Albert was a relatively small place ... Professionally it was great to be there and I learned a lot, but it was mostly for after-work reasons that we wanted to move someplace bigger. I had a good job but there was no one our age around – you know, people without kids who would do the stuff we wanted to do. There is one person from our law school class in Prince Albert, and there weren't people we could relate to except older well-established lawyers. (Saskatchewan)

Our daughter and her husband had been transferred out here; we were now alone in Montreal, and we came out here for the birth of one of their children. Within a week of when the baby was born, we started looking at houses, and within two weeks we had bought a house in Sherwood Park. My husband went back to Montreal to sell our house. It was that spur of the moment. But underlying that as well was the desire to get out from under the political situation. (Quebec)

I found that there was quite a bit of tension in Montreal where I was living. I am from Quebec City and they don't have that much tension. In Montreal there is tension between anglophones and francophones as both groups refuse to learn the other language. You even experience it in the stores, and when I left I was fed up with always being classified by language group. Then there is tension with those from other countries who feel that they are being forced to speak French. There is a lot of resentment between groups. I wanted to experience life elsewhere in an environment that is not so tense. (Quebec)

It was just around the time of the referendum and I guess I was too young to feel strongly about what was going on because I was in my own little world. But I did know that my possibility for success there was not great because I did not have flawless French. And when people did hear my accented French, they often switched to English. (Quebec)

We had a business in Cape Breton but it wasn't going anywhere. We had a non-union shop in a very union stronghold. We struggled with that and were getting by, but it was tough making a living, and we were burned out. (Nova Scotia)

We were tired of the French/English wrangling in Ottawa and really wanted an alternative in a smaller centre. Here we were able to establish our careers and that was what we were primarily hoping for. (Ontario)

Situational marginalization refers to the sense of social dislocation that a person experiences in her/his community of origin. It is the result of feelings of dissatisfaction (or, in its strongest form, alienation) that emerge in connection with the position she/he holds within that community. If there is no dissatisfaction, and no sense of marginalization occurs, there is little incentive to migrate. There are many things that may function as triggers for a person's dissatisfaction with roles, statuses, and relationships. Again, her/his dissatisfaction is with particular, not all, aspects of life in the community: hence the phrase "situational marginalization."

Box 4: Employment Marginalization

I am a teacher and they lay off teachers left, right, and centre in Nova Scotia, and you have to sub for six years before you can even be considered for a permanent job, and I wanted to get on with my life so Nova Scotia wasn't the place for me. (Nova Scotia)

I actually speak French but I have an English name. The problem is that they don't hire you if you have an English name. It's harder to get a job because you are not French. People don't believe that but it's true. There are a lot of jobs I applied for but was turned down because French was not my first language. (Quebec)

I was working for the government in Ottawa and there had been a whole bunch of layoffs. My job had changed quite a bit and I was not happy, so I wanted to make a change. (Ontario)

It was an easy decision. There was no work where I was in Dartmouth – at least none that would pay the same as out here – unless I wanted to be a waiter. I had a bunch of jobs with pay less than ten dollars an hour and I was close to welfare. Things for some people were very good in Nova Scotia, but for me they were very bleak. (Nova Scotia)

I was the first person in my family to have a university degree, but there was nothing around home for me. What would a woman do in a paper mill? So I had to come out here. I might have found something in Halifax, but if you didn't want to do retail, there were better opportunities for a woman out here. (Nova Scotia)

I felt like I wanted to make a change in my career. I was tired of doing the same thing, which I had done for seven years, and I felt like a caged animal and I wanted to get outside and do something different. I was an industrial mechanic at McCain's French-Fries in Borden. My marriage had broken up but that was two years before. (Prince Edward Island)

The decision to leave was based on where would be the best place for the advancement and enhancement of my career. I knew there were cuts coming in New Brunswick, and I had looked at going out of country but decided to try Alberta because of its growth … New Brunswick has greater competition for jobs and less pay. In New Brunswick, it was not so much that people did not have jobs but that they wanted to do better than they were doing. (New Brunswick)

The education you get is not relevant to small-town Canada. You get your education for a career and then you realize that what you have learned has no application to where you are from. (Prince Edward Island)

We decided to move because of lack of stability in work. I've had about ten different jobs in this calendar year. I was doing ship repair and the work would come and go. Working on the fast ferry meant that a lot of people said bad things [because of its reputation] and it hurt morale. (British Columbia)

I was lucky to get a job at a call centre when I graduated, but a lot of people can't find any job that pays more than eight or nine dollars an hour. Because I was bilingual, I got a better job that paid ten dollars an hour. The company was from Ontario and there were no opportunities for advancement. They didn't care. They just wanted to hire people at the lower wages. There was also a lot of favouritism at work, so where are you going to turn to? You felt you were lucky to get a job even if it paid nine or ten dollars an hour. Out here there is so much work in Alberta. I heard about other people who had moved here, about their jobs, and that they were doing well. (Prince Edward Island)

I finished my university courses and there were two or three job openings but twenty people in our class. If you were willing to move, you had more options, so moving west, for me, meant getting experience in my field so that I could eventually go back. Having five years of university, I didn't want to do what was left for me to do there. And to put it bluntly, I had a student loan coming out of my bank account and I had no money. Living with your parents when you are twenty-six and you can't pay your loans is crazy. You can find work doing labourer jobs or working retail, but when you go to university for five years, you want to use that education. The problem is that people who are in the jobs you want are there for years and you have to wait till they retire, or die, or move. There just aren't opportunities because the population isn't growing. (Prince Edward Island)

I was unhappy in my job because it was going nowhere and I was in a rut. I was living at home so things were cheaper, but I was not making good money and it was doing the same thing all the time. I called this friend I knew in Grand Prairie and I asked him if we could come out and stay with him for awhile. So I had someone to fly out with and we headed for Grand Prairie. (Nova Scotia)

There is one thing that really made us do the move. There is a lot of favouritism and cronyism or patronage. When you experience someone else getting a job that you should have got because you are better qualified, and you see that it is because they are related or they are friends. That's how people get jobs in Prince Edward Island. You see it every day. "Oh, so Joe Blow got a job there. Well, I didn't even think he had a high school education. Why didn't they hire me?" That was the last straw to us leaving, though we had talked about it a lot before. (Prince Edward Island)

It is a depressed economy back there, and you don't get paid at the level you should for the work you do. They don't pay you for the work you do, and they take advantage of you because they can replace you in five seconds. I was making $8.50 per hour and I was a retail assistant manager. I made a lot of money for them, so I went up to the manager one day and said: "I cannot work for this anymore. This is a retarded rate – I need a raise and I'm leaving if I don't get a raise." He said he couldn't give me a raise because then he would have to give all the others a raise. So I gave him my two weeks' notice. (Prince Edward Island)

Box 5: Special Case Secondary Migrants

[One group that experienced employment marginalization was comprised of refugee immigrants who had been in Canada for several years. For them, the key to migration was the enormous difficulty they had in finding any employment at all. Here are their experiences.]

I was in Toronto for two years and I learned English and went to school and couldn't find any work. If you didn't have any Canadian experience, it was hard to find work. All the time I went to agencies and nobody called me. So I heard there was work here in Brooks, and, when I came here, the first day I got here I got a job. (Ontario)

In Toronto, they gave me a lot of addresses to find work. And when I got there, there was no job. I was not lucky. I did not know too much English at that time and I know nothing about Canada. Toronto was too big and sometimes they give me addresses I don't know where it is. They tell me 'westbound' on the train and I don't know where it is. It was hard for me and here it is not so difficult. (Ontario)

I lived in St John's and Vancouver. I was in London, Ontario, for a long time and I couldn't find any job there. And I wanted to support myself. I met a lot of Sudanese there and many of them came to Brooks. So they called me and told me there was work here. A lot of people moved here from London. There was just no work there. Some people got jobs but the majority did not. (Newfoundland and British Columbia)

The work that I was doing in Vancouver paid low and all I could do was look after myself. I wanted to help my brothers and sisters back home because our father had died. I did janitorial work and the pay was not good. So I moved to Brooks, and since I have moved here, I sponsored all five members of my family to come here and now we are a big family here. But I left Vancouver as a woman all by myself. (British Columbia)

Box 6: Blocked Mobility

The situation in Manitoba was not bad if you were blue collar, but if you were in management and wanted to go anywhere, then you really had to leave. A lot of our friends like us were all leaving. People who were professionals (I have an MBA) and young were leaving because there people fight over the positions that are available but here you can come and pick because there is more available. (Manitoba)

There are jobs in New Brunswick but they are not career jobs. Call centres is work but those jobs don't go anywhere. Language is also a barrier to getting good jobs. Although most of us are bilingual, we are not French and you hear all the time that French people are picked first. Language was not the first reason why I left but indirectly it was a concern because of restricted employment opportunities. The real issue for me was that my anglophone friends were all leaving and to be the only anglophone left was not appealing. (New Brunswick)

My goal was to be a probation officer. There were three probation officers in my town, and they'll be there forever till they drop, so there was no chance. Every profession back home, the people who have been there for twenty years will be there for another twenty years, and the chances of you getting in there with them is impossible. (Nova Scotia)

We sold everything that we owned and packed up everything that would fit in our truck and got here and started looking for work. We did have jobs in Halifax but they weren't career jobs. There are some jobs there but there are a ton of people applying for them. We didn't want to be stuck where we were at, and wondering what life would have been like if we had moved, so we did it and tried to get some experience, and if it didn't work, we could just go back. (Nova Scotia)

Basically we moved here because of the kids. For the older people in Saskatchewan who have jobs, it's not a problem but the younger ones do have a problem. You can flip hamburgers if you want but to get anywhere is impossible. It seems like, in Saskatchewan, it is

> not what you know but who you know. Most of the young people were leaving anyway, so we thought we might as well go someplace where the kids would have a better opportunity. (Saskatchewan)
>
> In my work there was not a lot of opportunity in PEI. I was at the bottom of the pool, and it would have been awhile before I would have gotten real work in my field. There are only smaller hospitals in PEI, and people in the positions I wanted had many years to go before they retired. This is the way it is in a lot of fields, and I didn't want to wait that long till people retired. I didn't think I should have to, so we moved here. (Prince Edward Island)
>
> I didn't go to university for nine years to do what I was doing in Manitoba. I was working for the province but I wanted something based on my education, a little more challenging, and better pay. I was coasting there and look around for something better, but there was nothing there. (Manitoba)
>
> Even Saskatoon and Regina are pretty rural-based economies. The jobs tend to be more traditional, and there are not a lot of new technology jobs there. So it gives you a sense that if you want a different type of job, you have to go elsewhere to do it. If you stayed there, you could only go so far. (Saskatchewan)

If the first step in the marginalization process consists of dissatisfaction, the second step consists of the cognitive interpretation the migrant gives to her/his social context in the community of origin. The information processing referred to earlier becomes much more intense, structured, and purposive. *Cognitive marginalization* is an analytical response to the assessment of life chances within a community and it leads to the consideration of alternatives.[9] If situational marginalization is correlated with dissatisfaction, cognitive marginalization is correlated with distancing. *Distancing* allows the potential migrant to establish an emotional separation from her/his existing social context and to evaluate her/his position in relation to ambitions, values, and relationships from the perspective of personal choice. Typically, much of this is kept inside or only shared with a few significant others, but it is part of the process of weighing alternatives. Distancing is the process whereby both an intellectual evaluation and an emotional separation begin to occur in the mind of the potential migrant. It does not necessarily lead to migration, but it takes the potential migrant to the edge, which then makes a migration decision possible. Because this process occurs privately, it is not unusual for others to be surprised when the migrant suddenly announces her/his decision to leave. Distancing allows the decision to migrate to incubate and enables the migrant to prepare to handle the public challenges that such an announcement might produce, thus making it easier to leave.

Box 7 Cognitive Marginalization

I was doing my own research while I was at home back in Manitoba. I did not like the job I had at the bank and asked them for a different job. The bank where I worked had a hiring freeze on there whereas here they were actually looking for people. They said they had too many employees in Manitoba and people were not retiring fast enough. I checked it out and it was clearly different in Alberta. Because I had family to stay with here, it made the transition much easier. It gave me a place to live without rent for the first few months. (Manitoba)

I had to do all kinds of research because if I was wrong I would catch hell from my wife. I went to the library and looked at the Stats Canada publications and found the right evidence to migrate to Calgary. Then I thought, "Well, rents are nuts in Vancouver, and there's no work in the Okanagan. Calgary is near the mountains, and Edmonton is too far away from the mountains. Toronto and Ottawa had strong economies but rents were too high." (Manitoba)

We were trying to determine where to go and *Maclean's* magazine had a one-page spread on Calgary, and it seemed to be quite positive. We had a brother here and I had worked in Alberta for a few years in 1978, so we decided to go visit the brother and look at it. Within two weeks, I had several job offers so it was a no-brainer. (Nova Scotia)

The media – newspaper and magazine articles in particular – gave us this image of Alberta having a booming economy like corporate head offices. I thought I would have a lot of choice in terms of career opportunities in senior management and compensation packages. I thought Alberta [had] a gung-ho let's-get-it-done sort of attitude. In business, we were monitoring what was going on in Alberta all the time. I could almost sense the difference in attitude as soon as [I] crossed the border. It was not that Alberta was the promised land or utopia, but there was a different attitude with respect to work and everything else. (Saskatchewan)

Every day when I looked in the Halifax newspaper, there weren't many jobs to choose from, but when I looked at the *Calgary Herald* on-line, every day there were hundreds of jobs. In Halifax, people had a hard time finding jobs, and then it was probably part-time jobs. (Nova Scotia)

It was a deliberate decision on my part to come to Alberta. I researched from east to west. I went to one of the local libraries and I started reading all the papers from the Maritimes to Vancouver. I went through every province and evaluated what I know and how I felt about each place. When I got to the West, I discovered there wasn't much going on in Manitoba and Saskatchewan. But for two months I read the Saturday paper each week from Calgary and Edmonton, and every time I looked at the paper there was only good news, things were booming and there were jobs and there was always positive news. There were always two or three jobs at least that I could apply for. And I also had two friends in Calgary whereas I had nobody in Edmonton. I also looked at Vancouver, but it was over the Rockies and psychologically I couldn't handle that. It was just too far to go. It was just too much to cross the Rockies. (Quebec)

I went out and bought a *Calgary Herald* in Halifax before I even came here and I was looking for jobs. The Halifax paper has about two pages of ads and the *Herald* has about six or seven or ten. When you show someone that in Nova Scotia, their eyes just bug right out. It's mind-boggling to people there. (Nova Scotia)

Box 8: Distancing

It was difficult leaving the family – especially retired parents, and friends. It took six months to make up my mind but then I felt comfortable. (New Brunswick)

I was not happy for quite awhile and I did a lot of soul-searching before I left for about six months. (British Columbia)

We told our immediate family that we were considering the move. We came out here and the stuff in McKenzie town caught our eye before we got here. We got here, looked around, made some contacts, and then went back to Vancouver and started booking things and called the moving company. I got hired over the phone a couple of weeks later, loaded up the truck, and away we went. We didn't tell too many people because we didn't want them interfering with our decision. (British Columbia)

We made the decision jointly to come here. We had spent considerable time in school getting a good education, and we knew we had to move away eventually. It was a matter of where and when. I had looked for work for a year and it was a fight among the graduates in our program for the few jobs that were available. So by the time we left, we were mentally ready. (Newfoundland)

The mindset in British Columbia was bad and there was nothing but bad news in the media. Somebody is always on strike, there is always bad stuff about the economy, the bad stuff the premier is doing, and a lot of bigoted stuff. The cost of living was going up. In a nutshell, there was a negative environment in British Columbia at that time and you discussed it all the time with family and friends, acquaintances and partners, and at social functions and family functions. We knew we would leave long before we actually left. (British Columbia)

I had lost my job and my husband worked in Toronto and commuted home on weekends. When I lost my job, we knew then that we wanted to make a change so we could live together as a family full-time. We had a friend in Alberta who had been encouraging us to move here for about a year. We knew that if we moved closer to Toronto to be near my husband's work that we couldn't afford for me not to work due to the cost of living. We also both acknowledged that it would be better to be farther away from my mother-in-law. So as we thought about it over time, we knew what we had to do. (Ontario)

Quebec is like a ghetto. Look at the culture and the music. It's like they are closing themselves from the rest of the country and the world. And the people who are succeeding are the people who get out of there. People with the brains and abilities are going

> somewhere else. I don't even want to go back there because I feel I'm going to die. (Quebec)
>
> I just [decided] overnight. I got up in the morning and I said, 'I'm going to Alberta.' I thought I'd buy a plane ticket but I drove out. The car I drove in was in terrible shape and they said I'd never make it. But actually I had thought about it for months. (Newfoundland)

The point is that the act of migration is preceded by situational and cognitive marginalization, which are part of a releasing process that eventually allows the migrant to leave. Expectations, aspirations, disappointments, and conflicts are assessed and interpreted while, at the same time, alternatives are imagined and considered. Many migrants reported a period of considerable depression in the premigration phase, when they struggled internally to find the appropriate solution to the dilemmas that they faced.

MIGRATION AS A DECISION AND AS AN ACT

The actual decision to migrate, as well as the issue of when to go and where to go, is a matter of timing and the availability of options. The marginalization thesis might be considered a type of negative migration selection because it emphasizes push factors. What has been argued, though, is that, because migration involves uprooting, there must be a releasing mechanism that makes migration thinkable and possible. In order for migration to be a reality, there must be a destination and an actual departure. While conceptually, assessing these things may involve two different processes, they are clearly linked because dissatisfaction with a current domain must be based on some kind of comparison to a place where things may be different. Thus the process of disengagement is always in reference to potential options for re-engagement at a specific destination. This, however, is not a simple process either, and once the sense of marginalization sets in at the community of origin, it may continue for many years – even at the destination. In short, the migrant becomes a type of "marginal person" caught between the sending and receiving communities. Internal migrants may have smoother transitions between origin and destination than international migrants, but regional identities, cultural differences, and other adjustments cannot be overlooked.

In the cognitive marginalization process, distancing is promoted by the images the potential migrant develops of a destination; this makes comparisons possible and allows her/him to anticipate a destination and the role that might be played there. The potential migrant has to make a judgment about the cognitive distance between the place of origin and the destination in order to determine the latter's suitability.[10] Among the destination options, the preferred ones are those places where the migrant has some kind of ties and perhaps where a migration stream already exists. Rather than people weighing multiple destinations, destinations are, in a sense, pre-selected by those who have gone before and who can verify the conditions there. News accounts play a critical role in creating images of the destination, and migrants returning home to visit tell of their experiences.[11] Offers of assistance from friends and relatives at the destination provide information about where to go and where help can be obtained in the short-term. A relocation plan is socially constructed from the images, experiences, and assistance of others.

For independent migrants, the relocation process in itself is a marginalizing experience because it is entirely self-directed as migrants have to make all arrangements with no formal assistance. What makes the experience less anomic are the supports of the migration stream: earlier migrants providing advance information, regular contact by telephone and e-mail with those who have gone before, and a national society with enough mobility that the chances are great that relatives and friends of family (even if distant) can be located at possible destinations. Thus, the actual act of migration may normally be an individual act, but it is supported informally by connections from the place of origin, with the result that place of origin and destination are connected in some way. This support network was stronger for some people than it was for others; however, in moving to Alberta, the overwhelming majority of respondents reported some kind of informal relocation support at the destination, and this was almost always provided by someone originally from the place of origin or with ties to it (e.g., uncles, cousins). Thus, as the migrant arrived at the destination, she/he had a sense of being connected while still feeling like a newcomer and still being marginal. People without these connections were relatively few, though the degree of support they provided varied greatly. In any case, migration was still viewed as an individual act whose ultimate success depended on efforts by the migrant. Migrants had to learn how to mobilize social capital to their advantage in order to implement and facilitate the migration decision.

THE DESTINATION EXPERIENCE

Since migration is triggered by some form of dissatisfaction and the anticipation of resolving it in a new community, *situational integration* may be defined as the feeling of satisfaction that migrants begin to experience as the result of their new social position in their new community. If dissatisfaction is the trigger of situational marginalization, then satisfaction is the key feature of situational integration. As with situational marginalization, satisfaction is not likely to be experienced in all aspects of life at the destination, but it will be experienced in certain key respects. Obtaining an appropriate job may be satisfying, as may new job responsibilities and/or opportunities for advancement, new friends, new social groups, and so on. Some aspects of life in the new community may be more acceptable than others, but the key is that the migrant begins to feel integrated into some aspects of community life. With this comes a growing sense of satisfaction that the relocation has been successful. Of course, coming to feel integrated into a community is a long process – one in which getting a job is only the first stage.

Box 9: Situational Integration

[Migrants often had to resolve their transitional status within themselves, which opened the door to accepting the destination as home.]

I came to Alberta because I wanted to explore. I didn't want to be sheltered all my life. I wanted to explore myself in my job but also just to understand myself. If you move away from family, you get to explore yourself a lot more than if you are in that little nest. So I find that I am more independent now that I'm here. (Ontario)

I was walking through the mall at Christmas and I heard what sounded like Celtic Newfoundland music in the distance. All of a sudden, it hit me – like I had to move because I had been betrayed by my own province. That was the first time I had sort of put it in that perspective, and it helped me to put all that behind me. (Newfoundland)

I can't get over how well we were accepted. People bent over backwards to be sure we had help. Newfoundland is known for its hospitality and I didn't expect people here to be that friendly. We laughed about it and said it must be that half of Alberta is made up of Newfies anyway. I think it's because Alberta is growing and they are so used to having new people. I am guessing but I think a lot of people who we dealt with are not from here either so they remember what it was like to have just landed. (Newfoundland)

I've had ties with Calgary all of my life. I have several uncles and aunts here and my brother moved here about five years ago. I wasn't really happy with my job in Saskatchewan because it was a temporary full-time position that was sort of ongoing. My brother called me and said if I wanted a job in Calgary, there is one waiting here. So I called this guy and he offered me a full-time job with good pay. (Saskatchewan)

My parents won't move because they have good jobs. But I keep telling them that they and the people six feet under will be the only ones left ... There is nothing there for anyone under thirty, and I think about those kids in junior high school and it's sad to think that they will all have to pack up and leave ... I think it was best for me to come here. Most people say that but there are those who hate it here and can't wait to get their car paid off to go back. But I don't know why they want to do that because there is nothing back there for them. The only reason people want to go back there is family. But after you've seen the family, what are you going to do back there? (Newfoundland)

I have lost some of my socialist ideas and have become a champagne socialist. The capitalist in me is coming out more here. I think by coming here I wanted to prove to myself and to others that I could become something. (Newfoundland)

The interviews revealed large numbers of people who had experienced employment success that went beyond their wildest imagination. But there was also a clear recognition that this was only one step in having a favourable position within the community and that it was at best a partial form of integration. Indeed, it was still a form of marginalization. Integration that is partial is referred to as "situational" because some aspects of relocation may be deemed successful while other aspects are deemed troubling. The lack of meaningful relationships at the destination, a rejection of work values and long work hours, an inability to accept the local culture, a feeling of guilt caused by a sick parent or aging parents at home, along with missing friends, relatives, and the home culture can all contribute to a sense of *partialized integration*. When the integration is only partial, the destination is not considered to be home. On the other hand, the development of strong interpersonal relationships in the community, friendships at work, getting married or having children, or getting involved in local organizations can all contribute to a sense of integration that fuses positively with favourable employment. Situational integration can thus be the first stage of the process towards full integration, or it can be a form of partial integration that carries its own sense of marginality (see figure 18).

Box 10: Partialized Integration

[An important way to begin the integration process is through employment. A positive outcome in the search for a job predisposes the migrant to feeling much more at home at her/his destination.]

My image of Alberta was that as long as you had some kind of training, you were pretty well guaranteed work when you arrived. And that was pretty true in my case, though the job search did take two months. I had done a lot of research about possible companies where I would like to work in both Edmonton and Calgary before I even left, and I had about one hundred addresses and phone numbers when I moved. When I got here, I talked to a lot of people as well and ended up with a great job where I have been ever since. In general, I found job hunting much less discouraging here than at home because here work was available and you weren't just one of a hundred applying. Here I hear of people having a choice between three or four jobs and turning the others down, and you never ever hear of that at home. (Nova Scotia)

In order for me to get the job there I have here, I would have had to be between forty-five and fifty and would have had to have worked twenty-five to thirty years to get that kind of life. There is more movement here and you can advance quicker. So I thought I would come out here and climb the ladder. When I tell people in my trade back home what I am responsible for here, they can't believe it. (New Brunswick)

When I got here I used my BC work search strategy. There you take your resume and you copy it one hundred or three hundred times and you don't get any calls. Here I did that and I got so many calls I didn't know what to do with them. My biggest problem now is packing the different shifts of my two jobs into my schedule. I have more work than I have time for. My friend back home distributed 187 resumes with no response. Its different here and kind of shocked me. These are all entry-level and labour type jobs. But what struck me is that, after a month or so, I could look for a better job with better wages and that has a future. (British Columbia)

I knew someone from Ontario who had moved here so I called her to ask if I could stay with her for a couple of days when I arrived. And she found an apartment for me in her building so that helped. Then when I got here I went to Earl's and applied for a job, so I virtually got an apartment and a job all on the same day. (Ontario)

My brother owned a construction company in Calgary and he offered me a job. It was a pretty decent job and my wife and I talked about it and decided to take it. It was a new challenge and was something I had never done before. It was a definite step up from what I had been doing all my life, which was the same old rut. And our children were no longer at home. It was also a move for a lot more money. Being connected helped us to feel like we had a place here, and that helped us to feel at home much faster. (Manitoba)

In Newfoundland, they either claimed you were too well qualified or the job was already in essence filled in spite of the interview. The best I managed was an eight-dollar-an-hour job at an outbound call centre and that lasted two weeks. Here we work with a company that has 45,000 employees worldwide. We started here at ten dollars an hour, and by Newfoundland standards that was a lot. When I got eight dollars an hour there, the boss would point to the stack of resumes on his desk and say, 'I can hire anybody to fill your job.' Now I'm making a lot more here because I have moved up and [am now] in management. After two years of applying for jobs at home to no avail, and then to come out here and to get a job just like that ... you start to ask yourself what took us so long to decide to come here. (Newfoundland)

Back home, you work and do the same thing. Here they liked my personality and how I did my job, and they have given me promotions

> and sent me on more seminars than you could imagine. There it would take years to work your way up, and here I've done it in three years. At home, it's who you know and that's why you come out here – to get ahead. (New Brunswick)
>
> The job I had there paid $4.75 an hour, and here my first job paid ten dollars an hour and I was so excited to be doubling my money. (Newfoundland)
>
> I was educated and I wasn't working in anything that I was trained for. The options weren't there, and I couldn't do what I wanted to do there. I could have gotten a job with the provincial government or something like that, but that is not really a career move. When I left I wanted to see if I had what it took to run with the big boys, so you come out here and you work at a higher level and you work at projects that are more complex, and you prove to yourself that you can do it. I don't think I would be able to do that at home. (Prince Edward Island)
>
> I left Quebec after the referendum and was fed up with the politics game. My feeling was that you had to be an outstanding person to get a job in Quebec because there was too much competition. It is hard to climb the ladder there because the big cheeses at the top keep their seat and there is no room for you. My experience is that it is different here. This is a land of opportunity and … over there is a land of backstabbing because they are struggling with their job and struggling with their politics. (Quebec)
>
> I was working as a cook in Newfoundland and one day I asked myself, "Is this what I want to be doing twenty years from now?" That is why I left. I knew I was better than what that job had to offer so I just packed it in. I had a better job offer in New Brunswick but passed it up knowing that the culinary industry was better out West. I kept my nose to the grindstone initially, starting out with even less money, but now I am at the top of my profession. (Newfoundland)

If relationships in the destination community stabilize, and the social position of the migrant is considered satisfactory, cognitive integration can occur. *Cognitive integration* is the analytical response of the settled migrant to her/his social position in the destination community, and it enables her/him to adopt the new community as home. Unlike cognitive marginalization, which results in distancing, cognitive integration is triggered by a growing affectivity towards the destination. It is cognitive because, even though the attachment to the destination may grow, this is not done without various rationalizations regarding what is best "for our family," "for my career," or "for the future." In other words, the migrant develops a logical scheme that justifies an attachment to the new community. This may involve the job (e.g., seniority or its pension program), the fact that their children are settled in school, or the recognition that their place of origin lacks something that they now consider important. It might also involve the idea that migration had changed them in some way that led them to conclude that it would be difficult for them to return. The result of this is the mental acceptance of the destination and the reality that it is their new home. Often this recognition comes through going back home to discover that things have changed or that they have changed. With this comes the realization that the destination is now home.

Box 11: Cognitive Integration

My mother said maybe you'll luck out and get a teaching job back home, but to be honest I told her I don't really want that. I guess I want independence and want to run my own life and back there everybody knows me. My family is proud of me though, because I have a solid job here. All I know is that I doubt if I'm going back. (Ontario)

My mother says she is not going to have her grandkids three thousand miles away, so I guess it is either we move there or she moves here. When you have a small family, it's easier to get your parents to move here – but this is where our life is now. (Newfoundland)

Five years later, I'm now getting to the point of thinking of Alberta as home – to the extent that I can't see myself leaving here. When I look at BC and Saskatchewan, they have their problems. So does Manitoba. Ontario is too big. So when I look across Canada, Alberta is the best place to be. There's a good environment of growth here, and when people come in, it's very easy to catch on to that dream. Money can be had, opportunities are there, and it is easy to jump on the bandwagon. (New Brunswick)

> My daughter was part of the exodus from Quebec in the seventies, and it would be interesting to know how many moved here from there then. Now their parents are aging and they are moving here to be near their children. That's what we did so it is easier to fit in. (Quebec)
>
> We are connected to a lot of early retirement or retirement people here, and most have moved here because their children are here. The children come first and the parents follow later. And the taxes issue is a very common factor as well. (Manitoba)

While some migrants easily and quickly adapt to new locations (and thereby become fully integrated), there are many who have a kind of dual identity as they continue to identify with the community of origin. In this sense, integration is almost always partial and there is an identity tension that is never fully resolved.[12] Some continue to harbour thoughts about returning home at a later point. Attitudes of the receiving community are also critical to the migration outcome. Migrants can be made to feel like interlopers or "foreigners"; indeed, migrants might feel this way in any case simply because they are from elsewhere and do not fit in. I discuss this issue of "home" later, but it needs to be acknowledged that some people transfer identities quickly while others do not.

The idea of marginalization is built on the assumption that integration is an ideal end state. Integration means full participation and identification with a community. The problem is that, while embarking on a course of migration may be a response to marginality, the very act of relocation sustains this sense of marginality. New faces and new places juxtaposed with old identities and life patterns helps to perpetuate a sense of marginality, which is sustained by the acknowledgment of alternatives. This cognitive process begins at the place of origin as alternatives are considered, but it can continue at the destination as migrants repeatedly assess their decision to relocate. Over time, however, the migrant may have rationalized the relocation decision and outcome in such a way that there is both a subjective sense of satisfaction with her/his social position in the new community and a cognitive recognition that this is her/his new home.

EXPLANATORY VALUE OF THE PROCESSUAL MODEL

Understanding migration from the perspective of the migrant and as a process that begins before the act of migration and continues beyond arrival at the destination has important explanatory value. There are five reasons why this processual model is useful.

First, it helps us to understand the difference between a migrant and a non-migrant. It is difficult to become a volitional migrant if one does not assess one's place of residence as in some way inadequate. However, dissatisfaction is not enough: a sense of marginalization must result in the process of distancing and the consideration of alternatives.[13] A person who possesses little dissatisfaction, or who is dissatisfied but does not experience a sense of marginality and distancing, is not likely to actively consider migration. Migration occurs as the result of a personal evaluation that prompts the taking of great risks. As one man from Cape Breton put it, "Our situation was not unique. Most of the people were in the same boat like we were but the difference is we took a chance, and some people don't want to take a chance." Distancing enables the risk-taking that is required if migration is to occur.

Second, the processual model helps us to understand why some migrants stay at the destination while others return home. When migration occurs without the process described in the model, the migrant is not fully prepared for the relocation and returns home reasonably quickly because there is no personal rationale for staying away. For example, if friends talk someone into leaving with them, that person may go but may not be mentally prepared for the experience, thus returning after the sense of adventure is over. In some cases, the time away may be as little as a few weeks or months; this type of migrant is more like a visitor than a true migrant. As one mother from Truro, Nova Scotia, noted: "Our son went under pressure from us his parents because there were no jobs locally. But he was not prepared for the move and on the way back called to ask if he could return." If the migrant has not experienced a sense of marginality, she/he longs to return home and continue in the same patterns that existed before migration. The cognitive preparation for migration, which involves obtaining information and reviewing alternatives, is important. It changes the migrant's attitude towards the destination so that she/he can embrace the new community and begin the search for a suitable social position.

Third, the processual model helps us to understand why migration produces discord among people (especially couples) who migrate together. When one partner goes through this process and the other does not, the least marginalized partner constantly expresses feelings of regret about having left. As one migrant from Atlantic Canada put it, "I got roughly 3,600 miles of the silent treatment from my wife, and things were not pleasant until she got her first job here." In short, the wife left family and friends only reluctantly but was much happier once she had some basis for integration within the new community. Many couples reported differences of opinion about the necessity for migration; and, where distancing was a cognitive and joint process, the experience was more likely to be interpreted positively by both parties.

Fourth, the processual model also helps us to understand how migration can be a useful tool in the search for a more satisfying social location. Something is always learned from the migration experience – even if the migrant decides to return. The migrant may not be able to integrate into the new community, and this may lead either to another new start somewhere else or to a return home, where she/he may try again with the experience gained at the destination. Ironically, the migrant's success at the destination may even serve as the basis for returning home. For example, the young adult migrant who was motivated to relocate because of the need to assert her/his independence and to develop an autonomous identity may come to the point where she/he feels secure enough to return and deal with parental expectations. Or the worker who left the community because of lack of opportunity due to her/his inexperience may now return home with job experience that enhances the possibility of securing good work and gaining a position of respect in the social economy. In fact, House (1989, 113–18) has shown that internal migration plays an important role in skills development and employment experience, which then leads to the returning migrant's ability to play a much more visible role in community life. So whether the migrant stays or returns, she/he has much to learn through the experience of migration and its relationship to finding a satisfying social position. Indeed, some migrants learned much about the role of distancing and cognition upon returning home after their first migratory experience. This led them to try again when they were more prepared.

Fifth, the processual model allows us to see that migration is indeed a process and not just a simple matter of relocating from one place to another place. The migrant's evaluation of the departure community and the arrival community is rooted in connectedness and social position, which is what makes a location meaningful. Migration is more than a search for gainful employment. As Jobes (1992, 357) points out, "The choice of where to live is largely a decision about how one wishes to live, a decision involving more than money." Therefore, migration must be viewed as "innovating behaviour" in that it involves a personal search for a satisfying place within a community. However, the emphasis on process points out that the migrant's social position at the destination must be negotiated and that affectivity may take some time to develop, if it develops at all. Attachments to home and the realization that migration has brought about both gains and losses may support a position of partialized integration, which may continue indefinitely. Therefore, it should not be surprising that there is often considerable uncertainty about the permanence of the migration. From this perspective, migration involves transitioning behaviour, with no definitive beginning or end. Migration may mean new beginnings and going places, but it may also mean rupture, loss, regret, or even failure (Fielding 1992, 205–7). Migration may mean all of these things, either simultaneously or alternately. For all these reasons, long-distance internal migration cannot be reduced to a matter of changing location for work.

I discovered crucial evidence for this interpretation at the end of the in-depth interviews, when participants were handed a sheet with this open-ended question: "It is often said that migration occurs primarily for employment reasons. How well does this statement reflect your experience?" Somewhat surprisingly, only 26.6 percent agreed with this statement, while 73.4 percent disagreed with it. Some who agreed noted that they did not just come for any employment but, rather, for a specific type of job. The majority indicated that their move involved a wide range of factors. These factors involved, among other things, relationship issues, quality of life concerns, and ideological/political matters. While most study participants agreed that they would not have come to Alberta if the province had not had a robust economy, they did not interpret their relocation purely in employment terms. Economic explanations for internal migration miss important personal and social factors that serve as catalysts for migration.

CONCLUSION

The model I propose suggests that, in some ways, migration is a form of rejection because, for whatever reason, the migrant deems the community of origin as no longer suitable. An unsponsored migrant is much more likely than is a sponsored migrant to be initially prompted by negative selection. People need both a motivation to leave and a place to go, so push and pull factors must coexist if migration is to occur.

So what is the most important factor in Alberta's growth? Is it the push factor or the pull factor? The typical answer is the pull factor as most migrants say they were attracted by jobs. The problem with this answer is that it simplifies a complex process. In most cases, the migrant is not only searching for work but also for a solution to issues relating to personal dislocation. Migration is a strategy for solving one or more issues of social location, and, once the process begins, the tensions and uncertainties remain. The push and the pull factors are deeply intertwined, and one cannot exist without the other. Migration came about not just because of what was happening in Alberta but also because of what was occurring in the lives of individual migrants in their home communities. Blocked mobility or blocked opportunity in terms of work roles is only one part of the equation (albeit an important one). As Richard Florida (2002, 217–18) puts it, people move to places where there are opportunities to validate their identities as creative people. Perhaps the most basic function of internal migration is to provide an opportunity for individuals to renegotiate their position within society. Whether or not this renegotiation will be successful is of course uncertain.

7

Migration as Negotiating Place

A central question in understanding domestic migration concerns whether a move from one province to another or one region to another is really a significant disruptive event or whether it requires only minor adjustments because it take place within the same country. If the nation-state is a "place" shared in common, whose inhabitants have common identities and a common sense of belonging, then presumably migration within that entity is rather seamless – particularly in comparison to international migration, which presumes a more significant disruption marked by national borders that tightly regulate movement (Jacobsen 2002, 163). When national entities are rather small, it is possible that a common sense of place might be more likely to develop, although the experience of a smaller country like Switzerland, with its twenty-three distinct cantons, suggests otherwise. On the other hand, a country like Canada, which has the second largest territory in the world, has had to grapple with huge regional differences. This implies that "place" varies and does indeed matter. In other words, In Canada, even for the internal migrant, relocation can involve important transformations. This chapter explores the importance of place by examining how migrants negotiate their relocation.

THE PROBLEM OF PLACE

Migration is often viewed as exchanging one place for another, as though the physical place itself does not matter. Labour theories of migration, in particular, assume that places are merely objects or landscapes that can be exchanged for new places in the search for employment. When places are acknowledged to be different, they are typically viewed as settings because the fundamental differences between then are primarily understood to be cultural or social (Gieryn 2000, 466). Physiography is perceived as the backdrop to more important factors, such as economy, polity, language, and culture. Consequently, in any analysis of migration, the focus is primarily on its economic and social causes and consequences. Because it is assumed that the international migrant is more likely to experience socio-economic upheaval than is the domestic migrant, various forms of assistance are usually available to the former, not because of the place adjustments required but because of the socio-economic adjustments required. Conversely, it is assumed that the domestic migrant requires little assistance because she/he undergoes little socio-economic adjustment. This is because all residents share the same sense of place within the nation-state, which is the unit of analysis. In other words, place boundaries only seem to matter if they are international; and even then, the location itself is less important than is socio-cultural difference and the economic adjustment. At root, then, place is viewed as a rather neutral concept.

When place is acknowledged, it is often limited to serving as a unit of social organization (Fischer 1977, 140). Geographic areas are primarily containers that help classify people, the administrative units that organize them, or simply units for analysis. For this reason, sociologists are more likely to say that *who we are with* shapes us more than *where we are*. Context is understood to be more social than environmental. But the relationship between our external environment and our mental state has been clearly established (Gallagher 1993). Conditions of temperature, lighting, and physical arrangement have been shown to affect behaviour, and architecture shows how design affects interactions within physical space (Baldry 1999). Yet when it comes to migration, it is assumed that the social environment is the most critical and that humans somehow automatically adjust to their physical environment. Consequently, migration is more often viewed as a social problem than as a locational one.

When migrants talk about missing their home, it is almost always assumed that it is the people and the cultural patterns that they miss.[1] Physical objects like a rocking chair, a clapboard dwelling, a brownstone walkup apartment, a meandering river bordered by trees and teeming with fish, a uniquely laid out community with its streetscape and structures, or even a mountain with its crisp air and vistas or a seashore with its eerie dense fog and pounding surf are not important in themselves but only as places imbued with meaning because of the social interactions that have occurred there. The rocking chair is where grandma held you in her arms, the house is where you grew up, the river is where you fished in summer and skated with your friends in winter, the sidewalk is where you interacted with neighbours, the street is where you learned to drive, and the mountain/seashore is where you used to sit and think and dream. In each case, it is not the location itself that is considered important but the activity and the people associated with it (Marcus 1992, 111). Following from this, it is assumed that migrants miss people and are moved by memories associated with past experiences; their location of origin itself is of little relevance. Place-related issues are reduced to sociological issues.

UNDERSTANDING THE ROLE OF PLACE

In recent years, social scientists have begun to challenge the assumption that space or place is not critical to understanding human behaviour. Lefebvre, Foucault, Bourdieu, Giddens, Harvey, and Soja have each attempted to bring space back into the analysis of society. As Soja (1996, 46) notes, social reality is not just coincidentally spatial because there is "no unspatialized social reality" and "no aspatialized social processes." Instead, the traditional emphasis on time/history and the social, which was built on dialectics, needs to be replaced by a trialectic that takes account of space. Sociologists may have acknowledged the importance of place, but this has been done obliquely: space as "context." Context is understood as being comprised of social situations that occur in places that change over time. However, for the most part, the spatial dimensions of human action have been largely left to other disciplines in environmental science.

In order to disaggregate the spatial, Soja (1996) identifies three spaces: the physical, the mental, and the social. The first space is the real material world, the concrete things that can be mapped and that are physical. It often also involves those things that human activity has designed or produced. The second space involves the imagined representations of spatiality. Lefebvre would call this conceived space as it is tied to those who produce space (especially technocrats, scientists, and planners) and the discourse they use to express their ideas about it as they imagine it. The third space is the space of inhabitants and users and may be referred to as lived space. It is fluid and dynamic, full of interactive situations and struggles. But it is also a place for "Othering," for drawing from the physical and mental, the real and the imagined, and standing above both as "a strategic location to encompass, understand, and potentially transform all spaces" (Soja 1996, 11). Thus, the third space is a place for restructuring and changing space, and it is both real and imagined. It is "the creation of another mode of thinking about space that draws upon the material and mental spaces of traditional dualism but extends well beyond them in scope, substance, and meaning" (ibid.). The third space, then, is not just a space for living in a passive sense but, rather, a space for living in an active sense, involving reflections and actions that produce transformations. I propose to adapt this scheme in order to interpret migration as an intricate complex of physical, social, and mental factors.

TYPE 1: THE PHYSICAL BASIS OF PLACE

The aforementioned scheme can be applied in a strategic way to understand the importance of space in the migrant's experience. First, it points out that physical space, in both its natural (topography and landscape) and created (constructed and built) forms, has concrete manifestations that vary by location. Space is transformed into place because places do not exist in the abstract but are tied to a specific geographic location, which gives them character (Gieryn 2000, 464). Places are also different from space because that latter refers to sites that are devoid of meaning, whereas places are specific locations that have been socially defined and given meaning and emotion (Milligan 1998, 6; Altman and Low 1992, 5). Whether natural or created, places have been invested with meaning and interpretations (Gieryn 2000). An office building on Bay Street in Toronto (the financial hub of Canada) is not only likely to look different than an office building on Water Street in St John's (a centre of ocean administration), but its function and meaning is also likely to be very different, not only with regard to local residents but also with regard to national/international interpretations. The Churchill River (hydroelectric power), the Kelowna River (salmon spawning), the Niagara River (tourism), and the Old Man River (crop irrigation) may all be rivers, but the roles they play and what they symbolize are very different. It is this combination of the concrete physical aspects of space (with its variations in different locations) and the unique meanings attributed to each that transforms space into a unique place. Thus, migration from one location to another (whether internationally or domestically) requires learning the components and meanings of the new place, which are not likely to be interchangeable with the components and meanings of the old place.

Place, as a complex relation between people and the physical environment in which they live, is a locus for belonging and identity. A sense of place only emerges when the bond between people and place is strong, the converse of which is that when it is absent, there is a sense of placelessness (Relph 1976). In Canada, place is frequently related to province of residence. A migrant from Saskatchewan, for example, knows that her/his place of origin is a specific geographic setting with a unique topography consisting of prairie grass and lakes. It has an identifiable latitude and longitude, which makes it easily locatable and which differentiates it from other places. It has a specific name, which is reinforced through licence plates, mailing addresses, and political structures. But provinces are not the only form that places take. There are regions within provinces, counties, cities, residential areas, and households that are also places that are given meaning. A resident of northern Saskatchewan identifies more with forests than with short prairie grass, and a resident of Saskatoon has an urban identity that contrasts with that of the agriculturalist in another part of the province. Each location has its own unique physical character, which is enhanced by each location also being a place of memories (Milligan 1998, 2; Riley 1992). It is these attributes that overlay place with meanings and that contribute to the personal and collective identities of their residents. So places are not neutral; they engender loyalties and identities that have meaning for the inhabitant. People create meaningful places, and those places then act upon those people by giving them a sense of belonging and identity. This is the basis of what is called "place attachment," whereby a physical site is given emotional meaning not just because of its physical form but as the result of past interaction and accumulated experiences that has occurred there (Milligan 1998, 2; Gieryn 2000, 481). And just as it is possible to develop attachments to a place of origin, so it is possible to develop attachments to a destination. This occurs as the result of new experiences that may produce "dual place identities," a "primary place identity," a "secondary place identity," or a "between-place identity," with conflicting loyalties and a sense of being caught between two or more places.

Rather than viewing migration as a single act, this interpretation views migration as a process entailing the constant negotiation of place. If places are deeply intertwined with our identities and affective ties (see Tuan 1977), then changing places has a potentially profound personal effect with regard to who we are. So, on the one hand, place is imbued with all kinds of personal, social, and cultural meanings; but, on the other hand, it also provides a framework within which our own identity is created, sustained, and transformed (Cuba and Hummon 1993, 112). The question "Who am I?" is intricately related to the question "Where am I?" And, if identities are intimately related to place, then where you live, because it holds deeply rooted meanings, cannot simply be exchanged with someplace else.

Most migrants have a sense of place identity that emerges from their region of origin, which, in most cases is their place of birth. A migrant, in looking back, often develops an idealized or romanticized view of that place.[2] The negative is minimized and the place of origin is often referred to as "home." This is also the basis for comparisons with the destination, a place in which the migrants have had no prior history and that, therefore, seems "placeless" to them. In fact, some study participants commented that migrating to Alberta was like coming to a place with no history, which, in some ways made, them feel like pioneers – at least in terms of creating a new sense of place for themselves.

Empirical Evidence of the Importance of the Physical Aspect of Place

Landscape, or physical geography, was a major issue to many migrants, a fact that emerged in a number of different ways. For those who were having difficulty adjusting, landscape was a big part of that difficulty. Longing for physical aspects of place, especially among migrants from the Atlantic provinces, played a major part in adjustment, sometimes even to the point at which it trumped the social aspects.

> Alberta would be perfect if it had an ocean. It is the landscape that I'm homesick for because the people I care about I can stay in contact with. It's the ocean that I miss.

The features of the Alberta landscape that some cherished were negated in deference to the preferred physical environment at the place of origin.

> Alberta does not hold a candle to Nova Scotia for things to see. Like my friend said to me, you've seen one mountain and you've seen them all. (Nova Scotia)

> I have been here for nine months and I may be here for twenty years but I don't want to be. It's emotional and the landscape is the issue. I think people give up on Newfoundland too quickly and they should think about what they can give to it. I still want to live there and there is so much I love about it. (Newfoundland)

The rugged natural environment is compared with the created environment of city life.

> I'm changing my views about coming here. I grew up with the ocean and the wilderness and you can't find that here. I miss the isolation, so I'll probably go back to the East Coast. Leaving Newfoundland was the best option at the time, but I can't see myself staying here. Traffic is getting worse and worse here. (Newfoundland)

Whereas the ocean was important to people from the East Coast, others talked about air quality. Migrants from central Canada often compared the high humidity or damp cold of Ontario and Quebec to the dryness and freshness of the air in Alberta. Drier air and less smog were particularly singled out by asthmatics or people with similar respiratory problems.[3] Others seemed to miss the salt water and the dampness, which were absent in Alberta, while the prevalence of fog and rain in other parts of Canada had both supporters and detractors. In short, climate was not neutral: it often played a significant role in a migrant's assessment.

Another factor identified as important by many migrants was a big sky that was not blocked by trees – a characteristic feature of the western interior. For some, this feature avoided claustrophobia and was a major positive in their relocation. Perhaps the most dominant issue, though, was sunshine as Alberta has the most sunshine days of any province in Canada. Respondents linked the importance of sunshine to mood and disposition. Some migrants talked about experiencing symptoms that sounded suspiciously like those of seasonal affective disorder at their place of origin, and all such comments came from migrants from British Columbia.[4]

> People here are so much more positive. What makes a difference for me is the amount of sunshine that I get here in comparison to the Lower Mainland, where I grew up. It was not uncommon for me to be depressed ... I can't be depressed here. It doesn't last. The sun comes out and I feel like a million bucks.

> I think I'm one of the people who is affected by the rain and the fog, you know that disease where you don't get enough sunlight. I just love the sun here. And that has an effect on people's personalities too. People in BC don't want to believe this. They think they live in God's Country – Lotus land. You know it's minus 2 degrees and sunny and our kids are out playing. And it's plus 8 and raining there and they think that's better.

> We had had enough of the fog and the rain and we said, "What's wrong with going to a place that's cold and where the sun shines?" The idea of a climate change was actually appealing to us so that the kids could do outdoor things rather than being cooped up in the house or school because of rain. The kids were even excited about the snow.

> People are happier here than in Vancouver. There they would walk around with a sourpuss look. And here it is sunnier. I never went to a doctor but I think I was sort of depressed there, even my wife notices it.

> We had retired in British Columbia from Saskatchewan. The weather in the Okanagan was very depressing in the winter with the low-lying clouds. It made me feel depressed. This was a particular problem that women especially faced. I also felt cut off from my children in Manitoba by the mountains. It made me feel less comfortable there.

It is clear that geographical factors have social-psychological effects. However, mood was often linked to other factors as well, such as job stress or cultural issues.

> My wife had some depression in BC and I know that she is doing a lot better in Alberta. It's partly the weather and partly getting rid of the job stress.

> We like the Prairies. I couldn't live in a place where you don't see the sun. We like the cattle culture. This is our Canada. BC isn't our culture.

One couple talked about why they chose to live in Medicine Hat, a city on the plains, and they provided evidence that physical space played a big role in their choice of destination:

> We felt isolated in Thunder Bay and did not want to retire there. We wanted to live in a small city rather than a big one. We wanted to be where there was lots of light and the prairies were better than the mountains, which limited the light like in Thunder Bay. We like the dry climate. We chose Medicine Hat even though we knew no one here. (Ontario)

Sometimes elements of physical space were blended with other factors, such as the economy, and a deliberate effort was made to discover aspects of the new environment that could be considered attractive:

> When we left Vancouver Island, people couldn't believe it. Some are glad to see people leaving the island. Others couldn't understand why we would leave the scenery. But you can't eat the scenery. I think it was the sky that attracted me to Alberta. (British Columbia)

Some compared winters in other parts of the western interior with those in southern Alberta, and considered the latter, with its Chinook winds, to be much milder and to entail fewer mosquitoes in the summer.[5]

For some reason, migrants strongly associated living in Alberta with more outdoor activity than they were used to. Much of this seemed to be related to access to the mountains.

> I don't like crowds and being where there are lots of people, even though I lived in southern Ontario for a long time. In contrast, Alberta stands for openness and lots of space. I love the outdoors and it was such a turn on to come out here. For me it was an adrenaline rush. (Ontario)

> In Montreal you spend so much time in traffic that you just go home. Here the mountains are so close and we can drive to the mountains with our mountain bikes after work. I feel the outdoors is more important to life here. (Quebec)

> For me, it was a recreational decision because I wanted to be near the mountains. I used to come here on spring break for mountain sports like biking and hiking and skiing. My sister was also here but it was mainly for recreation that I chose Calgary. I like the mountains and that was my main reason. You can't make mountains in Manitoba. (Manitoba)

> There is one word to describe why we moved here and that is "lifestyle." We go out skating and hiking on the weekend. And when we come back from hikes, we often say "God, I like it here." We are more outdoors oriented here than we were in Toronto because access is much easier here. (Ontario)

What is intriguing is that, instead of Alberta's being perceived as a "prairie province" it is perceived as a "mountain province." Again and again, when asked how they decided on a destination, respondents reported that the mountains were a huge draw. In fact, only a few identified Alberta with flatlands and prairie – an image that is more consistent with descriptions of the Old West. There were some differences between migrants who settled in Calgary, where the mountains are easily accessible, and those who settled in Edmonton, where they are more distant. However, overall, Alberta was associated with mountains. Many talked about having visited the mountains prior to migration on family or skiing vacations. As one Saskatchewan man put it:

> Ever since I was young we would come to Alberta for skiing, and it helped develop an image that Alberta was glamorous and there was stuff happening here. Even now that I'm here, it hasn't changed because the big city has lots of options and its fun.

A migrant from Manitoba commented:

> When I was young, we went through Calgary every time we went skiing, so Calgary became associated with fun and good times. Then, in the summer, the mountains and Calgary became associated with vacation. So that was a positive image.

Coming to Alberta for vacations in the mountains meant that many migrants were favourably predisposed to the province and associated it with good times. Landscape was a major factor in positive lifestyle associations, and mountains were a far more prevalent image than were prairie or plains. On the other hand, some respondents acknowledged that there were real trade-offs as their place of previous residence also had important physical features. Alberta had the mountains, but it did not have sailing; the mountains were nice, but Manitoba had more lakes. The absence of lakes, beaches, and fall colours was often mentioned by migrants from central and eastern Canada. What is key is that the physical environment was an important element in their assessment of migration.

> I think it's a beautiful province and I'm proud of the geography here. Nothing else contributes to a greater sense of pride to me. (Ontario)

Geography was also important in that Alberta was sometimes viewed as attractive because of its central location in the Canadian West, which supported easier access to the other three provinces. Weekend trips to the neighbouring provinces were more possible from Alberta than from British Columbia, for example. Geography also played a role in the consideration of migration options. One person talked about how, when considering possible migration destinations, the Rocky Mountains served as a type of barrier:

> I also looked at Vancouver but it was over the Rockies and psychologically I couldn't handle that. It was just too far to go. It was just too much to cross the Rockies.

It is clear that the physicality of place was very important to migrants. It was not just backdrop or setting but, rather, was part of a complex of factors that affected how migration would be evaluated. The relationship of these factors to place negotiation and identity is discussed in the section entitled "The Lived Component of Place: Place-making" (see below).

TYPE 2: THE MENTAL IMAGERY OF PLACE

The second type of space refers to the fact that people who inhabit, use, or create spaces develop their own discourses to express their mental pictures of that space. People create cognitive maps of spatial environments to help them organize and recall what they know (Cadwallader 1992, 13). This is space as they imagine it and as formulated through their own worldview and experiences. It might be a place for making a living (e.g., "steeltown"), a place to make money (e.g., "boomtown"), a place in which to grow up (e.g., "my real home"), a place of alienation (e.g., "a hinterland"), or a place of belonging (e.g., "my people"). The discourse used by migrants represents the understanding they have of their community as a place (e.g., "dynamic," "depressed") or the image of the community as a place that has been constructed for them (e.g., "land of living skies" [Saskatchewan], "supernatural" [British Columbia]). The discourse of place represents images of that place. When a set of images of a place is put together, it forms a place-myth that characterizes a place in a way that, although usually stereotypical, is enduring. Places are arranged into hierarchies in which some have a higher status than others (e.g., "centre of the universe," "boondocks," "frontier," "core," etc.), and migrants learn this rhetoric, which functions as a form of labelling, of expressing stereotypes, biases, and differential evaluations. The migrant also has mental images of both the place of origin and the destination, and she/he develops a discourse to describe them – both prospectively (before departure) and retrospectively (after arrival). These mental images are interpretations of space, and they play a significant role in how migration decisions are made and evaluated.

What mental images do people develop of the place they want to leave and of the place to which they want to go? What mental images do they retrospectively develop about the place they left and the place they are in now, and what discourse do they develop to express those perceptions and evaluations? Furthermore, how do people in the sending place and the receiving place develop their own interpretations and images of migrants and the places from which they have come or the places to which they go?

At both the global level and the local level, space is not just physical geography but is recoded according to specific criteria in what Shields (1991, 29) refers to as "imaginary geographies." Some places are coded as sacred or dangerous, others are related to warm sentiments, while still others conjure up bad memories (Milligan 1998, 10). Some places may simply be regarded as the cumulative experience of multiple uneventful experiences. Places are coded according to the people who live there and the activities that take place there. Often it is personal associations related to emotions or experiences that interpret a place, but it can also be reflections on social arrangements of power or relations of production that structure one's image of a place. Images and myths develop about space, ranking it in relation to other space, giving it a sense of cultural order, but also reflecting the hegemonic order of the dominant images – the "ideas in currency" – that are afloat in any given society (Shields 1991, 14; Harvey 1989).[6] Regions in particular are susceptible to ranking and image building within a national society, with place images developing due to oversimplifying, stereotyping, stigmatizing, and labelling. These images serve an important referential function with regard to interpreting present, past, and future encounters. The development of these place images and metaphors serves as a kind of "intellectual shorthand" (Shields 1991, 46) to express what, in reality, are deeply complex matters. As a place develops a set of core images, these images are partial, with a tendency to exaggerate or understate, and they are difficult to dislodge even in the face of countervailing evidence. But because these place-myths are socially constructed, it is useful to know where they come from and whose interests they serve.

Through the course of national life, conflicts, and tensions, cultural differences, and inequalities create regional identities of subordination/

domination that are represented in images and stereotypes. Ridicule, teasing, and labelling are ways in which interregional relationships are presented and sustained, and nicknames play an important role in the imaging of regions. For example, the term "Newfie" may be considered derogatory when used by an Albertan as a negative stereotype, but it can be considered a term of endearment when used by an expatriate Newfoundlander who uses it to express solidarity with those from back home. Labels for people from Saskatchewan ("stubble jumpers," "gophers") or Manitobans ("flatlanders") can be either affectionate or derogatory, depending on who is using them and in what context. Prince Edward Islanders might be called "spud pickers" or "potato people," the province's wealth of potatoes being one of the few things that is publicly known about it. References to Albertans as "rednecks" or to Calgary as "cowtown" are often used by people from metropolitan Canada to ridicule the entire province. Labels used by Albertans to define British Columbia include "the left coast," "the wet coast," and "lotus land," reflecting both ideological and climatological perspectives, with BC being viewed as an abbreviation for "Bring Cash" (a reference to that province's higher taxes). While each of these labels contains an aspect of humour, there is also a sense in which such labels reflect interregional competition.

There is, in Canada, a social labelling of regional spaces that reflects power relationships between regions. In the course of this labelling, images are developed and sustained and are often difficult to change. These images can be contested, even though they have historical roots, and they serve as an important touchstone in the migration process. In fact, as Shields (1991, 47) argues, the discourse around images serves as the basis for individual decisions. Destinations are places that are "read" individually and collectively as cultural texts (Fielding 1992, 203). Few migrants have no picture at all in their mind about where they are going; rather, they have an image of that place – and that image is socially constructed. Whether or not it is accurate is another matter, but the image is very important in motivating the move and in anticipating the arrival. Such images are particularly important for the speculative migrant, for whom imagery is often the basis of hopes and dreams.

Many migrants experienced the tensions and dynamics of interregional relations. Even announcing the decision to relocate to Alberta prompted reactions in the home region that often reflected its position in the national hierarchy. Upon arrival in Alberta, migrants had to sort out their reactions to what they observed around them. A migrant from Ontario stated:

> Nobody ever says that, but the western inferiority complex led people to think that I thought I was better than they were. So they would get very defensive and it would come out as a superiority complex. People are always defending themselves as though it's a big rivalry, whereas in Ontario, we never even think of people in Alberta – let alone as a rivalry. Whatever they did in Alberta they did, and it was not part of our worldview.

The more dominant region may be interested in what is happening in the hinterland, but the latter appears minor in comparison with the former's overwhelming power. On the other hand, ascendance in the hinterland region is interpreted as a challenge to the heartland's hegemony, provoking airs of superiority on both sides as previously held images undergo change. Items such as the Alberta energy rebate – "Ralph bucks" (the $400 prosperity bonus) – and even the lack of a provincial sales tax creates a reaction outside the province:

> The striving mentality here has a bit of cockiness to it. It is almost like a Canadianized version of the American mentality. When Alberta is leading all growth industries, it's hard not to think that way. Even the absence of a provincial sales tax breeds a number-one mentality.

Migrants often encountered these markers of economic prosperity in Alberta ("going to the land of milk and honey"), which suggests that Canadians both inside and outside the province are struggling with its emerging image and its relations with other regions.

The emergence of Alberta as a growth pole in the national society involved socially constructed images and myths that deeply affected migrants. There was near universal agreement among participants in the study that images of Alberta were at least partially developed and sustained by the media. Headlines such as "Alberta Tops Nation in Growth" or "Thousands Flock to Alberta," along with human interest stories about people who had moved or the challenges in-migrants were facing, presented images of what was happening in the province. There was also some sense that what was happening in Alberta was a threat to existing regional power relations in Canada. Since the media were based in central Canada, migrants felt that these images tended to reflect the latter's vantage point. A migrant from Ontario noted:

> People in Ontario get all their images from the media. People there really believe that they are the dominant region and that that's the

> best place to live in Canada. So the question of why you have to leave Ontario is inconceivable to them because they have everything.

Before they arrived in Alberta, most migrants thought of it as entrepreneurial, capitalistic, and high energy: "the home of free enterprise." But this view was often dependent upon where the person came from. For example, a migrant from Ottawa thought Calgary was "pretty isolated" but that it was "more business-oriented" than Ottawa, which was "more government oriented." Another example of how region of origin played a role in developing images comes from a migrant from Newfoundland who was accustomed to a more ethnically homogeneous community:

> The thing we were worried about in coming here was the cultural differences. Like how do people use humour here? Or, like we know there are people here who we have never met before – like Ukrainians or Hutterites that we don't have back home – even Native reserves in such numbers. And we wondered how we were going to adapt, but it hasn't been like we thought it might be.

Alberta's image also involved oil and cowboys. Oil created images of "oil barons with silver belt buckles" and "streets paved with gold": getting rich was thought to be a possibility. For people who came from regions where young men typically went to Alberta to work on the oil rigs, the province meant fast money. The cowboy image was sustained by the reputation of the Calgary Stampede and the symbolic white Stetson. The media developed a mythology that saw Alberta cities as "hick-towns" with grain elevators always looming nearby. Perceptions that Alberta was more American than other provinces (one Manitoban referred to it as the "U.S. of A" ["the United States of Alberta"]) were sometimes expressed, and a migrant from Atlantic Canada thought of it as "big Texas North" because of its wide open skies.

The physical presence of the oil industry, with its wealth and risk-taking, fed an image of Alberta as "a land of milk and honey." This image attracted people to the province but it also created unrealistic expectations. It also promoted an image of Alberta as a place to try to make it but not as a place to stay. If booms created images, so did the notion of busts. The Klein government tried to change that image through the use of the promotional phrase "the Alberta Advantage," which implied that Alberta had developed an economic climate that was particularly good for business and, therefore, for putting down roots. This phrase captured the official discourse, which presented Alberta as a spatial location given a unique meaning by politicians and government administrators.

Empirical Evidence of Mental Images of Alberta

Potential migrants obtained images of Alberta in several ways, including through articles in newspapers or magazines. But word-of-mouth and the influence of friends and relatives were also important, and reports from migrants who came home to visit certainly helped to create images. These images were usually attractive, which, of course, helped to induce migration.

> When I thought of Alberta, I thought of oil and gas and jobs. That's what people talked about. People would say that you could get a job right away and that the jobs paid more. I don't know where people get that but that's what people were saying.

> We kept hearing about how rosy things were in Alberta. We heard about this through the media. But Edmonton also had posted some billboards in the Lower Mainland (BC) advertising Edmonton. Right outside Stanley Park there was a big billboard with Mayor Bill Smith welcoming people to move to Edmonton. It must have planted a seed because that was in 1997 or 1998. Then there was an article in the *Vancouver Sun* about a family that had moved to Edmonton, and they talked about how they liked it, the schools were good, and how they were very happy with their move. (British Columbia)

> Our image of Alberta was that it was a gold mine. That's where the money was. Ninety percent of people our age from home were coming out here. We got ITV from Edmonton and we would hear all those good things. We would also hear from other people who had come out and had been successful. We would hear all these stories from people who came out here for a few months and then come home, and then we would see them go out again, and we would hear all these stories, and that's what influenced us. (Newfoundland)

> Our image of Alberta was that it was more entrepreneurial, more active, and that it was energizing, and that it was a province with a

future. I'm not sure where we got that from – maybe it was the image of oil.

Graduates from our school were going to Ontario, but all of a sudden it changed. Pretty soon Jim was moving and Dan was moving and Joyce was moving – everybody was moving to Alberta. It was almost like tunnel vision – like that's the place to go. That's where the jobs were. And yet I said, "Look at those wing-nuts out there in Alberta – they are creating their own political party like they're more special than anyone else."

In PEI, people's families back home tell you all about how well their children are doing here, and maybe the success even gets bigger as the stories are told. But it gives you an idea, an impression about what life is like here. (Prince Edward Island)

We learned about Alberta and the way things are here primarily from people who move here. They come back and sort of recruit by saying it's a great place and there is lots of opportunity. I guess in that way I have also recruited back home.

I heard lots of stories of Alberta before I moved that [said that] everything was new. You get the image of this Mecca that is unbelievably progressive and where everyone is doing well and have nice houses. This was pretty attractive. (Nova Scotia)

These illustrations reveal how Alberta as a place became coded with meanings that enhanced the likelihood that the province would be a good destination. It is interesting that very few migrants mentioned any stereotypes of Alberta that were particularly negative or controversial, such as "rednecks" or "right-wing politics."[7] It is possible that these traits were considered irrelevant in the face of more compelling characteristics (e.g., the tax regime, conditions of prosperity). It seems that migrants simply selected place images that supported their decision to move.

As migrants interacted with the host society after arrival, they discovered that the place where they were from was coded –and usually not in a complimentary fashion – based on physical attributes. These traits involved gross generalizations (e.g., windy, rainy, flat) and ordered places according to rank, so that the destination appeared superior. For example, migrants from British Columbia were "escaping the rain" rather than moving from a milder to a harsher climate. In fact, arrivals picked up the regional stereotypes that were present in Alberta rather quickly. Some of these stereotypes involved referring to central Canada as "the East"; antagonism towards Ontario, especially Ottawa as the seat of government; and a lack of patience with Quebec. But migrants from central Canada were much less likely to report personal responses to this imaging than were migrants from the other provinces in the western interior and the Atlantic region. Images combined physical/geographical attributes with collective characteristics that reflected labelling and implicit biases, and they were received with mixed results.

> People sometimes joke about me being from Saskatchewan as a "ratlander," or "stubble jumper." I sort of got fed up with people saying it. It was not that they would carry on about it. It was just that everyone would mention it, and I got a bit tired of it. It was sort of a one-liner that I got tired of. (Saskatchewan)

> We are teased a lot about being from Saskatchewan, but we are well liked. We are teased about being "gophers," "flatlanders," and "stubble jumpers," or "car people" rather than "boat people," like the Vietnamese. (Saskatchewan)

> There is a lot of negativity here about the winters in Winnipeg, whereas to me it doesn't seem a lot different. When I say I'm from Winnipeg, they say, "Oh, it's windy there," and I say, "So, it's no different from here." People make those kinds of statements to me. To me, Manitoba and Alberta are very similar. (Manitoba)

> People here don't really know Saskatchewan. They only think about the south where it's flat, but they know nothing about the north where there are trees and lakes. I don't like it when people knock Saskatchewan. I can do that, but they can't. (Saskatchewan)

> When people hear you are from PEI, they seem to want to stop and talk. Sometimes when you are busy, you don't want that, but because you are from the other end of the country, people want to talk to you. They like the accent, or confuse it with Newfies, or tease us about being "spud pickers." (Prince Edward Island)

> People here have a very skewed view of the Maritimes. They think it is all rock and that everyone is poor and that people are all fishers.

This is a media image because we never felt while living in New Brunswick that it was a have-not province or that people were poor. People here consider it as the backwater of the country, but we don't feel that way. Yes, we were not fortunate to find work there, but it is a wonderful place to live and a great lifestyle. (New Brunswick)

I was always being introduced at work as from Nova Scotia. I would correct them and say, "New Brunswick." And they would say, "Well, it's all the same." So I would say that that would be like saying that Saskatchewan and Alberta are the same. It seems like anything east of Quebec is all the same. There is a huge ignorance of the Maritimes here – almost like Canadians and Americans. (New Brunswick)

Albertans know nothing about the East Coast. They think we are all Newfies and that we're all fishermen. They consider everything East Coast [to be] Newfie. If they started calling Newfies dumb, then I would take offence, but otherwise it doesn't bother me. (Newfoundland)

The image of Maritimers as lazy bums is a wrong image. There are lazy people there but there are also lazy people in Alberta. I don't think Albertans have a better work ethic than Maritimers, although they think they do. They get this from the media, but most of them don't really know because they haven't been there. There is a level of ignorance here about that. I think that there is little difference and people are the same everywhere and that you will always get a few of the extremes everywhere.

A "goofy Newfie" is somebody like Disney's Goofy. Somebody who laughs a lot and is sort of dumb. That comes from the ignorance in the oil patch where you have Newfoundlanders with little education making $72,000 as a roughneck with few social skills. Then it is just picked up by others as a careless generalization. (Newfoundland)

The attitude Albertans have of Newfoundlanders sucks. They make fun of your accent and they actually think it's funny. They think we're all alcoholics but we only drink on weekends. And all Albertans can think about is screech. That's how they label you. (Newfoundland)

Places were also coded in a manner that mixed physical attributes with socio-political evaluations. Again, coding was stereotypical, focusing on economic conditions, dispositions, and/or dominant activities:

> To me, Alberta is clean. BC always seems to be in a mess and Saskatchewan is always having a hard time with farmers. When I think of BC, I think of rain; and when I think of Saskatchewan, I think of dry and depressed. It's what you hear on the news and what you pick up from other people. Here it is not that way.
>
> There [are] a lot of people here from Ontario who don't stand up and admit that … a lot of people in Alberta feel mistrust in people from Ontario. You get the same old story about the energy program. People here don't like it when people from Ontario come here and try to tell them what to do.
>
> To me it was a matter of weighing the options. There was too much old money in the Maritimes. Toronto was too big for me. Vancouver was too expensive. Montreal taxes were too high. So what does that leave? In Alberta, taxes were minimal and there was no PST [provincial sales tax]. It seemed that there really were few options. And when you had the personal contacts we had here, Alberta just made sense.
>
> Ontario had never appealed to me and I think it was because Ontario seemed sort of conceited or arrogant. I feel there is a similarity between the West and the Maritimes and that is friendliness and the hospitality. That made the image of Alberta more positive.
>
> Some people in Ontario told us before we moved out here about that "let-easterners-freeze-in-the-dark" idea, so I expected people to make more derogatory comments about being from Ontario. But when it comes up that I am from Ontario, people just say, "Oh, that's nice," though sometimes I am teased in jest at work (most are from somewhere else anyway). We get more teasing about having lived in Ottawa and the federal government. (Ontario)

Places are clearly classified according to sweeping generalizations that often exaggerate one particular trait. There were no reports of these images being used in an antagonistic way, but perhaps they serve as a commentary on how the host society of Alberta reacted to being a magnet destination. For migrants, these mental pictures played a role in establishing place-myths that functioned to justify the choices they had made.

TYPE 3: THE LIVED COMPONENT OF PLACE – PLACE-MAKING

The third type of space is lived space, and it reflects how people struggle with their own relationship to the places in which they reside. Lived space builds from the two other types of space but moves beyond them to express the struggle that occurs when attempting to share space with others. Lived space is, profoundly, a space of transitions, in which meaning and location are continually being negotiated and evaluated. This process can be called place-making, with places taking on meaning through the identification and recollection of biographical experiences (Gieryn 2000, 472). There is no better illustration of someone engaged in this process than the migrant. Whether as someone who is considering leaving one place and who has images of the destination, or as someone who has already left one place and moved to another, the migrant stands outside both the sending and receiving communities. She/he occupies a type of "othered" position, constantly balancing the physical (real, concrete) and mental (images) aspects of both locations, constantly weighing and evaluating the appropriateness and consequences of her/his decision to migrate. It is in this third space that the migrant not only personally undergoes a transformation but also contributes to the transformation of the sending and receiving communities.

In this third space, the migrant is truly caught between the old and the new physical spaces, and she/he struggles with the mental images of the destination before departure and the realities of the new place after arrival. The realities of the destination as lived space reveal disappointments and unrealized expectations or, conversely, satisfaction and, even more, ambition. But migrants are also filled with regret and mixed emotions. How do leavers and newcomers struggle with their relations to the "old place" and the "new place"? How do they deal with this transitioning and change? How do they resolve dilemmas created by the relocation?

The Concept of Home

Perhaps the most basic struggle a migrant faces is with the location and identification of "home." For some, home is the place where you are born and raised (Brink 1995, 23). It may be a particular dwelling or landscape or community. In this sense, for a migrant, home is a fixed place of previous residence. But home may not simply be a structure or a location; it may also be an affective quality, a subjective state expressed in the phrase "home is where the heart is" (Rapoport 1995). This concept of home suggests that, if there are strong emotional bonds between parents, relatives, and friends in the region of origin, then this is where the heart is. But it also opens the door to the possibility that emotional bonds may be present at the destination and in other places as well. This more flexible concept of home is portable and suggests that, wherever you co-reside with significant others, that place can be identified as home. An even more flexible concept of home is represented by the phrase "home is where you find it," meaning that home is wherever you happen to feel comfortable. This idea suggests that attachment to place of birth/upbringing or to kin may be important but that it is not critical to the migrant's self-image and personal identity; rather, home is where she/he has her/his personal possessions, wherever that may be. Home as a fixed physical space is not as important – or, at least, is easily transferable.[8]

Box 1: Home

Home is where the heart is and my heart will always be in Ontario because that is where my family is. I have met a few kindred spirits but this is not where my roots are. (Ontario)

I've tried to make this home but it just can't be. Alberta is not part of my identity. It is hard to explain why you want the mist and the fog in your face.

I could live here for twenty-five years and I will never be an Albertan because that is not where my formative experiences were.

I still talk as though home is Quebec and "we" refers to the people in Quebec. My identity is where I grew up. Yet I would never move back there. (Quebec)

I don't know how permanent this is going to be but the bottom line is that you know you can always go home.

Many idealized/romanticized views of home are based on childhood memories (Porteous and Smith 2001, 63; Morley 2000, 19–20). In fact, the most common form of attachment to place is related to family love and security (Chawla 1992). Recollections of sites of play, memories of friends and experiences, and sounds and smells linked to specific "home" places often constitute emotional ties that cannot be erased. Returns to that place (whether as a visitor or as a return migrant) play a key role in the struggle to identify home. However, such returns are often disappointing because things are never quite the same. Others have grown up and moved on or at least moved into a different status (e.g., through marrying and having children). Other people age or die, buildings decay, and communities experience various forms of change. In any case, enough will have changed so that "it just doesn't seem like home anymore" – at least in some significant ways.

Furthermore, the experience of going away changed the migrant as well. She/he is exposed to different ideas, attitudes, and opportunities that make her/him a different person, often in subtle ways. Thus, while there may be initial euphoria over being back in a place where one feels comfortable and accepted ("home is where when you go there they have to let you in"), it may well be the case that being away has produced a different worldview that makes the returned migrant feel somewhat "out of place." In other words, not only has the interactional context changed but the interactional self has changed. One of the best examples of this is the migrant who returns "home" to retire. She/he soon discovers that she/he has been heavily influenced by the destination and has brought their reconstructed self back to the place of origin. Therefore, returning "home" is not as smooth and simple as it appears. Perhaps this is what stands behind the adage "You can't go home again." In short, migrants are often torn because they have emotional investments in two or more places, and in some significant way they are caught between them.[9]

Memories of a former home are unreliable gauges of how things are there now. Much of what we remember of the past is shaped by our current environment; what we remember is filtered and reinterpreted according to where we are and who we are with (Zerubavel 1996). Memories of physical sites are not fixed; rather, they are socially constructed, being added to, deleted from, and reinterpreted over time (Milligan 1998, 9). If a migrant is lonely at the destination, then the social ties of "home" are magnified – even if, before departure, the migrant may have found those ties worn, "old," and confining. This is a form of displaced attachment; that is, current unhappiness is displaced by a more positive attitude that the migrant had experienced at another point in time (Belk 1992, 47–8). If a migrant is making lots of new friends and having exciting new experiences at the destination, "home" is increasingly reinterpreted as something she/he has left behind. Upon raising children at a destination (or even considering doing so), "home" may suddenly take on a new meaning (though it is often encompassed by the desire to raise children in a similar environment to which the migrant was raised). If the migration has been successful, migrants may have a tendency to reinterpret past fond memories in a way that emphasizes the superiority of their new home over their place of origin. Given that the process of detachment is seldom complete, the migrant at least occasionally reflects upon her/his place of origin in ways that minimize the negative and emphasize the positive. In other words, memories of a place of origin are selective and often reflect the migrant's current situation and needs. These memories are not comprehensive, and, because they are fixed in time, they do not necessarily reflect current conditions in the home community.

Negotiating Place Identities from Origin to Destination

When the transfer from origin to destination is being processed physically, mentally, and socially, an identity disruption occurs that often results in homesickness (Brown 1992, 289). The migrant stands above her/his new environment, assessing it, determining its suitability, and locating her/himself within it. In this sense, the migrant is in an "Othered" position in which the struggle is to conform image with reality, expectations with actualities, and anticipation with actual experience. It is essentially, at least initially, a world of constant comparisons between the origin and the destination. Home is often identified as the place against which judgments about all other places are made. "This is better," "that is missed," "this is different," "that is lost," "I love it here," "I wish I could return" – all these emotions exist either simultaneously or alternately. Comparisons produce both joy and sorrow: joy over what is gained and sorrow over what is lost.[10]

Box 2: Homesickness and Its Resolution

When I came out here from Ontario the first time, I was lonely for my relatives and I kept thinking about how things were there when I was seven years old. But when we went back, we saw that everyone had their own families and we didn't belong in the same sense that I expected. We thought it would be good if the kids knew the relatives and all my friends were back there, and I realized this was no longer me and I had become an Albertan. I find peace in the mountains that they find in the trees and lakes. (Ontario)

About a year and a half ago, I got so homesick that I had to go home. But now I am completely the opposite. Things change and my friends from high school haven't changed at all in their thinking. When I went back I discovered that I couldn't live there anymore. I don't have as much in common with my friends there anymore because I moved away and I'm working here doing things they can't relate to. But my friends here can.

I got so homesick that I went back for eight months. But then after being there for awhile, I realized that I didn't like it. I knew I could come back and get a job because I had developed a good reputation.

I know a family from home that is moving back after Christmas. Their children don't want to go. They have no job to go to but they just want to go home. He is making twenty dollars an hour but she just doesn't like it here. Money isn't everything, and some people just do not like it here and are not happy. We told him he's nuts to leave and he said, "But why should we be unhappy?"

People who return go back because home is home. They are homesick and they want to be with family and friends. Some people are just not up to change. I had a hard time at first, more than my husband did, and he kept saying, "Look how well we're doing." But I missed home, where it was quieter and quainter.

Box 3: Transitional Identities – The "Othered" Position

I feel homeless in terms of my identity. I know I am no longer from Ontario but I am not quite here yet. (Ontario)

I will always be a Cape Bretoner so I don't know if I feel like an Albertan but I certainly have been Albertanized. (Nova Scotia)

We had no plan when we came out here and whatever happens happens. I would like to move back but I am torn and really don't know. I went back for three weeks at Christmas and in the summer, and I really couldn't wait to get back home – meaning Alberta. I really think I'm here for the time being but when I look at how I have grown and [how] people there haven't, I don't want to go back. I guess I am torn.

I call myself a transplant. When people ask me if I came from Alberta, I say I am a transplant, and then often they say, so am I! We are Albertans for sure – but a transplant.

I will always see myself as "a Maritimer living in Calgary" rather than "a Calgarian from the Maritimes" because I see my identity as based on being a Maritimer rather than where I am living.

We are always comparing Manitoba to Alberta. One is home and one is where I live.

I still think of myself as a Northern Ontario person because I have not been out here long enough yet. After all, that is where my roots are. But I don't get the impression that you have to have three generations here before you can say that you are an Albertan because everyone here is young. When you actually meet someone who is from Edmonton, that is rare, and I think most of Alberta is like that. (Ontario)

I went back for a wedding in which I was maid of honour and signed the register with my name and Fort McMurray, Alberta. and I said, "what did I do?" It was a startling moment but I guess Fort McMurray is my home now. I told my Mom and she looked at the book and started crying.

When I go home to visit I really want to stay there. It even brings tears to my eyes to say that since I want to go home so bad. But Calgary's OK too. There are opportunities here and you can't deny that. I'm happy that I came here but I'm not happy living here on a personal level.

I see myself as someone who lives here now but who is really from Montreal. I would never go back there until they change things. When I do go back to visit, I realize there is family but there is really nothing left of my old life there. (Quebec)

The first five years after migration comprise an arbitrary settlement period full of meandering between a sense of adventure and a sense of loss. In any case, it is difficult for the migrant to feel a sense of belonging at the destination. Migration into a closed society (i.e., a society in which there are few newcomers) entails difficulties with entrance and acceptance, while migration into an open society (i.e., a society in which there are many newcomers) is easier. This was clearly the situation in Alberta as newcomers found little difficulty in finding others who were also newcomers, often from the same general place of origin. Those who had positive experiences were highly likely to integrate quickly and to develop new community attachments (Hummon 1992, 258), thus no longer feeling like outsiders. As the result of interaction with others at the destination (a process known as locational socialization [Lofland 1973]), the migrant learns about the new place, new memories are created by fresh experiences, and a sense of rootedness, belonging, and place identity is enhanced. At the same time, while it appeared on the outside that locational socialization was relatively easy, it was quite typical to learn that migrants retained strong emotional ties to their place of origin – whether or not they ever hoped to return. It was not just that home was a physical place but also that it was a point of departure and an indelible personal orientation to the world (Jacobsen 2002, 3).

Box 4: Outside Identity

People are friendly but I found that drivers were more hostile to me until I switched my plates. They wanted me to go faster. People didn't treat me as being from another province as much as they considered me a small town dude, and they wondered how I would adjust to the big city. (Manitoba)

I sometimes feel like an outsider because it is harder to discuss things with anglophones, like politics or telling a joke. So I feel more comfortable being with those who speak French. (New Brunswick)

When people hear my accent, they ask where I am from. And they'll say, "Oh, I've been in Montreal," or they use some French words that help make it friendly. Or with your French thinking, you may say something that sounds funny and people will laugh as if you are telling a joke. But it has not been an obstacle. (Quebec)

When we got here, we learned that when we said we were from the east, people thought we meant Ontario. So when we said we were from the Maritimes, they would say we were Newfoundland. They don't know geography here. They are constantly telling us about people here who are also from Newfoundland and it turns out they are from another Atlantic province. People here don't know the difference between the Atlantic provinces. (New Brunswick)

People here think that everyone's on pogey back east. They think that everyone is on welfare or unemployment, which is not fair. I said if you believe that, then you are a bigger idiot than I have met in my entire life. (Newfoundland)

One thing people from Saskatchewan have in common is the Riders. A lot of my friends are from small towns and that assists in bonding too. It gives you the sense that we are all down-to-earth people and more genuine. (Saskatchewan)

It seems like in any larger workplace, there is a maritime contingent – you know, a couple from Nova Scotia and another or three from New Brunswick or PEI. It makes you feel comfortable because you can understand certain jokes that westerners don't get. We know people here who graduated from UNB and St Francis Xavier, and it makes everyone get along because we know these schools and people here don't necessarily. You run into people from back home all over the place. When you talk to a Maritimer, there is a sense of community. I learned one night at a bar that you don't say to people here that you are from back east. You say you are from the Maritimes because the feeling towards central Canada here is not always that good and people here refer to that area as the east. (Nova Scotia)

This book argues that migration is a process of detachment and reattachment in which the migrant interacts with the place of origin and the destination over a considerable period of time. It shows that a form of distancing occurs at the place of origin and that this begins the process of detachment, which is then deepened through the actual move and the entry into a new community. There is always a sense in which the migrant feels tied to the place of origin. That sense of identity can be fostered in a number of ways, such as by contact through telephone, the internet, or return visits. Telecommunications technology makes it possible for the migrant to be in two places at once; she/he is able to be at the destination while also, through phone or e-mail conversations, being at the community of origin. Much of what is discussed in such conversations is constructed from a common frame of reference between the migrant and the person back home. Return visits are more problematic in that, while it often feels good to be "home," this feeling is compromised by the knowledge that it isn't really home any more. In fact, many migrants claimed that going home was good medicine for the "migration blues" as it made them aware that their careers and new friends were somewhere else. On the other hand, return visits did frequently sustain the attachment to home, often leaving the migrant with warm feelings and strengthened emotional ties. The warm welcome experienced at home, the euphoria of seeing old friends, and the nostalgia created by visiting places with happy memories also provided a sense of belonging that reinforced place identity.[11]

A sense of identity that is tied to one's place of origin, which is seen as home, can be reinforced through interaction with other migrants who came from the same place. This is clearly most important in the initial stages of settlement, when contacts with people from home (typically earlier migrants) play a very useful role in helping people get established. It is typical for people to be drawn to those who come from the same place or same region. If they interacted at some point in the past, there is an immediate connection because of this *shared past* (Katovich and Couch 1992). Even if they hadn't known each other before, and had had many independent experiences in different contexts, as members of a group from the same region of origin they are bonded by a *common past*, and this allows new interaction. Using categorical identities such as being from Saskatchewan, Quebec, or the Maritimes provides both a sense of belonging and a sense of identity that is tied to a place of origin.

Shared or common pasts were celebrated not only through casual interaction or house parties but also through formal social clubs, which were established to foster socializing among people with a common place of origin. A backyard lobster boil provided the occasion for people of Maritime roots to get together, while formal organizations like the Maritime Reunion Association or the Saskatchewan Social Club organized events for other migrants. Professional athletic events such as NHL hockey or CFL football also provided an opportunity for people to express their loyalties and identities with their place of origin. It has often been stated that, particularly in Calgary, when certain teams were in town (most notably the Saskatchewan Roughriders but also other teams representing Canadian cities), at times it was difficult to know who the home team really was because the competition brought out people's original loyalties and identities. Other occasions, such as holidays (e.g., Thanksgiving) often provided an opportunity for people "away from home" to get together with others in the same position who otherwise would have been alone. Summer long weekends also provided opportunities for special events (e.g., town reunions) to be organized at the destination, often with the goal of raising funds for a project in one's home town.

All of these illustrations could be considered mechanisms whereby migrants, by linking the new place with the old place, made their new place of residence not only tolerable but also meaningful. This is the classic expression of place-making, and it has been well documented in the literature on international migration (Aguilar-San Juan 2005). I discuss the process of place-making further in chapter 10, but it begins by interacting with people from "back home" through just "hanging out" with them in homes or bars or coffee shops.[12] Often people who work at the same place or happen to come together for other reasons discover their common background and feel a sense of belonging together. One person's finding another person often results in the discovery that they know other people from the same region. Thus, through word of mouth, a network of ties is created that establishes a sense of community in diaspora. In this way, place of origin becomes the basis for interaction and for a common identity. In other words, the common condition of being absent from a home territory causes people to build social networks that bring in previously unknown people. These networks are built from a retrospectively shared location, which generates and reinforces a common identity.

IDENTITY SHIFTS

What is clear is that migrants must reconcile an old identity with a new location. This is similar to Castell's (2004, 8) idea of project identity because it involves the building of a new identity that redefines one's position in society and is a critical source of meaning.[13] The existence of an identity based on a place of origin different from the destination sustains the sense of distance that the migrant feels and reaffirms her/his position as an outsider. The question is, how important is that outsider identity to the migrant? It would be expected that this identity might be more important to the new arrival than to the long-term resident. But this depends on other factors, such as attitudes towards migration in the first instance, the importance of ties to home, plans for length of stay, abilities to adjust, and indicators of success at the destination. Some factors contribute to the reduction of an outsider identity. Promotions at work, buying your own home, having children at the destination, and becoming involved in community activities all facilitate a sense of rootedness. Becoming an Oilers fan or a Flames fan is often a good indicator that some rootedness is developing. Hummon (1992, 263–5) refers to this as "everyday rootedness" because it involves a simple attachment to community through daily activities. He distinguishes this type of rootedness from "ideological rootedness," which he ties to a more self-consciously articulated identification with the new community. This is a much deeper form of identification, and it may not develop unless it is triggered by some other factor.

Over time, the outsider identity softens and a dual place identity emerges. Some, however, do resist a new identity because they desire to return to their community of origin. For example, continuing to have out-of-province licence plates or restricting interaction with local people are both indicative that the migrant wants to return. Holding a place of origin identity and a destination identity simultaneously (though unequally), is one way in which the migrant begins to adjust to her/his new residence. The place of origin identity may be the primary identity, but, as rootedness begins to occur, the destination identity may become more primary. Factors that contribute to this rootedness are: elections (which require votes for local candidates and/or media discussions of local and national issues from the perspective of the destination region), the migration of other relatives (especially elderly parents) to the destination or the death of these significant others at the place of origin, and the development of a network of friends and membership in organizations at the destination. One example of a concrete way of symbolizing this dual identity involves the migrants who obtained an Alberta license plate but placed it within a licence plate holder inscribed with the words: "Home of my Heart: Cape Breton." All migrants seemed to hold a dual identity, although with varying degrees of strength. Changes/reversals in primary and secondary identities occurred over time.

Box 5: Place-making Identity Shifts

I consider myself an Albertan and not a New Brunswicker any more. That transformation happened when I had a child here and bought my first house. I have very little desire to go back even to visit because of the discomfort I am made to feel about having left. And I am defined as being successful and they don't like that. Most of my family is here now anyway. I have only limited contacts here with people from New Brunswick. (New Brunswick)

I developed a sense of belonging here by going to the Flames games, I have a Flames jersey. (British Columbia)

I've become an Oiler and Eskimo fan already and that helps me feel at home. But you have to learn what to say and not to say – like don't ever mention Trudeau. Now that I've adjusted, I don't think I would leave – even though my family is back there. I'd like to get my mom to move out here. (Ontario)

I don't know what it is but the Stampede image here makes rural people feel at home. I've grown to love it here pretty fast. I do want to move home sometime but unless something unforeseen happens, I'm quite happy to make this my home. (New Brunswick)

It seems to me that not many people really consider Calgary home and so the Stampede is a way of building a tradition for new people. There is a strange mix here of friendliness and strong business spirit. (Prince Edward Island)

I am still a French-Canadian and with my accent I can't hide it, but my wife and children are here now with me and we are making our life here so I guess I am an Albertan. I don't feel bad about that because there is a French community here that has been here for many years and I listen to the French radio. You can stay attached to the French side here if you want and I want to do that and make sure my children speak French too. (Quebec)

The presence of so many in Alberta born outside the province ensured that place of origin questions ("where are you from?") were often asked; and the occasional trip back home and interest in news about what was happening there seemed to preserve at least a residual identification with place of origin. In fact, this residual identity seemed to be quite powerful. Part of "who I am" is related to "where I am from," and all in-migrants who moved to Alberta as adults had a keen sense of where they were from. And, in large measure, where you are from is not primarily a matter of where you were born but where you grew up. While provinces can be very large and have many regional identities, "province" was the most persistent designator of locational identity. Cape Bretoners might feel a special kinship with other Cape Bretoners, but, at a great distance from home, they found that identifying with others from Nova Scotia, or even with Maritimers or "East Coasters," was a meaningful way of enlarging their boundaries while still retaining them. Part of the reason why an origin identity persisted was that the migrant had almost always left some family and friends (and sometimes property) behind, so there was always reason to return. Memories also refuse to die, which means that at least occasional trips to the place associated with these memories appeared justified.

Box 6: Intentional Identity Shifts

I think I considered myself an Albertan the minute I stepped off the plane. We made the choice to leave. In truth, I don't think we ever considered ourselves Quebecers, particularly as they define it now, even though we were born there. (Quebec)

I consider myself an Albertan now already, because it embraced me and took me in and got me a job right away. And through my first job, I hooked a better job, so I'm very happy. For the first time in my life I feel like I'm contributing and I'm useful. (Nova Scotia)

I consider myself an Albertan now but I have to fight for that within the French community. They don't like that. I have a tendency to assimilate but the French community does not like that and pressure you to do things with them. On my business card, I have a French side and an English side. I do not have the accent on my last name on the English side, but then I get pressure and I was told that I should present myself with the accent. When I do business in English, I want to present my English side. I don't want to play that politics game, I want to mix ... They also say don't speak in English with me, speak French. But I enjoy speaking English. I will speak what my reflex to say a sentence is and if you don't like it that it is in English, I don't like the pressure to speak French. (Quebec)

I came out here expecting to return home in a couple of years but now I am expecting to stay here permanently and go back only for vacation or to visit. I feel more secure here and there is nothing back there for us except our families. You don't see many young

> kids there or people our age at home. Here there are lots of kids and lots of young couples our age. (New Brunswick)
>
> I had never planned on staying or not staying. I just came out and I figured that if I didn't like it, I could go back tomorrow. Now I decided this is my home. At first I came here just for the money. I used to keep track of what was happening on the East Coast but now I don't know what's going on back there. We are in the process of buying a house now and I can't see myself going back unless I go when I retire. (Nova Scotia)

The strength of a migrant's origin identity seemed to vary with the place of origin. Places with a strong sense of collective identification (particularly the Atlantic provinces and Saskatchewan) were more likely to generate strong attachments to place of origin, and these were frequently articulated. When a strong place identity existed, expressions of loyalty seemed to consist of a developed stock of positive feelings about the place of origin that emerged to counter negativity. These expressions usually began at the place of origin as a way of handling the emotional struggles of departure and may even have been learned from those who had left earlier. Regions with a continuous pattern of out-migration seemed to possess a sense of siege, viewing external forces as a constant threat to their social economy. Comparatively speaking, it is this sense of external control that produced an underdog mentality in relation to other more dominant or prosperous regions or provinces. There is also a sense of abandonment that comes from community decline as rural areas and small towns struggle to survive, as buildings are abandoned, and as people leave. Rural depopulation and the virtual disappearance of fishing villages and agricultural towns evoke feelings of discouragement as smaller communities consolidate with larger communities that are only somewhat more viable. Thus, the migrant, who has already learned to develop a sense of solidarity in the face of more powerful forces at home, takes this way of thinking with her/him to the destination. This worldview is a coping strategy that has been learned at home and continues in the form of a regional identity once the migrant arrives at her/his destination.[14] But migration also sets in motion a process of reflexivity in which previously taken-for-granted elements of identity are rediscovered (Cohen 1985). Possessing a regional identity provides an important anchor as the migrant goes through the transitioning process (Rapport and Dawson 1998).

Box 7: Origin Identities in Relation to a Weak Economy

When you leave Saskatchewan, it is sort of like deserting your home. You know there is a problem and yet now you are contributing to that problem. And you don't want to be lumped into that category of people who say they hate Saskatchewan. Those people usually think they are too cool to associate with people from Saskatchewan. But we're not like that. We love Saskatchewan and never want to see anything bad happen to it. In fact, we are proud and patriotic about it. We want to talk about Saskatchewan and when we meet someone, the first thing we ask is where did you go to school and who do you know. And so everybody is here but when they want to get married, they go back home to Saskatchewan. (Saskatchewan)

Anybody from the Maritimes we feel comfortable with and I think it is because in comparison to this province, we all have an underdog feeling, and that gives us a discernible identity. And there is so much ignorance out here about the Maritimes that it forces us to stick together. (Prince Edward Island)

Being from Saskatchewan is like being the underdog. There is a sense of pride when you can compete. I speak of being from Saskatchewan with pride, but when you tell people where you are from, you don't expect to be taken seriously. You know, just because there are not a lot of people there and all that. I think there are a lot of character-building things about growing up there, so I use that to my advantage. (Saskatchewan)

I am not planning to go back at the moment, but once a Newfie, always a Newfie. I will always call Newfoundland my home if anyone asks me. I am happy to be here but I will always be a Newfoundlander. My uncles who are here all have the Newfoundland map or flag tattooed on their upper arms. I think things like that or Newfoundland bumper stickers or Newfoundland licence plates are a way to express your loyalty to Newfoundland. Newfoundlanders are patriotic just like Americans are. (Newfoundland)

I am very happy to be here but I'm not an Albertan. I will always be very proud to be from Saskatchewan. I think it comes from our socialistic roots where we work together and have pride. There is a spirit in Saskatchewan because we tend to band together. (Saskatchewan)

It is great to be able to say you are from PEI and I would never say anything else. But to badmouth it, I just wouldn't do it because that's where I'm from and I'm proud of it. (Prince Edward Island)

Place attachments did exist among people from provinces other than Saskatchewan or those in the Maritimes, but it appeared that those attachments were more individualistic than collective, and there was little sense of regional distinctiveness.[15] A migrant from Ontario or British Columbia, for example, may have strong attachments to their place of origin, but the collective expression of that attachment was much more low key and less related to a sense of inferiority.[16] A migrant from a province/region with a strong economy (e.g., Ontario) may know that there is a strong possibility that she/he will return, whereas a migrant from a region with a struggling economy may realize she/he will not likely return. Furthermore, the migrant from a region with a strong economy knows that her/his departure is less likely to affect that region than would be the case if it had a weak economy and experienced a constant outflow of people. As one respondent from Ontario noted:

Most people in Toronto couldn't care less if people are moving to Alberta. They would say that we have more than enough people here and so a few thousand moving to Alberta is nothing. It is not an issue for Ontario. The government might be concerned about the advantages of some provinces over others in attracting businesses but most individuals in Ontario do not see it as an issue.

But herein lies at least a partial explanation for why there are such variations in collective regional identities. Regions with weak economies generate a sense of guilt and/or sadness among out-migrants over leaving a declining area, and the origin identity not only compensates for the decision to leave but also provides a moral boost to those who were left behind, who may at least observe that those who leave have expressed their loyalty. Of course, the origin identity is also useful in creating community and group solidarity among migrants at the destination. As one woman from Saskatchewan noted:

We knew a lot of people here already – many who had moved from Saskatchewan a long time ago who were very welcoming. Actually

> most of the people we seem to meet are from Saskatchewan [laughs]. My husband wore a T-shirt with the logo from his school in Saskatchewan in a coffee shop here the other day, and someone came up to us and asked if we knew so-and-so. It's like every second person we run into is from Saskatchewan.

Migrants from regions/provinces with a strong economy do not bring this emotional baggage with them and are less likely to rally around regional symbols.

Box 8: Origin Identities in Relation to a Strong Economy

[Few migrants from these regions thought of their identity in regional terms. When they did, it was primarily in reaction to their anticipation of a negative comment relating to their community of origin's historic dominance.

I was told before I got here that I better get ready because people in Alberta hate people from Toronto and I would have a terrible time because everyone would hate me. So I was prepared to take the risk and was expecting some of that. (Ontario)

When I moved here, I got a funny reaction when I told people I was from Ontario so I stopped telling people where I was from. Now I just say I'm from the east. (Ontario)

THE DILEMMA OF HOME

Migrants, then, are people in transition. I have already described the dilemmas of that transition for the migrant who often longs for home at the same time as she/he is adjusting to the new place of residence. There are alternating periods of wanting to return home and wanting to embrace the new place – which only reopens the question of where home really is. If, on the one hand, home is the place from where you start, it can also be the place to which you want to return when you are away from it (Schutz 1945).[17] This means that you determine where home is according to where you feel comfortable. The experience of going home often means going to that place from where you started, which is often defined as the place where you grew up and where your parents/extended family live. In contemporary society, this, of course, is no longer a straightforward thing. However, going home (i.e., where you grew up or spent your formative years or lived the longest) is usually an illuminating experience. This is because, after migrating, you return home only to discover that things are no longer the same.[18] First of all, you yourself have changed and now see things differently. Having experienced life elsewhere provides a different lens on your own community, which no longer looks just as you remembered it when younger. Second, to return means to discover that things in the home community have likely changed. Your absence has meant that friends and relatives have had to build new networks of friends and that you are now an outsider. While you attempt to restart relationships or continue them, you discover that the parameters have changed and that you are now only a visitor or a guest. And if you do not indicate that your return home is permanent, there is little incentive for others to invest in a relationship with you. Besides, others at home are busy with their own activities, of which you are not a part. In short, after the first few days of euphoria about being home, you discover that this is no longer home. So if home is the place to which you want to return when you are away from it, upon returning you discover that it really is not home, that your new home is where you have your regular routine. Your picture of your home of origin is frozen in time; upon finding that it has changed, the more likely you are to feel that your new home is your real home.

Box 9: Migration as Temporary Absence

When we came here from Manitoba, it was with the idea that it was temporary and that we would go back depending on how we liked it. But [sigh] I don't know ... it is becoming more permanent but fifteen years from now I don't know. (Manitoba)

A lot of people come out here planning to work for eight months and then to go home, but our work in the city is not like that – it is permanent and not seasonal. (Newfoundland)

We are planning to be here for five years and then we are moving back to Halifax. I will never again move to a place where I don't know the city or don't know anyone. I'm pretty homesick. It was the right thing to come here because it will be better for us for our move back home. (Nova Scotia)

When we left, people said, "Oh, you'll be back, you'll be back" – because that is what people always used to do. But I hear some people here who said they would come for a year and it's twenty-five years later. It is also common to hear people say they will retire there. But you either have to go back before you have kids or you end up staying here. (Nova Scotia)

I was going to come here for two or three years and then go back to Ottawa. But now I was lucky to get married and have a child, but I miss home. (Ontario)

I always said I would go back but there is no plan to go back. I think I romanticize a lot about what I had when I grew up there. And it's home. But you have to have a plan if you go back, you just can't move back. The people I know who moved back were given an opportunity there to move back to. (Newfoundland)

Box 10: Commitment to Return

I will die there – come hell or high water. I have already stayed here longer than I said I would but I'll go back sometime. (Newfoundland)

We always knew when we left that we would go back. When? We don't know. It might not be till we're seventy, but we'll get back sometime. It's where we grew up and it will still be our home. (Nova Scotia)

I don't want to stay here forever, but I want to make the best of it. I'm trying to keep as positive as I can and experience as much as I can. I have only been here for a few months but he has been here for two years and we still get homesick. (Newfoundland)

If you came here with the attitude that you hate it and want to move back it will affect you. Our friends had a child here but they moved back and they said they didn't want the child to know it was from Calgary and wanted the child to feel like a Newfoundlander. (Newfoundland)

We thought my husband could work four weeks on and four weeks off and we could live in Newfoundland and he could commute to Alberta, but that is not how it works. I thought I was just coming for a visit, and when it wasn't happening that way I cried a lot. I will never call this home because we built our dream home back there and it is waiting for us. (Newfoundland)

We stay here because the novelty has not worn off yet and none of us have had an impending event [e.g., loss of job, a death at home, marriage] that would force us to consider returning. But our allegiance to Alberta is pretty shallow at this point. I sometimes wonder what that impending event will be for me. (Manitoba)

Box 11: The Return Dilemma

If you go home you are going to sacrifice something. You are either going to sacrifice money to gain family or you are going to stay here. Every year when I go home, people ask me when I'm coming back. Every time I tell them two more years. But I don't know. I think though that I would love to be home when I have kids. (Prince Edward Island)

When we were home two years ago, we bought a piece of land with the intention of building a house on it. But we are now no closer to going home than we were two years ago. We fight with it all the time: do you go home and take a cut in pay and also reduce your job mobility – or do you build your house here? I have a million miles to go with my job here and should I give that up? It is a lot to risk. What haunts me is going home and facing the reality that I can't make a go of it and I have to move back out here. It will be harder to move back if you by then have kids that have to be moved too. (Newfoundland)

We came here with the idea that it is going to be five years but I don't know now. We want to be closer to the kids – maybe Quebec or Ontario. If the family and kids were in Alberta, there would absolutely be no reason to leave. Even my job pays better here. (New Brunswick)

It was a good decision to come here because there are more opportunities. Sometimes it's hard to live here though because there is less family support. But when I was at home, I knew there was nothing there so I might as well try something different. We had no plan when we came out here and whatever happens happens. I would

> like to move back but I am torn and really don't know. I went back for three weeks at Christmas and in the summer, and I really couldn't wait to get back home – meaning Alberta. I really think I'm here for the time being but when I look at how I have grown and people there haven't, I don't want to go back. I guess I am torn. (New Brunswick)
>
> You can't get a job in Newfoundland after you finish your schooling. But if you go away for awhile and get some experience, then your chances of getting a good job back home are very very good. So what do you do if you discover that to move back you have to take a pay cut and pay more taxes? (Newfoundland)
>
> Lots of my friends have moved back home. They said they did it so why can't you. They are always after me to come home. But then there are others who wish they could move and didn't have the guts to do it. They have family to support and they know that if they move out here, they're on their own. Others are afraid they may not like it and will have to go back, and they are afraid of what they will come home to so it's easier to just keep things the way they are. (Newfoundland)

There are other variants to this scenario, but all have the same effect: what is home is no longer clear and, in any case, depends upon how one defines it. After accomplishing things while at the destination and taking on new roles, the migrant no longer finds it satisfactory to go back to the old roles – even should they be still available. Some migrants talked about how returning home was a problem because things and people at home had changed. But others complained that it was they who had changed while things at home had not. In any case, the very fact of migration had changed the migrant at least in some way, with the result that things could never be the same. Deciding to return permanently required serious adjustments and almost always entailed some element of regret as the migrant now had some pleasant memories associated with the destination.[19] On the other hand, deciding to stay at the destination also produced feelings of regret because of pleasant memories associated with the place of origin. Either way, once migration occurred, it had a personal impact that required many adjustments – adjustments that could perhaps last a lifetime – and produced an identity dilemma.

THE MYTH OF RETURN: THE DIASPORAN CONSCIOUSNESS

We have already seen that feeling marginalized in the community of origin does not mean that the migrant necessarily wants to leave. Even when leaving seems like the best option, it may still go against the migrant's deepest wishes. Because the migrant often still prefers the region of origin, and is only leaving due to social/emotional conditions that force her/him to consider other options, leaving can appear to be non-voluntary. People who leave under these conditions often take with them a diasporan consciousness – a sense of being one of many dispersed peoples living away from their homeland, to which they still feel strong attachments (Safran 1991). Upon arriving at the destination, migrants who possess a diasporan consciousness seek out others from the community of origin in order to rekindle and sustain their collective memories of their homeland. By making deliberate efforts to relate to their place of origin, either in a personal way or vicariously, migrant are able to sustain a sense of collective identity in spite of no longer being at home.

One of the key characteristics of a diasporan consciousness is the conviction that the current home is merely temporary and that the place of origin is the true home. This is the origin of the myth of return; that is, that someday, when conditions improve or when personal circumstances allow, one will return home.[20] This myth, of course, implies that all migrants should return home; however, in reality, only some do. Adherence to this myth is expressed through pledges of allegiance to the homeland and other symbolic means of demonstrating loyalty, whether return is likely or not.

Most migrants have a keen sense of having a place of origin but lack the emotional intensity towards it to possess a diasporan consciousness. Having fond memories of a region of origin is not the same as having memories that serve as a primary basis for identity. When the diasporan consciousness does not exist, the migrant still feels an attachment to place, but this is not something that is mobilized and collectively shared. Again, the diasporan consciousness seems to exist among migrants from regions where the sense of dispersal is the most acute; that is, where out-migration has been highly visible and has had a negative impact on the sending communities. In many diasporas around the world, a distinct consciousness often arose as the result of outsider status within the host society. In Alberta, this was seldom the case, although some "East Coasters" and, especially, Newfoundlanders experienced a reaction to their accents or good-natured teasing about their customs and habits. Otherwise, there was little evidence of hostile reaction to newcomers.

CONCLUSION

In Canada, geographic space is coded with all kinds of meanings. Images often contain elements of truth while also being gross generalizations. They do, however, play a major role in the migration process, and the migrant must learn how to relate images to realities. Migrants are involved in a form of negotiation when assessing and developing a sense of place, and this negotiation continues over time (Morley 2000, 54). The irony is that, whether a migrant stays or returns, the experience of migration creates a dilemma, with the migrant always straddling two places: the place of origin and the destination.[21] How the migrant deals with this dual place identity reveals much of the struggle and pain that she/he faces – struggle and pain that is never reflected in the aggregate statistics of migration data.

The more accumulated biographical experience a person has in a place, the greater the place attachment. Migrants are obviously in the process of accumulating biographical experience in a new place, but they also bring with them the accumulated biographical experience from the old place. Thus the migrant is repeatedly interacting with place and observing how material structures and personal and cultural interpretations are intertwined to affect their individual identity. For this reason, moving within a nation-state is far more nuanced than one would expect. What appears clear is that, while some migrants feel an attachment to the place of origin based on memories, others view the destination as a place in which to build their future.[22] When the migrant participates in the building of new communities at the destination,[23] there develops a kind of "existential fusion" (Zerubavel 1996, 290) between the her/his personal biography and the communities to which she/he now belongs, and the place-making process continues. It is in this "othered" condition that the migrant struggles to resolve the comparisons between place of origin and destination, in which sense of loss and sense of gain clash and must be resolved.

8

The Context of Out-migration

What role do conditions at the place of origin play in the decision to migrate to Alberta? It has already been established that people who migrate experience some form of marginalization in their community of origin; that is, some type of social dislocation occurs that renders the person open to the option of migration. How the migrant responds to those conditions reflects personal choices, but the conditions themselves play a role in impelling the migration. To emphasize personal choice is to accentuate the voluntaristic nature of migration. To highlight the conditions under which such a decision is made underlines the role that social context plays in the individual's decision to migrate. Migrants usually make a choice (consciously or unconsciously) about which of these two explanations is more prominent in their decision to relocate. When conditions in the region of origin are the dominant rationale in the decision to migrate, there is a clear sense that migration is involuntary or at least driven by underlying contextual factors over which the migrant has no control. The strongest way in which this notion of contextually forced departure is expressed in the literature is through the concepts of "exile" and "refugee." Are these concepts relevant to our ability to understand why migrants to Alberta were open to leaving their communities? How do conditions in the region of origin structure the decision to leave?

An exile is someone who feels forced to leave her/his homeland due to conditions that are beyond her/his control. Exiles seek other destinations as a remedy to their situation, but the place of origin is deeply cherished and they leave it wistfully. At the destination, there is some attempt to maintain at least some aspects of the original culture; above all, there is a strong sentiment, often ideologically driven, that focuses on notions of return. It is possible to be exiled by the authorities;

however, in the context in which we are interested, people are exiled more by conditions that are judged to be personally unfavourable.[1] When the conditions at the place of origin are given the primary weight in the decision to migrate, it is because relocation occurs reluctantly and the migrant feels like an exile. Persons who feel like exiles almost always hope to return.

Refugees have much in common with exiles in that their departure is also the result of conditions beyond their control. In other words, there is a sense of forced departure. The refugee, however, feels persecuted and is driven out by complex forces. She/he more or less concludes that her/his departure will be permanent because things at home are unlikely to change. The need to seek refuge occurs either because the community rejects the person or the person rejects the community. The exile anticipates returning whether or not conditions change, whereas the refugee is unwilling or unlikely to return because conditions are unlikely to change. Clearly, I do not use these two concepts in the same sense in which they are used in United Nations conventions, where they refer to threats to one's life, but they are heuristically useful in that they show how perceptions of structural conditions in the community of origin organize migration decision making.[2]

I use these two concepts because migrants to Alberta sometimes used them to describe their rationales for relocation. The implication was that they preferred not to migrate but that conditions in the region of origin forced them to do so. The notion of reluctant exiles has been used in a number of studies. Skeldon (1994, 12) uses it in relation to the people who migrated from Hong Kong in anticipation of its incorporation into China in 1997, but he also acknowledges that some migrants who had skills or capital were willing exiles because they perceived that relocation would lead to new opportunities. Berry (2000) uses the concept of exile to understand the internal migration of whites from the American South (e.g., Virginia, Arkansas, Georgia) to the North (especially the Midwestern states of Illinois, Michigan, Indiana, and Ohio) from the end of the First World War to the 1970s (the peak years were between 1945 and 1960). This migration was described as reluctant because participants did not want to relocate but were forced to do so because of economic conditions. Berry notes that many of these migrants had "divided hearts," being torn between their family of origin in the South and their family of procreation in the North, and that, as conditions improved in the 1980s and 1990s, a significant number of these migrants did return to the south to work, while others returned to retire or to be buried.

Reluctance to relocate in combination with a desire to return may be the typical pattern for exiles, but refugees view return as unlikely and are filled with anger at their forced departure. It is not my goal to maintain a strict separation between the concept of exile and the concept of refugee.[3] What is clear, however, is that while the notion of reluctant departure was a central theme for many migrants, among this group there was a difference between those who felt they left because something was missing in the community of origin and those who left because they were fleeing something. The first group is more akin to my description of an exile, whereas the second group is more akin to my description of a refugee. Sometimes study respondents used these terms explicitly, sometimes implicitly. I use these terms in order to demonstrate how conditions at the place of origin structure the perceptions of migrants and justify their decision to leave.

EXILES: RELUCTANT MIGRANTS

Exiles are driven out of their community of origin because of conditions that are beyond their control, the most typical one being linked to the economy. Persons who have no active role in the economy are forced to look elsewhere, even though other aspects of their lives in their community of origin may be quite suitable. Regions of the country in which the economy had soured or regions with little or no growth forced some people to migrate to Alberta. These migrants can be called "economic exiles" (indeed, some used this term to describe themselves) in that their choices were circumscribed by the lack of opportunity in their region of origin. Common themes among this group of people included engaging in long and discouraging job searches, existing within a social environment in which morale was low, and living in low-density communities that offered few options. People from big cities were somewhat less likely to feel pushed out due to lack of employment options.

> People who come out here have no other alternative. They live in a small place where there are seventy-five jobs but 500 people, and so you are driven out. A few years ago the prime minister said if you don't have a job then go somewhere else and a lot of people took him to heart. People have been doing that for years. They didn't need the prime minister to tell them that. (Prince Edward Island)

> Economic conditions in New Brunswick were horrible. The majority of the people are on unemployment insurance because the fishing

industry had collapsed. Even the fish plants only had work for a couple of months of the year. The suicide rate escalated enormously and the morale was very low. Economic conditions were so bad that we could have lost our house if we didn't leave. (New Brunswick)

People were pretty understanding when we left [northern] British Columbia. I think they just knew because so many other people were leaving anyway. Like, I wish we could stay and I felt really bad that we had to go. The fact that we almost had to go, like we had no choice, made me quite angry because I had to leave my home and I didn't want to. If everything had been going on all cylinders there, we would have stayed because we really liked it there. (British Columbia)

We feel like we were forced out. I would have left twenty years ago but my husband would never have left the island in a million years if he didn't have to. People tried to help us but there was nothing they could do. The union had all the good jobs sewed up. The only way my husband would even leave is if he was facing financial hardships and looking at welfare. And that forced him to leave within a week. (Newfoundland)

A sense of exile was also created by the inability to find work due to lack of experience:

It seems like you have to come away in order to get a job back home. It is really frustrating that you are qualified to get a job in Alberta but not at home. (New Brunswick)

These migrants moved away in order to facilitate a return:

If you move away and get experience in a bigger city – that's what I'm doing – getting experience, and then I'm going to go back to the East Coast ... If you stay in the region, you will never get a good job but if you move away then they want you. (Nova Scotia)

The sense of exile was strongest where the attachment to place was nourished by a strong local culture. This was often expressed through regional themes and songs of regret about having to migrate from the region (e.g., the Atlantic provinces [see chapter 13]). In other words, when attachment to place of origin was strong and was celebrated in such a way that it produced a sense of regional pride – particularly when the local culture had dealt with out-migration for a long time, yielding much collective regret about what was happening – it became clear to the out-migrant that her/his departure was not primarily a matter of personal choice but, rather, part of a collective fate that was shared by the entire home community. Reluctant migrants were likely to possess a group identity that kept alive their sense of loyalty and desire to return.

MIGRATION FLIGHT: SEEKING REFUGE

Another push factor of considerable importance involved the view that other conditions (usually non-economic conditions) were so unsatisfactory in the home community that fleeing was the only option. These conditions were striking in that they seemed to be rooted in a protracted struggle and produced strong feelings of hostility, fear, and anxiety that were akin to what is experienced by global refugees. Not surprisingly, the destination was evaluated in terms of whether or not it resolved those feelings. There was also a heavy ideological undertone to this sense of flight. In comparison to economic exiles, these migrants had largely given up on their home region and seldom talked about a desire to return.

Politics and Ideology

Ideological differences comprised a particularly striking push factor, given that Alberta possessed what was perceived to be a very different ideological climate from that found in the community of origin. This ideological difference was expressed in two ways. First, it was reflected in politics and government; second, it was reflected in attitudes towards work and personal achievement. The political/governmental perspective was more characteristic of migrants from Ontario and points west, whereas the attitudinal/lifestyle perspective was more typical of migrants from Atlantic Canada.

Ideology/politics was a major factor for many migrants because all provinces from Ontario westward had recently elected governments on the left. Alberta, in contrast, always elected governments on the right, and migrants often talked about fleeing left-wing governments. These migrants frequently referred to personal involvement in attempts to change the electoral results in their provinces of origin or merely lamented the fact that the results were not compatible with their way of thinking. There was no shortage of commentary about the recent NDP government in Ontario or the current (at that time) NDP governments in Manitoba and Saskatchewan. Because the NDP was in power in British Columbia during the study period and the province was struggling with both scandals and an economic downturn, it was not surprising that reaction from there was the strongest. In all cases, the one-party dominance of the Alberta government provided a very different ideological climate.

> If you believe that politics has affected the economy of British Columbia, then you could say I'm a political refugee. It is not that BC doesn't have the resources or the manpower or the brains, but the government had screwed up the principles of business they do not understand. And the attitudes of the government of Alberta are perceived to be better by a lot of people. (British Columbia)

> I didn't see Manitoba as being quite as progressive, meaning that I didn't see the province attracting other jobs. Even when there is a Conservative government there is a kind of socialist attitude that doesn't attract new businesses. I called the minister of finance on a talk show before I left and debated him over the number of people who were leaving and they couldn't admit it. That was kind of the final straw. They're not going to wake up. They're not going to change. The Conservatives were in power at that time but if we would have stayed until the NDP were elected, that probably would have done it for us too. (Manitoba)

> The NDP government in Ontario was a new experience for me and it scared me. That meant I had to go to Alberta. (Ontario)

> We sold our business in Saskatchewan and retired to British Columbia. The weather was nice and everyone seemed to be going there ... After we settled there, I was faced with a capital gain and my accountant told me we would be paying far less taxes in Alberta. So we first thought we would move for a year until the capital gains were dealt with. But the thing we didn't care for in BC was the government. The NDP was against my philosophy even in Saskatchewan and it was worse in BC. Taxes were higher and food costs were higher and we just didn't like it. (Saskatchewan/British Columbia)

> We are refugees, but for me I did come to Alberta to seek salvation because I wanted a major change. Some people come here seeking political asylum from government policies. (Saskatchewan)

> We saw the recession coming in Whitehorse and saw things going downhill. We saw the economy booming in Alberta and we saw that it was the only place where the government was doing something progressive. We were butting our heads against the government in the Yukon constantly over the various policies they had going on there. They were killing our own economy and we couldn't stand around and just watch that. Every time someone would try to bring in a new business there would be regulations against the business, and every industry that would come up would always raise environmental issues. You just can't run a place unless you have some kind of industry and there is so little of that anyway. (Yukon)

> I am a very philosophically and politically driven person. I like to think about things and I began to analyze what I thought were problems. I would not say I was in a depressed mood but I realized that a lot of my feelings were politically motivated. I grew up in a very socialist family that always served on committees of the CCF/NDP and I was brought up to believe that ideas mattered. But as I looked at it more closely, I could see that the intentions were good but that the results were bad. As I grew up, I would hear stories about evil Alberta and how its policies were business-oriented and always for profit and never for people. But as I matured I began to realize that profit was not a bad word and that it was necessary to keep people employed, and that the Saskatchewan way was wrong and was scaring away people with capital who wanted to expand. In small-town Saskatchewan, there is a negative image to being perceived to have more than the next guy and the idea is just to tax it away, which only keeps everybody poor. It took me awhile to understand all this. But when Klein came to power and began to articulate his ideas, I began to realize that there was an alternative and that's when I decided to move to Alberta. (Saskatchewan)

The second way in which this ideological difference was expressed involved the rejection of the dependency mentality, which was characteristic of regional economies that were stagnant or declining. There seemed to be some type of self-selection going on, in that migrants tended to be achievement-oriented and ambitious:

> I was laid off after the completion of the Confederation Bridge and I looked all over the Maritimes for work and it was a very bleak thing. I have friends who are strong believers in our social programs and I did not want to be one of those people. I did not want to get into that cycle. I know friends of mine who are third generation social assistance people and they don't really break that chain and live outside of that chain. That's all they really know. People became dependent on the handouts. I am not necessarily talking about welfare but about working just enough to get UI. The provincial government wants to get you off their rolls and on the federal UI so they get you some kind of work to a point. We just did not want to be part of that. (Prince Edward Island)

A returnee to Nova Scotia was convinced that self-selection determined who went to Alberta and stayed there:

> Albertans are more self-sufficient and that place attracts that kind of person. People go there and stay there because they don't want government handouts or because they want to open their own business. Back home, people want to depend on the government.

While Alberta was clearly more attractive to those who had an ideological affinity with right-wing policies, it was also apparent that a minority of migrants settled in Alberta despite, not because of, those polices:

> In 1996, the Harris government cut funding to public institutions, the unemployment rate was high at 10.6 percent, and there was no work in hospitals or universities at all. I had travelled all across the province looking for work in the administrative field. There was no work in Ontario and that is absolutely the only reason why I left. Politically I would have chosen any other province but Alberta, but Vancouver was out of my price range. My friends often voted NDP or Liberal, and when I said I was moving here they were aghast. I moved here out of desperation, to be honest, but I have bought my own place now so I expect to be here for awhile. But what I am hoping to do here is instill some of my liberal ways of thinking. (Ontario)

Some migrants returned to their region of origin because they did not like the ideological climate in Alberta (e.g., "I hated the competition in

Alberta and I went back to Saskatchewan because I knew the government would take care of me there" [Saskatchewan]). The issue of provincial political/ideological differences is discussed again later in the chapter, but there was no doubt that, for some migrants, political/ideological issues were major push factors.

Language Issues and the Quebec Nationalist Movement

It was clear that, with regard to migration, the nationalist agenda in Quebec produced a push effect, particularly with regard to anglophones. In view of the fact that the second migration wave to Alberta began in 1996, and that 30 October 1995 was the date of the second Quebec referendum, which was only narrowly won by the "no" side (50.6 percent to 49.4 percent), it was understandable that anglophone respondents from that province would emphasize the strength of this push factor:

> What really pushed me to leave was the referendum that took place in October 1995, and I just wanted to leave Quebec because I thought that anywhere would be better than there.

> The constant hassle of the political class and the academic class harping on language, language, and language. And I unfortunately am unilingual English. That was insurmountable. The area in which we lived used to be an English ghetto but by the time we left it had become French. I left friends I had had for sixty years but just to get out from under the politics didn't require a lot of soul searching. It grinds you down. It's constant. It never stops. Sometimes I felt like a second class citizen but I certainly felt like a minority. And we were treated differently.

> I'm French speaking but I'm glad I left because it's too much of a headache to deal with whether they are going to separate – will they do it this year or next year – and that will drive you crazy. Is it going to happen this time? And even if they do you don't know what is going to happen after they separate and that can drive you crazy not knowing what is going to happen.

> Getting out of Quebec was a dominating factor in my decision to leave. I was tired of it ... My health was getting really bad over the situation in Quebec. I had no energy and was feeling really bad. My

family had never seen me like that. I put in applications and went on interviews but I didn't speak the language and I did not feel comfortable in that environment. I knew there had to be something else. I felt the gun was at my head pushing us out. In that sense I was a refugee.

My reason for leaving Quebec was political. Although it was my home, I felt more and more unwelcome there because of the French-English situation. Every night on the news you would hear "language police measured letters on signs," and it drove me crazy. In the stores it wasn't so bad, but at work you would have to answer the phone in French first and in the elevator you never knew what language to speak. It was getting more and more annoying and it was making me angry. I felt like we weren't part of Canada. It was getting tiresome not feeling welcome in your own home. It was adding so much extra stress to everyday life. I was bilingual to a considerable extent but it still bothered me. We also always heard about how much more tax we were paying. And with the referendums, you never felt safe. When authorities such as police spoke to you in French, you always felt intimidated because you never knew where you stood.

It is nice to live in an English city. In Montreal it was so difficult, and as an anglophone you felt like an outsider even though I was born and raised there. It became more and more oppressive there and the politics drove me out. I was angry towards my own province for driving me out. In contrast, coming here and living in English was such a thrill that it took away some of that anger.

I wanted to leave ten years earlier than we did and I have no desire to go back. I feel much more at home here than I ever felt in Montreal, and it all comes down to the language. Even though I studied French and worked in French and could speak it pretty well, you still end up speaking to the other immigrants and English-speaking people in English ... When you are in an elevator in Quebec, you never talk to anybody. You never know if you should say hello in English or in French. You are always stepping on somebody's toes. So here people talk in elevators and to me that was a big thing.

There is no question that this kind of response was most typical of anglophones from Quebec. Many of these people were older and had migrated to Alberta because their children had already moved there in the first wave in the 1970s. At that point the parents still had good jobs, while their young adult children felt disadvantaged when attempting to find work in Quebec. By the late 1990s, many of those parents had retired, so relocating to Alberta was partially the result of the desire to be near their children and partially a response to what had been happening in their province. The nationalist agenda also repelled some francophones as well:

> People come here from Quebec for work and for a big change ... There was a recession and the referendum made me want to get out of there ... Things were getting worse and worse in Quebec. Now they are improving but not fast enough. I wanted to get out of there.

Quebec was not the only place that spawned an out-migration that was related to attitudes towards language. New Brunswick's decision to become a bilingual province (the only officially bilingual province in Canada) was also a push factor, particularly for unilingual anglophones in the north of the province:

> I had a good job back home and it paid well, but New Brunswick is bilingual and I was not bilingual so that limited my options. So I decided to move out here.

> I am from a French family but I don't speak French at all. One of the reasons I left is because I wanted to get away from all that language stuff. If you speak French, you have a better chance of getting a job. It seems to me the only way you get a job in New Brunswick is if you know someone, and the other way is through language. I can work as good as the next guy but that's the way it works.

One New Brunswick migrant provided a different twist to the role that politics played when comparing home with destination:

> I don't think politics had anything to do with most young people coming here. A lot of people just don't think about where they live in terms of the politics. But since I have been here, it's the politics that keeps me in Alberta.

Urban Factors

Another set of factors that caused people to flee involved their evaluation of urban diversity and congestion in their home communities.

Persons living in Canada's three largest cities often indicated that factors pertaining to living in a large metropolitan area were critical to their decision to leave:

> I had lived in Vancouver for twenty years and when we heard about how good things were in Alberta, it gave me that wistful feeling, a kind of homey kind of feeling. It is very hard to feel at home when half of the population is Asian and doesn't even speak English, and that was a huge influence for me. At the high school that was near us, there were only two white kids and most of the others didn't speak English and the prospect of raising my children in a situation where they didn't even have their own kind in the school ... And I heard this about other schools as well, so it seemed a much bigger problem in Vancouver than here. If there are foreign students here, they are forced to speak English because there are fewer of them. But there they didn't ever bother, and it became more of an in-your-face attitude of not wanting to comply with being a Canadian. I felt overwhelmed. And at times I felt like a stranger in my own country. I just felt more and more out of place and [felt] that in Alberta, I would be more with my own kind. We had foreign students living in our home and I enjoyed them very much, but when you really come down to feeling comfortable, you have to go where you feel most comfortable. (British Columbia)

> The density of the population has an impact on whether or not individuals can breathe or think or feel clear-headed given the congestion around you. The pace of the city was very high and the people were pushed to the point that there wasn't that friendly spirited quality. That was the biggest difference. I noted when we came here that there was a more relaxed pace and people had the time to be friendly, and they had space around their psyche in a way. In Vancouver, people constantly had to protect their psyche but here there was room to breathe. And I just felt so relieved to be here. (British Columbia)

> I just wanted to get out of Montreal. I hated it because it's crowded, polluted, and it's rainy. I just wanted to get out of there. People are stressed and not friendly. I liked it for the fun and excitement but not to live there. Politics are not important to me. I feel happier here than I did in Montreal. It is a quiet peace that is partially related to the lack of pollution and the friendliness of the people. It is also the length of daylight and the sun that to me is huge. I think I was sort of depressed before I came but here I am much happier. (Quebec)

> The pace in Ontario bothered us. We have a child who was affected by the pollution. Our jobs there were good so moving here was purely a lifestyle choice. We could afford to own a house in Alberta but not in the Toronto market. There was no wide open spaces and no blue skies. I felt claustrophobic there. (Ontario)

> I grew up in Toronto and loved it but I don't like the people there because they are rude and you can't talk to people. People are more affected by money out there. Then there is pollution and traffic, cost of living, car insurance, housing are all bad things there. It is just one mass of concrete from Niagara Falls to Kingston. Bedroom communities were just opening up one after another. That was part of what drove me away. The humidity without air conditioning is also bad. (Ontario)

> It's the cost of housing in Vancouver and the amount of time you spend in commuting every day. When we have a family, we want to be able to spend time with our kids, the quality time that will give them the morals we want to give them, and give them a sense of family. In the Lower Mainland, with both of us having to work in order to make the kind of money we needed, and the commuting time, that was the deciding factor in me making the move because of what I wanted our family to be. It was housing prices, commuting for two hours when you only live half an hour away, and the taxes, which give you the sense of getting beaten down every time you start to get ahead. Cultural diversity was not an issue. (British Columbia)

For these people, moving to Alberta's cities meant moving down the urban hierarchy to a smaller metropolitan area (although still a major city) that was much less complex and less costly than the ones with which they were familiar. Calgary and Edmonton, in particular, presented two new alternatives in a country dominated by three large metropolitan areas. While these Alberta cities lacked elements of street life, density, and sophistication that some migrants often missed, others liked the fact that they had a less dense population than did those they had left.

Conversely, moving up the urban hierarchy was viewed primarily in terms of new opportunities for work and leisure. Images such as those associated with the Calgary Stampede fostered familiarity and were much less pretentiousness than were those associated with Bay Street (in spite of the obvious presence of the oil and gas sector in Alberta's cities). In that sense, Calgary and Edmonton served as a new national meeting ground for those fleeing both large and small cities.

Other Issues

Leaving was much easier if it were compelled by strong feelings or if it could be justified in retrospect. Complaints about the place of origin covered a wide range of issues, some of which involved personal reactions to situations that others may not have thought problematic at all. For example:

> It always seemed ten degrees warmer in Medicine Hat. The crime rate was terrible in Regina. There is virtually no crime in Medicine Hat. Your insurance was constantly going sky high due to cars being stolen. I think Regina is the crime capital of Canada. The drug problem. When they closed the new Plains Hospital in Regina, that made my blood boil. They closed the best one down. Property taxes are much less here. The way things were going over there, we figured that the best thing we could do was to get out. And there was no light at the end of the tunnel. Things were always getting worse. (Saskatchewan)

Some people mentioned health issues as a factor in their move. If they came from big cities, they complained about smog and its effect on their breathing. Other people complained about allergies, pollens, humidity, and various other air-quality issues that they felt would be non-issues in Alberta.[4]

It was clear that broad contextual push factors played a huge role in setting the stage for migration. Not everyone in a place of origin viewed those factors in the same way as did the migrant. However, while individual assessments of these factors might vary, there is not doubt that those who left were powerfully influenced by them, often feeling as though they had been virtually forced to leave.

National Issues: Three Crises

It is important to assess the contributions of each province/region to Alberta's population growth and to link the out-migration from each province with contextual factors specific to that area. Before doing so, I identify three crises in specific sectors (fishing, farming, and forestry) that helped to set the stage for population movements.

We have already seen that agriculture underwent a substantial transformation that led to increasing farm size and to fewer farms, rural depopulation, and the disappearance of many small towns that were no longer viable. Mechanization and specialization combined with new biotechnologies and new agribusiness practices to change the structure of labour in rural areas. The Canada-United States free trade agreement negotiated in 1987, and broadened to include all of North America in 1994 (the North American Free Trade Agreement [NAFTA]), played an important role in consolidating these trends, particularly in supporting further integrating agriculture into large entities that were often under foreign ownership (Warnock 2003, 312). But the farm crisis could also be linked to the rapid rise in the price of wheat, which occurred in the 1970s and which led to higher land values and to farmers over-expanding through land purchases that greatly increased their indebtedness. Succeeding years of high interest rates, high energy costs, and variable grain prices led to massive economic difficulties with substantial personal and social costs (Jaffe 2003; Kubik and Moore 2003). Children of agriculturalists saw the problems, and, after concluding their education, they left the areas where they had been raised, moving to places that offered greater economic opportunity. Farmers continued to be forced off the land by these difficult conditions; also adversely affected were those whose businesses depended on a strong rural and small-town population base. The result was that, throughout Canada, rural areas provided many people who were eager to migrate in order to find a solution to their problems.

The second crisis occurred in the forestry industry. Forest harvesting was a staples industry whose health depended on export markets. These export markets experienced considerable volatility due to a series of booms and busts. This was particularly the case for British Columbia, which had the largest forest products industry in Canada. Forestry served as an important engine for British Columbia's economy, which was hit hard, especially in the late 1990s, when reinvestment stopped and job losses were significant (Hayter 2000, 65–103). The NDP government had been critical of forest industry practices for some time, and, upon being elected earlier in the decade, sought to restructure it by raising stumpage fees to ensure greater value to the public rather than to the corporate owners as well as to support the shift to more value-added commodity production. A new forest practices code was introduced in order to deal with environmental issues, but these changes brought extra costs to the industry (Pearse 2001).

The result was a massive slowdown in the industry and considerable acrimony among the various parties affected. This was exacerbated as the forest industry in Alberta lacked such regulatory reform, with the result that production increased in Alberta while it declined in British Columbia. Forest product communities in which closures took place produced a wide range of persons with various skills who were forced to look for new opportunities elsewhere. The proximity of Alberta, including the possibility of skill transference, enhanced the likelihood that some would choose that province as their destination. These people were often angry over government policies in British Columbia and in search of greater economic stability. All of this took place, of course, in the context of the softwood lumber dispute with the United States, which also deeply affected the industry.

The third crisis involved the fishing industry (Newell and Ommer 1999; Sinclair and Ommer 2006; Ommer 2007). It was experienced on both the Atlantic (particularly cod [Hutchings 1999]) and Pacific (particularly salmon [Gallaugher and Vodden 1999]) coasts in response to depleting stocks and to a commercialized/industrialized offshore fishery that used freezer trawlers and that profoundly affected local port economies.[5] The corporate restructuring of the fishing industry in the name of efficiency harmed independent fishers and small fish processors, making dispersed coastal communities and the livelihood of inshore fishers less viable. The crisis became particularly intense in the 1990s, with the closure of the cod fishery in 1992. The depletion of cod stocks due to mismanagement, corporate harvesting strategies, and foreign overfishing has been described as "the largest industrial shut-down in Canadian history" as 40,000 persons, from fishers to fish plant workers, were rendered unemployed in the Atlantic region (Canning and Strong 2002, 319). Newfoundland was hardest hit, with about half of all families affected being from that province; about 30 percent of those affected from in Nova Scotia.

A federal assistance program known as the Atlantic Groundfish Strategy (TAGS) provided income support and educational programs for displaced workers until 1998, but it was clear that this was only transitional and that it was not likely that the fishery would be reopened. This meant that large numbers of people were forced to look elsewhere for long-term survival, with the result that out-migration became a prevalent option. In some fishing communities, one-third to one-half of the residents expected that they would have to leave (Ommer 1998). While the moratorium in the industry did not necessarily mean that older people, whose ties and housing investments embedded them within their communities, would leave, but it certainly meant that younger people would do so (Canning and Strong 2002; Sinclair 2002). This crisis in the fishing industry played a huge role in the displacement of peoples not only inside this region but also outside these regions. When considering migration destinations, Maritimers were attracted to Alberta's strong economy in spite of the fact that the province was landlocked and farther away than the traditional destination of Ontario (Lycan 1969; Burke 1987).

These three crises served as major contextual push factors that contributed to population flows to Alberta. It is now useful to examine more closely the relationship between each province/region and Alberta as a destination.

MIGRATION FLOWS TO ALBERTA BY PROVINCE

It should not be surprising that, in both of the migration waves under review, by far the largest number of migrants to Alberta came from the two provinces with the largest populations: Ontario and British Columbia. In the first wave, it was Ontario that was the major origin province, and, in the second wave, it was British Columbia. What clues do we have that might explain why these two provinces played different roles in the two waves? What were the circumstances in both of these provinces as well as all other provinces that might help explain predilections to migrate?

Ontario

While Ontario has continued to be a significant destination for Canadians moving within the country, its relationship with Alberta has been especially interesting. Figure 19 shows that the out-migration from Ontario to Alberta reached a peak in the first wave in 1981 at 45,000 persons, and this peak has no counterpart in the second wave. Out-migration from Alberta to Ontario has remained rather steady at around 10,000 persons, with the exception of the period immediately after the first wave, when the recession occurred in Alberta. So except for the boom of the first wave and the bust that followed it, the population exchange between the two provinces has been relatively stable, although with more people moving to Alberta from Ontario than the reverse. This is significant because Ontario has always been a magnet destination, but it has also had high domestic migration outflows.

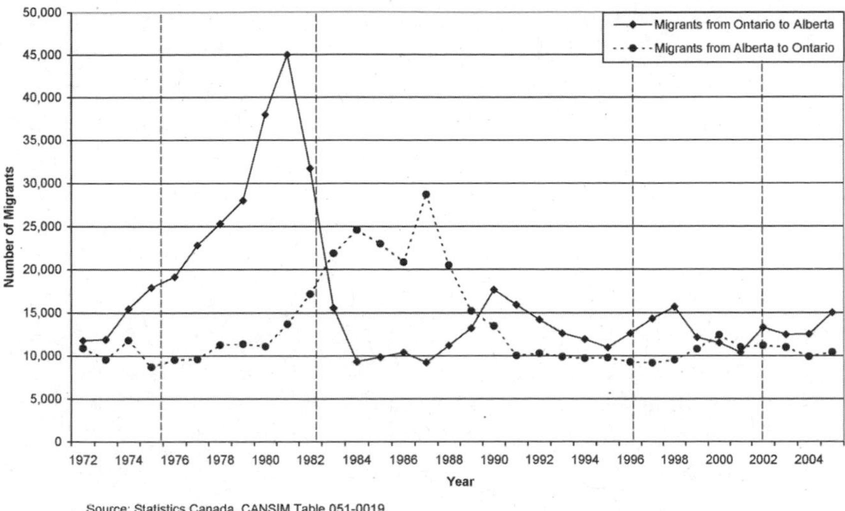

Figure 19 Migration Exchanges between Alberta and Ontario, 1972 to 2005
SOURCE: Statistics Canada, CANSIM Table 051-0019.

Ontario has been undergoing a process of deindustrialization as its economy is being transformed by globalization. The industrial economy that had been built on tariff protection has been under pressure, and many branch plants have been closed. In the early 1980s, the rate of economic growth in the province had slowed as high interest rates and inflation wreaked considerable havoc. The slowdown in the Ontario economy, then, provided a catalyst for people from that province to consider relocating. But there is a further consequence of this restructuring that is also of importance. Ontario had always been a buffer zone (Stone 1969, 65) or watershed province (Beaujot and McQuillan 1982, 153) in Canada. It had been the primary magnet in east-west migration flows and it had always been a barrier to flows to provinces on either side of it.[6] Now, the economic restructuring in Ontario meant that migrants from the Atlantic provinces might jump over Ontario and proceed directly to Alberta. This pattern, which began during the first wave, continued in the second wave.

It is interesting to note that the 1990s were difficult years in Ontario. The province elected its first NDP government in 1990. When the Harris Conservative government was elected in 1995, the decision was made to counter the mounting provincial debt with huge cutbacks and lower welfare benefits: this was known as the Common Sense Revolution (Whitaker 2001, 361–2). These drastic cuts generated considerable anger and worker displacement and resulted in a situation that was similar to what had occurred earlier in Alberta (Ibbitson 1997). The only difference was that the cuts took place first in Alberta, with those in Ontario coming two or three years later. The lag effect may have contributed to some migration between the two provinces. The wrangling between the two ideological approaches to governing in Ontario resulted in some migrants interpreting their out-migration in terms of this struggle. Here is one illustration of this kind of thinking:

> I left because taxes were going up due to the disastrous NDP government that gave Ontario an incredible amount of debt. Even municipal taxes were increasing. We left because I didn't like the tax structure. I'm a fiscal conservative and I don't like how the welfare system has destroyed society. I thought Klein had a lot of good ideas but the Toronto papers always made fun of Klein. We didn't go to BC because taxes were too high and it was too socialistic. In general, I'm nervous about NDP governments. I like it when debts are kept under control. (Ontario)

Whatever vacillations may have occurred in its economy, however, Ontario clearly remained the economic centre of the country, though perhaps somewhat differently positioned.[7] In particular, Alberta became a new option destination for internal migrants in a manner that challenged Ontario's former dominance.

British Columbia

Migration to British Columbia has played a major role in the westward shift of the Canadian population as the province has been a significant destination for internal migrants (though this migration does have peaks and troughs). British Columbia plays a somewhat different role in relation to Alberta than it does to the rest of Canada because the two provinces are neighbours. Population exchanges between them has always been high because of sheer proximity. Around 20,000 people a year, and sometimes more, relocate across these provincial borders in either direction (see figure 20). The two most notable spikes in out-migration from British Columbia seem to have occurred in parallel with the election of NDP governments in that province. People who migrated during these periods often articulated their relocation within this political framework.

The first major increase in out-migration was in 1974–75, when more people left British Columbia for Alberta than vice versa (see figure

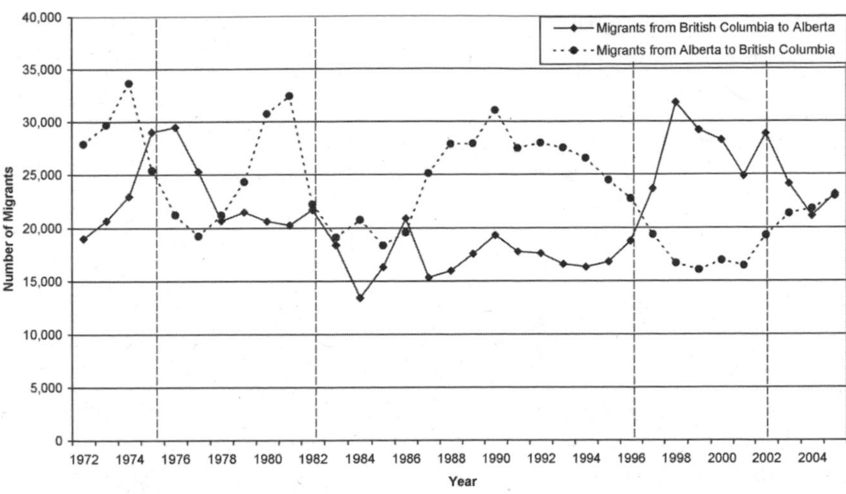

Figure 20 Migration Exchanges between Alberta and British Columbia, 1972–2005
SOURCE: Statistics Canada, CANSIM Table 051-0019.

20). These were roughly the years of the Barrett NDP government (1972–75). In the following years, the right-of-centre Social Credit Party served as a kind of an umbrella counter-entity whose aim was to keep the NDP out of power, and this it did until 1991, when the NDP were elected again under Mike Harcourt and were later led by Glen Clark until 2001. From the point of view of private capital investment and small business, the economic policies of the NDP, particularly in the Clark era, played a major role in stifling the economy, and there is evidence of capital flight to Alberta (Fairbrother 2003, 319–25). The economic effects of these policies were undoubtedly related to the spike in out-migration. For six years, from 1997 to 2002, out-migration from British Columbia to Alberta reached unparalleled levels (exceeding 30,000 persons in 1998) and far surpassed in-migration to British Columbia from Alberta. This is particularly striking because, during the late 1980s and early 1990s, the migration flow between the two provinces was tilted in British Columbia's favour. While out-migration to Alberta moderated slightly after 2001, in-migration to British Columbia from Alberta did increase after 2001 – ironically, the year the Liberals were elected. In terms of migration to Alberta from British Columbia, there thus appears to be some sort of correlation not only with the economy of Alberta but also with the governing party and economy of British Columbia. This was clearly evident in what many out-migrants from British Columbia had to say.

Immigration to British Columbia was another factor affecting domestic migration, particularly for those from the Lower Mainland. The decision of the British government to return Hong Kong to the Chinese government in 1997 played a major role in ensuring that Hong Kong immigrants would seek refuge for their capital. Many of them chose the Lower Mainland as a key location for investment. As a result, home ownership rates among recent immigrants were much higher in Vancouver than elsewhere in the country (Ley and Tutchener 2001). These arrivals changed the face of Vancouver, producing what some called "Hongcouver," and, combined with other factors, contributed to the high cost of housing in the area. In addition, the immigration of other East Asians into the Lower Mainland since the 1980s transformed the urban region into something quite different from what it had been when it was identified by its British roots (Cernetig 2001, 420–1). One study pertaining to the suburb of Richmond shows how the media played a role in creating a moral panic in 1995–96. The significant racial transformation of a previously Anglo-European community was described as producing cultural ghettoization and white flight (Deer 2006). By 2001, almost 40 percent of the population of the Vancouver Census Metropolitan Area consisted of foreign-born visible minorities. So, in addition to high housing prices, which served as an incentive for relocation for native-born people who were entering the housing market for the first time, racial diversity produced a type of white flight to Alberta as some neighbourhoods quickly became ethnic and racial enclaves (Ray, Halseth, and Johnson 1997).

> The issue was one of segregated cultures. It was like we were living in a foreign country living in Richmond. Business and services catered to the Chinese community predominantly. We found that their way of doing business in Canada overtook the marketplace and there was a paradigm shift from the values that I grew up with. And this caused us to look at other places.

> I grew up in Vancouver and the last few years it has been completely transformed. Living in Richmond was like living in Hong Kong. My parents are immigrants but things have now gotten out of hand and it happened so fast. We were so proud when we bought a new condo, and then we went to the first condo meeting and it was decided to hold the meeting in Chinese because that was the language of the majority of the people there. One man confronted my husband ... and it seemed like we were always broke there because of the high housing prices.

The inability to find affordable housing was clearly an issue for young adult migrants. Some less expensive housing was available in the Fraser Valley, but then a long commute became an issue. Both of these factors helped to stimulate the consideration of other options and became part of the discourse of those who moved to Alberta.

While the shift to service-sector employment in British Columbia and less dependence on staples production resulted in economic stability (Howlett and Brownsey 2001, 319), difficulties in the fishing industry and the softwood lumber industry played a role in supporting out-migration, especially outside the Lower Mainland. The out-migration from wood-producing areas of British Columbia (like Prince George) was directly linked to this staples downturn, but it also included other resource-based communities. The lack of employment options for young adults in the Interior (e.g., the Okanagan and the Kootenays) and on Vancouver Island also meant that there was a labour pool eagerly looking for new opportunities elsewhere.

> The thing that struck us the most when we first got here was all the signs you see everywhere about "Help Wanted." You never see that in BC. You pick up the Victoria newspaper and you are lucky if there is a page of jobs in there. The *Calgary Herald* would have ten to twelve pages. I went back and told people and they wouldn't believe it for if you had a job in BC, you were a lucky guy ... You get so sick of hearing of closings, or temporary shutdowns, or seasonal shutdowns, or another strike that you say there's gotta be something different.

It is important to know that the economy bounced back in British Columbia later in the first decade of the new millennium, but the economic stagnation of the latter part of the last decade of the old millennium meant that the options in Alberta served as a lure to people who were having unprecedented employment difficulties.

Box 1: Prince George
Prince George and "Beyond Hope"
The construction of three major pulp mills in Prince George in the 1960s and 1970s served as a major catalyst to the economy of that city. While there were ups and downs along the way, the city flourished along with the forestry industry until the 1990s, when new production and processing technologies began to change the industry. The province's introduction of a new code for forestry practices increased costs. Pressures to reduce costs and changing markets

(including the softwood lumber dispute with the United States) often produced temporary and even permanent shutdowns. This created economic disruptions for the community – disruptions that not only affected those employed in the industry but that also created multiplier effects that affected all aspects of the economy (Halseth and Halseth 1998).

One of the issues in British Columbia is that its two economies – one in the north and, to some extent, the Interior and one on the southwest coast – are very different from one another. The emphasis on people feeling alienated from the Lower Mainland, where the majority of the population is located, has created an artificial boundary at the community of Hope. Regional hostility is reflected in phrases such as "the world ends at Hope" or "there is no life beyond Hope." At times, this feeling of alienation has led British Columbians "beyond Hope" to look to Alberta as a more viable alternative. The downturn in the Prince George area economy accelerated around 1996, which was precisely the time when Alberta's economy began expanding. Skills in the lumber industry were easily transferable to similar operations in the Alberta communities of Grande Prairie or Hinton. Heavy equipment operators found jobs in construction or the Alberta oil sands. Edmonton especially benefited from migration from Prince George; in contrast, Calgary benefited from migration from the Kootenays. The fact that the new stumpage and forest code policies were associated with the provincial NDP government also added an ideological dimension to the assessment of the slowdown of the industry and the selection of Alberta as a destination.

Saskatchewan

We have already seen that Saskatchewan, Alberta's neighbour to the east, has experienced limited population growth since the beginning of rural depopulation after the Second World War. In only five years of the thirty-three-year period under review (1975 to 1977, 1982 to 1983) has Saskatchewan gained more people than it has lost through interprovincial migration, and the losses have been continuous since 1985. Around 7,000 to 8,000 people per year relocate from Alberta to Saskatchewan, but considerably more, with peaks of 16,000 to 18,000, have moved annually from Saskatchewan to Alberta (see figure 21). From 1972 to 2002, 361,000 people moved to Alberta at an annual rate of almost 12,000 per year. Almost 50 percent of Saskatchewan's

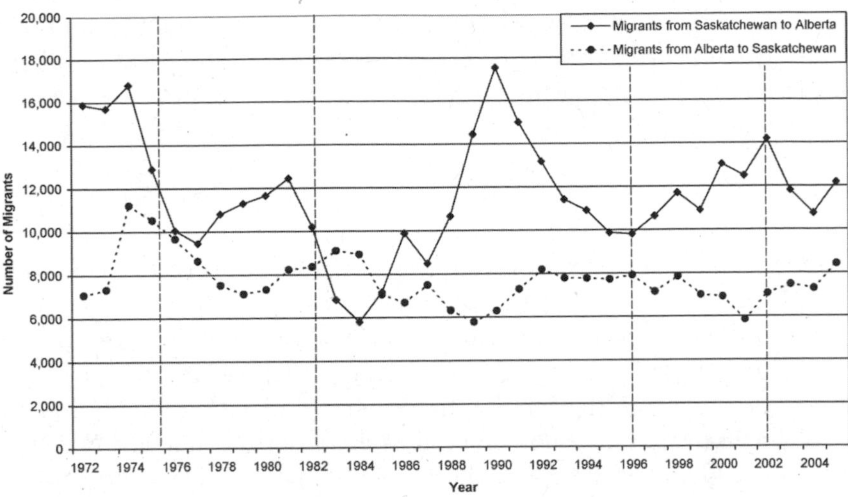

Figure 21 Migration Exchanges between Alberta and Saskatchewan, 1972–2005
SOURCE: Statistics Canada, CANSIM Table 051-0019.

out-migrants went to Alberta during the first wave, while almost 60 percent did so in the second wave (see table 11). Thus it is clear that Alberta has been the single most important destination of choice for Saskatchewan's out-migrants. Saskatchewan's losses to Alberta do not occur only during the two waves of growth in that province: they peak in 1974 and 1990. This suggests that it was not just what was happening in Alberta that was related to this out-migration but also what was happening in Saskatchewan. The only time when conditions in Alberta seem to have had an effect on out-migration from Saskatchewan was when the "bust" occurred after 1982, when more people moved to Saskatchewan from Alberta than vice versa.

Since Alberta and Saskatchewan both became provinces in the same year (1905), and Saskatchewan initially had an enormous population advantage, analysts have been striving to develop an explanation for why these two side-by-side provinces developed so differently (Brym 1978). Alberta has been the province with the expanding economy and Saskatchewan has been the province that has lost residents heavily and continuously through out-migration because economic development has not taken place at the same pace. It is not so much that Saskatchewan's economy has been declining as that Alberta's economy has been growing much more rapidly. The most obvious explanation for this difference is natural resources. Saskatchewan and Alberta both have oil and gas, but Alberta clearly has it in greater abundance and has become the centre for the industry in Canada.[8] Saskatchewan has much smaller deposits of these resources, but it also has high-grade potash and uranium. Potash extraction is not as capital- or labour intensive as oil and gas extraction, and it has few forward linkages. Uranium has uncertain and questionable markets. Oil and gas have elevated Alberta to a position of dominance relative to Saskatchewan because they have generated more employment, facilitated more urban growth, and attracted more in-migrants. It is not surprising, then, that many out-migrants from Saskatchewan have played a major leadership role in Alberta's petroleum industry (Jaremko 2006).

But if what was happening in Saskatchewan was even more important than what was happening in Alberta with regard to propelling out-migration from the former, then there must be factors within the province itself that have contributed to this population loss. Saskatchewan had a population over 900,000 in 1961, and while its population surpassed 1 million in 1986, it then fell below that mark and remained there. This means that Saskatchewan has seen little total growth over the last fifty years and; if it were not for growth through births, the province would be losing population at an even faster rate. Thus, there has been a depopulation trend throughout the province, and this has led to the loss of skilled labour and professional acumen. To the extent that agriculture has been a dominant industry in Saskatchewan it is not surprising that the transformation of that industry has contributed to out-migration. Pressures on the family farm have contributed to huge increases in farm debt, and the threat of bankruptcy or foreclosures has produced intense stress and family tensions, causing many to leave the farm (Bolaria, Dickinson, and Wotherspoon 1995; Schissel and Robertson 1998/99). As rural communities experience depopulation, they are unable to support essential services (such as in health care, education, and retailing), and this undermines their survival (Olfert and Stabler 1998/99). The ripple effect means that the province increasingly lacks the resources to support government services as well as adequate infrastructure. Given the fact that most out-migrants are young adults with a lifetime of tax paying the purpose of which was to support these services, the province loses doubly: both on the labour side and on the revenue side. Meanwhile, the employment growth in Alberta serves as a huge counter-weight to the limited range of employment alternatives in Saskatchewan. Migrants from Saskatchewan reflected on these issues continuously, complaining about the poor condition of the roads; the lack of jobs as teachers, nurses, accountants, and engineers; and the lack of diverse opportunities.

Many out-migrants from Saskatchewan mentioned the sharp differences in politics and ideology between the two provinces. The clash between the ideological left and right in Saskatchewan has mostly been resolved by the election of left-wing governments (formerly the Co-operative Commonwealth Federation [CCF] and now the NDP) (Wiseman 1996, 55). In fact, since the first election of the CCF in 1944, there have only been two periods of right-wing governments (1964 to 1971 and 1982 to 1991). The peculiar brand of agrarian socialism that developed in Saskatchewan is often said to be based on the consequences of drought and the Depression, which caused agrarians to band together for mutual protection and collective action. The question, of course, is whether this orientation plays any role at all in the province's inability to attract more investment.[9] In a recent set of interpretive pieces referring to the "heavy hand of the past," it is argued that this political perspective put the province on a path that emphasized social policy based on a grain economy – an economy that has since been massively transformed but for which there are few new alternatives. This perspective has not included strong policies for economic development, meaning that there has been little change in the province over time, especially in contrast to Alberta (Smith 2005). Marchildon (2005) notes that the psychological effect of this path has been that the optimism of the original settlers has transformed into the pessimism of those who live there now. Saskatchewan is infused with a myth that speaks of attachment to the land – a myth that began with the early settlers and that maintains that the province is a place of abundance and opportunity. Yet somehow it never reaches its potential (Eisler 2005). This recognition of the undeveloped potential of the province in the midst of limited growth has led many in Saskatchewan to accept the fact that out-migration is a lamentable necessity.

If Alberta stands for a small-"c" conservative orientation, Saskatchewan stands for an opposing orientation. The problem is that, since Alberta is the province with the expanding economy, it serves as a brain drain and labour drain for Saskatchewan residents who appear to have virtually no choice about relocation. This produces feelings of either inferiority or the inevitability of loss as people leave for new opportunities. It also fosters comparisons between the two provinces. There is no better place to observe this dilemma than in the biprovincial city of Lloydminster. The Alberta side of the city has experienced much more in-migration and home construction than has the Saskatchewan side. The asymmetrical spatial and economic development can be accounted for by the different political ideologies of the two provinces, with the Saskatchewan side providing housing and services that are more attractive to those with moderate incomes and the Alberta side providing housing and services to those with high incomes and who benefit from the province's tax policies (Bhargava 2000). Virtually all in-migrants to Alberta from Saskatchewan commented on this historical difference in political orientations.

A further issue is the growth of the Aboriginal population in Saskatchewan in comparison to the number of out-migrating Caucasians. The loss of non-Aboriginal young adults through out-migration who are in their child-bearing years and are soon to move into their most productive tax-paying years produces a unique situation when the birth rate in the Aboriginal population is increasing (Waiser 2005, 479). While the rural exodus of non-Aboriginals has involved leaving the province, the rural exodus of Aboriginals has almost exclusively involved migrating to Saskatchewan's urban areas (Smith 1997). Furthermore, provincial government planning documents released in 1999 projected that the Aboriginal school population was increasing at such a dramatic rate that it could reach almost half of the provincial school population by 2020. The *Saskatoon Star Phoenix* ran a series of articles early in the new millennium discussing these issues, and this came close to creating a sense of panic among non-Aboriginals.[10] This transformation was often noted by out-migrants to Alberta as a matter that concerned them, and it was also often intertwined with political criticisms such as the following:

> The problems in Saskatchewan were a shrinking population, increasing health care costs and increasing public expectations, a Native problem that would take a long time to deal with, and fewer people to pay the tax. I felt like things were only going to get worse in Saskatchewan. I came to the conclusion that socialist thinking was only perpetuating a downward spiral. There were a lot of tense suppers with my parents over a number of years. They were rooted in their ways with NDP thinking.

> I think we thought that Saskatchewan was really turning into a big welfare state. Natives didn't pay taxes, seniors don't pay taxes, and farmers don't pay taxes and when you take away those three s egments, you only have 40 to 50 percent of the tax payers left. So the province was not going anywhere and there was little future. I always supported the NDP but we are starting to become NDP bashers.

> People sort of feel here like they are losing their canopy. Government can't provide anymore. Yet people dig in their heels and say we are different from Alberta[, which] was initially settled by Americans, where everyone looks out for themselves. We are more caring. But we look at the shrinking population, and especially taxpayers, and it seems like maybe we can't do it. That is what puts fear into people. And when that is connected to the growing Native population and loss of new young tax payers, I think it does frighten people.

> Saskatchewan has lost a lot of taxpayers and community workers. Many of the more progressive thinkers left, and that really affects the communities there and makes it harder for the province to move forward. People who left were not satisfied with the status quo and were more entrepreneurial in spirit. They are not afraid of change, and while they appreciated their roots, they were not bound by them. And probably the other thing is that people were fed up with the politics. It sure seems to me that people started at least thinking about leaving when the Devine government was voted out in 1991 – at least that was the way I saw it. Romanow did cut back on the size of government but we never could develop the business structure. The politics and the economy seem to be tied together.

There is no doubt that some anxiety, maybe even paranoia, had been created in Saskatchewan and that this focused on the idea that a shrinking tax base due to out-migration placed the province in jeopardy, particularly in light of the concern that the contributions of the growing Aboriginal population would not significantly replace the contributions of those leaving. For this reason, employment and career development among First Nations had to become a major economic objective (Cuthand 1999). Some communities, like Prince Albert, were particularly successful in generating Aboriginal business activity through forming a partnership with twelve First Nations to establish the Prince Albert Development Corporation. This corporation had a high profile, owning businesses ranging from hotels to office buildings in Prince Albert and elsewhere, its purpose being to generate employment opportunities for First Nations people. The social structure of Saskatchewan was beginning to look much different than it had before. Some of this was the result of out-migration, and, in any case, it served as a catalyst to further out-migration by non-Aboriginals. Interviewees commented that border communities such as Lloydminster, and particularly Medicine Hat, attracted migrants who wanted to remain as close to Saskatchewan as possible but who preferred to live in Alberta in case the former was unable to fulfill its fiscal obligations. This was particularly the case for retirees, who wanted to be able to visit their home communities, friends, and relatives in Saskatchewan often but who preferred living in Alberta because they felt their future was more secure there.

The continuous stream of out-migration from Saskatchewan, particularly to Alberta, has given the two provinces, both of which were created 1905, a unique relationship. Alberta has become home to many former Saskatchewan residents, and proximity means that auto travel between the two provinces is relatively easy. As residents compare the prosperity of the two provinces, there have been calls, especially from Saskatchewan, for the two to merge. The contrast between the provinces, with one being a magnet for migration and the other losing migrants, becomes particularly acute during times of rapid growth in Alberta, and this nurtures feelings of helplessness and inferiority in Saskatchewan. Thus it was not surprising that, in 2002, the Government of Saskatchewan announced a marketing campaign, optimistically entitled "The Future Is Wide Open," that showcased what the province had to offer. It is unclear what the short-lived campaign accomplished, but it is clear that it attempted to challenge negative stereotypes outside the province and to create a new image of Saskatchewan – even if only in the minds of current residents. Realizing that expatriates were the best linkages to the province, a Saskatchewan ambassadors program was established in 2003 to encourage former Saskatchewan residents now living in Alberta to represent the province wherever they lived and to help to change its image. This approach was quite different from Manitoba's (see below) because it did not particularly target the return migration of former Saskatchewan residents but, rather, simply attempted to retain connections with them in a way that would benefit Saskatchewan. An electronic magazine called *Saskatchewan Connections* was published to facilitate this kind of communication. Out-migration was clearly acknowledged and accepted: the goal was to turn it into something positive.

More recent developments suggest some alterations of this pattern. Through changes in the commodities market, particularly energy and potash, the economy of Saskatchewan began to show a significant shift, with greater positive cash flows. In 2007, Saskatchewan experienced net positive interprovincial in-migration for the first time since 1984. Of specific interest, this was also the first year for some time in which slightly more people moved to Saskatchewan from Alberta than the reverse. It was also the year that the right-leaning Saskatchewan Party took the reins of government under the leadership of Brad Wall. While these events are outside the range of this study, it does suggest that some change may be occurring in that province that might affect future migration trends.

Manitoba

The other province in the western interior that has also consistently lost more population than it has gained through interprovincial migration is Manitoba. The fact that Alberta plays a critical role in Manitoba's gains and losses is verified in figure 22, which shows that population loss to Alberta corresponds closely with the boom and bust of the first wave of migration. But it also demonstrates that out-migration to Alberta was much stronger in the first wave than it was in the second wave. Since 1988, the out-migration to Alberta from Manitoba has continued to be stronger than the reverse migration, but it has been in the range of 5,000 to 6,000 people per year, as opposed to the 8,000 to 10,000 people per year in the first wave. Saskatchewan's loss to Alberta has, overall, been of higher volume than has Manitoba's, but Manitoba out-migrants often choose Ontario as their destination, whereas Saskatchewan out-migrants overwhelmingly prefer Alberta.

At first glance, there appears to be no particular relationship between the political party in power and out-migration from Manitoba as both the NDP and the Conservatives were in power during the time when out-migration was the highest in the mid- to late 1970s. The province was in the midst of a variety of economic adjustments, but the shift in power from the NDP to the Conservatives in 1977 and then back to the NDP in 1981 reflected a considerable ideological struggle and ongoing debate between ideas about redistributive justice and ideas about a market economy and how both could contribute to economic growth. Employment was an issue during this time, and the question was how to improve economic opportunities. After a fairly lengthy period of Conservative rule from 1988 to 1999, Manitoba again turned to the NDP, reaffirming the contrasts between the two ways of thinking. Persons who were staunch conservatives saw the election outcome as a catalyst for migration:

> The cruncher was the last election in Manitoba and what it would have meant. We looked at Alberta and we knew many people who had moved here and from word-of-mouth it seemed that

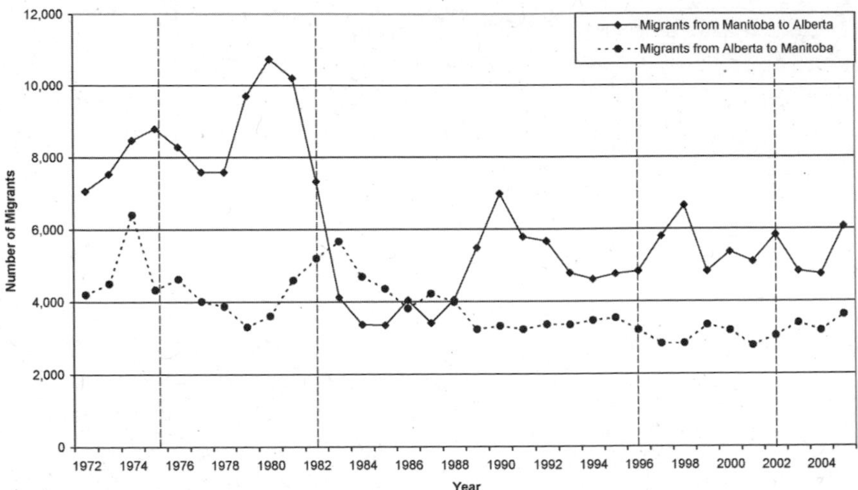

Figure 22 Migration Exchanges between Alberta and Manitoba, 1972–2005
SOURCE: Statistics Canada, CANSIM Table 051-0019.

> opportunities were higher and taxes were lower, which was better for professionals. The election of an NDP government meant that spending would take precedence over tax cuts and a better environment for businesses. The Conservative Party had done a lot for the province economically.
>
> Taxes were coming down under the Conservative government and the economy was getting better. Then the election, and I was really upset. I was a teacher and the teachers union sent a letter to every teacher and told them to vote NDP and it all seemed ridiculous.
>
> Opportunities at work were not as great as I had hoped and the election was the clincher for our decision to move. The Alberta government was more oriented to the future in being fiscally responsible and that suggested a better future where we wanted our children to live.

While Manitoba had a comparatively slow rate of economic growth, it did have considerable stability, low unemployment, and a surprisingly diversified economy centred on the metropolitan city of Winnipeg (Gonick 1990). The issue for Manitoba was not so much a matter of fighting decline as it was a matter of seeking to expand at a pace that was competitive with that of other provinces. Winnipeg had lost its once stellar position in the Canadian urban hierarchy and was struggling to compete for growth in the west against Edmonton, Calgary, and Vancouver. The loss of the NHL Winnipeg Jets in 1995 (Silver 1996) seemed to be symbolic of the dilemma that the province faced in attempting to raise its status as a major economic player, and migrants often referred to this as an indicator of why they had to consider other options.

As a response to the out-migration that had occurred, and in view of the desire to establish new momentum for the opportunities that did exist, in 2002 the Manitoba government announced an innovative "Manitoba Comebacks" campaign. The rationale for the campaign was based on the presupposition that former residents were the best target for in-migration and that they were more likely to be persuaded to return if it could be shown how much Manitoba had to offer. The most visible symbol of this campaign was a glossy magazine called *Manitoba Calling*, which highlighted major new developments and successes that made the province more appealing than ever before. This magazine was mailed to former residents free of charge. Five issues were published in 2002 and 2003 before it was discontinued. Other elements of the program included a "Home for the Holidays" initiative, which would put people coming home for visits in touch with potential employers. There is little evidence that this program had a significant impact, but it did show that the government was doing something to stem out-migration by heralding the opportunities that did exist.

Quebec

Since 1972, the Province of Quebec has continuously lost more population through interprovincial migration than it has gained. After the decade of the 1960s and the Quiet Revolution, which symbolized a new emerging Quebec, the 1970s were especially stormy years, particularly for anglophones. In 1970, the October Crisis – associated with the activities of the Front de Liberation du Quebec (FLQ), the invoking of the War Measures Act, and the symbolic transference of money from Montreal to Toronto by Brinks armoured cars – produced considerable concern that Quebec nationalism was creating instability in the province. The election of the avowedly separatist Parti Quebecois in 1976 and the passing of Bill 101 (which made French the official language of Quebec) in 1977 were clear statements about the shape the new Quebec was taking. As a result, out-migration peaked at 70,000 people in 1978. About two-thirds of this out-migration consisted of anglophones who were leaving what they considered to be a hostile environment (Caldwell and Fournier 1987). By far, the majority of this migration

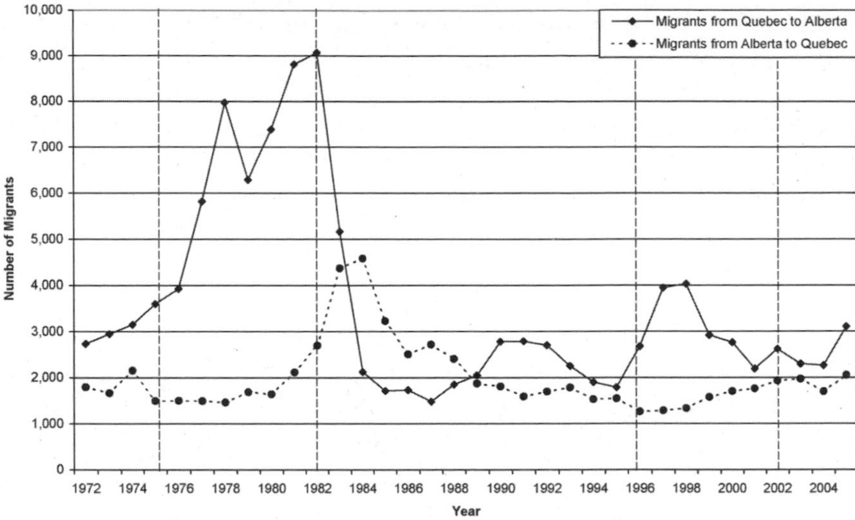

Figure 23 Migration Exchanges between Alberta and Quebec, 1972 to 2005
SOURCE: Statistics Canada, CANSIM Table 051-0019.

went to Ontario, but Alberta was also a destination. The migration to Alberta from Quebec reached its peak from 1978 to 1982 (see figure 23). However, even during this time period, the peak never reached 10,000 people annually – a total that was surpassed by all provinces to the west of Quebec. While some of the Quebec migrants that came to Alberta in the second wave were francophones, there were still more anglophones, although their numbers were diminishing, suggesting that the push from Quebec had either lessened or that Ontario was a far more preferable destination. Both conclusions are supported by the data. It is significant, however, that the 1995 Quebec referendum, in which the "Yes" vote was only narrowly defeated, did serve as another precipitating factor for out-migration among both anglophones and disaffected francophones (Lo and Teixeira 1998):

> I was born and raised French Canadian in Quebec, but I never became part of that Quebecois mentality. My university studies were all in English. I think Trudeau said it too but I don't feel like I am a victim. Whatever happened on the Plains of Abraham, you have to get over it. Quebecois are often whining about being victims but I never felt that way. I could float between the two cultures in Quebec but somehow I always felt more at home with the anglophones.

The political situation in Quebec, as has already been noted, played a key role in how migrants rationalized their departure for Alberta.

Atlantic Provinces

Limited economic development has meant that the Atlantic provinces have experienced out-migration (to "the Boston states," Toronto, the West) for many years (Levitt 1960; Brookes 1976; Choyce 1996; Bruce 1988). One migrant from the region put it this way:

> I think that the reason I left is because it's some kind of biological thing or what ... I look back in my family history and as far back as 1910 to 1925, my great grandparents were coming out here on harvest excursions. This was a special train that the CPR put on, and I think it was a fifteen dollars fare from the Maritimes to the Prairies. They were coming out here to help harvest the wheat ... and it's a pattern ... People always move from the east to the west. They first came by boat to Halifax and then they went west ... it's bred into us and ingrained into us ... go west. When people don't do as well as they should, [they] go west.

Attachment to the region, however, contributes to return migration in a manner that is seldom mentioned in interprovincial migration with regard to the other provinces.[11] Indeed, the evidence is that out-migration and in-migration in all four Atlantic provinces follow each other much more closely than is the case elsewhere in the nation, with perhaps greater out-migration from Newfoundland and Labrador. For the three maritime provinces (Nova Scotia, New Brunswick, and Prince Edward Island), out-migration has been closely shadowed by in-migration – a phenomenon that we had not observed with other provinces. The volume of migrants is much smaller than it is for the other provinces, which, of course is due to the fact that their base populations are so much smaller.

When the migration exchange between each Atlantic province and Alberta is examined, we see strong peaks that clearly demonstrate the net gain to Alberta in spite of the shadow effect of reverse migration in some years (see figures 24, 25, 26, 27). The existence of the two waves of migration is clear, but the strength of the first wave is the most dramatic. The actual volume of such migrants is considerably smaller than was the case with all other provinces, which reflects the relatively small

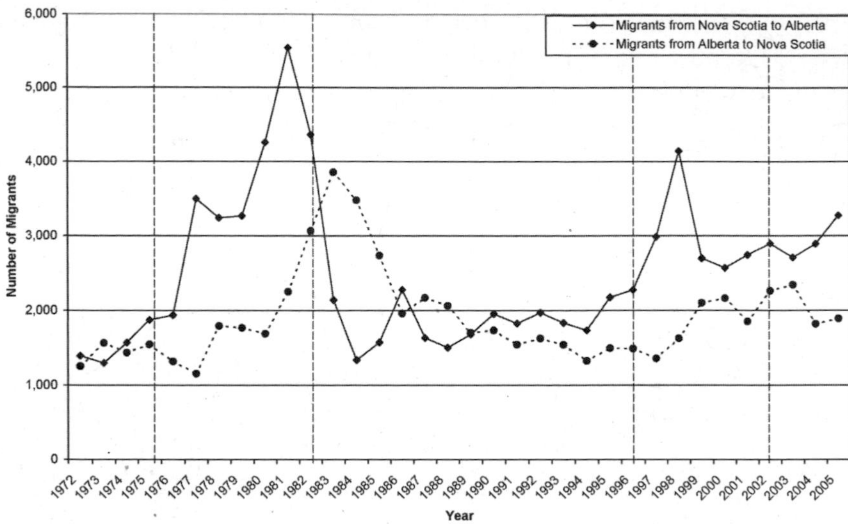

Figure 24 Migration Exchanges between Alberta and Nova Scotia, 1972 to 2005
SOURCE: CANSIM II, Table 051-0019.

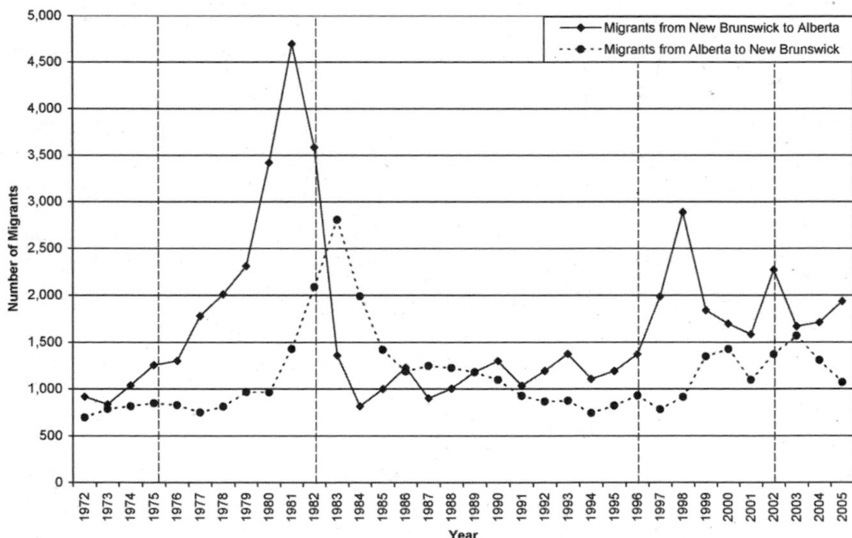

Figure 25 Migration Exchanges between Alberta and New Brunswick, 1972–2005
SOURCE: CANSIM II, Table 051-0019.

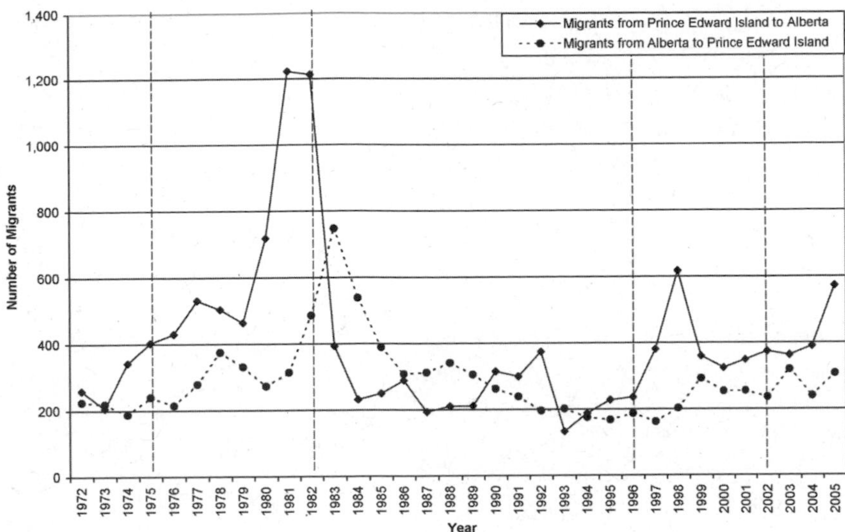

Figure 26 Migration Exchanges between Alberta and Prince Edward Island, 1972 to 2005
SOURCE: CANSIM II, Table 051-0019.

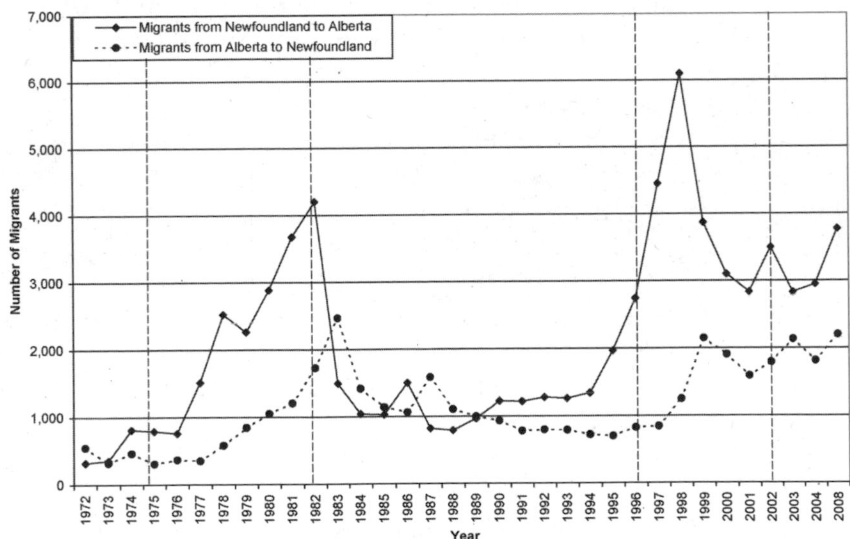

Figure 27 Migration Exchanges between Alberta and Newfoundland and Labrador, 1972 to 2005
SOURCE: CANSIM II, Table 051-0019.

populations of the Atlantic provinces but may also reflect the fact that Alberta is quite a distance.

Part of the Atlantic region, and yet different from the other provinces in important respects, is the Province of Newfoundland and Labrador, where out-migration exceeded in-migration in all but four of the thirty-three years under review. Again, there was some shadowing of in-migration with out-migration, but the gap between the two is much greater for most years, demonstrating that Newfoundland had experienced great population losses. Newfoundland's population loss through internal migration (over 100,000 persons) was much higher than that of the other Atlantic provinces (see table 1.3). Newfoundland also contrasts with the other Atlantic provinces in that the second peak of migration to Alberta is much stronger than the first peak and, in sheer numbers, exceeds the peaks of the other Atlantic provinces (see figure 27). All Atlantic provinces have two clear peaks in migration to Alberta that coincide with the two waves, but Newfoundland's second peak is much the stronger. This, of course, coincides with the collapse of the East Coast fishery, which hit Newfoundland particularly hard. The draw of home, though, remains clear as migration from Alberta to Newfoundland reached new heights in the post–2002 period. Thus, while Alberta certainly has a net gain from Newfoundland, the pull of home is strong (as it is in the other Atlantic provinces), with migration from Alberta to Newfoundland increasing after both the first wave and the second wave.

As already noted, the Atlantic provinces have not fared well within Confederation, resulting in an economy with little growth and considerable "transfer dependency"; that is, a dependence on various forms of federal funding (Matthews 1983; Finbow 1995; Savoie 1997). Some areas, like the Halifax metropolitan region, have done reasonably well; however, overall, employment has not been present in sufficient quantity to accommodate the population, especially young people emerging from postsecondary institutions with specialized skills. The turnover of people in existing jobs was not fast enough to accommodate the emerging labour force, and this led to an obvious labour surplus. Underemployment was a major issue as jobs were scarce, with various forms of job sharing providing part-time income or income for enough weeks to qualify for employment insurance. The so-called ten-to-forty-two syndrome (working ten weeks to qualify for forty-two weeks of unemployment insurance) supported community-based work sharing and seasonal employment, and this, in turn, discouraged labour mobility until the closure of the fishery (May and Hollett, 1995). The fishing moratorium, in combination with a restructuring of the newsprint industry, contributed to significant decline, particularly in many Newfoundland communities, especially outside of St John's (Norcliffe 2005). Many waited it out until the assistance programs ended, and then, beginning around 1997, migration became a much stronger option.

> The fishing villages are dying, as young people all have to go away. Many people even leave after high school. When you leave Newfoundland, many people hope you are going to come back, but in the back of their heart, they are not sure. When you have been highly educated, everyone knows you will have to leave. But it is the less educated that have usually stayed, but now it is hard for even them to stay. This produces a sense of loss, because as the population ages, who is going to be there to look after them? So as they look down the road, I don't think they project well to the future.

In many ways, the available labour pool in Newfoundland and Labrador was a good fit with the labour needs in Alberta. The closing of the shipyards in Marystown, for example, meant that many welders were available, and fishers transferred their carpentry skills to construction or became reliable labourers. Thus it was no surprise that Newfoundland and Labrador contributed disproportionately to the migration stream to Alberta from the Atlantic provinces.

Box 2: Nova Scotia and Labour Displacement
The displacement of workers through down-sizing or plant shutdowns was a major issue in some Nova Scotia communities. For example, Pictou County had three major employers (Michelin, Kimberley Clark, and Trenton Works). When Trenton Works (which manufactured railroad cars) laid off employees in 2000, it dropped from employing around 1,300 people to employing only 500.

A more critical economic struggle was experienced in Cape Breton, where coal mining and steel production had employed around 10,000 to 12,000 workers in the 1950s and 1960s. In fact, 13 October 1967 is often referred to as Black Friday, when 20,000 people marched in protest over the decision to close the mines and plants. The provincial and federal governments stepped in and rescued both operations, although at a reduced level, through two new Crown corporations: Sysco and Devco. Further downsizing took place beginning in 1992, with 4,000 employees being reduced to 1,650 by 1999. And, by 2001, coal mining and steel production had

> ceased displacing many workers and deflating the local economy. While many of the underground miners were labourers, they had a variety of trade-like skills that could be adapted to trade certification. Others working above ground or in steel were certified and could easily find work in Alberta. In general, most of these workers had at least some transferable skills, and, if they were not certified, they had a work ethic that made them potentially employable in Alberta if they decided to relocate.

The issue of language in relation to out-migration from New Brunswick has already been noted. New Brunswick is essentially divided by an east-west diagonal line from Grand Falls to Moncton (Lee 2001). North of that line, the population tends to be more French, Roman Catholic, and rural; south of that line, it tends to be more Protestant and urban. The traditional centre of power has been located south of the line. As the only officially bilingual (French/English) province in Canada, some New Brunswick migrants to Alberta expressed clear anxiety about the language issue and its relation to cultural conflict and employment policies. This was particularly the case in northern New Brunswick, where it was primarily anglophone young people who were open to out-migration. The requirement to hold a language proficiency certificate at an appropriate level tended to marginalize some anglophones, who were either unprepared for this kind of linguistic requirement or resisted it because they felt it put them at a disadvantage.

Given this historical experience of out-migration from the region, it was somewhat surprising to discover that in Alberta there was a strong pitch for former regional residents to return. "Come Home to a Career in Atlantic Canada" was the title of a forty-page newspaper magazine-type insert that appeared in Alberta newspapers in December 2006. A case was made for skilled and experienced workers to return to the Atlantic provinces not just for the opportunities but also because they were "home." Virtually every page of the document utilized the word "home," making the case for an Atlantic way of life that entailed lower costs and had the benefit of being lived near the ocean. The Atlantic region was portrayed as a place of new opportunity in which transferable skills honed in Alberta would be welcomed.

CONCLUSION

This chapter examines the push factors that prompted out-migration from each region of Canada. Clearly, these factors were not important to all migrants, but they set the stage for the consideration of migration and often played a role in a number of critical releasing factors. In each case, these dynamics contributed to the marginalization or dislocation of some persons, making them more amenable to out-migration. It was not that migration was the preferred solution but, rather, that many migrants felt pushed out. These were reluctant migrants. On the other hand, migrants were realistic and understood that relocating had its advantages. The fact that migrants were eager to leave to start over elsewhere should not be interpreted to mean that they necessarily wanted to go to Alberta. Nor should it be interpreted as an indication that they rejected their community of origin. Clearly, the social/political/economic conditions of the origin community were important elements in the decision to leave. In the next chapter, I show how migrants evaluated their destination.

9

The Migrant Encounters the Destination

If the context of the place of origin was important in the migration decision-making process, so was the context of the destination. Pull factors had to coexist with push factors in order for migration to occur. Reports of large numbers of people moving to Alberta helped to perpetuate an image of the province that, in combination with the imagery of wealth creation implied by oil and gas, enhanced the attractiveness of the province as a migration destination. This chapter attempts to analyze how economic conditions in Alberta shaped the experience of migrants, and it assesses the social psychological effects of this experience. It also discusses how an economy undergoing rapid expansion had a major impact on migration experiences and migration outcomes.

THE CONCEPT OF FRONTIER

Perhaps the most typical stereotype of Alberta is that it is a resource-driven hinterland on the western margins of the country. Its historic agricultural image as "the last best west" for agricultural homesteaders, followed by the discovery of oil and gas with its boom and bust reputation (which was often linked with the gold rush), helped to support the image of Alberta as a frontier.[1] For example, a 1980s film about Alberta, called *Riding the Tornado*, helped to perpetuate the notion of chaotic instability. While, in many ways, this image is a careless stereotype, it can be argued that the province's bursts of economic expansion do have traits similar to those found in a frontier – not a settlement frontier but an economic frontier (where one finds dramatic new growth).[2] Being a region that was relatively young, with a rapidly expanding population, and searching for its place as a more advanced economy, Alberta did possess a sense of being on the "edge" of expansion and development. And this made it feel like a frontier – at least in some respects. A frontier, in this sense, is not a previously unsettled area but, rather, an area that is proceeding quickly from one stage of development to another.[3] There are five characteristics of a frontier, and Alberta displayed all of them.

The first characteristic of a frontier involves sudden transformative change. The rapid influx of population to Alberta in the first wave, beginning in the 1970s, was merely a symptom of broader economic change. The sudden robustness of the economy generated spiralling effects, such as labour shortages, higher wages and house prices, and huge increases in infrastructural demands (e.g., schools and medical care). In many ways, it was a surprise and a shock to the national system as the rush of people and dollars to the Alberta economy produced an awareness that some kind of massive change was under way in which the province began to play a new role in the national fabric.[4] In many ways, the second wave seemed like déjà vu in that regard – only with greater intensity. Dramatically increased demand and growth-inducing change provided evidence that the province was a type of frontier as it rapidly underwent transformation from one stage of development to another. Calgary's and Edmonton's reaching the 1 million population mark was often considered symbolic of Alberta's having attained a new level of socio-economic significance. On the other hand, the collapse of the economy after 1981 also emphasized the frontier character of the province in that growth that was too rapid could be stopped and even reversed (Nikiforuk, Pratt, and Wanagas 1987). The implication was that regions with more mature economies were less likely to experience such dramatic swings, and the rapid changes in both directions supported the perception that Alberta was a province in which one would find frontier-like conditions.

The second characteristic of a frontier is that it is typically an area in which population inflows are chaotic and uncoordinated. It have already shown that the largest group of people moving into the province during the two waves were independent migrants who paid for their own relocation and who sought to do so as cheaply as possible. The automobile, the U-Haul trailer, and towing dollies, mini-vans, and trucks became the means of transport choice. Migrants often spoke of themselves as feeling like "hillbillies" because they packed all their possessions into their vehicle and then moved to Alberta. A male migrant from Nova Scotia put it this way:

> I have a small pickup truck that I had modified by getting the springs reinforced. I disassembled the furniture as little as it would go and loaded it up, and drove in six days. Every thing we had was in this old pickup truck so we had no startup costs when we got here.

Another migrant from Atlantic Canada spoke of renting a Ryder truck into which four people put their possessions; thus, they moved collectively yet independently. Others talked about selling their furniture before departure, or storing it, but then loading everything else into their vehicle before beginning their journey. A migrant from Newfoundland described the journey:

> I and my fiancée came in my own truck, my brother and his girlfriend and her younger brother came in their truck, my oldest brother and our first cousin travelled with my sister in her car, and our other first cousin and his two buddies travelled in his car, and then another guy from the town and his three friends were in their car. So five cars and fifteen people left the same small town in Newfoundland on the same day. That was just our community of 300 people alone – fifteen people leaving in one day. Out of the fifteen that came, five of us stayed and bought homes. The rest just worked seasonally and went back.

Migration of this nature had a somewhat tentative character, but it also implied a goal-directed rush to a destination that marshalled others in its wake. Of course, some migrants also arrived by plane and a few also travelled by bus; but they all gave the impression of arriving with all that they had. Migrants talked about financing this relocation through the use not only of their personal savings but also through loans from relatives and even banks.[5] This kind of migration was certainly different from employer-sponsored migration, where expenses were paid and various forms of relocation assistance were available. The sense of a frontier involves people coming and going – often with little supports – to try out the environment for themselves.

The third characteristic of a frontier involves the influx of a variety of population types. In the case of Alberta, this meant the development of greater population complexity from a previously smaller, more homogeneous population. If Alberta had at one time been characterized by a homogeneous agricultural economy, the growth of a more diverse and increasingly dense urban population changed that image. The two waves of in-migration did not begin that process by any means; rather, they intensified it. Professional workers and tradespeople were attracted to the province, but so were labourers, the unemployed, and even the homeless.[6] While domestic migrants were the largest group moving to Alberta, international migrants also began moving to Alberta in sufficient numbers to form their own communities in the province. As with many frontiers, migration to the new location often acts as a type of safety valve for people who had no place in their region of origin. We have already established that this was a major factor in the recruitment of migrants to Alberta, and migrants brought with them their cultural and personal differences. Alberta communities were often rapidly transformed by a flood of new residents, the result being that the province began to be comprised of a much broader range of people.

What is the range of types of people attracted to a frontier? Obviously there is a demand for a variety of workers from professional to blue collar in both the private sector and the public sector. Some of these workers are transferred to the province and others come as the result of national job searches. But there are many more who merely ride the wave to new locations of economic growth. For example, construction is a major employer in an expanding economy, and some construction workers are quite mobile, with walkup employment being typical. This type of worker is not necessarily committed long term to a particular worksite (or to the province) and may quit and return home or move on possibly to return again. One heavy-equipment operator who was interviewed for this study moved around the country without prearranged employment and only stayed as long he chose to do so. He claimed that his cell phone was his lifeline to family, who often did not have a clue where he was when he called them. This did not matter as they could always reach him by cell. Another group that was uncovered in this research was federal parole transferees who requested relocation because of the absence of work in their region of origin. At one level, this may appear as moving for work; however, there were many factors (such as court orders prohibiting interaction with a victim's family) that led parolees to leave small communities of origin. Many of these persons wanted to avoid those who were bad influences or those about whom they had supplied information (and therefore may have been interested in revenge). Still another group of people was composed of immigrants, particularly political refugees, who were admitted to Canada and assigned a destination only to discover there was little opportunity for them at that location. Elderly or retired parents who relocated to Alberta to be in the same place as their children made up another interesting category of in-migrants. The range of migrants to Alberta is much wider than this, but this brief list provides a sense of the many types of people who moved to Alberta.

The fourth characteristic of a frontier is that, because migrants are surrounded by newcomers like themselves, the frontier has the image of being an open society. Migrants do not feel labelled as outsiders by the host society nor do they feel that their migration status is in any way prejudicial to them. This was the experience of most migrants in urban areas in Alberta. As one person said:

> Everyone here seems to have come from somewhere else. It is just a matter of degree – who is the newest comer in the room. (Saskatchewan)

An Ontarian observed that:

> It felt like a big summer camp when I came here, or frosh week at university, because everyone had come here from all over at about the same stage I had.

A migrant from Saskatchewan stated,

> I know more people who have moved here from somewhere else than people who are from here. The first question I always ask is, "how long have you lived here?" You don't feel like this is a closed society.

Of course, not everyone was a migrant, but the way that migrants experienced Alberta minimized their sense of outsider status. As one British Columbian noted:

> there are so few native Calgarians that everyone is in the same boat as me. So no one can look down on me because they are probably an outsider too, who moved here in the last five years. That makes it a lot easier.

The migrant's feeing that they had moved to a more open society was always the result of comparisons between their destination and where they had previously lived:

> I lived in a community in British Columbia for five years and I never could break in and be accepted. But here there is no stigma attached

> to being a newcomer because you are the norm. There everyone has been there forever and here you fit much quicker.

Migrants from small communities or from communities with a declining economy often commented that, unlike newcomers in Alberta, newcomers in their respective home communities would have had a difficult time fitting in. A Newfoundlander noted:

> I never felt like an intruder, but I often think of if the shoe was turned and people were coming into Newfoundland to take jobs how we would feel.

A Quebecer observed that Alberta

> doesn't have the rigid structure that older provinces have. You have very few long-time Albertans. There is an openness to people moving in because people here see it all the time.

Most migrants encountered their new society through the workplace, where they often discovered many others who were newcomers. Furthermore, migrants were always discovering people from home or people they knew, and this reinforced their sense of being surrounded by other newcomers.

> I was working in this body shop and someone brought in a car and the file was marked "Churchill." I said, "Hey, that's my maiden name," and I asked where he was from, and it turned out to be my cousin who I hadn't seen for years. Everybody here is from somewhere. (Newfoundland)

In some work environments, migrants reported that the majority of workers were from somewhere else. And, even if that was not the case, a major topic among employees always concerned where people were from:

> When I think of people from my office, almost all are not from Alberta. They are from somewhere else. So I think it's tough to even know the true meaning of Alberta because it is a huge conglomeration of people. It helps to give you a sense of belonging when everyone else that you know is from somewhere else. You are just one of everyone else from somewhere else. (Ontario)

> There are so many transplants here that everyone is welcome. You are not invading someone's territory. It's sort of a mosaic of the country. (Nova Scotia)

The frontier effect involved the sense of openness that was the product of migrants constantly encountering other newcomers like themselves. Markers of being an outsider were not easy to determine:

> Most people I met did not even know I was not from here. Nobody even said she's from Saskatchewan, go away. (Saskatchewan)

> Most people had no idea that I was not from Alberta. I laughed when people asked me for directions. I never had any sense of being different from the people around me. (Quebec)

The fifth characteristic of a frontier is that it attracts people who are searching for a fresh start and who are eager to make the most of the opportunities that come their way. Because migrants felt that things were unsatisfactory in the region of origin, they anticipated that the destination would provide an opportunity to begin again with fewer encumbrances. Because frontiers supposedly have more newcomers than do other places, there is a sense that their social structure is more open and that they offer a more level playing field. As van Herk (2001, 3) notes, this quality supports an image of Alberta as "a place where pedigree is unimportant and migrants are encouraged to reinvent themselves." Success on the frontier, then, is intimately related to individual effort, personal achievement, and the adoption of a work ethic. Your past does not matter. Alberta was a new place with new opportunities, and success was largely dependent on one's ability to adapt and to work hard.

Because the range of work opportunities in Alberta was so vast, a first job was easy to obtain, and, over time, that job could be parlayed into another and another until the migrant reached the requisite degree of satisfaction. A migrant from New Brunswick noted:

> When I see so many people here from New Brunswick and other provinces, it reinforces to me that I have made the correct decision to come here ... I'm where everyone wants to be. I'm where the action is and I'm a part of it. I can compete. My life has changed drastically. My income has quadrupled. I have a tremendous grip on my life that I didn't have before.

The fact that many migrants came from places where such a range of opportunities did not exist, and where nepotism determined who received whatever limited work was available, made Alberta look like a new and promising frontier. The key, however, was that they recognized that the outcome of their migration was in their own hands and that, in large measure, whether or not their migration was successful depended on their own ability. Those who did not experience Alberta in this way were more likely to leave.

Hardships are expected on frontiers, but it is anticipated that they will be short term and eventually pay long-term dividends. This was especially the case for independent (unsponsored) migrants to Alberta who often came only with whatever belongings could be stuffed in a suitcase and with only enough money to get started. For those who succeeded, the sense of improvement in their situation provided a sense of upward mobility – even though it did not usually involve a change of class position. To go from sleeping on the floor to having a bed, or from renting an apartment to owning a house, or to move from part-time jobs with minimal benefits to a full-time job with full benefits, or to move from an entry-level job with an employer to a more responsible or professional position provided an individual migrant with some sense of upward mobility.[7] Migrants who experienced this kind of advancement tended to perceive it as confirmation of the fact that the independent pioneer spirit would eventually produce the rewards they had hoped for. Perseverance then became a significant characteristic of the migrant who stayed at the destination as opposed to the migrant who did not. But it is important to know that independent migrants were willing to start at the bottom and accepted the fact that migration would mean hardships. If they were able to see dramatic improvements in their situation, they were likely to view their migration as a success. Clearly, an overstatement but nonetheless representative of this kind of thinking is apparent in the words of the migrant who observed that "Fort McMurray has made more somebodies out of nobodies than any other place in North America." High pay provided a measure of success that was unattainable elsewhere in spite of the hardships and sacrifice required.

Box 1: Migration Means Starting Over: The Experiences of a Maritime Transplant

Bill came out to Alberta first. We had been married for about a year at home and we just were not making it as our jobs were just minimum wage. My husband went to the bank and got a loan so that he would have enough money to get out here and get established. He came out here with his brother-in-law and they got jobs right away. They got a basement apartment and slept on the floor in a sleeping bag on a piece of foam. They had no plates and no dishes and kept their food in a cooler. They mostly bought their food from vendors and didn't cook much. But he had a job and he liked the money he made so told me to come out too.

I arrived at 9:00 PM in the evening at the airport. I hardly recognized my husband. He had long hair and his ears were pierced – all things that he did not dare do in our small community back home. We went to the apartment and slept on the floor. We did that for five months, but I insisted that we go to Wal-Mart and buy a sheet as I did not want to lay on the carpet. Five months later we were given a mattress and laid it on the floor. We used paper plates and plastic knives and forks, and we reused them, even the paper plates by washing them after every use. We did that for six to seven months. Imagine eating spaghetti with plastic forks with the tongs all broken off. Sometimes we had food for supper but did not know what we would eat in the morning. When people heard that, they brought us food. That's when I said "get me back home. Having my parents bringing us food was way better than having strangers bringing us food." I still remember when we bought our first chair. It was the only chair we had. We took turns sitting in it and even sleeping in it.

We had no money because we had loans to pay back and bills to pay and rent was also a factor. Somebody gave us a television set and that was our big entertainment, but we even sold that to a pawn shop for twenty dollars when money got low. But things got better. First of all, Bill was a good worker and he kept getting raises because they liked how hard he worked. Second, we really had to learn how to divide up our money so that some money was applied to all our needs rather than just using it to pay bills and loans.

When we were married back in the Maritimes, people had set us up. We had been given beds, couches, kitchen table, a washer and other things. But when I left, there was no time to sell all this stuff so we just gave it all away. Coming to Alberta truly meant starting all over. The things we wanted to keep, we packed in three boxes and shipped out for seventy dollars. My husband was working seven days a week in the summer when I first arrived and he did that for a month straight with no days off. I didn't know anybody and I sat in the basement apartment and did not know what to do. Getting used to a big city was a real adjustment.

But it was worth it. When you see how far we have come, we feel really proud – and we did it all by ourselves. The bonus was the big cheque that Bill brought home. We had never seen a cheque that big. For Christmas, our gift to each other was another piece of furniture. This year we bought a new bed for ourselves from Ikea. We called home to tell our families about it and they said, "Wow!" (Prince Edward Island)

THE EXPANDING ECONOMY AS AN INTERPRETIVE CONCEPT

The most important factor in explaining the decision to move to Alberta and the outcomes of migration after arrival can be found in the fact that the time of strong in-migration was also the time in which Alberta's economy was rapidly expanding. An expanding economy supports a very different outcome for migration than a contracting, or even just stable, economy. An expanding economy creates a set of socio-economic conditions that allow migrants to evaluate their relocation in a positive way. It also results in their comparing the destination with their place of origin (and their situation in it) and evaluating it accordingly.

The idea of an expanding economy is a key interpretive concept that allows us to explain how structural conditions shape how people evaluate their life and how they think.[8] An expanding Alberta economy played a huge role in how migrants assessed their relocation, and it biased them towards viewing the move positively because it affected so many aspects of their life. Due to the availability of jobs, the structural condition of rapid economic growth supported quick partial integration into the social economy. Furthermore, an expanding economy also meant the potential to improve one's employment position. Thus, to the extent that employment (particularly employment potential in one's field) was a critical variable in the determination of self-worth and in obtaining a satisfactory position within the new community, an expanding economy provided great potential for a positive core baseline evaluation of migration.

An expanding economy can be contrasted with a declining economy or a stable economy. Many migrants made this type of comparison.[9] A community with an expanding economy has a different dynamic from a community with a static or declining economy. The psychology of an expanding economy is much different from that of a declining economy as it generates much more optimism. The variety of opportunities makes a significant contribution to mood elevation, which builds self-esteem and self-confidence. Two examples illustrate the point:

> I love the mountains and the weather and I love the drive and the energy of the people. You have a feeling that this is like New York where everybody has a drive and purpose in life. In Montreal, people like life ... but I'm sorry it's a depressing society there. You look down there, you don't look up. It is a less positive feeling. Maybe people here feel more confident because they have work and more money to spend. But they have much more purpose than I have ever seen. (Quebec)

> If you know there's more but you've lived in that rut back there, it is hard on you and your self-confidence. When you can go out and make money and get ahead, it is a self-confidence and self-esteem builder and does amazing things for your personality. That's freedom and independence. That's what being here has done for me. Before I came here I was at the lowest point in my life. You can't do things without money. It's depressing. It is hard to see a future if you are not working. (New Brunswick)

People who came from places where the economy was in the doldrums were quick to make comparative observation:

> We walked around the first summer we were here and we said, "Is it you or is it me or what? Do these people really seem happier here?" There is a real difference in the climate here. The economic climate is more upbeat and people seem more upbeat. I think we feel better about ourselves here. Even working for a company that is making money rather than losing money helps. (Quebec)

> I have found that where things are prosperous, people are happier and they are complaining less and less and BC was getting me down, especially in the North where there was a lot of unemployment and people were speaking on the negative side about conditions and the government. Every time you turn on the news, all you get is cutbacks and closures in the forest industry. It's in the newspapers and people are talking about it and it does become a bit depressing. (British Columbia)

Whether a rapidly expanding economy in itself brings happiness is questionable, but there is no doubt that it was a building block for migrants seeking to become established. A strong economy usually meant higher pay, and if there were higher costs, they were often ignored. As one observer noted, "People in Saskatchewan think the Highway #2 [between Edmonton and Calgary] corridor is nirvana because they know the pay is higher and that is where things are happening and that is where they want to be." (Saskatchewan)

An expanding economy also meant new positions and greater specialization:

> I was quite happy practising law in Regina and really didn't need to move. But if I would have known then what I know now, what I thought then was a very difficult decision would have been nothing because the career opportunities are much greater here, though I did not know that to any extent then. I call Calgary the best place to work closest to home. (Saskatchewan)

> They were constantly opening up new offices in Alberta. Every company I talked to in Ontario was opening up something new in Alberta and they were looking for people. When I heard that, I hustled out here. I had experience in several different fields and so I knew I would find something. (Ontario)

When the economy is expanding, change is all around and is often represented by new construction. Changes in the built environment provide the external symbols of new ideas and growth, which is often referred to as "an energy here that people feed off." It creates a sense of being at the heart of action, and this clearly has a psychological effect. Expansion is viewed as a barometer of well-being, even though these external elements may hide internal struggles and some may not feel the euphoria felt by others. Growth results in a feeling of optimism. This conclusion is supported by a 2001 survey of western Canadians, in which optimism about the future was the highest in Alberta and lowest in Saskatchewan, where the economy was not robust (Berdahl 2001).

In an expanding economy there is greater willingness to take risks because others are also risk-takers, and the mood becomes contagious, producing reliance on individual initiative, which supports a "can-do" attitude. Consequently, there is considerable faith in the private sector and, conversely, much suspicion of the public sector. The culture of prosperity nurtures a climate that is supportive of ambition. Expansion supports an entrepreneurial outlook, within which regulation and controls are viewed as restrictive. Thinking is structured by aspirations and dreams. The continuous arrival of new residents bolsters the sense of confidence that the society is "on the move." Enough people have experienced a sense of upward mobility that there is a sense of confidence in the future. Even if, technically, one does not experience upward mobility, the pay increase gives one a sense of prosperity:[10]

> My first pay cheque was for $700 and I couldn't believe it and went to my foreman and told him there must be a mistake. This was for only nine days work. He said, "No, it's right." So I went home and called my wife and told her to get out here. I worked for seven years at home and never once saw a pay cheque that big. (Newfoundland)

People frequently change jobs because there are lots of them and each one is usually in some way better than the last one:

> Alberta seems to be the land of milk and honey sort-of-thing. You know, you have one job in the morning and if you don't like it, you can get another one in the afternoon. (Manitoba)

> I was working a lot of seasonal stuff and term contracts in Sudbury and it was very frustrating ... [Here] we have each had three jobs in three years with great companies. I could switch jobs tomorrow if I wanted to. (Ontario)

Whether these job changes are actually occupational mobility (i.e., whether a change in class position actually occurred) may be another question, but the sense of mobility came from having a larger income and/or other tangible things – like a home or recreational items such as off-road vehicles, boats, and so on:

> A lot of people who had gone west would come back to town and they had nice trucks and other things, and naturally I thought if they can do it, I can do it. That is how I got the idea. Most of them thought they were coming for a year or two, but they ended up staying. The same thing has happened to me too and I've now got all the toys. (Ontario)

> I looked for work hard at home for eight months and got nothing. I came here and had five offers in five days. I was always promoted as rapidly as I could be. In my current job, I have moved through six levels already. The outrageous prosperity here means that I have seen "Help Wanted" signs all over the place and I have never seen that before in my life. I walked into the Employment Centre and there were 2,000 index cards on the wall, many for jobs paying seven to nine dollars an hour, and people were walking around saying there is nothing here. I said, "Wow, what a different mentality." The idea that there is nothing here is nuts. (Newfoundland)

COMMUNITIES WITH DECLINING ECONOMIES

In contrast to a community with an expanding economy, a community with a declining economy is comprised of people who are pessimistic and anxious about the future. There is considerable apathy, which is the result of a sense of powerlessness in the face of deteriorating conditions. Above all, this state of affairs seems to bother those with ambition who are not satisfied with the status quo:

> There was not only lack of work in Nova Scotia but also lack of ambition in the young people there. Many people would go to university but they would end up where they started from ... I was depressed ... There is a difference like night and day between Alberta and Nova Scotia. Ninety percent of the jobs down east are government-funded jobs so people support the Liberals. I feel things are economy driven here whereas it is government driven there. When you are down and out in Nova Scotia, that's pretty well the way it stays, whereas here I feel there is more hope and I feel less depressed. (Nova Scotia)

> Most of the people I worked with were either on UI or planning to go on UI in the near future. That is the way it is in the [Annapolis] Valley. I worked with mostly young people and they had no plans for anything more than their minimum-wage jobs. That was their goal – especially for young women whose husbands had factory jobs. There was a lack of ambition and I think I had more ambition. (Nova Scotia)

In communities where the economy is in decline, there is less willingness to take risks and, above all, there is a greater sense of dependence on the public sector to protect citizens. People are cautious, eager to preserve what is currently held, and resistant to change. People hold on to the jobs they have, and competition for scarce jobs becomes fierce (e.g., Burrill 1992).

> There is a colloquial saying back there about "hard times in the Maritimes," and what that means is it is hard to get employment. Getting by seems to be the way people think as opposed to laying down foundations for the future. There is not a lot of movement there in jobs so there is not a lot of positive motivation. I never had a lot of motivation to do new things, whereas here it's different. All of a sudden, I have this confidence to go out and do things whereas there I felt held back. Back there you stick with what works whereas here you can do a 180-degree turn and do something else. If you have a job there, you cling to it tenaciously and it develops a different mindset. Maybe it's not so bad if you are 40 but not if you are 25 to 30. (New Brunswick)

Other persons cannot find the jobs they want but settle for less in order to stay in the community. Nepotism often ensures that the jobs that are available go to the people at the core of the community. There may be a sense of pessimism that focuses blame on public figures or external factors to account for the condition of the community:

> In my region of New Brunswick, things were very depressed. People were always complaining to the government and about the government. For me it was depressing to have to deal with that mentality day after day. The difference in attitude is just totally different. There people expect it to rain and here people expect it to be sunny. Economic depression affects people mentally. You really notice it when you leave. (New Brunswick)

The constant departure of residents and, in particular, of young people (often the most qualified) brings with it a sense of the inevitability of decline:

> When you are in high school, if your parents aren't telling you, your friends are and they're telling you that you have to leave when you graduate. And you see it too – you see them leave. (Nova Scotia)

The return of former community members for visits only accentuates this sense of difference. They feel that the community never changes because little new development occurs and, when it does, it brings with it a greater dependence on the public sector.

COMMUNITIES WITH A STABLE ECONOMY

A community with a stable economy has the best of all worlds in that it has confidence in the future and a general sense of stability and well-being. There are few highs and lows and few problems caused by significant changes. Expansion is slow but orderly. The problem with a stable economy, however, is that it cannot accommodate all new entrants into the labour force (or even existing members of the labour force who are under-employed). New graduates find job opportunities, but these are limited in comparison to those found in an expanding economy. Others are looking for new challenges:

> We gave up a lot to move out here because our families are back there. But what we gained here was a sense of optimism. I had to pay my own way out here for the job interview and had to pay for my own hotel so it shows how far I was willing to go. But it was not just jobs here, but the type of jobs. We always had jobs back home but were looking for permanent jobs with real potential. That gave me a lot of confidence which I lacked before. (Ontario)

> [In Winnipeg] people fight over the positions that are available but here you can come and pick because there is more available. (Manitoba)

> They said at home that getting an education was the way to go if you wanted to make it. Then it turned out that you still had to leave. Here it is different. I'm using my education but it almost seems that those who don't have a good education are doing as well as those who do. (British Columbia)

> The big thing we heard was that the morale was different in Alberta because it was positive, young and dynamic. Ottawa seemed dull and in decline. That's what we were leaving. (Ontario)

> I made a very very rash decision to quit my job, to move to Alberta, and to try to get a job. I had a friend who had a friend in Calgary

> and she had a friend who was looking for someone with my background. I called that person and we did a two-hour interview over the phone and she called me two days later and said, "You've got the job, when can you start?" So I had to quit my job even sooner than I had said and find my way out here. I don't think that would even happen in Ontario because there is such a scramble for people and so many qualified people for jobs that there is lots of competition. To think I could have that kind of personal discussion over the phone to hire me was incredible. (Ontario)

Out-migration from a community with a stable economy may be much less noticeable than outmigration from a community with a declining economy, but it occurs at the margins of the labour force and often involves those looking for something different. The point is that a stable economy is still markedly different from an expanding economy, where the boundaries of growth are in stellar escalation. Both capital and people from stable economies are attracted to places where the economy is expanding rapidly.

DISTINCT ASPECTS OF THE ALBERTA ECONOMY

There were other aspects of the Alberta economy that served as pull factors. Alberta was perceived not only as a place with an expanding economy but also as a place that was very prosperous. Royalties from oil and natural gas provided revenues that created images of a flexible government. This became a highly publicized issue, especially as Alberta was paying down its debt and ultimately became the only jurisdiction in Canada to have no debt. This led to the assumption that the province was in a better position to provide for its citizens than were other provinces. For example, former Saskatchewan residents were discovered in Medicine Hat (near the eastern border of Alberta). These people wanted to be in Alberta because they thought that the government there was better positioned to provide services, but they also wanted to be able to easily return to Saskatchewan to visit:

> People from Saskatchewan like Medicine Hat because of the size ... And it is also closer to Saskatchewan. We are out of Saskatchewan but not that far away. People who move here are not just from the retail catchment area of the southwest but really from all over Saskatchewan. And then there is the mystique to coming to a place that has no sales tax.

Retirees who moved to Alberta sometimes expressed concern over government services. They felt more secure in Alberta and also preferred its tax structure. The perception was that Alberta's oil-based prosperity would be translated into better health care and more and better government services, which other provinces could not afford.[11]

At least partially because of its strong economy, Alberta also had a reputation for having lower taxes. Many migrants talked about taxes as being a significant factor in their decision to move to Alberta.

> There is a huge difference in taxes from what we paid in income taxes and property taxes in Manitoba to say nothing about the sales tax ... But there was nothing about Manitoba itself that encouraged us to leave. I always had it in the back of my mind that I wanted to move to a place where the tax structure was better. (Manitoba)

> Taxes are way better here than in New Brunswick and I like having no sales tax – but I guess it is really because I am a small "c" conservative." (New Brunswick)

While the idea that taxes were always lower in Alberta is debatable, it is clear that the absence of a retail sales tax was viewed as a bonus.[12] Since all internal migrants came from jurisdictions in which a sales tax was charged, for the first year or so these people would experience a sense of euphoria each time they made a purchase: "It was like getting a discount every time you bought something." In some cases, people from neighbouring provinces reported that, for years, they had travelled to Alberta to make tax-free purchases. This immediately gave migrants the sense that they had been right to leave their community of origin. One migrant gave the issue of taxation a different twist: "Taxes weren't an attracting factor for us to come here but they are a deterrent against going home" (Manitoba). Reflecting on higher taxes in other jurisdictions may have been a factor in some people's decisions regarding whether to stay or to leave.

The low rate of unionization in Alberta was an issue for some. Somewhat surprisingly, this was a pull factor for some migrants as it suited their ideological predisposition:

> The big difference between BC and Alberta is the difference that unions make because to me there are virtually no unions here. So this is a different way that people work here. I fit right in here because I always believed that you should get paid according to

> what you give to the company. In BC it doesn't work that way as, if you are in a union, everybody gets paid the same regardless of how much you work. If you have a work ethic here, then you can get somewhere and I like that. I have had four raises in two and a half years, so that shows how my own efforts made a difference. (British Columbia)

There was no evidence that migrants to Alberta were any more or less likely to have had a union background. What does seem to be the case is that independent migrants had a strong desire to make it on their own at the destination. While some may have preferred Alberta because unions were not so strong there, others slowly became converts to a non-union mentality because the expanding economy allowed them to experience success through their own efforts. An expanding economy allowed them to find their own niche, which provided a basis for the adoption of free enterprise thinking.

THE CONSEQUENCES OF AN EXPANDING ECONOMY FOR ALBERTA

As two pillars in the Alberta economy, agriculture and oil have played a major role in shaping the province. Mansell (1997, 21–2) argues that the agricultural industry and the petroleum industry were structurally similar in that both were highly capital-intensive, involved a high degree of risk, and were captive to volatile externally determined pricing. Thus petroleum and agriculture both contributed to a similar type of value system, and they reinforced each other. Individualism was a key element in this thinking, as was the idea that problems that did emerge were likely to be the result of factors external to the province. Thus, unity in the face of a perceived external attack was a much more dominant theme in Alberta politics than were internal conflicts between capital and workers. The values of risk-taking, individualism, entrepreneurialism, adversity, and the ability to make quick adjustments that militated against trade unionism came from working in petroleum and agriculture, which involved considerable risk-taking, multiple work units, a capital intensive atmosphere, and exposure to the vagaries of international markets. Where agriculture differed from oil was in the fact that, while both industries experienced wide fluctuations in market pricing, the payoffs in oil were potentially much more lucrative and dramatic. Of course, some of this free enterprise thinking was indeed mythological as government supports and/or industry incentives became part of the survival of both sectors.

In Alberta, oil and agriculture played a pivotal role in producing a mode of thinking supportive of free enterprise. The evidence presented in this chapter suggests that the process of migration involves self-selection and that the experience of migration, particularly to a place where the economy is expanding rapidly, reaffirms that these people support an individual work ethic and reap the rewards of their own initiative.

The central point about an expanding economy is that it provides the conditions that draw people who have other reasons to migrate. It becomes a beacon that attracts those who are available and open to relocating. But, more than that, an expanding economy enhances the chances of a successful migration, which then reinforces the idea that those with ambition and risk-taking traits are likely to be rewarded. Independent migrants are especially likely to feel affirmed by this process. Migrants who enter into an expanding economy, then, are likely to be self-confident and assertive, especially when the move has apparently worked in their favour. The experience also motivates them to be quite critical of those who lack such individual initiative and expect the government to support them. This was one of the reasons why some migrants became very critical of their home region if they felt that the people there were too dependent upon government assistance. In-migrants to Alberta during this era tended to support right-wing thinking because their own migration experience involved moving into an economy that was on an upswing.

The social psychology of the contrasts between a stagnant/declining economy and an expanding economy are significant. Regions with a declining economy had usually been in decline for some time. For example, as one leader in Cape Breton acknowledged, the decline of coal started in the 1960s, and from then on industries began to falter. Children born at that time were "raised with pessimism" so that "going away meant relief from that." In contrast, migrating to a place with an expanding economy produced optimism. This is not to suggest that all migrants were able to succeed, only that many appeared to do so, and they emerged from the experience with a stronger belief in individual initiative. A woman from New Brunswick commented:

> We were discussing this the other day. I know why people come to Alberta. It is because there are entrepreneurial niches here ... And even if you aren't entrepreneurial yourself, you can work for

> someone who is. This is a huge difference from home. Maybe those of us who come like the Protestant work ethic too much.

And, of course, in an expanding economy, that kind of work ethic is usually rewarded. Successful independent migration into an expanding economy thus helped to support a greater belief in the reliance on individual effort.

It would seem that a positive migration outcome resulted not so much from the fact that people had moved to Alberta as from the fact that they had moved to a place where the economy was rapidly expanding. On the other hand, whatever traits Alberta already possessed as the result of its own history were magnified by the structural conditions created by rapid growth and the in-migration that that supported. However, the shift to an overheated economy, especially beginning in 2005, created structural conditions that, potentially, would have a very different result. Not everyone succeeds on frontiers of economic expansion, and if Alberta were perceived as a more open society, this is certainly not something that should be equated with egalitarianism. In fact, some entered the province with very little and remained with very little. The segmentation of the labour market into those holding high-paying jobs (especially in the oil industry) from those holding low-paying service jobs created an increasing chasm between social classes (Krahn and Gartrell 1983). However, in contrast to older established regions of the country, where elites and "old money" were a matter of heritage, in Alberta an expanding economy meant that there was a lot of "new money" possessed by people who had suddenly become wealthy. The fact that many migrants experienced Alberta as an open society was due to the province's rapid economic growth and shortage of labour, which provided opportunities not found in declining or even stable economies. Because many migrants experienced career mobility, or at least income improvements, Alberta appeared to them to be a well chosen destination.

CONCLUSION

Alberta's rapid economic growth created an unequal playing field and set it apart from other provinces. Alberta was certainly not the only place that attracted internal migrants, but no other place had its dynamic and advantages.

The decision to migrate was an individual decision that required personal evaluations of both the place of origin and the destination in relation to one's goals. But the very experience of migrating independently and reasonably successfully reinforced the traits associated with moving to get ahead: ambition, mobility, and personal achievement, the core values with which Alberta has been identified. There does appear to have been some self-selection in migration, with the emphasis being on those who were more ambitious and entrepreneurial (Chiswick 2000, 61).[13] Migrants relocated independently and moved into an expanding economy with a wide range of skills and abilities rather than entering the labour force as an underclass. Because an expanding economy needs all kinds of workers, it is not just the educated who self-select for the move but also a wide range of workers. Furthermore, an expanding oil-based economy provides enough rewards for migrants that it tends to foster an increased belief in individual initiative, which, in turn, reinforces free enterprise thinking. If "where you live is who you are," then "where you go" is also "who you are" or "what you become." This is a provocative argument that is yet to be confirmed, but its outline seems to be present here.

10

Social Capital and Adjustment at the Destination

So far, the analysis has emphasized that internal migration is an individual act that takes place within a socio-economic context. The decision to migrate is related to some form of marginalization in the community of origin, but this does not mean that migration is a form of anomic behaviour. In fact, it is precisely the opposite. Migration is intensely social behaviour that involves social ties in the sending community as well as at the destination. Social capital is mobilized to assist in the migration process, from the decision to migrate to the actual migration to adjustment at the destination. This is especially the case for independent migrants, who need to feel connected and to have social support because, for them, migration is such risky behaviour.

In the pre-migrant stage, there is the need for information that will assist in decision making regarding both the wisdom of relocating and where to go. The plan to migrate is socially constructed, and it facilitates the migration from departure to arrival. The post-migrant needs contacts in order to settle –to find employment, housing, and friendship. The settled migrant then becomes an important contact for the newly arrived migrant. Since people are more likely to move to places where they already possess some social capital, it is clear that social ties play a significant role in where people move. Social ties are likely to play an important role in *where* a migrant will go, whereas personal decisions (that may well be socially conditioned) are likely to play an important role in *when* they will (Morrison and Wheeler 1978, 80).

The goal of this chapter is to demonstrate how the place of origin and the destination are linked through the use of social capital. By examining a variety of strategies adopted at the destination, I also show how this social capital can assist in the adjustment process.

THE MIGRATION STREAM

The important thing about internal migration is that there is usually considerable movement within a national society. The migration from one place to another is likely to have many precedents. The migration stream may be thin (with small volumes) or it may be strong (with high volumes) or it may be episodic: but it is continuous. For example, people have moved from Saskatchewan and Ontario to Alberta for many years, not just in the two waves that have been identified. They have also moved in the reverse direction. This means that most migrants knew someone in Alberta who had preceded them, whether thirty years ago or last month. In some cases, it was someone who had moved to Alberta in the first wave; in others, it was someone who had relocated earlier. These people could be relatives, friends, or friends of friends. In addition to having some kind of contact with someone who was already there, the migrant also often travelled with someone from home. Sometimes this phenomenon is referred to as "chain migration," but in this book the term "migration stream" is preferred because it emphasizes the fact that a multitude of types of ties existed, from strong to weak to vague, and that they were of varying volumes and strengths. The point is that migration to Alberta was not normally a move into anonymity.

Migration, then, was the result of spatial selectivity. Alberta was chosen as a destination because someone with whom a migrant had some kind of connection had gone there first, still resided there, and served as an important touchstone in the decision to move there. This practice of choosing a destination where family, friends, or someone known only vaguely has already settled has been referred to as the "beaten path effect" (Morrison 1977):

> When one person comes, they tell their friends, "Come out, come out, come out!" You can stay with me and this provides support and encouragement for the big move, which in some ways is not so difficult as a result. The happiness and encouragement of people here really makes a difference. (Ontario)

> First our daughter and son-in-law moved here, then we came. Then our son moved here followed by our son-in-law's parents, so we have quite a family contingent here now. You should have seen our Christmas dinner." (Quebec)

> Somebody told me that 40 to 60 percent of University of Saskatchewan grads come to Alberta. It's almost like a path that everyone follows like a cattle path. And it's not really a big jump because there are lots of people here that they know. And they can help you almost like an established community. You've got the networks here. My brothers are all here and only mom and dad are back home. It's not a leap of faith. (Saskatchewan)

> I came here because I knew a lot of people here and I knew it would be the closest to being a home away from home. And there were good opportunities here ... I had family and friends out here so it was no problem. You'll be well taken care of. You will have a great family base and friends here. (Prince Edward Island)

> I was in London, Ontario, for a long time and I couldn't find any job there. And I wanted to support myself. I met a lot of Sudanese there and many of them came to Brooks. So they called me and told me there was work here. A lot of them moved here from London. (Ontario)

In some cases, the migration stream was traced to parents who had been in Alberta at an earlier point but who had now moved back:

> It was pretty simple and it was a decision between my partner and I. A company told me they would hire me if I came to Alberta, and it meant a $10,000 raise from what I made before for a similar responsibility. I grew up in Ontario but I was looking for something a little bit different but not too culturally different. What made a difference though was that my parents were really supportive and that was because members of their family had come out here and done quite well. If I had not had their support it would have been a harder decision. (Ontario)

> My parents had come out here when they were young, and so my mom urged me to come out because, at my age, she said I could do a lot better here. I knew a couple people here but none of my close friends were here before I came out. Now that I am here, I know about 15 from my hometown in Edmonton and about 25 to 30 in Alberta. (New Brunswick)

Many elderly parents relocated to Alberta because their children had moved there earlier. In some cases, the move was made with reluctance:

> I never thought I would leave Quebec for political reasons. I never truly wanted to leave nor did I consider leaving but it was family that eventually got me to move to Alberta. Quebec separation is the only thing that would have forced me to leave. I lived in that beautiful old house [in Montreal] for thirty years, and I left a part of my soul there. But I will be buried there even though this in now my home. (Quebec)

> My daughter was part of the exodus from Quebec in the 70s, and it would be interesting to know how many moved here from there then. Now their parents are aging and they are moving here to be near their children. (Quebec)

> I was retired and my children were here. They did not move here directly from Quebec but had been in places like New York. So I decided to move to where they were. My friends didn't want me to come but since my children were here, I really didn't have a choice. I thought I better come while I had the energy. I didn't want my children to come and take me. (Quebec)

Migrants often talked about their move as something done independently, even though they were aware of many connections at the destination. They also had a sense of being part of a migration stream:

> I came out cold turkey in that I knew no one. I knew there were friends of friends here but I didn't contact them. The same year I came, others came as well and we sort of stayed in touch. But then in 97–98, a whole lot of people came out here. People with technical backgrounds got jobs quickly but so did others. You always read in the newspapers back home that there were tons of jobs in Alberta. So when someone comes out here and gets a decent job, that gets back to friends or members from their class, and pretty soon everyone floods out here. Most of these people are single, but if their parents ever are out of work, then they come too. I know a number like that. (New Brunswick)

> It takes one person, a leader, to leave and then others follow out of curiosity. If they can do it, I can do it. It gave them courage. They need a security blanket of other people ... A lot of people out here from PEI have been friends for years and years. One person moved and it just kept going. Everyone I know out here I either went to school with them for twelve years or whatever – there are not a lot of people here from there that I just met. (Prince Edward Island)

Migrants from Manitoba spoke of how the linkage with people from back home enabled them to build a friendship network:

> Most of my close friends in Alberta are Manitobans. I am working so much that I don't have time to make new friends any other way. So I sort of fall back to my friends from Manitoba. Most of my best friends had already moved here so that made a big difference in me even coming here. And if you find one person form Manitoba, you then find five others.

Just knowing there were people from back home at the destination was often comforting for migrants – whether or not they got together regularly. Because of the significant number of other migrants, people did not need to interact with many of the host society:

> We are now Albertan. But we don't really know what an Albertan is because we haven't met many. For our generation, all our friends are from elsewhere. (Ontario)

The flip side of the observation that migrants felt that everyone was new and that there were few native-born Albertans is that there were many there from their own region of origin, and this reduced the sense of strangeness. A Saskatchewan migrant noted:

> I get that small town kind of feeling in Alberta because I am always running into people from Saskatchewan. I was in a coffee shop in an office tower and I was waving to people who went by all the time. These were all people from home, and I like that because it makes you feel at home. But in another way, it's kind of sad.

The anonymity of being in a strange place was reduced through contact with others who had a similar place of origin. An East Coaster explained how region of origin fostered sociality even when previous personal ties were lacking:

> I probably still would have moved here if I did not have friends here but it made the move a lot easier. At least 50 percent of my friends here are from home or the Maritimes in general whom I did not know before. I don't know what it is but if you're from the Maritimes you feel more comfortable even if you just met them.

> You know that they understand because they are coming from the same scenario. (Nova Scotia)

One of the interesting ways in which the sense of being part of a migration stream was experienced on a daily basis was through observing out-of-province licence plates. Migrants themselves often viewed these sightings as evidence that others were moving here, were "checking things out," or were visiting friends and family who had moved here. Furthermore, since provincial regulations in Alberta only required a rear licence plate, this left the front plate as a convenient place for advertisements for one's home region/province. Albertans often identified these persons as "one-eyed bandits" because the front plates gave the impression that they were longing for home and would return there once they had made enough cash. But for migrants themselves, these plates helped them to identify each other.

> We have a licence plate with a Nova Scotia flag on the front of our vehicle instead of an Alberta one. I wave at them all every time I see one. It looks like half of Nova Scotia lives here. In fact, I gave one to a friend for a wedding gift. (Nova Scotia)

This kind of plate was particularly common among Nova Scotians and Newfoundlanders, for whom it provided a sense of community in diaspora.

> We have a Newfoundland licence plate on the front of our car and people are always coming up to me to ask me where we are from. Every time we go out it is always, "'So where you from?" It is always other Newfoundlanders wanting to talk. (Newfoundland)

> It gives me a sense of a "touch of home" when I run into people from Nova Scotia and we talk. I'll be driving down the road and I'll see a Nova Scotia licence plate and I'll try to get beside them to see if I know them, and there have been a couple of times where I have. (Nova Scotia)

Newfoundland maps on the back window of the car and bumper stickers that read "Proud to be a Newfie" also served the function of community building. They allowed home loyalties to be expressed and also enabled interaction with other migrants.

The sense of a migration stream was particularly obvious when migrants travelled independently and utilized connections with those who had gone before. There were also instances in which migrants travelled together. Finding someone else to migrate with makes migration less daring – especially if it involves long distances: "Some friends and I were talking and one guy said he was going so the rest of us said we would go too" (Manitoba). This was particularly a pattern among young adults. For example, clusters of young people, all of whom came from the same town, were discovered in various places in Alberta. Places such as St Stephen, New Brunswick; Brandon, Manitoba; Creston, British Columbia; Dalhousie, New Brunswick; and Stephenville and Deer Lake, Newfoundland seemed to produce groups of young people who travelled together. In any case, the existence of a migration stream established a destination and provided the social support necessary to ensure that migration was not an anomic act.

Box 1: Social Capital at Three Alberta Destinations

FORT MCMURRAY

Fort McMurray was a particularly popular destination for migrants from Newfoundland. Some claimed that Newfoundlanders could handle the more isolated northern location of the city because they were accustomed to the sense of isolation that comes with living in Newfoundland. Others claimed that the terrain around Fort McMurray was similar to that in western Newfoundland and that this facilitated adaptation. As one person pointed out, "The fact that Newfoundland television stations are available here on cable almost makes it seem like we are at home."

Migration flows from the northern peninsula and the west coast of Newfoundland to Fort McMurray seemed to be particularly heavy. The closure of a board mill plant in Stephenville some years earlier meant that many had lost jobs as pipefitters, millwrights, machinists, electricians, and welders, and the oil sands was an attraction for this experienced labour pool. The program in heavy equipment operation at the College of the North Atlantic, a trade school in Stephenville, also helped to support a pipeline of people who were immediately employable. An official from Stephenville reported that they knew of eighty to one hundred young adults in Fort McMurray from their community alone: "Many of them are only out of high school a couple of years and try their luck finding a job but they hang out together. Living there is a cross between going camping and having a continuous party. They do that for a year or two and then get serious about doing something with the rest of their life." The community of Port aux Basques, the site of the ferry crossing to the mainland, had also experienced significant job loss when the ferry system was made more efficient, and there was a labour pool of welders, electricians, plumbers, and instrumentation people who could no longer find adequate work there. Their skills, of course, were in high demand in Fort McMurray. This included men in their fifties who had retired early or men who were looking for better pay.

The first stream of Newfoundlanders to Fort McMurray began in the 1970s, with the emergence of the Suncor plant. This meant that there had been Newfoundlanders in the city for thirty years, and other Newfoundlanders joined them. With the advent of the second wave of migration, the collapse of the fishery back home, in combination with expansion in the oil sands, provided added incentive for migration to Fort McMurray. And it is beyond dispute that the city was attractive to Newfoundlanders because others from "down home" were already there. In fact, a man in Port aux Basques made this observation about his son, who was considering a move there: "Not only would he have relatives there for twenty years but he would have a network of friends. Our family is the only one of my brothers and sisters left in Newfoundland, so if my son goes, I am not sure what the future is for us here." It is therefore no wonder that Fort McMurray was often referred to as Newfoundland's second largest city. The flow of migrants to that city has been particularly striking.

MEDICINE HAT

Because of its proximity to the Saskatchewan border in southeastern Alberta, Medicine Hat had a particular appeal to people from Saskatchewan. Persons in the adjacent agricultural communities and from places like Swift Current and Maple Creek had long been attracted to Medicine Hat for shopping (locals sometimes referred to them as "Skatchers") because of Alberta's lack of a provincial sales tax. People particularly concerned about the health of the economy in Saskatchewan and its ability to support an aging population wanted to move to Alberta, but they also wanted to be close to their home communities. A section of the city with new condominiums built especially for retirees, many of whom were allegedly agriculturalists from Saskatchewan, was jokingly referred to as the "wrinkle ranch." Thus, moving to Medicine Hat meant being in Alberta in the company of other persons from Saskatchewan and still having easy access to social networks back home.

BROOKS

The town of Brooks lies between Calgary and Medicine Hat on the Trans-Canada Highway. Originally an agricultural community made possible by an extensive irrigation system, the community was transformed by the discovery of a productive gas field in the 1970s. The community, however, was turned on its head when IBP purchased and expanded an existing meat (beef) packing plant called Lakeside Packers on the edge of the city in 1996 and became its largest employer, with about 2,700 employees. Perhaps the most significant change for Brooks involved the lack of local labour to staff the meat packing plant. The plant had at first attracted labour from British Columbia and Saskatchewan, and later a large influx of Newfoundlanders arrived. The hard labour and piecework demanded of workers meant that turnover was high and that there was a constant demand for new workers. Increasingly, immigrants (and particularly refugees) who could not find employment elsewhere in Canada gravitated to Brooks. At various times there has been a huge sign on the highway advertising the need for hundreds of workers ("to be filled immediately"). Refugees from Sudan and Somalia who had been dispersed by the Canadian government to cities across the country, and who had difficulty obtaining employment in those locations, formed a particularly large group in Brooks. The City of Brooks was transformed from an agricultural town into an immigrant-receiving centre by 2001.[1] Relocating to Brooks often occurred through social networks among these new arrivals, and the cultural clash they experienced with the host community often led to considerable clustering and mutual support networks.

SOCIAL CAPITAL AND MIGRATION ADJUSTMENT

Relationships with other people provide important social capital needed to facilitate migration, but these ties were particularly important after arrival at the destination. There are two kinds of social capital that are relevant to this analysis (Putnam 2000, 22–3). *Bonding social capital* refers to the dense ties that reinforce in-group identities and that are inward-looking, occurring among people sharing similar characteristics. We have already seen how nuclear or extended family members or others from the place of origin play a key role at the destination in helping the migrant establish a sense of community. This type of bonding social capital may also be useful in other forms of migration transitioning as it provides both moral and material aid (e.g., a temporary place to sleep, assistance in job searches). These ties tend to be insulating and to provide comfort in a strange environment. *Bridging social capital*, on the other hand, tends to be more outward looking and involves people who are lacking intimate relationships. This type of social capital assists the migrant in making connections with a neighbour (at origin or destination) or a friend of a friend or the relative of someone with whom he/she works. These are the "weak ties" (Granovetter 1973) that exist in many social circles and that can be very helpful with regard to information diffusion. While bonding social capital was important to some migrants, bridging social capital was important to almost all migrants. Both types of social capital were critical in three areas: housing, employment, and friendship formation.

Social ties were particularly important in the settlement period immediately after arrival, when finding housing was the first task. An Atlantic coast migrant talked about her offer to people back home:

> When I go back there ... what we do offer is free accommodations for a month if they want to come out here. I won't cook for them but they can stay with us. We even have a niece with us now. Anyone who wants to come out here for the opportunity gets a free month. (Newfoundland)

These social ties are not primarily based on reciprocity but on expected behaviour. An Ontario migrant observed:

> This is the first year that we have not had another family member living in our house from back east. We had his nephew, we had my nephew. It's typical here to look after relatives, family, or cousins, you look after them when they come here. (Ontario)

A Nova Scotian illustrates how moving independently still utilizes bridging ties:

> I came out here all by myself ... I told my mom that I was thinking of going out here and she told one of her friends who then called her son in Alberta and he called me. He offered help and advice (Nova Scotia)

Others combined this type of contact with their own innovative ways of obtaining housing:

> As a young adult, I made my own decision ... so I drove out with mom and dad ... But first we stayed with our cousins and everyone was staying on air mattresses all over the floor. (Newfoundland)

> When I got here, I had a friend of a friend who let me stay on his couch for a week. Then I stayed with a relative for a couple of weeks. I borrowed a car from someone from home and took my applications all over the city. I faxed stuff for free from the manpower office. (Manitoba)

Migrants from Ontario reported this housing trajectory:

> At first we lived in a motel where we paid by the week. Then we got an apartment to share for four people. Then we had six of us so we rented a whole house. People were always coming and going so finally we split up and each got their own apartment. After we started a family, we bought a house and now we almost always have someone staying in our basement. (Ontario)

Migrants who entered the province without sponsorship or paid expenses had to be innovative in finding housing, especially in a tight housing market. Bridging ties and bonding ties were both important in providing transitional housing.

Relatives or friends also played a role in helping migrants find work:

> One day I said to my dad, I've had enough of this, I've got to move out West. My dad told my uncle I said that, and he told my cousin, who then told his brother-in-law who lived in Alberta and who I didn't know from a hole in the ground. He happened to have an opening that was tailor-made for me. So I found my job in Alberta in true PEI fashion, which is word-of-mouth and who you know. They just helped you along. (Prince Edward Island)

> My best friend here is a guy who grew up down the street from me back home. There are probably twenty from back home here. I am not in touch with all of them but sometimes I hear about them when I call home. They'll say so-and-so just went out there, or so-and-so just came back. I just heard that there are eight people from back home in Swan Hills working at that waste treatment plant. One guy found a job there and others followed. (New Brunswick)

> I didn't think I really knew anyone here but then my parents gave me the phone number of the cousin of someone from our church back home. His dad had come to Alberta a long time ago. So I called him and he told me about a place that was hiring. That is how I got my job. (Manitoba)

A Prince Edward Island migrant noted that "the fact that there were people here to stay with and to help you get started helped to make coming here possible." This is not to imply that all migrants had such ties, but most did. Weak ties sometimes produced nothing, but in other cases they produced useful tips and suggestions – even if the relationship did not go any further. Sometimes just knowing that there were people from their home region that they could call on if needed played a major role in helping migrants through the adjustment period, whether or not they actually contacted these people.

The interviews suggest that assisting migrants always involved generalized reciprocity, meaning that providing assistance occurred with little sense of mutual obligation. Instead, migrants helped each other because they had gone through a common experience, even if at different times. Providing a place to live or a bed to sleep in during the transitional period was the most common form of assistance offered, but other forms included tips on jobs, permanent housing, and/or contacts. The giver of assistance had no expectation of payback. Thus the experience of migration served as a bridge that linked migrants over time through the provision of mutual assistance, the purpose of which was to facilitate the settlement phase of the migration process.

ADAPTIVE STRATEGIES

The fact that most migrants saw Alberta as an open society did not mean that there were not challenges to living in an unfamiliar environment. For example, drivers with Saskatchewan plates were sometimes self-conscious when they were honked at for driving erratically (which they did because they didn't know where they were going), and assumed that this had happened because of their being from another province. Other migrants picked up the fact that some westerners did not have warm feelings about central Canada or the federal government.

> People would find out that I was from down east. But as soon as they discovered that that did not mean Toronto but the Maritimes, they treated me and responded to me much differently. That's when I started to identify myself as a Maritimer because of the cordial response it received. (New Brunswick)

Francophone Quebec migrants typically feared that their English-language skills would not be adequate or that they would be labelled in some way.

> There are people who say that we would be treated badly because of the referendum and that it is all because of rednecks. But nobody ever came to me and said you are a French speaker and I don't like you or don't want to do business with you or serve you. (Quebec)

Some migrants did experience teasing and were drawn into debates about issues (e.g., the federal government, Quebec separatism, or Maritime culture) relating to their region of origin. East Coasters, in general, thought that Albertans were largely ignorant of their culture, history, and geography, and they sometimes experienced negative stereotyping.

> It's weird to be here and to discover that no one knows anything about your part of the country. And everyone calls you a Newfie just because you are from Atlantic Canada regardless of what province you're from. It's humorous to me but often Maritimers get mad about it. (Nova Scotia)

On occasion interviewees referred to feeling stigmatized and fighting a sense of inferiority, "which is why we are willing to work harder to prove we are more responsible" (Newfoundland) Newfoundlanders were the most likely to express these feelings.

There is, then, some sense of a struggle between insider/outsider status, and this can result in what has been referred to as marginalization. Migrants who experienced this struggle developed strategies to help them adapt. In analyzing the interviews, six adaptive strategies that reflect the pro-social nature of the migration experience in Alberta were uncovered. Not all migrants utilized such strategies: they were more prominent among those who came longer distances and those who strongly identified with their place of origin.

The first adaptive strategy involves residential clustering with people from back home. The need for housing meant that contacts that could help the migrant find housing were crucial, and this enhanced the possibility that people with similar backgrounds might live near each other. If this strategy were to occur, it was most likely to occur at the time of arrival. Perhaps the strongest expression of this kind of strategy occurred among Newfoundlanders. One Newfoundland migrant in Edmonton described his arrival experience this way:

> When four of us got off the plane at the airport, we stood there and said, "What do we do?" We lived in a motel for a month in Leduc, then in a motel in Nisku, then [in] another motel on Calgary Trail for a month until we got established. When you are dropped out of nowhere, you don't have a clue. I had never been off the Island or even across Newfoundland, and then to be here by yourself. But since we got an apartment, there has been at least 100 from back home who have passed through our place. At one time, we had twenty people staying in a two-bedroom apartment. The apartment manager was from Newfoundland and she used to party with us. When you are from Newfoundland, you have an instant group. People can't understand how you would take people you barely know into your house, [but] because they are from Newfoundland, you feel safe to have them there. (Newfoundland)

This was not typical of migrants, but it does point out that living near someone with whom one has connections can assist with the adjustment process. Residential clustering can also occur through choosing to locate in a community in which it is likely that one will find people from back home. Again, Newfoundlanders provide the strongest example of this phenomenon. Migrants from the west coast of Newfoundland were more likely to be found in Fort McMurray, while migrants from the Burin Peninsula were more likely to be found in Brooks:

> My boyfriend moved here so that's why I came. He has lots of family here and then everybody started coming up from our hometown. There are about 1,100 people here from our hometown of 10,800. A whole bunch of us lived together in one house and there were

waiting lists for apartments and the only way we got one was because we knew somebody. Then we would tell our friends and pretty soon there were lots of us living there (Newfoundlander in Brooks)

When I was a kid there were 700 to 800 people in Grand La Pierre. Now there is probably less than 400 to 500 there. I did not complete high school but most people had to move away if they did. I would guess there are at least 100 people here from this small town. Nobody knows how many there are here from the Burin Peninsula, but there might be up to 1,000 – 500 to 600 anyway. Eighty- to 90 percent of the Newfies who are here are from the Burin Peninsula. We try to live near each other as much as possible. (Newfoundlander in Brooks)

Newfoundlanders from the south shore (Irish Loop), Conception Bay, and St John's (townies) were more likely to settle in Edmonton or Calgary. To the extent that this type of concentration is the result of a common destination choice, it is yet another form of residential clustering. Clustering of this nature was more likely to occur when migrants came from a great distance. Fort McMurray was unique in that by far the majority of its population was from somewhere else. As one East Coaster put it:

There are so many Maritimers here that it doesn't even seem foreign. We took Fort McMurray without even firing a shot. And if you are not careful, we'll take over the whole damn province. (Nova Scotia)

Within each destination, clustering sometimes occurred as the result of connections made through housing searches, and, in the big cities, this showed up in clustering in specific areas. Such areas include Mill Woods in Edmonton (see Burrill's [1992, 203] reference to "townie houses")[2] and the clustering of young Saskatchewan adults in apartments in an area known as the Beltline in Calgary:

There are a lot of people from Saskatchewan who live in this area around 17th Ave in perhaps a ten-block radius. These are all low-rise apartments and condos with lots of stores and restaurants and it's really like a village in the city. We know about a couple hundred like ourselves. We like living close to the downtown and close

> to the action. It's a patio lifestyle for young adults. But it is also sort of like living in a small town because you walk everywhere. (Saskatchewan)

Some minor clustering of francophones was discovered in Calgary and Edmonton in particular apartment complexes. Overall, however, this type of clustering was not typical of most migrants, who found housing wherever it was most suitable.

The second type of adaptive strategy involves the creation of home territories. A home territory refers to the transformation of semi-public space into a gathering place for those from a common place of origin.[3] This type of space was likely to be a restaurant/bar or clubhouse, where interaction could regularly occur among those with a common background.[4] But it could also be a "travelling pack" comprised of people who hang out together regularly and who take their sense of community with them anywhere they go. For example, a group comprised of young adults from Stephenville, Newfoundland, who had attended the same high school and postsecondary school hung out together at different places in Fort McMurray. They did not colonize one bar or restaurant as their own but, rather, moved around to different places and carried their sense of community with them.

The sense of home territory being realized at a consistent location and at regular times was facilitated by the Maritime Reunion Association in Calgary and the Newfoundland Club in Fort McMurray, who set up parties and pub nights that provided informal activity and a sense of belonging. Much more typical was the identification of privately owned restaurant/bars as hangouts for people from a particular region of origin. Restaurants/bars such as Da Rock, Mudders, Screech and Schooner, Skipper Billy's, and the Atlantic Trap and Gill were favourite hangouts for Maritimers – places where they could socialize and listen to East Coast music. A wine bar in Calgary called The Newt became a regular Wednesday-night meeting place for Quebecers and other francophones in Calgary, although it was used by other patrons as well. A restaurant owned and run by a Newfoundlander in Fort McMurray served Newfoundland favourites, and this attracted East Coasters. Several bars in Calgary became known as Saskatchewan meeting places:

> I went to this local pub called Classic Jack's and half of the people in there were from Saskatoon. It is a pretty diverse group that goes there, but it is true that there are three or four groups from Saskatoon that go there. (Saskatchewan)

Some of these bars provided food and drink in a down home atmosphere and often featured guest entertainers from the region of origin – something that always drew a large crowd. Others just became regular stops on particular nights for people who shared a common region of origin. There were reports of smaller groups that got together on a quasi-regular basis at a particular hangout for a short period of time but then drifted apart.

Another version of the "travelling packs" involved people from home who would get together on weekends for leisure pursuits. Hikes, picnics, skiing, or car trips to tourist spots in the area with others from one's home region were frequently reported.

The third adaptive strategy involves patronizing retail establishments that cater to in-migrants. The Newfoundland Store in Calgary brought in specialty goods from home (e.g., Purity products, salt beef, salt pork), and its existence assuaged the sense of social distance Newfoundlanders felt in a new province. Other stores, such as a local IGA in the Mill Woods section of Edmonton, established a special section of Newfoundland products to accommodate the demands of new arrivals. The arrival of a fast-food chicken franchise (Mary Brown's) from Newfoundland, first in Fort McMurray and then in other Alberta cities, was also a clear indication of Alberta's anticipation of a migrant market that could serve as a base that could then be expanded to local patrons. Special events such as the Calgary Stampede made a point of including East Coast artists on one of its performance stages. In short, numerous efforts were made to ensure that new arrivals would feel connected in Alberta. Note, however, that most of these special efforts were directed to people who brought to the province a strong regional home identity: these people were primarily from the East Coast and Saskatchewan (and, to a lesser extent, Quebec). No evidence was found of similar products and events being directed to migrants from Ontario or British Columbia.

The fourth adaptive strategy involves the creation of voluntary organizations in which migrants could socialize with those from back home. Clubs and organizations played an important role in generating in-group activity among migrants. While it was impossible to develop a detailed inventory of such organizations, there were some that had a particularly high profile. For example, throughout the year, the Saskatchewan Social Club in Calgary organized many events (e.g., cabarets, pub crawls, and games) that provided an opportunity for people from Saskatchewan to socialize with one another:[5]

> As soon as you meet someone from Saskatchewan you just have to ask where they are from because everybody knows everybody. The club jump-starts your friendship building. It is a stepping stone to building friends. (Saskatchewan)

At least two summer picnics called Saskatchewan Communities Reunions were held near Calgary, with "flying banners" of every Saskatchewan community represented. The biggest rallying point, however, were the visits of the Saskatchewan Roughriders football team to the city to play the Calgary Stampeders. These games were always guaranteed sellouts. Pre-game and post-game partying, and travelling to the stadium by bus from party headquarters, provided unlimited opportunity to express loyalty to Saskatchewan and to sustain home-town feelings. Dressing in green and sharing "Rider Pride" became hugely symbolic of fidelity to one's province of origin.

Traditionally, religious organizations have played an important role in supporting interaction among international migrants. There was little evidence of such organizations having played a similar role among origin group migrants to Alberta, with one exception.[6] The Salvation Army is a particularly strong church in Newfoundland. About one-third of one local suburban Salvation Army church in Calgary was composed of people with a Newfoundland background, and a Fort McMurray church also had numerous Newfoundlanders in attendance (although not to the degree that might be expected). Most churches found that migrants were young, had other options, were busy becoming economically independent, and were uncertain about putting down roots in Alberta. Young adults are less likely than are other age cohorts to participate in religious organizations. As one Salvation Army pastor described it, when Newfoundlanders came with their parents, it was the parents and older people who were more likely to get involved in the organizational activities of the church: "Young people were more enamoured with the multitude of options that they had here which they did not have in the outport communities." He noted that "if all Newfoundlanders who migrated here went to church, we would have a big crowd." However, since Newfoundlanders tend to stay with the religion into which they are born, "[they] show up at the church here when we least expect it" and whenever there is something special being offered, like a jig's dinner or the celebration of a birth. According to the pastor, Newfoundlanders come "out of the woodwork" then because they know the church has a special tie with them.

Another example of how internal migrants cluster around a specific religious organization may be found in the case of francophones and the French Roman Catholic church:

> Our support network here is all francophone. We went to the French church and it started from there and people introduced us to others. After church we go for coffee and then meet other people and from there developed a circle of friends. We socialize with those friends, go camping on weekends, and see each other regularly. And they are all francophones. I had no idea I would find francophones here. I thought we would be the only ones to speak French in Calgary. And there are more francophones coming all the time. I even got my job through meeting people at church. (Quebec)

Religious organizations can play an important role in this kind of clustering if the migrants speak a language that differs from that spoken by most residents of the host province. Since language was not an issue for most internal migrants, there was little to propel this type of clustering. Instead, migrants made choices about religious involvement in the same ways as did members of the host society.

Migrants from Manitoba were much less organized than were migrants from other places, though again football games often became rallying points ("I loved being a Bomber fan in Calgary because it gave us a reason to get together"), and occasional activities were organized (e.g., the Brandon Boys Golf Tournament). Manitobans, however, did have a unique cultural form of group interaction known as the Saturday "Manitoba Social." Derived from Ukrainian culture, the idea was to throw a party for an engaged couple; serve rye bread, sausage, and cheese; engage in circle dancing; and take up a collection in order to help the couple pay for wedding expenses. The Manitoba Social often involved selling tickets and winning door prizes and was easily transformed from a wedding celebration into a Saturday night get-together for former Manitobans, whatever the occasion might be. Its very name served as a rallying point for ex-Manitobans. For people from Manitoba who understood this tradition, the Manitoba Social provided an opportunity to meet with people from home.

I have already referred to a formal organization called the Maritime Reunion Association (MRA). This organization had its own building, an older two-story house near the centre of Calgary. The MRA was initially founded in the first wave of in-migration in the early 1980s, when plans for a lobster feed for 1,200 people in a local arena required a special liquor permit (Burrill 1992, 199–204). This event created the momentum that eventually led to the acquisition of the house as a gathering place for people from the East Coast. It also established a tradition that later became commonplace: that of ignoring the provincial differences between people from the Atlantic provinces and developing a sense of camaraderie through the use of the all-inclusive term "East Coasters." However, the MRA played no other role for in-migrants, limiting itself to socializing and offering the potential to make connections through partying. As a result, it had no structure to keep it going over time, and, when East Coasters found other outlets for socializing, the organization withered and eventually died early in the twenty-first century. In Fort McMurray, the Newfoundlanders Club was very active in its space in a strip mall, which included a dining-room serving Newfoundland specialties and featuring visiting Newfoundland bands.[7] Many of these organizations had a loose concept of membership and existed only to plan occasional events. For example, the Prince Edward Islanders Club, or the Friends of the University of Prince Edward Island (UPEI) met only once a year. One of the attractions of the gathering involved meeting other islanders who were in Alberta. It was clear, though, that connecting with people from home was not dependent on such organizations and, to the extent that in-migrants sought such connections, formal organizations were not necessary.

It should be noted that most migrants did not feel the need to establish special organizations to cater to people from their place of origin.[8] Most joined existing organizations and got involved in activities that helped them to integrate into the host community. Many migrants reported joining churches, sport groups, hobby clubs, and fraternal organizations as a way of meeting new people and feeling part of the community. On the other hand, many also reported that settling in took far too much energy and time to engage in joining behaviour of any kind.

The fifth adaptive strategy involves the workplace as a place where friendship formation begins. In fact, other than children, who facilitated friendship formation among migrants who shared childcare activities, the workplace was the single most important facilitator of new friendships:

> There is a lot more socializing through work here then in Ottawa. The workplace was a great way to meet people. And the demographics here of young people supports that 90 percent of the people I know are not from Alberta and they are really open to get to know you. (Ontario)

A British Columbia migrant noted that he "had never been one to pal around with people I work with, but here I have made a lot of friends through work." In some workplaces, the employment of people from the same region of origin helped to facilitate this kind of interaction:

> Being with people from Manitoba is not something we search for but it just happens. In my training group at work, it turned out that three of us were from Winnipeg, and when we found out we were all from Winnipeg, we made Winnipeg jokes – like we are all cheap and use coupons in restaurants, and we all sat together and it was kind of like a bonding thing. And we made fun of where we grew up. One fellow was from Transcona, and we said it was a different planet. (Manitoba)

A Saskatchewan migrant also pointed out that the workplace provided a place to meet other migrants:

> In our company, there are about twenty-five from Saskatchewan out of a total of 180 employees. A lot of my other friends at work are from Manitoba. The Calgary people already have their social life, so those of us from elsewhere tend to hang out together. And if they are from Saskatchewan, you can always find something in common. (Saskatchewan)

Often employers who needed to hire more people and who had had a good experience with a migrant from a particular place would deliberately seek to hire others from the same region. Current migrant employees were sometimes asked to recruit other people from back home.

The sixth adaptive strategy involves informal gatherings in homes. These gatherings were extremely important with regard to socializing with others from home. A unique example follows:

> We pretty well hang out with just Newfoundlanders. On the weekends we just have everybody over and there are usually ten to twelve here. We are all from CBS [Conception Bay South], and having house parties is pretty regular. Sometimes we go out somewhere but we don't have to. Newfoundlanders love to just relax together in our houses. Sometimes someone will cook a jig's dinner on Sundays. The supermarkets are starting to carry Newfoundland products now, like Millwoods IGA. We can buy Black Horse and Blue

> Star – both Newfoundland beers here. I think they are trying to accommodate us here. (Newfoundland)

Large Newfoundlander house parties (sixty to eighty people) were often reported in Fort McMurray. One Newfoundland family in Brooks reported this kind of family socializing on a daily basis:

> When we have a family get-together here, we are eighteen all told. They are all cousins and nieces and nephews. Every evening we visit with family. Like I might go to the gym to work out but then I go to visit a niece or nephew. Our nephew is the first born Albertan in our family. (Newfoundland)

Holidays served as a good opportunity for migrants to socialize. Being away from home, migrants were often conscious that many established residents had family close by or an established network of friends with which to celebrate the occasion. In contrast, migrants had each other. For example, in Calgary, thirty to forty people from Inverness County, Nova Scotia, always had turkey dinner together at Thanksgiving. Informal socializing in homes with other expatriates could occur at any time, but holidays were often an especially good time to seek others from one's place of origin.

Francophone migrants had additional reasons for wanting to socialize with other francophones:

> My Quebec friends here are so important that if they had not been here when I needed them, I would have moved back. They are my real friends ... When I wanted to find French friends, I went to the organized events but now we just get together informally. When I needed to speak French, I went there and that was how groups sort of formed. (Quebec)

One interesting variation in the role of the home in facilitating interaction was expressed by a migrant from Manitoba:

> I moved into a new neighbourhood and it was easy to meet new people. If you move into an older neighbourhood, people are more set in their ways. There are so many new neighbourhoods here that it seems more welcoming. Everyone is new here and they are all in the same boat. (Manitoba)

Newly built suburbs in the two rapidly expanding Alberta cities of Calgary and Edmonton served as locations for considerable socializing among young families, who were made more aware than ever that they were not the only new residents in Alberta.

LACK OF SOCIAL CONNECTEDNESS

It is important to acknowledge that not all migrants were able to establish satisfactory social ties in Alberta. The evidence is fairly overwhelming that migrants who lacked social ties at the destination were the most likely to struggle and to be unhappy. Migrating independently and being part of a migration stream did not mean that people were able to establish social connectedness. The lack of family and friends was a particular issue for some people, making days like Christmas particularly troubling: "I spent my first Christmas here all alone and I remember waking up and planning when I was going to go back to Ontario." A British Columbia migrant commented:

> It has been hard to come here alone but I don't regret it. You have to have friends to get friends and that has been hard not to have family to turn to. But when you don't know anybody you spend a lot of time with people you can tolerate rather than people you actually connect with. It's getting better.

A Quebecer noted, "It has taken me about three years to create a circle of friends and acquaintances. The first year and a half was rough." Migrants talked about going to gyms, bars, laundromats, and even fast-food restaurants to meet people. The age group that had the most difficulty consisted of older people who were not in the labour force. Women over fifty who were essentially trailing their husband, and seniors who had relocated to Alberta because their children were now here, were especially vulnerable in that respect. Elderly persons who had lost their spouse and who were transplanted so that they could be near their children were particularly isolated as the entire family was busy with their activities. Relocation was often hard for this group of people. On the other hand, older couples who were still able to get involved in community activities were somewhat happier, even though they also lamented the losses that went with the move. It seems that relocating to be with children solved one set of problems only to create another.

Earlier, I indicated that out-migration from the community of origin was, in some instances, prompted by the desire to escape the clutches of family and friends. But the reverse was true as well, and often people back home did not understand the full consequences of relocation for the migrant.

> People considered it normal for young people to leave. In fact, they almost look up to us for that. They said, "Wow – you're living this fancy life out here near the mountains and with lots of money and low taxes." And [they think] that we are whooping it up out here with a great life. But the reality of it is that all we have out here is our jobs – we have no family and no support system. So prosperity out here has come at a very high price. (Ontario)

It was rare for migrants to have no contacts at all among themselves. What was more typical was not having the right social relationships and missing home. But there was considerable variation with regard to the degree to which migrants needed or utilized contacts with people from home. What is striking, however, is the role that the workplace played in friendship formation at the destination.

CONCLUSION

Migrants were clearly not loners, even though they may have migrated independently. They all learned how to mobilize social capital in the place of origin as well as at the destination in order to facilitate a successful adjustment. The easiest way to mobilize social capital was to utilize contacts from home. These contacts were available as the result of a migration stream that had existed for many years. Various adaptive strategies were used, some of which were based on the migration stream, others of which involved embracing existing organizations and activities within the community. The place of employment was a particularly effective place in which to build social capital both with people from the place of origin and with other new migrants. Perhaps signalling the partial integration that occurred at this early stage of arrival, some migrants continued to use connections with others from their place of origin in order to successfully adapt to their new life in Alberta. Other migrants attempted to blend in as quickly as possible, did not feel disadvantaged as new migrants, and could easily balance their interstitial position between origin and destination.

11

Women and Migration

Somewhat unexpectedly, as the research proceeded, it became clear that gender played an interesting role in internal migration and that this role needed to be explored.[1] Previous research on women and internal family migration has tended to be male-focused and, therefore, concludes that women usually passively follow their male partners. When we focus on the independent (unsponsored) migrant rather than on the corporate migrant, it becomes apparent that all women, and partnered women[2] in particular, have a sense of control over the migration process and, therefore, initiate and benefit from it. While some women may follow men, it is also possible that they may have their own labor force interests at the destination. When women play an active role in migration decision making, this contributes to greater satisfaction with relocation.

When analysts discovered that migration is not gender-neutral behaviour but, rather, a process that reflects gendered family relationships, the door was opened to assessing migration as an interpersonal and interactional phenomenon. The implication was that the relationship between migrants themselves must become part of the migration investigation. It was not that relationships in migrant families had been previously ignored but, rather, that women were assumed to be followers of male providers (Jacobsen and Levin 2000; Nivalainen 2004). There is reason to suspect that things have changed and that women play a different kind of role than they did in the past – especially when their migration is unsponsored. This analysis focus on partnered women, although occasional comparisons are made with single women who are migrants.

THE ROLE OF WOMEN IN FAMILY MIGRATION

Relationships traditionally received less attention in the migration process due to the assumption that, when women migrated with men, they did so as "followers" of men or "in association" with them (Bielby and Bielby 1992; Kanaiaupuni 2000). Gender was largely ignored as women were subsumed under the category "family migration" (Boyd 1989) and were treated more as migrant's wives than as female migrants in their own right (Brettell and Simon 1986). The patriarchal model of gender/family relations assumed that the true migrant was a male who was in search of economic betterment. This model placed women in the position of accompanying family (Houstoun, Kramer, and Barrett 1984). Such an economic perspective was reflected in Mincer's (1978) pioneering study, which introduced the concept of the "tied partner" who moved because the relocation was assessed in terms of the net economic benefit accruing to the family as the result of the male partner's earnings. Since Mincer's work, there has been much research that has pointed out that male-induced migration disadvantages women through the acceptance of patriarchal gender norms in family relations (Bonney and Love 1991; Halfacree 1995).

Much of the thinking about couple relationships in internal migration has been shaped by company-paid relocation. Corporate employers promise upward mobility, increased pay, and higher job status (usually to their male employees) but with little regard for families (Pinder 1989). The impact on women of being tied movers results in a sense of powerlessness that suggests that the move was either forced on them or, at best, was being made only reluctantly due to acquiescence to traditional roles. Hendershott (1995), for example, argues that male-induced moving for work produces harmful effects on women, such as psychological dysfunction. She refers to this as the "spousal mobility syndrome." Victimized by the myth that homemakers are transportable, married wives and mothers were shown to bear the emotional and social costs of the move, which were often traumatic (Ammons, Nelson, and Wodarski 1982; Leon and Dzuegielewski 1999).

However, with the growth of female participation in the labor force, and, particularly, the presence of women in full-time jobs and professional work, has come the growth of dual income or dual career couples/families. Among the outcomes that have been studied are commuter marriages, married women who are themselves corporate relocatees, and the development of more egalitarian attitudes towards marriage. At least some of the negative migration effects for women that have been identified in the past might have been due to the "trailing mother" with young children rather than simply to "the trailing wife" (Bailey and Cooke 1998; Cooke 2001). Women now may forego or delay childbearing, have fewer (or no) children, or may themselves have labour force interests. These developments suggest that women may no longer be merely victims, accessories, passive facilitators, or reluctant movers, being seen merely as adjuncts to the labor force. On the contrary, partnered women may have their own labor force interests at the destination, and this may lead them to be active decision makers in a move that they can view as positive.

ISSUES IN ANALYZING WOMEN'S ROLE IN MIGRATION

For persons in relationships, migration must contain at least some elements of negotiation. Jacobsen and Levin (2000) suggest that, in spite of the fact that a higher-earning spouse may have a bargaining advantage, migration is best represented as "intrahousehold bargaining." Similar to other decisions pertaining to work/family roles, migration reveals patterns of power in marital relationships (Zvonkovic, Greaves, Schmiege, and Hall 1996). Power in these instances is usually invisible and involves acquiescence to gender roles (e.g., a belief in the preeminence of a husband's career or acceptance of the rationality of corporate decision making). However, what may emerge as "apparent consensus" (Komter 1989, 209) between persons negotiating relocation may actually conceal underlying contention. For example, Whitaker (2005) discovered that women in husband-induced corporate-paid moves tended to view the decision process as consensual because they decided not to refuse to move, even though they did not agree with the decision to do so and were unhappy. So the question becomes: are decisions about migration that are made independently different from decisions about migration that are employer-induced?

The key difference between a sponsored move and an independent move is that, in the latter, the migrant has a greater sense of control. Bearing all the costs and risks of relocation in the face of an uncertain outcome places the responsibility for the move on the shoulders of the migrant, who simultaneously feels both vulnerable and in charge. The key, then, is control, which suggests that migration can be an assertive act.

The interactional nature of migration, particularly with regard to the role played by women, is often obscured by the use of survey or aggregate data in panel studies, which understand gender as a statistical category (Pedraza 1991; Abdo 1997). The use of quantitative data hides the motivations and meanings of migration behaviour that remains hidden and does not consider the impact of interpersonal relationships (Boyle, Cooke, Halfacree, and Smith 2001). If the goal is to understand how women migrants perceive their behaviour, then we need to conduct qualitative interviews. This will enable us to appreciate that migration involves a complex process of negotiation – a process that is not reducible to economic costs and benefits (Jobes, Stinner, and Wardwell 1992).

Gender roles had not been a primary focus of Phase 1 of this study, but the data gathered suggested interesting and unanticipated interpersonal dynamics on the part of women migrants. Women participants were recontacted by telephone for a supplementary interview that explicitly focused on gender issues and migration. Many first phase participants had moved and could no longer be found, but we did interview forty women. Married women were somewhat less likely to have moved since the first interview and, therefore, are more strongly represented in the subsample than are single women. The data presented are based on information received from all women who participated in Phase 1 of the study plus information received in supplementary interviews with a subsample of forty.[3] The focus is primarily on partnered women, but the experience of single women is also included when relevant.

MIGRATION AS RELATIONSHIP CHANGE

For almost all women in the study, whether partnered or single, and regardless of age, migration was not just about employment and income but also about changed relationships. Migration was intimately tied to relationships in the region of origin as well as at the destination. Becoming a migrant changed the way women understood themselves, and this, in turn, affected their relationships with others. Very seldom were relationship changes expressed in a non-emotional way. Many expressed concerns about leaving parents or an elderly mother (or feeling they could now leave because a parent had died). Some said that their family in the place of origin had made them feel that they had betrayed or abandoned them by moving. Others felt they needed to distance themselves from their parents, in-laws, or old friendship networks. Relocation had its painful aspects and created many persisting dilemmas, which, in turn, were often reconciled by promising eventually to return.

Young adult women expressed the need for change as something consistent with coming of age.

> There comes a time in your life when you have to go away and not depend on your family. I needed time to develop me. Yes, I needed a good job but that was not ultimately why I left. It was time to go and be changed. (Ontario)

Some claimed that their family supported their migration as an act of independence: "I was very close to my family, but it was time to break from that mould, and they encouraged me to make a new life for myself" (Nova Scotia). The fact that migration was not just a job search but something deeper was expressed as follows:

> It has been important for us to come here as a couple because we have been able to discover ourselves apart from our family. I have learned and grown so much about who I am. (British Columbia)

A 25-year-old young woman from Saskatchewan said that migration had been a liberating experience:

> Leaving my home province has unleashed a beast in me because I have experienced new things. Because of that I am even more willing to venture out even further. Who knows where I will go next?

A somewhat older but single woman said:

> I thought about leaving for about a year and I felt I needed a change in my environment. I felt I was stagnating. I had been around the same people for so long, and if I changed my surroundings, that would be the impetus to make some decisions. I needed to make a big change. I was tired of my city and I wanted different opportunities. (Ontario)

Two other women made these observations:

> Most people at home were caught in a rut and couldn't leave, so we decided to leave before that happened to us ... It was just time to experience something new. We had outgrown our community. (Nova Scotia)

> We needed a new start. We thought moving would do that.

Those who did not have such a positive attitude towards relocating probably did not migrate or had already returned home. One retired woman who moved to Alberta because her daughter was there saw the relocation as an opportunity to enhance the mother-daughter relationship rather as an event that resulted in loss of relationships at home.

The evidence noted above illustrates that there were many non-economic relationship-related reasons for migration that moved beyond the typical explanation of migration for work. Push factors, which create what Mincer (1978, 759) calls "locational disequilibrium," included relationship changes such as those involved in graduating, getting married, divorcing or breaking an engagement, being laid off or being underemployed, and so on. Pull factors were also related to relationships (e.g., having contact with people at the destination who offered assistance, the exciting prospect of developing relationships with new people). The point is that migration was always interpreted in the context of relationship change, and these changes were typically viewed more positively than negatively.

MIGRATION AS AN EMPOWERMENT PROCESS

In spite of the emotional burden of migrating, it was far more typical for women to talk about how relocating was a growing experience and led to intense self-development. A woman from the Atlantic provinces observed her own experience this way:

> I drove across the country by myself. When I got here I stayed at a friend's place but I was still by myself. My car had 300,000 kilometres on it and was held together by duct tape. I looked around and all of a sudden I was petrified. I realized that my life was going to start now. I called a friend and she just said, "You drove across the country by yourself, and now you're afraid to leave your apartment?" It really was empowering that I did it all by myself. (Newfoundland)

The initiative and assertiveness demanded by relocating and re-establishing oneself often led to the development of new skills. Partnered women talked about the planning, coordination, and budgeting required for such a move as well as the need to speak to strangers and to deal with bureaucracies, all of which required a certain boldness. The result of this kind of activity was to produce greater confidence in their ability to navigate society in order to obtain the ends they desired. Typical statements included these from two women in their twenties: "I seek out new opportunities more as the result of moving here" (Nova Scotia) or "I'm a stronger person because I am more independent" (Quebec). While many struggled with not being near family, others talked of the need for more distance and independence and how the process of migration supported the development of a more independent self.

THE ROLE OF WORK AND CAREER IN FEMALE MIGRATION

In contrast to women who were compelled to move because of their husbands' work, the most consistent finding was that, with the exception of retired women, about 80 percent of the women viewed migration as a mechanism for personal improvement, if not social mobility, through new employment options. Such a finding held true for all women regardless of marital status, and even stay-at-home mothers were pleased to know that work opportunities were there if they wanted them. Such perceptions were rooted in feelings of blocked mobility in the region of origin, and relocation offered a sense of hope for the future. Women with postsecondary education, in particular, talked about moving "to advance my career," "to find a job in my field," "to do what was best for me professionally." Almost one-half of the study participants lamented the fact that they were unhappy with their jobs at origin because there was "no room to move up and that was not what [they] had gone to school for." The dissatisfaction with their former employment often had to do with its not being a "real job," meaning that it either did not have enough hours or (more likely) that it was not a job upon which a career could be built. One married professional woman stated:

> I was in a very low-paying job that was related to my field but was more technician's work, so it was level one with no place to go and very low pay. I was working in a position that was well below what I was qualified to do ... I had been applying for professional positions that were related to my background for about four years with no success. (New Brunswick)

Women often expressed frustration with the fact that positions in their field were occupied with people who were not retiring fast enough. A 30-year-old woman expressed her concern in these terms:

> My goal was to be a probation officer. There were three probation officers in my town and they'll be there forever till they drop so there was no chance. Every profession back home, the people who have been there for twenty years will be there for another twenty

> years, and the chances of you getting in there with them was impossible. (Nova Scotia)

Blocked mobility, then, seemed to be a major factor in the decision to move.

Employment itself was not the issue but, rather, significant work for which they had received training, or for which they had a keen interest, or that was important to their self-identity. Migration was necessary in order to "get ahead." With regard to the region of origin, the perception was that "if you stayed, you could only go so far," or "if you wanted work at home, you needed experience, so you go away to get experience in your field." A 50-year-old woman noted:

> We sold everything and moved out here. It was a big decision to leave the family behind. But there were no opportunities for ME there. (Ontariy)

Another woman said:

> He wanted to move so I began to look into what there was for me there. That is when I came to accept the idea when I could see how I could benefit too. (Quebec)

Clearly, women evaluated the success of the relocation in terms of their own career interests.

Employment was critical to women's evaluation of migration. They talked about how fast they found work or how they started at the bottom and worked up, moving from one job to another. A 40-year-old woman said:

> Coming to Alberta was a very happy time for us because I had a job and he had a job after too much unemployment and uncertainty. (Newfoundland)

Notice that this woman's job was just as important as was her partner's job: "We considered going back home but there was only a job for one of us." Women believed that relocating to a region that had an expanding economy was a very affirming thing to do. One woman in her late twenties, who had had eight jobs in five years in Alberta, claimed that each one was better than the next. She noted: "The job situation here really makes you feel wanted, and it gives you a sense of confidence" (Saskatchewan). At the same time as partnered women felt that the move had a satisfactory employment outcome for them, they still believed that the male partner's employment was critical in the relocation. As one woman in her thirties noted: "I was happy to come and was unemployed for only three weeks. But it would be laughable to think that we moved just for my job" (Ontario). Clearly, partnered women were under no illusions that the interests of their male partners could be ignored.

MIGRATION AS A PROCESS OF NEGOTIATION

In most cases, the actual decision to migrate required time to germinate. Many women reported thinking about relocation for over a year or more. Some women were very systematic with regard to making their decision, using newspapers, libraries, and the internet to check economic conditions and job ads at the destination; others were more influenced by social contacts.

For partnered women especially, migration was almost never an impulsive decision. Occasionally, a woman would express surprise that her male partner suddenly mentioned that they should leave, but typically such a decision was made in the context of repeated discussions. Underemployment was almost always a catalyst in these discussions. Many expressed feelings of depression regarding their circumstances, and this led the couple to conclude that a change was necessary ("We had no choice. We had to move"). A 43-year-old woman stated:

> I followed him because there was not work for him at home. I had a job as a legal secretary but it was not secure so I followed him. It took six months to make up my mind but then I felt comfortable with it. And I am happy with my job here. (Nova Scotia)

These women almost always expressed their acceptance of the decision to move, maintaining that their interests and concerns had been considered.

Many women felt that they had skills that were easily transferable, and this helped them accept the implications of their partners' feelings about the move. A 27-year-old rationalized her role in the decision to move as follows:

> In my field, I can find work anywhere. I had a job and was quite happy, but my husband could not find work. Things were going OK

> for me but I couldn't look at just me. I had to look at the two of us. I saw it as an opportunity for us to grow together. (New Brunswick)

Some women accepted the fact that they might soon be leaving the labour market to have children and used that as a rationale for why their partners' interests had to be considered first. But there was always the idea that the right destination should be chosen so that, if the woman wanted to work later, there would be opportunities.

Women whose husbands were in construction explicitly came under the category of women who moved because their husbands moved. Construction worker families were accustomed to moving to where there was construction. Women who were part of these male-initiated moves almost always accepted it in what they considered to be the interests of the family. A 42-year-old woman said:

> I moved here because my husband moved here. I lost my career but it was a step up for my husband so it was better for all of us. (British Columbia)

Or, to put it another way, women would consider the impact of their husbands' unhappiness on their own happiness, and this would convince them to move: "I had a good job that I really enjoyed but he was so unhappy that it made me unhappy" (Manitoba). Clearly, women in relationships with men had to consider the interests of those with whom they were partnered and had to assess how relocation would affect their relationship.

What is particularly important is that these illustrations indicate not just that partnered women felt the need to compromise but also that this compromise meant that both parties were active in the labour force:

> I had a job but my husband didn't. So I figured he had a right to work too. We picked Alberta because we both thought we would be able to find good jobs. Ironically, my husband got a job right away, but I had trouble. (Ontario)

Unsponsored women migrants were much more likely than were partnered women in sponsored moves to expect the decision to relocate to be beneficial in terms of their own employment.

When asked who initiated the idea of moving, most women could identify who did so, but succeeding discussions involved shifting positions. A 34-year-old woman provides the best illustration of this type of dialogue:

> He initiated the idea of moving, but wasn't going unless I agreed. We talked for a year or so about it, but we put it off until the conditions were right, until everything fell into place. Then several things happened, and I ended up being the one who felt most strongly about leaving. (Quebec)

One woman admitted that she was the one who wanted to move and that, after discussing it over a long period of time, "he eventually went along with it" (Nova Scotia).

In many cases, it was not so much who proposed the idea of relocation as what transpired over the gestation period that was of importance. A woman noted that it was mainly her husband's idea to relocate and that, during the two years that they considered the option, she lost her job, which convinced her that moving was necessary even though it would be very hard for her:

> We worked like a team. He went ahead and bought the new house and I stayed behind and sold the old house and packed up. I think, though, that I had to deal with more of the emotional things about leaving because he had already moved on. (British Columbia)

Women whose husbands relocated first often expressed such feelings (Magdol 2002). In general, though, who initiated the idea of relocating was not important because, after months of consideration, the other partner almost always worked through how her or his own employment interests would be addressed.

MIGRATION: THE ISSUE OF INFLUENCE AND POWER

Information gleaned in Phase 1 of the study suggested that the question of who initiated the idea of migration was more significant than had been anticipated. Consequently, a more specific question was asked in the second interview, and the results were surprising. Of the forty women interviewed, twenty-eight were classified as either married or in a serious relationship. Fully 46 percent (13) of those partnered women felt that they had been the primary influence in the move, 25 percent (7) felt the decision was entirely joint, and only 29 percent (8) felt that the male had been the dominant force in the move. Among these respondents, overall, women felt quite powerful. This is reflected in the following statements: "He initiated the idea of moving but, in the end, I felt most strongly about it" (Nova Scotia); "I initiated the move. He didn't come happily" (Ontario); "He never would have elected to come here by himself, but when I said I was moving, he agreed to come along easily" (Saskatchewan); and, "We both really wanted to do it and worked out the details together" (Prince Edward Island).

Instead of being the drag in migration, women were often the initiators. When women played that role, their ability to be assertive within their dyadic bond was clear. To be sure, some women who wanted to move were less assertive, such as a 45-year-old woman who exclaimed: "I would have left twenty years earlier but my husband didn't want to leave. He finally felt forced out because of the economy" (Nova Scotia). However, at the other end of the assertiveness continuum, one woman noted: "In our relationship, I am the one who instigates things" (Newfoundland). Boyfriends sometimes followed girlfriends who migrated with girlfriends. One young woman recounted her own experience by noting:

> My boyfriend was more sentimental about not going and preferred to stay. But I said, "come on, are you going or am I going by myself?" (Newfoundland)

A 29-year-old woman pointed out that, because she was so committed to relocating, her seven-year relationship with a man ended. A number of other single women indicated that moving either ended a relationship or followed the breakup of a relationship. As one woman in her twenties noted about her boyfriend:

> Basically it was my idea to move as I knew that I could do better financially. But I am also more outgoing and adventurous. It was either he came with me or it was over. I would have gone no matter what. (Ontario)

Within partnered relationships, some women played a dominant role, even to the point of initiating the move.

ASSESSING THE OUTCOME OF MIGRATION: CONTROL

For most women, the assessment of the decision to migrate was intimately related to the extent to which they had some control over the decision. All single women felt that they had control, whereas those who were partnered had to deal with the dynamics of their relationships. The data unequivocally demonstrate that, for partnered women, the overall assessment of the move is much more likely to be positive if they were actively part of the decision-making process. In contrast, one woman who did not have that control expressed remorse:

> I have been here for six months and I may be here for twenty years, but I don't want to be. I try to keep as positive as I can and experience as much as I can. (Newfoundland)

Resignation and unhappiness was strongest when women felt that they did not have any choice in the migration:

> My husband came out to work and I thought I was just coming for a visit and when it wasn't happening that way, I cried a lot. I will never call this "home" because we built our dream home back there and it is waiting for us. Whenever I buy anything here, I always imagine how it will look in our house back home. (Newfoundland)

One of the key symbols of tension was the home that partnered women, in particular, may have reluctantly left behind. Such attachments almost always suggested a negative assessment of the migration. On the other hand, when partnered women viewed their migration more positively, it was because they felt that they had made a decision to establish a new home at the destination: "I feel this is home now because we are building a new house and a baby is on the way" (Manitoba).

In contrast to corporate-sponsored migration, which comes with many forms of assistance to partnered women, unsponsored migration required initiative, and this contributed to the sense of control women experienced. Typical are references to enhanced personal/couple skills:

> This had to be a team effort because everything depended on the two of us. (Quebec)

> You can't do things as you always did and that forces you to be persistent and figure things out for yourself. He needed me and I needed him or it would not have worked. (New Brunswick)

A successful migration was considered a challenge, and it required constructive energy.

There is no question that the small number (18 percent) of women who only moved because their husbands wanted to move were the least satisfied. Negative feelings were often repressed in order to support husbands or to rationalize the move in terms of what was in the best interests of the family. Women who had strong attachments to parents or grandparents, or to children or grandchildren back home, would comment "my heart is not here" or "back there is where my heart is and that is where I want to be." When husbands/boyfriends were working long hours and overemphasized the acquisition of money, the gulf between the emotional aspects of life and the monetary benefits of the move, created tensions in relationships, were accentuated. Regardless of marital status, from time to time the social costs of separation from family and friends and the emphasis on "getting ahead" economically led to expressions of emotional ambivalence about the move among all women.

CONCLUSION

The use of qualitative interviews allowed us to understand the dynamics of migration decision making from the perspective of partnered women. In doing so, it helps us move the debate about the gendered consequences of migration beyond income and labour market outcomes (Marsden and Tepperman 1985; Morrison and Lichter 1988). At the same time, a few limitations should be acknowledged. The emphasis in this chapter has been on hearing the voices of women in relation to the migration process. This, obviously, leaves out the men. It is also possible that those who viewed their migration more positively were overrepresented. Women who had more negative outcomes or who felt trapped by the move and did not adjust may have either returned to the place of origin or not participated in the study. There were also few families with older children in the sample. This is unfortunate, as their presence would have added another level of complexity to the evaluation of decision-making processes and outcomes. The experiences of ethnically diverse groups and all social classes were also omitted from the study design.

Our discussion, however, does advance our understanding of the role that partnered women play in domestic migration. By focusing on the independent mover, women who initiate and benefit from migration are easily identified. The results challenge the assumption that women are always losers or subordinates in internal migration (Jacobsen and Levin 2000). They are also a corrective to a previous study done on migrants to Alberta, which suggested that three-quarters of women migrants followed their spouses and played a subsidiary role in the husbands' decision to migrate (Shihadeh 1991). Our results are consistent with findings elsewhere (Jacobsen and Levin, 1997) that indicate that single women can be major gainers from migration; however, our results broaden these findings to include partnered women who benefited from migration as individuals. The fact that 88 percent of the women who participated in the second interview considered the move to be positive from a personal employment perspective supports this point. So, in contrast to the corporate mover, who focuses on employment continuity for one partner (usually the husband [Shaklee 1989]), independent movers are more likely to look for opportunity for both partners, and this enhances the likelihood that the outcome of the migration for women will be duly considered. Thus, one spouse has no particular advantage over the other as both experience discontinuities in labour force participation, and this creates a greater sense of equality with regard to the evaluation of the move.

Because the independent mover carries all the responsibility and risks of relocating, couple dynamics are more likely to come into play and women are more likely to have a voice. In comparing women's experience with migration according to marital status, women without partners would be expected to be much more likely to feel a sense of control in migration than would partnered women (Boyle, Cooke, Halfacree, and Smith 2001). The data here point out that even partnered women who are independent movers exercise power and influence in the decision to move and are therefore more likely to be satisfied with the outcome. Such moves particularly appeal to women who have labour market interests and who are ready to take control (Markham, Macken, Bonjean, and Cander 1983). The sense of departure control (i.e., when to move or where to move) helps to create what McCollum (1990, 223) calls "authentic choices," which then extend to feeling a sense of personal control and responsibility at the destination.

These results indicate that relational considerations are important factors in the migration process. And, instead of focusing only on outcomes at the destination, analyses must begin at the place of origin. Partnered women clearly understand migration as altering their role in a variety of relationships. While the idea of joint decision making in migration might mask male dominance (e.g., Zvonkovic, Greaves, Schmiege, and Hall, 1996), partnered independent movers require a more collaborative process in order to maximize the success of a move in which the sense of "self-imposed powerlessness" (Whitaker 2005) among women is less likely to occur. In addition, it has also been demonstrated that active participation in the decision to migrate not only increases women's satisfaction with the move but also allows them to see the growth potential of the move so that they are less likely to consider themselves the trailing spouses. These results suggest that, potentially, migration can be empowering for women – "a catapult for growth and change" (McCollum 1990, 34).

There appeared to be few differences between men and women with regard to the sort of restlessness and dissatisfaction that prompted migration. Employment issues, among a whole range of other factors, can create a sense of marginality in the community of origin. Both genders in a partnered relationship experience something similar, although they may not experience it equally. But the crucial finding is that women in partnered relationships are less likely to feel marginalized when their migration is unsponsored and therefore are not as prone to be male-driven as are their counterparts in sponsored relationships. Clearly, women are more likely to adapt better at the destination when migration serves their own interests.

The give-and-take required by compromise in decision making may be creating some symmetry in migration decisions (Smits, Mulder, and Hooimeijer 2003). What is needed now is a more thorough analysis of the interactional dynamics between both partners. These findings do not suggest that the "tied mover" has been eliminated. However, unsponsored migrant women in partnered relationships have been shown to have much more initiative, power, and control in migration than was previously acknowledged.

12

The Internet and Migration

An important discovery in this research is the role of the computer in the migration process. Many migrants made reference to the importance of computer-mediated communication (CMC) for searching, connecting, and generally facilitating migration, from the pre-migrant stage to the final stage of settlement and adaptation. This chapter explores how and why the computer was significant in migration.[1]

After learning from migrants about the importance of the internet, we developed a research strategy that led to an examination of websites suggested by respondents as well as websites discovered through the use of search engines, using keyword searches such as "away," "homecoming," "reunion" by province of origin. Snowballing was conducted based on the top twenty matches, and message boards, chat rooms, and guest books were discovered, often with links to other sites. Through bulletin boards and chat rooms we made requests for websites relating to migration from a region of origin. We kept a log of all sites during a six-month period in 2002, and these sites were monitored regularly throughout that period. The data found in these web searches provided rich evidence of the role that CMC provided to persons who became migrants.

The results of the interviews in the main study suggest that those who migrated the longest distances (i.e., from Atlantic Canada) were most likely to make reference to multiple forms of computer usage. Furthermore, the result of the web searches indicated that attempts to connect migrants with province of origin were also most likely to be found among persons from the Atlantic provinces, where out-migration has been a long tradition and where proud provincial identities are strong. By far the largest internet traffic occurred with the Province of Newfoundland, which serves as the primary focus of this chapter.

MIGRATION AND CYBERSPACE

One of the compelling aspects of CMC is that, in being asynchronous and disembodied, it transcends the limitations of time and space. Geographical boundaries and time zones often appear irrelevant to interaction that is based on electronic connectors. CMC can support interaction that is rooted in or sustained by a real community, but it can also be a virtual community linking people without a basis in physical space. CMC can build bridges between people previously known or unknown and separated in time and space, and it can sustain those relationships without physical contact. All of these traits make the computer of particular interest in the study of migration because it can play a powerful role in overcoming the "friction of distance" (Champion and Fielding 1992, 122). How does the migrant use the internet? How is distance mediated by CMC?

Migration formerly meant a radical break from place of origin to destination (Faist 2000). The lack of rapid forms of communication meant that long-distance migration in particular was disruptive to social ties and former cultural traits. Return visits and continuous contact were cumbersome at best and often expensive. Migrants then established real communities at the destination (e.g., ethnic villages), where those who shared a common origin gathered to facilitate adjustment to the new location.

More recently, the idea of transnational communities linking origin and destination has supplanted the old idea that migration meant a sharp break from the home community (Castles and Davidson 2000). Migrants are now much more likely to continue to retain strong ties to their region of origin, and complex transnational relationships are developed, with homelands serving as important symbolic anchors for dispersed peoples (Safran 1991; Van Hear 1998; Cohen 1997). Boundaries now are perceived to be more permeable at the same time that there has been an erosion of territory as the pre-eminent marker of community (Jacobsen 2002, 14). The new markers are more fluid and portable, and may have both local and translocal dimensions. One of the key factors supporting this transformation has been the revolution in communications. Not only is it possible to return home more often for real visits (e.g., via air travel), but it is also possible to maintain continuous contact with home by virtual visits. Reduced rates for telephone was the first step in that direction, but CMC has more recently played a major role in sustaining ties to place of origin. Thus, due to choices available through participation in virtual communities in cyberspace, homelands are no longer just a memory supported by an occasional contact but, rather, are an intimate aspect of daily living.

The internal/domestic migrant does not have to cross an international boundary, and movement back and forth to the place of origin might be easier than it is for international migrants, but often other dynamics of the move are quite similar to those encountered in international migration. There is usually a keen sense of a place of origin, along with a sense of loyalty related to that place. There is the need for adjustment to a new regional culture and to the sense of being "out of place" (Cresswell 1996). It might be hypothesized that shorter-distance moves, even when they cross provincial boundaries, are not as likely to be as disruptive as are longer distance moves within the same country. Indeed, our research found that the use of the computer for other than e-mailing seemed to take on greater significance the farther the migrant had to travel to come to Alberta. This fact may not only be a function of the physical distance from Atlantic Canada to Alberta but also a reflection of the social, cultural, and economic distance represented by these two locations (Burrill 1992). As people belonging to societies with rich traditions and a strong sense of belonging, Atlantic Canadians may experience migration quite differently than do other provincial migrants and may share some similarities with international migrants.[2] Migrants from Newfoundland, in particular, claimed that CMC played an important role in their lives as it facilitated contact with home.[3] The sense of cultural identity that exists among Newfoundlanders suggests that there may be crossover value in linking the findings presented here to the findings pertaining to international migrants.

Newfoundland is unique in a number of ways. The province joined Canada in 1949 somewhat reluctantly, after a history of responsible government (and much later than Confederation, which occurred in 1867). The intense loyalty that Newfoundlanders feel to their homeland has produced an emergent ethnicity that is rooted in distinctive speech patterns and word meanings, vibrant myths and folklore about the past, and a pervasive group consciousness (Hiller 1987; Overton 1996, 45–61; Jackson 1984). All of this has occurred in the context of economic underdevelopment and dependency as well as frustrations over external political and economic control (House 1985; Sinclair 1988; Matthews 1983). While out-migration has long been an issue, though seasonal or short-term (House 1989), the fishing moratorium, which was imposed in 1992, ultimately led to a stronger wave of out-migration. Thus, Newfoundlanders are a people with a strong collective sense of belonging who, at the same time, have become vulnerable to pressures to relocate.

UNDERSTANDING THE INTERNET IN THE CONTEXT OF THE MIGRATION EXPERIENCE

The migration experience can be understood by classifying the different types of CMC with each phase of migration. For the purpose of this analysis, only CMC that enables a sender and receiver to connect are examined. Four categories of internet usage are identified (search tool, e-mail, bulletin board systems, and chat rooms), all of which were part of a computer-supported social network (Wellman et al. 1996) and of relevance to migrants.

The search tool is a totally instrumental means of obtaining information using websites, search engines, or online stores. E-mail is an asynchronous but private form of CMC that is free of the limitations of time and space since messages can be sent and received anytime from anywhere. Bulletin board systems (BBS) are also asynchronous because messages can be posted for a long time and have large audiences; but they lack privacy. Readers and senders on the BBS appear to be more proactive in their attempt to recruit and build relationships as they not only announce but also chat. Last, chat rooms are synchronic because they run in real time, are organized around topics or themes, but only continue as long as the participant is in the room. It is important to note that these four categories all connect to each other. For instance, search tools lead to BBS's, and chats will often lead to private e-mail's among users. CMC is not used in one exclusive format, and the use of one format often enhances the use of other formats. Yet all formats have a distinct function, and the function of each can be described and analyzed for the migrant.

The use of the internet and its functions vary at different points in the migrant experience, which we have divided into three phases. The *pre-migrant* has not yet moved and is still located in her/his place of origin. The pre-migrant is considering the possibility of moving and typically is seeking information and linkages to assist in making the decision to move or has already made the decision and is looking for the informational supports to facilitate the move. The *post-migrant* has completed the move but has been away from the community of origin or, conversely, has been located in the new destination for fewer than five years. While five years is a somewhat arbitrary time frame, it suggests a reasonable period of adaptation. The third phase focuses on the *settled migrant*, who has been located at the destination for more than five years. Obviously, not all migrants move only once, and some may return while others who return may migrate again. Nevertheless, this typology did seem to represent the majority of our study participants.

However, as a typology, it is only meant to provide a framework for interpretation. It is also important to acknowledge that not all migrants use the internet and that, even when they do so, not all migrants use it in the same way or at all phases of the migrant cycle. However, the purpose and experience of online usage characteristically changes with each phase, and the goal of this discussion is to sketch the functions, roles, and abilities of the internet in each phase of the migrant experience.

Central to this discussion is the fact that the computer now provides a resource to migrants that was previously unavailable. E-mail obviously makes it possible for migrants to communicate with a wide range of people in a speedy and cost-effective way both for instrumental (e.g., job seeking) and affective (e.g., contact with relatives and close friends) purposes. But the use of the computer as a search tool is perhaps one of its most powerful functions, and from here bulletin boards and chat rooms can be found. All four of these computer uses were relevant to all categories of migrants, but one reason why we were able to determine that the computer was specifically important to Newfoundland migrants involves the identification of bulletin boards created specifically for Newfoundland expatriates.

Another important variable is the existence of some permanent entity that helps to maintain the site over a long period. In the case of Newfoundland, the monthly magazine and cultural trade organization called the *Downhomer* (www.downhomer.com) fostered the preservation of cultural artifacts and music and also helped to sustain Newfoundland's ties with expatriates. One of the unique aspects of Newfoundland culture is the importance of the kitchen as a place for warm interaction. So the existence of a BBS called "The Kitchen" provided a location in which it was possible to monitor computer-based interaction over a period of several months. It was here that ample evidence could be found regarding how important the computer was for migrants from Newfoundland, it was here that it was possible to assess the role it played in their lives. From this location, it was also possible to find chat rooms and both to observe conversations and to engage in conversations between Newfoundlanders at home and abroad.

THE COMPUTER AND THE MIGRATION CYCLE

Table 19 identifies twelve cells relating the four types of computer usage with the three phases of migration. Each column in the table is discussed vertically in order to demonstrate how the different types of computer usage vary with different phases of the migration cycle.

THE PRE-MIGRANT

The first column identifies the *pre-migrant*, who is essentially information-seeking and finds the computer enormously useful in obtaining information, making contacts, and obtaining assistance and advice about the possible move. It is in this phase that the computer as a search tool is particularly valuable. The pre-migrant can learn about the destination, its weather, its tourist attractions, its dominant industries, and job postings through both narrative discussions and pictures that helped to stimulate pre-migration excitement. For example, the City of Calgary website, which includes links to employment and information on "Living in Calgary," reported that more than 50 percent of its visitors were from out of province (www.gov.calgary.ab.ca). In particular, the number of Newfoundland visitors to the site increased five timcs its normal rate on the pages that included job postings.

E-mail addresses of possible contacts might be located using search tools, but e-mail addresses of people who had successfully relocated and who could assist with housing and/or employment (perhaps as a distant relative or simply as "a friend of a friend") were also important. Chat rooms were especially useful for informal interaction with regard to job searches and in attempts to find accommodations. Potential migrants could lay out their problem or concern, and many people responded with advice, suggestions, and offers for contacts. It became clear that chat rooms provided real support and not just virtual support as people not only exchanged information but also discussed feelings and shared observations between earlier migrants and those still back home.

The desire to give and receive information online supports precisely what Jones (1995) considered to be the basis of a virtual community. In almost all cases, these discussions were between people previously unknown or, if contacted by e-mail, were perhaps distant relatives. However, as Granovetter (1973) has noted, these weak ties are often more important than strong ties because they bridge social groups with different pools of information and contacts and play a key role in enhancing social capital and opportunity. The opportunity to discuss feelings and concerns about migration in a personal manner, particularly in chat rooms, suggests that there may also be cathartic value in this kind of interchange. Later in the migration cycle, illnesses were often discussed in a way that mobilized support, and birthdays were often celebrated. In general, though, the pre-migration experience online was purely instrumental; that is, it was concerned with what can be learned that would assist with the decision to relocate and facilitate the relocation itself. And the computer was particularly useful (as opposed to the telephone, which was more likely to presume a prior and more meaningful relationship) when relationships between sender and receiver were distant.

THE POST-MIGRANT

The *post-migrant* adds a new dimension to the use of the computer in that, while the pre-migrant uses the computer to look forward to the move, the post-migrant uses it not only as a tool to help her/him integrate into the new community but also as a means of looking backward, of staying in touch with the community of origin. The migrant is now in a position to use the computer more skilfully to learn about the new community because personal contacts and site visits complement what she/he learned via information and pictures on the internet. For example, information and gossip about potential employers are now available in real time, which then makes the use of the computer for the exploration of websites much more purposeful. Even leisure activities at the new residence are facilitated by the information contained on the internet. Whereas telephone information calls were often either automated or difficult to gain access to, internet information was immediate.

The backward "gaze" of the computer facilitates the maintenance of old ties. The acquisition of news about the place of origin via newspaper websites was particularly important. Many of our study participants read the home newspaper online every day not only as a way of staying in touch but also as a way of dealing with homesickness. The frequency of such newspaper reading online seemed to drop off over time, but many indicated that, even three or four years later, they still occasionally read the local home paper on the internet. Some respondents also mentioned using government websites (e.g., civic, county, or provincial) to find information on what was going on back home. Migrants who hoped to return to their region of origin were specifically interested in keeping up with what was going on at home, not only in terms of the news in general but also in terms of employment news or news about the economy. This was often a supplement to gossip or information received via telephone, which was often sketchy but that could be confirmed or given more substance through internet surfing.

E-mail was a quick, efficient, and cost-effective way to keep in touch with relatives and friends back home (especially via group e-mails to cousins, aunts/uncles, former classmates, friends, and so on). When the migrant knew of others who had also relocated, regardless of the destination, e-mail was an important means of staying in touch. In sum, e-mail, and the use of attachments (including documents and pictures), played a key role at this stage in the migrant's remaining connected to the community of origin. E-mail addresses are one of the easiest pieces of personal information to obtain (Mann and Stewart 2000) and can be found through search tools, BBS's, and mutual friends in chat rooms, thus enabling the migrant to retain old ties or rediscover lost ties. Young adults who often lived in a variety of places for short periods of time until they settled down found this form of communication particularly useful. Announcements on bulletin boards were also helpful in finding others of similar origin. Chat rooms took this process even further by providing an opportunity for synchronous discussion between people who shared a common background. These discussions, often making use of Paltalk (one Paltalk group name was "Newfie buddies"), might include both migrants and non-migrants, or they might include only migrants from a specific location or migrants who have settled in a particular location. This often occurred thanks to roll calls or to general appeals to persons using the net in specific locations (e.g., "Hart's Cove Roll Call," "Hello to Anyone in Alberta from Central Newfoundland," "Anyone from Happy Valley-Goose Bay, or Eastport Here," "Welcome 2 All Newfies from St. Lawrence Who R Living Away"). One appeal to people with ties to the community of Seal Cove produced sixteen responses in four days from different people who were from Seal Cove or were currently living there. Another chat was labelled "Baie Verters in Alberta, Come on Down!" and drew twenty-one responses from people from the town of Baie Verte, Newfoundland, who were living in Alberta. The sense of a common background and culture legitimized the chat and provided substance to the discussion.

The backward gaze of the post-migrant is a powerful element of computer use in this phase of the migration experience. There is a sense of rebuilding that is the result of emphasizing a sense of continuity between the new and the old. The desire for virtual contact with home might facilitate adjustment to a new place or, conversely, wistfully support the desire to return. For example, some migrants noted that internet postings of pictures from scenic locations back home increased homesickness, whereas others noted that they only fed a sense of nostalgia. The virtual aspect of the computer led some respondents to claim that the computer helped them to feel that, in a significant sense, they were "at home" ("I love being able to go back home right in my own living room") when, physically, they were at a considerable distance from home. The existence of web cams at recognizable Newfoundland locations and available on the internet heightened this sense of telepresence: "It is great because while I'm not there, it sort of makes me feel like I'm there."

For both the newly settled migrant and the well-settled migrant, CMC is particularly powerful in creating a perceptual illusion of non-mediation so that what occurs is not mediated but real. The cyberspace Newfoundland Kitchen utilizes hyperreality online:

> The Newfoundland Kitchen has always been a meeting place for family and friends to exchange thoughts and news, the center of any social event, sing-a-long or party. We would like for you to use the kitchen to meet new friends and keep in touch with old friends, thank people for random acts of kindness, wish them a happy birthday or anniversary ... So come on in, help yourself to a cup of tea, pull up a chair and enjoy the company!

The concept of a kitchen in cyberspace that seemed so real that, in a chat room, participants could pretend to drink tea in the kitchen, reminisce about past memories and life, and not have to bother with making a meal or doing the dishes was striking. Participants could visualize "going back home right in their own living room." The chat room gave the migrant a sense of being connected to home when she/he was actually not at home. One interviewee noted that www.downhomer.com (the home of "The Kitchen") "keeps us together wherever we are." CMC creates a sense of personal warmth and realism, and its ability to transport the migrant back ("You are there"), or to bring another place to the migrant ("It is here"), or to bring migrants together ("We are together") makes it a particularly useful tool for the migrant who sought to retain or rediscover ties with their place of origin (Lombard and Ditton 1997).

THE SETTLED MIGRANT

If the backward gaze of the migrant in the post-migrant phase is often borne out of a longing to return, a feeling of homesickness, or a desire to stay connected, the *settled migrant* is usually reasonably well adapted to her/his destination and wishes to rediscover a lost or neglected connection to home. If return to home had been a lively option before, it is dimmer at this point, perhaps deferred or even abandoned. Yet the glory of the past connection is sustained or revived into a lively tie. For migrant Newfoundlanders of earlier eras, before the prevalence of the internet, the online community may have been discovered only after they had been away from home for many years. For those whose former identity had lapsed, rediscovering genealogical roots was often incredibly important, and there were many sites that attempted to assist migrants in locating lost family and friends. Search tools were especially helpful, and bulletin boards were primary mechanisms for rediscovering and reattaching. It was quite typical to find BBS's that contained multiple messages in each string of persons recounting old relationships ("if you're from Brighton, I knew your mother"). Sometimes bulletin boards announced a search for particular people or people from a particular location. At other times, Newfoundland cuisine or the desire to use Newfoundland lingo served as the basis for discussions in chat rooms. In short, the computer facilitated the development of a virtual community of Newfoundlanders whether at home or in diaspora.

It is important to note that study participants seldom identified the computer as a replacement for telephone communication, even though it may have been cheaper. Telephone usage appeared to be particularly significant for family members (such as parents and close friends) to whom the intimacy of hearing a voice and its tone was important (Wellman et al. 1996, 218). There were respondents, however, who had gone to great lengths to overcome the intimacy barrier of the computer, even to the point of purchasing webcams so that people could not only talk to each other on the internet but also see each other. The telephone may be more intimate, but it was not nearly as effective in developing new relationships as was the computer (Putnam 2000, 169).

THREE TYPES OF ONLINE RELATIONSHIPS

The study of migration yields new evidence of how online and offline relationships are supported by CMC (Garton, Haythornthwaite, Wellman 1997). Three types of relationships occur among migrants online: new ties, old ties, and lost ties. *New ties* refer to the need of the migrant to establish relationships with people previously unknown and in which the computer plays the connecting role. New ties are almost always essentially instrumental in that they are important in both the decision to relocate and in the mechanics of adjustment. The pre-migrant establishes new ties to assist in finding housing or employment. The post-migrant needs to get established and become integrated into the new community, which includes not only developing new ties with persons at the destination as well as with other expatriates at the destination. The settled migrant seeks to establish new ties with people who share a common heritage. The computer is extremely useful in developing new ties online.

The computer is also helpful with regard to retaining and nourishing *old ties* as it enables one to sustain an identification with the home community. Keeping in contact with family and friends from the region of origin helps to perpetuate the sense of belonging, regardless of whether return is contemplated. The computer makes it easier to maintain old ties in the post-migration phase because the real basis for the relationships is still fresh and vibrant. So if new ties are essentially instrumental, old ties are primarily affective, dealing with emotional linkages, reminiscence, and often childhood and family history. In the settled phase, old ties are often harder to rediscover than they are in the post-migration phase, though they always have the potential of being revived.

CMC also plays a valuable role for the migrant in rediscovering *lost ties*. Study participants often told of reconnecting when people had lost contact with one another, especially when both parties to a relationship had relocated. Internet users mentioned using search engines, message boards, guest lists, and chat rooms as ways of finding lost ties and reconnecting with them. They noted it was "so easy to use the internet to find people ... and I have been found that way as well by people I have lost touch with." The internet helped migrants, regardless of how long they had been away (one participant said it had been twenty-six years), to rebuild old relationships. The potential for rediscovering lost ties through the computer is probably one of the most effective developments of the cyber age. Little evidence was found that online relationships produced new real-time relationships. But the evidence was overwhelming that online relationships helped to sustain earlier and/or continuing offline relationships. Furthermore, online relationships based on place of origin were in themselves often considered to be as real as real-time relationships because of the affectivity associated with in-group feelings.

THE INTERNET AND THE VERIFICATION PROCESS

The creation of relationships online, and particularly in chat rooms and BBS, is not without complications, primarily due to the anonymity of the internet (Walther 1997). Participants can present themselves in any way they desire, and issues of identity concealment and deception are crucial (Donath 1999). Online "signals of identity" (Donath 1999, 30) are important as a means of authentication, but they are clearly interpretive, few in number, and prone to be deceptive. The fact that CMC users frequently build stereotypical impressions of their communication partners with relatively meagre information but according to whatever signals they are given is known as "overattribution" (Walther 1997, 346). Within the virtual community, connections are made based on the assumption of truth and honesty, but these connections are also subject to various forms of verification.

It is significant that Newfoundland migrants and non-migrants using the internet developed their own system of verification, which allowed the interchange to become more prosocial and even hyperpersonal (Walther 1997). Verification was accomplished through a series of questions that elicited information a person would know only if she or he had come from Newfoundland and its specific communities. In the Newfoundland chat rooms, authentication occurred through place of origin questions such as "Where are you from?" In one chat room, new members were virtually ignored until their place of origin was revealed. Further verification then occurred via an additional hierarchy of questions that attempted to identify specific things about that community that were likely known only to an insider. One of the most reliable methods of accomplishing this involved asking who someone's parents were or asking if she/he knew particular people. Landmarks, Newfoundland talk, and aspects of Newfoundland culture were discussed in a manner that made being an insider critical to being part of the conversation. Once this process of verification occurred, it was not unusual for the communication to move to a deeper level and eventuate in the discussion of things that were often quite personal.

The affectivity of the tie was also related to the duration of the online relationship. The same Newfoundland online users were often found in the same chat room at the same time every day, and it was evident that there were huge emotional gains in connecting with other islanders. When a short-term relationship occurred, it was usually purely instrumental. The pre-migrant, for example, may have logged on for help with her/his move and, once relocated, may not have logged on again. This short-term contact failed to reach the hyperpersonal stage. But the overattribution based on Newfoundland origins enabled the migrant to gain help easily because the virtual community of Newfoundlanders online had a strong territorial identity.

Mitra (1997) identified discursive strategies among South Asian Indians on the internet, and such strategies were also an important means of creating boundaries of exclusion and inclusion among Newfoundlanders. The use of "Bay talk" (the dialect of people from outport Newfoundland communities) was part of some messages (e.g., "Okay b'ys, I's heere. I gots to tell ya, me new puter says 'ello to me and everyt'ing") and is a badge of authenticity and patriotism. The somewhat humorous identity of one chat leader as the "Codfadder" was an ingenious reference to Newfoundland's historic dependence on codfish adapted to virtual interaction. Reference to local dishes such as "seal flipper pie," "Newfie stew," "weggies," or "cod tongues" are elements of Newfoundland culture known only from within. Loyalty to "the Rock" (as Newfoundland is affectionately called) and the desire to return were repeatedly expressed. All of these elements built in-group solidarity and warmth. As one chat participant put it, "This place reminds me of the Cheers song, 'sometimes you want to go where everyone knows your name and they're always glad you came.' You always get a warm welcome in here." Another participant said the chat made her feel closer to Newfoundland even though she did not see herself "being able to visit anytime soon." Thus, in an interesting way, the virtual community and the real community were blended in absentia.

THE DIASPORIC ONLINE COMMUNITY

The very nature of CMC is that it supports the existence of a "digital diaspora" through homesteading on the net as "new communitarians" (Naficy 1999, vii; Rheingold 1993). But is there any difference between diasporic online communities and other forms of online communities?

Diasporic peoples have an acute sense of being removed from an original home of which they have a vivid memory and to which they continue to relate either personally or vicariously (Safran 1991; Cohen 1997). This is not to suggest that all migrants necessarily have a diasporan consciousness but that, for those who chose to relate to the homeland, CMC could be particularly useful. Bromberg (1996) argues that it is especially isolated individuals who desire this connectivity, and the feeling of isolation may be particularly strong for migrants who come from a place with a strong cultural identity that is considerably different from that found in their new home. While we have little evidence that Newfoundlanders felt isolated in Alberta, they all had strong place attachments to Newfoundland, and many of them longed to return some day. While this place attachment was rooted in accumulated biographical experience (Gieryn 2000, 481), it was also the case that rootedness based in Newfoundland as a parent's place of birth was important to earlier migrants and second-generation migrants. In sum, both place of birth and previous residence were compelling factors in establishing the virtual community for Newfoundland migrants, and, because place of origin was the defining characteristic for participation, no previous face-to-face interaction was necessary.

The second characteristic of the Newfoundland virtual community is that it links people in place with those out of place. In other words, the migrant is connected with the non-migrant, the diaspora with the homeland, almost seamlessly. There is a telepresence (Steuer 1992) that literally allows the user to feel present in alternate space through the interactivity and vividness that the net provides. On some websites, there were images of home and pictures of family and friends that enhanced the vividness of the computer experience for the migrant. Migrants were encouraged to listen to Newfoundland radio stations online, particularly if they were dedicated to Newfoundland music and culture. Newfoundland music, videos, and cultural artifacts were available for purchase online. Steuer's concept of telepresence helps us to understand how and why migrants might actually become "addicted" to visiting message boards and chat rooms and/or posting messages. CMC takes the migrant back home by creating and sustaining images through recipes, slide shows, community profiles, and humour, all of which sustain an atmosphere of hyperreality. As has already been noted, the interactivity and depth of the communication is sometimes so intense that the virtual connectivity is perceived as real rather than as only online.

It is possible that these unique characteristics of the diasporan migrant predisposed them to involvement in online communities. Diasporic peoples may at times feel isolated, homesick, or marginalized. Miller and Slater (2000) have shown how expatriate Trinidadians used the internet as a platform from which to deal with their marginalized position on the global stage. Similarly, Mitra (2001) has shown how South Asian Indians use the internet as a way of being heard. CMC may be a vehicle of empowerment, but it can also be a counterpoint to loneliness and depression by enabling people to indulge their nostalgia, rediscover their roots, and take advantage of opportunities to form connections. The online community sustains the prior identity (even if only in a fragmented sense) and can empower that identity. Instead of being the alien outsider in a strange land, the migrant is enabled by the online community to be a member of a shared community. As one chat participant stated:

> Here I am living in Edmonton for four years now and I am looking at Newfoundland through a computer screen. I miss home very much and would like to visit again soon. I didn't understand what my grandfather used to mean when he said, "You can take the man out of the bay, but you can't take the bay out of the man." Now I do know what he means. Everyone that is from Newfoundland should put their shoulders back and hold their head high like I do and be proud of where you are from.

There was no better illustration of how a migrant might feel as an outsider in a new society than the discussions found on the internet regarding how Newfoundlanders felt about being labelled as "Newfies". Chat strings were examined in which participants discussed their feelings about this term, differentiating its use by outsiders (seen as a putdown) from its use by insiders (seen as a term of endearment). Newfoundlanders expressed pride in this identity in spite of what others might say. The frequency with which this topic occurred suggests that CMC plays a significant role in helping Newfoundlanders deal with their unique identity, in handling negative stereotypes, and in providing a sense of solidarity.

In some ways, then, forming an interest community on the basis of place of origin promotes a form of cyberbalkanization. There is a sense of exclusivity based on prior residence and/or place of birth, which means that there are rigid requirements for belonging to the virtual community – requirements that prevent others from joining and that separate the in-group from the out-group. Unlike Bromberg's (1996) analysis of the isolated individual and Dimaggio et al.'s (2001) analysis of hypersegmentation, our analysis found no clear evidence that participants in the Newfoundland virtual community substituted interaction with others in their new place of residence with in-group interaction in cyberspace. However, at the very least, we can hypothesize that the Newfoundland virtual community provides a vital thread of continuity between the old residence and the new residence and that it assists in helping the migrant deal with the identity issues raised by relocation.

CONCLUSION

It is clear that the internet is not used primarily to build a virtual community based on previous face-to-face interaction. Nor is the online community independent of a community that exists in physical space; instead, CMC builds an online community from a generalized sense of belonging (as slippery and mythological as it may be) based on a group identity and a territorial homeland, and reinforces it through online interaction. An online discussion yielded this observation:

> When you are of Newfoundland descent, you are born into a very large geographical family that goes from one end of the island to the other. You never have to worry about meeting a stranger or of being alone. You only have to say you are from Newfoundland and you will immediately be contacted by Newfies everywhere to ask how they can help you and will be treated as one of the family because in the eyes of the true Newfoundlander, we are all family no matter where we may roam. Newfoundlanders never think of people as strangers but as friends they haven't met. It is a great feeling to know that you are never alone and that there's a whole island and world of Newfs out there waiting to talk to you a total stranger as if you were family. It's hard to explain because it's a feeling and people just react to the feeling.

This sentiment, if widespread (and we believe it is), is easily supported by CMC and is particularly conducive to interaction and reinforcement in cyberspace. The end result, to use Wellman's (2001) words, is that cyberspace has become cyberplace. Consequently, it is no surprise that internet usage may be more common among these migrants than among migrants from other provinces. It is this strong in-group feeling that is enhanced by computer usage.

The continuing importance of the internet through the various stages of the migrant experience is consistent with the notion developed in this book that migration is not just an event but also a process that continues over time. In particular, the internet assists the migrant through the various phases of resettlement, adjustment, and identity shifts required by her/his marginal position. The evidence also reinforces the importance of the role of networks and contacts in fostering and facilitating migration. CMC transforms the migration experience through new ways of developing social capital, and this contribution can continue long after settlement at the destination.

This chapter focuses on migrants from Newfoundland because they revealed a higher usage of the computer for a variety of purposes than did other migrants. However, migrants from many other provinces also used the computer for searching and connecting. Not all migrants were computer users, of course, but it is clear that, for those who were, it was a powerful resource. Online participation was an important means of increasing social capital. CMC clearly strengthened the capacity of individuals to command resources through participation in various networks (Portes 1995, 12). The virtual community provided a variety of forms of social capital both online and offline, and this assisted in the transitions concomitant with migration. Migrants' use of the computer at each stage of the migration process clearly demonstrated the nature of the network society (Wellman 2001), with its loosely coupled and spatially dispersed networked individualism.

13

The Three Island Thesis: Folk Culture and the Myth of Return

As we have already seen, some of the most interesting features of the migration flow to Alberta have come from the Atlantic provinces. While migrants from other provinces were much more numerous than were migrants from the Atlantic provinces, the impact of out-migration on the latter seemed to be much more significant, and, at the same time, East Coast migrants brought to Alberta something that other migrants did not. This phenomenon seemed to be most strongly represented on the three islands of the Atlantic region – Newfoundland, Cape Breton, and Prince Edward Island. This chapter develops the thesis that migration from these islands is shaped by their island-character as places where out-migration repeatedly occurs. It shows how the myth of return emerges in this context and how it engenders a folk culture that helps people deal with the ambiguities and struggles involved in the migration process.

THE THREE ISLANDS

The three islands of Atlantic Canada are unique within Canada in that they engender intense loyalty and a sense of collective identity. Each of them has a unique history and culture in spite of their similarities as island communities. All of them were settled by people of Celtic origin. Newfoundland is the biggest in terms of land surface (110,000 square kilometres) and in terms of population (510,000). Cape Breton is about one-tenth the size of Newfoundland in area, and Prince Edward Island is about one-twentieth the size of Newfoundland. Both smaller islands have similar population sizes, though Prince Edward Island (138,000) is slightly smaller (Cape Breton 147,000) and is the smallest province in Canada both in terms of territory and population. Cape Breton is not a province but, rather, is part of the Province of Nova Scotia. Newfoundland, Nova Scotia, and Prince Edward Island, in conjunction with New Brunswick, make up the Atlantic region.[1] Individually, they are the smallest provinces in Canada, both in terms of land surface and in terms of population, by a considerable margin.

Cape Breton is different from Newfoundland and Prince Edward Island not only in that it is not a province but also in that it is an appendage to the more dominant section of the Province of Nova Scotia, which is focused around Halifax. The island at one time had a flourishing coal and steel industry, but, through the last half of the twentieth century, both collapsed. The result is that Cape Breton has felt powerless and marginalized both within Nova Scotia and in relation to the rest of Canada. In contrast, as provinces, even though they are island communities, Newfoundland and Prince Edward Island have a stronger structural presence within the national framework. Nevertheless, their role within Confederation has always been at a comparative disadvantage to that of other provinces, which are larger and have stronger economies. The collapse of the fishing industry only reinforced this sense of disadvantage. All these island communities had limited catalysts for new economic growth, but expectations were particularly high for economic renewal through energy resources in Newfoundland.

All three islands possess a distinct sense of boundary in that they are surrounded by water and refer to the rest of Canada as "the mainland." Reaching Newfoundland from the Canadian mainland requires a ferry ride of six to eight hours from Sydney (itself on the island of Cape Breton) and then it is still a long drive to the capital city of St John's, which is located on the east side of the island. Cape Breton is separated from Nova Scotia by the Strait of Canso and was not connected to it until the Canso Causeway was built in 1955. Prince Edward Island required ferry service to get to the mainland until the completion of the Confederation Bridge in 1997. Whether the distance was great or small, the sense of separation from the mainland helped islanders to promote an awareness of being a distinct people.

Prince Edward Island is known as the birthplace of Confederation, which occurred in 1867; ironically, however, the province delayed entering Canada until 1873, when conditions were perceived to be more favourable. Cape Breton Island, as part of Nova Scotia, was one of the founding parties to the establishment of Canada in 1867. But islanders were always conscious of the fact that their island was a peripheral region to the more populous mainland of Nova Scotia and Halifax. Newfoundland, on the other hand, only decided to enter

Confederation, by the thinnest of margins, in a referendum held in 1949. In all three cases, islanders feel that Confederation has not been particularly helpful to their economic growth and that, if anything, economic development has lagged, with the result that they experience high unemployment rates while the more powerful parts of the country maintain their hegemony over them.[2] The combination of geographic separation, persistent powerlessness on the national scene, and rich local histories has reinforced a sense of cultural distinctiveness and collective identity that has resulted in a unique island mentality (Bartman 2000).

ISLANDS AND THE MYTH OF RETURN

One of the unique characteristics of islands is that they experience out-migration but little in-migration (unless there are new opportunities to absorb new residents). None of these islands has experienced much in-migration, with the exception of the prime years for the steel industry in Cape Breton and the war years in Newfoundland. On the other hand, they have all experienced much out-migration. Going away was connected with seeing more of the world and overcoming the insular nature of the island, but it was also connected with finding work. Going away was typical behaviour, but going away implied coming back. In fact, the idea of return was a powerful sentiment deeply ingrained in island culture.

Around the late nineteenth and early twentieth centuries, out-migration from these three islands became quite typical. Heading west in Canada was one option, but relocating to New England, or what was called "the Boston states," was also common. Seasonal migration to work on the "lake boats" (on the Great Lakes) or the railroad, or "harvest excursions" to the west ensured that families would retain their island residence because this form of labour migration was seasonal and primarily involved men (MacDonald 2000). Others moved their families or relocated as single young adults to begin new families at the destination. In any case, these islands have experienced repeated out-migration, and the notion of return became a pivotal part of their interpretive apparatus.

The idea of return may be labelled a myth because it is not simply true or false but, rather, represents a set of assumptions that persists within the local culture. The first element of the myth of return is that it consists of a generalization that has not been confirmed in any detail. Indeed, careful attention to individual cases would reveal that not everyone returns. But enough people do return to ensure that the myth persists as a generalized truth. In spite of the fact that return does not always happen, people act as though it does. The most basic assumption in the myth of return is that leaving is temporary. This was certainly the case when men left the island for seasonal work, but it persists even when time spent away from the island is much longer.

The second element of the myth of return is that being absent from the island for a long period of time is not voluntary but, rather, occurs because the individual has no other choice. Return is always assumed to be the preferred choice, but particular conditions delay it. These conditions (e.g., the lack of well-paying jobs on the island or the lack of jobs in one's area of expertise) are the result of external forces that prevent the island from reaching its full potential. For their part, people on the island feel strongly that things there could be conducive to migrants' returning, but, due to external factors that are beyond their control, they feel powerless to change the status quo. On the other hand, the migrants bring great prestige to the island due to what they are accomplishing while away – making "good money" or having "great jobs" – all of which reflects favourably on the island character. These accomplishments demonstrate the goodness of the formative influence of island life. But they also show that islanders abroad function as ambassadors of island life; therefore, their absence is not in vain and can be applauded. It is always understood that being away is in no way a rejection of island culture but, rather, purely a response to economic conditions. If migrants do not return, it is always due to extenuating conditions (e.g., having grandchildren at the destination) rather than to a direct or indirect rejection of the island.

The third element of the myth of return is that island life is superior and preferable to life lived elsewhere. The island produces a special breed of persons not found elsewhere. Island society is based on family, and everyone cooperates for the good of the community. While the island cannot satisfy all one's needs, it satisfies one's most basic need – the need to belong. The island is not just a place but a community and it brings with it a sense of unity (even if this unity is itself a myth). It is this primordial identity that is at the root of the myth of return: islanders share a common origin, a life marker, that is not replaceable by life on the mainland. Island life is better not just because the island is where you come from and where you belong but because its quality of life is superior to that found anywhere else. And the most important quality of island life is found in community.

The in-group feeling that is so much a part of island thinking originates with being born on the island. Thus, one does not choose to be an islander, one is born an islander. Persons who move to the island can never be fully accepted. In order to accommodate this mode of thinking, a migrant from Newfoundland tried to do the next best thing: "We went back to Newfoundland to have our son baptized there so that he would be rooted in Newfoundland." Among people who live on the island, the world can be neatly divided into two groups: those who were born there and those who are "from away." Newfoundlanders routinely use the term "come from aways," or "CFA," to refer to those who are not genuine islanders. On the other islands, as well, there is an awareness that birth is a marker of belonging. Because islands are not recipients of large-scale movements of population, outsiders are relatively easy to identify.

Islanders never accept the fact that migrants might not come back. Expatriate islanders may put down roots somewhere else, but the discourse demands that they will always return when the appropriate goal has been met (e.g., "after I make some money," "when I retire," or "when I've had enough"). Islanders who remain on the island do not accept that someone might be away for good (e.g., "I don't think they will ever come back, but I hope they do," or "I know they want to come back if they could"). In other words, islanders "never say never," even though coming back may be improbable. Even the annual summer pilgrimages ("the geese come back in April, the relatives come back in July and August") or occasional vacation visits are taken as evidence that the myth of return is true. The myth is also supported by public comments made by returnees (whether permanent or visitors) that glorify island life and speak warmly of its attributes – especially in comparison to the mainland.

In Canada, the myth of return is strongest in Newfoundland, Prince Edward Island, and Cape Breton. Even though many people have left these islands never to return, the myth persists. A humorous story that circulated through Prince Edward Island told of a new entrant to heaven who received a guided tour and discovered a group of unhappy people locked in a metal cage. St Peter informed the new entrant that the unhappy people were all from the island and that, "if we let them out, they will all try to go back" (Weale 1998, 20). This illustrates the power of the idea that life on the island is better than life anywhere else.

The myth of return is an ideology that bridges the migrant and the home community. It is a way for the disappointment and attrition felt by the home community to be brought together with the remorse and guilt felt by those who have left. Thus, the myth is useful to both stayers and leavers. Leavers need a mythology to deal with their outsider status at the destination and their longing for home (Overton 1996, 49); they need a way to explain their departure to those who stay. But stayers also need a way to deal with the "out-migration trauma" (Weale 1992). The myth of return provides a discourse that enables islanders to deal with the dilemmas and alienation experienced by both migrants and the community of origin as the result of out-migration. It is useful to migrants in their new destination, where they feel very much in transition, as well as to those at home, who are searching for ways to connect with their absent community members.

Out-migrants are assumed to want to retain their island identity wherever they might reside in the diaspora. In order to facilitate this connection, magazines or newsletters such as the *Cape Bretoner* (Cape Breton), the *Downhomer* (Newfoundland), and the *Maple Leaf* (Prince Edward Island) were produced (the *Downhomer* outlasted the other two). These publications expressed warm sentiments about social gatherings, usually held in homes, called "ceili" (Irish) or "ceilidh" (Scottish) and pronounced "kaylee." These gatherings took place both at home and in diaspora. These "kitchen parties" made significant use of the fiddle and step-dancing and were important symbols of island culture, creating affectionate feelings of belonging. It is noteworthy that all three of the islands have experienced a cultural renaissance over the last thirty years, in which attention to music and the arts and local history have sustained a sense of island identity (Hiller 1987).[3]

THE RETURN MYTHOLOGY AMONG MIGRANTS TO ALBERTA

In almost every interview, islanders living in Alberta supported the myth of return, which has four elements. The first element involves the idea that leaving is considered temporary. A Cape Bretoner saw it this way:

> When you do go away, you always consider it temporary and not home. It is just something in your spirit that makes this home and makes you want to come back.

This connection to the island involved an intense belief that was both mysterious and real. It was also inwardly compelling. As one Prince

Edward Islander noted, "I will die there – come hell or high water. I have already stayed here [Alberta] longer than I said I would, but I'll go back sometime." Another Islander put it this way: "I say you always come back one way or the other – either in a box or on your own." Viewing going away as something short-term avoided having to deal with a sense of finality, and this was easier on both the migrant and those in the home community:

> There were others who had already moved to Alberta from Cape Breton and it seemed like it just was a natural step for people for at least five years and then [they would] come back. My brother said, "Ya, but you'll never come back." I think that was a threat from my family. But everybody said, "O, you'll come back. Stay a year or two but you are too much of a Cape Bretoner to stay there." (Cape Breton)

A Newfoundlander said: "Everyone knows you don't leave because you want to leave. So if you have to leave, it makes sense that you want to come back." Coming back was a dominant theme and was associated with intense loyalty to place. Not only was leaving considered temporary but it was also considered to have been undertaken reluctantly, and this tempered any sense of having rejected the island.

The second element of the myth of return involves the idea that there is a relationship between the island as a physical place and the collective identity that emerges from the sense of community. An island, being surrounded by water, is a bounded territory. This bounded character links its inhabitants with the distinct characteristics of the physical place. Consequently, the sea is an important element in island mythology: "If a Newfoundlander can't smell salt in the air, they eventually have to move back." Many Prince Edward Islanders, when discussing their desire to return, talked about the need to "see" the water. Newfoundlanders, in particular, had an affinity to the island's unique rocky terrain, often referring with much affection to "the Rock." Migrants saw physical features as compelling factors in their own identity, and this stimulated the desire to return. A phrase oft-repeated by Newfoundlanders regarding those who did return was: "You can take a Newfoundlander off the Rock, but you can't take the Rock out of the Newfoundlander." The physical characteristics of the island were part of the mystery of belonging, making return natural and, indeed, almost inevitable (at least according to the myth). This imagery is particularly notable in view of the fact that Alberta was a land-locked province – a fact that sharpened the contrast for those whose identity was deeply associated with being "people of the sea."

The third element of the myth of return involves the idea that return is endemic but not necessarily immediate. A Newfoundlander acknowledged that the timeline for return was very fuzzy:

> We always knew when we left that we would go back. When? We don't know. It might not be till we're seventy but we'll get back sometime. It's where we grew up and it will still be our home.

The desire to return was often coupled with the desire to raise children at home, and this often brought about a fear of repeating the same cycle:

> I feel comfortable here but I don't want to put my roots down too deep. It's great for now but if I have kids, I think I'd like to go back. But if I go home just to have kids, they'll just grow up and leave. Then what?

The acknowledgment that part of the reality of living on an island was that people were always leaving meant that going back would probably only result in the cycle once more being set in motion for the next generation. Because leaving occurred so frequently, and because some did return at varying stages of the lifecycle, there was sufficient reason to utilize the discourse of return, even though the time of return was unknown and could be far in the future. For most people, the promise to return was a statement of possibility whose probability was unknown: "I don't know when we will return but that is the way we always talk." In short, return was an important part of the migration discourse even when it was unclear when it might occur.

The fourth element of the myth of return is that it is utilized even when the possibility of return is full of dilemmas. While return was the objective, there was always the fear that adjustments may have already been made at the destination:

> The longer I am here, the more difficult it is to go back home where I thought I wanted to be. And it is not just economically, but the lifestyle, such as doing stuff in the mountains or the urban life here for social and leisure activity. (Cape Breton)

> You can't get a job in Newfoundland after you finish your schooling. But if you go away for awhile and get some experience, then

> your chances of getting a good job back home are very very good. So what do you do if you discover that to move back you have to take a pay cut and pay more taxes? (Newfoundland)

A woman from western Prince Edward Island reflected on her own struggle.

> I had a dream once that we went back to PEI and we got back into the same cycle of having nothing, and I said, "Oh no, why did we do that when we were doing so well?" And when I woke up, I knew where that came from because I really did want to go home but knew what would happen if we did.

This type of reflection indicates that migrants were often quite realistic and that they did not overly romanticize island life. In fact, the things they might idealize when in Alberta may well have been precisely the things that had prompted them to leave:

> It's a double-edged sword. There is a strong sense of family and community there. On the other hand, you get sick of being identified by who your father is and it sort of makes you feel trapped there. In my case, you just decide early on whether you are going to stay or whether you are going to leave, and I decided to go where there were more options. I just felt I had to get off the Island. (Prince Edward Island)

An Islander who hoped to return acknowledged:

> It's a funny thing in PEI that people can't wait to get off the island and go to a big city to become anonymous. That is in reaction to PEI, where everybody knows your business. The smaller the community in PEI, the more it is that way, and I couldn't wait to get out of there.

PEI's migrants, being from the smallest island, were particularly concerned about escaping the social constraints of the island. Yet, as with other islanders, once they were away, they became more aware of the island's advantages and its relationship to their personal identity. Needless to say, this was one more dilemma with which islanders struggled.

Islands, then, breed intense loyalty and belonging while at the same time standing for limited opportunities. Realism often conflicted with the return discourse. If the economic implications of returning were negative, one compromise was for parents or extended family to relocate to Alberta rather to have the migrant family return (i.e., "bringing the Rock to Alberta"). A mother from Newfoundland said she came to Alberta because:

> My two sons are here in Calgary and I just retired back home ... I decided to make some extra money so I came here to Alberta to work. In about a year or two, I will really retire. I want to go back, but if my sons start having children here, then I might have to stay. And I'm not sure what this says about my loyalty. But I will always go back to visit.

This statement reflects how the return myth could be sustained even when return was not likely; that is, through the promise to visit home. Occasional visits home were always full of nostalgia, which, when expressed upon return, helped to sustain the myth in the home community:

> My son came home and told us how wonderful it was to be back and see everybody and see all the places he used to play, like his tree house and the schoolyard. He said he could not return home to live right now but this was the next best thing. (Cape Breton)

So islanders always return – even if only for short visits. One of the most strategic times to visit was when weddings were being held as it was then easy to see many people. There were reports of weddings of couples now living in Alberta who returned to get married back in Newfoundland in order to honour the parents and friends of the bride and groom. Often Newfoundland friends living in Alberta would also return for the event, ensuring that it would be an emotional high for all.

The nebulousness and endurance of the notion of return was clearly expressed by one island migrant who viewed returning as being connected to the hope that someday life on the island would make it more likely that they could go home:

> The best way to characterize Newfoundland people is a phrase they used, "living in hopes." When a fisherman puts down the net, you live in hopes that today's catch will be better than yesterday's. Your whole life is based on hoping that someday things will be different.

> So even when you go away, you live in hopes that some day things will be better in Newfoundland and you can return.

Here it is clear that responsibility for return does not rest with the individual but, rather, that it is related to the structural conditions affecting island life. Return is rationalized in many different ways. If it is not permanent return, then it is a return for visits. And, in any case, utilizing the return discourse demonstrates a commitment to the myth of return that keeps it alive. In spite of its limitations, the myth of return endured.

Many migrants to Alberta from other places in Canada talked about the possibility of returning to their home region at some point in the future. This was not unique to Atlantic Canadians. What was unique to migrants from the three islands was the pervasiveness of the idea of return even when the possibilities of return were extremely remote. Migrants from other locations in Canada were more likely to admit that the door had been closed, that they were not going back, and that, if anything, they were more likely to move elsewhere should relocating become necessary. For some of these non-island migrants, moving back was a real possibility and whether they did so or not had to do with personal preference. In any case, for these people migration did not come with the same psychological/cultural baggage as it did for Atlantic Canadians, and there was less need for a discourse to deal with their limited options in the region of origin.

One of the intriguing aspects of this research involved discovering that a folk culture had emerged on these islands and that it expressed the mixed emotions associated with migration to Alberta, along with the ultimate desire to return.

THE FOLK CULTURE OF MIGRATION TO ALBERTA

It should not be surprising that migrations deeply affect both giving regions and receiving regions and that this would be represented in art, song, and literature. Armstrong (2004), for example, has pointed out that, through works of fiction, cultural intellectuals play a unique role in interpreting a region's experience with migration. In examining the fiction produced in Atlantic Canada since the Second World War, themes such as a critique of distant urban destinations and how they affect migrants and returnees, and the problems produced by the search for identity and a sense of "home," are easily uncovered (Keefer 1987). Armstrong argues that the writing of cultural intellectuals reflects many of the dilemmas the region faces regarding the wisdom of staying or leaving as well as the nostalgia and criticism that the migration experience evokes. The work of Alistair MacLeod has been particularly expressive of the fears and excitement of leaving the Atlantic region, especially focusing on the constant desire to return.[4] Fiction is just one cultural representation that may arise; folk songs may also emerge in response to migration.[5] The following discussion demonstrates how the context of Atlantic Canada, particularly the three islands, generated a folk culture in relation to migration. First, however, it is important to examine how migration to Alberta has been expressed more generally in Canadian folk culture.

SONGS AS FOLK CULTURE IN THE EARLY MIGRATION TO ALBERTA

It is interesting to note that there is a folk culture in song about migration to Alberta that precedes the migration described in this book. Francis (1989a, 160–2, 177–9) describes the folk songs that developed in the western interior among the earliest settlers and that reflected their experiences and feelings, difficulties and challenges. Usually a popular melody was given new words to express the frustration produced by the ideals and expectations of the new land amidst the realities of poor crops, bad weather, and financial stress. One song, entitled "Hurrah for the Palliser" (referring to the Palliser triangle described in chapter 2), lamented the struggle of homesteading:

> Hurrah for the Palliser, land of the free
> Land of the wheat rust, grasshopper, and flea
> I'll sing and I'll praise it, I'll tell of its fame
> While starving to death on my government claim. (162)

Another song, entitled "Alberta Land," made reference to the lack of rain and the cold weather which challenged expectations.

> We reached the land where we were told
> Was chocolate soil and full of gold
> And naught was known of storm or cold
> Alberta Land, Alberta Land. (177)

It is not known how widespread the knowledge of these songs was in Alberta during the settlement years, but they reflect the frontier experience of the migrant, irrespective of from where that migrant had come. Later songs, however, had a clearer comparative frame of reference, relating the place of origin in relation to the destination. Two songs became popular in the 1960s and 1970s in which Alberta was still implicitly portrayed as rural and frontier-like, as a place to make a new start away from urban Ontario. Both of these songs became well known in Canada because of the national reputations of their performers, and they emerged out of the country/folk music genre. "Four Strong Winds" is associated with Ian and Sylvia (Ian Tyson and Sylvia Fricker) and, for a time, virtually served as an Alberta anthem. It represents the strong relationship between Alberta people, the land, and the climate, and it highlights the migration theme:

> Four strong winds that blow lonely, seven seas that run high,
> All these things that don't change, come what may.
> But our good times are all gone,
> And I'm bound for moving on.
> I'll look for you if I'm ever back this way.

The song goes on to say that it is best to go to Alberta in the fall, when the "weather's good," and that the singer has friends who can help with getting a job; but there is still a certain sadness about leaving. The wistfulness of the tune, its easy melody, and the popularity of Ian and Sylvia and their folk/country music made this song a Canadian favorite.[6] Another one of Tyson's songs, "Old Alberta Moon," includes the refrain:

> So gas up your Chevy, and head 'er way out west
> To the land of golden opportunity
> You'll get a first-hand education of how the cowboy rocks and rolls
> With that old Alberta moon thrown in for free.

The second major song of that era was recorded by Gordon Lightfoot, a folk singer from Ontario who wrote "Alberta Bound" in the early 1970s. The refrain of this ballad was also easily sung and presented life in the western province as starkly different from that in the big city. Leaving was related to the need for a new start, and the Alberta landscape and people were the primary attraction. The refrain, well known and easily singable, repeatedly referred to being "Alberta bound."

> Alberta bound, Alberta bound
> It's good to be Alberta bound

Alberta bound, Alberta bound
It's good to be Alberta bound

All of the above songs suggest that Alberta is rural and open and can be contrasted with the big cities in central Canada. This was largely the result of the experiences of the writers or singers, who were either from Ontario or who had lived there. Moving to Alberta was related to lost love or separation from loved ones, and, in some way, Alberta always represented a different landscape, a different lifestyle, and a new start. There is little sense that these songs were written in response to a large-scale migration of any kind; rather, they seem to be idiosyncratic expressions of individual situations. But they do reflect how, at that time and within the national context, Alberta was viewed as a western frontier.

FOLK SONGS AND ISLAND MIGRATION

A very different picture of Alberta is contained in songs that emerged from the Atlantic provinces a bit later and in which Alberta was compared not with the big city but with the sea and harbour communities. These songs were often filled with lament about what was left behind rather than joy at what was found at the destination. They expressed considerable sadness regarding the experience of out-migration, and most of them originated in one of the three islands. A number of older songs from Prince Edward Island deal with migration to the "Boston states" (e.g., "The Boys of the Island"), and there are many sad farewell songs, such as "Prince Edward Island, Adieu" and "Farewell to Nova Scotia" (Ives 1999, 19–20, 230–3). But the songs that deal most explicitly with Alberta come from Cape Breton and Newfoundland, and they began to emerge in the 1970s (the time of the first migration wave to Alberta) and continued through to the turn of the twenty-first century. In this era it was not the rural view of Alberta that predominated in the lyrics but the urban view: the big city with its oil-based economy could be compared with the small towns and the fishing economy back home. The inability of the fishing economy to provide full employment was one issue, but so was the collapse of the cod fishery, especially towards the end of the century. The Irish Descendants recorded a plaintive lament called "Will They Lie There Evermore?" It speaks of the days when fishers used to return to the bay loaded down with fish, while now the fishing equipment just lies on the shore because there is so little to catch. It is not surprising that it asks questions about what it was that turned the ocean "as lifeless as a stone" and whether the sea would "revive once more."

The collapse of the fishery provoked the writing of many songs that reflected the sadness and starkness of a weakened industry – an industry that had once been the base of a thriving Atlantic economy. It was this collapse, of course, that served as the impetus for out-migration, which, in turn, prompted further song-writing.

THE DILEMMAS OF MIGRATION

The weakened economies of these Atlantic communities created real dilemmas as people who loved their way of life were forced to reconsider their futures. Another sad song by the Irish Descendants, entitled "The Rock and a Hard Place," tells the story of an unemployed man who felt he had to leave his home and go to Alberta in order to support his family but who is torn by the fact that his wife did not want to leave and would not go with him. He details the emotional pain of packing up and hearing his wife cry during the night as she tries to sleep beside him. He feels caught between a rock and a hard place. The next morning, when he gets up to leave, he starts his car but just can't drive away. He turns the engine off and goes back into the house, but with no idea of where he will find work if he stays. He refuses to become a migrant because the personal costs are too high. The refrain is as follows:

the rock and a hard place there's no in between
one holds my work the other my dreams
cause she won't go with me and I just can't stay
the rock and a hard place I guess that's our way.

Another song tells the story of a man who lost his job because of downsizing at the plant in which he worked. He hitches up a U-Haul trailer and drives across Newfoundland to Corner Brook and eventually takes the ferry to the mainland and then on to Toronto and Alberta, and maybe eventually Fort McMurray. The song is called "U-Haul Trail" and was written by Don Crewe.

Now I'm looking back at Gander, disappearing in my rear-view mirror
If I keep pushing 90, I might be reaching Corner Brook by eight
I'll make up some time on that lonely stretch from Robinson to Wreckhouse
And catch the midnight ferry for a hundred miles across the Cabot Strait

Some songs played on the comparison between Alberta and the Atlantic region. Stan Rogers wrote a song called "The Idiot," which plays on this kind of comparison, particularly that between being unemployed but living by the sea and being employed in Alberta but working on refinery row. The narrator could have gone on welfare back home but decided to leave, claiming that this probably made him an idiot because he had given up the freedom to roam the woods and fish the streams for a different kind of freedom.

> So bid farewell to the Eastern town you never more will see.
> There's self-respect and a steady cheque in this refinery.
> You will miss the green and the woods and streams and the dust will fill your nose.
> But you'll be free, and just like me, an idiot, I suppose.

Another one of Rogers' songs, "Free in the Harbour," reflects on how the fish are now free in the harbour because the fishers have left to make their money in Alberta.

A song written by Ron MacEachern, "Go Off on Your Way," tells of the pain suffered in many communities in Cape Breton when people have to say goodbye to members of their families. The song lists many of the last names of these people and comments:

> Go off on your way now and may you find better things
> Don't wait around till you have no fare to leave
> All the best if you're stayin', all the best if you should choose to leave
> Here's to kindness on your journey, here's to joy in your new home.

The song ends by noting that, even though some might return, people are leaving daily. The narrator notes that he would probably be a millionaire if he were given one penny for each person who experienced a broken heart because of the pain caused by migration. It was understood that many people had to leave. And, in spite of the pain and social disruptions that this caused, they were always wished the best. But these wishes were given in a way that left no doubt about how negatively the communities were affected by this out-migration.

LIFE AT THE DESTINATION AND THE MYTH OF RETURN

Since one of the popular destinations of migrants from Atlantic Canada was the oil sands of Fort McMurray, it is not surprising that they would write songs that reflect this experience. A local group of expatriates who call themselves the East Coast Connection wrote a song entitled "Tarsand Fever," in which the refrain is:

> Tarsand fever from my head down to my toes
> In the north lands of Canada, province of the rose
> Tarsand fever building in my bones
> For the rest of my life, Alberta I will roam.

The implication here is that life at the destination is hectic and perhaps even exciting. At the very least, it captivates migrants who are seeking economic betterment with its promise of significant rewards.

Kenzie MacNeil from Cape Breton understood this process and wrote a song called "Bound to Alberta," which reflects the reality of people missing home but, ironically, being caught up in the Alberta economy. The issue of return was a key factor in this dilemma:

> Maybe I'll go home again
> When the time is right
> Maybe I'll just settle down, the feeling's hard to fight
> As long as work is steady and old friends can still be found
> To Alberta, I'll be bound.

Not surprisingly, longing for home and the idea of return are intertwined in the lyrics of these songs. Returning was often idealized as the best end result. Cyril MacPhee wrote a song entitled "And We'll All Come Back Again," which includes the refrain "Like we've never gone away." The implication is that return is the expected outcome and that reintegration would be almost seamless. Another song, "Harbour Town," talks of leaving Alberta, after having been there for ten long years and having shed many tears, to return to the sea, to the harbour town filled with friends and family, and to "a simpler life." Songs like this fit the myth of return, and their popularity helps to maintain it.

MIGRATION HUMOUR

Migration, of course, always provided difficult situations at the destination, and one way of dealing with these was through humour. For example, the best jobs in Fort McMurray were with the major oil companies (especially Suncor and Syncrude) rather than with a contractor or in the service industry. The East Coast Connection (based in Fort McMurray) wrote a song ("Looking for a Woman with a Syncrude

Job") in which the man tries to get a job with Syncrude and fails. He is working hard to pay the bills but struggles and concludes that the next best thing to being employed there himself would be to try to get involved with a woman who had a Syncrude job. The song, of course, is even more humorous because of the unbalanced sex ratio in Fort McMurray, which would make finding a woman with that kind of job very difficult.

> So I'm thinking that they won't hire me, I'll do the next best thing
> I'll find a woman working there and she'll pay for the ring
> No more will I be broke or busted or will I cry or sob
> I'll be hooked up to a woman with a Syncrude job

Of course, the woman was supposed to own her own home and have a fancy car, a hefty bank account, credit cards, go to church on Sundays, and not frequent bars. And it would be even better if she worked night shifts so that he could party with the boys. The humour continues with him acknowledging that his love is easily "buyable" under these conditions – as long as the buyer holds a Syncrude job.

Migrants often joked about what it meant to be an East Coaster in Alberta. One of the most interesting songs was Simani's "Saltwater Cowboys," which deals with a Newfoundlander struggling to maintain his identity in a different culture. It seems that the Newfoundlander in Alberta is "a new kind of breed" in that "rubbers and the sou'wester caps" are traded for "rodeo boots and big Calgary hats," and they learn to "talk Newfie in a soft-Texas style." But "You can't fool your old man by dressin' like that. You're still just a Newfie in a Calgary hat."

Two examples of migration humour come from a music and comedy production called "The Rise and Follies," which was performed all over Cape Breton in the 1980s.[7] One involves a hilarious dialogue on the Canso Causeway, which separates Cape Breton from Nova Scotia. A man was just leaving Cape Breton for Calgary and the other was just coming back, and they meet on the causeway. The person leaving for Calgary asks what life is like there, and he learns that there is so much partying that the returnee "hasn't slept all night in two years." They then discuss the toll on the causeway and laugh about how you have to pay to cross to Cape Breton but that "you are always free to leave." The fellow coming back claims that Calgary is full of Cape Bretoners and, furthermore, that, even though they did not know each other before, they discovered that they shared lots of relatives and friends in Cape Breton. In other words, migration was not an anonymous process, and home was still the place where you were best connected.

The other comedy sketch occurs in the suburban Calgary home of a Cape Breton couple who are visited by a representative of "the Upper Middle Calgary Residential Committee." The representative informs the couple that they have some annoying habits, which must stem from their Cape Breton background, and that they are now expected to keep their grass more carefully trimmed, not to expose their laundry in public (hanging wash outside), and to keep their children quiet and under control. After enduring this harassment for awhile, the couple decides that they are moving back to Cape Breton. The presentation is done with considerable humour, but it is clear that, for these islanders, Calgary represents urban sophistication and that they long for the warmth of home.

CONCLUSION

The three islands of Atlantic Canada make an interesting contribution to our understanding of migration to Alberta in that they reveal themes that were not typical among migrants from other parts of Canada. The pervasiveness of the notion of return is so deeply ingrained in Atlantic Canadians that it finds expression in various forms of folk culture. At the very least, this demonstrates that out-migration is a painful experience for both the migrant and the home community. Overton (1996, 129) argues that the songs that are generated are not so much oriented towards fantasizing about the past or serving as a symbolic link to home as they are towards expressing alienation with life at the destination and a desire for something more. This explanation may be partially true for islanders, for they may experience considerable dissatisfaction with the destination. On the other hand, it is important to understand that Atlantic folk culture expresses all of the dilemmas of being a migrant. Destinations as well as places of origin are never simply good or bad but, rather, are fraught with numerous dilemmas. Migration meant uprootedness and restlessness that brought with them numerous gains *and* losses. Furthermore, the vision of the islands represented in these songs often reflects an idealized past that no longer exists (particularly since the collapse of the fishery) but that provides solace to people in far-away places during times of discouragement. At the very least, these songs helped to sustain connections to "home" and to the past. And they provided a sense of rootedness regardless of whether migrants would return for short-term visits, full time, or not at all. Mostly, they provided an outlet for the emotions associated with out-migration.

14

The Effect of Migration on Origin Communities

Destinations that receive migrants are always keen to know whether migration to their region is permanent or only temporary. Will migrants to Alberta stay or will they leave? But the same question is also asked by the region of origin. Will those who leave stay away or will they return? The answer to this question affects both places deeply. This chapter focuses on the place of origin, analyzing the impact of out-migration on that community. But with every out-migration flow there is also a return migration, so the question of who returned and under what conditions is also addressed. In examining the experience of returned migrants as well as the community of origin's reaction to them, we show how readaptation was often more difficult than expected. We focus on staying or returning as the two basic options for migrants because the study revealed few instances of migration to a new place.[1]

THE IMPACT OF OUT-MIGRATION ON COMMUNITIES OF ORIGIN

For many years, the issue of out-migration and restricted economic development in some regions of Canada has been the basis for national redistributive policies known as equalization payments. Regions with slower growth were given special payments from the federal government in order to provide more adequately for their existing population. This, among other things, aimed to stem the flow of out-migration from those regions. Such policies have had limited success. The well-known economic analyst of the Maritime region and vociferous advocate of regional development for that region, Donald Savoie (2006), understood how communities of origin were affected by out-migration. Indeed, this is clear in the title of his book: *Visiting Grandchildren*. His point is that those who had to leave would not just be coming back to visit parents and grandparents who were left behind but, rather, that they would eventually come back to visit their grandchildren who had now returned to live and work in a prosperous region. In other words, instead of being the casualty of out-migration, these regions would see a brighter day through in-migration flows to a healthier economic region.

Out-migration may deeply affect any community. The degree to which a community is affected is not only a function of how many leave but also of the size of the community and the strength of its economy. Small communities whose resources are thin and whose organizations are limited may find that out-migration reinforces their precariousness. Larger communities that depend on a single industry that may be in the midst of decline or restructuring or that have a limited range of opportunities may lose population in the normal course of events and still survive. But they have little to entice new in-migration to counter their losses. Communities in which the economy is strong, on the other hand, whose cities are large and getting larger through migration, may be more or less unaware of any out-migration that does occur. In short, some communities were more aware of their population losses to Alberta than were others. In particular, residents of the densely settled urban regions of southern Ontario and the Lower Mainland of British Columbia were much less aware of how out-migration to Alberta affected them and, in fact, were more likely than were residents from elsewhere to minimize what was happening in Alberta:

> Most people in Toronto couldn't care less if people are moving to Alberta. They would say that we have more than enough people here and so a few thousand moving to Alberta is nothing. It is not an issue for Ontario. (Ontario)

A migrant from the Lower Mainland put it this way:

> People in BC like to think of Alberta as a hick town. Many of them can't see themselves stooping down to come to Alberta, which is a problem for them. (British Columbia)

People in these strong urban regions possessed a sense of regional superiority, viewing Alberta almost as a hinterland upstart. With millions of people in their cities and provinces, whatever out-migration to Alberta occurred from their communities had little impact. Ironically, then, the places that contributed the most to Alberta's population growth through migration (Ontario and British Columbia) were, due to their large populations, the least likely to be affected by out-migration. On the other hand, places that were more likely to lament the out-migration of their population to Alberta provided fewer people overall but were heavily affected by their loss.

INTERPRETING OUT-MIGRATION

Passive Acceptance

Regions with a stagnant, slow-growing, or declining economy were particularly vulnerable to out-migration and were greatly affected by it. Those who remained were required to develop an interpretive framework for what was happening to their community. One response to out-migration was a feeling of powerlessness and vulnerability. The outward trend was accepted as inevitable due to the limited options in the home region. The out-migration of young people was understood as being just what young people do – either for adventure, or education, or personal development. Often parents and educators encouraged their children to develop professional or career interests without fully recognizing that doing so almost necessitated out-migration ("Now that our young people are going to colleges and universities, they expect something more than local jobs can provide" [New Brunswick]).

> We raise 'em and educated 'em at a good university, and then send them out because there was nothing here for them. And for people who are watching everyone go, it's really frustrating. (Saskatchewan)

In short, career specialization almost always required relocation. It might be that the education for that career required relocation, but it was also likely that, even if that education had been available in the region, the requisite jobs were not. As one parent lamented:

> We didn't raise our children for them to leave. We raised them to make a contribution here. We had no idea that becoming a professional would automatically mean that they would have to leave. (Manitoba)

Higher education or specialized education implied relocation, which contributed to what was acknowledged as a brain drain or labour drain, often of the most capable from within the community (Edmondson 2003). This might be lamented but was often understood as merely inevitable, and it was accepted that there were limited opportunities within the community.

An interesting illustration of how the inevitability of out-migration was acknowledged but then turned into something positive by a region losing population is the Saskatchewan Roughriders' establishment of Riderville.com in 2002. The football team recognized that its local fan base was being affected by out-migration, but it also knew that former Saskatchewan residents were loyal to the province and cheered for the team. As was noted, "You can take the fan out of Saskatchewan but you can't take Saskatchewan out of the fan." Riderville was the website for "Rider Nation," an implied collectivity of out-migrants who acknowledged their roots by cheering for the team based in their home province and supporting it in other ways regardless of where they lived. The promotional phrase "You moved. Your heart stayed" captures the essence of a diasporic community. The online community was launched in Calgary ("Saskatchewan's biggest city") because it was estimated that 225,000 people who lived in Calgary were either from Saskatchewan or had strong family ties in that province. In this instance, out-migration was accepted as a fact but reworked and presented as a potential asset.

When out-migrants are young people who do not have an established place within the community the impact is acknowledged but is not immediately devastating. A youthful Ontario migrant observed:

> People would sort of rationalize our decision by saying, "You are just going out there for some fun but you are coming back, aren't you?" They assumed that we were just coming back where the family was, and we said, "Well maybe, if it doesn't work out, but we are leaving." (Ontario)

Leaving is what young people do, and it is not as threatening as is the leaving of older people. A woman from Newfoundland recounted her experience:

> When I left, my mom was acting really strange because I knew she didn't want me to go. But when I went back this summer, I had only been there one day and she was going off to her activities in the evening. I said, "Mom, are you going out and leaving me?" and she said she didn't want to disappoint her friends. It bothered me for

> about five seconds but I was glad that she had adjusted to me not being around anymore. (Newfoundland)

Most of the impact of the out-migration of young people is long term and is felt through the loss of those who would have married and had children within the community, thus ensuring the viability of its schools and local businesses.

The impact is far stronger when out-migrants are adults who have established positions within the community. Three residents expressed their feelings about out-migration from their communities:

> In the last ten months, seven families have left our community for Alberta. Most of these people were businesspeople (car dealer, accountant, contractor, investment consultant, hotel owner) in our community, and they were supporters of the Conservative Party or Reform Party. Many of them had children who had already moved to Alberta ... People around here are not surprised when people leave, but I would say the general feeling is one of disappointment. They are not angry but are sad to see that we are losing so many good people ... Here everybody has their place and when someone leaves, their place is filled by contraction. For those who leave, they get to expand out of their former place, and that is probably more exciting for them than for us who are left. (Saskatchewan)

> If you leave, there is a bigger reaction if you were a farmer and gave up on the family business. But if you were not a farmer and lived on a smaller farm, your leaving did not impact the community as much. When the number of farmers starts shrinking, that has a greater impact on the town. Or if we had shut down a small business, that would have had an impact. But that is not the way it is for most young people who leave. (Saskatchewan)

> All the young people are leaving my town and that leaves the older people. The plant reopened but with fewer jobs and they are held by older people, so what happens when they retire? One of my friends' husbands had a good job but she wanted to leave because all of her family had moved out here, so now they've gone too. People who grow up together, stick together, and sometimes even leave together. (Nova Scotia)

When entire families migrate and leave the community, when a generational cohort leaves, or when business owners and entrepreneurs leave (especially if they close down their businesses), the community is much more likely to feel discouraged and devastated than when young people leave. When the departures are felt in terms of the loss of capital, new ideas, and capable leadership rather than just in terms of the loss of people, the impact of out-migration is startling.

Blame and Attribution

Passive acceptance is one way in which communities responded to out-migration. However, the most common interpretive frame involved blaming the provincial and/or federal governments for the fact that people had to leave. Such frames were especially likely among remaining family members. Two types of thinking were typical: (1) residents thought that conditions in the past were much better than they were in the present and that something happened – something for which governments were at least partially to blame – that caused the region to decline; (2) residents thought that the region had enormous potential but that governments were not taking advantage of it. In either case, people have to leave, and this is perceived as being the government's fault:

> With the business failures here, every street has a home for sale and it has a domino effect. It is devastating and you get angry. You have to blame somebody so you blame the government. Why do they let this happen? (Newfoundland)

Establishing blame helps people in declining or stagnant regions to explain what is happening to their communities.

The Home Community and the Migrant

Communities at a greater distance from Alberta and with weaker economies often tended to idealize that province in a manner that produced a strong sense of regional inferiority, with all of the emotions that this evoked. People sometimes described Alberta through the use of such phrases as: "paved with gold" (referring to its streets), "promised land," and "land of milk and honey." This imagery was often perpetuated by how those who stayed interpreted the behaviour of those who left. A New Brunswicker noted:

> When I go back, I am treated very differently at home. I think they think we have money because I send money home to my mother. Then people say, "Oh, she can afford to send money home and she

flies home." I also send clothes home, so it creates an illusion that I have all this money. (New Brunswick)

Their ability to fly across the country supported images of Alberta migrants as prosperous jet-setters – no consideration was given to the possibility that saving for the trip may have been a priority. Migrants who returned to Atlantic Canada with new cars or trucks, new recreational vehicles (e.g., quads) – so-called "toys" – fostered such distorted images. A young adult Nova Scotia migrant told of his experience:

> When I got my first job, I called my mom and dad right away, but then they got worried that I might not come back because the rate of pay was too good. But they were pretty proud of me and told everybody back home. When others heard that, everybody else wanted to come out too. No recruiting company was needed. (Nova Scotia)

Exaggerated ideas about the nature of life in Alberta created considerable unrest among some people in the communities of origin. At its strongest, such interpretations could be referred to as a "crabpot syndrome" (i.e., mocking those who try to better themselves). People who left were viewed as being too ambitious, as climbers, as money-grabbers, and at least some in the community viewed these out-migrants as embracing values that elevated them above their home community, which they no longer thought to be good enough for them. Here is one example:

> I consider myself an Albertan and not a New Brunswicker any more. That transformation happened when I had a child here and bought my first house. I have very little desire to go back even to visit because of the discomfort I am made to feel about having left. And I am defined as being successful and they don't like that. Most of my family is here now anyway. (New Brunswick)

A Nova Scotian engaged in considerable reflection about how she thought her home community reacted to her:

> I've always found that when you are home, you are always a product of whatever everybody believes you are. You are a product of people's perceptions. You kind of fall into that rut when you become what people think you are and you believe that. Me coming

> out here has given me the opportunity to be my own person. At home, people don't want to see other people do well. They just want the status quo. (Nova Scotia)

The tensions that migration produced were also reflected in the experience of this Newfoundlander:

> If you do go away and even come back on vacation, you often get a lot of flack that you were not committed to Newfoundland, and then there is the attempt to put you down, that if you've gone to the mainland, you must think you are a big shot and are a helluva success. Yet if you stayed there, it was just because of some bloody strong-mindedness and not a sense of realism. (Newfoundland)

It is clear from these examples that leavers felt that communities often had a hard time dealing with too much out-migration. People who stayed in the community sensed that going away meant taking on a different status that made local people feel inferior. Thus, the desire to ridicule ("you'll never last") those who left, even if not done publicly, was an attempt to maintain solidarity among those who remained behind. One returnee found herself talking about her experiences in Alberta a lot, even though she had resettled in her province of origin.

> At work I have to be careful not to say much because they always sarcastically tease me about being from the land of milk and honey where everything is better. There is enormous jealousy here about anything to do with Alberta because people see so many leaving. (Nova Scotia)

Many migrants understood this thinking more clearly when they returned for a visit, only to find that they received a muted welcome. Migrants brought home a different way of thinking, a different set of experiences, and had a new set of social networks at the destination – all of this distanced them from their former friends. What was perhaps more important was that, regardless of whether the migrant was aware of this difference, local residents in the home community were very likely to perceive her/him that way. A twenty-something male adult migrant from New Brunswick recounted his experience:

> Of the people who stay, everyone wants to see you fail because they can't leave. When you return, my friends frowned upon me and

> treated me like a deserter. And I really got a dose of that. It was almost hostile. They look at you as though you think you are better than them, and it's really petty. It's because you choose to leave. They look down at you because they think you think the choice they have made to stay is a bad one.

Hearing that someone who left had been successful implied that those who had stayed had made a poor decision. The implication was that leaving was better than staying. The departure of a friend also meant that those who remained had to close ranks and, unless the migrant was going to return permanently, there was little reason to reinvest in the relationship. Migrants reported mixed feelings about home visits, which were often bittersweet experiences.

Some migrants knew that they had developed a "know better" attitude towards their home community. One returnee remembered how former community members talked when they were in Alberta:

> The worst kind of people in Alberta are ex-Saskatchewan people. They were often bitter and angry and talked bad of Saskatchewan. Sometimes they write letters to the local paper and complained about the Saskatchewan government and wanted to change it. They also complained about the taxes. It bothered me to hear them always complain and criticize Saskatchewan. (Saskatchewan)

These comments indicate that migrants had an air of superiority about having left, and this provoked a defensive reaction among those people who had not.

There were other ways in which out-migrants created a sense of uneasiness in the home community. Migrants who considered their relocation to Alberta successful often encouraged others to move as well, and this was not always appreciated by the home community:

> I am always trying to get everybody to move here and sometimes my friends and relatives in Manitoba and Saskatchewan don't like to hear that. It's because I feel more comfortable here. The weather is more temperate and it is the politics that is most of it. I enjoy it here so I think everybody else would enjoy it too. Sometimes people show me their property tax sheet in Saskatchewan and I say to them, "Why would you want to pay that much?" (Saskatchewan)

Another study participant told about her attempt to recruit a woman back home:

> And she said. "I am so sick and tired of you guys who moved to Alberta telling us everything is better there." She let me have it for about five minutes because she is tired of hearing this kind of thing. People will often say, "Well, you might not pay for sales tax but you pay user fees for everything so you are no better off there than in Saskatchewan." I'm starting to get lots of comments like that, even if I don't talk about it. (Saskatchewan)

Leavers not only threatened home communities by leaving but also by talking about how things were better in Alberta and actively trying to recruit others to join them. Reports of "success" at the destination, whether given by migrants themselves or by their parents back home were easily interpreted as bragging, and this often led to resentment and/or disillusionment among those who remained in the community of origin.

Out-migration clearly affected some communities more than others. Communities that consistently lost people to Alberta often struggled with interpreting that loss. Burrill (1992) has argued that the psychology and culture of people in the Atlantic region of Canada has been greatly affected by the continued stream of out-migration. It has bred a sense of inferiority, with the regional culture being denigrated by the destination, and with everything of importance being found in the "away" locations. The continual bleeding of talented people has threatened the existence of many regional communities, not just those in Atlantic Canada, and has negatively affected many families.

MIGRATION ECHO

One of the key aspects of migration within a national state is that return migration is relatively easy. In fact, migration back and forth is not unusual. If return migration occurs, then it is clear that the community of origin may not be permanently affected by out-migration. The questions, of course, are: how many, who returns, and under what conditions? Assuming that economic conditions continued to be stable and attractive at the destination (which they were for migrants to Alberta during our study timeline), it might be expected that return migration would be smaller and flatter than out-migration. Return migration that shadows out-migration with a lag time of a year or two appears like a migration echo (an echo being associated with something that has been sent out but returns, though in a diminished form).[2]

The migration echo may be the result of personal choice or it may be a massive collective response to changing conditions. If it is the result of personal choice, it usually occurs within a year or two of the initial migration. It occurs because many migrants consider their initial migration to be a temporary experience, experiment, or adventure. Migrants also sometimes relocate with a plan to stay three to five years and then return home. Return migration may also reflect differences in the ability to adjust, adapt, or succeed at the destination. In each of these instances, the return is a matter of individual choice. The second kind of return migration is more structural and is usually more dramatic, being the result of some kind of downturn in the economy at the destination. We have already established that the wave of migration that occurred in the late 1970s-early 1980s resulted in a post-boom outflow after 1982. Tepperman (1983) found that people who moved to Alberta were five times more likely to leave than were people who were born there. Arrivals were more likely to move again because they had already moved. In addition to changes at the destination, it is also theoretically possible that return migration may represent improved conditions in the place of origin.

It appears that, in domestic migration, there will always be some who will return to the place of origin within a year or two. Internal migrants apparently have a clear sense of a "home region," which provides a continuous anchor throughout the migrant's life. Reasons for return include economic necessity or lifecycle issues. In contrast to international migration, where the costs of relocation make return migration more difficult, in internal migration return to the home region is always a possibility. The fact that benefit plans, such as pensions, unemployment insurance, and healthcare, are national and portable strengthens that possibility.

Demographic Evidence

A migration echo refers to the migration flow that occurs when a province that has received significant migration from another province experiences a rise in the reverse flow. Under the conditions mentioned earlier, this flow is smaller than the initial migration flow, leaving a net gain to the destination province. This phenomenon can be observed through an examination of the migration exchange between Alberta and each province.[3] Figure 19 shows that a spike in in-migration to Alberta from Ontario occurred from 1975 to 1982 but that it was followed by an increase (though a smaller one) in out-migration to Ontario from 1981 to 1987. Something similar could be said for 1996 to 1998, when the in-migration was much weaker but when it was also followed by a rise in out-migration in 2000. British Columbia demonstrates a similar pattern. Figure 20 shows that a spike in in-migration to Alberta from British Columbia was followed by an even higher spike in out-migration to British Columbia from Alberta in 1980–81. Similarly, an increase in in-migration to Alberta from British Columbia from 1996 to 1999 was followed by an increase in out-migration to British Columbia beginning in 2002. It is important to know that there is no way of determining whether the migration echo is necessarily made up of returnees (especially in the case of British Columbia), but the fact that out-migration follows somewhat after in-migration suggests that this is at least part of the cause.

This pattern might be expected in relation to these two high-destination provinces, but what about other provinces? When Alberta's relationship to Saskatchewan is examined, in-migration to Alberta spikes from 1977 to 1979, and out-migration from Alberta to Saskatchewan increases from 1981 to 1984; in-migration to Alberta increases from 1988 to 1990, and out-migration increases from 1991 to 1992; in-migration to Alberta increases from 2000 to 2002, and out-migration to Saskatchewan increases from 2002 to 2004 (see figure 21). The dates vary a bit for Manitoba, with in-migration to Alberta increasing from 1979 to 1981 and out-migration to Manitoba rising from 1981 to 1983; in-migration to Alberta rises from 1996 to 1998, and out-migration to Manitoba rises from 2002 to 2004 (see figure 22). The pattern is most noticeable in the migration exchange between Alberta and Quebec in the same time period of the first wave and immediately thereafter, with much less of an effect during the second wave (see figure 23). Heavier in-migration to Alberta from the Atlantic provinces (see figures 24, 25, 26, and 27) in both waves is followed by heavier out-migration to the region in succeeding years. In short, the stronger in-migration to Alberta, as represented in both waves, was generally followed by heavier out-migration than otherwise occurred (presumably back to the province of origin). One can reasonably infer that a significant portion of this migration is indeed return migration shadowing the initial flow only in a reverse direction.

There has been a particular interest in assessing out-migration and in-migration in the Atlantic region. The analysis of migration exchanges, particularly from Atlantic Canada, has concluded that, traditionally, the predominant destination has been Ontario. Out-migrants from Atlantic Canada have been younger and better educated than return migrants, who tended to be older and poorer educated (Hiscott 1987c; Hou and Beaujot 1995). Or, to put it another way, out-migration was motivated more by employment or economic factors, whereas return migration was based on factors such as family, lifestyle, personal preferences, or a desire to be with one's own people. Most of the migration to the Atlantic provinces has consisted of return migration rather than primary migration. This is partly due to the fact that many migrants had no intention of remaining at the destination and were not constrained in that decision by economic factors such as lower incomes at home (Gmelch and Richling 1988). Out-migration was also related to a long history of seasonal or short-term migration from the region (Gmelch 1980; Gmelch 1983; Richling 1985; Hiscott 1987a, 1987b; Sinclair and Felt 1993; MacKenzie 1985, 2002). Newfoundlanders who returned appear to have been motivated less by economic self-interest and more by attachment to a way of life in which individual income was not as important as household and non-cash income (House 1989; Gmelch and Richling 1988). As we have noted, there is no question that Atlantic Canadians, particularly Newfoundlanders, often spoke of returning home.

The collapse of the fishery, however, left such a pattern more in doubt as outport communities had been considerably weakened. As one migrant to Alberta noted, "My family at home is just scraping by and if that is what it means to go home, I'm not going" (Newfoundland). The combination of greater distance between Alberta and the Atlantic region and the fact that there was less to return to became a significant block to return migration. Yet return migration did continue to occur as some coastal communities demonstrated considerable resilience (Ommer 2002), and it was especially prompted by the ownership of a home or the acquisition of cash, which enabled a comfortable lifestyle. There was some sketchy evidence that people who moved back to regions where out-migration was continuous might also be people who moved back for good jobs. An examination of Public Use Microdata Files revealed that, in the migration exchange, people who moved to the Atlantic provinces and Saskatchewan from Alberta tended to have lower incomes when they returned than did those who moved to Alberta from these places. On the other hand, people who had higher incomes (over $110,000) in these locations included those who had come from Alberta in the past five years. We have no way of knowing whether all these in-migrants were returnees or persons who had been poached from Alberta, but this provided at least some indirect evidence that some people who moved in the reverse direction did so to gain higher levels of income. This provides some support for the idea that there were returnees who came back to the home province with skills and experience that made them more competitive for higher-level positions (cf. Sinclair 2003, 214–16).

Newfoundland made an attempt to track this more recent migration exchange through medicare registrations (Newfoundland Statistics Agency 2001). Evidence of considerable repeat migration was uncovered as almost one-third of respondents had moved from the province at least once before. When comparing out-migration with in-migration, almost half had left the province to look for work, whereas less than 4 percent returned to look for work. Returnees were much more likely to return if they had a job to go to, but personal/family or retirement reasons also prompted return. Those who returned were much more likely to be married (or living common law) and were better educated than were those who left. The implication is that if marginality were a primary reason for leaving, then feeling integrated into the community through employment or social connectivity was a primary reason to return. On the other hand, among all migrants, one of the primary drawbacks to returning was a reluctance to take a lower-paying job than the one they held in Alberta. To many, taking a major cut in pay was unthinkable.

Return, then, is a complex phenomenon. What we do know is that some communities lose more people than they gain through migration and that the return rate for these communities is lower than the leaving rate.[4] In contrast, the return rate is much higher for people who come from urban communities, where the options are more diverse. The question then is, why and under what conditions does return migration occur?

A REFERENCE GROUP THEORY OF RETURN MIGRATION

It has already been pointed out that migrants repeatedly compared the destination with the place of origin. In the first instance, this occurred purely as a natural response to the need to adjust. Indeed, there was an excitement to migration as there was much that was new and challenging at the destination. The adventure of exploring and discovering at the new location often yielded many comparisons that were positive and sometimes even thrilling, providing the migrant with the sense that the move had been a wise decision. New recreational opportunities, new eating establishments and watering holes, new scenery, different newspaper and media outlets, and meeting new people provided a sense of exhilaration that enhanced the migrant's ability to see the move as an adventure, even if it had not been undertaken with that in mind. On the other hand, some things were viewed negatively. Different roadways and grid patterns could be a challenge. They could also be intimidating, especially at rush hour. Adjusting to a different climate (or altitude) or a different political culture was not always easy. According to one British Columbia migrant:

> The Alberta I came to had user fees, higher insurance rates, and I had to take a decrease in pay. It wasn't nearly as lucrative as the media had made it out to be. (British Columbia)

Above all, migrants deeply missed people, landmarks, and events back home and made daily comparisons between the destination and what they were accustomed to. This dilemma of the new and the old, the unfamiliar and the familiar, gains and losses was part of the everyday life of the migrant, especially in the time period right after arrival.

The migrant continually assessed the consequences of the migration and evaluated it. The conclusions that were arrived at were shaped by the social group that provided the frame of reference for the migrant's personal analysis. While it was possible that the migrant might evaluate the move independently, in most cases, there were significant others in the migrant's life who helped to provide a yardstick for the evaluation. These significant others may have been parents, relatives, friends, co-workers and peers, neighbours, people with whom the migrant grew up, or people with whom the migrant shared organizational affiliations. The people with whom the migrant interacts most heavily serves as the *reference group* in migration evaluation. The reference group may be at the destination and it may also be at the place of origin. A reference group refers to people with whom an individual has social relationships and who provide her/him with a sense of belonging and identity. More important, reference groups provide benchmarks for the evaluation of migration and shape the way the migrant assesses the outcome of relocating. The ultimate strength of a reference group is related to the ability of a migrant to find a satisfactory social position at the destination. As we see below, reference groups may change in strength over time, and they may compete with each other, thereby producing considerable conflict.

The reference group approach to migration evaluation is very important because it enables us to understand how assessments about the migration are made and, ultimately, whether the migrant stays at the destination, returns, or moves yet again. If the reference group is at the place of origin, and remains there, there will be constant pressure for the migrant to return home. For example, a migrant from Quebec stated:

> I was born and raised in Quebec and ... grew up with the Quebecois identity. No one in my family speaks English except me. They didn't understand why I wanted to live so far from home and in an English environment. They keep asking when I am coming back. I am trying to decide whether being with them is important enough for me to go back. (Quebec)

If the primary reference group is made up of parents, family, or friends at origin, this will be fundamental to how well the migrant adjusts. Where migration from the region of origin was viewed as legitimate but temporary, or where migration was frowned upon, there were strong pressures to return. Where migration was considered acceptable and it was expected that individuals would go where it was most suitable for them, there were few pressures to return. If the community of origin was important to the migrant and she/he retained the home community as her/his frame of reference, she/he may reside at the destination but not really live there. In some ways, it was as though such migrants never left home. A female migrant from Ontario stated emphatically:

> When I moved here, I had no intention of staying, and what I have done is build a wall around myself and don't even want to look at the broader picture of what's behind what I see. I came with the view that I was leaving so I am not even opening myself up to a lot of the opportunities that could possibly be open to me. (Ontario)

While it might be natural for these feelings to be expressed in the period immediately following migration, the long-term maintenance of home as the point of reference retards adjustment at the destination and facilitates return migration.

On the other hand, if the reference group was no longer at the place of origin but at the destination, the adjustment was much easier. For example, a migrant from Quebec who felt uncomfortable there observed:

> I think I considered myself an Albertan the minute I stepped off the plane. We made the choice to leave. In truth, I don't think we ever considered ourselves Quebecers, particularly as they define it now, even though we were born there. (Quebec)

A Nova Scotian commented:

> About a year and a half ago, I got so homesick that I had to go home. But now I am completely the opposite. Things change and my friends from high school haven't changed at all in their thinking. When I went back I discovered that I couldn't live there anymore. I don't have as much in common with my friends there anymore because I moved away and I'm working here doing things they can't relate to. But my friends here can. (Nova Scotia)

Adopting a new reference group at the destination, however, was not without conflict. Consider the francophone who felt caught between conflicting reference groups at the destination:

> I consider myself an Albertan now but I have to fight for that within the French community here. They don't like that. I have a tendency to assimilate but the French community does not like that and pressure you to do things with them. On my business card, I have a French side and an English side. I do not have the accent on my last name on the English side, but then I get pressure and I was told that I should present myself with the accent. When I do business in English, I want to present my English side. I don't want to play that politics game, I want to mix. I do not feel the way they do and they look at you that it's not OK. They also say don't speak in English with me, speak French. But I enjoy speaking English. I will speak what my reflex to say a sentence is and if you don't like it that it is in English, I don't like the pressure to speak French. They like to act like they are still in Quebec but we're not. (Quebec)

In some ways then, the long arm of the region of origin was felt even at the destination. The migrant was torn between the expectations of the old reference group and those of the emerging one.

Community of origin can also function as a reference group through lifestyle comparisons: "What was my life like back there and what is it like here?" The first feeling of migrants who were underemployed or unemployed in their region of origin was a sense of elation over being employed in Alberta. Repeatedly we heard the refrain: "I am happy here because I am working." Such comparisons between destination and origin verified the importance of meaningful and productive work with regard to one's social position. Along with the new social position at the destination came material benefits that also served as the basis of favourable comparisons with the home community. A woman from New Brunswick made this comparison:

> We had a house all picked out back home for $75,000 and we couldn't get mortgage approval. Here we bought a house for $170,000 and we got approved right away. We moved out with one car that we could hardly make the payments on, and now we have two cars. That is progress. (New Brunswick)

The migrant then compared her/his social position in the community of origin with her/his social position at the destination. If the comparison was satisfactory, there was no desire to leave. Family and friends back home also provided a standard by which to compare the success of the migration. For example, having a higher income than peers or family back home could help justify staying at the destination. A woman from Nova Scotia came to this conclusion:

> People usually go home because they are homesick. When I first came out here, my father was heartbroken and I knew that. But now he sees how well I'm doing and how much I'm making and he understands that I would not be able to live as well at home. I'm not going home to take a pay cut. I'm not going home to be poor. (Nova Scotia)

The father's ultimate acceptance of the economic benefits of the move was important to this migrant. Migrants also compared the availability of things like home ownership or discretionary spending on entertainment at the destination and at the community of origin. The result of this evaluation could affect their decision to stay or return. But there were tough tradeoffs. For example, working long hours at the destination may have led the migrant to compare this with a more leisurely pace back home. Hearing about family get-togethers back home might resurrect feelings of social deprivation that would activate an interest in returning. When the community of origin provided the reference group for a migrant, everything at the destination was evaluated through that interpretive lens.

If, on the other hand, the migrant's reference group was at the destination, then a new set of alternatives arose. The first alternative was that the migrant's primary reference group was other migrants from the home region. These migrants all faced similar challenges, and success in dealing with these was measured by how others fared. If others were doing well and the migrant was doing just as well or better, then the migration was deemed successful. If, on the other hand, others were doing well and the migrant was not, either efforts were redoubled or doing less well was interpreted as a signal that the migration had been a failure. One migrant compared herself to other migrants and concluded that it had been very hard:

> After being here for two and a half years, it has been a real struggle. Looking for work and my husband being laid off ... at the end of the month we can't seem to get ahead, our housing is so much more expensive. We are not doing as well as our friends. (Saskatchewan)

This negative evaluation was at least in part a reaction to the successes of her comparison group – others who also migrated. Migrants who were unhappy, even despite some measure of success, and who returned home for visits or constantly talked of home may influence others to feel less sure about their decision to remain at the destination. Thus, some reference groups at the destination became very unstable – even to the point of disintegration as members slowly left and returned home. Although some would stay, they would do so with a new reference group made up of those committed to staying.

The second alternative was the creation of a new reference group at the destination. These may have consisted of peers, co-workers or other professionals, neighbours, or just new friends (including boyfriends/girlfriends and their families). Establishing new social ties that then became a new reference group made previous reference groups either secondary or residual, sometimes usurping home ties altogether. A migrant from Newfoundland made this observation:

> We originally came here for five years, but you know what, no one is there anymore. Our friends are here. And more than that, our children were born here, and this is home to them now, and all our friends are here, so going back does not make any sense. (Newfoundland)

Some migrants moved into this adaptive mode fairly quickly, and this enabled them to "feel right at home." For others, progress in this direction moved in fits and starts or was delayed, happening only eventually. In all of these instances, adjustment and integration could proceed because the migrants had few encumbrances and much social support.

The new reference group could be made up of other migrants, regardless of place of origin. As one person noted, "Alberta is now my home but we are not from here so we bond with others who have also moved here" (Ontario). The mutual experience of migration may cause people to bond together to work through the adjustments:

> I have a group of friends here now and we said we would not go home unless everybody else would go home. Twenty-five of us were together for Canada Day weekend and we said if everyone else was going home, we'd go home too. (Nova Scotia)

The longer a migrant stays away from the community of origin, the more likely the community at the destination will provide the reference group. Proximity does become a factor with regard to sustaining ties that are strong enough to enable people to serve as a reference group. To be out of touch with a reference group at home heightens the likelihood that it will soon no longer be adequate as a reference group. An Atlantic migrant observed:

> This has been a very positive experience for us, but what I don't want to see is that we are here so long that any chance of going back is closed off. We are already beginning to feel a bit distant from home. It is sort of scary because if our child is here much longer, he will be an Albertan, and for us to uproot him would not be fair either. (Newfoundland)

It is important to underscore the fact that reference groups were not static entities. Parents or family in the community of origin may die or the old reference group may be diluted, and this may influence the migrant's decision not to return. The act of migration itself also transforms the migrant, and this means that the fit changes for both sides. A New Brunswick woman concluded:

> I would like to move back but I am torn and really don't know. I went back for three weeks at Christmas and in the summer, and I really couldn't wait to get back home – meaning Alberta. I really think I'm here for the time being, but when I look at how I have grown and people there haven't, I don't want to go back. I guess I am torn. (New Brunswick)

The life situations of peers at origin may have changed as well, with the result that they have developed a new reference group to which the migrant was now marginal.

Migrants may have multiple reference groups, and this can create considerable conflict, particularly when they straddle the origin community and the destination. For example, family in the community of origin whose approval was important to the migrant may have repeatedly been encouraging return migration at the same time as professional peers at the destination offered the migrant other expectations and rewards. These cross-pressures often left migrants feeling torn and compromised, often eager to return home, yet also eager to do things that destination peers were doing (e.g., many migrants felt that satisfying their reference group at home meant spending most vacation time there, whereas their peers at the destination talked of vacation trips to other places). When a primary reference group back home is replaced by a primary reference group at the destination, this is often very painful for those at home as such a shift is experienced as a form of rejection. As one migrant from New Brunswick noted, "We have been more successful job wise here than we ever thought, but this success has come at a very high price family-wise." Thus, one reference group might be sacrificed for another reference group, producing a very painful situation. A francophone Quebecer expressed this struggle and the sense of guilt that it produced:

> Yes I do have a great job and I do have great friends and I like the environment here. But I have sacrificed a lot in terms of my family, like when your father calls you and says we are all sitting around the table and celebrating your aunt's birthday. I hate it when he does that. (Quebec)

Some migrants openly acknowledged the resolution of these conflicting feelings. A migrant from Manitoba claimed that she

> felt very positive about being here, and sometimes I feel bad that I don't have more homesickness or have a feeling of betrayal of leaving people behind, but we almost have a feeling of freedom from all the large family demands. We have new friends here. (Manitoba)

Feeling conflicted about migration sometimes led migrants to exist in a suspended state between place of origin and the destination:

> I don't want to get involved in the community because then it would be harder to leave. I want to be free to leave. I came out here for five months, and four years later I'm still here with a permanent

> contract. I don't want to stay but I'm also afraid to go back and be uprooted again. That's not all. Coming here maybe was the biggest mistake of my life because I left a seven-year relationship that ended when I came out here. (New Brunswick)

Many migrants may be described as incipient returnees because strong allegiances at home ensure that the potential for return always exists. This was particularly the case when family was persuading the migrant to return but the economic benefits of being in Alberta were still strong:

> There are two reasons why I would go home – family and family. But when you go home you don't know what the end result will be and whether you will have to pack your bags to go back to Alberta. (Newfoundland)

> If you go home you are going to sacrifice something. You are either going to sacrifice money to gain family or you are going to stay here. Every year when I go home, people ask me when I'm coming back. Every time I tell them two more years. But I don't know. I think though that I would love to be home when I have kids. (Nova Scotia)

> We stay here because the novelty has not worn off yet and none of us have had an impending event [e.g., loss of job, a death at home, marriage] that would force us to consider returning. But our allegiance to Alberta is pretty shallow at this point. I sometimes wonder what that impending event will be for me. (Ontario)

It is clear that, for many migrants, home still provided an important reference group. This pull, however, was at least somewhat neutralized by the economic benefits of remaining in Alberta:

> What makes it good to be here is that we are not struggling financially ... On the other side, though, if there was a downtime in the oil patch, we could just load up our truck and go back and not have to worry about selling everything. (Nova Scotia)

For persons whose reference group was still at the place of origin, it was conceivable that any reversal of their economic situation would serve as the justification for a return home.

RETURN MIGRATION

So who are the migrants that return? Put simply, they are people for whom a social group at home has continued to serve as their primary reference group. In going away, migrants learned that their social location in their community of origin was more important than they previously thought and they were prepared to try again. Two migrants from Ontario who longed to return put it this way:

> Home is where the heart is, and my heart will always be in Ontario because that is where my family is. I have met a few kindred spirits, but this is not where my roots are. I am an Ontarian forever. That will always be. I just live in Alberta. I have every intention of not being here in five years. It's because I will never belong. (Ontario)

> I've got a place here so this is my home for now. It's not by choice but it's the only place I've got to go until I go back where I belong. But I'm not out here by choice either, for when I left Ontario, I only had $180 in my pocket. Everybody has bad luck from time to time and it hit me in 1999 in Ontario. So I came out here (Ontario)

A hairstylist in Saskatchewan who returned from Alberta was more metaphorical in her evaluation:

> Moving to Alberta is like taking a plant and pulling it out by its roots and replanting it in Alberta. Sometimes the conditions are right and the replanting takes hold and you thrive. But other times, the soil is not right there and you begin to die. Those are the people who have to return home. (Saskatchewan)

Replanting at the destination meant being socially integrated into the new community in some way. Failure to thrive there meant a lack of such integration, which compelled the need to leave. In any case, the primary dynamic in a return to the place of origin was the idea of "coming home." By definition, coming home meant returning to the place where you belonged, and it represented a preferred alternative to staying at the destination or seeking another destination. A returnee in Halifax said:

> I left Alberta because there was no culture and no sense of community. Here I had a sense of belonging and that is what I wanted. (Nova Scotia)

Another study participant put it this way:

> I came back because of the quality of life ... [the job I got] is not as good as what I had but it does not matter because this is where I belong. In the long run, quality of life is more important than money. (Manitoba)

Coming home implied a social context and perhaps also a landscape that trumped other things considered significant, like money or material possessions. It was also possible that this discourse masked other reasons for returning

One of the intriguing questions about return migration was whether it was the result of failure or whether other, more positive, factors were involved. In other words, was the return propelled by push factors at the destination or pull factors at the region of origin. When push factors were emphasized, they were understood in terms of the failure to find a satisfactory position within the community at the destination. Reference group issues were usually central. The inability to find acceptance in a work group; the inability to succeed in a work group; the failure to find adequate employment; the feeling of being lonely, isolated, or unconnected; and/or the inability to relate to the culture of the destination all served as push factors for return. Two illustrations make this point. The mother of an Atlantic returnee noted:

> My son went out there but he found that it was hard to break in. Here everyone knew who his dad was, and they treated him differently. So he came back. He didn't last. (New Brunswick)

At home, her son had a sense of belonging that could not be achieved at the destination. The comments of a returned male from Pictou County, Nova Scotia, also illustrate this point:

> I never landed a job with a good future or I might have stayed. But the baby was due and my wife wanted to go back to our family. (Nova Scotia)

Lacking adequate employment and feeling the need to be connected to family due to the birth of a child made the social ties at home all the more important.

The foregoing illustration indicates that there may be sociological pull factors from the region of origin. Parents, grandparents, friendship networks, and a sense of belonging to a local community can be strong incentives to return – even at the cost of lower financial rewards. Perhaps the single most important reason that people gave for return migration was family. In some cases, elderly parents needed care; however, for young couples, the compelling factor in returning was to be near family when they had children. One woman from Winnipeg put it this way:

> I flew back five times in one year to see my family. I knew when I started a family I wanted to move back, to move close to my family. Being in Alberta showed me money isn't everything and family is. My husband was not as enthused about moving back. If he had stayed, he could have done much better financially. (Manitoba)

A recently returned Nova Scotian noted:

> We wanted to raise our child among family. Financially it is hurting because we only have job prospects rather than a firm job. But here we have grandparents for daycare and not an independent caretaker. (Nova Scotia)

In a surprising number of cases, returning for family reasons was also related to working in a family business or in a business that had family connections:

> I left to get away from connections and to make it on my own. But I have come back because the connections [particularly in business] my family has here gives me a higher profile in the community. (Saskatchewan)

A Prince Edward Islander remarked:

> My father has fishing gear and all the licences and we have a blueberry farm and I have a share in that. So I have something valuable to go back to. (Prince Edward Island)

Sometimes the retirement of parents meant that there was now a place for a son or daughter in the family business.

Returning home meant that reference group ties were stronger in the community of origin than at the destination. The social networks at home, both those with strong ties and those with weak ties, provided a sense of belonging that was missing at the destination. And if the migrant failed to have a meaningful reference group at the destination, she/he had a tendency to idealize life at home as being safe and comfortable with well-established networks. Thus, push and pull factors operated at the same time.

Job loss offers a good example of how push and pull factors could operate conjointly. If there was ever a time to consider return, it was when the migrant lost her/his job.[5] Being unemployed could be considered as failing at the destination, and this could prompt return. But being unemployed also provided the occasion to contrast the destination with the social capital at the place of origin:

> When I got laid off in Alberta, it caused me to rethink. I did not have enough connections there, whereas in Manitoba, I feel like I have connections all over. That sealed it for going home. (Manitoba)

Very few migrants interpreted their return migration as a personal failure; rather, they developed rationalizations that denigrated the destination and lauded the place of origin. There were a number of issues that could be framed so that the destination could be rejected and the place of origin accepted. For example, people who were unable to generate a strong enough income or to establish new ties in Alberta interpreted their departure as a cost-of-living issue: "I left because of the cost of living. People in Alberta are too preoccupied with making money and I found that disheartening (Saskatchewan). A Summerland, British Columbia, returnee put it this way:

> Everybody keeps saying that you can make more money in Alberta, and you can. But not every job is like that, and if you are not lucky enough, you are better off at home with family near. (British Columbia)

Migration almost always turned out to be the wrong decision when it failed to have adequate financial rewards (Dupuy, Mayer, and Morissette 2000, 26). This only accentuated the need for family support, which was easier to come by at home.

Another prominent rationalization for returning concerned the pace of life in Alberta. Returning home seemed one way of getting off the treadmill of working long hours in order to maintain a meaningful lifestyle:

> I didn't want the competitiveness of Alberta and the twelve-hour workdays. I want a slower pace, and I want to take a step back and prepare long-range for retirement. (Saskatchewan)

Unsponsored migrants who had jobs with low pay and who worked long hours at one or more jobs came to associate living in Alberta with a hectic work schedule. In other cases, the shortage of labour meant that employers asked employees to work long hours. For these people, returning home provided relief from a lifestyle in which their survival depended on redoubling their efforts. Alberta was characterized by people driven by achievement and upward mobility ("getting ahead" and "making money"), and the returnee often saw her/himself as a different type of person. As one returnee noted:

> Alberta is a Petri dish for a certain kind of person. People who go there and stay there think differently. Maybe all of a certain type go there. (British Columbia)

A returnee from Atlantic Canada who repeated the migration cycle several times noted:

> There is a totally different culture there than here. The corporate culture is not what I am used to so I just do short stints and come home. (New Brunswick)

In contrast, the home community is presumed to offer a very different kind of lifestyle:

> In Alberta, everyone just wants to get ahead, whereas here you can enjoy life. (Manitoba)

Another way to look at this is through the lens of the lifecycle:

> It is just a matter of where you are in life. Young people have to get away, and when they start making babies, their attitude changes. Then they look for a safe place to raise their family. (Ontario)

Migrants who returned to small communities sometimes used the phrase "culture shock" to describe their reaction to the demands of work life, big-city living, and a racially diverse population. Some migrants felt anonymous in big cities as they were accustomed to small-town living, and this created a sense that the home community was "where we belong." One female returnee who was having a difficult time adjusting to life in Alberta told of having won a trip for a family of four to Disneyland while living in Edmonton. She wanted to return home so badly that she converted the trip to five one-way tickets to Newfoundland. She told her family, "No, we're not going to Disneyland. We're going to Newfoundland." The frenzied bustle of Fort McMurray was too much for people accustomed to a slower pace. Some admitted that they were not prepared for the pace of life in Alberta but that, having once experienced it, if they ever returned, they could probably handle it much better. In any case, people who came to Alberta without the support of those at home often viewed returning as a welcome relief.

If, as I have shown, some left their province of origin for political reasons, it stands to reason that some would return for political reasons. The region of reference for these people was their home region, where political values were often more congenial to their own thinking:

> My dreams for more meaningful employment were really realized here, but I want to go back to Ontario because this province will never mesh with my liberal values. (Ontario)

> We did not want to live in a one-party democracy. We are staunch NDPers. Here [Saskatchewan] there is lower car insurance and no medicare premiums. People are good neighbours and take care of each other; Alberta has become so urbanized and aggressive, but here people take time for you and care for each other. (Saskatchewan)

> I did not like the competitive spirit in Alberta. I was in the carpet business and there was a lot of competition and I had to drive all over the city for jobs. I decided that I wanted to go to a place where the government would take care of me. (Saskatchewan)

In other instances, it was unclear how adjustment difficulties and homesickness were related to politics. But note that family and political values could be intertwined:

> I hated Alberta and I hated Klein. I even left my girlfriend there because I hated it so much. You might get paid more and gas is cheaper but you drive more. This is where my family is anyway, and I was the only one who was away. (Ontario)

The rationales for returning were often as complicated as were the rationales for leaving.

For a multitude of reasons, migration was not always successful, and, therefore, return migration always remained a significant option. The inability to adjust, adapt, or accept the destination was not the only reason to return home. Some migrants claimed that they had always planned to return. A New Brunswick migrant observed:

> I have established a time frame now and I think in another year I want to go back. I'm still half there. It tore me in half to leave. I have family there and good friends there to whom I am closer than most people are to their siblings. Those ties are very close to me, and I am extremely close to my family. (New Brunswick)

Upon departure for Alberta, most migrants had some sort of plan in which returning home was at least a fallback position. For some, going away was part of a plan to make life in the community of origin more satisfactory. This might be accomplished through earning money to buy a house back home or other material things. Two Maritimers made the following observations:

> The idea is to stay here long enough so that you can be mortgage free when you move back to PEI. We debate with ourselves about whether we should invest in a house while we are here because we are throwing away a lot on rent. (Prince Edward Island)

> I came out here to pay off my debts. I've enjoyed my time out here but I would like to get back to the Maritimes somewhere. (Prince Edward Island)

Persons who already owned a home in the community of origin had a major incentive to return:

> I thought I was just coming for a visit, and when it wasn't happening that way I cried a lot. I will never call this home because we built our dream home back there and it is waiting for us. (Newfoundland)

Some migrants left to obtain professional experience but always intended to return. A migrant from Halifax said:

> I had an MBA, but to get a job there you needed experience so that's why I think people move out to the West – to get experience so that

> they can then move back and get the jobs that they want. (Nova Scotia)

A Cape Bretoner described his plan this way:

> I am a third-generation coal miner and everybody I grew up with was in either steel or coal ... I was in this coal industry for over twenty years and decided that I should get into a career that would give me the best chance of employment in Cape Breton. I thought it would be teaching, so I went off to get my education degree. But because there was not a lot of retirements, it will be awhile till I can get hired in Cape Breton so I thought I would come out here to get experience. At my age, in the late forties, that was my best opportunity. I think a window will open up in two to three years at home, but, in the meantime, the best opportunity for me is in Alberta. (Nova Scotia)

The decision to have children or to school them in the community of origin was also an issue in returning. Wanting to educate children in the region of origin was a very clear indicator that that was where the primary reference group was located. Other, more long-term migrants, would return upon retirement because the region of origin was where their friends and family resided. For all of these persons, migration had built within it a plan for return. Whether that plan was fulfilled or not, it did play a role for many migrants. In other words, returnees were not just people who had rejected the results of migration; they were also people who had always intended to go home.

For some people, migration was part of an empowerment strategy whose goal was always to return. For example, going to Alberta might be part of a strategy to get job experience so that they could return home and be qualified for the employment they desired, or it might be a way of making money that they could then bring home. Surprisingly, a significant number of migrants talked about moving to Alberta so that they could pay off their debts ("I left with a \$65,000 debt and it is now down to \$5,000 after two years in Fort McMurray" [Newfoundland]). Alberta stood for job opportunities that were not available at home and for fast cash:

> A lot of young people go to Alberta to make money. They call it "to work on the rigs," but maybe they do and maybe they don't. The idea is to make some serious coin and then come back here to do what they want to do. (Ontario)

A man from Saskatchewan explained why he left and why he returned:

> My wife and I moved to Calgary right out of school when the important things in life were jobs, entertainment, and opportunities. There were more jobs in our field in Calgary than all of Saskatchewan. We stayed in Calgary for five years and moved up in our careers, working hard and getting nowhere. We moved from one rental home to the next. When our priorities changed to family, children, and a stable home, we decided that Regina is where we wanted to be. Six months after moving back we bought our first house and pay less than half of what we were paying for rent. We came back with more experience and had an easier time finding jobs ... Moving to Alberta was a great thing, but moving back was the best thing we have ever done. (Saskatchewan)

With regard to her experience in Calgary, a Newfoundland woman said:

> I started as a receptionist and worked my way up to an account manager in six years. I learned on the job and worked my way up ... Without our experience in Alberta, we would never have been able to come home and do what we are doing today. (Newfoundland)

Whether returning was planned or not, some people saw how it could be empowering. They realized that they could sell their homes at inflated prices in the hot Alberta economy and bring the proceeds to a lower-cost economy, where they could live debt free:

> In Alberta, I would have to work for us to make it. I did not want to do that. So we sold our home and after we paid off our mortgage, we were still able to buy a home here and be debt-free. (Nova Scotia)

As one Prince Edward Islander from Charlottetown put it:

> Maritimers have a saying that if you have to go away, don't come back empty-handed, meaning work hard while you are away and bring the proceeds back with you. (Prince Edward Island)

In all these ways, returning could contribute to empowerment. And it is important to recognize that these types of positive outcomes did occur.

THE ACTUAL EXPERIENCE OF RETURNING

The actual experience of returning was often was very different from what was expected. Returnees may have had a difficult time fitting in because they were caught between the worldview of the place of origin and that of the destination (cf. Sinclair 2003, 217–20). While for some the big city may have meant anonymity, for others the smaller community back home meant confinement. Here are some laments:

> I feel like I am more like a Calgarian. People there are from everywhere and are transient and need to make friends. Here they don't need you. (New Brunswick)

> My wife wanted to come home to family so I came too. But when I left Winnipeg, I just wanted to get out because it was an older city. I felt Calgary was younger, more vibrant and alive. Now that I am back, the socialist government drives me nuts, the tax situation is brutal, and there is too much complacency. My experience in Alberta told me Manitoba was wrong. So I think I want to move back. (Manitoba)

Going away had the potential of changing migrants in some way:

> It took awhile to fit in [even though this is where my brothers and sisters are] because, at heart, we had become westerners to an extent. (Ontario)

Fitting in back home was not always easy, and differences were often quickly noted.

An older woman from Nova Scotia talked about feeling lonesome and homesick because she could not hear the ocean where she lived in Stony Plain (a suburb of Edmonton). She went back to Nova Scotia for a wedding and people there talked her into coming back:

> But now I have been here for one year and I'm torn. Now I think I'm sorry because I did get accustomed to it. The attitude is different there. On top of that my daughter and grandchildren are there but my other family and friends are here. (Nova Scotia)

Discovering that social ties were in both the community of origin and the destination produced considerable conflict.

Conflicted feelings also resulted from making comparisons between the origin community and the destination community. One person who eagerly anticipated returning home to Atlantic Canada perceived an unexpected difference between an expanding economy and a stagnant economy:

> There is an attitude difference here that is more doom and gloom and people are always blaming the government. People in Alberta are more upbeat and never sit around and talk about how bad things are. I think the attitude here rolls in with the fog and makes you feel pretty draggy. (Newfoundland)

A male returnee to Regina spoke of the difference between Saskatchewan and Alberta:

> If it wasn't for all my family back here, I wouldn't have come back. I think they give you a blood test in Alberta and if you have any socialist genes, they just punch you right back to Saskatchewan. (Saskatchewan)

A female returnee from Prince Edward Island made a different comparison:

> The adaptation coming back was harder than I expected. Here everybody always knows everybody and everything and that is oppressive. The good things are also the bad things. You go to the store and everybody knows you, but there are days in which you don't want that. (Prince Edward Island)

Persons who returned to small communities, where the contrast between the destination and the home region was most striking, were especially likely to make this kind of observation. On the other hand, a return to a major regional metropolitan centre such as Halifax was more likely to be satisfactory.[6]

The evaluation of the consequences of returning was never straightforward and simple. Migrants were sometimes conflicted because the pay was better and work was more plentiful in Alberta than it was at home. On the other hand, they longed for the lifestyle of their home region. Such persons were aware that something was being sacrificed.[7] A Prince Edward Islander observed:

> It is bittersweet. It is the good of the small town versus the opportunities of the big city. I liked Alberta but I want to be here. (Prince Edward Island)

While in some instances there was clear unanimity between couples and family members with regard to moving back, in others there was disagreement. One spouse may have wanted to return while the other did not:

> My husband found it better in Alberta but our son missed Saskatchewan and this influenced my husband to move back. He is less happy here now but we are more happy. (Saskatchewan)

A wife of a couple from Halifax described their struggle this way:

> He was more okay with being away, but I did not like being away. He would say, "Oh, just another year," and then "just another year." Then we started to think about buying a house. I wanted to be home because of family. I would get calls from the birthday parties and they would say, "We miss you," and I would be depressed for days. I always knew in the back of my mind that we would not be staying.

Such conflicts often provoked family stress:

> In a lot of families, it is a real tug of war. One spouse wants to go and the other doesn't. It works that way for leaving here but also for coming back too. (British Columbia)

Furthermore, it was not unusual, in hindsight, for families/couples who did return to have second thoughts. The rationale for returning may have been convincing at the time, but there were always gains and losses. A Newfoundlander who returned home with her husband because they wanted to raise their family at home observed:

> I have second thoughts every second day. If I was in Alberta now, I would be crying that my family would not be seeing the baby growing up. But I left a great job and great friends in Alberta. So what are you to do? (Newfoundland)

Migrants whose adaptation at the destination was not positive were, of course, the least likely to express a sense of loss upon returning home. Persons who returned primarily for family reasons were the most likely to wonder if they had made the right decision.

> We had been thinking of returning [to Prince Edward Island] for several years. But now that we are here we realize that Alberta had sort of become our home. One and a half years later, we still have questions about our decision, and now we are thinking about the potential for the future for our children here. (Prince Edward Island)

Migration clearly changes people in some way, and, in many ways, returnees discovered that they were divided people, caught in a web of decisions that were not clear cut, with a piece of them still residing in Alberta. A government officer in Newfoundland put it this way: "Some people who come back to retire come to the realization that home is now Alberta. "It's not how I remember it," they say. Some can't reconcile their past ideas with current realities."

It was not surprising that return migrants felt unsettled for a long time. Just how long depended on the degree of distancing that she/he experienced and on whether the marginality experienced before migration had been resolved by coming home.

THE REACTION OF THE COMMUNITY OF ORIGIN TO RETURNEES

Communities that repeatedly lose population appear to be caught in a dilemma about returnees. On the one hand, they are proud of local persons who go away and "make it big" as this seems to reflect positively on their community. But if the person has not succeeded while away, then her/his return could be a sign of failure. The many diverse meanings of leaving and returning are expressed by this Newfoundland migrant:

> If someone leaves and is a big success, then people say they made the right decision and it reflects glory on Newfoundland. Going to the mainland is a way of finding out if you are better than other people who have stayed. But if you come back and didn't make it away, that sort of reflects on Newfoundland too, meaning that you failed. (Newfoundland)

On the other hand, welcoming the returnee was seen as a validation that home was still home (e.g., "Maritimers always come back."). Returning was also viewed as socially restorative to the community. As a returnee from Cornwall, Prince Edward Island, noted: "People said it's good to have you back where you belong."

Home communities could often sense that returnees were having difficulty settling in and that they were constantly making comparisons. One returnee even admitted that he was being quite critical of the home community and was trying to change it:

> I came back for the lifestyle and to take care of my parents. But going to Alberta changed me and I brought back the Alberta attitude, which is a more Americanized attitude towards business. In Manitoba, they just hum and haw and debate. In Alberta, they are more entrepreneurial and more willing to stick their necks out. People who come back bring that Alberta attitude with them. That is what I am trying to do here. (Manitoba)

This kind of attitude was at times resented, but it shows that fitting in upon return was not always easy.

A community constructs its interpretation of out-migration by examining the rationales of those who decide to return. The return migrant, of course, has to have a publicly acceptable explanation for why a decision was made to return. It was more likely for the migrant to say that the destination was rejected because the home community was better than to say that she/he came home because she/he had somehow failed. A francophone Quebecer who had trouble with English in Alberta "used the excuse of the rednecks" to explain why he returned to Quebec, where he no longer felt at a disadvantage. Common criticisms of the destination, such as high costs, pace of life, or commuting time, were picked up by residents of the home community and used to stereotype the destination, providing a justification for why they themselves would not/should not leave.[8]

Sometimes community members built their interpretation of the migration experience from regular contacts with migrants who lamented being away. Hearing about how much they missed home and missed particular people often created images of migrant unhappiness. A New Brunswick woman said she had returned from Alberta because she "did not want to die in a foreign land" and was in touch with people still in Alberta "who desperately wanted to come home but felt trapped." Clearly these are people for whom the community of origin served as a significant reference group.

Home communities often also got caught up in other stereotypes that inflated the strengths of the destination. A New Brunswick returnee noted:

> People couldn't believe we came back and were incredulous that we left the place where the streets are paved with gold. So we told them that we learned that money isn't everything. (New Brunswick)

Even here there was a moral lesson that reinforced the positive attributes of the home community. As a school principal in Saskatchewan exclaimed:

> It's the media that does it. The media gives the image that Alberta is the pot at the end of the rainbow, and they hype it too much because the pot is still full of crap like everywhere else. (Saskatchewan)

Downgrading the destination ("People leave here with great expectations ... and when they get there, they discover it is not so great" [Ontario]) was one reaction that helped the host community understand why returning was a good idea. The difficulty in sorting myth from reality was a difficult issue for many home communities.

One type of returnee of specific interest was the person who came back to retire. Obviously, this kind of population exchange had a huge impact on both sending and receiving communities. If Alberta was the magnet for younger high-earning and tax-paying citizens while the home community was the magnet for older citizens who were no longer paying taxes and who depended on a range of government services, the implications of this return are significant. Retirees often justified their return by criticizing life in Alberta:

> The speed of life in Alberta is fierce. You wake up in the morning running. (Newfoundland)

Retirees were inevitably attracted to the home community by the presence of siblings or other family members and friends. This type of person likely made regular visits to the home community, with the result that ties remained strong. Most of the retirees whom we encountered had gone to Alberta in the 1970s and 1980s, so they were not part of the second wave of migration. The home community gladly welcomed such persons but could not help but realize that the return of older persons was considerably different from the return of younger persons. In fact, the return of retirees tended to reinforce the idea that the community was not suitable for people wanting action and opportunity.

CONCLUSION

The decision to return to the community of origin, like the decision to leave it, was complex. However, there was usually one overarching factor that explained the return, and that was that, in some sense, the home community still provided the person with her/his primary reference group. In other words, the migrant was dissatisfied with her/his social location at the destination and wanted to return to the region of origin, where there was still adequate social capital to enable them to establish a more satisfactory social position.

Return migration had different meanings for different people. While for some people return signified failure, for others it was part of an empowerment strategy. Return was also a basis for conflict, with integration into the community of origin often being much more difficult than expected, and returnees in family units often had different interpretations of the wisdom of return. For some, migration was essentially an adventure for which there had been little preparation, and return was almost taken for granted. Migrants who felt marginalized at the place of origin only to discover that they felt the same way at the destination had clearly not found a more satisfactory position within the community. Regardless of the reason for migrating in the first place, if the migrant's primary reference group remained at the place of origin, then return was much more likely. Of course, this did not mean that, upon return, the migrant's evaluation of the gains and losses involved in coming home did not create new struggles and dilemmas.

The impact of out-migration on some communities was critical. The loss of young adults of child-bearing years created a huge gap in the social structure of these communities. The loss of people with ideas, energy, enthusiasm, and entrepreneurial skills also had a long-term impact. One entrepreneur who moved to Alberta discussed the different ways in which he had invested in his home community (including employing over one hundred people) only to see things fall apart as the community declined. He then retorted:

> I know this [Alberta] is a different place and I'm going to set up successful businesses here. Just watch me! (Newfoundland)

There is no doubt that, regardless of community type, migration involved the transference of skills, labour power, and even capital from the home region to Alberta. It also meant that, once a person became a migrant, she/he was continually negotiating her/his position, whether at the destination or upon return to the community of origin. And, in spite of this chapter's focus on return migration, it was also recognized that, once migration occurred, there was a strong probability that the migrant would never return.

15

Reassessing Migration

Allowing migrants to Alberta to share their experiences provided useful information that supported the construction of an interpretive framework for how and why migration occurred. As a further check on what was uncovered through the in-depth interviews, a follow-up survey provided an opportunity to explore statistically some of the key questions that emerged in the exploratory interviews and that help to specify factors in the migration selection process.

The study as originally designed aimed to uncover the meanings and motivations of migration, and this required in-depth interviews. As the data collection proceeded, the major issues came into sharper focus, which facilitated the construction of an instrument to measure the perceptions of migrants quantitatively. Phase III of the study involved a mail-out follow-up survey in 2003 to all participants in Phase I (see Appendix). While the length of time in Alberta was still not long, given the fact that all participants had arrived between 1996 and 2001, it did provide a second look at how migration was evaluated. This chapter reports the results of this aspect of the study and attempts to relate it to earlier findings.

Due to the fact that many participants in the study had probably already moved, many of the original participants were no longer at their declared place of residence, and the response rate was only 48.4 percent (n = 165). Given the fact that this sample cannot be considered fully representative of all individuals interviewed previously, the results should be interpreted with some caution. However, the fact that the conclusions from the survey data were highly similar to the earlier qualitative interviews suggests that the survey data is valid. In essence, the converging evidence between the two data sources builds a strong case for the conclusions of this research project.

We used a scale that asked participants to state their reaction to thirty-four brief statements clustered into six categories: (1) Leaving Where You Previously Lived, (2) Choosing Where to Move, (3) Comparing Alberta with Your Home Province, (4) Evaluating Your Decision to Relocate, (5) Experiencing Life in Alberta, and (6) Returning to your Home Province. Participants were asked to indicate whether they strongly agreed, somewhat agreed, neither agreed nor disagreed, somewhat disagreed, or strongly disagreed with each statement on a five-point Likert scale. For our purposes, those who strongly agreed or somewhat agreed could be usefully combined, as could those who strongly disagreed or somewhat disagreed, to reflect a tendency to accept or reject a statement. Where it is useful to indicate the strength of agreement with a statement, the response differences between "somewhat" and "strongly" agreeing or disagreeing will be indicated.

WHY DID MIGRANTS LEAVE THEIR PLACE OF ORIGIN?

One of the key questions addressed by this research is why people were prepared to leave their place of origin. The general expectation was that it was the opportunities that were present in Alberta that served as the magnet for the relocation, and this is where the emphasis in explaining the migration stream is usually placed. But there was also reason to suspect that there may have been push factors in the region of origin that may have facilitated the move. Six statements were designed to tap into this question of relocation motivation. In view of the fact that internal migration could be considered by some (and particularly young adults) as an adventure with a positive motivation, respondents were asked to respond to the statement "When I left my home province, it was largely for adventure." Forty-four percent agreed with this statement, although considerably more somewhat agreed (34 percent) than strongly agreed (10 percent) . An almost equal number (45 percent) disagreed, with the remaining 10 percent neither agreeing nor disagreeing. There were more who strongly disagreed (26 percent) than who strongly agreed (10 percent). The standard deviation of 1.41 confirms that there was considerable variability around the mean (3.16), suggesting that, while some may have come to Alberta for adventure, there were many who did not. And even for those who did come to Alberta for adventure, most felt that that was only part of the motivation. So overall, adventure appears to be a weak explanation for migration.

A similar situation was found with regard to the statement, "I left my home province because I had little choice." A standard deviation of

1.51 (mean = 3.41) again indicates considerable variation among respondents. However, while 35 percent agreed, 54 percent disagreed with the statement, and those who strongly disagreed (37 percent) were more numerous than were those who strongly agreed (15 percent). Thus, while some felt that they had no choice in leaving, that group was smaller and much softer in these convictions than was the group who felt it had a choice in leaving. This suggests that most of our study participants did not feel like victims but, rather, were active decision makers in their migration. A somewhat validating response was also obtained to the statement, "It upsets me that I had to leave my home province." The standard deviation of 1.43 (mean = 3.23) again suggests the existence of a range of responses supported by 39 percent agreeing and 44 percent disagreeing. Only 12 percent strongly agreed that leaving upset them, while 29 percent strongly disagreed that leaving upset them. So, in spite of the variation of responses, among those agreeing that leaving was upsetting, there were more who only moderately agreed that this was the case. If reluctance had been a more dominant feature of this migration, the intensity of agreement with this statement would have been much stronger. The fact that so many also disagreed with the statement suggests that, on the whole, these migrants are not persons who have been emotionally overwhelmed by their need to relocate or upset that they had to leave.

What is much more dramatic, however, is the strength of agreement to the statement, "The political and economic atmosphere back home was negative." Here fully 70 percent agreed with this statement, with 40 percent strongly agreeing (mean = 2.12). Only 15 percent disagreed with it at any level of intensity (somewhat or strongly). This suggests that the political and economic environment in their region of origin, as it pertained to them, played a significant role in their decision to relocate. When responding to the statement, "I actually felt depressed before I moved here," a much smaller percentage agreed with it (26 percent) than disagreed with it (54 percent), including a solid 41 percent that strongly disagreed (mean = 3.61). It is important to note that depression was an issue for some persons (9 percent strongly agreed and 17 percent somewhat agreed). But it was clearly not a major issue for most respondents, especially for the large number who strongly disagreed. It might also be concluded that the 21 percent who neither agreed nor disagreed felt that the idea of pre-migration depression was irrelevant.

Another possible reason for migration may have been a difference in ideology or worldview between the migrant and those back home, and this may have served as a push factor. So we included a statement that read: "One of the reasons I left home was because the people there think differently than I do." Twenty-two percent agreed but 59 percent disagreed (mean = 3.73). Again, the percentage of those who strongly agreed with the statement (8 percent) was much weaker than the percentage who strongly disagreed with it (43 percent). This would suggest that, for most respondents, ideological or worldview differences may not have been at the root of the relocation. On the other hand, the fact that almost one-quarter of the respondents interpreted their migration as at least partially caused by such an explanation is worth noting.

Adventure, depression, and ideological differences were not dominant push factors in migration, but they did play a role for a minority of respondents. About two in five did leave for adventure, and one in four felt depressed before they moved. About one in three felt that they had little choice in the necessity to relocate, and two in five were upset that they had to leave their home province. One in four were prompted to leave by the fact that they had a different worldview from those at their place of origin. Thus, while the emotional upheaval of leaving or the sense of migration as non-volitional behaviour was much more muted (or even rejected) than expected, there were clearly mixed reasons for people wanting to leave. For most people, a negative political and economic atmosphere appears to have been the strongest causal factor in out-migration. There are grounds to conclude that relocation was, in large measure, prompted by the perception of politico-economic conditions in which a variety of other factors were also at work. These factors, however, did not remove the sense of volition that most migrants felt about their decision to relocate (in contrast to feeling pushed out by circumstances). The implication is that migration was intentional behaviour, the goal of which was the attainment of some type of personal objective.

CHOOSING WHERE TO MOVE

How do people who have decided to leave go about choosing where to move? One possibility is that they decide to move to places where they already know people. When respondents were asked whether they agreed with the statement, "I came to Alberta because of people I knew who were here already," 56 percent agreed with and 39 percent disagreed. A relatively high standard deviation of 1.64 points out that there is considerable variation among the respondents. In sum, for the majority, relational ties played a role in people's choice to move to Alberta.[1]

Another component of the choice to move to Alberta may have been the appeal of making more money. When asked to assess the statement, "I am here just for the money," there was a definite tendency to reject this assertion, with a higher mean of 3.53 and a lower standard deviation of 1.29. Fifty-five percent disagreed with the statement, and 26 percent agreed with it; among those who agreed, only 7 percent strongly agreed. Perhaps the statement was too strong, but there appeared to be a reaction to the idea that money was the primary motivation for most migrants. And, for those for whom money was important, there was a reluctance to interpret the migration purely in monetary terms.

A third possibility in the choice about where to move pertained to worldview. In response to the statement, "I moved to Alberta because my way of thinking was closer to the way people think here," more disagreed (49 percent) than agreed (33 percent). Among those who disagreed with this statement, more strongly disagreed (33 percent) than somewhat disagreed (16 percent). While the standard deviation reflected considerable variability (1.45), it is clear that, for many, a perception of more compatible thinking with people in Alberta was not a critical factor in the choice to move there. Interestingly though, one-third of the respondents did indicate that such ideological similarities were important to them. This was a slightly stronger response than received from those who said they left their region of origin for ideological/worldview reasons.

There is, then, some support for the idea that people moved to Alberta because they knew people there already, but there is less support for the fact that people moved to the province just for the money or because the worldview of Albertans was similar to theirs. Between these two latter responses, however, it is clear that a significant minority did relate to the idea that Alberta's worldview was closer to theirs.

COMPARING ALBERTA WITH THE HOME PROVINCE

A dramatic result of this analysis is that participants overwhelmingly concluded that the move to Alberta resulted in their being financially better off ("I am economically better off by being in Alberta"). Fully 82 percent agreed with the statement, including almost 60 percent who strongly agreed. In contrast, only 5 percent disagreed with the statement. This result is not surprising because migrants who remained in Alberta would obviously be the ones most likely to feel this way. Migrants who were not better off were much more likely to have already left and probably did not participate in the survey. But the strength of this conclusion is indisputable (mean = 1.65, standard deviation = .94).

One interesting question is whether this economic well-being also translated into greater comparative trust for Alberta politicians ("I trust politicians here more than I trust politicians back home"). Perhaps of first significance is the fact that 41 percent neither agreed nor disagreed with this statement. Politics was perhaps not on their radar. Of those who remained, only slightly more disagreed with this idea (34 percent) than agreed with it (25 percent). In short, there was no clear confirmation that being in Alberta had a significant effect on migrants' building a comparatively greater trust in Alberta politicians (mean = 3.18, standard deviation = 1.23).

It might also be asked whether this overwhelming sense of economic well-being might enhance the comfort level with being in Alberta, particularly in relation to the region of origin. In response to the statement, "For me, coming to Alberta was in some sense like coming home," there was considerable variation (mean = 3.07, standard deviation = 1.35). Thirty-five percent agreed with that statement and 40 percent disagreed. Respondents demonstrated a similar level of variability with regard to the statement, "When I go back home to visit, I feel like I don't belong there anymore" (mean = 2.94, standard deviation = 1.34). Forty-one percent agreed and 37 percent disagreed. The statements are indeed quite strong and seemed to have provoked two opposing response streams. The comparison of place of origin with destination is most strongly reflected in the responses to the statement, "When I hear about life back home, I am glad that I did not stay there." Forty-six percent agreed with that statement, whereas only 26 percent disagreed with it. A much lower mean (2.51) points out the tendency for respondents to agree that life at their destination was preferred, which would make sense in light of the fact that so many felt that they were economically better off in Alberta.

In sum, our respondents tended to agree that they were much better off economically in Alberta, which would be consistent with the comparative observation that they were glad that they did not stay in their region of origin when they heard about life back there. However, the more contrasting responses to the other items suggest that, while they clearly tap important feelings for some respondents, for others they do not. Keeping this in mind, one in four did agree that they trusted Alberta politicians more than they trusted those back home; one in three agreed that going to Alberta was like coming home; and two in five agreed that, when they go back home to visit, they feel like they do not belong there anymore. There is, then, a sense in which a significant minority of our respondents had developed a comfort level with living in Alberta that went beyond economics, particularly when it was contrasted to where they lived before. On the other hand, there is roughly an equal-sized group that did not share those feelings.

EVALUATING YOUR DECISION TO RELOCATE

One of the important purposes of the follow-up survey was to understand how migrants later evaluated their decision to relocate to Alberta (varying from two to seven years). The first statement in this section attempted to uncover those who regretted the move ("In retrospect, I wish I would have stayed in my home province instead of moving to Alberta"). Perhaps the most noteworthy thing about the response to this statement is that it was overwhelmingly rejected, with only 7 percent agreeing and 84 percent disagreeing (mean = 4.33, standard deviation = .98). The converse of that statement identified those who had a much more positive assessment of their relocation ("I feel that my decision to move here was a good one"). Ninety-two percent agreed with that statement and almost three-quarters of all respondents strongly agreed (mean = 1.39, standard deviation = .80). Only 3 percent disagreed, suggesting that this follow-up sample tapped primarily those for whom the move was considered successful.

The attempt to identify those for whom the outcome of the migration was less successful was made through the statement, "I am disappointed because my expectations in moving here have not been met." This statement focused on determining whether there was a disconnection between expectations and actual outcomes. Seventy-seven percent disagreed that this was their evaluation, including 53 percent who strongly disagreed (mean = 4.21, standard deviation = 1.02). Only 7 percent agrced, which was very similar to the percentage who agreed with the earlier statement about regretting the relocation. Most of these respondents felt that their expectations had been met. Two more positive statements followed, both of which had similarly high levels of agreement. "Being in Alberta makes me feel good" resonated well with respondents, with 78 percent agreement and only 7 percent disagreement (mean = 1.89, standard deviation = .98). The sense of feeling increasingly comfortable in Alberta was assessed through the statement, "I feel more at home in Alberta the longer I am here." Eighty-two percent agreed and only 9 percent disagreed (mean = 1.88, standard deviation = 1.05).

The summation statement, or conclusion, was contained in the assertion, "I think I am probably in Alberta permanently." In spite of the high level of agreement that moving to Alberta had been a good thing, and that Alberta was a place that made migrants feel comfortable, there was some slippage regarding whether the move was to be considered permanent. Only 59 percent agreed with the statement, while 28 percent disagreed. The mean of 2.47 and standard deviation of 1.37 suggests a much higher level of variability than was present in the other items in this section. Of course, we do not know why some migrants concluded that their migration to Alberta might not be permanent; however, in spite of their high levels of satisfaction with Alberta, there is clearly a group whose members do not expect their migration to be permanent. On the other hand, the majority do intend to remain in the province.

The interesting thing about the items in this section is that all of them, except the last one, polarized the responses in the direction of a positive evaluation of their migration to Alberta. The strength of this assessment is conveyed in the fact that "strongly" agree or "strongly" disagree always had the highest level of support. This positive evaluation of the migration experience, however, did not necessarily translate into the conviction that Alberta would be a permanent home. It might be surmised that there are personal/family matters that are perceived as moderating factors, in spite of other indicators of migration satisfaction.

EXPERIENCING LIFE IN ALBERTA

Two aspects to experiencing life in Alberta were measured in this section: the first deals with work and career; the second deals with social ties.

In the interviews, migrants often talked about the range and sequence of jobs that they had in Alberta after arrival. This often led migrants to view their current job as quite different from the type of job that they might aspire to in the future. However, the most straightforward question focused on the present: "I am really happy with my current job". Given the fact that the evidence suggests that these respondents were happy with their decision to move to Alberta, it could be expected that they would be reasonably happy with their current job, and this is indeed the case. Seventy-seven percent agreed with this statement, including a majority who strongly agreed (mean = 1.89, standard deviation = 1.02). Only 7 percent disagreed. Migrants were overwhelmingly satisfied with their employment. The second work-related statement allowed us to assess the move from a career point of view: "It has been a good career move for me to come to Alberta." Fully 82 percent agreed with that assessment, including the 62 percent who said they strongly agreed (mean = 1.61, standard deviation = .94). There was thus overwhelming satisfaction with the career outcomes of the move.

Two further statements were included in order to determine how migrants felt about the consequences that this career outcome had for them personally. In response to the statement, "Since I moved here, I feel like I put in too many hours working," there was considerable variation (mean = 3.16, standard deviation = 1.25). Thirty-two percent agreed with this statement, though only 10 percent did so strongly; 40 percent disagreed, with 28 percent neither agreeing nor disagreeing. These results suggest that too much work is a problem for about one-third of the sample; however, even with this group, it is not considered a serious problem. The conception of Alberta as a place demanding long hours of work is certainly not borne out by this sample (although it does not control for regions such as Fort McMurray, where long work hours were more typical).

Another way of assessing the importance of work for our respondents was to place it in the context of the Alberta economic environment: "I feel like work and making money dominates people's thinking in Alberta." Forty-nine percent stated that they agreed with this statement, and only 20 percent disagreed with it, suggesting that work and economic betterment was a major theme of life in the province (mean = 2.59. standard deviation = 1.18). But it is also significant that almost one-third (30 percent) neither agreed nor disagreed that money and work dominated life in Alberta. It is interesting that, when migrants were asked to respond to the statement, "The lifestyle in Alberta appeals to me," 85 percent agreed and only 9 percent disagreed (mean = 1.86, standard deviation = .95). While the meaning of lifestyle was not defined, these results suggest that there was no strong negative reaction to the dominant way of life in Alberta and that migrants must have found some acceptable work-leisure balance.

There is also a social aspect to experiencing life in Alberta that pertains to interaction with people back at the place of origin or with people from the place of origin living in Alberta. When asked to assess the statement, "Keeping in touch with people back home is very important to me," 82 percent agreed (mean = 1.69, standard deviation = 1.03), while only 7 percent disagreed. The evidence is clear that most migrants maintain ties with people in their region of origin and that these ties are important to them. Of course, the strength or regularity of those ties was not measured. But how important are such ties at the destination? Are ties with persons from the region of origin also important there?

When presented with the statement, "People from home who live in Alberta are an important part of my life here," 52 percent agreed and 27 percent disagreed. Twenty-two percent neither agreed nor disagreed, suggesting that the respondents were split over whether friends from home were important to them at the destination (mean = 2.64, standard deviation = 1.43). Keeping in touch with people back home is of overwhelming interest to these migrants, but doing so at the destination is of less importance – though the majority of respondents prefer to do so. One might assume that maintaining contact with relatives back home is what keeps the responses to the first statement high and that, in some important ways, migrants establish new friendship networks at the destination. But it is significant that half of the respondents found people from home in Alberta and that these relationships were an important part of their lives.[2]

Interaction with people from the region of origin might also be linked to the extent to which migrants felt that there were barriers to their social integration into life in Alberta. The statement, "I feel like I am an outsider in Alberta," was meant to assess the extent to which migrants felt welcome or, conversely, experienced a sense of strangeness. Seventy-four percent disagreed that they felt like an outsider in Alberta, with the largest segment (45 percent) feeling "strongly" about that (mean = 4.05, standard deviation = 1.09). In contrast, only 12 percent agreed with the statement (including only 3 percent who strongly agreed that this was the case). In short, while ties to people back home are important to almost all migrants, ties with other migrants from back home are less important in the destination community – at least for some. While about one-half of the respondents said that ties with people from their region of origin were important at the destination, the fact that only 12 percent felt like an outsider suggests that migrants do not feel a sense of exclusion and that they tend to experience Alberta as a more open society.

Overall, then, migrants were satisfied with their relocation to Alberta from the perspective of their current job and from the perspective of their career. About one-third felt that they worked too much, and about one-half thought that work and making money dominated the thinking of people in Alberta. But when migrants were asked to assess their lifestyle in Alberta, there was clear satisfaction. One of the reasons for this satisfaction may be that, while they had strong ties to their community of origin, they also felt very much at home and did not feel like an outsider in their new place of residence. For those who wanted ties with other newcomers, from home or elsewhere, their availability provided the support that they needed; however, friendship formation and inclusion did not appear to be a problem.

THE PERMANENCE OF MIGRATION

How do these migrants perceive Alberta in relation to their place of origin? Is there a sense that this migration was only temporary? Was return to the region of origin at some point contemplated? The respondents were asked to measure the urgency of return by selecting one of three possibilities: as soon as possible, in the long-term, and upon retirement. In response to the statement, "I would like to return to my home province as soon as possible," only 13 percent agreed, while 72 percent disagreed (mean = 3.95, standard deviation = 1.21). Clearly, among those in this group, there is no overwhelming desire to return soon. Respondents were also asked to indicate whether their "ultimate goal was to return to their home province." A larger group (27 percent) agreed that that was their goal, but 56 percent disagreed (mean = 3.57, standard deviation = 1.44). When the desire to return was measured according to the statement, "I expect to retire in the region where I came from," the percentage agreeing increased yet again to 35 percent (mean = 3.23, standard deviation = 1.50). Only 44 percent disagreed, while 21 percent were unsure or ambivalent.

There are several ways of looking at this data. One is that, while there was an increase in the desire to return over the three phases (immediate, ultimately, retirement – from 13 percent to 35 percent), only one-third of the respondents considered moving back at any phase. This suggests that return migration, for this group at least, was not a strong possibility and that, for most of these migrants, there was little desire to return home. On the other hand, the fact that one in eight wanted to return home soon, one in four wanted to ultimately return home, and one in three wanted to return home for retirement suggests that, even though these migrants assessed their decision to relocate to Alberta as a good one and felt that they were better off for being in the province, this did not imply a permanent commitment to reside there. Another way of looking at this is to see that, for many of these migrants, province of origin continued to be a residence option even once they had left. In short, at least at this point, migration did not imply closing the door to return – though this was a minority point of view and may have reflected wishful thinking more than a realistic assessment.

Three statements were included whose purpose was to determine the reasons that people moved back home. Rather than measuring this in an intensely personal way, the goal was to understand why (or under what conditions) they or others might consider returning home. One way of measuring this was to propose that some had difficulty adjusting and preferred the more familiar surroundings of home ("Most people who return home do so just because they are homesick"). Almost half (46 percent) of the respondents agreed with this statement, while only 15 percent disagreed (mean = 2.60, standard deviation = 1.00). Thirty-nine percent neither agreed nor disagreed. It is clear that difficulties adjusting and longing for home may be part of the picture, but the majority of respondents felt uncomfortable with this explanation and either rejected it or were unsure. Another way of putting the adjustment problem was to imply that those who returned home were reacting to the environment in Alberta, which may have been too competitive for them ("People who return home just can't cope with the competitive environment in Alberta"). Only 18 percent agreed with this statement, while 46 percent disagreed and 37 percent neither agreed nor disagreed (mean = 3.46, standard deviation = 1.10). It is clear that these migrants did not see the competitive environment in Alberta as the primary driver in people's desire to return home and that the reasons for return were either very different or much more complicated.

Finally, since many of the migrants were young adults and entry-level professionals who may have viewed Alberta as a good place to get started in their careers, we presented the statement: "My work experience in Alberta will help me get a better job back home should I choose to return." Note that this statement did not ask if this was their plan but, rather, focused on the role that being in Alberta *could* play in their ability to return home successfully. Over half (57 percent) agreed with this observation, while only 19 percent disagreed (mean = 2.44, standard deviation = 1.29). Those who disagreed or who neither agreed nor disagreed (25 percent) may have come from locations where the skills or job experience that they had developed in Alberta were not related to what was available in their home economy. Otherwise, it was clear that job experience in Alberta was considered a huge benefit in relocation back home, although the benefit may vary with the place of origin.

In sum, these respondents were not eager to return home soon, but some hoped to do so at some point in the future. The percentage of respondents desiring to return home increased in the long term, including for purposes of retirement. However, even at that, the majority did not expect to return to their region of origin. Most migrants perceived the reasons why people would return home as quite complex and not reducible to factors such as homesickness or the competitive environment in Alberta (though the former was stronger than the latter). The majority thought that their work experience in Alberta would help them in finding employment back home if they did return, but it was also clear that many were not convinced of this, probably because they came from places where their skills were not in demand.

GENDER, AGE, AND MARITAL STATUS

A two-tailed t-test of significance (at the .05 level) was used to assess the importance of gender, age, and marital status in explaining response differences. Gender was not a critical variable, with two exceptions. Somewhat surprisingly, men were somewhat more likely than women to be upset that they had to leave their home province, but they were more likely than women to trust politicians in Alberta than politicians at home. None of the other response differences was statistically significant.

Respondents in the youngest age category (20–29 years of age) were less likely to view Alberta as their permanent residence than were those over 30 years of age. They were more likely to have come to Alberta for adventure or to claim that they had just come to Alberta for the money. They were also more likely to keep in touch with people back home and to want to associate with people in Alberta who were from back home. Consequently, it was not surprising that they were less likely to agree that going to Alberta was like coming home, less likely to agree that they did not belong at home when they returned to visit, and less likely to agree that when they heard about life back home that they were glad that they had not stayed there. They were also less trusting of Alberta politicians and were much less likely to have moved to Alberta because their way of thinking was closer to what they perceived to be the way of thinking in Alberta. It follows that they were less likely to say that being in Alberta made them feel good or that their stay in Alberta would probably be permanent. On the other hand, they were more likely to see that going to Alberta was a good career move and that it would help them get a better job back home. They tended to think that work and making money tended to dominate people's thinking in Alberta and were more likely to think that they had been working too much since arriving there. They were much more likely to think that they would return to the region of origin either soon, eventually, or for retirement than were those over 30 years of age.

Age, then, was an important factor in that migrants under 30 felt much more strongly attached to home than did those over 30, and their stay in Alberta was much less likely to be considered permanent. This is an important point in light of the fact that persons under 30 are much more mobile. It also suggests that those over 30 who migrate are much more definitive in their migration because, as people age, they are presumably much less mobile. However, when they do migrate, it is the result of serious reflection on their position in the community of origin, with the result that when they choose their destination they do so with care and commitment.

If age is a critical variable, then it is not surprising that marital status is also significant. It would be expected that single persons would have much in common with persons under 30, and indeed that is the case. Single people were less likely to consider Alberta their permanent residence than were married people, and they were more likely to have come for adventure rather than to leave a negative political and economic atmosphere back home. They were more likely to be motivated by the fact that they had friends who were already in Alberta. Keeping in touch with home or friends from home in Alberta was therefore much more important for them than it was for married people. Political/ideological issues, like trusting Alberta politicians more or agreeing with the thinking of people in Alberta, were much less important to them than they were to married people, and they were also more likely to feel more at home in their region of origin and had to have more interest in staying there. Single people, though, were more likely to agree that their decision to move to Alberta was a good one and they were somewhat more likely to be happy with their job (although both single and married were happy with their jobs). Singles were also somewhat more likely to want to return home and thought that their Alberta experience would help them get a better job when they did so.

Thus, somewhat paradoxically, single younger persons (under 30) were more tied to home than were married persons over 30. This is a surprising finding in that it would normally be expected that older persons and persons who were married had stronger roots in the region of origin. On the other hand, for this older group, migration was a highly rationalized act, while for younger singles it was often seen as temporary and as a rite of passage. In the long run, younger migrants may elect to stay in Alberta; however, their initial decision to migrate was not the product of the same careful rationalization that went into the decision of older migrants.

There was another finding that was not unexpected. It is often observed that Atlantic Canadians have a different attitude towards migration than do other Canadians, and being from Atlantic Canada did indeed make a difference.[3] In comparison to migrants from other parts of Canada, they were less likely to consider Alberta their permanent residence and were more likely to be upset that they had to leave their home province. They were more likely to acknowledge that they were better off economically by being in Alberta, but they were less likely to view their migration as motivated by adventure. They were more likely to say that people from home were an important part of their life in Alberta, and, therefore they were less likely to say that going to Alberta was like coming home. The desire to return home occurred on a gradient in that Atlantic Canadians were much more keen about returning home than were migrants from other parts of Canada; however, the intensity of that desire increased over a longer period of time. In other words, fewer wanted to return "as soon as possible" than wanted to "ultimately return" or even wanted "strongly" to return upon retirement. Atlantic Canadians were also much more likely than were other Canadians to see a return home as the result of being homesick.

THE END RESULT OF MIGRATION

One of the important questions in any study of migration is whether the destination is considered permanent. Migrants might choose to return to the place of origin at some point in the future or they might eventually decide to relocate somewhere else (this is known as onward migration). Persons who migrate once are much more likely to migrate again, so there is always the possibility that the migrant will try other destinations. From the point of view of the host society, which in this case was Alberta, it is useful to know whether migrants intended to stay. In the first phase of the study, participants were asked if they intended to make Alberta their permanent home. In response, 53.4 percent said that they expected to remain in Alberta and that this province was their destination; 12.9 percent said that they had no plans to remain in Alberta permanently, although they did not indicate whether return migration or onward migration was their expectation. One-third (33.7 percent) of the participants, though, were unsure about their future plans. In short, half of all migrant respondents expected to remain in the province. While the group that was sure that it would not stay was proportionately quite small, there were a substantial number of migrants who were unsure.

In the follow-up survey of Phase III, a slightly higher percentage (59 percent) thought that they would remain in Alberta permanently. One-quarter to one-third of all respondents expected to return to their region of origin to reside at some point in the future (perhaps as late as retirement). Thus it was clear that the idea of return remained alive – even if at this point the possibility was a long way off and maybe only rhetorical. Furthermore, no question was asked to explicitly tap interest in onward migration, but the responses from Phase I and Phase III seem to suggest that migrants to Alberta did not think of their migration simply as one step towards another destination. And, if they did not stay in Alberta, they were more likely to think about returning to their region of origin.

The important questions, then, are: what are the characteristics of those who are more likely to return? And how do they differ from those who are most likely to stay. It has already been shown that age and marital status are statistically significant as predictors of permanence, whereas gender is not. Pearsonian product moment correlations between key variables were completed, and those that were significant at the .01 level facilitated the construction of a profile of the expected returnee (i.e., migrants who did not expect to stay in Alberta because they wanted to return home) and the expected retainee (i.e., migrants who expected to remain in Alberta).

THE EXPECTED RETURNEE

It would not be surprising if people who were "upset that they had to leave" and people who felt that they "had little choice but to leave" were the most interested in returning. And, when the two variables were correlated, we found that this was indeed the case. People who felt that they left their region of origin because they had little choice were more likely to be upset that they had to leave (r = .51). They were more likely to feel depressed before they left (r =. 32), and they also saw the political and economic atmosphere at home as being negative (r = .32). Migrants who were upset that they had to leave were more likely to feel that people from home were important to their life in Alberta (r = .32) and were less likely to say that moving to Alberta was like coming home (r = -.35). Being upset about leaving was also correlated with wanting to return soon (r = .38), eventually wanting to return (r = .41), and wanting to retire at the place of origin (r = .37). So wanting to return was related to a lack of control over leaving and to being depressed about having to do so. It makes sense, then, that these migrants were more likely to spend time with people from home while in Alberta and were much less likely to view coming to this province as being like coming home. The negative attitude at the time of migration seems to have a continuing impact on the assessment of migration and the desire to return.

Another way of stressing the importance of migration motivation is to look at whether money itself was the primary motivation to relocate. Persons who came to Alberta "just for the money" were less likely to feel good being in Alberta (r = -.30) and were more interested in returning home either soon (r = .41) or eventually (r = .36). So it appears that understanding migration motivation as the result of having little choice, of being upset, or moving just for financial reasons was more likely to produce a migrant who wanted to return. The corollary of this observation is that those who chose to leave did so more deliberately, with an established rationale and justification that enhanced their likelihood of staying at the destination.

THE EXPECTED RETAINEE

Migrants who expected to remain in Alberta were much more likely to feel that they were economically better off in Alberta (r = .45) than were migrants who expected to leave, and they were also more likely to be glad that they no longer lived in their place of origin (r = .44). Their depression before migration had a very different basis than did that of the expected returnee who was simply unhappy about having to leave. When migrants who thought that they would live in Alberta permanently felt depressed before migration, that mood was correlated with their feeling that they thought differently than did people at the place of origin (r = .36). Feeling negative about the political and economic environment back home was also correlated with believing that people there thought differently than they did (r = .37), being depressed before leaving (r = .38), and believing that their move to Alberta was taking them to a place where the thinking was closer to their own (r = .31). Migrants who expected to remain in Alberta also felt that they didn't belong when they went home to visit (r = .31) and were more likely to state that they were glad that they were not back home (r = .30).

Migrants who said that they migrated at least partially due to their having a different worldview from those at home were more likely to think that the way of thinking in Alberta was closer to their own (r = .65). They also felt that moving to Alberta was like coming home (r = .52), and they were glad that they had not stayed in the community of origin (r = .51). Not surprisingly, they were less likely to feel that staying in touch with people back home was important to them (r = -.33) and were more likely to feel that they did not belong at their place of origin when they returned to visit (r = .40). They were also more likely to trust Alberta politicians more than they trusted politicians at home (r = .38). Conversely, being in Alberta made them feel good (r = .32), more at home (r = .31); and they were more likely to consider their stay in Alberta as permanent (r = .35). Interestingly, they were also more likely to view returnees as people who could not cope with the competitive environment in Alberta (r = .31). It is not surprising, then, that these people were not much interested in returning home either soon (r = -.31), eventually (r = -.34), or upon retirement (r = -.36).

These correlations do not establish causation but they do point out that migrants who *chose* to leave their place of origin were more likely to consider Alberta as their permanent residence when they felt some kind of alienation with regard to their home environment. Having a different worldview, being despondent about conditions at home, and/or not feeling close to people back home increased the likelihood that migrants would feel more comfortable and at home in Alberta. These persons were obviously less interested in returning under any conditions. These conclusions were clearly retrospective as migrants made them after they had settled in Alberta, and it is not known to what extent they were held prior to relocation. It also appears that these migrants experienced a sense of distancing and differentiation with regard to their region of origin.

MIGRATION MARGINALIZATION

The migrant who wanted to return felt alienated or marginalized at her/his destination. The migrant who expected to stay in Alberta, conversely, felt alienated or marginalized at the region of origin. This sense of alienation served to legitimate whatever course of action the migrant preferred. Three factors at the destination help to explain the migrant's choice.

The first factor emphasizes social ties. People for whom staying in touch with people back home was very important were more likely to stay in touch with people in Alberta who were from back home (r = .40). Persons who maintained these social ties were more likely to want to eventually return home (r = .32) or return home to retire (r = .330). They were the most convinced that their work experience in Alberta would get them a better job back home upon their return (r = .31). They were also less likely to feel out of place when they visited back home (r = -.30) and were less likely to feel glad that they were not at home when they heard about life back there (r = -.37). Also not surprisingly, migrants who felt that it was important to keep in touch with other migrants in Alberta who were from back home were also more likely to want to eventually retire in their region of origin (r = .34). Various social ties with home clearly reinforced the lack of belonging to the destination community and the sense of attachment to the place of origin. Conversely, the lack of such ties or their relative unimportance reinforced the lack of belonging to the region of origin and the sense of attachment to the destination.

The second factor pertains to worldview. Those migrants who felt they had a similar worldview to those in Alberta were far more likely to be happier there than were those migrants who did not. Such persons were more likely to trust Alberta politicians more than those at home (r = .56), no longer felt like they belonged in their home region when they visited there (r = .46), were glad that they had not stayed there (r = .60), and were more likely to feel that going to Alberta was like coming home (r = .60). Being in Alberta was more likely to make them feel good (r = .46) and to be appreciative of its lifestyle (r = .42), especially the longer they remained there (r = .45). This led them to perceive their relocation to Alberta as permanent (r = .46). This obviously meant that they were less likely to feel like outsiders (r = -.36), and they had little interest in returning to their place of origin at any time (r = -.40). These persons were also more likely to view returnees as people who could not cope with the competitive environment in Alberta (r = .42). In important ways, then, appreciating the fact that Alberta was different from the place of origin enhanced the likelihood of feeling aliened from the latter and resulted in greater acceptance of the former as a permanent residence.

The third factor pertains to economic well-being. Migrants who felt that they were economically better off in Alberta were more likely to think that their relocation was a good decision (r = .32) and that it was a good career move (r = .55). They were much more likely to disagree that their expectations had not been met (r = -.42) and were more likely to be glad that they were not back home (r = .33). Clearly, comparative economic prosperity was highly significant in positively evaluating the migration destination.

There is, then, a significant relationship between positively evaluating/experiencing life in Alberta and having less interest in returning to the home province. If going to Alberta was like coming home, then it makes sense that persons who felt that they did not feel at home when they visited their province of origin (r = .34), would prefer Alberta politicians (r = .50), and would be glad that had not remained at home (r = .61). On the other hand, people who wished that they had not moved or whose expectations were not met were less likely to feel at home in

Alberta. They were more likely to feel like outsiders, were unable to relate to the lifestyle of Alberta, and wanted to return to the community of origin.

These conclusions were confirmed through t-tests. It would be expected that people who considered their migration to Alberta to be permanent would differ considerably, on a whole range of responses, from those who did not consider their move to Alberta that way or who were unsure about it. Those who considered Alberta as their permanent residence were more likely to feel that they left home because people back there thought differently than they did, and they were much more likely to agree that their move had been motivated by their ideological congruence with the thinking in Alberta. They also had greater trust in Alberta politicians, which meant that going to Alberta was in some sense a homecoming, so they were glad that they had not stayed in the community of origin. They were more likely to feel at home in Alberta, to feel good about being there, to appreciate the lifestyle, and to not feel like outsiders. On the other hand, migrants who saw their relocation to Alberta as temporary or who were unsure of their continued residence there were more likely to have closer attachments to home. None of the work variables (e.g., happy with job, career move, work dominates, too much work) were statistically significant. It stands to reason, then, that people who considered their migration to Alberta as more permanent would be those who felt comfortable with the political and economic environment and who felt that work was not the only important factor in their move.

DISCUSSION

The qualitative interviews had already pointed out that migration was a complex phenomenon, and meanings and motivations for migration were not easily reducible to simple causes. The quantitative data reported in this chapter reaffirm this conclusion as most statements evoked a wide range of responses, suggesting that care must be taken in interpreting the results. What is clear, however, is that most migrants understood their position in the social and political economy of their home region as problematic. To the extent that it is possible to identify a single reason why migration was considered, it is this. Some migrants felt upset that they had to leave, or felt that they had no choice, or were depressed before leaving. But even more felt positive about relocating – not only because they no longer felt comfortable at home but also because they saw migration as an opportunity for a fresh start. Their migration was of their own volition. It is interesting that money, in and of itself, was not a prime motivator for moving to Alberta. This suggests that a more satisfactory social position was more important than mere monetary reward.

It was also clear that most of the respondents were overwhelmingly satisfied with their migration to Alberta. Comparisons that they made with their life back home led them to be glad that they had not stayed there, convinced them that their decision to move to Alberta was the right one, and resulted in their expectations being met. They felt more at home in Alberta and found that its lifestyle appealed to them. Undoubtedly, part of the reason for this was that they were now economically better off. They not only had more money, however, they also had a more satisfactory social position. Most migrants were happy with their job and viewed going to Alberta as a good career move. That money was not everything is evidenced by the fact that only three in five thought that they would stay in Alberta permanently. There were clearly multiple factors in the decision to stay, and perhaps what migrants considered a satisfactory social position evolved over time.

The idea that Alberta is an open society was supported by the fact that respondents overwhelmingly reported that they did not feel like outsiders there. Some of this comfort level came from the fact that many knew people who were already in the province and maintained contact with those from the home region who lived there. As expected, most maintained regular contact with people back home, which, for some, kept alive the notion of return.

There was often a strong minority position with regard to many of the indicators, and this cannot be ignored. For example, a minority did move reluctantly and were upset about it, only relocating to Alberta for the money. Some were upset about the fact that work and making money dominated life in Alberta. Some did feel like outsiders and were not comfortable in Alberta. It would be expected that those who were less likely to remain in Alberta would come from this group. These minority positions were very important in the correlations.

CONCLUSION

People whose migration to Alberta included some form of distancing from their region of origin were more likely to feel satisfied with their decision to relocate. This meant that they had assessed their place in the political/social economy of their own region and had decided to leave. Migrants were more likely to accept their new location if they felt they had some choice in the move. Those who went through the dissatisfaction/distancing process were more likely to have a positive evaluation of their move and had few regrets about having relocated. Migrants over 30 years of age and those who were married were more likely to have gone through this process. Persons under 30 and single persons were less likely to have experienced this type of dissatisfaction and distancing and were more likely to want to return home.

There were other implications to the age and marital status divide. Migrants under 30 were more likely to have moved for adventure and to see coming to Alberta as a good career move that might help them get a better job back home. Persons over 30 years of age (and especially married persons), on the other hand, were more likely to have felt marginalized in their home region, often having an unsatisfactory place in the social economy and/or disagreeing with the dominant worldview there. They were also more likely to trust Alberta politicians and to feel that going to Alberta was like coming home. While the economic implications of being in Alberta were the same for those on both sides of the age and marital divide, those over 30 were much more likely to interpret their relocation ideologically. Age and marital status, then, appear to be significant factors in determining whether the migration process involved a calculated decision, which, in turn, was likely to make the migration more permanent.

While gender was not a significant factor, region of origin was important. Migrants from Atlantic Canada were much more likely to want to return home and were more likely to understand the concept of homesickness.

In sum, persons who were more likely to see their migration to Alberta as permanent were likely to be over 30 and married and to have felt marginalized in their home region. They were more likely to feel that they had chosen to leave, to feel at home in Alberta, and to agree with that province's worldview. On the other hand, persons who wanted to return were less likely to feel that they had control over their departure and/or were under 30 and saw the move as an adventure. If the migrant who expected to stay in Alberta was more likely to feel marginalized at the place of origin, the expected returnee was more likely to feel marginalized at the destination.

16

Conclusion

Behind the research reported in this book is the observation that the in-migration that Alberta experienced towards the end of the twentieth century and into the new millennium represented a significant moment in Canadian history. While interprovincial migration in Canada was not new, the direction, cause, and flow of this migration was new. This migration seemed to symbolize important shifts within Canadian society. This being the case, migration to Alberta provides a window on a particular period in Canadian life.

This study was conducted at two levels: the micro level and the macro level. By adding the focus on the individual migrant to aggregate level data, my goal was to understand migration from the point of view of the migrant so that it would be possible to more fully understand when and why migration occurred. This was the micro level of analysis from which we built a theory to explain internal migration. The macro level of analysis placed what was occurring in Alberta within national and international contexts. National societies are always changing as the result of new developments and new issues that challenge the status quo. Throughout *Second Promised Land*, there have been numerous hints that changes in Canadian society are reflected in migration to Alberta. In addition to the micro perspective, what this book offers is a study in macro-sociology, taking into account not only domestic migration to Alberta but also how this affects Canada as a nation-state and how this is connected to global forces.

The goal of this chapter is to review the findings and implications of this study at both the micro-level and the macro-level. Specific emphasis is given to how migration to Alberta both contributes to and reflects a changing Alberta and a changing Canada.

THE MICRO PERSPECTIVE

A major contribution of this study is that it argues that the analysis of internal migration, which begins with the individual migrant rather than with migrant aggregates, produces invaluable insights. The interviews with migrants demonstrate that emphasizing "moving for work" simplifies a complex process because it only acknowledges economic factors and accentuates the importance of the destination. What is needed is an approach that links both the region of origin and the destination. Migrants themselves acknowledged that, with regard to reasons for relocating, "moving for work" had the greatest legitimacy in the public realm; however, as they reflected more deeply, a wide range of reasons for moving came to the surface – reasons that the simple response "moving for work" seemed to mask. This is confirmed by the fact that, at the end of the interviews, only about one-quarter of migrants said that they had moved primarily for reasons of employment. While people would not migrate to a place where employment options were limited, it became clear that a broader constellation of factors were at work and that these served as releasing agents with regard to the decision to relocate. Whether due to changes within the broader community or changes within the individual or both, a sense of dissatisfaction emerged with regard to how the migrant viewed her/his social position within the community of origin. This dissatisfaction had a marginalizing effect that resulted in her/him beginning a process of distancing, which then made migration possible.

The key in this analysis is the idea of marginalization, which was the product of some aspect of a person's life within the community of origin being considered unacceptable. She/he then began to see migration as a potential solution to the desire to have a more satisfactory social position. It is possible that marginalization may be caused by unemployment or underemployment, but even these economic factors need to be understood from the perspective of the individual's social location in the community. The lack of a productive role in the social economy of a community, as evaluated through the lens of career ambitions, the desire for meaningful work, and/or the utilization of skills, can have a devastating effect on one's sense of self-worth. Social location may be related to monetary rewards but it is also related to more than that. Other important issues in social location relate to, among other things, lifecycle, interpersonal and familial concerns, and conflicts over worldview. When any of these factors had a marginalizing effect on an individual, the door was opened for an attempt to resolve this condition through migration.

The argument, then, is that migration is a mechanism whereby individuals may attempt to locate themselves more satisfactorily within a social community. The process begins in the community of origin and continues at the destination. The study of migration links the sending and receiving communities by examining how social position is perceived, experienced, and negotiated in both communities. Migration is not an act but a process that involves continuous evaluations – even at the destination, where it must be determined whether the problem of social location has been adequately addressed. This is particularly the case because all migration involves gains *and* losses, both of which must be resolved in the evaluation. Migrants also experience marginalization at the destination and develop strategies to overcome it. An adequate, though partial, integration usually begins with finding satisfactory employment. This is an important first step, but it is not the only step, in obtaining a satisfactory position in the new community. Negotiating identity and shifts in identity based on place were often part of the process. As has been demonstrated, the idea of return served as an interesting counterpoint that allowed migrants to deal with the transitional nature of their migration, pending the satisfactory and permanent resolution of the issue of social location at the destination. In most cases, this was an ongoing issue and was not easily resolvable, especially given the fact that a satisfactory social location was not just about employment.

By focusing on the individual migrant, it has been possible to understand more clearly who migrates and why, and who returns and under what conditions. The social-psychological approach developed here understands the migrant as a member of a community from which she/he must disengage as well as a member of a new community with which she/he must re-engage. Moving for work did not occur in a social vacuum. The emphasis on social position provides an interpretive apparatus that can account for a wide range of situations that individuals considered unsatisfactory and that might prompt migration. When these situations facilitated distancing and the consideration of alternatives, people could become migrants. Without undergoing this process, people were not likely to migrate; and, if they did do so, they were more likely to return. But return could also take place when experience at the destination enabled the migrant to acquire a more satisfactory position in the community of origin. It also provided a fall-back position for those who had unsuccessfully integrated into the destination community. The focus on the individual migrant also facilitates an understanding of how the search for a more satisfying position in the destination region may be partially resolved in the early years but may continue for many years.[1]

This study breaks new ground in focusing on the unsponsored migrant, for whom the risks of migration were much greater and where the mobilization of social capital was much more informal than it was for the sponsored (i.e., "transferred") employee. Unsponsored migration involved independent risk-taking behaviour but not anomic behaviour. Bridging ties were very important with regard to facilitating a successful migration, and social ties at the destination played a strategic role in the adjustment process. Whereas the computer was not a factor in previous migration eras, the internet now serves as a useful tool for migrants with regard to generating and mobilizing social capital. It is also important to recognize how social capital, as understood through reference groups, plays a significant role in shaping integration into the new community or, in contrast, in fostering return. In addition, the focus on unsponsored migrants provides new insights into how women have a much more powerful role in the migration process than was previously thought.

THE MACRO PERSPECTIVE

As has been noted, a major presupposition of *Second Promised Land* is that this is not just a study of Alberta but an analysis of various macro-level dynamics within Canadian society and beyond. Since the focus of the analysis is on interprovincial migration, the national context is assumed, and changing migration patterns within Canada provide empirical support for the fact that the society is undergoing some modification. Migration is not only a matter of demographic shifts, it is also a matter of addressing differences in regional economies, cultures, and worldviews. Migration represents significant shifts in which worldviews that were previously marginalized become increasingly prominent. Migration also reflects global forces – forces over which provincial and national jurisdictions have little control. The internationalization of the energy industry played a huge role in demonstrating how globalization has dramatically changed Alberta's fate. Thus, the flow of interprovincial migration involves far more than people moving within Canada: it involves recognizing how global forces are changing both Alberta and Canada.

As has been demonstrated, the rise in energy prices at the world level has been a critical economic stimulus to Alberta. It was not only what was happening with price on the production side (as represented by OPEC and the Middle East) but also what was happening to it on the consumption side as the increased demands from places like India and

China created new interest in Alberta as the provider of a scarce commodity. As the price of oil rose and the demand increased, investment in energy production in Alberta rose exponentially. Investment decisions by international oil conglomerates and entrepreneurs with multinational operations played a major role in intensifying investment in the province. While these investments were at first measured (though supportive of growth), nothing increased their pace and intensity more than the construction frenzy in the oil sands, beginning around 2003. As external investment in the province accelerated, it was no exaggeration to say that Alberta had little control over its economy. As investment increased, the demand for labour also increased, and this supported more in-migration. All of this was outside national or provincial control.[2] Thus, while, on the one hand, Alberta was a beneficiary of these investments, it was also a victim, particularly as growth spiralled beyond the point of the province's being able to provide housing and services to the incoming population, many of whom were now being actively recruited rather than making independent decisions to relocate. The point is that it was the insatiable global demand for energy, and the investors, all of whom sought to benefit from this demand, that drove the economy and prompted more in-migration. This is a macro-level factor, and it played a huge role in what was occurring in Alberta. If there had been no increase in oil prices beginning in the 1970s, Alberta may have had a healthy economy but it would not have sparked the new investment needed to support the two waves of interprovincial migration that we have discussed.

Alberta also needs to be understood in terms of its position within Canadian society. Canada is currently structured in such a way that Ontario is its core. Ontario is demographically the largest province, and Toronto is Canada's dominant city. The dual power of Ontario and its neighbour Quebec (Canada's second largest province) ensured that these two provinces contained the majority of the Canadian population, and this has translated into power and influence. Indeed, these two provinces have largely controlled the national agenda. While the Atlantic region once had flourishing industries, these were lost as the result of economic concentration in central Canada. The Atlantic region was the birthplace of Confederation, but, over time, it lost its political and economic influence; and, with that, it lost many of its people.

With the two central Canadian provinces firmly in control, the West was settled with the idea that it would play a supporting role as a hinterland to central Canadian interests. The fact that many protest movements and political realignments have come from the West can be considered evidence of its attempts to resist subordination. British Columbia has been somewhat less oriented to central Canada than has the western interior, where the perception of being a captive market to central Canadian interests has always been high. Among the three interior provinces, Alberta clearly grew faster than did Saskatchewan and Manitoba, and it has been the beneficiary of out-migration from these two provinces. This meant that Alberta's growth was often perceived as being due to population redistribution within the region. For example, it was often assumed that Alberta was the primary destination of former Saskatchewan residents ("Will the last one out please turn out the lights?"). But this view of Alberta marginalized it, categorizing it solely in regional terms. The two waves of migration discussed in this book changed that perception. To the extent that Alberta became a migrant destination for the entire country, migration contributed to the restructuring of Canadian society. Ontario no longer served as the barrier to east-west migration that it once had been. In becoming a national migrant destination, in combination with other elements of economic change, Alberta could no longer be viewed as a hinterland. Disturbing the status quo, however, was painful, and it was intriguing how often the refrain "Oh, it's just oil" was used as a way of minimizing Alberta's migration growth. If this growth were simply due to oil, then Alberta's hinterland status had only been slightly and/or temporarily amended by a non-renewable resource – as powerful as that resource may have been.

The Canadian West had symbolized great hopes for the expansion of the Canadian nation. The extension of the central Canadian dream of a nation from sea to sea, which rivalled the kind of expansion experienced in the United States, was predicated on the role that the West would play in building the country (Owram 1980, 218). That view, however, was built on the expectation that agriculture would be the backbone of the new society, and it provided the myths of promise and success that were often challenged by the difficult realities of settlement. No one who had understood the West in these terms could have predicted the kind of uneven development that would occur, in which a non-renewable resource (in combination with other factors) would serve as a springboard for unprecedented levels of growth and change in one province alone. It would have been difficult to predict that a landlocked province in the western interior could be in anything but a subsidiary position to the centres of demographic, economic, and political power in central Canada.

Yet, what has emerged in Alberta is challenging the way Canadian society has always been understood. The financial advantages accruing to one province, the new-found sense of power that comes from owning and managing a strategic global resource, and the rapid growth of its population has crushed the old stereotypes of the province's role in Confederation. In spite of industrial decline in central Canada, no one is under any illusion that Canada is being radically transformed by what is happening in Alberta. But it *is* being transformed – even if only in small steps. Obviously, it is too much to visualize Alberta's emerging as a new fulcrum in Canadian society. But there is a clear sense in which Alberta has redefined its role within Canadian society and has attempted to retool the national agenda. The rapid economic expansion that Alberta experienced has played a role in rewriting its understanding of how Canada is now configured. As has been playfully said many times, Albertans now sometimes think that the rest of the country can be reorganized from Alberta's perspective. Saskatchewan and Manitoba have become the "Near East," Ontario and Quebec "the Middle East," the Atlantic provinces "the Far East," and British Columbia "the Far West." While this is obviously over the top, it does communicate a significant point: not only has Alberta been changing but Canada has been changing as well, and this is so at least partially because of what is happening in Alberta. And in-migration to Alberta is a reflection of that fact.

SPECIFYING TRANSFORMATIONS

This is not the place to identify all of the changes that have occurred in Alberta or in Canada over the two waves of in-migration. Others with more expertise in political and policy analysis can take up this task. What can be done is to outline some of the ways in which in-migration to Alberta has helped to change this province as well as to transform Canada.

How In-migration Changed Alberta

First, and obviously, migration increased the population of the province. Alberta's population more than doubled since 1971 (the beginning of the new era for the province, as discussed in chapter 2), and there was a net growth of 600,000 people in the ten years from 1996 to 2006. This growth was not just the direct result of internal migration; it was also the indirect result of the birth rate of those who migrated. Because so many of the migrants were young adults in the prime of their childbearing years, in-migration to Alberta had a double impact. This meant that Alberta not only had the highest in-migration rate in the country but also the highest birth rate. Consequently, as long as this population characterized Alberta, the growth of the province would proceed at a pace quite different from that of provinces that lost their young adults through out-migration.

Second, because this in-migration largely came from other parts of Canada rather than from international destinations, Alberta became a virtual mixing bowl of Canadians. This removed any sense of insularity that might otherwise have developed, and it made the province a meeting ground for Canadians from all over the country. It removed any thought that Albertans had a common agrarian background and blended people with a variety of occupational interests and regional cultural experiences. Many new residents could not relate to old stereotypes of the province because they brought a different regional cultural background with them.

Third, in-migration played a significant role in the urbanization of the province. It propelled the population of both of Alberta's two major cities over the million mark, and it contributed to the growth of metropolitan galaxies, with small towns and outlying areas being seen as part of the urban region. It played a role in increasing the size of smaller centres such as Red Deer and, particularly, contributed to urbanization in the provincial north in Grande Prairie and Fort McMurray. The increasing dominance of Edmonton and Calgary in the province, along with a more prominent role in Canada, meant that these cities had become more outward-looking rather than inward-looking.

Fourth, the experience of receiving so many migrants amidst an expanding economy played a role in transforming Alberta's perception of itself. Regular reports in the media trumpeted these gains through migration in a way that altered how Albertans understood their own province. Interacting with newcomers provided constant reminders that there must be something desirable in Alberta – something that made others choose to come there. The psychological and political consequences of this fact contributed to the erosion of Alberta's long-held hinterland mentality. This, along with an accelerating economy, tended to create a new sense of power in which Albertans no longer held so tightly to the old perceptions of western alienation. And for some, the flocking of people to Alberta served to verify that the province was a special place within Canada. In short, in-migration contributed to replacing the underdog mentality with a new collective self-confidence that sometimes bordered on arrogance.

Fifth, to the extent that independent migrants succeeded in Alberta, their experience lent credibility to the idea that Alberta was a place that welcomed risk-taking and individual initiative. An expanding economy supported income growth, which was then linked to perceptions of upward mobility, which migrants contrasted to their personal position at the place of origin. To feel rewarded for being a risk-taker and to experience a sense of achievement at the destination led newcomers to understand Alberta as a different sort of place. If Alberta had been previously perceived as at least somewhat different in that it had a more free enterprise ideological perspective than did the other provinces, then migration put an experiential stamp on this sense of difference. This point is explored more later in the chapter.

How Internal Migration to Alberta Changed Canada

First, internal migration to Alberta contributed to the continued westward shift of the Canadian population. Alberta's population growth rate was the highest in Canada, particularly from 1996 onwards, and this ultimately led, in 2006, to Alberta's share of the Canadian population surpassing 10 percent. In combination with the incremental growth occurring in British Columbia since the 1950s, the percentage of Canada's population living in the two far western provinces continued to climb and was approaching one-quarter of the nation's population. If internal migration means that one region must lose population while another region gains population, the slow but steady movement west clearly changes the dynamics of the country. To the extent that British Columbia's economy strengthened by the middle of the first decade in the new millennium, so that both Alberta and British Columbia were receiving in-migrants while Ontario was losing people through internal migration, migration westward was continuing to be a factor of national significance.

Second, migration growth in Alberta accentuated the significant differences that existed between the three provinces of the western interior. Whatever commonalities may have existed between these provinces in the twentieth century, when the wheat economy defined the region, has now been lost, and the tendency of the national discourse to link all three "Prairie" provinces must be considered archaic. By 2007, energy hydrocarbons were having new significance in the other western provinces, creating a basis for a new commonality; however, Alberta continues to play the more dominant role by a considerable margin.

Third, the fact that Alberta grew primarily through internal migration illustrates how Canada was being remade from within. The country was being remade from without through international migration, but this impact was primarily being felt in the biggest cities, particularly Toronto and Vancouver. Major immigration-receiving areas became considerably different from regions that did not receive such influxes of population. In contrast, the fact that Alberta became a destination of choice for internal migrants, and that Atlantic migrants were prepared to jump over Ontario (formerly the typical destination for out-migrants from that region) to come to Alberta, was a matter of considerable significance. Migration to Alberta had become a national phenomenon, and this opened the door to Alberta's playing a very different role on the national stage. The fact that gross migration to Alberta was even higher than net migration meant that the province became a part of the experience of many Canadians throughout the country, which, in turn, elevated its profile. There is perhaps no better illustration of this transformation than the fact that the twenty-second prime minister of Canada, Stephen Harper, was an Ontario resident who migrated to Alberta in the first wave in 1978. He was first elected as an MP from Alberta as a member of the western-based Reform Party and became prime minister as the leader of the new Conservative Party of Canada in 2006. It is interesting that a migrant from Ontario to Alberta would return to his home province (Ottawa, Canada's capital, is located in Ontario) advocating what was widely understood as a western perspective on Canada as a nation.

Fourth, the image of migration to Alberta as a type of "black gold rush," in which making money and seeking prosperity were key themes, perpetuated images of the province as a different kind of place. This was particularly so in contrast to declining regions that continually lost population and/or in contrast to regions that just held their own. On top of the images of the white hat and the urban cowboy was added a new layer of oil men and technocrats who were simultaneously risk-takers and comfortable corporate entrepreneurs, with large salaries and big profits. Venture capital linked easily with venture migration, free enterprise effortlessly connected migrants to a strong achievement orientation, and capitalism merged with individual capital accumulation, thereby uniting the Alberta environment and the migrant in both reality and myth. On the national scene, the result of these images was that Alberta became much more closely tied to free enterprise principles, which differentiated it from provinces with a more collectivist orientation.[3] This is a point to which we will return.

Fifth, in-migration to Alberta provided further evidence to Canadians that the province was challenging the status quo in interregional relations. The economic advantage that some parts of the country had over other regions of the country was a long-standing issue in Canadian society. The hegemony of central Canada allowed Ontario, in particular, to become a major magnet for migration destination, far exceeding other provinces. And this has been so for a long time. The new-found economic expansion occurring in Alberta demonstrated once again how economic advantage was related to migration streams. Royalty payments and government budget surpluses, in combination with significant job creation and strong tax yields, produced a province with economic leverage that beckoned people from everywhere. National societies are all vulnerable to transformations when some regions develop economic advantages and others do not. And, if that advantage is lost, there is nothing to stop people from migrating again within their own country. The implication is that Alberta possessed unprecedented drawing power but that there was nothing permanent about this migration flow. Economic changes might occur that would prompt new migration to other regions.

The emergence of Alberta into a new position on the national scene demonstrates that the core/hinterland pattern could only be transformed when regional dependencies were altered. As has already been noted, Alberta, along with much of the rest of the West, was in a dependency relationship with central Canada. Ontario, on the other hand, solidified its hegemony by not depending on its hinterland alone but by becoming the location for American branch plant industries and the preferred location for international capital operating in Canada. In other words, Ontario benefited nationally to the extent that it became a strategic location for foreign capital. The role of the Autopact, which allowed American automakers to assemble automobiles in Ontario (and, to some extent, in Quebec) that would be sold on both sides of the border illustrates the importance of external factors that enabled Ontario to develop economically in a way that other provinces did not (Courchene 1998). It might also be said that British Columbia at least partially transformed its hinterland pattern by developing an external orientation as well through becoming more involved in Asian trade. In a similar way, but with a different commodity, Alberta developed an advantage not shared by other provinces in that energy hydrocarbons were in demand internationally. This made the province very important to the global economy and less dependent on central Canada. While in some ways this growth could be minimized by pointing out that it occurred primarily because of a nonrenewable resource (which would mean only short-term prosperity), energy hydrocarbons did allow Alberta to break loose from its sense of dependence on central Canada. Where this is leading is still unclear, but Alberta's significance nationally has risen primarily because of the international importance of its dominant commodity. Hydrocarbons gave Alberta the power to challenge old interregional relations, and in-migration was a manifestation of this.

In-migration played a significant role in changing the image of Alberta on the national front. Energy hydrocarbons certainly altered the image of the province, but so did reports of migration and rapid population growth. Outside the province, particularly in the largest metropolitan areas in Canada, the image of Alberta as an unsophisticated hinterland lingers. The relatively sudden aggregation of wealth and opportunity in one region startled the status quo in which the newfound power in Alberta was both a threat and an unfair advantage. The swagger emerging from the province clashed with that of other regions, which had long possessed their own sense of superiority within the national society. Stereotypes of Albertans as "urban cowboys" clashed with their ambitions as "national agenda makers." In-migration symbolized not just the redistribution of people but the redistribution of power. All images, of course, are fluid and subject to change by unfolding events and socio-economic circumstances (Francis 1992, 734); however, images of place do serve as important framing devices. And it is for this reason that migration growth contributed to changes in the image and role of Alberta at the national level, which then began to change how Canadians understood their own society.

INTERPRETING THE OUTCOME OF THIS MIGRATION FLOW TO ALBERTA

Based on the research presented here, it is now possible to sketch the core argument for how and why these migration flows have affected Alberta and Canada. Some of our conclusions require more empirical testing, but together they provide a provocative interpretation of what has occurred. It is important to understand that what we say here does not apply to all migrants; rather, what we describe is an overall effect.

One of the key interpretive themes of this study is that a region with a rapidly expanding economy provides an unusual context for internal migration. While it has been argued that there is a difference between a rapidly expanding economy and a boom economy, the two concepts do blend in that both represent largely positive economic conditions.[4] It has been argued that an expanding economy is not just a context but an interpretive concept because it drives the migration process and explains the outcomes of migration in a very powerful way. An expanding economy not only serves as a magnet in the redistribution of people but it also tends to ensure that the migration will be successful. An expanding economy is an important explanatory variable in that it increases the likelihood that migration will be a positive experience because it offers employment opportunities that lead to perceptions of well-being and/or upward mobility. An expanding economy means that migrants do not compete with members of the destination community for employment because there are more than enough jobs to go around. An expanding economy means that the host society appears to be more open because migrants are surrounded by other migrants like themselves. More extreme boom conditions (such as occurred after 2005) may have created competition for scarce resources (e.g., housing, transportation), but, generally, such competition did not result in the alienation of newcomers. In short, Alberta's expanding economy not only attracted migrants from across the country but also increased the likelihood of their success. Following the argument developed earlier, this does not mean that the migration flow could simply be described as labour migration but, rather, that the nature of the economy created a particular climate that was conducive to more positive migration outcomes.

It has already been established that independent, or unsponsored, migrants are people who have taken an enormous risk in relocating by venturing out on their own without formal supports. They have made a calculated, personal decision to leave, and this has required considerable initiative on their part. They have embarked on housing and job searches, which sometimes required enormous patience and boldness, in a strange place. This does not mean that they did not have any social ties to assist them (some had more informal supports than others), but, in general, independent migrants had to be enterprising people with a determination to succeed. Many failed in this process or aborted it and returned home. But those who stayed on often achieved an enormous sense of success. Succeeding in the job search, moving from one job to another that was better, attaining promotions, obtaining jobs unlikely to be obtained at home, receiving pay raises, and/or watching others experiencing similar things were all more likely in an expanding economy. Similar things happened when the economy shifted into boom-mode, although under these conditions scarcity and the high cost of housing made job enhancements somewhat less appealing.

Experiencing a successful outcome at the destination had a considerable impact on independent migrants. Migration was interpreted as promoting change and personal growth. A New Brunswick migrant's comments sum up the feelings expressed by many:

> People back home always ask, "When are you coming back?" They almost seem resentful that we are not coming back. They ask questions like, "Do you actually like it there?" or "Why would you like it there?" I don't know why they say that. But one thing I know is that we are growing more for being here. For them, everything is the same. They never change. Nothing changes for them. (New Brunswick)

Migration often had a comparative element, with people who migrated comparing themselves favourably with peers who did not. Migration was interpreted as a boost to personal development. Furthermore, the enormity of the challenge of relocating independently created considerable self-satisfaction. A Manitoban put it this way:

> There is a sense of accomplishment from living here – that you have achieved something. There is a certain sense of accomplishment that you established yourself from somewhere – to pick yourself up and relocate and re-establish yourself because no one here knows you in the job market. To go back and say you have done that makes you feel good. (Manitoba)

The personal initiative required by such a move, and the sense of satisfaction that resulted, meant that migration was self-validating. In other words, migration had a deeply personal impact.[5]

There is often considerable debate about whether and to what extent Alberta is different from other provinces in Canada. When measuring attitudes of Albertans' towards a wide range of public policy issues, they are not strikingly different from those of people in other regions of Canada (Gibbins, Archer, and Drabek 1990, 229–38; Barrie 2006; Berdahl 2006). However, the *perception* that Albertans are ideologically distinctive in a political sense or that they possess a unique political culture is a view that is widely shared.[6] Provincial political elites have sharpened that sense of difference because there are "institutional incentives" (Pickup, Sayers, Knopff, and Archer 2004) for doing so, and the national media have also promoted a discourse of difference through constant repetition. Alberta, then, is often seen as an outlier in

Canadian life in that it advocates more free enterprise thinking and gives more credence to individual initiative. In reacting to Alberta's subordinate position within Confederation, activists have made repeated efforts to redesign the province through new internal policy initiatives as well as through attempting to remake Confederation in the province's own image. Barrie (2006) argues that certain formative experiences in the history of Alberta created a background of populist ideas (such as direct democracy and consensus politics) as well as a suspicion of Ottawa and partisan politics. To the list of formative events (e.g., various expressions of political experimentation such as the United Farmers of Alberta, Social Credit, West-Fed, Reform, Canadian Alliance, and/or the discovery of oil at Leduc in 1948) that have helped to make Alberta different within the Canadian context we must now add these two waves of internal migration.

The nature of the energy industry, with its high rewards and its resultant multiplier effects on the provincial economy, has created an unusual environment in which economic expansion heightens support for ambition, individualism, and competitive capitalism. If rapid economic expansion in Alberta was not enough to provide support for a discourse of difference, then the experience of migrants themselves (especially of those who considered their migration successful) helped to create a perception that Alberta was different from the rest of Canada. Using a broad brush, the difference can be explained as follows. People migrated to Ontario because it was a long-time hegemon and because they wanted to find their niche in a province that had incredibly diverse opportunities. Migration to British Columbia (especially to the Lower Mainland) occurred at least in part because the climate attracted many who were older and who brought their capital with them. Alberta, on the other hand, served as a "promised land" where independent migrants were risk-takers and sought a new start.[7] The expanding economy enabled migrants to find out that the discourse of difference was real and that Alberta did indeed possess a different type of regional culture. Thus, in-migration must be understood as another example in a long line of actions that helps to sustain a sense of regional difference both inside and outside Alberta. It has also, in the process of creating a different kind of society, played a role in replacing ideas of powerlessness, inferiority, and alienation with ideas of power, superiority, and innovation (cf. Francis 1992, 726–31).

Because independent migration is self-selective, focusing on those who possess the initiative and work ethic to make the move successful, those who chose to do so blended easily into the destination. Those who moved were those who were most motivated to ensure that their migration was not in vain. This is especially true of migrants who were married and over 30 years of age. So it was not just that Alberta attracted a particular type of person but that it retained a particular type of migrant – one who succeeded at the destination and experienced some distancing from the place of origin. And if the migration was rewarded, the characteristics of the migrant (e.g., hard work, initiative) that led to this were reinforced as she/he was integrated into the new regional culture. There is, then, a relationship between self-selection and where people choose to migrate.[8] The phrase "where you go is who you are" implies that there is some kind of synergy between the migrant and their destination.[9] Alberta attracted a particular type of person and retained a particular type of migrant – those who had succeeded and could then easily embrace Alberta's apparent values.

The expanding economy that Alberta experienced in both the first and second wave of migration conveyed images of a location that promised rewards for those with confidence in individual effort, risk-taking, ambition, and entrepreneurialism. Alberta, then, became a place imbued with particular meanings. These emerged at the outset of the migration cycle and attracted and retained people predisposed to appreciate them. The expanding economy provided an environment that verified the choices of those migrants who self-selected, and this contributed to the sense that Alberta was differed from the rest of the country (or at least from the migrants' experiences in their region of origin). People who migrated to Alberta *chose* to leave their home communities and defined their successful integration at the destination by embracing and reinforcing its major characteristics. So migration did not just mean population growth for Alberta and population loss for origin regions, or the shifting of population within the nation-state; rather, it meant the transplantation of people with particular attitudes and/or with sufficient positive experiences that allowed them to feel rewarded in the new environment and to interpret their relocation in a particular way. Migration to Alberta changed both the province and the regions of origin, but it also changed the nation-state. Some self-selection may have occurred at the region of origin, but further self-selection occurred at the destination, and this was the result of those who chose to stay having their positive feelings about Alberta reinforced. To that extent, in-migration contributed to making Alberta a different place.

For Alberta to become a promised land, it needed migrants who were discontent with their present but who had a vision of a better future. As in the past, such visioning was replete with myths that often contrasted sharply with reality (Francis and Kitzan 2007). Not all migrants experienced a successful integration at their Alberta destination.[10] There were those who returned because they found the environment inhospitable for one reason or another, those who had no intention of staying anyway, and those who engaged in onward migration. There were also those who were trapped in continuing marginality in Alberta and for whom migration had led to little improvement. There was also always the possibility that indicators of apparent success, with which a migrant to Alberta might identify, could later be reinterpreted in the light of losses. And there was always the possibility that the bloom might fall off the "rose" (the wild rose is Alberta's provincial flower) if retrenchment occurred within the economy and many were left disillusioned. Issues of environmental harm caused by energy production could choke the industry and drastically affect the province. Sudden economic downturns could dramatically transform faith in free enterprise. Thus, while the in-migration to Alberta that has been examined here has played a role in transforming the province and transforming Canada, there is reason to wonder what new realities might arise, creating new migration flows and new cycles of change.

We have focused on a particular point in time, and the outlines of a new era already appear on the horizon. The shift from an expanding economy to a boom economy became clearly evident in 2005 as in-migration reached even higher levels over the next two years as the result of aggressive recruitment strategies. Housing shortages drove up housing costs, traffic congestion increased, infrastructure could not keep up with demand, the crush in healthcare created wait-lists, and the negative consequences of rapid growth became more apparent. While in-migration was high, out-migration was also increasing (e.g., in 2007, for the first time in many years, more people moved to Saskatchewan from Alberta than the reverse), suggesting that boom conditions might not be conducive to continued upward growth or to migration retention. In addition, new economic growth in other provinces (e.g., Saskatchewan, Nova Scotia, and Newfoundland) has resulted in unanticipated opportunities for new migration, while Ontario has struggled. The economic downturn in the fall of 2008 brought a fresh element of uncertainty, which might easily affect the migration stream. This reminds us that migration within a national society is dynamic, not only one way, and not a once-and-for-all situation. We now await the next phase of change.

Appendix: Methodology

The major question with which this project had to grapple was how to study internal migration in a way that would reveal what we wanted to know about it. If the important thing about migration was the number of people moving to and from Alberta and their place of origin, those data were available. Statistics Canada had quantitative data in both the census and the annual demographic statistics that provided the evidence that was needed to verify the volume of internal migration involved in Alberta's growth. This, of course, made movers into numbers and minimized understanding migrants as people in social contexts. What was needed was an understanding of why people moved, how they decided where to go, how they perceived the outcomes of their migration, and, above all, what migration meant to them. Rather than imputing meaning and motivations indirectly from demographic statistics, there was an acute need to understand the migration process from the migrant's perspective (Fielding 1992, 207), and this served as the driving focus of the study.

A three-stage study design was established in order to understand the experience of migration. The first stage (Phase I) sought a sample of in-migrants to Alberta who were willing to discuss their migration experience in open-ended semi-structured interviews. The second stage (Phase II) included interviews in the regions from where migrants originated in order to determine how people in these communities felt about the out-migration to Alberta and how it had affected them. A second goal of this phase was to locate persons who had migrated to Alberta but had since returned, for if it was important to know why people had left the community in the first place, it was also important to know why some out-migrants had returned. The third phase of the study sought to determine the outcome of migration by re-interviewing the same migrants in Alberta from Phase I two to three years later.

PHASE I (SEPTEMBER 2000-JULY 2002)

In-depth interviews of one hour or more in length were carried out with 341 migrants throughout the province, using a maximum variation sampling technique to ensure a range of origins (rural, small towns, cities) and destinations (all urban, though some were small urban centres) were included. There were no straightforward methods for obtaining a random sample of participants for the study, so, throughout the province, we utilized public service media announcements in local communities and a respondent-driven sampling methodology (a variant of snowball methods [see Heckathorn 1997]) within communities of significant growth. The goal was to obtain thirty participants from every province of Canada. Potential participants for the study called a toll-free number and a call-back preliminary interview established eligibility for participation based on date of arrival, minimum age, and whether the move had been made independently. Only persons who had arrived in Alberta from 1996 onwards were allowed to participate in the study as 1996 was deemed to be the start of this wave of in-migration. Study participants had to be at least 20 years of age at the time of migration (this was in order to eliminate those who had just graduated from high school). Participation was limited to those who were unsponsored migrants (i.e., people who bore the costs of relocation personally as opposed to those who made employer-sponsored moves). No offer for study participation was rejected if eligibility requirements were met. In some cases, couples who migrated together participated in the study, but otherwise volunteers participated as individuals. There were also several group interviews involving persons who had all migrated to Alberta separately but who became friends after arrival, usually because of a common region of origin.

Semi-structured interviews usually took around one hour and were organized around four themes: the decision to leave the region of origin, the decision about where to relocate, experiences in relocating/adjusting at the destination, and the evaluation of the decision to relocate. Subset questions guided the interviewer in all four categories. Interviews were tape-recorded and responses were coded and stored in twelve major categories (nodes) using the computer program NUDIST, which allowed the data to be retrieved and compared along common themes among all cases. At the conclusion of the interview, participants were also offered the opportunity to put in writing their own assessment of why they migrated and the effect that it had on them.

Representativeness of the Sample

Since there was no systematic way of obtaining a representative sample, how close was the sample that was generated to the characteristics of all in-migrants to Alberta? In short, is the sample on which this study is based a reasonable representation of all interprovincial migrants who came to Alberta during this time period? Table A provides the data to assess this question.

The goal was to interview at least thirty persons from each province in order to provide adequate evidence of experiences and observations from different parts of the country. Therefore, there was no attempt to weight the sample according to the population size of each province or according to the size of the in-migration pool from that province. This meant then that British Columbia, in particular (but also, to some degree, Ontario and Saskatchewan) was underrepresented in the sample. On the other hand, the Atlantic provinces were overrepresented in the sample, with some interesting justification, because out-migration from this region had a greater impact on place of origin than did out-migration from other regions. The relocation from Newfoundland to Alberta (which involved travelling a huge distance), and from an ocean culture to a land-locked culture, was particularly intriguing. Another point to note is that the representation from the Territories was very small in the sample. Since migration from the Territories represented a very different phenomenon (due to the large number of temporary/contract workers who moved and then returned and/or to the large number of permanent residents who move south temporarily for study or medical care) no special effort was made to include them. They were also a very small part of the migration flow. However, five persons from the Yukon are part of the sample, and none of these was a contract worker. Migration to and from the Territories seemed to be driven by a variety of factors that were unique to those locations.

In terms of year of arrival, 1996 and 1998 are somewhat overrepresented in the sample, and 2001 is somewhat underrepresented. For our analysis, the second wave concluded in 2002, and there were no respondents who migrated to Alberta in that year (even though interviews were conducted then). Respondents who participated in the study in 2002 had all migrated earlier as that was the last year in which inter-

Appendix Table A Measures of representativeness of sample and subsample to actual migrating population

Year of Arrival	*Total In-Migrants*	*Sample*	*Subsample*	*% In-Migrants*	*% Sample*	*% Subsample*
1996	57,037	63	31	13.6%	18.5%	18.8%
1997	70,333	48	22	16.8%	14.1%	13.3%
1998	86,307	84	39	20.6%	24.6%	23.6%
1999	70,932	60	34	16.9%	17.6%	20.6%
2000	70,721	55	28	16.9%	16.1%	17.0%
2001	64,129	31	11	15.3%	9.1%	6.7%
Total	419,459	341	165			
Age of Migrants						
20–29	28,070	171	69	47.3%	50.1%	41.8%
30–39	16,008	77	31	27.0%	22.6%	18.8%
40–49	7,843	50	33	13.2%	14.7%	20.0%
50–59	3,563	28	21	6.0%	8.2%	12.7%
60+	3,895	15	11	6.6%	4.4%	6.7%
Total	59,379	341	165			
Gender						
male	32,395	173	67	54.6%	50.7%	40.6%
female	26,984	168	98	45.4%	49.3%	59.4%
Total	59,379	341	165			
Region of origin						
NFLD.	6,099	47		7.2%	13.8%	
P.E.I.	617	30		0.7%	8.8%	
N.S.	4,143	38		4.9%	11.1%	
N.B.	2,889	26		3.4%	7.6%	
QUE.	4,027	40		4.8%	11.7%	
ONT.	15,679	48		18.6%	14.1%	
MAN.	6,651	30		7.9%	8.8%	
SASK.	11,694	35		13.8%	10.3%	
B.C.	31,789	42		37.6%	12.3%	
YK	850	5		1.0%	1.5%	
Total	84,438	341				
Atlantic	13,748	141	51	16.3%	41.3%	30.9%
Not Atlantic	70,690	200	114	83.7%	58.7%	69.1%
Total	84,438	341	165			
Marital Status						
Single	97,065	176	73	51.0%	51.6%	44.2%
Married	93,260	165	92	49.0%	48.4%	55.8%
	190,325	341	165			

NOTE: Statistics for age, gender, and region of origin are based on the peak year of migration to Alberta, which was 1998. All statistics are based on persons 20 years of age and older for both the in-migrant population to Alberta and the sample population.

SOURCE: Statistics Canada, CANSIM Tables 051–0012, 051–0019 and 2001 Census, Cat no. 97F0008XCB01002.

views were conducted. It might be expected that those who arrived earlier would have been more interested in volunteering for the study or more likely to be available for participation. In any case, year of arrival did not become an important variable for this study, but all of the core years are represented.

The ages of the sample are a very close fit with the age ranges of all in-migrants to Alberta. The youngest age category (20–29) is somewhat overrepresented and the oldest age category (60+) is somewhat underrepresented. In terms of gender, females are slightly overrepresented and males are slightly underrepresented. The marital status of the sample is almost identical to the marital status of all in-migrants.

The methods utilized to develop the sample produced more respondents from larger centres, which is where most in-migrants settled. While respondents were found in some smaller places, they were usually coded with the larger centre (e.g., Sylvan Lake with Red Deer, Red Earth Creek with Grande Prairie). Calgary was more strongly represented in the sample than Edmonton; however, unlike Edmonton, Calgary was also a particularly strong destination in the second wave. People connected to the tourism industry in Banff/Canmore and Jasper were deliberately eliminated from the study as the seasonal and temporary migration to those locations was radically different from the migration that was the focus of this project.

In sum, the sample is reasonably representative in age, gender, and marital status, and the rationale for region of origin in the sample has been justified. The restriction of study participants to unsponsored migrants could not be compared to available data as Statistics Canada has no way of distinguishing sponsored from unsponsored migrants. Since internal migration (rather than immigration) was the focus of the study, recent immigrants had to have lived in Canada for at least two years before moving to Alberta in order to participate. Given the recruitment methods used for participation in the study and the reluctance of immigrants to volunteer to participate due to language or other issues, few secondary migrants were involved. The sampling method utilized was not a successful recruiting mechanism for the participation of visible minorities, who formed a small part of the sample but who were also a small part of the migration flow.

PHASE II (FALL 2002/SPRING 2003)

Interviews with migrants who made Alberta their destination often raised issues about what life was like in their communities of origin, how people at the place of origin reacted to the out-migration to

Alberta, and how this out-migration affected their communities. In the interviews in Phase I, interviewees were asked for recommendations about who in their origin communities should be contacted regarding these matters for competent comment. A press release about the study and its objectives was sent out to the media in all other Canadian provinces, asking for input about this impact. Assistance was also requested in identifying persons who had migrated to Alberta but had since returned to their region of origin. These two methods provided opportunities to talk to a wide range of people on research visits to places from where migration to Alberta had been significant from the point of view of the home community. As a result of the press releases, the principal investigator in this study was invited to participate on radio talk shows and to do countless media interviews throughout the country, which resulted in a diversity of other contributions to the study, at least in part because the toll-free telephone line was always made available for further input.

Site visits to these communities meant that many formal interviews and informal discussions were held with a wide range of people, from community leaders to persons encountered "on the street" from St John's, Newfoundland, to Prince George and Victoria, British Columbia. There was less media interest in providing input for this study in Quebec and Ontario, where migration to Alberta had a less noticeable impact, but the flood of calls to the first radio talk show in which we participated in St John's demonstrated how noticeable this migration was to other Canadians not only there but also in other provinces. This media involvement opened doors to new information that could not have been obtained in any other way. In total, ninety-five additional interviews were held with people across Canada on the topic of migration to Alberta. One hundred and three interviews were held with people who had left Alberta and returned home. And forty-two additional interactions were held with people as the result of radio talk shows. None of these interviews/interactions followed a particular interview schedule. Due to the limitations of the data collection, the conclusions and evidence presented here are not thorough, but we do provide a window on issues concerning migration from sending regions and offer very valuable information to supplement more formal data collection.

PHASE III (2003)

A follow-up contact was made with all participants in Phase I in order to find out how migrants evaluated their decision to relocate to Alberta several years later. In contrast to Phase I, which consisted of lengthy personal interviews, Phase III of the research involved written responses through both a survey and a mail-out that offered the opportunity for open-ended comments and reflections. Forty-three statements, using a five-point Likert scale, were grouped into six categories – (1) Leaving Where You Previously Lived, (2) Choosing Where to Move, (3) Comparing Alberta with Your Home Province, (4) Evaluating Your Decision to Relocate, (5) Experiencing Life in Alberta, and (6) Returning to Your Home Province) – and this provided important corroborative data.

Many participants had moved and could no longer be found but 48.4 percent (n = 165) responded. These responses are referred to as the subsample, and Table A also reports on the characteristics of this group. In terms of year of arrival, the subsample matches reasonably closely with both the sample and the total universe of in-migrants, with the exception of 2001. The range of ages of the subsample is reasonably close to the sample, although older people (50+) were somewhat more likely to respond. The major difference between the sample and the subsample is that women were more likely to respond to the follow-up survey (59 percent versus 49 percent in the sample and 45 percent of all in-migrants). It is likely that these were married women because married women were somewhat overrepresented in the subsample (56 percent), which also suggests that this group was the most stable and least likely to have moved. So if there is a slight bias in the subsample, it is towards women who were older and married who were either more likely to be locatable or who took the time to respond to the mailing.

A second aspect of Phase III is the invitation to women to volunteer for a supplementary interview on gender issues and migration. This may have contributed to the slight overrepresentation of older married women. Forty women were re-interviewed by telephone in order to focus more specifically on how migration had affected them. The results of this work are reported in chapter 11.

Methodological Issues

There are a variety of issues with which this type of research must grapple. One is the issue of retrospective rationalizations, or recalling only those aspects of the relocation that fit the current personal perspective of the interviewee. However, Gmelch (1992) argues that migration is a disruptive event and is therefore likely to be recalled with more vivid detail than are some other events. The issue of selectivity in recalling the past is a matter for which there can be few controls. On the other hand, the migration was indeed relatively recent in relation to the time of the interview ,which should have enhanced the ability to recall more detail. Whether the interviews yielded a well-rounded picture of all aspects of the migration experience, of course, is a moot point. Undoubtedly some post-migration reflections were new interpretations.

A further question could be raised about what motivated people to volunteer to participate in the study. In discussing this question with participants after the interview was over, it became clear that one of the motivations for participation involved the opportunity to verbalize personal feelings about a demanding if not traumatic event. It often appeared to the interviewers that the interview provided an opportunity for the migrant to work through her/his own feelings (Hiller and DiLuzio 2004). Interviewers had the sense that an enormous amount of honesty was being heard at the interview table. Since participants came forward to volunteer their involvement in the study, it seemed that interviews served as a type of migration therapy, where feelings and observations were readily offered to the interviewer, who was seen as a neutral person. While we cannot be definitive about this, there was a sense that, instead of providing a massaged version of the migration experience, the study participant was providing a very open version of the real issues.

Because it was impossible to obtain a larger and more comprehensive sample, and because the purpose of the interviews was to understand migration from the migrant's perspective, the goal of the interviews was systematic exploration for the purpose of discovery rather than for the confirmation of hypotheses. This, of course, did not preclude developing a model or organizing the material into generalizations in order to more clearly understand migration behaviour. Taking this approach also supported the goal of the study, which was to place these micro/personal migration experiences into a macro context in which migration to Alberta told a larger story about a changing Canadian society.

It would be a mistake not to mention that the principal investigator received input from numerous other sources once the subject of the research was made public. E-mails were received from people who were not part of the study but who were deeply affected by this migration. People were constantly being encountered in a variety of places, and their stories provided further verification and supplementation of what the formal data had provided. In many ways, living in Alberta "as a sociologist" during this period was like being engaged in a constant laboratory experience These experiences, however, did add to the liveliness of the research project and the public interest in it. The wide-ranging input received was preserved in quotations – some of which are included in this book. The quotations reported here are only a small sample of some of the responses received and are referenced by originating province. They demonstrate how migration is a real life experience.

Lead Interview Questions

1. **"Can you tell me how you decided to leave your place of origin?"**
*This is a very important question and you should probe as many factors as possible in this decision.

2.(a) **"How would you describe the conditions in your region of origin at the time you decided to leave it?"**
Before you left
*How did you evaluate conditions in the area in which you used to live before you moved?
*How would you describe the mood of your friends and acquaintances regarding conditions in the region before you left?
*How had you and your friends typically understood your region in the context of the rest of Canada?
Since you left:
*How would you now evaluate conditions in the area in which you used to live?
*What is the mood of your friends and acquaintances there now?
*How do you now understand your region of origin within the context of the rest of Canada."

(b) **"What factors in your region of origin contributed to your decision to leave?"**
*This is similar to #1 although the emphasis here is on region of origin rather than personal reasons.

3.(a) **"How was your decision to leave received by people in your region of origin?"**
*Were you the only one who thought of leaving?
*How did you explain to others why you were leaving?
*How was your decision received?"

*How did you ever think you were being disloyal by leaving? Did others think so?
*Did you consider your decision to leave as permanent or temporary?

(b) **"What impact did your decision to leave have on your region of origin?"**
*This might be less appropriate for people from larger communities.

4.(a) **"How did you come to decide where you were going to move?"**
*What were the destination options and what preconceived images did you have of them?
*How did you obtain information about destination options and your eventual destination?
*What did you expect life would be like in your destination region? How did those expectations compare with what you were experiencing in the region in which you currently lived?
*Did anyone influence you in your decision about where you would move?

(b) **"What images did you have of your destination before leaving and how did it compare with your place of origin?"**

5. **"How did you travel to your destination and how were other people involved with your move?"**
*What means of transportation did you use? *Did you travel alone?
*If your family also came to your destination, did you travel together and arrive at the same time?
*How much did you take with you? Did you use a professional mover or a rental moving conveyance?
*Did you go directly to this destination or did you stop elsewhere to explore opportunities there or even live for awhile somewhere else?

6.(a) **"How did you compare Alberta with your region of origin when you first arrived?"**
When you first arrived:

*How did you evaluate conditions in your destination region?
*How did you compare it with your region of origin?
*What adjustments did you think you would have to make to this new region?

(b) **"How do you now compare Alberta with your region of origin?"**
*How do you now evaluate conditions in your destination region?
*How do you now compare it with your region of origin?
*In what way is your destination region different and how did you adjust to it?

7. **"How did you try to get established in your new location?"**
*What procedures did you follow to get established?
*Did you find employment relatively soon, and if so, how? Are you satisfied with this employment?
*How did you establish social networks and social supports? Are you satisfied with the networks you have established?
*Did you seek out others from your region of origin? Are you still in touch with them?

8. **"How do you think you were treated as a newcomer?"**
*When you arrived (or do you now) feel like an outsider in any way? Did it ever seem to you like you had moved to another country and were in some sense a foreigner?
*Do you feel you were treated like an outsider by locals or identified by them in terms of your region of origin?
*Did you experience any local resentment to your move to this destination?
*What sorts of experiences led you to feel at home or to miss your region of origin?

9. **"In hindsight, do you think that your decision to move to Alberta was a good one?"**
*Do you feel that leaving your region of origin was still the best option?
*Do you feel that you chose the right destination?
*How much do you keep in contact with your region of origin?

*How do people "back home" now evaluate your decision?
*Do you think you will ever go back? Would you go back if you could? How often do you go back for visits?
*If you felt forced to move, do you have any resentments about that? Do people back home have any such resentments?
*Do you think of yourself now primarily in terms of your region of origin or your new region of residence?
*What has this experience taught you about the nature of Canadian society?

Phase III
Alberta In-Migration Study
Follow-up Survey

This survey is meant to be a follow up to our initial interview with you and seeks to determine how you now evaluate your decision to relocate to Alberta. Please use the scale to the right and darken the bubble of the answer that best reflects your position.

	Strongly Agree	Somewhat Agree	Neither Agree nor Disagree	Somewhat Disagree	Strongly Disagree
A – Leaving Where You Previously Lived					
1. When I left my home province, it was largely for adventure.	①	②	③	④	⑤
2. I left my home province because I had little choice.	①	②	③	④	⑤
3. It upsets me that I had to leave my home province.	①	②	③	④	⑤
4. The political and economic atmosphere back home was negative.	①	②	③	④	⑤
5. I actually felt depressed before I moved here.	①	②	③	④	⑤
6. One of the reasons I left home was because people there think differently than I do.	①	②	③	④	⑤
B – Choosing Where to Move					
1. I came to Alberta because of people I knew who were here already.	①	②	③	④	⑤
2. I am here just for the money.	①	②	③	④	⑤
3. Keeping in touch with people back home is very important to me.	①	②	③	④	⑤

4. People from home who live in Alberta are an important part of my life here.	①	②	③	④	⑤
5. I moved to Alberta because my way of thinking was closer to the way people think here.	①	②	③	④	⑤
C – Comparing Alberta With Your Home Province					
1. I am economically better off by being in Alberta.	①	②	③	④	⑤
2. I trust politicians here more than I trust politicians back home.	①	②	③	④	⑤
3. For me, coming to Alberta was in some sense like coming home.	①	②	③	④	⑤
4. When I go back home to visit, I feel like I don't belong there anymore.	①	②	③	④	⑤
5. When I hear about life back home, I am glad that I did not stay there.	①	②	③	④	⑤
D – Evaluating Your Decision to Relocate					
1. In retrospect, I wish I would have stayed in my home province instead of moving to Alberta.	①	②	③	④	⑤
2. I feel that my decision to move here was a good one.	①	②	③	④	⑤
3. I am disappointed because my expectations in moving here have not been met.	①	②	③	④	⑤
4. Being in Alberta makes me feel good.	①	②	③	④	⑤
5. I feel more at home in Alberta the longer I am here.	①	②	③	④	⑤
6. I think I am probably in Alberta permanently.	①	②	③	④	⑤
E – Experiencing Life in Alberta					
1. I am really happy with my current job.	①	②	③	④	⑤
2. I feel like I am an outsider in Alberta.	①	②	③	④	⑤
3. The lifestyle in Alberta appeals to me.	①	②	③	④	⑤
4. It has been a good career move for me to come to Alberta.	①	②	③	④	⑤

5. I feel like work and making money dominates people's thinking in Alberta.	①	②	③	④	⑤
6. Since I moved here, I feel like I put in too many hours working.	①	②	③	④	⑤
F – Returning To Your Home Province					
1. I would like to return to my home province as soon as possible.	①	②	③	④	⑤
2. My ultimate goal is to return to my home province.	①	②	③	④	⑤
3. I expect to retire in the region where I came from.	①	②	③	④	⑤
4. Most people who return home do so just because they are homesick.	①	②	③	④	⑤
5. People who return home just can't cope with the competitive environment in Alberta.	①	②	③	④	⑤
6. My work experience in Alberta will help me get a better job back home should I choose to return.	①	②	③	④	⑤

Table 1 Interprovincial In-migration and Net Migration by Province, 1972–2002

Province	*In-Migration*	*Net Migration*	*% of all In-Migrants*
Newfoundland and Labrador	274,339	–108,827	2.7
Prince Edward Island	101,496	5,604	1.0
Nova Scotia	585,524	–2,939	5.8
New Brunswick	439,671	–10,401	4.4
Quebec	808,562	–480,312	8.1
Ontario	2,573,022	125,964	25.7
Manitoba	587,844	–158,295	5.9
Saskatchewan	584,629	–180,358	5.8
Alberta	2,107,330	346,760	21.0
British Columbia	1,965,558	480,759	19.6
Total	10,027,975		100.0

SOURCE: Computed from Statistics Canada, CANSIM Table 051–0012.

Table 2 Interprovincial In-migrants by Province, 1972–2002, 2003–2005

	Canada	*NL*	*PEI*	*NS*	*NB*	*PQ*	*ON*	*MB*	*SK*	*AB*	*BC*
1972	395,432	12,391	4,316	22,711	20,190	38,011	108,168	26,017	19,831	61,331	75,424
1973	396,138	11,822	4,327	25,225	20,689	36,142	97,666	29,441	21,167	63,529	78,874
1974	437,549	13,133	4,947	26,245	21,811	41,175	100,684	33,487	27,887	73,083	89,182
1975	411,709	12,333	5,337	26,782	24,072	37,225	85,175	29,608	29,697	79,075	74,976
1976	375,351	11,699	4,268	24,512	22,898	32,562	81,717	26,356	28,299	77,821	58,567
1977	356,769	8,171	3,879	20,669	15,785	28,617	86,883	22,788	23,691	81,211	58,119
1978	363,393	8,316	3,864	20,128	15,131	23,960	97,015	20,646	20,637	83,200	63,730
1979	360,289	8,414	3,633	19,726	14,969	25,477	86,491	18,927	20,779	87,649	67,805
1980	374,434	9,333	3,204	18,003	13,916	21,935	79,533	18,645	20,428	101,936	81,734
1981	399,488	9,118	3,465	19,465	14,013	24,341	80,248	21,604	22,603	113,640	84,311
1982	352,442	9,393	3,298	19,329	14,190	20,764	84,736	21,480	21,867	95,156	55,860
1983	301,707	9,705	3,375	19,021	14,656	21,122	87,034	20,119	20,810	56,884	44,133
1984	275,051	6,271	2,932	16,712	12,497	23,854	90,802	16,797	18,592	38,564	43,306
1985	272,017	5,982	2,889	17,201	11,075	25,048	87,084	16,988	16,289	43,598	40,566
1986	290,045	6,045	2,806	17,615	11,547	25,767	89,694	17,518	15,639	54,116	44,426
1987	305,778	7,951	2,685	17,042	12,073	24,958	104,626	17,403	16,416	42,860	54,176
1988	320,897	9,259	3,255	18,177	13,005	26,544	99,220	17,767	14,454	48,977	64,194
1989	330,581	10,105	3,384	19,404	14,300	28,045	89,035	16,170	14,216	58,680	71,212
1990	357,118	10,705	3,436	20,328	15,201	30,229	84,130	18,049	15,748	70,860	82,183
1991	321,238	10,346	2,815	18,713	13,780	25,457	73,780	16,581	16,665	63,360	73,813
1992	316,253	9,266	2,937	18,361	12,715	25,116	70,813	15,955	17,796	59,647	77,695
1993	302,869	7,558	2,649	17,707	11,671	25,550	66,385	15,848	17,258	54,069	78,763
1994	288,908	6,580	2,688	15,259	10,725	23,777	64,625	15,253	16,828	51,763	76,549
1995	284,968	6,406	2,514	15,299	10,853	23,056	66,902	15,890	16,814	51,247	70,783
1996	291,285	7,005	2,882	16,263	11,770	22,556	69,059	15,075	17,411	57,037	66,959
1997	292,857	6,962	2,694	15,878	11,230	20,437	69,978	13,883	16,771	70,333	59,432
1998	309,234	7,392	2,570	16,304	10,904	20,513	75,216	14,906	18,697	86,307	51,524
1999	276,930	7,995	2,579	15,529	10,470	19,506	72,821	13,985	15,200	70,932	43,300
2000	285,817	8,400	2,662	16,272	11,286	20,989	78,903	14,075	14,556	70,721	43,465

Table 2 continued

2001	269,220	7,499	2,567	15,313	10,539	21,341	74,516	12,623	12,985	64,129	43,338
2002	290,490	8,784	2,639	16,331	11,710	24,488	70,083	13,960	14,598	75,615	47,159
Total	10,206,257	274,339	101,496	585,524	439,671	808,562	2,573,022	587,844	584,629	2,107,330	1,965,558
Mean (1972–2002)	329,234	8,850	3,274	18,888	14,183	26,083	83,001	18,963	18,859	67,978	63,405
2003	274,899	9,198	2,686	16,686	11,233	24,272	64,236	13,707	15,172	64,627	48,078
2004	261,380	8,397	2,570	15,087	10,690	23,727	57,186	13,301	14,551	60,822	50,406
2005	288,668	10,007	2,975	16,251	10,947	26,502	62,189	14,879	16,406	70,730	53,119

SOURCE: Statistics Canada, CANSIM Table 051–0012.

Table 3 Net Interprovincial Migration by Province, 1972–2002, 2003–2005

	NL	*PEI*	*NS*	*NB*	*PQ*	*ON*	*MB*	*SK*	*AB*	*BC*
1972	864	349	–586	384	–21,637	14,462	–8,880	–18,995	4,190	28,088
1973	–777	782	4,851	2,102	–19,754	940	–5,489	–16,524	5,498	27,193
1974	–2,719	821	1,014	2,269	–12,581	–9,802	–1,656	–10,472	2,911	31,505
1975	543	1,334	2,422	6,037	–10,361	–28,194	–6,119	697	23,155	9,615
1976	132	456	3,639	5,907	–13,354	–18,932	–4,982	5,296	26,579	–5,035
1977	–4,223	292	–1,195	–161	–27,986	–5,363	–3,001	3,263	34,084	5,801
1978	–4,229	610	–285	–1,284	–45,466	7,934	–5,054	–2,504	32,674	18,316
1979	–3,412	18	–546	–1,184	–30,382	–5,878	–11,094	–2,674	34,490	22,211
1980	–3,543	–471	–2,448	–2,947	–29,636	–24,280	–13,884	–4,564	42,242	41,067
1981	–4,243	–1,046	–3,345	–4,975	–23,476	–33,932	–8,847	–3,604	45,991	39,008
1982	–4,522	–814	–736	–1,968	–27,189	–1,101	–1,976	151	30,914	7,046
1983	1,286	671	3,778	3,286	–23,557	25,292	2,292	3,401	–14,276	–611
1984	–2,492	466	2,663	1,792	–16,358	40,304	–946	2,277	–33,579	6,424
1985	–3,697	205	2,172	–815	–7,674	33,953	–894	–1,874	–19,484	–1,967
1986	–5,697	–177	–268	–2,182	–4,774	32,722	–1,943	–7,021	–5,131	–3,727
1987	–4,660	–247	–1,144	–2,016	–5,285	46,133	–3,230	–5,654	–32,444	9,493

Table 3 continued

1988	−3,380	353	−1,285	−2,027	−8,103	30,497	−5,640	−12,364	−18,752	21,614
1989	−1,790	317	564	−481	−7,821	8,351	−9,421	−17,165	−1,308	29,421
1990	−2,021	−41	−45	72	−7,125	−10,138	−9,874	−19,928	9,159	39,984
1991	−711	−544	573	928	−13,093	−10,947	−7,687	−11,783	8,647	34,108
1992	−1,669	−237	306	−253	−12,552	−11,045	−7,641	−8,481	2,983	38,004
1993	−3,078	654	96	−1,402	−8,420	−14,189	−5,544	−6,348	−1,181	40,099
1994	−4,952	622	−1,887	−671	−8,758	−9,420	−4,614	−5,431	−1,630	37,871
1995	−6,974	349	−2,741	−813	−8,947	−2,841	−3,220	−3,652	−556	29,291
1996	−7,436	638	−1,245	−369	−12,626	−2,822	−3,566	−2,161	7,656	22,025
1997	−8,134	136	−1,648	−1,263	−17,436	1,977	−5,873	−2,794	26,282	9,880
1998	−9,490	−416	−2,569	−3,192	−16,958	9,231	−5,276	−1,940	43,089	−10,029
1999	−5,695	193	201	−1,244	−13,065	16,706	−2,113	−4,333	25,191	−14,484
2000	−4,263	104	−270	−1,183	−12,146	22,369	−3,456	−7,947	22,674	−14,610
2001	−4,493	165	−2,077	−1,530	−9,442	18,623	−4,323	−8,410	20,457	−8,286
2002	−3,352	62	−898	−1,218	−4,350	5,354	−4,344	−8,820	26,235	−8,556
Total	−108,827	5,604	−2,939	−10,401	−480,312	125,964	−158,295	−180,358	346,760	480,759
Mean	−3,511	181	−95	−336	−15,494	4,063	−5,106	−5,818	11,186	15,508
2003	−1,683	165	510	−843	−1,829	637	−2,875	−5,141	11,903	−1,037
2004	−2,027	144	−772	−760	−822	−6,935	−2,565	−4,521	10,606	7,865
2005	−1,875	−222	−473	−1,650	−2,332	−8,375	−3,832	−4,583	16,615	7,456

SOURCE: Statistics Canada, CANSIM Table 051–0012.

Table 4 Rates of Natural Increase, Net International Migration and Net Interprovincial Migration by Province

	Natural Increase	*Net International Migration*	*Net Interprovincial Migration*
First Wave: 1975–1982			
NL	13.0	0.8	–5.2
PEI	7.5	1.4	0.4
NS	6.7	1.6	–0.4
NB	8.5	1.2	–0.1
PQ	8.1	2.8	–4.0
ON	7.1	6.1	–1.6
MB	7.9	4.5	–6.6
SK	9.3	2.1	–0.5
AB	11.8	5.5	16.3
BC	7.1	6.5	6.5
Second Wave: 1996–2002			
NL	1.8	0.3	–11.4
PEI	2.7	0.6	0.9
NS	1.9	1.4	–1.3
NB	2.2	0.3	–1.9
PQ	3.2	3.0	–1.7
ON	4.6	8.4	0.9
MB	4.2	2.3	–3.6
SK	3.8	0.5	–5.1
AB	7.0	2.5	8.3
BC	3.8	7.6	–0.9

NOTE: Rates are per 1,000.

SOURCE: Computed from Statistics Canada, CANSIM Table 051–0001 and 051–0004.

Table 5 Interprovincial Out-migrants, Canada and Provinces, 1972–2002

	Canada	*NL*	*PEI*	*NS*	*NB*	*PQ*	*ON*	*MB*	*SK*	*AB*	*BC*
1972	395,432	11,527	3,967	23,297	19,806	59,648	93,706	34,897	38,826	57,141	47,336
1973	396,138	12,599	3,545	20,374	18,587	55,896	96,726	34,930	37,691	58,031	51,681
1974	437,549	15,852	4,126	25,231	19,542	53,756	110,486	35,143	38,359	70,172	57,677
1975	411,709	11,790	4,003	24,360	18,035	47,586	113,369	35,727	29,000	55,920	65,361
1976	375,351	11,567	3,812	20,873	16,991	45,916	100,649	31,338	23,003	51,242	63,602
1977	356,769	12,394	3,587	21,864	15,946	56,603	92,246	25,789	20,428	47,127	52,318
1978	363,393	12,545	3,254	20,413	16,415	69,426	89,031	25,700	23,141	50,526	45,414
1979	360,289	11,826	3,615	20,272	16,153	55,859	92,369	30,021	23,453	53,159	45,594
1980	374,434	12,876	3,675	20,451	16,863	51,571	103,813	32,529	24,992	59,694	40,667
1981	399,488	13,361	4,511	22,810	18,988	47,817	114,180	30,451	26,207	67,649	45,303
1982	352,442	13,915	4,112	20,065	16,158	47,953	85,837	23,456	21,716	64,242	48,814
1983	301,707	8,419	2,704	15,243	11,370	44,679	61,742	17,827	17,409	71,160	44,744
1984	275,051	8,763	2,466	14,049	10,705	40,212	50,498	17,743	16,315	72,143	36,882
1985	272,017	9,679	2,684	15,029	11,890	32,722	53,131	17,882	18,163	63,082	42,533
1986	290,045	11,742	2,983	17,883	13,729	30,541	56,972	19,461	22,660	59,247	48,153
1987	305,778	12,611	2,932	18,186	14,089	30,243	58,493	20,633	22,070	75,304	44,683
1988	320,897	12,639	2,902	19,462	15,032	34,647	68,723	23,407	26,818	67,729	42,580
1989	330,581	11,895	3,067	18,840	14,781	35,866	80,684	25,591	31,381	59,988	41,791
1990	357,118	12,726	3,477	20,373	15,129	37,354	94,268	27,923	35,676	61,701	42,199
1991	321,238	11,057	3,359	18,140	12,852	38,550	84,727	24,268	28,448	54,713	39,705
1992	316,253	10,935	3,174	18,055	12,968	37,668	81,858	23,596	26,277	56,664	39,691
1993	302,869	10,636	1,995	17,611	13,073	33,970	80,574	21,392	23,606	55,250	38,664
1994	288,908	11,532	2,066	17,146	11,396	32,535	74,045	19,867	22,259	53,393	38,678
1995	284,968	13,380	2,165	18,040	11,666	32,003	69,743	19,110	20,466	51,803	41,492
1996	291,285	14,441	2,244	17,508	12,139	35,182	71,881	18,641	19,572	49,381	44,934
1997	292,857	15,096	2,558	17,526	12,493	37,873	68,001	19,756	19,565	44,051	49,552
1998	309,234	16,882	2,986	18,873	14,096	37,471	65,985	20,182	20,637	43,218	61,553
1999	276,930	13,690	2,386	15,328	11,714	32,571	56,115	16,098	19,533	45,741	57,784
2000	285,817	12,663	2,558	16,542	12,469	33,135	56,534	17,531	22,503	48,047	58,075

Table 5 continued

2001	269,220	11,992	2,402	17,390	12,069	30,783	55,893	16,946	21,395	43,672	51,624
2002	290,490	12,136	2,577	17,229	12,928	28,838	64,729	18,304	23,418	49,380	55,715
Total	10,206,257	383,166	95,892	588,463	450,072	1,288,874	2,447,058	746,139	764,987	1,760,570	1,484,799
Median	316,253	12,394	2,986	18,186	14,089	37,668	80,574	23,407	23,003	55,920	45,414
Mean	329,234	12,360	3,093	18,983	14,518	41,577	78,937	24,069	24,677	56,793	47,897

Table 6 Percentage Distribution by Age of Interprovincial Migrants, Alberta, 1981 and 1998

	In-migrants		*Out-migrants*		*Net Exchange*	
	1981	*1998*	*1981*	*1998*	*1981*	*1998*
0–4 years	6.8%	0.1%	8.0%	0.1%	5.0%	0.1%
5–9 years	7.1	6.6	7.8	7.6	6.1	5.7
10–14 years	5.6	5.7	6.1	6.1	4.9	5.3
15–19 years	16.3	9.8	9.3	7.5	26.5	12.1
20–24 years	23.5	19.1	20.2	16.1	28.5	22.2
25–29 years	14.4	13.9	15.6	13.2	12.6	14.6
30–34 years	9.6	11.1	10.6	11.2	8.2	10.9
35–39 years	5.8	7.8	6.2	8.7	5.2	6.9
40–44 years	3.6	5.6	4.0	5.8	3.1	5.4
45–49 years	2.0	3.6	2.7	4.3	1.0	3.0
50–54 years	1.6	2.4	2.4	3.0	0.3	1.8
55–59 years	1.2	1.8	2.3	2.7	–0.3	0.9
60–64 years	1.0	1.4	1.9	1.6	–0.5	1.2
65–69 years	0.6	1.2	1.5	1.5	–0.6	0.8
70–74 years	0.4	0.8	0.7	1.1	–0.1	0.4
75–79 years	0.3	0.6	0.3	0.6	0.1	0.6
80–84 years	0.1	0.4	0.2	0.4	0.1	0.4
85–89 years	0.0	0.2	0.1	0.1	0.0	0.3
90 years and over	0.0	0.1	0.0	0.1	0.0	0.0
Total Percent	100.0	100.0	100.0	100.0	100.0	100.0
Total Number	113,334	84,977	67,341	42,534	45,993	42,443

1998
mean age of Canadian interprovincial migrants *28.49*
mean age of Albertan interprovincial in-migrants *27.30*
mean age of Albertan interprovincial out-migrants *28.36*
mean age of Albertans *34.60*
mean age of Canadians *36.80*

SOURCE: Statistics Canada, CANSIM Table 051–0012; Annual Demographic Statistics 2003, Tables 1.16 and 1.25.

Table 7 Ages of Interprovincial Migrants to Alberta by Province of Residence 5 Years Ago, 2001

	Canada	*NL*	*PEI*	*NS*	*NB*	*PQ*	*ON*	*MB*	*SK*	*BC*
5–9 years	8.2	6.5	3.1	6.1	8.0	8.0	9.0	8.4	7.4	8.7
10–14 years	6.7	5.8	5.4	7.4	6.0	7.3	6.8	6.8	6.7	6.6
15–19 years	6.5	6.1	3.8	5.3	7.1	7.0	6.2	6.4	7.3	6.4
20–24 years	13.9	20.7	28.0	17.4	16.3	12.4	11.7	13.2	17.4	12.6
25–29 years	15.8	23.6	24.1	23.2	19.7	14.2	16.0	16.4	16.8	13.3
30–34 years	11.8	13.3	17.2	11.3	11.3	10.0	12.8	11.2	10.1	12.2
35–39 years	10.4	8.0	6.1	9.6	10.6	11.6	11.2	10.8	9.2	10.8
40–44 years	8.1	6.0	3.4	8.4	8.3	9.0	8.5	7.7	6.9	8.4
45–49 years	5.9	4.1	0.8	4.5	5.8	6.6	6.5	5.9	5.2	6.2
50–54 years	4.3	3.4	4.2	3.4	3.0	4.6	4.1	5.0	4.0	4.5

Table 7 continued

55–59 years	2.6	1.3	1.1	1.3	1.6	2.7	2.3	2.2	2.4	3.2
60–64 years	1.8	0.5	1.1	0.5	1.0	1.6	1.6	1.9	1.9	2.2
65–69 years	1.3	0.2	0.0	0.7	0.5	1.3	1.2	1.5	1.8	1.5
70–74 years	0.9	0.3	0.8	0.1	0.2	1.2	0.8	1.1	1.0	1.2
75 years and over	1.7	0.3	0.0	0.9	0.5	2.5	1.5	1.3	2.0	2.1
Total	100.0	100.0	100.0	100.0	100.0	100.0	100.0	100.0	100.0	100.0

SOURCE: Computed from Statistics Canada, 2001 Census, Catalogue no. 97F0008XCB01005.

Table 8 Sex Ratios of Interprovincial Migrants to and from Alberta Compared to Canada for the First and Second Waves

Year	*In-migrants to Alberta*	*Out-migrants from Alberta*	*Migrants in Canada*
1975	106.7	105.0	106.1
1976	106.7	105.0	106.2
1977	122.1	110.4	113.5
1978	121.2	115.1	113.3
1979	119.6	113.5	111.8
1980	123.2	109.9	113.3
1981	122.5	112.8	113.7
1982	117.8	115.2	111.9
Average	*117.5*	*110.9*	*111.2*
1996	105.9	105.0	105.8
1997	108.6	105.6	106.7
1998	116.2	105.4	108.6
1999	114.0	107.5	106.3
2000	109.3	109.5	105.6
2001	109.4	107.1	105.3
2002	112.9	106.4	105.0
Average	*110.9*	*106.7*	*106.2*

SOURCE: Computed from Statistics Canada, CANSIM Table 051-0012.

Table 9 Sex Ratio of Interprovincial Migrants to Alberta by Province of Residence 5 Years Ago, 1981 and 2001

	1981	*2001*
Newfoundland and Labrador	121.2	118.3
Prince Edward Island	121.1	155.9
Nova Scotia	126.5	116.3
New Brunswick	136.4	119.8
Quebec	126.1	104.4
Ontario	122.2	104.6
Manitoba	111.4	103.0
Saskatchewan	104.2	97.8
British Columbia	102.3	106.7
All Migrants	115.7	105.9
Sex ratio of total Canadian population		

SOURCE: Statistics Canada, 1981 Census, Catalogue no. 92-907, Table 2, Catalogue no. 92-901, Table 1; 2001 Census, Catalogue no. 97F0008XCB01005.

Table 10 Destination of Interprovincial Migrants by Province of Origin, 1975–1982, 1996–2002, by Numbers

	Origin										
Destination	*NL*	*PEI*	*NS*	*NB*	*PQ*	*ON*	*MB*	*SK*	*AB*	*BC*	*Total*
First Wave, 1975–1982											
NL		1,112	11,425	5,260	5,134	39,278	3,021	731	6,435	3,251	75,647
PEI	1,152		7,284	4,399	2,084	10,506	890	471	2,513	1,427	30,726
NS	14,694	7,373		26,835	15,909	65,550	5,572	2,719	14,584	14,165	167,401
NB	6,996	4,556	25,846		27,764	48,586	3,545	1,618	8,688	6,705	134,304
PQ	4,551	977	10,195	19,827		134,563	6,814	3,173	14,091	18,987	213,178
ON	39,552	7,471	58,475	41,764	262,121		54,363	22,432	92,368	96,465	675,011
MB	4,412	964	5,854	4,273	10,299	62,311		27,533	33,565	28,234	177,445
SK	1,426	490	3,508	2,512	4,893	32,071	36,785		67,371	35,455	184,511
AB	18,622	5,486	27,988	20,360	52,867	227,880	70,188	88,763		188,480	700,634
BC	6,820	1,857	18,871	9,457	39,574	161,469	50,303	41,294	196,784		526,429
Total	98,225	30,286	169,446	134,687	420,645	782,214	231,481	188,734	436,399	393,169	2,885,286
Second Wave, 1996–2002											
NL		954	7,938	2,875	1,515	22,327	1,023	673	10,364	4,894	52,563
PEI	1,625		4,451	3,038	835	5,037	264	250	1,590	1,303	18,393
NS	13,541	4,235		16,863	6,369	39,349	2,977	1,963	12,851	12,389	110,537
NB	4,744	2,754	16,816		12,948	23,966	1,695	911	7,865	5,488	77,187
PQ	1,619	630	6,008	13,628		93,544	3,368	1,917	10,848	17,111	148,673
ON	36,734	4,768	46,461	28,590	160,185		35,297	16,081	73,334	104,127	505,577
MB	1,606	240	3,008	1,801	3,745	29,700		16,329	21,290	18,972	96,691
SK	1,272	240	1,775	1,103	1,879	12,270	17,559		49,725	22,166	107,989
AB	26,600	2,641	20,318	13,634	21,139	89,860	38,393	82,711		185,362	480,658
BC	6,654	1,113	12,060	5,656	25,818	118,473	25,200	23,920	127,403		346,297
Total	94,395	17,575	118,835	87,188	234,433	434,526	125,776	144,755	315,270	371,812	1,944,565

SOURCE: Statistics Canada, CANSIM Table 051–0019.

Table 11 Destination of Interprovincial Migrants by Province of Origin, 1975–1982, 1996–2002, by Percentages

Destination	*NL*	*PEI*	*NS*	*NB*	*PQ*	*ON*	*MB*	*SK*	*AB*	*BC*
First Wave, 1975–1982										
Newfoundland and Labrador	%	3.7	6.7	3.9	1.2	5.0	1.3	0.4	1.5	0.8
Prince Edward Island	1.2		4.3	3.3	0.5	1.3	0.4	0.2	0.6	0.4
Nova Scotia	15.0	24.3		19.9	3.8	8.4	2.4	1.4	3.3	3.6
New Brunswick	7.1	15.0	15.3		6.6	6.2	1.5	0.9	2.0	1.7
Quebec	4.6	3.2	6.0	14.7		17.2	2.9	1.7	3.2	4.8
Ontario	40.3	24.7	34.5	31.0	62.3		23.5	11.9	21.2	24.5
Manitoba	4.5	3.2	3.5	3.2	2.4	8.0		14.6	7.7	7.2
Saskatchewan	1.5	1.6	2.1	1.9	1.2	4.1	15.9		15.4	9.0
Alberta	19.0	18.1	16.5	15.1	12.6	29.1	30.3	47.0		47.9
British Columbia	6.9	6.1	11.1	7.0	9.4	20.6	21.7	21.9	45.1	
Total	100.0	100.0	100.0	100.0	100.0	100.0	100.0	100.0	100.0	100.0
Second Wave, 1996–2002										
Newfoundland and Labrador	%	5.4	6.7	3.3	0.6	5.1	0.8	0.5	3.3	1.3
Prince Edward Island	1.7		3.7	3.5	0.4	1.2	0.2	0.2	0.5	0.4
Nova Scotia	14.3	24.1		19.3	2.7	9.1	2.4	1.4	4.1	3.3
New Brunswick	5.0	15.7	14.2		5.5	5.5	1.3	0.6	2.5	1.5
Quebec	1.7	3.6	5.1	15.6		21.5	2.7	1.3	3.4	4.6
Ontario	38.9	27.1	39.1	32.8	68.3		28.1	11.1	23.3	28.0
Manitoba	1.7	1.4	2.5	2.1	1.6	6.8		11.3	6.8	5.1
Saskatchewan	1.3	1.4	1.5	1.3	0.8	2.8	14.0		15.8	6.0
Alberta	28.2	15.0	17.1	15.6	9.0	20.7	30.5	57.1		49.9
British Columbia	7.0	6.3	10.1	6.5	11.0	27.3	20.0	16.5	40.4	
Total	100.0	100.0	100.0	100.0	100.0	100.0	100.0	100.0	100.0	100.0

SOURCE: Computed from Statistics Canada, CANSIM Table 051–0019.

Table 12 Percent Distribution of Interprovincial Migrants to Alberta, Percent Moved to Alberta in Last Five Years, and Percent Born in Another Province for Select Alberta Destinations, 1981 and 2001

	All Interprovincial Migrants to Alberta (%)		*Moved to Alberta in Last Five Years (%)*		*Born in Another Province (%)*	
	1981	*2001*	*1981*	*2001*	*1981*	*2001*
Medicine Hat	1.6	2.3	13.5	9.2	36.3	36.2
Brooks	0.5	0.9	17.7	19.2	36.2	40.2
Lethbridge	1.5	2.0	9.5	7.4	24.0	25.2
Calgary	38.0	39.7	20.4	10.1	39.9	32.5
Red Deer	2.5	2.7	18.5	9.8	34.6	32.5
Camrose	0.3	0.3	9.0	5.2	20.0	21.7
Edmonton	29.0	25.4	13.2	6.6	51.6	23.8
Lloydminster AB	0.7	0.9	26.7	16.0	66.0	69.9
Grande Prairie	1.5	2.0	20.4	13.1	32.7	31.4
Fort McMurray	4.2	3.0	46.0	17.1	57.4	46.7
Wetaskiwin	0.4	0.4	14.1	8.3	24.9	25.5
Alberta	———	———	15.1	8.2	29.2	27.6

SOURCE: Statistics Canada, 1981 Census, Catalogue no. 95–945 (Vol. 3, profile series B) and Catalogue no. 93–933 (Vol. 3, provincial series, Table 9); 2001 Census, Catalogue no. 95F0357XCB01004 and no. 95F0008XCB01002.

Table 13 Hypermobility Index for CMA's and Provinces, 1981 and 2001

		1981	*2001*
Newfoundland and Labrador	**63165**	**110.3**	**124.3**
St. John's	22645	121.0	132.3
Prince Edward Island	**15665**	**178.5**	**117.4**
Nova Scotia	**107290**	**151.0**	**119.5**
Halifax	60570	224.3	170.2
New Brunswick	**73690**	**143.9**	**102.4**
Saint John	12375	141.5	102.0
Quebec	**182185**	**44.9**	**25.6**
Québec	14605	23.9	21.7
Montréal	108920	64.8	32.2
Ontario	**433105**	**73.0**	**38.4**
Ottawa-Hull	75140	131.5	71.5
Toronto	146560	67.1	31.5
Manitoba	**103780**	**162.0**	**94.0**
Winnipeg	66355	174.8	100.3
Saskatchewan	**110135**	**151.7**	**114.3**
Regina	24410	184.0	128.5
Saskatoon	30585	215.4	137.4
Alberta	**365035**	**235.1**	**124.1**
Medicine Hat	8035	210.7	131.5
Brooks	2760	268.6	241.4
Lethbridge	7990	159.3	120.6
Calgary	141780	324.7	150.3
Red Deer	9300	272.2	139.7
Camrose	1400	142.8	97.5

Table 13 continued

Edmonton	98625	239.1	106.4
Lloydminster (AB)	3050	383.6	236.0
Grande Prairie	6775	312.7	185.4
Wood Buffalo	9550	611.6	224.7
Wetaskiwin	1365	203.3	126.1
British Columbia	**327045**	**142.1**	**84.5**
Vancouver	136545	119.5	69.4
Victoria	34770	178.8	113.3

NOTE: The hypermobility index measures the number of interprovincial movements in and out of a province/city, regardless of origin or destination. Movements in and out are treated equally regardless of whether there is a net gain or a net loss. It is calculated by adding together all interprovincial in-migrants and out-migrants to either a province or city and dividing the total number of movements by the total population of the province or city times one thousand. The index expresses the extent to which the population is in flux due to interprovincial migration. Cells that are shaded identify provinces/cities for whom the index reflects a net loss in interprovincial migration.

SOURCE: Computed from Statistics Canada 1981 Census Catalogue No. 92–907 Tables 1 and 3; 2001 Census Catalogue No. 97F0008XCB01009.

Table 14 Change in Number of Farms and Size of Farms, Western Interior 1921–2001

	1921	*1931*	*1941*	*1951*	*1961*	*1971*	*1981*	*1991*	*1996*	*2001*
Number of Farms										
Manitoba	53,252	54,199	58,024	52,383	43,306	34,981	29,442	25,706	24,383	21,071
Saskatchewan	119,451	136,472	138,713	112,018	93,924	76,970	67,318	60,840	56,995	50,598
Alberta	82,954	97,408	99,732	84,315	73,212	62,702	58,056	57,245	59,007	53,652
Size of Farms										
Manitoba	274	279	291	338	420	543	639	743	784	891
Saskatchewan	369	408	432	550	686	845	952	1091	1152	1283
Alberta	353	400	434	527	645	790	813	898	881	970

NOTE: Size of farms is average farm size in acres.

SOURCE: 2001 Census of Agriculture: farm data and farm operator data, full release, catalogue no. 95F0354XCB.

Table 15 Rates of Components of Growth for Alberta and British Columbia, 1972–2002

	Birth Rate		*Death Rate*		*Rate of Natural Increase*		*Immigration Rate*		*Rate of Net International Migration*		*Rate of Net Interprovincial Migration*	
	AB	*BC*	*AB*	*BC*	*AB*	*BC*	*AB*	*BC*	*AB*	*BC*	*AB*	*BC*
1972	17.3	15.0	6.4	7.7	11.0	7.2	4.9	8.0	2.9	6.4	2.5	12.2
1973	17.2	14.6	6.2	7.6	10.9	7.0	5.4	9.5	3.4	7.9	3.2	11.5
1974	16.6	14.1	6.2	7.7	10.4	6.4	7.9	13.5	4.5	10.9	1.7	12.9
1975	16.9	14.5	6.3	7.8	10.7	6.7	8.7	13.4	5.8	11.2	12.8	3.8
1976	17.4	14.2	6.2	7.5	11.2	6.7	8.5	10.0	6.4	8.3	14.2	–2.0
1977	17.4	14.1	5.9	7.1	11.5	7.0	7.1	6.6	5.4	5.3	17.5	2.3
1978	17.2	14.0	5.9	7.2	11.3	6.8	5.8	5.4	3.6	3.7	16.2	7.0
1979	17.4	14.3	5.7	7.2	11.7	7.1	4.3	4.7	2.2	3.1	16.4	8.3
1980	17.3	14.2	5.6	7.0	11.7	7.2	7.8	8.1	6.5	7.0	19.3	15.0
1981	18.0	14.5	5.6	7.0	12.5	7.5	8.1	8.1	6.9	7.2	20.0	13.8

Table 15 continued

1982	18.6	14.9	5.5	7.0	13.1	7.8	8.7	7.7	6.7	6.4	13.1	2.5
1983	19.0	14.6	5.3	7.0	13.7	7.6	5.7	5.3	3.6	3.8	–6.0	–0.2
1984	18.8	14.8	5.3	6.9	13.4	7.9	4.5	4.9	2.4	3.4	–14.0	2.2
1985	18.3	14.6	5.4	7.0	12.9	7.6	4.1	4.1	2.3	2.5	–8.1	–0.7
1986	18.2	14.1	5.6	7.1	12.6	7.0	3.8	4.1	2.3	2.7	–2.1	–1.2
1987	17.6	13.8	5.5	7.0	12.2	6.9	4.4	5.2	2.3	3.8	–13.3	3.1
1988	16.9	13.4	5.6	7.3	11.3	6.2	5.2	6.6	3.3	5.5	–7.6	6.9
1989	17.3	13.6	5.5	7.1	11.8	6.6	6.0	7.7	4.4	6.7	–0.5	9.2
1990	17.1	13.7	5.5	7.1	11.6	6.7	7.1	8.1	5.5	7.0	3.6	12.2
1991	16.4	13.4	5.5	7.0	10.9	6.3	6.9	9.1	5.0	8.1	3.3	10.1
1992	16.2	13.3	5.5	7.0	10.7	6.3	6.5	10.0	3.6	8.0	1.1	11.0
1993	15.4	12.9	5.6	7.2	9.8	5.7	7.1	11.5	4.4	9.5	–0.4	11.2
1994	14.8	12.6	5.8	6.9	9.0	5.7	6.7	13.4	4.3	11.6	–0.6	10.3
1995	14.3	12.4	5.7	7.0	8.5	5.5	6.0	12.2	3.6	10.6	–0.2	7.8
1996	13.9	12.1	5.7	7.0	8.1	5.1	5.0	12.3	2.9	10.8	2.8	5.7
1997	13.2	11.5	5.9	7.0	7.3	4.5	4.9	13.5	2.4	10.9	9.3	2.5
1998	12.9	10.9	5.8	7.0	7.1	3.9	4.0	10.2	1.7	7.3	14.9	–2.5
1999	12.9	10.6	5.7	6.9	7.2	3.7	3.8	8.5	1.8	5.7	8.5	–3.6
2000	12.6	10.3	5.7	6.9	6.9	3.4	4.3	9.1	2.4	5.9	7.5	–3.6
2001	12.2	9.9	5.8	6.8	6.4	3.1	5.3	9.7	3.1	6.7	6.7	–2.0
2002	12.2	9.8	5.7	7.0	6.4	2.8	5.3	9.2	3.2	6.3	8.4	–2.1
Mean rate	16.2	13.3	5.7	7.1	10.4	6.1	5.9	8.7	3.8	6.9	4.8	5.3
2003	12.3	9.7	5.9	6.9	6.4	2.8	4.3	7.7	2.8	5.7	3.8	–0.2
2004	12.2	9.5	6.1	7.1	6.1	2.5	5.3	8.7	3.9	6.7	3.4	1.7
2005	12.6	9.5	6.1	7.1	6.5	2.5	5.3	9.5	4.1	7.8	5.1	1.8

NOTE: Rates are per 1,000.

SOURCE: Computed from Statistics Canada, CANSIM Table 051–0001, 051–0004.

Table 16 Components of Growth for Alberta and British Columbia, 1972–2002

	Natural Increase		*Net International Migration*		*Net Interprovincial Migration*	
	AB	*BC*	*AB*	*BC*	*AB*	*BC*
1972	18,598	16,680	4,933	14,826	4,190	28,088
1973	18,846	16,677	5,825	18,806	5,498	27,193
1974	18,201	15,632	7,944	26,650	2,911	31,505
1975	19,270	16,820	10,573	28,046	23,155	9,615
1976	20,992	16,997	11,951	21,087	26,579	–5,035
1977	22,421	18,032	10,432	13,543	34,084	5,801
1978	22,821	17,762	7,285	9,782	32,674	18,316
1979	24,484	18,944	4,563	8,321	34,490	22,211
1980	25,608	19,681	14,144	19,289	42,242	41,067
1981	28,592	21,153	15,758	20,374	45,991	39,008
1982	31,014	22,499	15,790	18,288	30,914	7,046
1983	32,724	22,121	8,593	11,176	–14,276	–611
1984	32,107	23,265	5,709	9,971	–33,579	6,424
1985	30,926	22,745	5,527	7,330	–19,484	–1,967
1986	30,677	20,957	5,552	7,988	–5,131	–3,727
1987	29,628	20,909	5,700	11,484	–32,444	9,493
1988	27,698	19,211	8,189	17,147	–18,752	21,614
1989	29,419	21,004	10,958	21,366	–1,308	29,421
1990	29,585	21,945	13,897	23,171	9,159	39,984
1991	28,209	21,330	13,079	27,277	8,647	34,108
1992	28,236	21,774	9,506	27,879	2,983	38,004
1993	26,054	20,330	11,694	34,009	–1,181	40,099
1994	24,336	20,946	11,628	42,757	–1,630	37,871
1995	23,373	20,708	9,712	40,089	–556	29,291
1996	22,564	19,881	8,078	41,882	7,656	22,025
1997	20,615	17,715	6,763	42,986	26,282	9,880
1998	20,554	15,709	4,912	29,256	43,089	–10,029
1999	21,294	14,822	5,416	22,870	25,191	–14,484
2000	20,786	13,925	7,257	23,947	22,674	–14,610
2001	19,607	12,552	9,432	27,312	20,457	–8,286
2002	19,936	11,569	9,888	25,788	26,235	–8,556
Total	769,175	584,295	280,688	694,697	346,760	480,759
% of net growth over period	55.1	33.2	20.1	39.5	24.8	27.3
2003	20,299	11,825	8,935	23,544	11,903	–1,037
2004	19,622	10,429	12,358	28,186	10,902	7,333
2005	21,539	10,462	14,667	35,842	34,423	8,214
2006	21,679	10,898	19,397	37,942	57,105	3,779

SOURCE: Statistics Canada, CANSIM Table 051–0004, ADE Catalogue No. 91–215

Table 17 Employment in Calgary and Edmonton by Sector and Percentage Change, 1994–2004 (numbers in thousands)

	Calgary				Edmonton			
	1994	*2004*	*Number Change*	*Percent Change*	*1994*	*2004*	*Number Change*	*Percent Change*
Total employed, all industries	403.2	598.3	195.1	48.4%	431.2	556.3	125.1	29.0%
Goods Producing Sector	93.9	142.1	48.2	51.3	83.9	126.7	42.8	51.0
Agriculture	2.2	2.7	0.5	22.7	3.3	4.5	1.2	36.4
Forestry, Fishing, Mining, Oil and Gas	30.5	33.7	3.2	10.5	8.6	12.4	3.8	44.2
Utilities	3.2	3.0	–0.2	–6.3	5.1	5.9	0.8	15.7
Construction	28.1	52.2	24.1	85.8	26.3	51.7	25.4	96.6
Manufacturing	30.0	50.5	20.5	68.3	40.7	52.2	11.5	28.3
Services Producing Sector	309.3	456.1	146.8	47.5	347.3	429.5	82.2	23.7
Trade	65.6	91.9	26.3	40.1	76.1	89.4	13.3	17.5
Transportation and warehousing	24.7	36.4	11.7	47.4	21.4	30.0	8.6	40.2
Finance, insurance, real estate and leasing	27.5	36.1	8.6	31.3	27.4	31.1	3.7	13.5
Professional, scientific and technical services	31.4	63.4	32.0	101.9	26.1	36.5	10.4	39.8
Business, building and other support services	14.6	27.8	13.2	90.4	11.3	20.0	8.7	77.0
Educational services	29.2	29.7	0.5	1.7	31.4	41.0	9.6	30.6
Health care and social assistance	31.7	48.3	16.6	52.4	48.7	61.3	12.6	25.9
Information, culture and recreation	17.4	31.8	14.4	82.8	22.9	24.6	1.7	7.4
Accommodation and food services	30.6	43.9	13.3	43.5	26.7	39.5	12.8	47.9
Other services	21.1	28.1	7.0	33.2	22.5	24.9	2.4	10.7
Public administration	15.6	18.7	3.1	19.9	33.0	31.3	–1.7	–5.2

Source: Calculated from Statistics Canada, CANSIM Table 282–0057

Table 18 Employment in Alberta by Selected Sector and Percentage Change, 1994–2004

	1994	*2004*	*Number Increase*	*Percentage Change*
ALL SECTORS	1,078,547	1,472,331	393,784	36.5
GOODS PRODUCING INDUSTRIES	231,715	357,534	125,819	54.3
Forestry	3,759	3,347	–412	–11.0
Oil and Gas Extraction	63,907	89,385	25,478	39.9
Construction	58,820	116,493	57,673	98.0
Construction of Buildings	12,797	24,904	12,107	94.6
Residential	5,525	12,714	7,189	130.1
Non-Residential	7,272	12,189	4,917	67.6
Civil Engineering/Infrastructure	13,962	31,579	17,617	126.2
Building Trades	32,061	60,011	27,950	87.2
Manufacturing	92,824	136,008	43,184	46.5
Non-Durable Goods (eg. food, beverages)	45,043	57,041	11,998	26.6
Durable Goods	47,780	78,966	31,186	65.3
Wood Product (eg. doors, windows)	6,712	11,567	4,855	72.3
Fabricated Metal (eg. boilers)	11,274	20,547	9,273	82.3
Machinery (eg. mining)	7,962	17,008	9,046	113.6
SERVICE PRODUCING INDUSTRIES	846,832	1,114,797	267,965	31.6
Trade	192,712	265,860	73,148	38.0
Wholesale Trade (eg. food, building)	60,028	77,487	17,459	29.1
Retail Trade (eg. consumer products)	132,683	188,373	55,690	42.0
Transportation/Warehousing	55,921	75,389	19,468	34.8
Finance and Insurance	36,843	44,528	7,685	20.9
Real Estate	20,964	30,256	9,292	44.3
Professional, Scientific and Technical	48,038	92,102	44,064	91.7
Administrative and Support Services	31,450	60,898	29,448	93.6
Educational Services	87,503	99,687	12,184	13.9
Accommodation and Food Services	94,211	111,239	17,028	18.1
Health Care Services	109,251	125,131	15,880	14.5
Other Services	43,396	62,681	19,285	44.4
Arts, Entertainment, Recreation	21,696	31,683	9,987	46.0
Public Administration	71,292	69,665	–1,627	–2.3

SOURCE: Computed from Statistics Canada, CANSIM Table 281–0024

Table 19 Types of Computer Usage in the Three Phases of Migration

	Pre-Migrant	*Post-Migrant*	*Settled Migrant*
Search Tool	Searching for a wide range of information about the potential destination. Function: Exploration and discovery to facilitate migration destination adjustment.	More skillful use of Internet to obtain information about new community. Mechanism to obtain news from home. Function: Facilitate integration to new community and retention of ties to home community.	Using the Internet to research for connections to place of origin in multiple forms. Function: rediscover-ing an eroding identity in diaspora.
E-Mail	Formal and informal contact with previously known or unknown persons. Function: Evaluate migration prospects and mobilize assistance. Establishing new ties	Primarily used to maintain home contact and to establish/retain contact with other migrants. Function: Retaining ties to home but helps build ties among migrants.	Communicating with people from home particularly to share life histories and genealogies. Function: Reconnect with family/ community ties.
BBS	Obtain information regarding contacts, employment, housing, or other basic needs. Function: Information gathering through formal postings.	Making announce-ments that reconnect people where migration broke ties. Function: Response to loss of real attachments by being proactive in trying to connect.	Locating friends and family from home and reviving aspects of home culture. Function: rediscovering, reattaching, and searching for new relationships.
Chat	Obtain advice from earlier migrants and discuss feelings and observations. Function: informal interaction in preparation for migration.	Maintaining contact and sustaining home ties. Function: Seeking substitutes for real presence.	Finding old friends and creating new friends based on shared background. Function: Seeking the warmth of personal observations and assessments of others.

Notes

CHAPTER ONE

1 Fischer used the county as the definition of a local move, so a long-distance move is merely from one county to another. This is not a measure of interstate moves. In contrast to most Canadian cities, many American cities, such as New York, Boston, and Chicago, border two or more states, which affects the meaning of interstate moves.

2 Muller and Espenshade (1985, 25) point out that migration has been so dominant in California's history that at no time has the majority of the state's population gain ever occurred as the result of natural increase.

3 From 1996 to 2004, Alberta's retail sales growth was the highest in Canada; retail sales per capita, disposable income per capita, and the proportion of disposable income spent in retail stores were also considerably higher than the national average. See "Provincial Retail Trade since the Turn of the Millennium, 1996–2004," Statistics Canada catalogue 11–621-mie2005032.

CHAPTER TWO

1 This image of the Prairies is perpetuated in a variety of ways, including through literature such as Wallace Stegner's popular *Wolf Willow*, which offers his account of growing up in the Cypress Hills area in the southwestern part of Saskatchewan.

2 The term "western interior" can be found in numerous places in the literature (e.g., Warkentin 1964, 3; Friesen 1984, 3–4) and is often used as a synonym for the Prairies. Friesen, for example, acknowledges that there are three distinct landscapes in the region, of which the prairies are only one; however, he still refers to the region as "the Prairies" and the three provinces as "the Prairie provinces." "Western interior" is a more accurate term because it is more geographically correct; it does not just focus on one of the region's physical

landscapes. Furthermore, it provides a context within which to understand the region, which has been transformed by urbanization and economic diversification and moved beyond the Prairie agricultural economy.

3 For an economic analysis of the differences between the Alberta economy and the British Columbia economy, see Chambers (2001).

4 For a good discussion of the region, its characteristics, and names used to describe it, see Kaye and Moodie (1973).

5 The one exception was migrants from the United States, who already had experience in dryland farming (Hansen 1940, 219–43).

6 Britnell (1939:6) estimated that, in 1939, about two-thirds of the settled areas in Saskatchewan were on the grass-covered plains.

7 Kaye and Moodie (1973) combined the two areas using the term "prairie-parkland," but their focus was on the Canadian plains rather than being an attempt to include all of the territory of the western interior, which, even at the time of their analysis, consisted of northern locations like Flin Flon, Thompson, Prince Albert, and Fort McMurray.

8 This is an adaptation of an argument made by Friesen (1999, 10–11). However, his point about the West shifting from two Wests to one West with four regions is not part of this argument. There is no attempt here to argue for any unitary notion of the West.

9 Note that the high birth rate in Alberta is not caused by the fact that women in that province have more children but, rather, by the fact that the comparatively large young adult population, including women of child-bearing age, means that the crude birth rate is higher than it is in other provinces.

10 For a good discussion on how agribusiness transforms rural life, see Edmondson (2003).

11 Melnyk (1999, 85–115) notes that the landscape has been allowed to define the Prairies only at the cost of ignoring the fact that cities have always been a part of the region. In fact, he argues that now the five major cities of the region act as prisms, organizing the region conceptually into five city-states.

12 The concept of the Calgary-Edmonton corridor as an "economic tiger" is an idea that emerged in the twenty-first century. For an interesting analysis of this concept, see "The Calgary-Edmonton Corridor," TD Economics Special Report, 22 April 2003.

13 The nature of these common interests is difficult to specify. Historically, they have been built on a reliance on resources for the strength of the economy, concern over transportation, and, perhaps most important, a sense of disempowerment in national affairs (Gibbins and Arrison 1995). A 2001 study provided survey data to support the fact that most western Canadians think of themselves as living in a region that is distinct from the rest of Canada (Berdahl 2001).

14 One of the intriguing issues in the last part of the twentieth century involved the strong Reform/Alliance/Conservative support in the West at the federal level as opposed to the strong NDP support at the provincial level (at least in British Columbia, Saskatchewan, and Manitoba). Both these federal and provincial stances in the West were sharply different from what was happening in the rest of the country (McCormick 2001, 402–3).

15 As Gibbins (1980, 202) puts it: "When regional concerns could be more readily identified a cabinet minister could speak for the region by addressing those concerns; to speak for wheat was to speak for the West. Now broad regional concerns and regional spokesmen are both harder to find." For a good discussion of Manitoba's changing role and how left-wing ideology affected that province, see Gonick (1990).

16 Wiseman (1996, 30), for example, refers to the fact that British Columbia's frontier economy was more corporate than agrarian because it was based on mining and lumbering and was sponsored by big corporations. This empowered workers and resulted in a unique brand of left-right struggle that is even more ingrained in British Columbia than it is in the other western provinces.

17 In spite of the fact that grassroots value differences between the provinces are not great, political elites have played a major role in articulating differences in provincial identities (Barrie 2006). Barrie argues that the free enterprise theme was first articulated in Alberta by Ernest Manning in 1944 but that the words and actions of Alberta's premiers have not always been consistent with free enterprise ideologies.

18 The defeat of the NDP by the Liberals in British Columbia in 2001 was perceived as an attempt to create a more business-friendly environment, similar to that in Alberta.

19 Emery and Kneebone (2005) argue that these differences may be more of degree than of real political ideology as economic policies between the western provinces usually became similar over time.

20 Alberta's previous experience with ideological differentiation occurred in the 1940s and 1950s in the Manning years, when the province's agenda was in sharp contrast to that of Saskatchewan, which focused on agrarian socialism.

21 Population numbers in brackets are from the 2001 census.

22 For a good discussion of the rise and fall of Winnipeg's role in the region, see Phillips (1981).

23 For a similar shift in the oil business from New York to Houston in the United States, see Feagin (1988, 84).

24 By 2002, Calgary not only had more corporate head offices than Vancouver but it also more head office employees (Statistics Canada, the Daily, 8 December 2003).

25 Calgary is also the Canadian headquarters for Greyhound Canada.

26 Calgary is also the Canadian corporate headquarters for the large grocery retailer Canada Safeway.

27 This was all the more intriguing because, at that time, Alberta also had the highest college and university tuition of any province in western Canada. See also University of Calgary Office of Institutional Analysis Project Report 2386, "Interprovincial Migration of University Students: An Alberta Perspective."

CHAPTER THREE

1 For many years, Statistics Canada used a residual method that explained the difference between births and deaths and total population as net migration. This obviously did not allow a distinction to be made between international migration and interprovincial migration. Place of birth was an important census question and did serve as a measure of the extent to which people moved, but it was only a vague indicator of migration flows because it did not distinguish between someone who had arrived one year ago and someone who had arrived fifty years ago. In 1961, Statistics Canada began to ask each respondent where he or she had lived five years ago, and this became an indicator of mobility. In 1991, a second question was added, and it asked where a person had lived one year ago. A much more sensitive indicator is reported in the Annual Demographic Statistics, which are based on income tax files. This data source is only available from 1972 and, because of its greater accuracy and sensitivity, is the major statistical data source for this study.

2 The position taken here is that in-migration data are a more robust indicator of the impact of demographic change than are net migration data, which underplay the volume of new arrivals and their impact on the receiving society. Goldstein (1976) questions the concept of the "net migrant," which he labels both mysterious and misleading. On the other hand, net migration does provide a summary statement of the balanced net effect of in-migration and out-migration.

3 Newbold's (2007) research on immigrants who had arrived in Canada in 2000–01 found little evidence of interprovincial mobility during their first six months in the country. While this time period after immigration is not long, it does confirm that whatever mobility was likely to take place focused on the three major cities in Canada so that immigrants could reside near co-nationals. These immigrants showed little predisposition to move to Alberta.

4 The Public Use Microdata File from the 2001 Census (Statistics Canada catalogue #95M0016XCB, Individuals File) provides useful data based on a 2.7 percent sample for variables for which the full census does not gather information. This data source provides additional information about educational attainment, income, employment, and other variables pertaining to interprovincial migrants who moved in the five-year period prior to the 2001 census.

5 Statistics Canada (1982, 1983) analyzed the characteristics of migrants to Alberta based on the 1980 Labour Force Survey. Its studies concluded that about one-quarter of the working-age population were migrants, the majority of whom were between 20 and 44 years of age, predominantly Canadian-born, and somewhat better educated than non-migrants.

6 It is unclear as to why this is the case. It is possible that, since the resource boom was attributed to oil and gas, which has experienced huge fluctuations in market price, moving to Alberta was considered to be more temporary and risky and, therefore, less appealing to women or families. Coming to Alberta might be considered a short-term opportunity to make big sums of money. Another explanation might be that there was an employment cluster in the oil and gas industry, which supported labour such as rig work, seismic work, or pipeline work – forms of work that do not normally engage women. However, this is not totally convincing as the heaviest migration was to the biggest cities, suggesting that the draw was urban-based employment, which is not as male dominant as is employment in the oilfields.

7 While the majority of in-migrants went to the province's largest cities, it is important to know that in-migration also touched other Alberta communities, such as Whitecourt, High Level, Sylvan Lake, and Olds. The absolute numbers may not be large, but in-migration clearly also affected small communities. In fact, this may be a neglected aspect of this study because, in both 1981 and 2001, 17 percent to 19 percent of the total number of in-migrants went to these smaller communities. A large number of in-migrants in the mountain park communities of Banff/Canmore and Jasper were temporary, seasonal, and adventure-based, and these were purposely excluded from this study.

8 Table 13 is not a perfect measure of this change, but it does provide some sense of how movement in and out is relative to the overall size of the population. The one cell for which there is no ready explanation is the one that shows the positive size of the index for Saskatoon in 1981. Clearly, cities with smaller populations that experience high movements in and out will have a higher index, and in this case it is positive, though with only small net growth. What did occur was a high level of movement both in and out.

CHAPTER FOUR

1 There is no attempt here to argue that the influence of the major centres had waned or that American companies were less important in Canada than they had been. Much research in the industry was still carried on elsewhere, and much decision making was still based in Houston. But the industry in Canada had become much more complex, and Canadian expertise played an increasingly important role.

2 An interesting comparison is with Silicon Valley, where Saxenian (1994) explains the dynamism and growth of that area in relation to the existence of dense social networks and a flexible open labour market that promotes experimentation and entrepreneurship in high technology rather than depending on vertically integrated corporations. The agglomerations of skill, venture capital, and supplies is rooted in a horizontal network of specialists in the region.
3 The Small Explorers and Producers Association of Canada is based in Calgary and has over 450 members.
4 The Petroleum Industry Training Service (PITS) is located at Nisku and provides training for blue-collar workers seeking employment on oil rigs. It offers a variety of courses, from petroleum engineering and field production to environmental issues such as spill response. While it is not the only such training facility in Canada, attending it is one of the most direct ways of entering the fieldwork part of the industry, which often appealed to young males. It also trains people from other parts of the world for work in their own countries.
5 For an interesting comparison, see Joe Feagin's (1985) discussion of how the global context changed Houston's role in the oil industry.
6 City population figures here were provided by Alberta Municipal Affairs based on 2006 data.
7 It is difficult to be precise about the populations of many growing communities in Alberta because of the shortage of housing, which meant that many dwellings were occupied by more people than was allowed under zoning regulations. This, in turn, meant that efforts were often made to hide the true number of people residing in a dwelling, rendering census counts inaccurate (nowhere was this more problematic than in Fort McMurray). So federal census counts were often considered to have major undercounting problems. To this we must also added problems associated with general workforce transiency as well as with how to account for work camp inhabitants who were contract workers.
8 This observation may vary with location of residence. For example, it is almost impossible to be unaware of oil sands activity in Fort McMurray. In cities like Edmonton or Calgary, the oil and gas industry is not part of the daily life of most residents.
9 Saskatchewan and Manitoba have also had low unemployment rates.
10 Chun argues that, because migration increases employment, governments that want their region to grow should induce migration if it does not occur.

CHAPTER FIVE

1 One of the best illustrations of this tendency to focus on the economic is Stone's classic (1969, 131–2) study of internal migration in Canada. Stone

fully acknowledged that not all migration was economically motivated and that migration involved a complicated set of influences; however, having said that, he then proceeded to focus only on economic factors.

2 For an anthropological approach that takes a similar perspective, see Brettell (2003) and Gmelch (1992). Their emphasis on understanding migration from the inside relies upon the use of life histories, oral narratives, and/or migration stories.

3 An older account that contains similar elements can be found in Ritchey (1976).

4 "Meaningful labour" is defined here as: a better job than the one held before, work in one's field, a new job that opens up other options, work with more status, work in an important industry, or work particularly valued by an employee. In the interviews, most migrants discussed their relocation in these terms rather than purely in terms of wages.

5 This phenomenon is viewed from a political economy perspective in the discussion of core-periphery relations (see below).

6 A good example of this phenomenon is the Canadian Employee Relocation Council, which exists to support and manage workforce mobility among employers.

7 Flowerdew (1992, 135–6) argues that, in the United Kingdom, most econometric studies assume that labour migration is speculative, whereas, typically, most contemporary long-distance migration is likely to be contracted. One study that uses data from a labour force survey found that about half of interregional moves involved no change of employer at all (Gordon 1992, 121). It can be assumed that this pattern occurred in normal conditions as opposed to conditions of an expanding economy.

8 Compare Tepperman (1985, 53), who estimated that, in the 1970s, only about 12 percent of male migrants to Alberta were job transfers. Further support also comes from the study by Currie and Halli (1989), who found that migration to Edmonton during the first wave (1980–81) was more likely to be driven by job opportunities (i.e., consisted of independent migrants), whereas migration to Winnipeg, a slow-growth city, was more likely to be driven by job transfers.

9 U-Haul, for example, had very low rates for persons wanting to take equipment out of Alberta as the company needed to get rid of the surplus of equipment from one-way rentals to Alberta.

10 Some migrants had contacted employers in Alberta who promised them work before they left their community of origin. However, if this was just a loose or verbal arrangement and no expenses were paid to relocate, these persons were allowed to be part of the study.

CHAPTER SIX

1 Compare Stinner (1992), who also refers to social location as structuring migration intentions.

2 This approach is particularly relevant to studies of internal migration, although it may also have relevance to international migration. It is an alternative to two-worlds theories of migration (which imply huge gulfs between sending and receiving societies) and to tabula rasa myths (which imply that migrants enter their destination wanting to be assimilated) (Jackson 1969, 2). The linkage between origin and destination is continuous and ongoing. See also Moon (1995, 520) who interprets migration as a subjective response and as a perception of social structure.

3 Morrison and Wheeler (1978, 82) speak of the "allure of elsewhere" and its "idealized possibilities." According to them, novelty may be as alluring as economic opportunity."

4 For a review of the critiques of asking people why they move, see DeJong (1999).

5 Reflexive progression is the complex, discursive activity whereby the respondent, at the encouragement of the interviewer, refines thoughts and observations as the interview unfolds. This process is thought to be necessary because initial observations are invariably guarded or superficial, and probing allows the interviewee to be more reflective and to engage in self-discovery, thereby producing more accurate responses. This approach is developed more fully in Hiller and DiLuzio (2004).

6 This is somewhat different from McHugh's (1984) argument that a subjective norm must be present, with the potential migrant's being influenced by what significant others think about relocation.

7 For a similar point, see Brettell (2003, 27).

8 Cadwallader (1992, 13) refers to this process of information organization and evaluation as the construction of a cognitive map.

9 Compare Richmond (in Van Hear 1998, 43) who distinguishes between the reactive migrant whose relocation is dictated only by events, with minimal choice and planning, and the proactive migrant, whose decision to relocate is based on rational calculation and planning.

10 Cadwallader (1992, 41) discusses the concept of cognitive distance, but we apply it in a somewhat different way.

11 See, for example, the 12 February 2001 edition of *Maclean's* magazine, with the headlines "Alberta Bound: A Booming Economy Is Drawing Workers from across Canada."

12 Goyder (1995) found that internal migration was socially disruptive, with the result that migrants were less likely to be satisfied with their life than were native-born non-migrants.

13 It is interesting that Oded Stark (2006), an economist, also understands migration as being related to dissatisfaction in a social community. However, for Stark, the discontent emerges from having an income lower than others, which leads to feelings of relative deprivation. Stark is right in placing the migrant within a community context; however, as an economist, he limits discontent to monetary factors and does not see the broader social processes that are at work.

CHAPTER SEVEN

1 Porteous and Smith (2001, 6) note that it is common to accept the idea that we are attached to people but that it is much less common to accepted the idea that we can be attached to a place on its own.
2 Shils (1978, 405) argues that place attachment is primarily articulated in response to actual departure or threatened displacement rather than to migration itself. While migration might intensify place attachment at one level, it is also likely that such sentiments existed prior to migration and, conversely, that (paradoxically) migration contributes to the lessening of place attachment.
3 It was difficult to determine the role that these climatological factors played in personal health and their relationship to the assessment of migration. What was clear, however, is that any improvement in health at the destination was credited to the relocation.
4 The link between mood and sunlight is clearly established as seasonal affective disorder. However, it is unclear why migrants from British Columbia frequently brought up this issue while migrants from the Atlantic provinces (especially Newfoundland), where rain, fog, and coolness are also omnipresent, did not.
5 The point is that, in comparison to the rest of the western interior, southern Alberta was considered to have milder winters. On the other hand, all of the western interior has more severe winters than does most of the rest of southern Canada, but this was hardly ever mentioned by in-migrants. Perhaps a study of out-migrants would have uncovered this point.
6 Lefebvre (1995, 120) refers to space that is a material reflection of the social relations of production as a "concrete abstraction."
7 This was less true in the post–2005 period, when economic growth turned into a boom with its attendant housing shortages and higher costs.
8 Not everyone feels an attachment to place that produces what Hummon (1992, 271) calls "uncommitted placelessness." For example, there is a small core of construction workers comprised of men who demonstrate only a fleeting interest in place and who go by themselves to wherever their work takes them. Clearly, those people for whom one place can easily be substituted with another have a low degree of place attachment (Milligan 1998, 7).

9 It is important to note that, not only does attachment to place have many different dimensions but there are also many different ways in which people can feel this attachment. As well, different people express their attachment in different ways (Fischer 1977, 156).
10 The problem of place attachment is that any discontinuity in rootedness to place always involves the experience of loss (Milligan 1998, 28)
11 It is possible to overplay these positive emotions on returning home. While most migrants did identify at least some positive associations with a return visit, they also often had negative experiences. For example: "I was disillusioned because buildings or things that I remembered so positively were not nearly as impressive to me now. The house looked smaller and the neighborhood seemed old." Others reported negative emotions upon encountering people or situations that they were glad to have left. For others, discovering that their friends were no longer there or were busy with their own lives reinforced the fact that they were now outsiders.
12 A restaurant in Edmonton that catered to Newfoundlanders was, indeed, called "Back Home."
13 As Castells (2004) puts it, the roles that people play organize function, but identity is much more important because it is a source of meaning. So the roles that migrants play at a destination may be important, but the identity that they build is a critical source of meaning. Who am I in relation to where I am from and where I am now?
14 Conrad and Hiller (2001, 3) argue that there is some support for the fact that Atlantic residents have a low sense of efficacy because they accept that it is "their lot to struggle rather than to arrive" but that they combine this viewpoint with "regional pride and relentless optimism."
15 Compare Marger and Obermiller (1987), who studied Maritimers in Toronto and concluded that an emergent ethnicity was much more difficult to develop when a sense of distinctiveness was weak.
16 The one exception we discovered in the Province of Ontario involved people who came from Sudbury, which, ironically, is also a declining community. The other location in which people displayed this sentiment was Prince George, British Columbia, which was struggling at the time with the decline of the lumber industry. However, there was much optimism that things in Prince George would improve in the future. Perhaps it is the sense of having left others behind in a struggling community that generates strong expressions of loyalty and an emotional reaction similar to the guilt one might feel upon abandoning a sinking ship. While this is putting it too strongly, it is true that expressions of loyalty serve to counter flagging spirits.
17 It is interesting that Schutz's early analysis of the homecomer remains relevant to any examination of this phenomenon.

18 For a good discussion of the problems of returning home to Newfoundland, see Sinclair (2003).

19 Bad experiences at the destination, on the other hand, served to make the return home much easier.

20 The myth of return is discussed in more detail in chapter 13.

21 This line of thinking parallels recent discussions about transnational identities among immigrants that look at how migrants go back and forth between place of origin and destination and maintain multiple loyalties.

22 Milligan (1998, 2) distinguishes between meaning given to a place because of memories in the interactional past and expectations based on the interactional potential of the new place.

23 Zerubavel (1996, 286) refers to these thought communities, where we learn to interpret our experiences as mnemonic communities.

CHAPTER EIGHT

1 The exile is subject to, and defined by, a unique combination of enforced and self-imposed migration.

2 I acknowledge that these concepts have been adapted for use in this study and that the discussion has benefited greatly from the work of Skeldon (1994).

3 Burrill (1992, 202) provides a quotation that serves as an interesting illustration of how some Maritime migrants felt that their situation was comparable to that of international refugees, whose departure was also involuntary: "We're economic refugees. If you come here from Laos or Indo-China ... they give you all kinds of benefits. They help you get organized. What the hell do they do for the Maritimers that come here?"

4 It must be recognized that the relationship between health issues and climate is a very individual matter. Whereas moving to Alberta seemed to be a solution for some people, move away from Alberta seemed to be a solution for others.

5 Two major research projects were undertaken on this issue. On the Atlantic coast, the project was called Coasts Under Stress but there is analysis from both coasts in Sinclair and Ommer (2006) and Ommer (2007). On the Pacific coast, another research project was still in process at the time of writing and was called the Resilient Communities Project.

6 Ledent (1990, 60) describes Ontario as the "hinge" of the nation's population exchanges because, although people left it to go east and west, there was little cross-fertilization throughout Ontario from east and west.

7 Courchene (1998) describes Ontario's changing position during this period as less dependent on the Canadian economy as it was becoming a regional state within the North American market.

8 It needs to be noted that Saskatchewan also has additional oil and gas potential, as represented by the discovery of the Bakken deposit, which has spurred the development of new technologies to extract oil from shale.

9 Emery and Kneebone (2005, 18) point out that there is little evidence that Saskatchewan's socialist policies undermined the economy's productive capacity, but it has resulted in a higher dependency ratio.

10 See Deer (2006) for a discussion of how the media can create a sense of moral panic by discussing issues in a particular way.

11 Dupuy, Mayer, and Morissette (2000, 8) have pointed out that migration from rural communities in western Canada occurs with much greater regularity than it does in Atlantic Canada, in spite of the fact that labour conditions in rural areas are not better in the Atlantic region.

CHAPTER NINE

1 For an interesting discussion of the frontier nature of oil booms as it relates to Texas towns, see Olien and Olien (1982). One of the differences between oil booms and other mineral booms is that the former are much more labour intensive in the exploration phase, whereas the latter are more labour intensive in the production stage. Classically, frontier-like conditions were more associated with exploration than with production.

2 This discussion benefited greatly from the work of Murray Melbin (1987).

3 Compare the work of S.D. Clark, who explored the sociology of development on early Canadian frontiers (Hiller 1982, 65–6). Clark argued that a frontier was not necessarily associated with a period of early settlement or the furthest line of settlement but, rather, with places where economic growth was dynamic and had sociological consequences.

4 In 1980, a conference was held at the University of Alberta entitled "Power Shift West: Myth or Reality?" that symbolized this sense of structural change and evaluated it. See *Canadian Journal of Sociology* 6 (1981):165–83.

5 One Prince Edward Islander claimed that his banker observed that every year he approved at least one hundred loans for travel to Alberta, sometimes just for seasonal work, which would be paid back from the earnings accrued in that province.

6 So-called homeless people were interviewed and included in the sample. In every case, these were people who were attracted to the province by the reputation it had developed as the place where things were happening. Some of these people were fleeing situations at their place of origin and had personal problems; others just had difficulty finding adequate employment.

7 For a discussion on the debate about what kind of mobility occurred among migrants to Alberta during the first wave, and based on an analysis of the

1980 Labour Force Survey, see Tepperman (1985). My use of the term "mobility" refers to both a general improvement in life conditions and a change in social position (which was particularly the case among those coming to Alberta in entry level professional jobs). The first sense of mobility was probably the most common.

8 As noted earlier, an expanding economy is to be distinguished from a boom economy, where employment may be plentiful but where other conditions of life (such as housing) are more problematic. The field research upon which this study was based took place during economic expansion rather than during boom conditions.

9 The important point is not that these are conclusive assessments of these communities of origin but, rather, that they represent how migrants recalled them.

10 Tepperman (1985) has argued that migration produces little occupational mobility and "leads to changes or improvements that are more imaginary than real." It may be true that, for some, migration brought few status gains, but the significant increase in income had definite rewards. An expanding economy also offers niche jobs at high levels of pay.

11 Whether these expectations were well founded, of course, was another issue. Alberta's infrastructure and government services were not keeping up with the population growth. It was also clear that, in matters such as health care, there were provincial variations in the provision of specialized services. The Alberta health care program, for example, had a more generous treatment program for children with autism than did other provinces, and some migrants took advantage of this difference.

12 As an example of this kind of debate, it was pointed out that, although Alberta may not have had a retail sales tax, it charged for health care premiums, and this washed out the difference. Respondents often debated at great length as to whether the cost of living (including taxation) was higher or lower in Alberta in comparison to their region of origin.

13 Bennett (1973, 193) concludes that a form of behavioural selection did occur in the settlement years up to the 1960s. He argues that people who came and people who stayed were more likely to be agriculturalists who were "consumption-deferring, patient, cautious, conservative operators."

CHAPTER TEN

1 Some estimates suggest that as many as seventy languages were represented in the meat-packing plant, and this, of course had an impact on the community of Brooks. The other large beef-packing plant in Alberta (Cargill) was located in High River, a community very close to Calgary, which minimized the

impact on the host community because labour, especially immigrant labour, had easy access from the city.

2 A resident from Conception Bay South in Newfoundland reported keeping track of how many people from her community lived in Mill Woods in Edmonton; in 2002, there were 136 people from Conception Bay living in Mill Woods. This kind of record keeping was typical of migrants from communities all over Newfoundland.

3 The concepts of "home territory" and "colonization" are adapted from Lofland (1973).

4 Compare Burrill (1992, 41), who discusses big Saturday-night dances in Boston that brought migrant Maritimers together with bands such as the "Inverness Serenaders" from Cape Breton.

5 The Saskatchewan Social Club was organized in the early 1990s to facilitate camaraderie among people from Saskatchewan. Membership required either having lived or having worked in Saskatchewan, but affiliate members (who lacked that background) were also welcome. The club had about 150 members early in the millennium, though membership varied from year to year. It also published an occasional newsletter called the *Sasquatch*.

6 Burrill (1992, 92–8) refers to churches in Boston that catered to migrant Maritimers: First Presbyterian attracted many Prince Edward Islanders, United Presbyterian in Newton attracted many Cape Bretoners, and Tremont Temple was even referred to as "the Canadian church."

7 A Newfoundland club had been established in Cambridge, Ontario, when Ontario was the primary destination for Newfoundlanders. They reported crowds of up to 10,000 from all over southern Ontario for Canada Day parties. However, interest declined over time as the younger generation was born in Ontario and the desire to maintain contact with Newfoundland waned.

8 An earlier study of Maritime migrants to Toronto concluded that, while there was a sense of common identity among these migrants, there was a weak sense of consciousness as a distinct group supported by institutional structures (Marger and Obermiller 1987). This is similar to my findings.

CHAPTER ELEVEN

1 This chapter is an adaptation of Hiller and McCaig (2007).

2 For the purposes of this analysis, "partnered women" are defined as married and unmarried women attached to men.

3 See the appendix for a discussion of the three phases involved in the research design.

CHAPTER TWELVE

1 This chapter is an adaptation of Hiller and Franz (2004).

2 We were able to discover two online guest books that were explicitly directed to people from Cape Breton Island in Nova Scotia. One of them was maintained by the *Cape Bretoner* magazine. These guest books operated like a bulletin board chat but without the same organization and detail as was found on the Newfoundland sites. While the sense of loyalty and group identity in Cape Breton approaches that found in Newfoundland, we were unable to discover a similar community in cyberspace. We were also unable to find a similar cyber presence for Quebec expatriates to Alberta, although one website was identified as being for people wanting to leave Quebec (www.quitterlequebec.com). An electronic newsletter distributed by the Calgary chapter of the French-Canadian Association of Alberta was used to announce events for French speakers, but it did not include opportunities to interact online. It also sought to promote ties between French speakers whatever their origins rather than to link only those from Quebec.

3 It is interesting that the Household Internet Use Survey 2001, reported by Statistics Canada in the *Daily*, 25 July 2002, indicated that Alberta (along with British Columbia) had the highest (65 percent) regular internet use of all households in Canada and that Newfoundland had the lowest (50 percent).

CHAPTER THIRTEEN

1 Not only is New Brunswick not an island but it also lacks a sense of being a homogeneous distinct community. One of its unique features is that it is divided into two constituencies: francophones in the north and anglophones in the south.

2 Newfoundland's unemployment rates have been the highest in Canada. Cape Breton, due to the collapse of its industries, has had a much higher unemployment rate than has the rest of Nova Scotia. Unemployment has been less of an issue in Prince Edward Island, but concern about out-migration can be seen in a report by the Institute of Island Studies entitled *A Place to Stay? The Report of the Prince Edward Island Population Strategy '99, Population Strategy Panel* (Charlottetown: Institute of Island Studies, 2000).

3 One interesting example of this phenomenon is the publication of the *Dictionary of Newfoundland English* in 1982.

4 The two publications of particular relevance to this theme are *The Lost Salt Gift of Blood* (1976) and *No Great Mischief* (1999).

5 Berry (2000) has shown how migration from the American South to the North was reflected in music, particularly bluegrass and gospel. The migration experience produced a wide range of songs that dealt with the loneliness of separation from home (e.g., "Daddy and Home" by Jimmie Rodgers, "Detroit City" by Mel Tillis), the guilt of leaving, and a desire to return (e.g., "Carry Me Back to the Mountains," "That Silver-haired Daddy of Mine," and "Homecoming").

6 "Four Strong Winds" was voted the number one all-time Canadian song in a CBC Radio One audience poll in 2005. Later, this song was also sung by other artists as well.

7 I am grateful to Kenzie MacNeil for drawing my attention to these forms of popular culture emerging from Cape Breton and for providing me with copies of the music.

CHAPTER FOURTEEN

1 It is possible that migrants may choose to move elsewhere rather than to go back to the region of origin; however, in our fieldwork, we were unable to discover such persons. We also encountered little field evidence of serial migration. Most of the migration observed was directly from the region of origin to the Alberta destination and from the destination directly back to the region of origin. This may be a different pattern than that which occurred during the first wave because, as Tepperman (1983) found, people born east of Quebec were more likely to stop-over in another province on their way west. This meant that their move involved a two-step migration, whereas people from Ontario west were more likely to have only a one-step migration. Most of the migration in the second wave was one-step, including that from the East Coast.

2 Currie and Halli (1989, 43) note that migration to slow-growth areas is more likely to result in return migrants.

3 Using in-migration and out-migration data between two provinces offers only a crude measure of return migration because there is no guarantee that the reverse flow are all returnees. However, if there is an atypical upswing in reverse flow migration between two provinces, an argument can be made that it is likely that many of the migrants are returnees.

4 Dupuy, Mayer, and Morissette (2000) found that, at most, one in four leavers returned to their community of origin if they came from a rural community.

5 Loss of employment or a downturn in economic conditions was a significant catalyst for return. But even in this case reference group theory is applicable. Chapter 3 shows how out-migration from Alberta increased after the first wave in 1982 as the economy in that province went into a tailspin. In our

interviews there were hints that, in spite of job loss, people whose primary reference group was in Alberta were more likely to remain in the province than were those whose primary reference group was elsewhere. Kennedy and Mehra (1985) argue that migrants are more likely to stay when they have strong social networks at the destination to help them deal with economic instability.

6 Returning did not necessarily mean going back to a home town but relocating to a large city in the home region. Upon leaving Alberta, many migrants from the Atlantic region relocated to Halifax, which is the region's biggest city.

7 One report was received from a mother in Atlantic Canada, who said that her son had committed suicide because he was lonely and could not adapt but that he had not wanted to come home and live from pay cheque to pay cheque.

8 A good example of this was the Retirement Cape Breton program, which encouraged people to retire in Cape Breton. Their brochure highlighted the lifestyle of smaller communities in contrast to the lifestyle of big cities: "To escape your hectic lifestyle ... To be greeted on the streets by perfect strangers ... To enjoy a high quality of life ... that is unrivalled."

CHAPTER FIFTEEN

1 The response may have been higher if the question had been worded differently. As worded, causation in migration may have been attributed too strongly to knowing people already in Alberta, when other factors may have been more prominent in the respondent's mind.

2 Note that the statement did not attempt to measure the degree of importance of ties with people from back home at the destination at different points in time. For example, it is possible that such ties were important during the first month or two after arrival but that, after two or three years, they were not. The statement only refers to the current status of such friendships.

3 In order to increase the number of cases in a category, two categories were created: Atlantic (participants from all four Atlantic provinces) and non-Atlantic (participants from all the other provinces).

CHAPTER SIXTEEN

1 There is some emphasis in the literature on how migration has disruptive effects on both the migrant and the host community. Goyder (1995), for example, argues that internal migration in Canada results in lower life satisfaction in places where migration is high. The notion of social disruptions in energy boom-towns is also a controversial topic of a thematic issue of the

Pacific Sociological Review 25 (3): 1982. The thesis developed here does not examine incidences of social breakdown (e.g., crime, spousal abuse, etc.) but, rather, the coping strategies of migrants. In other words, the emphasis is more on the migrant as an active agent in the migration process rather than as a victim of the process.

2 The question of control was intensely debated in the post–2005 period, when the pace of investment reached feverish levels (particularly in the oil sands), leading to calls for more controlled growth supervised by the Alberta government (as opposed to letting the market determine the pace of growth).

3 This was particularly true in the time period of this study but has been less true in succeeding years, with neighbouring provinces all shifting more to the right.

4 This distinction was made partially to accommodate the time period under investigation, but it was also made to point out that recruitment under boom conditions meant that the competition for scarce resources could result in the outcomes of migration having problematic aspects.

5 It is important to re-emphasize that not all migration to Alberta had positive outcomes, and this point will be made again later in the chapter. What is argued is that an expanding economy enhanced the likelihood that an outcome could be positive. An expanding economy also attracted those who were unable to succeed in such an economy.

6 It is interesting that most interpretations of this sense of difference are linked to migration – but of a different kind. In this case, it is immigration from the United States into Alberta in the early settlement period that brought progressivism and populism into the province, which then clashed with traditional conservatism in Canada. This is often understood as the origin of Alberta's unique political culture.

7 Compare Fielding (1992, 209) who referred to the southeast of England as the "escalator region" of that country because it attracted young adults who were upwardly mobile, which then attracted investment from companies looking for that kind of person. Accelerated promotions meant high levels of income at an early age, which, in the long term, often led either to burnout or to a rejection of the lifestyle in the long-term.

8 I am indebted to the work of William Michelson (1977) and his theory of environmental choice for this interpretation.

9 To that phrase might also be added, "Where you stay is who you are."

10 This is not a study of the province's growing inequality; however, it is important to note that many migrants came to Alberta with high hopes (and sometimes unrealistic hopes) that were shattered by their experiences of poverty and homelessness. It is important to note that viewing a migration as successful is open to considerable interpretation – even from an economic perspective.

References

Abdo, N. 1997. "Gender Is Not a 'Dummy': Research Methods in Immigration and Refugee Studies." In Status of Women Canada, *Gendering Immigration/Integration: Policy Research Proceedings and a Selective Review of Policy Research Literature 1987–1996*, 41–50. Ottawa: Status of Women Canada.

Aguilar-San Juan, Karin. 2005. "Staying Vietnamese: Community and Place in Orange County and Boston." *City and Community* 4: 37–65.

Akerman, Sune. 1978. "Towards an Understanding of Emigrational Process." In *Human Migration: Patterns and Policies*, ed. William H. McNeill and Ruth S. Adams, 287–306. Bloomington: Indiana University Press.

Alberta Agriculture. 1997. *Agriculture in Alberta*. Edmonton: Alberta Agriculture.

Alberta, Government of. 1961. *Graphs of Growth*. Edmonton: Bureau of Statistics.

Allen, Richard, ed. 1973. *A Region of the Mind: Interpreting the Western Canadian Plains*. Regina: Canadian Plains Studies Centre.

Altman, Irwin, and Setha M. Low, eds. 1992. *Place Attachment*. New York: Plenum.

Ammons, P., J. Nelson, and J. Wodarski. 1982. "Surviving Corporate Moves: Sources of Stress and Adaption among Corporate Executive Families." *Family Relations* 31: 207–12.

Anisef, Paul, and Michael Lanphier, eds. 2003. *The World in a City*. Toronto: University of Toronto Press.

Archer, Keith, and Roger Gibbins. 1997. "What Do Albertan's Think? The Klein Agenda on the Public Opinion Landscape." In *A Government Reinvented: A Study of Alberta's Deficit Elimination Program*, ed. Christopher Bruce, Ronald Kneebone and Kenneth McKenzie, 462–85. Toronto: Oxford University Press.

Armstrong, Christopher J. 2004. "Migrant Imaginings and the Atlantic Canadian Regionalisms." In *Canadian Migration Patterns: From Britain and North America*, ed. Barbara J. Messamore, 245–62. Ottawa: University of Ottawa Press.

Bailey A.J, and T.J. Cooke. 1998. "Family Migration and Employment: The Importance of Migration History and Gender." *International Science Review* 21: 99–118.

Baldry, Chris. 1999. "Space the Final Frontier." *Sociology* 33 (3): 535–53.

Bhargava, Gura. 2000. "A City Divided by Political Philosophies: Residential Development in a Bi-provincial City." *American Journal of Economics and Sociology* 60 (1): 317–73.

Bantjes, Rod. 2005. *Improved Earth: Prairies Space as Modern Artefact, 1896–1944*. Toronto: University of Toronto Press.

Barr, Brenton M. 1972. "Reorganization of the Economy since 1945." In *The Prairie Provinces*, ed. P.J. Smith, 65–82. Toronto: University of Toronto Press.

Barrie, Doreen. 2006. *The Other Alberta: Decoding a Political Enigma*. Saskatchewan: Canadian Plains Research Center.

Bartman, Barry. 2000. "Patterns of Localism in a Changing Global System." In *Lessons from the Political Economy of Small Islands*, ed. Godfrey Baldacchino and David Milne, 38–55. Charlottetown: Institute of Island Studies.

Bartram, David. 2005. *International Labor Migration: Foreign Workers and Public Policy*. New York: Palgrave Macmillan

Basran, G.S., and David Hay, eds. 1988. *The Political Economy of Agriculture in Western Canada*. Toronto: Garamond.

Beaman, Jay, and Carol D'Arcy. 1980. "A Typology of Internal Migration." *Canadian Studies in Population* 7: 9–20.

Beaujot, Roderic, and Don Kerr. 2004. *Population Change in Canada*, 2nd ed. Oxford: Don Mills.

Beaujot, Roderic, and Kevin McQuillan. 1982. *Growth and Dualism: The Demographic Development of Canadian Society*. Toronto: Gage.

Belk, Russell W. 1992. "Attachment to Possessions." In *Place Attachment*, ed. Irwin Altman and Setha M. Low, 37–62. New York: Plenum.

Bennett, John W. 1973. "Adaptive Strategy and Processes in the Canadian Plains." In *A Region of the Mind: Interpreting the Western Canadian Plains*, ed. Richard Allen, 181–99. Regina: Canadian Plains Studies Centre.

Berdahl, Loleen. 2001. *Looking West: A Survey of Western Canadians*. Calgary: Canada WEST Foundation.

– 2006. *Political Identities in Western Canada*. Calgary: Canada West Foundation.

Berry, Chad. 2000. *Southern Migrants, Northern Exiles*. Chicago: University of Illinois Press.

Berton, Pierre. 1984. *The Promised Land: Settling in the West 1896–1914*. Toronto: McClelland Stewart.

Bielby, W.T., and D.D, Bielby. 1992. "I Will Follow Him: Family Ties, Gender-role Beliefs, and Reluctance to Relocate for a Better Job." *American Journal of Sociology* 97 (5): 1241–1267.

Bolaria, B. Singh, Harley D. Dickinson and Terry Wotherspoon. 1995. "Rural Issues and Problems." In *Social issues and Contradictions in Canadian Society*, 2nd ed., ed. B. Singh Bolaria, 419–43. Toronto: Harcourt Brace and Company.

Bonney, N., and J. Love. 1991. "Gender and Migration: Geographical Mobility and the Wife's Sacrifice." *Sociological Review* 39: 335–48.

Bott, Robert D. *Our Petroleum Challenge: Sustainability into the 21st Century*. Calgary: Canadian Centre for Energy Information.

Boyd, M. 1989. "Family and Personal Networks in International Migration: Recent Developments and New Agendas." *International Migration Review* 23 (3): 638–70.Boyle, P., T.J. Cooke, K. Halfacree, and D. Smith. 2001. "A Cross-national Comparison of the Impact of Family Migration on Women's Employment Status." *Demography* 38: 201–13.

Breen, David H. .1993. *Alberta's Petroleum Industry and the Conservation Board*. Edmonton: University of Alberta Press.

Brett, J.M. 1982. "Job Transfer and Well-being." *Journal of Applied Psychology* 67 (4): 450–63.

Brett, J.M., and A.H. Reilly. 1988. "On the Road Again: Predicting the Job Transfer Decision." *Journal of Applied Psychology* 73 (4): 614–20.

Brett, J.M., L.K. Stroh, and A.H. Reilly. 1993. "Pulling up Roots in the 1990s: Who's Willing to Relocate?" *Journal of Organizational Behavior* 14 (1): 49–60.

Brettell, Caroline. 2003. *Anthropology and Migration: Essays on Transnationalism, Ethnicity, and Identity*. Walnut Creek, CA: AltaMira Press.

Brettell, C.B., and R.J. Simon. 1986. "Immigrant Women: An Introduction." In *International Migration: The Female Experience*, ed. R.J. Simon and C.B. Brettell, 3–19. New Jersey, NY: Rowman and Allanheld.

Brink, Stephen. 1995. "Home: The Term and the Concept." In *The Home: Words, Interpretations, Meanings, and Environments*, ed. David N. Benjamin, 17–24. Aldershot: Avebury.

Britnell, G.E. 1939. *The Wheat Economy*. Toronto: University of Toronto Press.

Brookes, Alan J. 1976. "Out-migration from the Maritime Provinces, 1860–1900." *Acadiensis* 5 (2): 26–55.

Bromberg, H. 1996 "Are MUDs Communities? Identity, Belonging, and Consciousness in Virtual Worlds." In *Cultures of Internet: Virtual Spaces, Real Histories, Living Bodies*, ed. R. Shields, 143–52. London: Sage.

Brown, Barbara. 1992. "Disruptions in Place Attachment." In *Place Attachment*, ed. Irwin Altman and Setha M. Low, 279–304. New York: Plenum.

Brubaker, Roger 2004. *Ethnicity without Change.* Cambridge: Harvard University Press.

Bruce, Harry. 1988. *Down Home: Notes of a Maritime Son.* Toronto: University of Toronto Press.

Brym, Robert J. 1978. "Regional Social Structure and Agrarian Radicalism in Canada: Alberta, Saskatchewan, and New Brunswick." *Canadian Review of Sociology and Anthropology* 15: 352–72.

Burke, Mary Anne. 1987. "Migration between Atlantic Canada and Ontario, 1951–1985." In *Canadian Social Trends*, Statistics Canada Catalogue 11–008E.

Burnet, Jean. 1951. *Next Year Country: A Study of Rural Social Organization in Alberta.* Toronto: University of Toronto Press.

Burrill, G. 1992. *Away: Maritimers in Massachusetts, Ontario and Alberta.* Montreal: McGill-Queen's University Press.

Cadwallader, Martin. 1992. *Migration and Residential Mobility: Macro and Micro Approaches.* Median: University of Wisconsin Press.

Caldwell, Gary, and Daniel Fournier. 1987. "The Quebec Question: A Matter of Population." *Canadian Journal of Sociology* 12: 16–41.

Canning, P., and C. Strong. 2002. "Children and Families Adjusting to the Cod Moratorium." In *The Resilient Outport*, ed. R.E. Ommer, 342–8. St. John's: ISER Books.

Card, B.Y. 1960. "The Canadian Prairie Provinces from 1870 to 1950: A Sociological Analysis." Calgary: Dent, 1960.

Carroll, William K., and R.S. Ratner. 2005. 'The NDP Regime in British Columbia, 1991–2001: A Post Mortem.' *Canadian Review of Sociology and Anthropology* 42 (2): 167–96.

Castells, Manuel. 2004. *The Power of Solidarity*. London: Blackwell.

Castles, Stephen. 2003. *The Age of Migration: International Population Movements in the Modern World*, 3rd ed. London: Guilford Press.

Castles, Stephen, and Alastair Davidson. 2000. *Citizenship and Migration: Globalization and the Politics of Belonging*. New York: Routledge.

Cernetig, Miro. 2001. "The Far Side of the Rockies: Politics and Identity in British Columbia." In *A Passion for Identity: Canadian Studies for the 21st Century*, 4th ed., ed. David Taras and Beverly Rasporich, 413–26. Scarborough, ON: Nelson Thomson Learning.

Chambers, Edward J. 2001. *An Evaluation of the Two Provincial Economies in the Post FTA/NAFTA Period: Restructuring in Alberta and British Columbia.* Edmonton: Western Centre for Economic Research.

Champion, Tony, and Tony Fielding, eds. 1992. *Migration Processes and Patterns.* Vol. 1: *Research Progress and Prospects.* New York: Belhaven Press.

Chastko, Paul. 2004. *Developing Alberta's Oil Sands.* Calgary: University of Calgary Press.

Chawla, Louise. 1992. "Childhood Place Attachments." In *Place Attachment*, ed. Irwin Altman and Setha M. Low, 63–86. New York: Plenum.

Chiswick, Barry R. 2000. "Are Immigrants Favourably Self-selected?" In *Migration Theory: Talking across Disciplines*, ed. Caroline B. Brettell, 61–76. New York: Rutledge.

Choldin, Harvey M. 1973. "Kinship Networks in the Migration Process." *International Migration Review* 7: 163–75.

Choyce, Lesley. 1997. *Nova Scotia: Shaped by the Sea.* Toronto: Viking Penguin

Chun, Jinsuk. 1996. *Interregional Migration and Regional Development.* Aldershot: Avebury.

Clark, William A.V. 1981. "Residential Mobility and Behavioral Geography: Parallelism or Interdependence." In *Behavioral Problems In Geography Revisited*, ed. K.R. Cox and R.G. Golledge, 182–205. New York: Methuen.

– 1998. *The California Cauldron: Immigration and the Fortunes of Local Communities.* New York: Gilford Press.

Coates, Kenneth, ed. 1985. *The Alaska Highway: Papers of the 40th Anniversary Symposium.* Vancouver: UBC Press.

Cohen, Anthony P. 1985. *The Symbolic Construction of Community.* London: Routledge.

Cohen, Robin. 1997. *Global Diasporas: An Introduction.* Seattle: University of Washington Press.

Collins, Robert. 1994. "The Sun Would Shine Forever." In *Alberta in the 20th Century.* Vol. 3: *The Boom and the Bust*, 2–17. Edmonton: United Western Communications Ltd.

Conrad, Margaret, R., and James K. Hiller. 2001. *Atlantic Canada: A Region in the Making.* Toronto: Oxford University Press.

Conway, J.F. 1983. *The West: The History of a Region in Confederation.* Toronto: James Lorimer and Company.

Cooke, T.J. 2001. "'Trailing Wife' or 'Trailing Mother'? The Effect of Parental Status on the Relationship between Family migration and the Labor-market Participation of Married Women. *Environment and Planning* 33: 419–30.

Cooper, Barry, and Mebs Kanji. 2000. *Governing in Post-Deficit Times: Alberta in the Klein Years*. Toronto: University of Toronto Press.

Courchene, Thomas J. 1970. "Interprovincial Migration and Economic Adjustment." *Canadian Journal of Economics* 4: 550–76.

– 1998. *From Heartland to North American Regional State: The Social, Fiscal, and Federal Evolution of Ontario*. Toronto: University of Toronto Press.

Cresswell, T. 1996. *In Place, Out of Place: Geography, Ideology, and Transgression*. Minneapolis: University Of Minnesota Press.

Cross, Philip, and Bowlby, Geoff. 2006. "The Alberta Economic Juggernaut: The Boom on the Rose." *Canadian Economic Observer,* September, 3.1–3.12.

Cuba, Lee, and David Hummon. 1993. "A Place to Call Home: Identification with Dwelling Community and Region." *Sociological Quarterly* 34: 111–31.

Currie, Raymond F., Shiva S. Halli. 1989. "Mixed Motivations for Migration in the Urban Prairies: A Comparative Approach." *Social Indicators Research* 21: 481–99.

Cuthand, Doug. 1999. "Province's Future Hangs on Native Development." *Saskatoon Star-Phoenix*, A5.

Dawson, C.A., and Eva R. Younge. 1940. *Pioneering in the Prairie Provinces: The Social Side of the Settlement Process*. Toronto: Macmillan.

Day, Katherine May. 1989. "Government Policies, Unemployment Rates, and Interprovincial Migration in Canada." PhD diss., University of British Columbia.

Deer, Glenn. 2006. "The New Yellow Peril: The Rhetorical Construction of Asian Canadian Identity and Cultural Anxiety in Richmond." In *Climbing Space: Racialization in Canadian Cities*, ed. Cheryl Teelucksingh, 19–40. Waterloo: Wilfrid Laurier University.

DeJong, Gordon F. 1999. "Choice Processes in Migration Behavior'. In *Migration and Restructuring in the United States*, ed. K. Pavita and S. Davies Withers, 273–93. New York: Rowan and Littlefield.

Diaz, Polo, and Paul Gingrich. 1992. "Crisis and Community in Rural Saskatchewan." In *Rural Sociology in Canada*, ed. David A. Hay and Gurcharn S. Basran, 36–50. Toronto: Oxford.

Dimaggio, P., E. Hargittai, W.R. Neuman, and J.P. Robinson. 2001. "Social Implications of the Internet." *Annual Review of Sociology* 27: 307–36.

Doern, G. Bruce, and Glen Toner. 1985. *The Politics of Energy: The Development and Implementation of the NEP*. Agincourt, ON: Methuen.

Donath, J.S. 1999. "Identity and Deception in the Virtual Community." In *Communities In Cyberspace*, ed. M.A. Smith and P. Kollock, 29–59. New York: Routledge.

Dupuy, Richard, Francine Mayer, and Rene Morissette. 2000. *Rural Youth: Stayers, Leavers and Return Migrants*. Statistics Canada Analytical Study Series 2000152e.

Edmondson, Jacqueline. 2003. *Prairie Town: Redefining Rural Life in the Age of Globalization*. New York: Rowman and Littlefield.

Eisenstadt, S.N. 1954. *The Absorption of Immigrants*. London: Routledge and Kegan Paul.

Eisler, Dale. 2005. "The Saskatchewan Myth." In *The Heavy Hand of History: Interpreting Saskatchewan's Past*, ed. Gregory P. Marchildon, 67–85. Regina: Canadian Plains Research Centre, University of Regina.

Emery, J.C. Herbert. 2006. "Alberta 1986: The Bloom Comes off the Wild Rose Province." In *Alberta Formed-Alberta Transformed*, ed. Michael Payne, Donald Wetherell, and Catherine Cavanaugh, 159–74. Calgary: University of Calgary Press.

Emery, J.C. Herbert, and Ronald D. Kneebone. 2005. *Mostly Harmless: Socialists, Populists, Policies and the Economic Development of Alberta and Saskatchewan*. Technical Paper No. TP–05003. Calgary: Institute for Advanced Policy Research.

Epp, Roger, and Dave Whitson, eds. 2001. *Writing off the Rural West*. Edmonton: University of Alberta Press.

Fairbrother, Malcolm. 2003. "The Freedom of the State? Recent NDP governments and a Reply to the Globalization Skeptics." *Canadian Review of Sociology and Anthropology* 40 (3): 311–29.

Faist, T. 2000. *The Volume and Dynamics of International Migration and Transnational Social Spaces*. Oxford: Clarendon Press.

Feagin, Joe. 1985. "The Global Context of Metropolitan Growth: Houston and the Oil Industry." *American Journal of Sociology* 90 (6): 1204–30.

– 1988. *Free Enterprise City: Houston in Political-Economic Perspective*. New Jersey: Rutgers University Press.

Fielding, Tony. 1992. "Migration and culture." In *Migration Processes and Patterns*. Vol. 1: *Research Progress and Prospects*, ed. T. Champion and T. Fielding, 79–95. New York: Belhaven Press.

Finbow, Robert. 1995. "Atlantic Canada: Forgotten Periphery in an Endangered Confederation." In *Beyond Quebec: Taking stock of Canada*, ed. Kenneth McRoberts, 61–80. Montreal: McGill-Queen's University Press.

Finnie, Ross. 1998a. "Interprovincial Mobility in Canada: The Effects of Interprovincial Migration on Individuals' Earnings." *Human Resources Development Canada*, W–98–5E.

– 1998b. "Interprovincial Mobility in Canada: A Longitudinal Analysis." *Human Resources Development Canada*, W–98–5E.

– 1999a. "Inter-provincial Migration in Canada: A Longitudinal Analysis of Movers and Stayers and the Associated Income Dynamics." *Canadian Journal of Regional Science* 22 (3): 227–62.

– 1999b. "The Patterns of Inter-provincial Migration in Canada, 1982–95: Evidence from Longitudinal Tax-based Data." *Canadian Studies in Population* 26 (2): 205–34.

Fischer, Claude. 1977. *Networks and Places: Social Relations in the Urban Setting*. New York: Free Press.

– 2002. "Ever-More Rooted Americans." *City and Community* 1: 175–93.

Florida, Richard. 2002. *The Rise of the Creative Class*. New York: Basic Books.

Flowerdew, Robin. 1992. "Labour Market Operation and Geographical Mobility." In *Migration Processes and Patterns*. Vol. 1: *Research Progress and Prospects*, ed. Tony Champion and Tony Fielding, 135–47. New York: Belhaven Press.

Fowke, Vernon. 1957. *The National Policy and the Wheat Economy*. Toronto: University of Toronto Press.

Francis, R. Douglas. 1992. "Changing Images of the West." In *The Prairie West: Historical Readings,* 2nd ed., ed. R. Douglas Francis and Howard Palmer, 717–39. Edmonton: University of Alberta Press.

– 1989a. *Images of the West: Responses to the Canadian Provinces*. Saskatoon: Western Producer Books.

– 1989b. "In Search of a Prairie Myth: A Survey of the Intellectual and Cultural Historiography of Prairie Canada." *Journal of Canadian Studies* 24 (3): 44–69.

Francis, R. Douglas, and Chris Kitzan. 2007. *The Prairie West as Promised Land*. Calgary: University of Calgary Press.

Franklin, Rachel S. 2003. "Geographic Domestic Migration across Regions, Divisions, and States: 1995–2000." *Special Reports*. N.p.: United States Census, 2000.

Frey, William H. 1996. "Immigration, Domestic Migration, and Demographic Balkanization in America." *Population and Development Review* 22 (4): 741–63.

– 1999 "Immigration and Demographic Balkanization: Toward one America or Two?" In *America's Demographic Tapestry: Baseline for the New Millennium*, ed. J.W. Hughes and J.J. Seneca, 78–100. New Brunswick: Rutgers University Press.

– 2002. "US Census Shows Different Paths for Domestic and Foreign-Born Migrants." *Population Today* 30 (6): 1, 4–5.

Frey, William H., and S. Alden. 1988. *Regional and Metropolitan Growth and Decline in the United States*. New York: Russell Sage.

Friesen, Gerald. 1984. *The Canadian Prairies: A History*. Toronto: University of Toronto Press.

– 1999. *The West: Regional Ambitions, National Debates, Global Age*. Toronto: Penguin/McGill Institute.

Gallagher, Winifred. 1993. *The Power of Place: How Our Surroundings Shape our Thoughts, Emotions, and Actions*. New York: Poseidon Press.

Gallaugher, Patricia, and Kelly M. Vodden. 1999. "Tying It Together along the BC Coast." In *Fishing Places, Fishing People: Traditions and Issues in Canadian small-scale fisheries*, ed. Dianne Newell and Rosemary E. Ommer, 276–97. Toronto: University of Toronto Press.

George, M.V. 1970. *Internal Migration in Canada*. Ottawa: Dominion Bureau of Statistics.

Gibbins, Roger. 1980. *Prairie Politics and Society: Regionalism in Decline*. Toronto: Butterworths.

Gibbins, Roger, and Casey Vander Ploeg. 2005. *Investing Wisely*. Calgary: Canada West Foundation.

Gibbins, Roger, and Sonia Arrison. 1995. *Western Visions: Perspectives on the West in Canada*. Peterborough, ON: Broadview.

Gibbins, Roger, Keith Archer, and Stan Drabek. 1990. *Canadian Political Life*. Iowa: Kendall/Hunt Publishing Company.

Gieryn, Thomas F. 2000. "A Space for Place in Sociology." *Annual Review of Sociology* 26: 463–96.

Gilpin, John F. 1984. *Edmonton: Gateway to the North*. Windsor: Windsor Publications.

Gmelch, George. 1980. "Return to Migration." *Annual Review of Anthropology* 9: 135–59.

– 1983. "Who Returns and Why: Return Migration Behavior in Two North Atlantic Societies." *Human Organization* 42: 46–54.

– 1992. *Double Passage: The Lives of Caribbean Migrants Abroad and Back Home*. Ann Arbor: University of Michigan Press.

Gmelch, George, and Barnett Richling. 1986. "The Impact of Return Migration in Rural Newfoundland." In *Return Migration and Regional Economic Problems*, ed. Russell King 185–97. London: Croom Helm.

Gmelch, George, and Barnett Richling. 1988. "We're Better Off Home: Return Migration to Newfoundland Outports." *Anthropology Today* 4 (4): 12–14.

Goldstein, Sidney. 1976. "Facets of Redistribution: Research Challenges and Opportunities." *Demography* 13 (4): 423–34.

Gonick, Cy. 1990. "The Manitoba Economy Since World War II." In *The Political Economy of Manitoba*, ed. Jim Silver and Jeremy Hall, 25–48. Regina: Canadian Plains Research Centre.

Gordon, Ian. 1992. "Modelling Approaches to Migration and the Labour Market." In *Migration Processes and Patterns*. Vol. 1: *Research Progress and Prospects*, ed. Tony Champion and Tony Fielding, 119–34. New York: Belhaven Press.

Goyder, John. 1995. "Migration and Regional Differences in Life Satisfaction in the Anglophone Provinces." *Canadian Journal of Sociology* 20 (3): 287–307.

Granovetter, Mark. 1973. "The Strength of Weak Ties." *American Journal of Sociology* 78: 1360–80.

Grant, Shelagh D. 1988. *Sovereignty or Security? Government Policy in the Canadian North, 1936–1950*. Vancouver: UBC Press.

Garton, L., C. Haythornthwaite, and B. Wellman. 1997. "Studying On-line Social Networks." *Journal of Computer-mediated Communication* 3 (1), available at <http://jcmc.huji.ac.il/vol3/issue1>, viewed May 2003.

Gray, Earle. 2005. *The Great Canadian Oil Patch: The Petroleum Era from Birth to Peak*, 2nd ed. Edmonton: June Parren Publishing.

Gray, James. 1979. "Boomtime: Peopling the Canadian Provinces." Saskatoon: Western Producer.

Greenwood, Michael J. 1975. "Research on Internal Migration in the United States." *Journal of Economic Literature* 13: 397–433.

Greenwood, Michael J., Peter R. Mueser, David A. Plane, and Alan M. Schlottmann. 1991. "New Directions in Migration Research." *Annuals of Regional Science* 25: 237–70.

Halfacree, K.H. 1995. "Household Migration and the Structuration of Patriarchy: Evidence from the USA." *Progress in Human Geography* 19: 159–82.

Halfacree, K.H., and Paul J. Boyle. 1993. "The Challenges Facing Migration Research: The Case for a Biographical Approach." *Progress in Human Geography* 17 (3): 333–48.

Hall, David. 1977. "Clifford Sifton and Settlement Policy, 1896–1905." In *The Settlement of the West*, ed. Howard Palmer, 50–85. Calgary: University of Calgary, Comprint Publishing Company.

Halseth, Greg, and Regine Halseth, eds. 1998. *Prince George: A Social Geography of BC's Northern Capital*. Prince George: UNBC Press.

Hansen, Marcus Lee. 1940. *The Mingling of the Canadian and American Peoples*. Vol. 1. Toronto: Ryerson Press.

Hanson, Eric J. 1958. *The Dynamic Decade: The Evolution and Effects of the Oil Industry in Alberta*. Don Mills, Ontario: T.H Best Printing Company, Ltd.

Harris, J.R., and M.P. Todaro. 1970. "Migration, Unemployment, and Development: A Two-sector Analysis." *American Economic Review* 70 (1): 126–42.

Harrison, Trevor, and Gordon Laxer. 1995. *The Trojan Horse: Alberta and the Future of Canada.* Montreal: Black Rose Books.

Harvey, David. 1989. *The Condition of Post-modernity: An Enquiry into the Doings of Cultural Change.* Oxford: Blackwell.

Hay, David A. 1992. "Rural Canada in Transition: Trends and Developments." In *Rural Sociology in Canada*, ed. David A. Hay and Gurcharn S. Basran, 16–35. Toronto: Oxford.

Hayter, Roger. 2000. *Flexible Crossroads: The Restructuring of British Columbia's Forest Economy.* Vancouver: UBC Press.

Heaton, Tim, Carl Fredrickson, Glenn Fuguilt, and James Zuiches. 1979. "Residential Preferences, Community Satisfaction and the Intention to Move." Demography 16 (4): 565–73.

Heckathorn, Douglas. 1997. "Respondent-driven Sampling: A New Approach to the Study of Hidden Populations." *Social Problems* 44 (2): 174–99.

Helliwell, John F. 1996. "Convergence and Migration among Provinces.' *Canadian Journal of Economics* 29, special issue (April): S324–30.

Hendershott, A.B. 1995. *Moving for Work: The Sociology of Relocating in the 1990s.* New York: University Press of America.

Hesketh, Bob, ed. 1996. *Three Northern Wartime Projects.* Edmonton: Canadian Circumpolar Institute and Edmonton and District Historical Society.

Hiller, Harry H. 1982. *Society and Change: S.D. Clark and the Development of Canadian Sociology.* Toronto: University of Toronto Press.

– 1987. "Dependence and Independence: Emergent Nationalism in Newfoundland." *Ethnic and Racial Studies* 10: 258–73.

– 2007. "Gateway Cities and Arriviste Cities: Alberta's Recent Urban Growth in Canadian Context." *Prairie Forum* 32: 47–66.

Hiller, Harry H., and Linda DiLuzio. 2004. "The Interviewee and the Research Interview: Analysing a Neglected Dimension in Research." *Canadian Review of Sociology and Anthropology* 41 (1): 1–26.

Hiller, Harry H., and Tara M. Franz. 2004. "New Ties, Old Ties and Lost Ties: The Use of the Internet in Diaspora." New Media and Society 6: 731–52.

Hiller, Harry H., and Kendall S. McCaig. 2007. "Reassessing the Role of Partnered Women in Migration Decision-making and Migration Outcomes." *Journal of Social and Personal Relationships* 24 (3): 457–72.

Hiscott, Robert. 1987a. "A Profile of Employed Migrants between Atlantic Canada and Ontario." In *Canadian Social Trends*, Statistics Canada Catalogue 11–008E.

– 1987b. "Determinants of Marginal/Central Work World Employment for Recent Atlantic Canada-Ontario Migrants." Queen's paper in Industrial Relations.

– 1987c. "Return Migration from Ontario to Atlantic Canada: A Comparison of Returning and Non-returning Migrants." *Canadian Review of Sociology and Anthropology* 24 (4): 586–99.

Howlett, Michael, and Keith Brownsey. 2001. "British Columbia: Politics in a Post-staples Political Economy." In *The Provincial State in Canada*, ed. Keith Brownsey and Michael Howlett, 309–33. Peterborough, ON: Broadview Press.

Hou, Feng, and Roderic Beaujot. 1994. "The Differentiation of Determinants among Return, Onward, and Primary Migrants in Canada." *Canadian Studies in Population* 21 (1): 1–19.

– 1995. "A Study of Interregional Migration between Ontario and Atlantic Canada, 1981–1991." *Canadian Journal of Regional Science* 18 (2): 147–60.

House, J.D. 1980. *The Last of the Free Enterprisers: The Oilmen of Calgary.* Toronto: Macmillan.

– 1985. *The Challenge Of Oil: Newfoundland's Quest for Controlled Development.* St John's: Institute of Social and Economic Research.

– 1989. *Going Away … And Coming Back: Economic Life and Migration in Small Canadian Communities.* St John's: Memorial University.

Hummon, David M. 1992. "Community Attachment." In *Place Attachment*, ed. Irwin Altman and Setha M. Low, 253–78. New York: Plenum.

Hunt, Gary L., and Richard E. Mueller. 2004. "International and Interregional Migration in North America: The Role of Returns to Skill." In *Canadian Migration Patterns: From Britain and North America*, ed. Barbara J. Messamore, 229–44. Ottawa: University of Ottawa Press.

Houstoun, M.F., R.G. Kramer, and J. Mackin Barrett. 1984. "Female Predominance in Immigration to the US Since 1930: A First Look." *International Migration Review* 18: 908–59.

Hutchings, Jeffery A. 1999. "The Biological Collapse of Newfoundland's Northern Cod." In *Fishing Places, Fishing People: Traditions and Issues in Canadian Small-scale Fisheries*, ed. Dianne Newell and Rosemary E. Ommer, 260–75. Toronto: University of Toronto Press.

Hutchinson, Brian. 1994. "5,000 to 75,000 in 12 Years." In *Alberta in the 20th Century*. Vol. 3: *The Boom and the Bust*, 88–117. Edmonton: United Western Communications Ltd.

Ibbitson, John. 1997. *Promised Land: Inside the Mike Harris Revolution.* Scarborough: Prentice-Hall.

Ironside, R.G. 1984. "Rural Alberta: Elements of Change." In *Environment and Economy: Essays on the Human Geography of Alberta*, ed. B.M. Barr and P.J. Smith, 95–110. Edmonton: Pica Pica Press.

Islam, Muhammed N. 1985. "Self-selectivity Problems in Interregional and Interindustry Migration in Canada." *Environment and Planning A*, 17, 1515–31.

Ives, Edward D. 1999. *Drive Dull Care Away: Folk Songs from Prince Edward Island*. Charlottetown: Institute for Island Studies.

Jacobsen, David. 2002. *Place and Belonging in America*. Johns Hopkins University Press.

Jacobsen, J.P., and L.M. Levin. 1997. "Marriage and Migration: Comparing Gains and Losses from Migration for Couples and Singles." *Social Science Quarterly* 78 (3): 688–709.

– 2000. "The Effects of Internal Migration on the Relative Economic Status of Women and Men." *Journal of Socio-Economics* 29: 291–304.

Jackson, F.L. 1984. *Newfoundland in Canada: A People in Search of a Polity*. St John's: Harry Cuff Publications.

– 1969. "Migration: Editorial Introduction." In *Migration*, ed. J.A. Jackson, 1–10. Cambridge University Press.

Jaffe, JoAnn. 2003. "Family Labour Processes, Land, and the Farm Crisis in Saskatchewan." In *Farm Communities and the Crossroads: Challenge and Resistance*, ed. Harry P. Diaz, JoAnn Jaffe, and Robert Stirling, 137–48. Regina: Canadian Plains Research Center.

Jansen, Clifford J., ed. 1970. *Readings in the Sociology of Migration*. New York: Pergamon Press.

Jaremko, Gordon. 2006. "Saskatchewan Spawning Oil Leaders." *Calgary Herald*, 9 September, C5.

Jasper, James M. 2000. *Restless Nation: Starting Over in America*. Chicago: University of Chicago Press.

Jobes, Patrick. 1992. "Economic and Quality of Life Decisions in Migration to a High National Amenity Area." In *Community, Society and Migration in America*, ed. Patrick C. Jobes, William F. Stinner, and John W. Wardwell, 335–62. New York: University Press of America.

Jobes, Patrick C., William F. Stinner, and John M. Wardwell. 1992. *Community, Society, and Migration: Non-economic Migration in America*. New York: New York University Press.

Johnson, Hans P. 2002. "Leaving California." *California Journal* 33 (6): 40–3.

Jones, S.G. 1995. "Understanding Community in the Information Age." In *Cybersociety: Computer-mediated Communication and Community*, ed. S.G. Jones, 10–35. Thousand Oaks: Sage.

Junor, Sean. 2004. *The Price of Knowledge: Access and Student Finance in Canada*. Ottawa: Canadian Millennium Scholarship Foundation.

Kanaiaupuni, S.M. 2000. "Reframing the Migration Question: An Analysis of Men, Women and Gender in Mexico." *Social Forces* 78 (4): 1311–47.

Kanter, Rosabeth Moss. 1977. *Men and Women of the Corporation*. New York: Basic Books.

Katovich, Michael A., and Carl J. Couch. 1992. "The Nature of Social Posts and Their Use as Foundation for Standard Action." *Symbolic Interaction* 15: 25–47.

Kaye, B., and D.W. Moodie. 1973. "Geographical Perspectives on the Canadian Plains." In *A Region of the Mind: Interpreting the Western Canadian Plains*, ed. Richard Allen, 17–46. Regina: Canadian Plains Studies Centre.

Keefer, Janice Kulyk. 1987. *Under Eastern Eyes: A Critical Reading of Maritime Fiction*. Toronto: University of Toronto Press.

Kennedy, Leslie W., and N. Mehra. 1985a. "Effects of Social Change on Well-being: Boom and Bust in a Western Canadian City." *Social Indicators Research* 17: 101–13.

– 1985b. *Moving to Get Ahead: Does It Pay?* Edmonton Area Series Report No. 45, Population Research Laboratory, Department of Sociology, University of Alberta.

Kneebone, Ronald D., and Kenneth J. McKenzie. 1997. "The Process behind Institutional Reform in Alberta." In *A Government Reinvented: A Study of Alberta's Deficit Elimination Program*, ed. Christopher Bruce, Ronald Kneebone, and Kenneth McKenzie, 176–210. Toronto: Oxford University Press.

Krahn, Harvey, and John W. Gartrell. 1983. "Labour Market Segmentation and Social Mobility in a Canadian Single Industry Community." *Canadian Review of Sociology and Anthropology* 20 (3): 322–45.

Komter, A. 1989. "Hidden Power in Marriage." *Gender and Society* 3: 187–216.

Kubik, Wendee, and Robert Moore. 2003. "Farming in Saskatchewan in the 1990s: Stress and Coping." In *Farm Communities and the Crossroads: Challenge and Resistance*, ed. Harry P. Diaz, JoAnn Jaffe, and Robert Stirling, 119–33. Regina: Canadian Plains Research Centre.

Lamont, G.R., and V.B. Proudfoot. 1975. "Migration and Changing Settlement Patterns in Alberta." In *People on the Move: Studies on Internal Migration*, ed. Leszek A. Kosinski and R. Mansell Prothero, 223–36. Canada: Methuen.

Lautt, Melanie L. 1973. "Sociology and the Canadian Plains." In *A Region of the Mind: Interpreting the Western Canadian Plains*, ed. Allen, Richard, 125–51. Regina: Canadian Plains Studies Centre.

Laxer, James. 1983. *Oil and Gas: Ottawa, the Provinces, and the Petroleum Industry*. Toronto: James Lorimer.

Ledent, Jacques. 1990. "Canada." In *International Handbook on Internal Migration*, ed. Charles B. Nam, William J. Serow, David F. Sly, 47–62. New York: Greenwood.

Lee, Philip. 2001. *The Life and Politics of Frank McKenna*. Fredericton: Goose Lane.

Lefebvre, Henri. 1995. *The Production of Space*. London: Blackwell.

Lemann, Nicholas. 1991. *The Promised Land: The Great Black Migration and How It Changed America*. New York: Knopf.

Leon, A.M., and S.F. Dziegielewski. 1999. "The Psychological Impact of Migration: Practice Considerations in Working with Hispanic Women. *Journal of Social Work Practice* 12 (1): 69–82.

Ley, David, and Judith Tutchener. 2001. "Globalization and House Prices in Canada's Gateway Cities." *Housing Studies* 16 (2): 199–223.

Lipset, Seymour Martin. 1968. *Agrarian Socialism: The Cooperative Commonwealth Federation in Saskatchewan – A Study in Political Sociology*. California: University of California Press.

Liaw, Kao-Lee. 1990a. "Joint Effects of Personal Factors and Ecological Variables on the Interprovincial Migration Pattern of Young Adults in Canada: A Nested Logic Analysis." *Geographical Analysis* 22 (3): 189–208.

– 1990. "Neutral Migration Process and Its Application to an Analysis of Canadian migration Data." *Environment and Planning A* 22: 333–43.

Lisac, Mark. 1995. *The Klein Revolution*. Edmonton: NeWest Press.

Lo, Lucia, and Carlow Teixeira. 1998. "If Quebec Goes ... The "Exodus" Impact?" *Professional Geographer* 50 (4): 481–98.

Lofland, Lyn H. 1973. *A World of Strangers: Order and Action in Urban Public Space*. New York: Basic Books.

Lombard, M., and T. Pitton. 1997. "At the Heart of It All: The Concept of Telepresence." *Journal of Computer-mediated Communication* 3 (2), available at <http://jcmc.huji.ac.il/vol3/issue2/>, viewed May 2003.

Long, Larry. 1988. *Migration and Residential Mobility in the United States*. New York: Russell Sage Foundation..

Low, Setha M., and Irwin Altman. 1992. "Place Attachment: A Conceptual Inquiry." In *Place Attachment*, ed. Irwin Altman and Setha M. Low, 1–12. New York: Plenum.

Lu, M. 1998. "Analyzing Migration Decision Making: Relationship between Residential Satisfaction, Mobility Intentions, and Moving Behavior." *Environment and Planning A*, 30, 1473–95.

Luo, L., and C.L. Cooper. 1990. "Stress of Job Relocations: Progress and Prospect." *Work and Stress* 4 (2): 121–8.

Lycan, Richard. 1969. 'Interprovincial Migration in Canada: The Role of Spatial and Economic Factors.' *Canadian Geographer* 8 (3): 237–54.

MacDonald, Edward. 2000. *Of You're Strong Hearted: Prince Edward Island in the Twentieth Century*. Charlottetown: Prince Edward Island Museum and Heritage Foundation.

MacGregor, J.G. 1967. *Edmonton: A History*. Edmonton: Hurtig.

Mackenzie, A.A. 1985. "Cape Breton and the Western Harvest Excursions, 1890–1928." In *Cape Breton at 200: Historical Essays in Honour of the Island's Bicentennial, 1785–1985*, ed. Kenneth Joseph Donovan, 71–83. Sydney: University College of Cape Breton Press.

– 2002. *The Harvest Train: When Maritimers Worked in the Canadian West, 1890–1928*. Wreck Cove, NS: Breton Books.

Mackintosh, W.A. 1934. *Prairie Settlement: The Geographical Setting*. Toronto: Macmillan.

Macpherson, C.B. 1953. *Democracy in Alberta: Social Credit and the Party System*. Toronto: University of Toronto Press.

Magdol, L. 2002. "Is Moving Gendered? The Effects of Residential Mobility on the Psychological Well-being of Men and Women. *Sex Roles* 47 11/12: 553–60.

Mann, C., and F. Stewart. 2000. *Internet Communication and Qualitative Research: A Handbook for Researching Online*. London: Sage.

Mansell, Robert L. 1997. "Fiscal Restructuring in Alberta: An Overview." In *A Government Reinvented: A Study of Alberta's Deficit Elimination Program*, ed. Christopher Bruce, Ronald Kneebone, and Kenneth McKenzie, 16–73. Toronto: Oxford University Press.

– 2002. "The Alberta Economy: Changes and Challenges." In *Alberta's Fiscal Frontiers: The O'Brien Years and Beyond*, ed. Bev Dahlby 75–104. Edmonton: Institute for Public Economics.

Mansell, Robert L., and Michael B. Percy. 1990. *Strength in Adversity: A Study of the Alberta Economy*. Edmonton: University of Alberta Press.

Mansell, Robert L., and Ronald Schlenker. 2006. *Energy and the Alberta Economy: Past and Future Impacts and Implications*. Calgary: Institute for Sustainable Energy, Environment, and Economy.

Marchildon, Gregory P. 2005. "The Great Divide." In *The Heavy Hand of History: Interpreting Saskatchewan's Past*, ed. Gregory P. Marchildon, 51–66. Regina: Canadian Plains Research Centre, University of Regina.

Marcus, Clare Cooper. 1992. "Environmental Memories." In *Place Attachment*, ed. Irwin Altman and Setha M. Low, 87–112. New York: Plenum.

Marsden, Lorna R., and Lorne J. Tepperman. 1985. "The Migrant Wife: The Worst of All Worlds." *Journal of Business Ethics* 4: 205–13.

Marger, Martin N., and Phillip J. Obermiller. 1987. "Emergent Ethnicity among Internal Migrants: The Case of Maritimers in Toronto." *Ethnic Groups* 7L 1–17.

Markham, W.T., P.O. Macken, C.M. Bonjean, and J. Corder. 1983. "A Note on Sex, Geographic Mobility, and Career Advancement." *Social Forces* 61 (4): 1138–46.

Massey, Douglas. 1999 "Why Does Immigration Occur? A Theoretical Synthesis." In *The Handbook of International Migration: The American Experience*, ed. Charles Hirschman, Philip Kasinitz, and Josh Dewind, 34–52. New York: Russell Sage Foundation.

Massey, Douglas., Joaquín Arango, Graeme Hugo, Ali Kouaouchi, Adela Pellegrino, and J. Edward Taylor. 1994. "An Evaluation of International Migration Theory: The North American Case." *Population and Development Review* 20 (4): 699–752.

– 1998. *Worlds in Motion: Understanding International Migration at the End of the Millennium*. Oxford: Clarendon Press.

Matthews, Ralph. 1983. *The Creation Of Regional Dependency*. Toronto: University Of Toronto Press.

May, Doug, and A. Hollett. 1995. *A Rock in a Hard Place: Atlantic Canada and the UI Trap*. Toronto: C.D. Howe Institute.

McCollum, A.T. 1990. *The Trauma of Moving*. Newbury Park, CA: Sage.

McCormick, Peter. 2001. "Power and Politics in Western Canada." In *A Passion for Identity: Canadian Studies for the 21st Century*, 4th ed., ed. David Taras and Beverly Rasporich, 401–12. Scarborough, ON: Nelson Thomson Learning.

McGinnis, D. 1977. "Farm Labour in Transition: Occupational Structure and Economic Dependency in Alberta, 1921–1951." In *The Settlement of the West*, ed. Howard Palmer, 174–86. Calgary: Comprint Publishing Company.

McHugh, Kevin E. 1984. "Explaining Migration Intentions and Destination Selection.' *Professional Geographer* 36 (3): 315–25.

McKenzie-Brown, Peter, David Finch, and Gordon Jaremko. 1993. *The Great Oil Age*. Calgary: Detselig.

Melbin, Murray. 1987. *Night on Frontier: Colonizing the World after Dark*. New York: Free Press.

Melnyk, George. 1999. *New Moon at Batoche: Reflections on the Urban Prairie*. Banff: Banff Centre Press.

Messamore, Barbara J. ed. 2004. *Canadian Migration Patterns: From Britain and North America*. Ottawa: University of Ottawa Press.

Michelson, William. 1977. *Environmental Choice, Human Behavior, and Residential Satisfaction*. New York: Oxford University Press.

Miller, D., and D. Slater. 2000. *The Internet: An Ethnographic Approach*. Oxford: Berg.

Milligan, Melinda S. 1998. "International Past and Potential: The Social Construction of Place Attachment." *Symbolic Interaction* 21 (1): 1–33.

Mincer, J. 1978. "Family Migration Decisions." *Journal of Political Economy* 86 (5): 749–73.

Minister of Industry. 2004. *Canadian Agriculture at a Glance*. Catalogue no. 96–325-XPB.

Mitra, A. 1997. "Diasporic Web Sites: Ingroup and Outgroup Discourse." *Critical Studies in Mass Communication* 14: 158–81.

– 2001. "Marginal Voices in Cyberspace." *New Media and Society* 3 (1): 29–48.

Moon, Bruce. 1995. "Paradigms in Migration Research: Explaining 'Moorings' as a Schema." *Progress in Human Geography* 19 (4): 504–24.

Morley, David. 2000. *Home Territories: Media, Mobility, and Identity*. New York: Routledge.

Morrison Peter A. 1977. "The Functions and Dynamics of the Migration Process." In *Internal Migration: A Comparative Perspective*, ed. Alan A. Brown and Egon Neuberger, 61–72. New York: Academic Press.

Morrison, Peter A., and Judith P. Wheeler. 1978. "The Images of Elsewhere in the American Tradition of Migration." In *Human Migration: Patterns and Policies*, ed. William H. McNeill and Ruth S. Adams, 75–83. Bloomington: Indiana University Press.

Morrison, D.R., and D. T. Lichter. 1988. "Family Migration and Female Employment: The Problem of Underemployment among Migrant Married Women." *Journal of Marriage and Family* 50 (1) : 161–72.

Muller, Thomas, and Thomas J. Espenshade. 1985. *The Fourth Wave: California's Newest Immigrants*. Washington, DC: The Urban Institute Press.

Morton, W.L. 1973. "A Century of Plain and Parkland." In *A Region of the Mind: Interpreting the Western Canadian Plains*, ed. Richard Allen, 165–80. Regina: Canadian Plains Studies Centre.

Munton, A.G. 1990. "Job Relocation, Stress, and the Family." *Journal of Organizational Behavior* 11 (5): 401–06.

Munton, A.G., N. Forster, Y. Altman and L. Greenbury. 1993. *Job Relocation: Managing People on the Move*. Chichester, UK: John Wiley and Sons.

National Energy Board. 2000. *Canada's Oil Sands: A Supply and Market Outlook to 2015*. Ottawa: National Energy Board.

Nakosteen, R.A., and M. Zimmer. 1982. "The Effects on Earnings of Interregional and Interindustry Migration." *Journal of Regional Science* 22: 325–41.

Naficy, H., ed. 1999. *Home, Exile, Homeland: Film, Media, and the Politics of Place* . New York: Routledge.

Newbold, K.B. 1996a. "The Ghettoization of Quebec: Interprovincial Migration and Its Demographic Effects." *Canadian Studies in Population*, 23 (1): 1–21.

– 1996b. "Income, Self-selection and Return and Onward Interprovincial Migration in Canada." *Environment and Planning A*, 28: 1019–34.

– 1998. "Out-migration from California: The Role of Migrant Selectivity." *Geographical Analysis* 30 (2): 138–52.

– 2007. "Secondary Migration of Immigrants to Canada: An Analysis of LSIC Wave 1 Data." *Canadian Geographer* 51 (1):58–71.

Newbold, K. Bruce, and Kao-Lee Liaw. 1994. "Return and Onward Interprovincial Migration through Economic Boom and Bust in Canada, from 1976–1981 to 1981–86." *Geographical Analysis* 26 (3): 228–45.

Newfoundland Statistics Agency. 2001. *Preliminary Report of the Survey of Out-migrants and In-migrants*. St. John's: Government of Newfoundland and Labrador.

Newell, Dianne, and Rosemary E. Ommer. 1999. *Fishing Places, Fishing People: Traditions and Issues in Canada's Small-scale Fisheries.* Toronto: University of Toronto Press.

Nikiforuk, Andrew, Sheila Pratt, and Donald Wanaqas, eds. 1987. *Running on Empty: Alberta after the Boom.* Edmonton: Newest Press.

Nivalainen, S. 2004. "Determinants of Family Migration: Short Moves vs. Long Moves." *Journal of Population Economics* 17: 157–175.

Norcliffe, Glen. 2005. *Global Game, Local Arena: Restructuring in Corner Brook, Newfoundland.* St John's: ISER.

Norrie, Kenneth H. 1992. "A Regional Economic Overview of the West Since 1945." In *The Prairie West: Historical Readings*, 2nd ed., ed. R. Douglas Francis and Howard Palmer, 697–714. Edmonton: University of Alberta Press.

Olfert, M. Rose, and Jack C. Stabler. 1998. "Economic and Demographic Characteristics of the Pecos Area." *Health and Canadian Society* 5 (2): 287–308.

Olien, Roger M., and Diana Davids Olien. 1982. *Oil Booms: Social Change in Five Texas Towns.* Lincoln: University of Nebraska Press.

Ommer, Rosemary E. 1998. *Final Report of the Eco-research Project: Sustainability in a Changing Cold-ocean Coastal Environment*. Memorial University of Newfoundland.

– 2002. *The Resilient Outport: Ecology, Economy, and Society in Rural Newfoundland.* St John's: ISER Books.

– 2007. *Coasts under Stress: Restructuring and Social-ecological Health*. Montreal: McGill-Queen's University Press.

Owram, Doug. 1980. *Promise of Eden: The Canadian Expansionist Movement and the Idea of the West, 1856–1900*. Toronto: University of Toronto Press.

Overton, James. 1996. *Making a World of Difference: Essays on Tourism, Culture and Development in Newfoundland*. St John's: Institute of Social and Economic Research.

Packard, Vance. 1972. *A Nation of Strangers*. New York: David McKay.

Palmer, Howard. 1990. *Alberta: A New History*. Edmonton: Hurtig.

Pandit, Kavita, and Suzanne Davies Withers, eds. 1999. *Migration and Restructuring in the United States*. Lanham, MD: Rowman and Littlefield.

Parra, Francisco. 2004. *Oil Politics: A Modern History of Petroleum*. London; I.B. Tauris and Company.

Pearse, Peter H. 2001. *Crisis and Opportunity in the Coast Forest Industry*. Vancouver: Report to the Minister of Forests on British Columbia's Coastal Forest Industry.

Pedraza, S. 1991. "Women and Migration: The Social Consequences of Gender." *Annual Review of Sociology* 17: 303–25.

Phillips, Paul. 1981. "The Prairie Urban System, 1911–1961s: Specialization and Change." In *Town and City: Agents of Western Canadian Urban Development*, ed. Alan F.J. Artibise, 7–30. Regina: Canadian Plains Research Centre.

Pickup, Mark, Anthony Sayers, Rainer Knopff, and Keith Archer. 2004. "Social Capital and Civic Community in Alberta," *Canadian Journal of Political Science* 37 (3): 617–45.

Pinder, C.C. 1989. "The Dark Side of Executive Relocation." *Organizational Dynamics* 17 (4): 48–58.

Porteous, J. Douglas, and Sandra E. Smith. 2001. *Domicide: The Global Definition of Home*. Montreal: McGill-Queen's University Press.

Portes, Alejandro. 1995. *The Economic Sociology of Immigration: Essays on Networks, Ethnicity, and Entrepreneurship*. New York: Russell Sage Foundation.

Portnov, Boris. 1999. "The Effect of Regional Inequalities on Migration: A Comparative Analysis of Israel and Japan." *International Migration* 37 (3): 587–615.

Proudfoot, Bruce. 1972. "Agriculture." In *The Prairie Provinces*, ed. P.J. Smith, 51–64. Toronto: University of Toronto Press.

Putnam, Robert D. 2000. *Bowling Alone: The Collapse and Revival of American Community*. New York: Simon and Schuster.

Ram, B., Y. Edward Shin, and Michel Pouliot. 1991. *Canadians on the Move.* Statistics Canada Catalogue Number 96–309E.

Rapoport, Amos. 1995. "A Critical Look at the Concept 'Home.'" In *The Home: Words, Interpretations, Meanings, and Environments*, ed. David N. Benjamin, 25–52. Aldershot: Avebury

Rapport, N., and Andrew Dawson, eds. 1998. *Migrants of Identity: Perceptions of Home in a World of Movement.* New York: Berg.

Ray, Brian K., Greg Halseth, and Benjamin Johnson. 1997. "The Changing Face of the Suburbs: Issues of Ethnicity and Residential Change in Suburban Vancouver." *International Journal of Urban and Regional Research* 21 (1): 75–99.

Rasporich, Anthony W., and Henry C. Klassen, eds. 1975. *Frontier Calgary: Town, City, and Region, 1875–1914.* Calgary: McClelland and Stewart.

Relph, Edward C. 1976. *Place and Placelessness.* London: Pion.

Resnick, Philip. 2000. *The Politics of Resentment: British Columbia and Canadian Unity.* Vancouver: UBC Press.

Rheingold, H. 1993. *The Virtual Community: Homesteading on the Electronic Frontier.* Reading: Addison-Wesley.

Richards, John, and Larry Pratt. 1979. *Prairie Capitalism: Power and Influence in the New West.* Toronto: McClelland and Stewart.

Richling, Barnett. 1985. "You'd Never Starve Here: Return Migration to Rural Newfoundland." *Canadian Review of Sociology and Anthropology* 22 (2): 236–49.

Richmond, Anthony H. 1993. "Reactive Migration: Sociological Perspectives on Refugee Movements." *Journal of Refugee Studies* 6 (1): 7–24.

Riley, Robert B. 1992. "Attachment to the Ordinary Landscape." In *Place Attachment*, ed. Irwin Altman and Setha M. Low, 13–35. New York: Plenum.

Ritchey, P. Neal. 1976. "Explanations of Migration.' *Annual Review of Sociology* 2: 363–404.

Roach, Robert. 2002. *Beyond Our Borders: Western Canadian Exports in the Global Market.* Calgary: Canada West Foundation.

Robinson, Chris, and Nigel Tomes. 1982. "Self-selection and Interprovincial Migration in Canada." *Canadian Journal of Economics* 15 (3): 474–502.

Roseman, Curtis C. 1983. "Labour Force Migration, Non-labour Force Migration and Non-employment Reasons for Migration." *Socio-Economic Planning Science*, 17, 303–314.

Rosenbaum, James E. 1983. *Careers in a Corporation: the Internal Stratification of an Organization.* New York: Academic Press.

Safran, William. 1991. "Diasporas in Modern Societies: Myths of Homeland and Return." *Diaspora* 1 (1): 83–99.

Sandefur, Gary D. 1985. "Variations in Interstate Migration of Men across the Early Stages of the Life Cycle." *Demography*, 22 (3): 353–66.

Savoie, Donald J. 1997. *Rethinking Canada's Regional Development Policy: An Atlantic Perspective*. Canadian Institute for Research on Regional Development.

– 2006. *Visiting Grandchildren: Economic Development in the Maritimes*. London: University of Toronto Press.

Saxenian, Annales. 1994. *Regional Advantage: Culture and competition in Silicon Valley*. Cambridge: Harvard University Press.

Schachter, Jason S. 2004. "Geographic Mobility: 2002–2003. " *Current Population Reports*. N.p: US Census Bureau.

Schissel, Bernard, and Audrey Robertson. 1999. "Hope and Fear: Rural Sustainability and Family Violence." *Health and Canadian Society* (special edition) 5: 225–42.

Schutz, Alfred. 1945. "The Homecomer." *American Journal of Sociology* 50: 369–76.

Schulman, Norman, and Robert Drass. 1979. "Motives and Modes of Internal Migration: Relocation in a Canadian City." *Canadian Review of Sociology and Anthropology* 16 (3): 333–42.

Seldon, James. 1973. "Postwar Migration and the Canadian West: An Economic Analysis." In *Prairie Perspectives 2: Selected Papers of the Western Canadian Studies Conferences, 1970, 1971*, ed. Anthony W. Wasporich and Henry C. Klassen, 154–70. Toronto: Holt, Rinehart and Winston.

Sell, Ralph R. 1992. "Individual and Corporate Migration Decisions." In *Community, Society and Migration in America*, ed. Patrick C. Jobes, William F. Stinner, and John W. Wardwell, 221–53. New York: University Press of America.

Sell, Ralph R., and Gordon F. DeJong. 1983. "Deciding Whether to Move: Mobility, Wishful Thinking and Adjustment." *Sociology and Social Research* 67 (2): 147–65.

Shaklee, H. 1989. "Geographic Mobility and the Two-earner Couple: Expected Costs of a Family Move." *Journal of Applied Social Psychology* 19 (9): 728–43.

Sharpe, Sidney, Robert Gibbins, James H. Marsh, and Heather B. Edwards, Heather B., eds. 2005. *Alberta: A State of Mind*. Toronto: Key Porter Books.

Shaw, R. Paul. 1985. *Intermetropolitan Migration in Canada: Changing Determinants over the Decades*. Statistics Canada, Catalogue 89–504E

Shields, Rob. 1991. *Places on the Margin: Alternative Geographies of Modernity*. New York: Routledge.

Shihadeh, E.S. 1991. "The Prevalence of Husband-centered Migration: Employment Consequences for Married Mothers. *Journal of Marriage and the Family* 53 (2): 432–44.

Shils, Edward. 1978. "Roots – The Sense of Place and Port: The Cultural Gains and Causes of Migration." In *Human Migration: Patterns and Policies*, ed. William H. McNeill and Ruth S. Adams, 404–26. Bloomington: Indiana University Press.

Silver, Jim. 1996. *Thin Ice: Money, Politics and the Demise of the* NHL *Franchise*. Halifax: Fernwood.

Sinclair, Peter R. 2002. "Leaving and Staying: Bonavista Residents Adjust to the Moratorium." In) *The Resilient Outport: Ecology, Economy, and Society in Rural Newfoundland*, ed. Rosemary E. Ommer, 289–318. St John's: ISER Books.

– 2003. "Moving Back and Moving In: Migration and the Structuring of Bonavista." In *Retrenchment and Regeneration in Rural Newfoundland*, ed. Reginald Byron, 199–225. Toronto: University of Toronto Press.

Sinclair, Peter R., Heather Squires, and Lynn Downton. 1999. "A "Future without Fish? Constructing Social Life on Newfoundland's Bonavista Peninsula after the Cod Moratorium." In *Fishing Places, Fishing People: Traditions and issues in Canadian's Small-scale Fisheries*, ed. Dianne Newell and Rosemary E. Ommer, 321–39. Toronto: University of Toronto Press.

Sinclair, Peter R., and Lawrence F. Felt. 1993. "Coming Back: Return Migration to Newfoundland's Great Northern Peninsula." *Newfoundland Studies* 9: 1–23.

Sinclair, P.R., ed. 1988. *A Question Of Survival: The Fisheries and Newfoundland Society*. St John's: Institute Of Social And Economic Research.

Sinclair, Peter R., and Rosemary E. Ommer. 2006. Power and Restructuring: Canada's Coastal Society and Environment. St. John's: ISER Books.

Sjaastad, Larry A. 1962. "The Costs and Returns of Human Migration." *Journal of Political Economy* 705: 80–93.

Skeldon, Ronald, ed. 1994. "Reluctant Exiles? Migration from Hong Kong and the New Overseas Chinese." London: M.E. Sharpe.

Smart, Alan. 2001. "Restructuring in a North American City: Labour Markets and Political Economy in Calgary." In *Plural Globalities in Multiple Localities: New World Borders*, ed. Martha Rees and Josephine Smart, 167–93. Lanham: University Press of America.

Smith, David. 1997. *Saskatchewan and Aboriginal Peoples in the 21st Century: Social Economic and Political Changes and Challenges*. Regina: Federation of Saskatchewan Indian Nations

– 2005. "Path Dependency and Saskatchewan Politics." In *The Heavy Hand of History: Interpreting Saskatchewan's Past*, ed. Gregory P. Marchildon, 31–50. Regina: Canadian Plains Research Centre, University of Regina.

Smith, P.J. 1972. *The Prairie Provinces*. Toronto: University of Toronto Press.

– 1984. "The Changing Structure of the Settlement System." In *Environment and Economy: Essays on the Human Geography of Alberta*, ed. B.M. Barr and P.J. Smith, 16–35. Edmonton: Pica Pica Press.

– 2001. "Alberta: Experiments in Governance – From Social Credit to the Klein Revolution." In *The Provincial State in Canada*, ed. Keith Brownsey and Michael Howlett, 277–308. Peterborough, ON: Broadview Press.

Smits, J., C.H. Mulder, and P. Hooimeijer. 2003. "Changing Gender Roles, Shifting Power Balance and Long-distance Migration of Couples." *Urban Studies* 40 (3): 603–13.

Soja, Edward W. 1996. *Thirdspace: Journeys to Los Angeles and Other Real-and-Imagined Places*. Malden, MA: Blackwell.

Speare, Alden, Sidney Goldstein, and William H. Frey. 1972. *Residential Migration and Population Change*. Bellinger: Cambridge.

Speare, Jr., Alden, Frances Kobrin, and Ward Kingkade. 1982. "The Influence of Socioeconomic Bonds and Satisfaction on Interstate Migration." *Social Forces* 61 (2): 551–74.

Stabler, Jack C., and M. Rose Olfert. 1996. *The Changing Role of Rural Communities in an Urbanizing World: Saskatchewan – An Update to 1995*. Regina: Canadian Plains Research Centre.

Stabler, John, and M. Rose Olfert. 2002. *Trade Center Systems in the Canadian Prairie Region*. Saskatoon: University of Saskatchewan.

Stamp, Robert. 1984. "The Emergence of Alberta as a Geopolitical Entity." In *Environment and Economy: Essays on the Human Geography of Alberta*, ed. B.M. Barr and P.J. Smith, 5–15. Edmonton: Pica Pica Press.

Stark, Oded. 2006. "Inequality and Migration: A Behavioral Link." *Economics Letters* 91 (1): 146–52.

Statistics Canada. 1982. "Characteristics of Migrants to Alberta and British Columbia, 1976–1980." *Labour Force Survey*, Research paper no. 28.

– 1983. "On the Move: Results of a Special Survey on Migration." *Labour Force Survey*, Report no. 35.

Stegner, Wallace. 1962. *Wolf Willow*. New York: Viking.

Steuer, J. 1992. "Defining Virtual Reality: Dimensions Determining Telepresence." *Journal of Communication* 42 (4): 73–93.

Stimson, Robert J., and John Minnery. 1998. "Why People Move to the 'Sun-belt': A Case study of Long-distance Migration to the Gold Coast, Australia." *Urban Studies* 35 (2): 193–214.

Stinner, William F. 1992. "Community Attachment and Migration Decision Making in Non-metropolitan Settings." In *Community, Society and Migration in America*, ed. Patrick C. Jobes, Willian F. Stinner, and John W. Wardwell, 47–82. New York: University Press of America.

Stone, Leroy O. 1969. *Migration in Canada: Regional Aspects*. Ottawa, DBS.

– 1974. "What We Know about Migration in Canada: A Selective Review and Agenda for Future Research." *International Migration Review* 8: 267–81.

– 1979. *Occupational Composition of Canadian migration*. Statistics Canada.

Taft, Kevin. 1997. *Shredding the Public Interest: Ralph Klein and Twenty-five Years of One-party Government*. Edmonton: University of Alberta Press.

Taylor, R.C. 1969. "Migration and Motivation: A Study of Determinants and Types." In *Migration*, ed. J.A. Jackson, 99–133. Cambridge University Press.

Tepperman, Lorne. 1983. *The Social Costs of Rapid Turnover: Patterns of Migration to Alberta in the 1970s*. Research Paper No. 143, Centre for Urban and Community Studies, University of Toronto.

– 1985. "Musical Chairs: The Occupational Experience of Migrants to Alberta, 1976–80." *Social Indicators Research* 16: 51–67.

Thompson, John Herd. 1998. *Forging the Prairie West: The Illustrated History of Canada*. Toronto: Oxford University Press.

Thrush, Glen. 1999. "Something in the Way We Move." *American Demographics* 21 (11): 48–55.

Toneguzzi, Mario. 2006. "Home Values Gain 50% in One Year." *Calgary Herald*, 7 February, D1.

Trovato, Frank. 1986. "The Relationship between Migration and the Provincial Divorce Rate in Canada, 1971 and 1978: A Reassessment.' *Journal of Marriage and Family* 48: 207–16.

Trovato, Frank, and S.S. Halli. 1983. "Ethnicity and Migration in Canada." *International Migration Review* 17 (2): 245–67.

Tuan, Yi-Fu. 1977. *Space and Place: The Perspective of Experience*. Minneapolis: University of Minnesota Press.

Tupper, Allan, and Roger Gibbins, ed. 1992. *Government and Politics in Alberta*. Edmonton: University of Alberta Press.

Uhlenberg, Peter. 1973. "Non-economic Determinants of Non-migration: Sociological Considerations for Migration Theory." *Rural Sociology* 38 (3): 276–311.

United States. 2003. *Statistical Abstract of the United States*. Washington, DC: Bureau of Census.

Van Herk, Aritha. 2001. *Mavericks: An Incorrigible History of Alberta.* Toronto: Penguin.

Vanchon, Mark, and Franscis Vaillancount. 1999. "Interprovincial Mobility in Canada, 1961–1986." In *Canada: The Sate of the Federation, 1998–1999*, ed. Harvey Lazar and Tom McIntosh, 101–22. Montreal: McGill-Queen's University Press.

Vandercamp, John, and E. Kenneth Grant. 1976. "The Economic Causes and Effects of Migration: Canada, 1965–71." *Economic Research Council.* Catalogue EC22–48.

Van Hear, N. 1998. *New Diasporas: The Mass Exodus, Dispersal and Regrouping of Migrant Communities*. Seattle: University of Washington Press.

Voisey, Paul. 1988. *Vulcan: The Making of a Prairie Community*. Toronto: University of Toronto Press.

Waiser, Bill. 2005. *Saskatchewan: A New History.* Allston, MA: Fitzhenry and Whiteside.

Walther, J.B. 1997. "Group and Interpersonal Effects in International Computer-mediated Collaboration." *Human Communication Research* 23 (3): 342–69.

Warkentin, John. 1973. "Steppe, Desert and Empire." In *Prairie Perspectives 2: Selected Papers of the Western Canadian Studies Conferences, 1970, 1971*, ed. Anthony W. Wasporich and Henry C. Klassen, 102–36. Toronto: Holt, Rinehart and Winston of Canada.

Warkentin, John, ed. 1964. *The Western Interior of Canada*. Toronto: McClelland and Stewart.

Warnock, John W. 2003. "Industrial Agriculture Comes to Saskatchewan." In *Farm Communities and the Crossroads: Challenge and Resistance*, ed. Harry P. Diaz, JoAnn Jaffe, and Robert Stirling, 303–22. Regina: Canadian Plains Research Centre.

Weale, David. 1992. *Them Times.* Charlottetown: Institute of Island Studies.

– 1998. *A Long Way from the Road.* Charlottetown: Acorn Press.

Weeks, John R. 1996. *Population: An Introduction to Concepts and Issues*, 6th ed. Belmont: Wadsworth.

Weir, Thomas R. 1972. "The Population." In *The Prairie Provinces*, ed. P.J. Smith, 83–98. Toronto: University of Toronto Press.

Wellman, B. 2001. "Physical Place and Cyberplace: The Rise of Personalized Networking." *International Journal of Urban and Regional Research* 25: 227–52.

Wellman, B., J. Salaff, D. Dimitrova, L. Garton, M. Gulia, and C. Haythornthwaite. 1996 "Computer Networks as Social Networks:

Collaborative Work, Telework and Virtual Community." *Annual Review of Sociology* 22: 213–38.

Wetherell, Donald E, and Irene R.A. Kmet. 2000. *Alberta's North: A History, 1890–1950*. Edmonton: University of Alberta Press.

Whitaker, Elizabeth Ann. 2005. "Should I Stay or Should I Go Now: Wives' Participation in the Decision to Move for Their Spouses' Jobs." *Michigan Family Review* 10: 88–109.

Whitaker, Reg. 2001. "Revolutionaries out of Ontario: The Mike Harris Government and Canada." In *A Passion for Identity: Canadian Studies for the 21st Century*, 4th ed., ed. David Taras and Beverly Rasporich, 355–73. Scarborough, ON: Nelson Thomson Learning.

White, P., M. Michalowski, and P. Cross. 2006. "The West Coast Boom." *Canadian Economic Observer* 19 (5): Statistics Canada Catalogue no. 11–010-XIB.

Whitely, A.S. 1932. "The Peopling of the Prairie Provinces of Canada." *American Journal of Sociology* 38 (2): 240–52.

Winer, Stanley L., and Denis Gauthier. 1982. "Internal Migration and Fiscal Structure." Catalogue 22–109, Economic Council of Canada.

Winson, Anthony, and Belinda Leach. 2002. *Contingent Work, Disrupted Lives: Labour and Community in the New Rural Economy*. Toronto: University of Toronto Press.

Wiseman, Nelson. 1996. "Provincial Political Cultures." In *Provinces: Canadian Provincial Politics*, ed. Christopher Dunn, 21–62. Peterborough: Broadview.

Wolpert, Julian. 1965. "Behavioral Aspects of the Decision to Migrate." *Papers of the Regional Science Association* 15: 159–69.

– 1966. "Migration as an Adjustment to Environmental Stress." *Journal of Social Issues* 22 (4): 92–102.

Zerubavel, Eviatar. 1996. "Social Memories: Steps to a Sociology of the Past." *Qualitative Sociology* 19: 283–99.

Zimmerman, Carle C., and Garry W. Moneo. 1971. *The Prairie Community System*. Canada: Agricultural Economics Research Council of Canada.

Zvonkovic, A.M., K.M. Greaves, C.J. Schmeige, and L.D. Hall. 1996. "The Marital Construction of Gender through Work and Family Decisions: A Qualitative Analysis." *Journal of Marriage and the Family* 58: 91–100.

Index